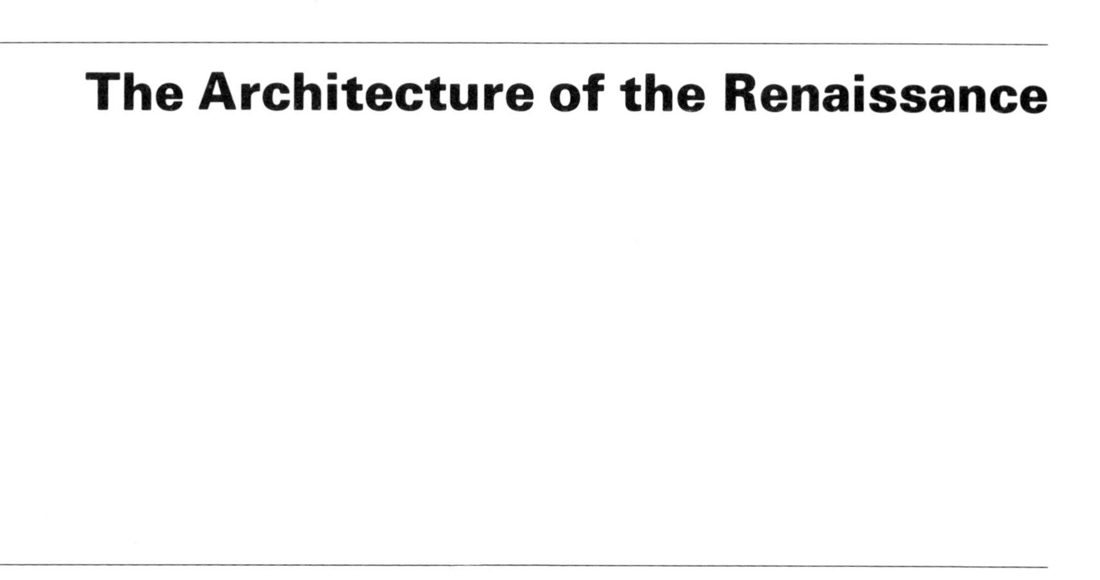

The Architecture of the Renaissance

By the same author

The Origins of Modern Town Planning

History of Modern Architecture

The Architecture of the Renaissance

Leonardo Benevolo

Volume II

London and Henley
Routledge & Kegan Paul

First published in Italy in 1968 as
Storia dell'Architettura del Rinascimento

Translated from the second revised
Italian edition, 1973
by Judith Landry
This English translation first published
in Great Britain in 1978 by
Routledge & Kegan Paul Ltd
39 Store Street, London WC1E 7DD and
Broadway House, Newtown Road,
Henley-on-Thames, Oxon RG9 1EN
Filmset and printed in Great Britain by
BAS Printers Limited, Over Wallop, Hampshire

British Library Cataloguing in Publication Data

Benevolo, Leonardo

The architecture of the Renaissance.

1. Architecture – History
I. Title II. Landry, Judith
724'.1 NA500

ISBN 0-7100-8036-0

Contents

Volume II

655 *'The human figure in demonstration of the voice, the elements and perspective' from Caporali's edition of Vitruvius, 1536*

five

The crisis of sensibility

From the fifteenth century onwards theoreticians of architecture repeated that architecture was a science, and that it included the whole group of technical skills that could modify the setting for human life; the fullest enumeration of these techniques is to be found in the proem to Alberti's treatise: the architect's province ranged from buildings to carts, mills, watches, aqueducts, ships, engines of war and fortifications. Later this list became shorter or was recited without conviction because individual technologies were organized independently and a specialist literature grew up for each one. On the other hand, the assertion of the scientific character of architecture was repeated with increasing emphasis and was expounded in the early seventeenth-century treatises in the scholastic language of the time. Scamozzi wrote:[1]

> 'In the abstract, architecture makes use of number, size, materials, natural movements and the other parts through speculation; and it also uses discrete and continuous quantities, and proportions, and equivalences, just exactly as the Mathematician and Physicist and Metaphysicist do; indeed it so closely approaches these first, that where they end, there the principles of Architecture fade . . . and for this reason the Ancients . . . called it a Science, and put it in the class of Mathematics.'

To emphasize this 'speculative' character of architecture, Federico Zuccaro, quoting Plato, observed: 'The ultimate essence of Architecture consists not only in building, but extends also to observations of the heavens, building of sundials, and war-engines.'[2]

There was nothing new in these statements which had been repeated ever since classical antiquity. What was new was that from 1589 Galileo was at work studying the laws of mechanics, pointing his telescope towards the heavens in 1609 and publishing *Nuncius sidereus* in 1610; in the following decade Descartes in his stove-warmed room had the revelation of the new 'marvellous science', Kepler stated the laws of movement of the planets and Bacon wrote his *Novum organum*.

Modern science, which was then being born, did not enter the framework of traditional physics or metaphysics, and used mathematics in a way completely different to that spoken of so far by philosophers and artists from Leonardo to Scamozzi and Zuccaro: 'Men of science', Lionello Venturi has written, 'refined the scientific method for the study of nature, and thus rendered the artistic doctrine of nature useless and outmoded';[3] their work no longer had anything in common with the work of artists, but threatened architecture's claim to a scientific or objective nature – and indeed threatened the similar claim of drawing, begetter of all the arts – i.e. the conceptual nucleus of the artistic tradition developed over the past two centuries. The emphasis given to this thesis in the writings of the time reveals a new concern with its validity which had appeared incontrovertible during the previous period.

To grasp the critical nature of this particular turning-point, which was to alter the cultural perspective of all artistic activity from now on, one must examine the course of the transformation in its various phases and components.

In chapter 4 we described the detachment of specialized technologies – surveying, mechanical constructions, hydraulics and fortification – from traditional architecture. The same happened with the scientific notions traditionally included in the apprenticeship of the figurative arts. Anatomy was an independent science from the time of Vesalius onwards and the study of the human body was perfected by the specialists who successively occupied his Chair at Padua from 1546 to 1625: Colombo, Fallopius, Fabrizio, Casserio, van der Spiegel; this research no longer found an outlet in art but in physiology, stimulated by Harvey who in 1628 published his discovery of the circulation of the blood. The treatises on the natural sciences were written by specialists, and their illustrations – from Andrea Cesalpino's *De plantis* (1583) to the manual of Casserio and van der Spiegel (1627) – were no longer the province of painters but that of professional engravers. Perspective – which continued to be part of artistic literature, in the form laid down by the treatise-writers of the late fifteenth and first half of the sixteenth centuries (Piero della Francesca, Gaurico and Pélerin) – was studied with scientific rigour after the middle of the century by Commandino (in the *Commentario* to Ptolemy's planisphere of 1558) and by Jean Cousin (in the *Livre de perspective* of 1560) and was systematized definitively by Guidobaldo del Monte in the *Perspectivae libri sex* of 1600, independently of any artistic intent.

At this time the notion of perspective space as something single, infinite, measurable and distinct from the objects placed in it became a philosophical hypothesis, in antithesis to the Aristotelian one, and later a postulate of the new scientific research.

In 1557 Scaliger used the word *spatium* as synonymous with *locus* and *vacuum*, giving the Aristotelian physical terms meanings completely different to their original ones.[4] In 1586 Telesio clearly defined the new notion of space as an entity independent of the bodies that occupy it (*moles*):[5]

'Space can become the receptacle of any being, and in the case of the beings occupying it withdrawing or being driven away, it does not withdraw and is not driven away, but remains perpetually identical, ready to receive all the beings which replace the others, and promptly assumes the dimensions of all the beings that are placed in it, and is always similar to the things that are placed in it, but is never identical with any of them, nor identified with them, but completely different from all of them.'

In 1585 Bruno celebrated the same concept in poetic form:[6]

'Henceforth I spread confident wings to space,
I fear no barrier of crystal or of glass;
I cleave the heavens and soar to the infinite.'

In 1593 Patrizi compared this notion with the principles of Aristotelian ontology and brought the antithesis into the open on the metaphysical plane as well; space was neither substance nor accident, but 'a substantial extension subsisting for itself, not inherent to anything'.[7]

In the second half of the sixteenth century pocket watches were perfected with the invention of the regulator and pyramid and were produced by rational methods, turning from exceptional objects into everyday implements; soon afterwards, for the aims of pure research, scientists invented precision clocks, from Galileo's (1581) to Huygens' 'pendulum clock' (1656). The possibility of measuring the course of time exactly, independently of physical phenomena, influenced the representation of space and confirmed the philosophers' notion of it as pure extension. Thus in the seventeenth century Gassendi and Newton, by synthesizing the arguments of the philosophers and the discoveries of the scientists, defined the new concepts of space and time as 'well-known to all'.[8] The idea of a system of proportional ratios independent of absolute measurements – which for two centuries had functioned as the conceptual basis for the figurative arts and architectural planning – became the basic postulate of the new mechanical conception of the world:[9]

'But because the parts of space cannot be seen, or distinguished from one another by our senses, therefore in their stead we use sensible measures of them. For from the positions and distances of things from any body considered as immovable, we define all places . . . and so, instead of absolute places and motions, we use relative ones; and that without any inconvenience in common affairs.'

Today we are in a position to assess the continuity between the notion of perspective space established by the artists of the fifteenth century and the developments of the philosophical and scientific thought of the late sixteenth century; but the artists of this period did not perceive the connection between the researches mentioned so far. The organization of culture which emerged from the middle of the sixteenth century onwards excluded direct confrontation between the work of artists, technical experts and scientists, and made improbable the kind of exchanges of stimuli which had taken place at other times, e.g. between Brunelleschi and Paolo Toscanelli or between the Neoplatonists of Careggi and the artists at the time of Lorenzo the Magnificent.

It is therefore largely pointless to seek for any direct relationship between the contents of art and science; the Carracci and Caravaggio were contemporary with Galileo and Bellarmino, Poussin with Descartes and Rembrandt with Huygens, but they moved in different worlds and communicated with one another not through their experiments, but in the mutual division of labour. On this last point the repercussions of the birth of modern science were decisive; in fact the synthesis between invention and research, between beauty and truth, which was typical of traditional artistic theory and praxis, was no longer tenable, at least not with the same significance. Art was no longer underwritten by objective penetration into the reality of the external world, because this reality was now accessible to, and analysable by, other methods endowed with another kind of cogency. Nature emerged as cognizable and controllable through the analytical study of its processes, not artificially, through the illustration of its visible forms. The measurement of objects was no longer an approximative value, definable with the traditional projective methods, but an exact one, to be obtained with arithmetical calculation and checked with the appropriate instruments.

All this threatened not the content of artistic experience, but its theoretical value and the civil use to which it could be put; it brought up, for the first time ever, the problem of the purpose of art, which had not arisen in the previous period when art performed a primary function of approach to, and incorporation in, the visible scene, and had at its service a wide range of techniques of production and communication, whose utility needed no demonstration, since they were continually used in everyday life.

Artistic culture reacted in two ways to this situation: by accentuating its internal formalism, and attributing its historical rules with a conventional, indisputable value; or by renouncing these rules and shifting its field of action from the intellectual sphere to that of feelings and emotions.

Giampaolo Lomazzo, in *L'idea del tempio della pittura* (1590), described the artistic legacy of the sixteenth century as a well-proportioned building, where the seven columns corresponded to the seven main painters (Michelangelo, Gaudenzio Ferrari, Polidoro, Leonardo, Raphael, Mantegna and Titian), associated with the seven planets and corresponding metals; the interest in individual cases, which was dominant in Vasari's *Lives* published a generation earlier, was replaced by a preoccupation with classifying and generalizing, which came from a new defensive attitude. The word 'idea', which is the key term of the intellectualist tradition of the sixteenth century, appears with significant regularity in the titles of treatises by Federico Zuccaro and Scamozzi, already mentioned (*L'idea de' pittori, scultori et architetti*, 1607; *Dell'idea dell'architettura universale*, 1615).

The eclectic programme implicitly put forward by Lomazzo was enlarged upon by the Carracci who began their careers in the 1590s. The well-known antithesis between the Carracci and Caravaggio gives a clear idea of the two possible outcomes of the crisis: intellectual pursuit of the idea, and emotional pursuit of reality. Lionello Venturi, following up the observation already quoted, has written:[10]

'Fifteenth century Florentine painting is inconceivable without the painters' faith in their interpretation of nature. There was then a world of ideas which became art, because art was regarded as the best way to understand reality. But Caravaggio . . . could no longer have this faith in the scientific character of his work; his Mannerist education had warned him only too well of human artifice. Furthermore his manner of feeling was too direct and powerful to adapt itself and follow other people's devices, and possibly exaggerate them further. He therefore rebelled against the Mannerist tradition and wanted to return to nature. But how? Lack of faith in scientific truth prevented him from having any ideal guide; he had to fall back upon the passions, emotions, and sensations, and give up the "idea".'

The great painters of the seventeenth century – Zurbarán, Velazquez, Rembrandt and Frans Hals, belonging to the following generation – followed the course taken by Caravaggio, as Venturi explains. In this way the illustration of sensible experiences and the analysis of feelings could be pushed well beyond the traditional limits, and supplied common experience with a new contribution, complementary to that of science and technical knowledge. Artistic research concentrated on the group of values that scientific research was eliminating from its field of investigation.

In prevailing artistic culture, however, the most advanced experiments were no longer able to direct the whole course of production. The individual communication of feelings remained uncertain and prey to innumerable cultural and institutional difficulties; for this reason it inevitably moved into collective communication, and individual states of mind were reduced to models of social behaviour. In this way the two outcomes of the crisis tended to merge: the pursuit of emotions was disciplined by the intellectual norms of propriety, decorum and etiquette; art became the world of persuasion and of the calculation of emotional effects.

Freedom and licence found their pendant in a plethora of precepts and conformism. Even in 1556 Daniele da Volterra, who covered up the nudes in Michelangelo's *Last Judgment* at the order of Pope Paul IV, earned himself the nickname Braghettone (person

656 *The* Crucifixion of St Peter *by Caravaggio. S. Maria del Popolo, Rome*

wearing wide breeches, i.e. tramp); but the treatises on religious art published after the conclusion of the Council of Trent, from that by Cardinal Paleotti[11] to that by Federico Borromeo,[12] laid down a large number of rules of propriety, apart from the elimination of nude figures, and progressively conditioned both general feeling and the opinions of the majority of the artists; in 1652 Pietro da Cortona wrote a treatise on painting in collaboration with the Jesuit Ottonelli,[13] and in 1668 Lebrun was in a position to lay down a detailed code '*à dessiner les passions*'.[14]

Before placing the field of experience which directly concerns us, i.e. architecture, within this framework, we must consider two more aspects of the general situation: the handicap of the various arts *vis-à-vis* this common tendency and the social circumstances which affected this turn of events.

Venturi observes that among the visual arts – painting, sculpture and architecture – only painting could freely follow a realistic and emotional tendency, both because of the quality of its instruments and because it had behind it the Venetian tradition of the sixteenth century. One might add that the repertoire of the figurative arts – painting and sculpture – depended upon natural models, even if modified and rectified by tradition, and therefore admitted recourse to nature against tradition (this was Caravaggio's programme); but architecture had a repertoire of artificial forms codified only by tradition and history, which therefore could be broken down only by historical criticism, not by naturalistic criticism, and it was consequently more stable. Furthermore the whole repertoire of the visual arts, with all the weight of the rules elaborated during the previous two centuries, was far more rigid than that of literature – which was being modified and enriched along with the general vocabulary of the various European languages – and that of modern music, which was emerging at this time, as it became disengaged from the norms of polyphony.

Lastly one must bear in mind that the parties involved in the cycle of the production and enjoyment of artistic goods were themselves changing.

The wars of religion and the price revolution hastened the dispersal of the Renaissance ruling class. The increase in the importing of silver from America began in 1544, after the discovery of the mines of Peru and Mexico, and reached its peak in the second decade of the sixteenth century; the rise in prices began around 1550 and continued uninterruptedly, in the various countries, until it reached a maximum between the first two decades of the seventeenth century. Soon afterwards, in 1618, began the Thirty Years' War which developed into a great public calamity in some countries of central Europe and produced the greatest fall in population after the epidemics of the fourteenth century. The social consequences of these events, and of the other changes that were concentrated into the early seventeenth century (the crisis of sixteenth-century large-scale capitalisms; the restoration of neo-feudalism; the new class-based, anti-revolutionary character of the political concert of the great powers; the growth of bureaucracy; the new organization of trade and also of what has been called the 'revolution in consumption';[15] the introduction of the potato and maize from America and of rice from Asia; the cultivation of sugar in the islands of the Atlantic; the spread of the new stimulants – tea, coffee, tobacco, rum) will have to be considered as terms of comparison for the architectural events in the chapters to come. For the moment one need note only that the new ruling classes – the sovereigns with their courts and bureaucratic machinery, the merchants and nobles who came in for the great new riches, the new religious orders and the new clergy – had largely lost competence and confidence in cultural production, and were no longer valid partners for artists; at the same time the lower classes began to lose the feeling of solidarity with the ruling classes and their cultural symbols. In 1416 the

657 *The* Surrender of Breda *by Velazquez. Prado, Madrid*

discoveries of Latin manuscripts, announced by Poggio Bracciolini from St Gall in his letters to Niccoli, were greeted in Florence as popular events; in 1599 the summary of Campanella's trial – in the strange mixture of Latin and the vernacular which would have horrified the two fifteenth-century humanists – stated that '*Mauritius Rinaldus dixit de auditu a Campanella* . . . that he wanted to have all Latin books burned, because it was confusing to people who don't understand them'[16] (and one cannot help being reminded of Renzo's similar protest which Manzoni had him make in 1628). Now poets and writers were using and refining ordinary language; in 1623 Galileo published his most important polemical work in the vernacular, so that it should be read by a wider public; but artists, and in particular architects, were bound to the Latin of the rules and standardized forms of preceding centuries, and were not in a position, except incidentally, to provide a popular type of artistic production.

The simultaneous crisis of patrons and users influenced the artists' work and set up differential limitations among the arts.

As far as the users were concerned, we must consider both the extent of the contact and their degree of participation in the works of the artists. Cervantes, Lope de Vega, Shakespeare and Monteverdi were active at the same time as El Greco and Caravaggio; their works circulated in a more restricted circle – among people who could read, or appreciated music, or went to the threatre – while painters' pictures were before everyone's eyes in churches; but they brought a series of far more direct stimuli to the general sensibility. The skill of painters, sculptors and architects had almost no parallel in the active experience of the public; it could be admired, not imitated. But the skill of writers and musicians, however sublime, concerned words and the singing and playing of instruments, which belonged to everyday life and could be cultivated by an infinitely easier process. Furthermore the spread of music and writing was ensured by efficient systems of notation, while buildings, paintings and statues had to be seen on the spot and could be reproduced only very imperfectly.

As far as the patrons were concerned, one need observe only that the work of sculptors and above all of architects depended upon commissions from a very restricted class; the work of painters could be financed by a somewhat broader one, and the freedom of pictorial research was sometimes linked to the specific make-up of this class, as in Holland; literature and music required a much lower financial commitment and, however anticonformist it might be, found suitable channels of circulation more easily. Furthermore the public theatre – which was becoming organized at this time and of which we shall say more later on – was the first example of high-level artistic production which depended only on a special organization of its users. Shakespeare, Lope de Vega and the Italian opera writers did not need the patronage of the powerful, or enjoyed it only incidentally; their place was taken over by figures such as Richard Burbage, Shakespeare's manager, who did not represent the public but interposed himself between artists and public with a new role.

In weighing up these circumstances one must take into account that the words 'freedom' and 'anticonformism' belong to a more recent vocabulary, not to the seventeenth century. Art and literature registered the crisis of models of behaviour that occurred in the second half of the sixteenth and the first half of the seventeenth centuries in varying ways, but they did not consciously enlarge upon it; they did not seek a breaking-point, but a point of stabilization. The nature of this research on the crisis was not critical, but rhetorical, and its structure was dependent on the elements of Aristotelian rhetoric which from the end of the fifteenth century constituted the 'blueprints of *humanitas*, the forms of the mental structure of the cultured man'.[17] The categories of rhetoric were *inventio*, *dispositio* and *elocutio* which corresponded to the categories of poetics, mimesis, pathos and the marvellous; Alberti, who based himself on Cicero, Seneca and Horace, transferred the distinction between 'story', 'composition' and 'ornament' into figurative culture (with the oscillations we talked of in chapter 1), but in the treatise on painting he was already inverting the discussion of the expressive means (Books I and II) in relation to that on content (Book III) and in the treatise on architecture he concentrated discussion on the relationship between 'walling' and 'ornaments'. This tendency finds a parallel, in literary terms, in the crisis of *inventio*, which was transferred from rhetoric to dialectic, and in the reduction of *dispositio* to *elocutio*, which was at the root of the antinomy between an autonomous conception of rhetoric (Speroni)[18] and a heteronomous one (Patrizi);[19] literature and the arts thus took the full brunt of the

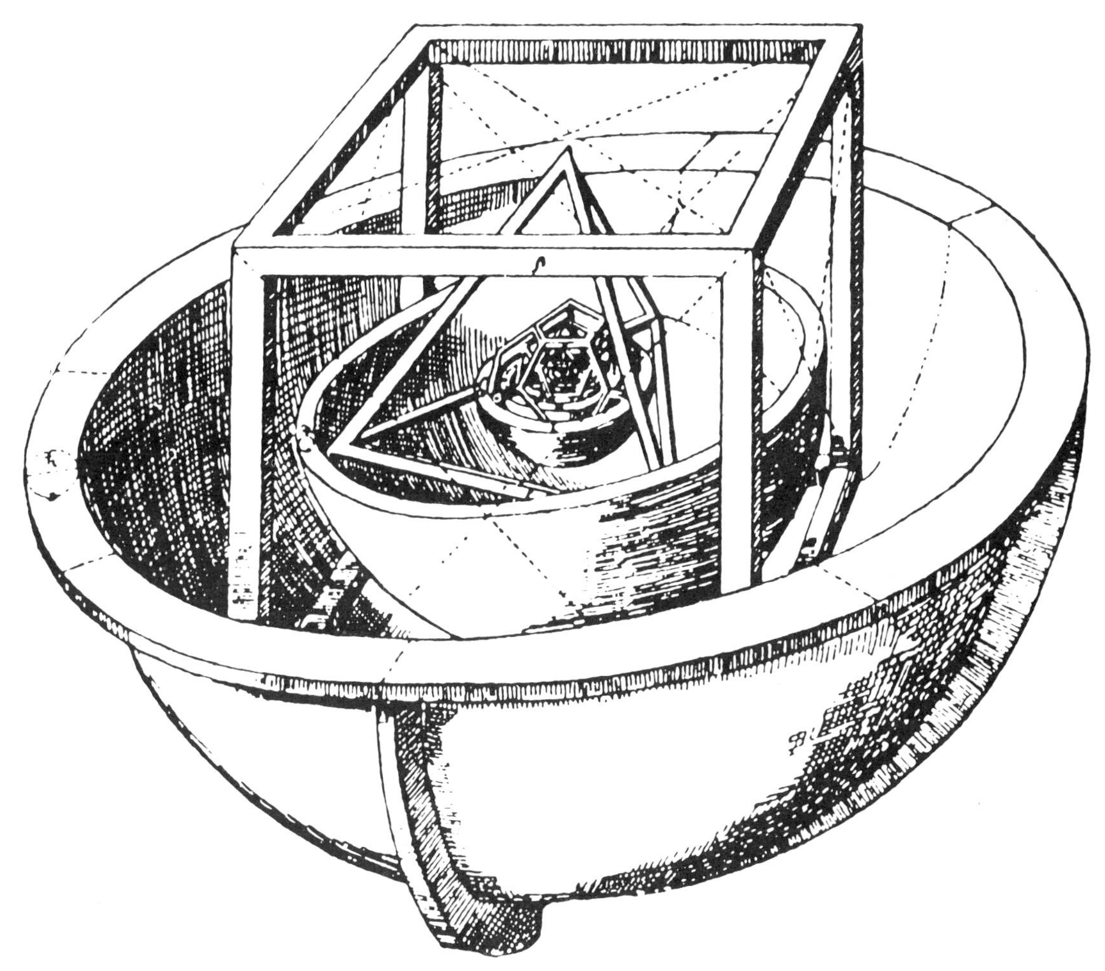

658 *An illustration from Kepler's* Mysterium cosmographicum*: the regular bodies which define the extent of the orbits of the planets*

doctrinal and moral controversies of the late sixteenth century, such as that between hedonism and moralism (this was the case with Torquato Tasso and Ammannati).

The social significance of the crisis of *inventio* has been pointed out: in Aristotelian theory *inventio* depended upon moderation, verisimilitude, propriety, hence upon public opinion, which was analysed in its typical judgments. These values foundered during the social changes of our period, and left the instruments of rhetoric suspended over a void of opinion, filled on each separate occasion by a series of specific requirements, which ranged from reasons of state to the aspirations of a certain class, group or individual.[20]

But in the seventeenth century neither literature nor the arts were in a position to discuss these needs dialectically, as was to happen in the eighteenth century; while the theoreticians of literature (Matteo Pellegrini,[21] Baltasar Gracián,[22] Pierre Corneille[23]) and of art (Gian Pietro Bellori,[24] Marco Boschini[25]) proposed a combination between *docere* and *delectare*, which were the two poles of the conflict that arose at the time of the Reformation and Counter-Reformation, artists and men of letters themselves took every possible liberty provided that representation exactly re-established, in form, the psychological harmony and satisfaction ultimately denied it in content.

The rise of science removed from the system of the arts its main argument for stability and social utility, i.e. its value as a vehicle for knowledge; artistic mimesis could no longer be the imitation of reality and had to become the imitation of emotions. The moment they became separated, there seemed to be no communication between these two lines of activity; scientific mentality did not enter the sphere of the arts, at least until the late seventeenth century, and the imitation of emotions remained a practical, useful mimesis, non-scientific and therefore non-revolutionary. In fact for a long time scientific research remained a heterodox affair, far from being an inherent part of the social and cultural system; one need think only of the difficulties experienced by scientists in the first half of the seventeenth century, the result not only of political or religious conservatism, but primarily of the structure of a society which demanded a formal perfection forgotten or questioned in the field of morals; long before he came up against the Holy Office, Galileo announced his discoveries of 1609 in Latin riddles, and Descartes took as his personal motto the phrase '*larvatus prodeo*'.

But this is not all. Descartes' attempt to establish the certainty of philosophy with the very method of scientific certainty – 'as two and two make four' – led to the doctrine of clear and distinct ideas which, in its turn, could be interpreted in a rhetorical way: the criterion of truth, in fact, was the serenity with which one might possess certain concepts, certainty against recurrent doubt.[26] Kepler practised experimental research, but did not accept the incompleteness which was typical of this research, and felt the need to imagine the new cosmic system in a form as complete and harmonious as the traditional one; the Neoplatonic flavour of the arguments put forward in *De harmonice mundi* was no longer a logical and aesthetic ideal – corresponding to the moment when the two attributes were still fused, and valid as a plan of action for all society – but an aesthetic ideal, which survived the distinction that had come to be made between the two fields of experience, and which had a far more restricted social range. In fact at the time of Ficino and Copernicus, the contemplation of the music of the spheres was a stimulus to enquiry and to the examination, by means of calculus, of the processes of the physical world; the ruling class, by encouraging this idea, was managing the general interests of Renaissance society. But at the time of Kepler and Descartes this same contemplation was an alternative to the scientific research already embarked on, which eliminated the spheres and refuted discussion of universal harmony or moved it to another level. The new ruling class, on which both artists and scientists depended, was concerned to preserve this ideal as an evasive diversion, as an element of cultural distinction or as an instrument of social preservation; in any event it certainly behaved as a class which managed its own interests and developed a bureaucratic or competitive relationship with the other classes.

In the seventeenth century the principle of emotional satisfaction, which seemed incontestable in every field of culture, acted as a factor of social discrimination, and kept most activity, even the most open-minded and 'popular', remote from the interests of the common people. The 'Roman housewives' battle for milk', of which Brecht speaks,[27] remained free from the scientists' criticism and out of reach of the artists' consolation. The ills that afflicted the lives of the majority in the seventeenth century were no different from those monotonously encountered in previous centuries: plague, war and famine;

if they now made up a sorrier picture,[28] this was due partly to the fact that culture offered what Cervantes called a 'false comfort'.[29] Conservatism, which corresponded to the interests of the ruling classes, was largely accepted as a general habit and was not subject to any organized challenge.

The work of the artists, precisely because it was carried out in the institutional forms established in the sixteenth century, ended by overturning its civil function: the relation between art and manners, which in Raphael's day served to introduce an element of coherence and general communicability into art, now served to introduce an element of hierarchical stabilization into manners, i.e. it covered the crisis of moral and social affairs with artistic form. This withdrawal, which became more pronounced during the course of the seventeenth century, was the starting-point for the so-called artistic 'revolutions' and prevented them from proceeding to their extreme consequences.

For this reason Galileo's tragedy does not resemble those of the innovating artists, and the risk inherent in the scientists' research – a real risk, if a man ventured out upon unknown ground and did not know in which direction he might be led – found no parallel in the artists' research, however bold and undogmatic.

Renewal and tradition in architecture

Architecture has a peripheral position in the picture we have been attempting to describe. In comparison with the other arts, architecture was weighed down by the system of heaviest restrictions:

1 The architectural repertoire was based on a system of conventional forms and found its models in history – i.e. in the monuments of classical antiquity – rather than in nature; it could therefore be contested only by a critical study of history, the conceptual instruments for which did not yet exist.

2 Works of architecture enjoyed the greatest publicity; they were before everyone's eyes, indeed they formed the physical setting in which town-dwelling communities lived. But now the architect's skill found no direct parallel in the experience of the spectators who were excluded from all active participation in the layout of the urban scene.

3 The commissioners of works of architecture were a small fraction of the community, particularly in the large centres. There existed a very rigid parallel between the cultural level of works of architecture and the social level of those who commissioned them which – particularly in the first half of the seventeenth century – excluded any relation between court building and popular building that was not one of hierarchical subordination.

These limitations explain the greater stability of architectural culture, the delay with which it registered the consequences of the figurative innovations and polemics that appeared between the end of the sixteenth century and the beginning of the seventeenth, the impossibility of a comparison with the crucial experiments of literature and music. The position of architecture at this vital turning-point in European culture is well exemplified by the collaboration between Ben Jonson and Inigo Jones; architecture was capable of producing a set that was noble, eloquent, picturesque and conventional for the singularities and eccentricities of the play to be enacted: a generic background for the specific passions evoked by poetry.

Neither did the dates correspond; while Caravaggio died in 1610, El Greco in 1614, Cervantes and Shakespeare in 1616, Marino in 1625 and Gongora in 1627, Bernini began his career as architect in 1624, Borromini and Pietro da Cortona in 1634, and the 'heretical' European architects – Guarini and the Spaniards, Germans and French – in the second half of the seventeenth century.

But the history of heretical or innovating experiments is almost impossible to trace, because of their very close ties with orthodox or conservative ones. Furthermore, emphasis on innovating artists, who complicated or transformed classical planning models, would give this type of option undue pre-eminence over ones adhering to the classical tradition.

In reality the crisis of architectural culture, which was coming to a head during the 1620s, consisted in the collapse of the objective criteria of choice typical of recent tradition; these objective criteria were replaced not by other criteria of the same kind, but by tendentious proposals, and often by a number of conflicting and complementary ones; the outcome of this crisis was not the formation of a new common repertoire, as an alternative to the previous one, but the start of a debate for an indefinite period.

The field of religious architecture registered the change of cultural options most clearly. In Catholic countries the last objective and uniform model of a religious building was that defined by Vignola in the Gesù in Rome (1568) and diffused throughout the world by the Society of Jesus, between the end of the sixteenth century and the first half of the seventeenth (Figs 659–60). The main architects responsible for this were Father Étienne Martellange (1568–1604) in France – he was in Rome from 1590 to 1604, and later designed the Society's churches at Avignon (1620), Blois (1625) and Paris (1625) and became a sort of inspector of Jesuit buildings throughout the kingdom – and in Spain Francisco Bautista, who designed the church of Toledo in 1628, and began to supervise the church of the imperial college in Madrid in 1629. The generation of progressive architects who began their careers between 1630 and 1660 opposed this model with a wide range of ground plans, including repetitions of the classical central plans of the High Renaissance: the four-armed octagon as in Borromini's S. Agnese (1652), the Greek cross as in S.Luca by Pietro da Cortona (1634)

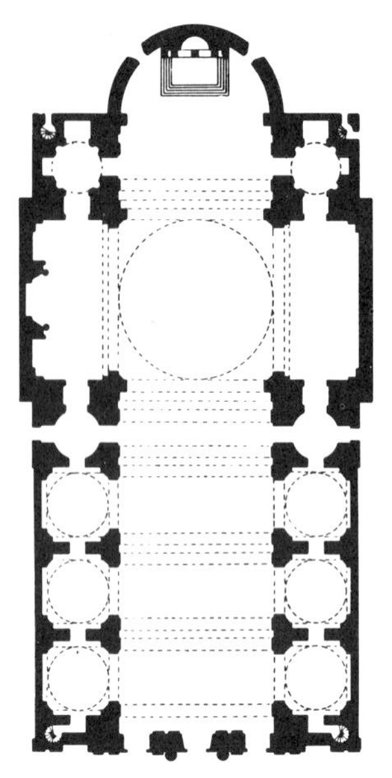

659 *Plan of S. Ignazio, Rome*

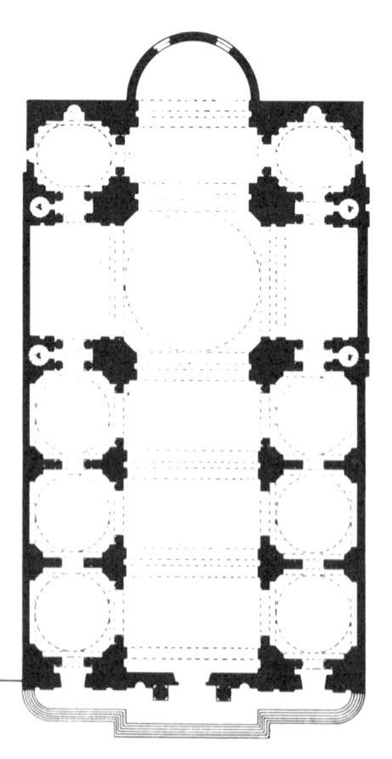

660 *Plan of the Gesù, Rome*

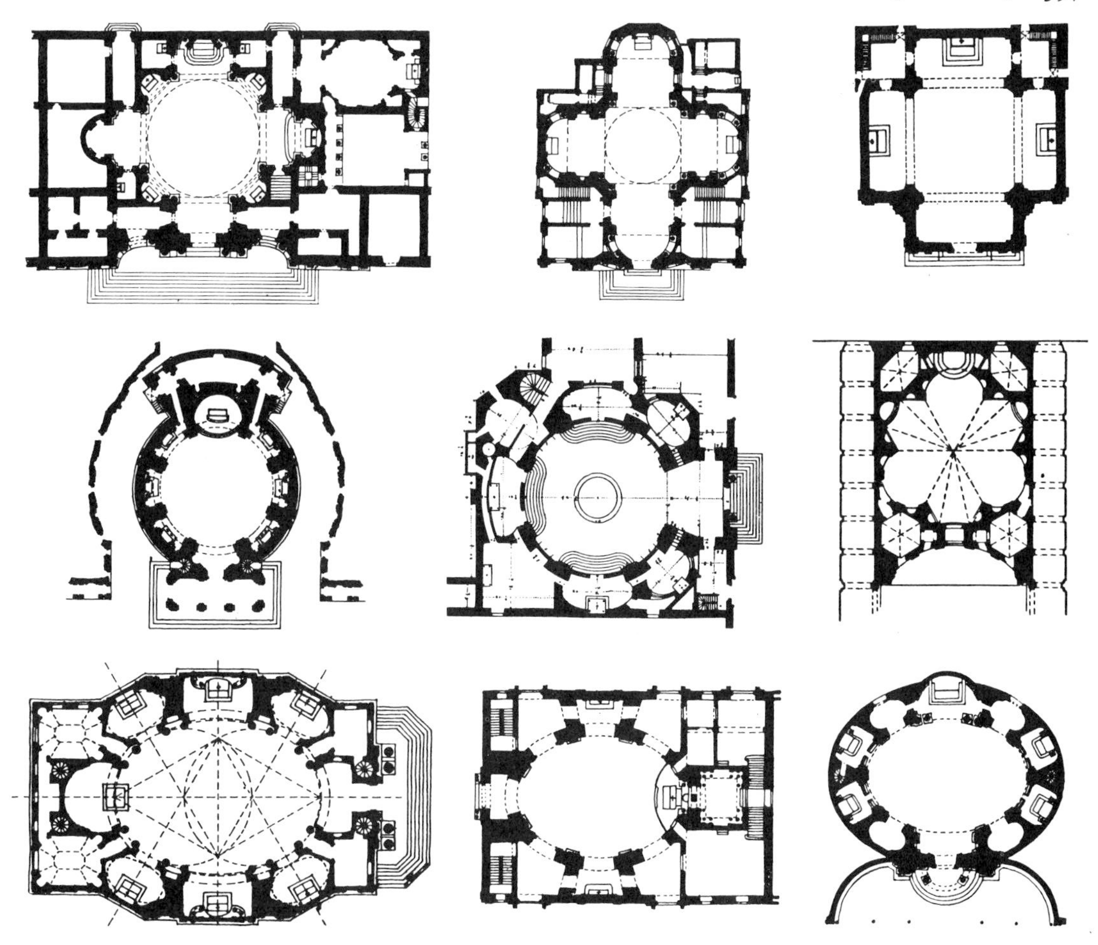

661–669 *Nine plans of seventeenth-century Catholic churches*
1 S. Agnese, Rome 2 SS. Luca e Martina, Rome 3 S. Tommaso, Castelgandolfo 4 The Assunta, Ariccia
5 The Visitation, Paris 6 S. Ivo, Rome 7 S. Carlo alle Quattro Fontane, Rome (as planned)
8 Desamparados, Valencia 9 S. Andrea al Quirinale, Rome

and in S. Tommaso in Castelgandolfo by Bernini (1658), the rotunda as in the Visitation by F. Mansart in Paris (1632) and the Assunta at Ariccia by Bernini (1662); anamorphic versions of them: the elongated octagon with four apses as in Borromini's S. Carlino (1634), or with four arms in the church of the Collège des Quatre Nations in Paris by Le Vau (1668), the oval in S. Andrea al Quirinale by Bernini (1658) or in the church of the Desamparados in Valencia by Martinez (1652); the original geometric inventions of Borromini (S. Ivo, 1642), of Guarini (S. Lorenzo, 1666; S. Filippo Neri, 1679) (Figs 661–9) or, at the other extreme, the intentional repetition of a medieval type of distribution and construction in the Paris parish churches of the seventeenth century, St-Roch by Lemercier (1653), St-Sulpice by Gittard (1655), St-Nicolas-du-Chardonnet attributed to Lebrun (1656), St-Louis-en-l'Île by Le Vau (1664).

Similarly in the Protestant countries, architects who had to find forms suited to the buildings for Protestant churches produced an enormous variety of types, not justified by diversities of function or structural require-

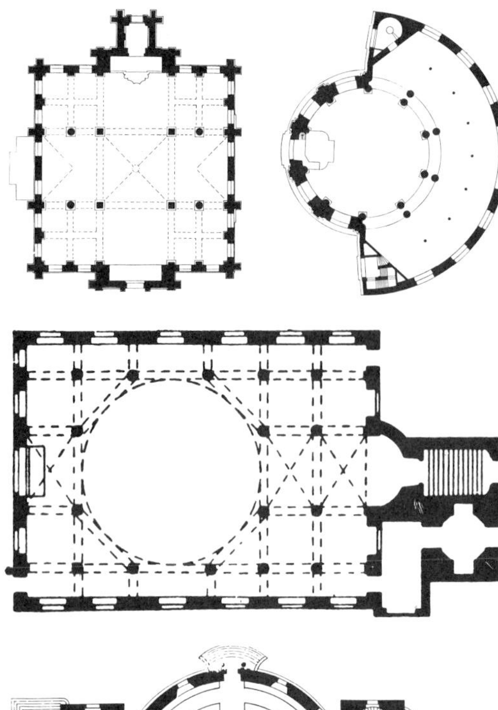

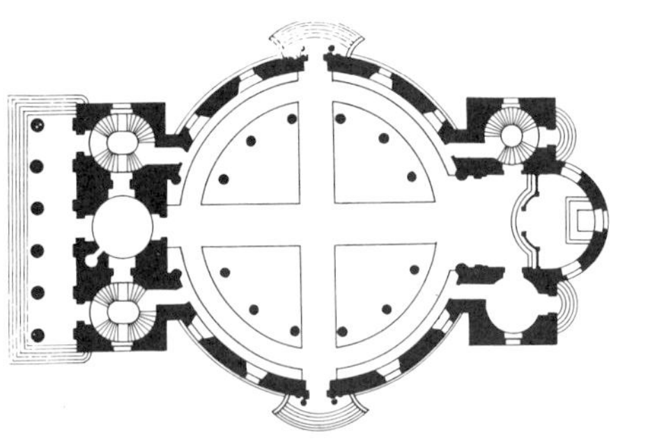

670–673 *Four plans of Protestant churches*
1 Nieuwe Kerk, Haarlem 2 Nieuwe Lutherse Kerk, Amsterdam 3 St Stephen Walbrook, London 4 A project for St Martin-in-the-Fields, London

ments, but by the opening up of the architectural debate; sometimes the range of building types was the result of the work of a single designer, for instance Wren who rebuilt the London churches after the fire of 1666.

The result of these experiments was not a new integrated movement, to be opposed to the Renaissance movement or to be characterized by a new adjective, for example 'baroque' (we have so far avoided using this insidious term and shall continue to avoid it) but the emergence, in the unitary field of architecture, of a sphere of elusive decisions subjected to sudden vacillations, for which from now on the word 'art' was to be reserved, in a more restricted sense. In this field an unlimited variety of stylistic decisions was current, ranging from the absolute conservation of classical models to the invention of completely new ones, from the continuity of recent tradition to the conscious return to past ones, including late Gothic, as in Bohemia. The organic nature of this field of choices was maintained by the very intuitive character of the cultural approach; when in the eighteenth century this character disappeared and was replaced by historical reasoning, the various groups of choices became incommunicable.

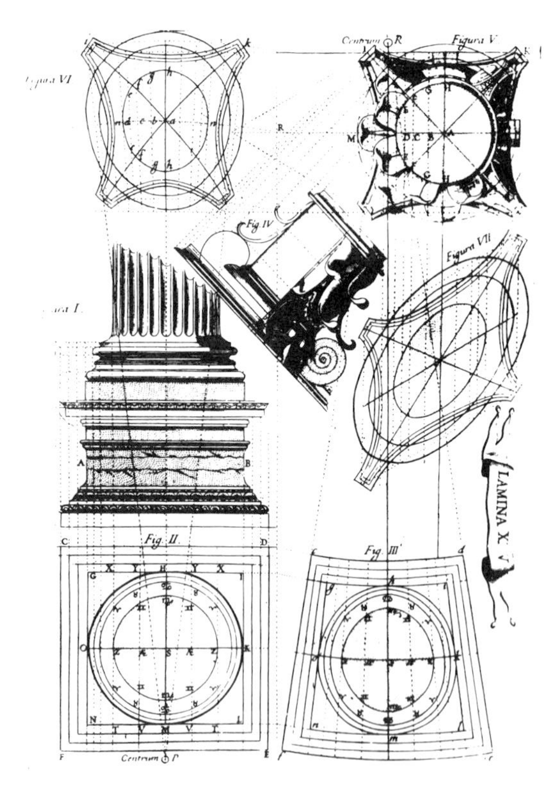

674 *A plate from Caramuel's treatise,* Architectura recta y obliqua *(written in the early seventeenth century), Vigevano, 1678*

The chief experiment in this cultural state of affairs took place in Rome in the second third of the seventeenth century, and influenced almost all similar European experiments; we shall talk first of this and then of the others.

The Roman school

At the funeral of Sixtus V, in 1590, the catafalque of the great Pope was decorated by the young Lombard architect Carlo Maderno (1556–1629), who was then beginning his career working for Domenico Fontana.

In the following decades work went ahead to complete the great works begun by Sixtus V, especially in the eastern part of the city; Fontana and Flaminio Ponzio built the two chapels at the sides of S. Maria Maggiore, Maderno restored the convent of S. Susanna (from 1597 to 1603) (Fig. 676) and built the church of S. Maria della Vittoria (1605), giving monumental form to the square of S. Bernardo already dominated by Fontana's impressive Acqua Felice. The intense building activity of this period regularly made use of the building types established in the late sixteenth century: for churches the model of the Gesù (1568) was repeated in S. Maria in Vallicella (1575) (Fig. 675), S. Girolamo degli Schiavoni (1585), S. Giovanni dei Fiorentini (1588), S. Andrea della Valle (1591), S. Nicola da Tolentino (1614), S. Isidoro (1622), SS. Domenico e Sisto (1623), S. Ignazio (1629); for palazzi the model was the Sangallo block, made flexible and freed from the canons of symmetry by Fontana – in the Lateran palace (1586) – and by Martino Lunghi – in Palazzo Borghese (1605) (Fig. 677); in the first years of the seventeenth century Giacomo della Porta built the Villa Aldobrandini at Frascati, a last, perfect repetition of the sixteenth-century type dominated by a single axis according to the principal line.

Conformity in architectural production contrasts, at this period, with the innovations

675, 676 *Façades of S. Maria in Vallicella and S. Susanna, Rome*

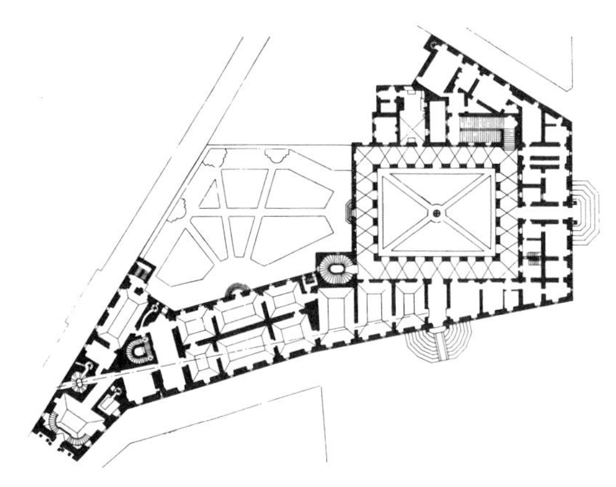

677 *Plan of Palazzo Borghese, Rome*

and debates in figurative production. Rome was the capital of the arts, the goal of the greatest Italian artists – Caravaggio arrived about 1590, Annibale Carracci in 1595, Mochi in 1600, Pietro Bernini in 1603 – and of a large number of foreigners, from the Flemish Romanists of 1572 onwards: Rubens from 1601 to 1602, Callot in 1608, Ribera in 1610, Vouet and Claude Lorrain in 1614, Duquesnoy in 1618, Poussin in 1624 (and, among the architects, Jacques Lemercier in 1607, Inigo Jones in 1613). It was also a moment of ideological and scientific controversies: in 1600 Bruno's trial was held, in 1603 Federico Cesi founded the Accademia dei Lincei, the first European scientific institution.

The first important architectural problem that could not be solved by traditional methods arose in 1607, when Paul V came to complete the façade of St Peter's.

The structures of Michelangelo's organism had been completed by Giacomo della Porta, who died in 1602; between 1603 and 1606 the inner mosaic decoration of the dome was carried out, under the direction of the cavalier d'Arpino (Fig. 678). All that remained to be built was the body of the façade which implied the laying out of the space in front of the basilica, still occupied by the old projection with the Benediction Loggia. In 1586, on the open space in front, more than 250 metres from the façade anticipated by Michelangelo, Fontana put up the obelisk which was to settle the lie of the piazza.

Michelangelo's plan did not consider the layout of the surrounding space, and artists who have tried to imagine this space – such as those who decorated Sixtus V's library – spontaneously transported the monument into an imaginary landscape, eliminating all the adjacent buildings (Fig. 335). Thus Michelangelo's façade was not a concrete image, that could be linked with the city setting, but functioned only as a complement to the building taken in itself; similarly the façade – like the rest of the external architecture – is independent of the internal organism, and acts as a compact base for the volume of the dome, with which it retains a projective relationship, interpretable in many different ways. It is therefore understandable that sixty years later, when the Neoplatonist cultural climate still operating at the time of Paul III had faded, the problem should have been examined on the basis of the new sensibility to landscape, and of the pressure for functional utility and the interest in typological regularity: hence the decision by Paul V to lengthen the church, transforming the Greek cross into a Latin one and bringing to St Peter's the longitudinal type that had become canonic during the last forty years.

It is true that respect for the letter of Michelangelo's plan was still very strong, and indeed was felt most strongly by the most cultured representatives of the patron class, such as Maffeo Barberini, the future Urban VIII.[30] But by now it was a conventional homage, and the very organization of that plan provided the starting-point for the last variant; in fact all that was required was to keep the form of the façade fixed as an extension of the giant order which runs round the perimeter of the church, and vary its position, bringing it forward as much as necessary to develop a longitudinal block in front of the cruciform organism. This correction changed the conditions of the dome's

678 *Interior of the dome of St Peter's, Rome*

679 *The interior of St Peter's, transformed by Maderno*

visibility and produced a new problem, though of the same nature as those created by Michelangelo with the decisive choices of 1546; it did in fact sacrifice the close-up view of the dome, and posed the more complex problem of a long-distance view, not fixed but variable and connected with the whole urban fabric of the Borghi.

Having taken the decision to prolong the organism – which seems to have met with more objections in clerical circles than among artists – Paul V organized a competition for its architectural realization in 1607, postulating that the basilica must occupy all the space of the old St Peter's; it should be noted that in this way the distance between façade and obelisk was reduced to about 180 metres, and the premise was established for laying out of the square in front of the building.

The competition, in which Flaminio Ponzio, Girolamo Rainaldi, Domenico Fontana, G. A. Dosio and Ludovico Cigoli took part, was rightly won by Maderno, who interpreted the data of the problem in the most coherent way.

Inside, the architect prolonged the barrel-vaulting of the front arm, distinguishing the new structure from the old with a small indentation, and placed a series of communicating chapels at the two sides: this was the Jesuitical organism, ingeniously adapted to the new dimensions; Michelangelo's architectural covering was continued on the outside, around the new block – because of its two-dimensional character it lent itself conveniently to following any course the masonry body might take – and the façade was produced by the slightest accentuation of the

680 *The entrance hall of St Peter's*

relief of the giant order, with the great fluted columns protruding beyond the pilasters. The unusual proportion of the façade, wider than it is high, was intentional and emphasized by the lateral sections – on which the campanili were to rise – so that it does not seem to be a frontal composition, but a continuation of the architecture that ran all round the perimeter, as in Michelangelo's plan; the dome thus remained visible from the piazza, though more or less hidden according to the distance, and a range of views from the various parts of the square was established, one of the greatest virtues of the scheme; only later, from the end of the seventeenth century onwards, was this to be considered a defect, and it gave birth to the idea of an axial road, to restore the original graphic positioning of the dome above the façade at an infinite distance. In this space, then undefined, Maderno placed a fountain which was the re-elaboration of a previous fountain by Bramante; Bernini moved it – together with a second identical fountain – to the transversal axis of his organization.

As in the façade of S. Susanna, completed in 1603, Maderno demonstrated his specific ability in accepting traditional typologies, modifying and loosening their rigidity with a subtle combination of detail. But now he did something more, i.e. he established the spatial theme of the piazza, developed fifty years later by Bernini.

The new façade of St Peter's, begun in 1607, was finished in 1612. Soon afterwards the interior details of the church were begun,

681 *The façade of St Peter's*

682, 683 Aeneas and Anchises *by Bernini. Villa Borghese, Rome*

and this occupied the best Roman artists until the middle of the seventeenth century. The order in which the work was done shows that the great subject was tackled by degrees, with significant hesitation. First, under the pontificate of Paul V the decoration of the portico was completed; a multitude of stuccoers and stonemasons were working at the orders of Maderno and Antonio Buonvicino, including the young Francesco Borromini (1599–1667), who arrived in Rome in 1614. Only after 1623, when Cardinal Barberini became Pope Urban VIII, was conclusive work carried out on the decoration of the enormous space, which the main architects of the Renaissance, from Bramante onwards, had helped to define.

Bramante's Greek cross, with the tomb of St Peter as its centre, made it necessary to place the main altar in the middle of the building; the altar was marked by a baldacchino, which was exactly under the dome and had to bear comparison with the great surrounding space. Urban VIII entrusted this difficult task to the twenty-five-year-old Gian Lorenzo Bernini (1598–1680), already known as the author of the marble groups for the villa of Cardinal Borghese (Figs 682–3) and the restoration of S. Bibiana.

Bernini worked on the design of the

684 *Bernini's baldacchino in St Peter's*

685 *Bernini's baldacchino in the central space of St Peter's*

baldacchino from 1624 to 1630, and supervised its execution – together with his contemporary Borromini, promoted to the position of assistant – from 1630 to 1633. In this short time the two artists, rivals for the rest of their lives, contributed together to defining the splendid *macchina* which is virtually the manifesto of the new Roman artistic culture.

The position in the ground plan – of decisive importance, because it did not coincide with the vertical axis of the cupola, but was shifted towards the back – was fixed by Maderno, who placed the hollow of the Confessio to correspond to the axis, and therefore introduced a longitudinal organism into the centre of Bramante's and Michelangelo's cross, clearly linked to the new general organization of the church. Bernini interpreted and underlined this decision by choosing a rectangular plan, thus firmly differentiating the view along the nave from that along the transverse arms; furthermore, from the very beginning he conceived the expedient of the four free columns, spiralling like those of the *pergula* of the old basilica. Borromini – already less interested in spatial problems, and a phenomenal inventor of details – possibly suggested the form of the top with the dolphin-shaped scrolls, which firmly prevent the baldacchino from looking like a traditional building structure (Figs 684–5).

Although it uses a large number of earlier points of inspiration, this organism is com-

686, 687 *Bernini's decoration in St Peter's: general view and a detail*

pletely novel in its open structure, made up of free and separate elements, and in the rigorous monochrome treatment of the gilded or burnished bronze, which helps to suspend it in the atmosphere of the surrounding space. The relation between forms and air is also emphasized figuratively: the festoons which hang from the top are slightly bent, as if moved by a breath of wind. In this way the baldacchino is freed from the crushing architectural tutelage of Bramante's cross, and emerges as an accessory of Maderno's newly orientated space.

From 1629, when Maderno died, Bernini supervised the interior decoration of the whole church and settled the recurrent motifs, realized subsequently by a host of craftsmen: the niches of the four piers, with the gigantic

statues, topped by the loggias where the old twisted columns were incorporated; the marble encrustations on the supports of the lesser arches, with the medallions isolated against a yellow-brown marble background; the stucco statues between these same arches and the main cornice; the doorways to the side rooms, with the columns in pink Cottanello which, together with the gold and the white marble, define the overall tonal register of the setting, against which the bronze work placed at the focal points stands out: the baldacchino, and at the end St Peter's chair designed in 1656, which has as a further background the yellow and orange stained glass window representing the dove in the aureole.

Once the plurality of architectural scales conceived by Bramante had been destroyed, this decoration, with its broad spacings and rigorous control of colours, managed successfully to mediate between the gigantic scale of Michelangelo's architecture and the normal scale of the furnishings and people, and is of crucial importance in the general effect (Figs 686–7). The main expedient chosen by Bernini was to give the figurative elements – the statues in the niches, the figures of the *putti* around the medallions, etc. – a scale halfway between the human and the architectural, which could take the lengthy views imposed by the vastness of the building, and which appears gigantic only when seen from close to, often with a suggestive crescendo effect; this scale also dominates the later minor schemes, such as the tombs of the Popes, for which the artist gave two memorable models: the tomb of Urban VIII (1639–47) and that of Alexander VII (1671–8), where the combination between architecture, sculpture and applied arts is superb (Figs 688–9).

The part played by Bernini was equally decisive for the layout of the exterior.

From 1642 onwards he designed the two campanili at the ends of the façade, and also considered a partial rebuilding of Maderno's

688, 689 *The two tombs for Urban VIII and Alexander VII in St Peter's by Bernini*

façade, i.e. the demolition of the two end wings in favour of two towers isolated from the base upwards; this approach was not forceful, and indeed derived from a conventional desire to give the façade more normal proportions, interrupting the continuity of the architectural covering which runs all round the church. Bernini finally decided to build two light superstructures, consisting of free-standing elements, as for the baldacchino; in the course of their execution, in the first years of the papacy of Innocent X (1644–55), the foundations gave way and the new structures had to be demolished. Bernini retained the position of architect of St Peter's, was strongly criticized, but limited his work to the decoration of the interior, and only under Alexander VII (1655–67) did he once more assume responsibility for the exterior layout, now turning his attention to the whole open space in front of the church.

The fundamental data in this scheme are:

1 The distance of the obelisk from the façade, still very considerable although reduced by Maderno; as far as Fontana was concerned the obelisk served only to indicate an axis of indefinite length, and did not generate a problem of proportion of the longitudinal view with the transversal ones. But what the new feeling for landscape required was a coherent three-dimensional arrangement of the spaces defined on paper at the time of Sixtus V.

2 The obstruction caused by the wing of S. Damaso in the apostolic palazzi; this wing extended considerably at the left side of Maderno's façade, and fixed a limited width for the first part of the piazza; the overhead corridor of Alexander V which led to Castel S. Angelo started from beyond this building, but further from the axis of the church, and it, too, limited the width of the second part of the square.

3 Maderno's façade, being brought forwards in relation to the transept of the church, obscured Michelangelo's dome to a varying extent depending on the distance, as we have pointed out; cupola and façade could no longer appear simultaneously except at a very great distance, i.e. under abstract conditions which did not concern the Roman culture of this period. On the other hand, the interval between dome and façade could be measured optically from an intermediate distance, the more precisely, more oblique the view, through an obvious application of Thales' theorem, familiar to the visual culture of the time.

The campanili which were to have stood at the end of the façade would have helped to close in the fan of views converging on the dome, and would have been aligned with the intervening buildings that limited the space, likewise converging, available for the piazza, putting the façade clearly into relation with the piazza. (Probably Bernini, though having had to give up building the campanili, took the considerations of 1642 as a point of departure, and was all the more determined to exclude the possibility of executing them in the future; but the two clocks put in their place by Valadier, being almost contained within the height of the façade, suggest a broadening of the range of views over the whole arc of the horizon, and in fact, in every distant view – for instance that from the hills of the left bank – they fail to connect church and piazza, and the dome is left to stand out as a free volume on a flat base.)

Starting from these elements, and incorporating a series of projects already previously worked upon (by Ferrabosco, Rainaldi, etc.), Bernini conceived the piazza as divided into two spaces: the first, in the shape of a trapezium, was framed by two solid wings, similar to those in the engravings of 1607 with the plan of Maderno's façade, but diverging towards the façade as well as being distorted into a parallelogram, to follow the slope of the ground; once beyond the obstacle presented by the wing of S. Damaso, the architectural order of the two wings continues in the form of a free colonnade, and curves to form two arcs, of which one is almost at a tangent with the corridor of Alexander V. In this way a second, oval, space with four centres is created around the obelisk, only partly enclosed by the colonnade because the landscape and surrounding houses remained visible above the top or between the shafts of the columns. This space is rendered independent by its unusual surround, by the striking presence of the transversal axis – marked by the obelisk and two fountains – and above all by the lie of the land, adapted so as to break up the uniform slope of the Vatican hill like an enormous flight of steps. In fact, beyond the introduction of the two wings, the colonnades run almost level, and the original slope is balanced by a conical counterslope which isolates the obelisk, with its circle of bollards, in the centre of a hollow; the shaping of the ground, also emphasized by the eighteenth-century paving in large radial sections, makes the form of the oval space perceptible, indeed physically verifiable, and gives it a three-dimensional substance much greater than that deriving from the modest height of the colonnade, considered in relation to the great intermediate surface area. Thus this space, though open and permeable to the surrounding landscape, can take comparison with the solid mass of the church, whose measurements it reproduces (about 200 by 150 metres) and acts as a linking element between church and city; the gigantic scale of the church, rendered absolute and unique by Michelangelo's contribution, is here reversed, translated into a void around which the usual and normal-sized (though grandly spaced) elements of the urban scene, palazzi, houses and, in the background, hills, all stand. The colonnade only partially obscures the view of these elements from the square, and breaks off to the front, allowing the

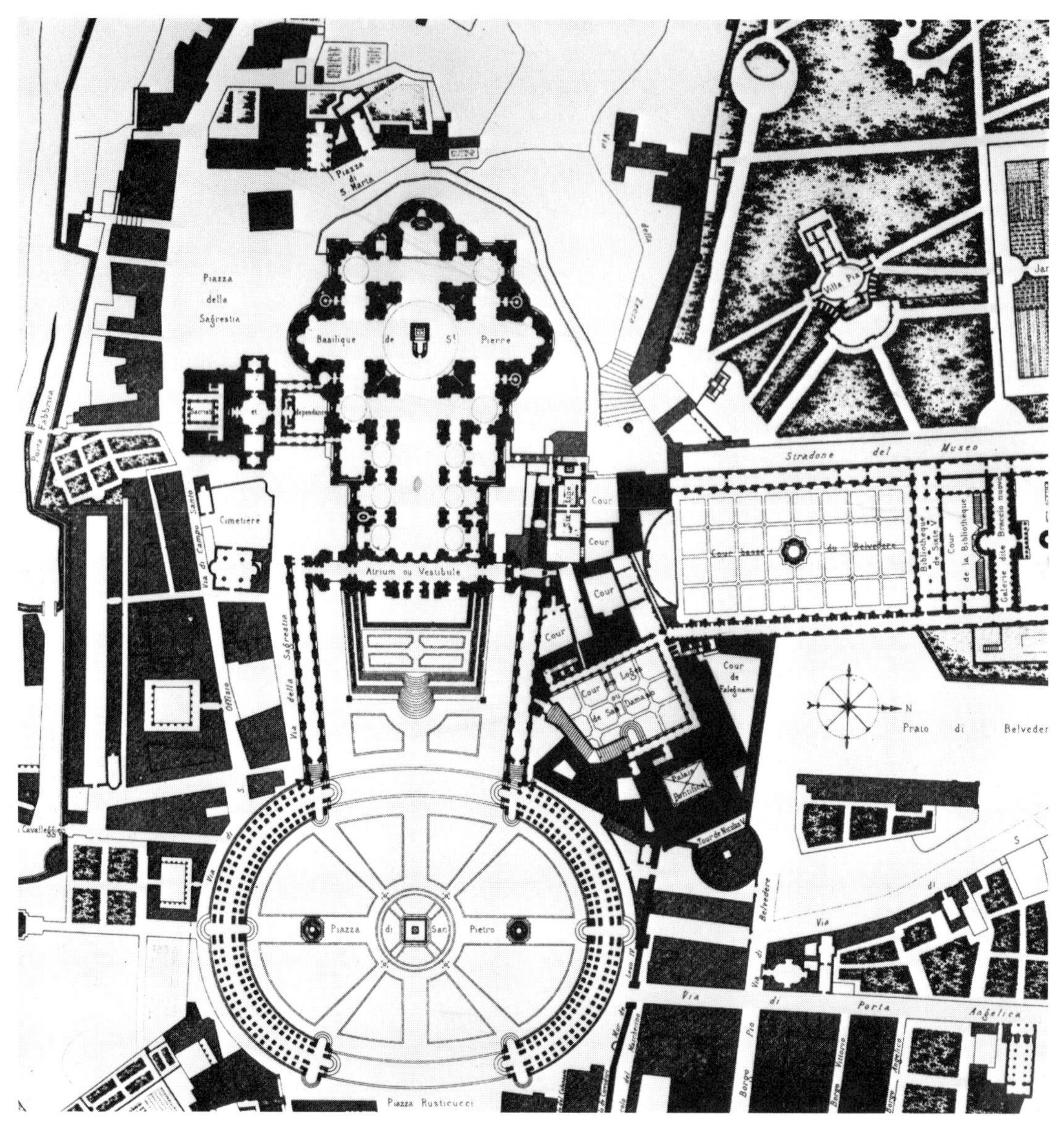

690 *General plan of St Peter's square (from Letarouilly)*

houses of piazza Rusticucci to appear at the end of the great space.

The solution of this point of juncture, so consistent with the whole, was the result of an omission; initially Bernini planned the complete closing in of the oval with a third arm of columns; in 1667 he decided to set back this arm towards piazza Rusticucci, to create a small antepiazza, and to allow the observer to appreciate the overall form of the oval, before crossing its perimeter. During his travels in France Bernini pointed out to the seigneur de Chantelou that buildings on a central plan required an entrance somewhat set back, because as soon as they entered people immediately took a few steps forwards, and

691 *Aerial view of St Peter's square*

692 *St Peter's square, looking towards the city before the opening of via della Conciliazione*

found themselves right inside, before having given the building an overall glance; in 1658 he applied this reasoning to S. Andrea al Quirinale, and now he extended it – as Wittkower observes[31] – to the oval of the piazza; none the less the death of Alexander VII, in the same year, caused the execution of the third arm to be delayed, and it was not by chance that Bernini and his successors left the architectural layout of this part incomplete; in fact the depression of piazza Rusticucci also achieved the effect of preparation intended by Bernini and allowed people a momentary glimpse of the circle of the colonnades from the outside before entering the intermediate space. Furthermore, the irregularity of the houses acts as a preparatory contrast to the regularity of the piazza; thus a continuous and dramatic gradation was established between the popular tone of the buildings of the Borghi and the supremely aristocratic tone of the church, which no designer, up to the present day, has felt confident enough to alter.

Bernini's piazza, opened up between city and basilica, is a gigantic linking instrument and must be considered in terms of the activities that take place there. We have seen that the square is primarily a ground-level arrangement, where the paving counts at least as much as the architecture; this paving is often covered by a dense crowd, and its concave form helps to present the multitude to itself, as in theatres, i.e. to guarantee each person a position in and overall vision of the

693, 694 *St Peter's square: view from an air balloon at the beginning of this century and view from the steps of the basilica towards piazza Rusticucci before its demolition*

movements in which he is involved. For the first time a large-scale architectural scheme was dependent on the free movements of the crowd, rather than upon the set movements of important personages.

This was the last Roman scheme on the gigantic scale prescribed by Bramante, Michelangelo and Domenico Fontana, commensurate with the scale of the ancient monuments. But Bernini rightly interpreted the attempt to adjust the modern city to the scale of the ancient one as an interrupted attempt, and accepted the co-existence of the monumental scale with the ordinary one; indeed he took the contrast between the monument and the district of ordinary houses as the main theme of his composition. Thus he wound up the Utopia of Julius II and Bramante and fixed once and for all the character of modern Rome – that of permanent contrast between the aristocratic and the popular tone. This extremely exact historical judgment remained valid almost until the present day, and spanned the rise and fall of classicism; but it gradually made the image of the city alien to the rest of European culture; Rome became the city of ruins and monuments in the midst of hovels, of pomp and poverty, and as early as the eighteenth century it already 'did not seem like a capital';[32] it was a city where artists and writers came to seek not the models of the present but the memories of the past, indeed the concept of the past as irretrievable, the concept of the rancour of time and the fickleness of fortune.

695 *The crowds in St Peter's square*

Let us look more closely at the relationship between Bernini's layout and the two visible elements of the church – façade and dome. The façade is subject to the exceptional scale imposed by Michelangelo, and already Maderno, to resolve the problem of the entrance openings, had to introduce a second and much lower order between the supports of the giant one; this forms the architrave of the central openings and the imposts of the two side ones. The cornice of Bernini's order which surrounds the piazza runs at a level with the cornice of the second order by Maderno, and thus is correctly independent of the scale of Michelangelo. But the divergence of the two straight wings, seen from the oval space, prevents one from grasping this parallel and foreshortens the length of the two wings considerably, i.e. causes the façade to seem closer and lower than it is in reality, and makes it comparable to the rest of the architectural décor which surrounds the piazza. Naturally, as one walks towards the church this effect diminishes and, emerging from the oval, one can grasp the real relation between wings and façade, dominated by this correspondence of level, which is expressed in a clear hierarchical subordination. As one comes closer still, the blunted corner of the façade hides the interpolation of the two wings and annuls even this effect of subordination, allowing only Michelangelo's structure, transcribed by Maderno, to stand out.

The dome itself is always partly hidden by the façade; the result – as we have seen – is an

696 *The crowds in the side arms of the colonnade*

extremely significant gradation of impressions, which accentuates, rather than diminishes, the presence of the dome in the space of the piazza. First let us consider the range of effects along the longitudinal axis. While one is in the space between the two straight wings the dome is invisible; when one enters the oval only the lantern can be seen and from the foot of the obelisk the whole bulk emerges, though without the drum; going still further away, at the end of the oval one can see part of the drum, just enough to gain a clear idea of its shape. The view from the obelisk was possibly calculated by Maderno, and the effects in the oval anticipated and supervised by Bernini; the fact is that, walking backwards from the beginning of the oval to the centre, the main bulk of the dome comes into view progressively and exactly, i.e. a precise parallel is established between the enclosed form of Michelangelo's hemisphere and the open form of Bernini's funnel; the latter acts as a projection and open air development of the former.

This range of effects varies according to the distances along the longitudinal axis, and each effect is common to all the points situated on a single line perpendicular to this axis; the observer, in fact, is not invited to proceed along the middle axis, but rather along the edges of the square, where the colonnades present themselves as continuations of the two entry roads coming from the Borghi into piazza Rusticucci. Thus Bernini's layout accentuates the importance of the oblique views, which – as we have already noted – make it possible to compare dome with façade and thus measure the distance of one from the other. Furthermore the variety of the oblique views confirms the dominant position of the dome, upon which the whole range of possible views converges; in fact every oblique view, while it remains axial *vis-à-vis* the round dome, does bring about a foreshortening of both the façade – as Argan[33] observed – and, even more so, the system of wings and porticoes, i.e. it underlines the character of the dome as the fixed centre of an endlessly variable landscape.

The disastrous opening up of via della Conciliazione (1936–50) has largely eliminated both the gradation of the effects along the longitudinal axis and the balance between axial and oblique views. In fact it has introduced a long-distance view, in which the succession of elements well-spaced in depth has been flattened into a two-dimensional image, and Bernini's arrangement has been intercepted by the lateral buildings, allowing Michelangelo's composition – cupola and façade – to stand out in its original abstractness; it has emphasized the axial approach unduly, reducing the colonnades to secondary wings, and the oval to an extended road; it has given piazza Rusticucci an aristocratic character, and has even given the new palazzi a ridiculous imitation of the cornice of the colonnades. The main work of modern classicism, which sums up the whole cycle of experiments from Bramante to Bernini, has been resolutely mutilated as recently as thirty years ago, despite the weight of historical studies and rhetorical exaltation that had accumulated on the matter.

Bernini's layout, though complex, was carried out with surprising economy of means; the design of the colonnades is very simple and was arrived at after the rejection of a large number of more elaborate variants (with arches and pilasters; with doubled columns, etc.); in the definitive version the richness of effects is obtained not by the complications of the frontal motif, but by the superimposition of four rows of columns, at different distances, and always variable from different points of view. The most problematic point of juncture was that between the semi-circles and straight wings; in fact the motifs at the ends of the semi-circles are aligned according to the main lines of the wings, and are distorted obliquely in relation to the fronts of the colonnades; but despite the divergence of the wings they none the less form obtuse angles with the semi-circles and the end motifs are therefore obliquely placed towards the outside, reinforcing the illusion produced by the wings. The wings contain two galleries, the northern one acting as a grand entrance to the Vatican palaces; in 1664 Bernini laid out the Scala Regia on a continuation of it, and its further rise acts as a backdrop to the long sloping space, and simulates a depth greater than the real one with the trick of perspective convergence.

Bernini's work on St Peter's is so important because it assumed and co-ordinated all earlier parts into a new organism; if indeed one can justly name an author of the great monument, it can be none other than Bernini. He rejected a further break in the continuity of the work, as Bramante and Michelangelo had done, in two different ways, in the sixteenth century; he set himself – with a totally new retrospective sense – to understand the long story of its building, to unify the various partial contributions and to present the mother church of Christianity as a synthesis of all past history. A coherent architectural itinerary leads the visitor from the poor houses of the Borghi to the sublime culmination of the bronze throne, at the end of the basilica. The remains of the Constantinian church have been retained and integrated, as far as possible, in the new arrangement, and the whole range of symbolic associations thought up in the last two centuries (from the Biblical likenesses of Nicholas V and his men of letters to the geometrical and cosmic harmonies of Bramante, the philosophical metaphors of

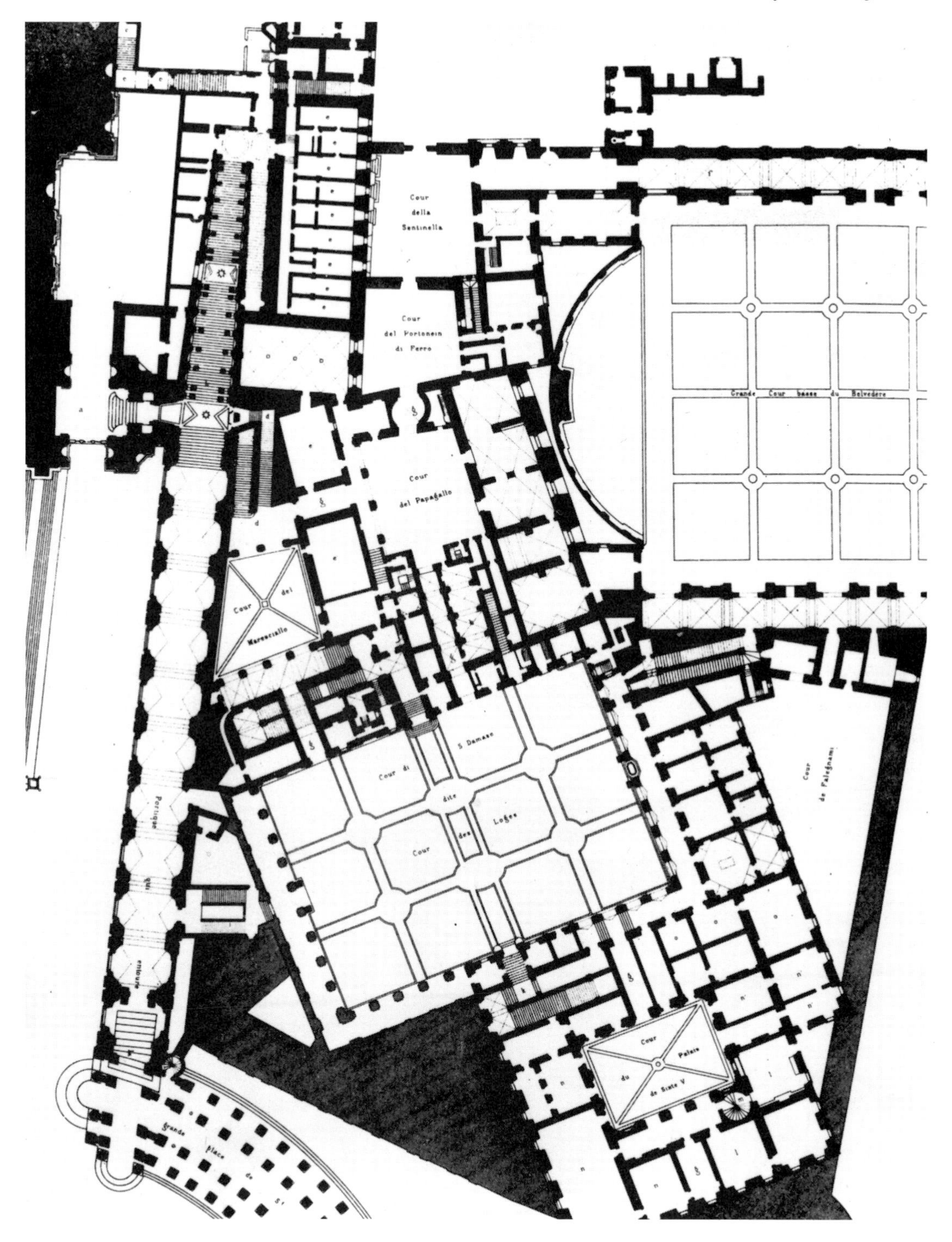

697 *The new entrance to the Palazzi Vaticani from the Scala Regia (from Letarouilly)*

Michelangelo and the rhetorical metaphors of seventeenth-century culture – for instance the image of the colonnades as open arms, also illustrated in a drawing by Bernini; and from the extra-historical value of the classical forms to the historical meanings attributed to the single elements, for instance the vine-covered columns of the baldacchino, associated with the memory of the temple of Solomon) were accepted not as alternative tendencies, but as elements of a continuity that was interesting as a whole. Bernini understood that the moment of exclusive hypotheses was over; architectural classicism could only lay out the background – noble and generic – for the human vicissitudes which succeeded one another over the years, and were now evaluated in their temporal structure.

Bernini's contributions to St Peter's extended over his entire life and form his most convincing work for that very profound sense of history with which they were fitted into this ancient undertaking. Meanwhile he was immensely active both as an architect and as a sculptor: in 1629 he succeeded Maderno on the building of Palazzo Barberini and realized the three-storeyed loggia between the two projections, brilliantly combining the model of the palazzo with that of the sixteenth-century villa; he contributed to the layout of piazza Navona for Innocent X, with the idea of the series of three fountains; under Alexander VII he designed many very important public works, including three centrally planned churches – S. Andrea al Quirinale (1658), Ariccia (1662) and Castelgandolfo (1658). In his sculpture he was seeking finesse and extreme differentiation of treatment of the marble – already found in his youthful groups for Camillo Borghese (1618–23): *Aeneas and Anchises*, with its insistent comparison of the bodies of the three characters, child, adult and old man; *Apollo and Daphne*, with the two figures windswept from running, and the female one contrasting with the bark of the growing tree; he attempted a physical representation of religious ecstasy – in the St Teresa (1644) and in the statue of the blessed Albertoni (1674) – and also the expression of a completely personal feeling – in the figure of *Truth uncovered by Time* (1646–52); but in architecture he intentionally kept away from extreme effects and oversubtle distinctions. He ran the whole gamut of the classical repertoire with sublime liberty, without inventing fundamentally new devices and without compromising by imprudent handling the unvarying nature of the standardized elements, those guardians of classicism's stability in time; but with unfailing certainty he discovered the variant suited to each occasion and each place and smoothed out all the consequences of his intervention, always re-establishing the continuity of the setting.

On this basis Bernini organized a vast group of workers: his studio and workshop functioned as a thriving business. The activity of his pupils – Giacomo Antonio Fancelli, Lazzaro Morelli, Francesco Baratta, Antonio Raggi and his son, Paolo Bernini – before and after the death of the master, confirmed the historicity of his approach, and multiplied its consequences over a vast field. Thus Bernini's approach was not only stated but was substantially translated into reality; the repertoire codified in the last half century was reabsorbed, as an individual case, into a broader repertoire which utilized the whole range of classicism made available in a new historical vision and could have the most varied imaginative elaborations. The coherence of this production was based on the harmony between Bernini and his pupils in so far as they were sharing in a living tradition, operating in a well-defined area; for this reason Bernini's classicism, unlike Raphael's, was not suitable for export beyond the confines of Rome and was more fatally subject to progressive exhaustion, as the intuition of traditional historical continuity became more difficult with the passing of time. The organization of the actual work – based on

698 *St Peter's throne*

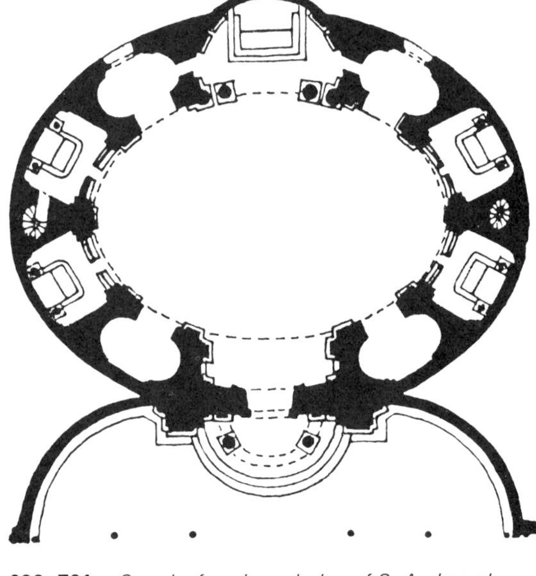

699–701 *Cupola, façade and plan of S. Andrea al Quirinale*

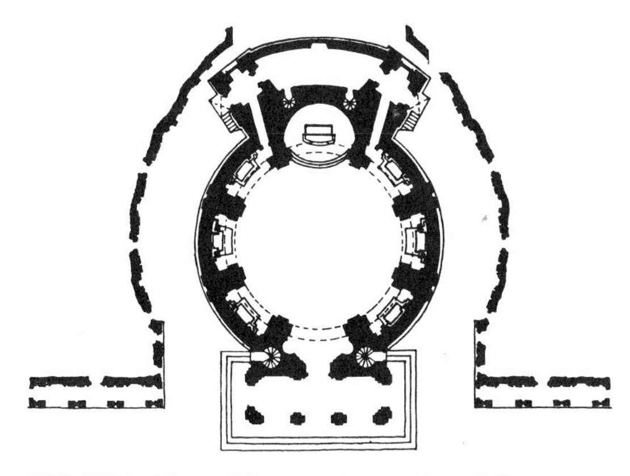

702, 703 *View of the cupola and plan of the Assunta, Ariccia*

personal and simultaneous control of the architectural décor – was still the old one, and was not such as to be able to stem the deterioration of habits through the usual channels of transmission.

But Pietro da Cortona (1596–1669) and Francesco Borromini developed a completely different thesis. The two artists arrived in Rome almost at the same time; Pietro da Cortona came from Tuscany in 1612 and obtained rapid success as a painter, particularly in the decoration of large architectural spaces; Borromini came from Ticino and was a distant relative of Maderno's, worked from

704, 705 *Façade and detail of the interior of the Assunta, Ariccia*

706–708 *Façade, interior and plan of SS. Luca e Martina, Rome, by Pietro da Cortona; note the relationship between external and internal architecture*

1614 as a stonemason and from 1630 as assistant to Bernini on St Peter's and Palazzo Barberini.

In 1634 Pietro da Cortona was elected principal of the Accademia di S. Luca, and soon afterwards began to build the church of SS. Luca e Martina, for the Academy; in the same year Borromini obtained his first commission as an independent architect from the Trinitarians, for the convent of S. Carlo alle Quattro Fontane.

For S. Luca Pietro chose the Greek cross plan, in intentional revolt against recent tradition and looking back to the models of the High Renaissance; however, the distributive type was merely a starting-point, because all the care of the architect was lavished on the plastic articulation of the

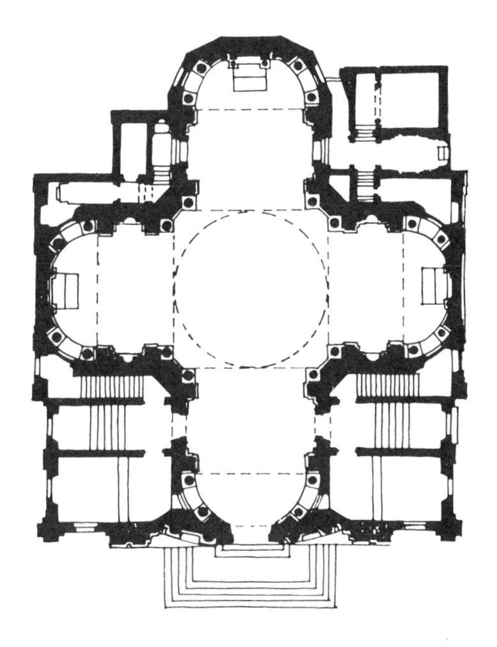

empty space, free from any relationship with the articulation of the volume. In fact the walls of the crossing, bare of chapels or secondary spaces, are broken up by a series of protruding or receding elements – pilasters, columns and niches – grouped according to an independent law and such as to alter the character of the space completely; in this case the church seemed to have been created by compressing an architecture of greater overall dimensions into a small space, with repeated foreshortenings, and the solid walls acquired an illusory depth, emphasized by the perfectly conceived expanses of decoration (Figs 706–8).

The models for this architecture were the compositions of church façades, from the Gesù (c. 1575) to S. Susanna (1603), where the intensification of motifs and the representation of depth through foreshortening were justified by the singular character – both in terms of perspective and of ceremonial importance – of the façade in relation to the rest of the building. The transfer of this mode of composition from the façade to the internal walls of a church indicates the rejection of the traditional distinctions, and attributes to an enclosed space the expressive intensity hitherto reserved for a frontal composition set in external space.

In the façade of S. Luca the architect introduced a direct representation of the internal space significantly reversed; the façade is curved, as if by the pressure from the apse behind it, and becomes a volume, rather than a flat composition.

In the convent of the Quattro Fontane Borromini, with the patience of a true craftsman, began to divide up the small plot in order to obtain from it the church dedicated to S. Carlo, the cloister, the various rooms needed by the community and even a garden. The church – whose perimeter is restricted by the presence of the blunted corner of the fountain – was based on another distributive model of the High Renaissance, the domed space with four apses, here emphatically elongated. Borromini, too, aimed at characterizing this space with the same intensity as S. Luca, but without employing the already known range of associations between pilasters and columns, linked to the frontality of planes and hierarchy of traditional spaces: he did not want in any way to emphasize the hierarchy between the main space, under the dome, and the secondary spaces of the apses, and he placed an order of columns on the walls which made it possible to resolve the intersecting and intermediate point of the apses in the same way. The articulation of this rhythm was achieved by anamorphosis – which, as a mathematical problem, was engrossing Father Mersenne's friends (including Descartes, Maignon and Niceron[34]) in Paris at just this time – i.e. by the various distortions of the elements running from the longitudinal to the transversal axis, their homological relationship remaining recognizable and emphasized by subtle decorative devices (for example, the different shapes of the capitals placed on a convex stretch of the perimeter, with the scrolls reversed, and of those placed on a concave stretch, with the scrolls placed normally).

On this already elaborate scheme Borromini laid out a remarkable system of decorations, largely invented or modified in relation to the traditional types, so as to reduce to a minimum the diversity between the main elements – i.e. the parts of the architectural order – and the secondary ones. The use of plaster and stucco in place of natural materials – here as in S. Luca – helped further to equalize this diversity and to bring out the excellence of the approach, in relation to the physical quality of the structures (Figs 709–10).

The account by Father Juan de S. Bonaventura of the work on S. Carlo recalls the polemics aroused by this unusual building; 'the rivals of Sr. Francesco Borromini' criticized him, saying that 'his buildings are beautiful, but involve vast expense':[35]

709 *Interior view of S. Carlo alle Quattro Fontane by Borromini, Rome*

'The first item, that they are beautiful, and of extremely ingenious architecture, even his rivals admit, and it is true; the second is false: as one can clearly see in the building of this church, whose expense is not as much as twelve thousand scudi, with all its perfection of masons, stuccoers, ironworkers, carpenters, painters, tile-workers and lampmakers. . . . It is indeed true that his buildings cost a great deal, and since they must be estimated according to their Value, rise to great sums; but this is not a result of the expenses of the Patroni delle Fabriche, nor yet of the material or multiplication of days . . . but of the art, ingenuity and method that the said Francesco employs in his buildings,

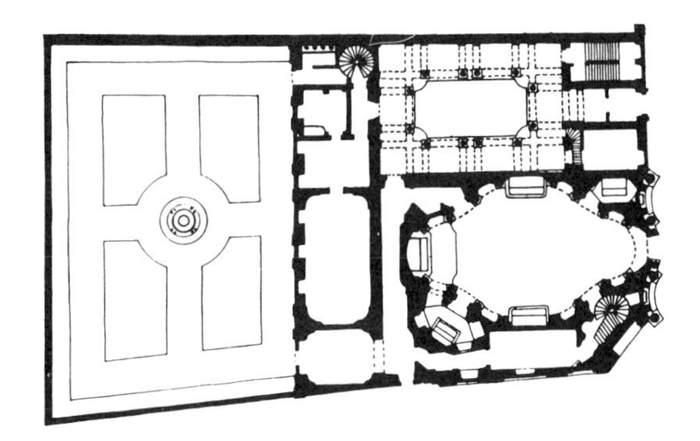

710 *Plan of the convent of S. Carlo alle Quattro Fontane*

arranging the material in such a way for the artificers, that that work, which should take many days, is made extremely easy even though in fact it is very difficult, and they perform it as though it were smooth and straightforward: Because the said Francesco himself guides the bricklayer's trowel, the stuccoer's palate-knife, the carpenter's saw and the stone-carver's chisel, the tile-worker's hammer and the ironworker's file. So that the Value of his buildings is great; but not their expense, as his rivals criticize: for this comes from no other source than the industry of his genius.'

S. Luca and S. Carlo, despite the differences in taste and in degree of departure from traditional models, indicated a basically similar tendency, in contrast to that of Bernini. It aimed at attaining, in architecture, the same degree of personal involvement and intensification of effects obtained previously in literature and the figurative arts; it required a maximum of expressive tension on all occasions, and aimed at an unusual product, a precious isolated exception, and all the more valid the less it was affected by the environmental context. This tendency asserted an equally unusual historicity of its own, and excluded the openness to all history of Bernini's classicism; it was not concerned with the general thread, but with some past experiments – such as that of Michelangelo – set in an intentional present; in this way it aimed at salvaging the hypotheses that had been discarded, the possibilities excluded from the historical process, rather than the solutions confirmed by experiment. The work of architecture was designed bearing in mind a generic public, rather than a specific circle; it was to be a novelty, like a book or musical score, and brought the personality of the author into the foreground, into a direct dialogue with the public.

But in architecture the institutional obstacles – the shadow cast by the client, the complication of the executive process – and stylistic obstacles – the unvarying nature of the classical repertoire – made this thesis almost untenable. Furthermore not even Borromini, who was certainly the most committed, was inclined to pay the price of a total break, i.e. to accept the precarious, imperfect and inconclusive character of a truly unbiased mode of research, and here lay the weakness of his position; his most original works had always to conclude harmoniously, to be perfectly finished in every detail, to allow no contradiction to persist. Thus neither Borromini nor Pietro da Cortona was in a position to replace existing tradition by a new experiment; they could only presuppose it, and oppose it with an internal polemic, destined to be short-lived.

The problem of duration, in fact, was the hardest of all for the two architects beginning their careers in the 1630s. It is worth noting that their architectural careers began in 1634, the year after Galileo's trial; if perhaps the anticipation of a great cultural revival, widespread earlier in other fields, did influence their work, undoubtedly this hope was already on the point of collapse. The Roman ruling class offered growing resistance to every kind of innovation and dominated architects' opportunities in the most rigid way, and architects had no alternative routes available to them, unlike Galileo who published his *Nuove scienze* in Leiden in 1638.

Faced with these difficulties the two artists, whom we have so far presented in a parallel fashion, reacted in two different ways. Pietro da Cortona, connected as a painter to the cultural establishment of the time, devoted himself to architecture only sporadically, and was increasingly less committed; in 1656 he designed the façade of S. Maria della Pace, and in 1658 that of S. Maria in via Lata, interpreting two different environmental situations with extraordinary finesse and making use of Bernini's great example, but he gave up the policy of realizing a new and self-sufficient space that had been stated with S. Luca. This policy was followed up only in the theoretical plans for piazza Colonna and the enlargement of piazza del Gesù, manifestly unconcerned with possibilities of actual implementation. In a letter of 1646,[36] the artist, now fifty years old, lamented having 'always had bad luck in those matters' (i.e. architecture) and regards this situation as irredeemable; 'If I do have any regrets, it would be that I have not been able further to study the profession of painting. Architecture serves me only for my amusement.'

Borromini, on the other hand, pursued his architectural programme unremittingly and indeed relied upon his specialization as pure architect, the result of an executive apprenticeship rather than of the practice of the figurative arts. He chose his clients from the lesser religious orders, less drawn to the traditional noble models, and worked for the court only for a brief period, under the pontificate of Innocent X, even then becoming involved in serious disagreements; he subordinated his private life rigidly to his professional activity, and even, on many occasions, gave up reasonable recompense, so as not to sacrifice his artistic freedom; he made various friends among his clients, for instance Virgilio Spada and Juan de S. Bonaventura, but did not rely on any responsible collaborator and worked alone, like Michelangelo whom he chose as his model.

But similarity with the lot of Michelangelo or of other artists in conflict with society was only partial; Michelangelo's vocation or Caravaggio's misadventures were the product of a human difficulty that preceded the cultural one and which was reflected only partly in their work as artists; Borromini, on the other hand, suffered the consequences of a purely artistic difficulty and ended by sacrificing his destiny as a human being to this difficulty, to the point of suicide in 1667; this very suicide, in fact, revealed the falsity of his position and was the prototype of the professional dramas to be experienced by

711 *Façade of S. Maria della Pace, Rome, seen frontally from the access road*

712 *Façade of S. Maria in via Lata, Rome, seen from the Corso*

avant-garde artists from this moment onwards, brought into being by a conception of art as unconditional commitment.

Borromini's career from 1634 to 1667 was impressively consistent; after the convent of the Trinitari he built the Filippini house (1637–43), completed the Palazzo della Sapienza (1642–62) and the Propaganda Fide (1647–62), carried out the restoration of S. Giovanni in Laterano (1646–9) and the transformation of S. Agnese in piazza Navona (1652–7); his last work was the façade of S. Carlino (1664–7).

The church of S. Ivo alla Sapienza, executed in the middle of this cycle of experiments, is his most successful work (Figs 713–20). The design is absolutely independent of traditional models, not only in its unusual hexagonal plan, but because the hexagon and six surrounding lobes, alternating in shape, can in no way be distinguished as main space and secondary spaces. In fact the wall is decorated with an order of pilasters which meet sharply between one lobe and the next, and do not anywhere give form to the hexagonal prism. The entablature of the order exactly repeated the perimeter of the plan, and the ceiling springs directly from this perimeter, its dome shape gradually attenuated with the convergence of the arches upon the circular opening of the lantern.

This time the plan was not the result of the manipulation of a regular model, but of an original geometrical construction which employs regular figures in a new combination: two interlocking triangles which form a star with six points, replaced or blunted by six circles. This figure, clearly recognizable, dominates the horizontal section of the space at all heights, but since the roof curves upwards until its level coincides with the horizontal, the effect of the figure on the shape of the ceiling gradually decreases, and finally merges with the circle, from which the lantern springs.

Here too, as in S. Carlo, the articulation of the space is achieved by anamorphosis, but

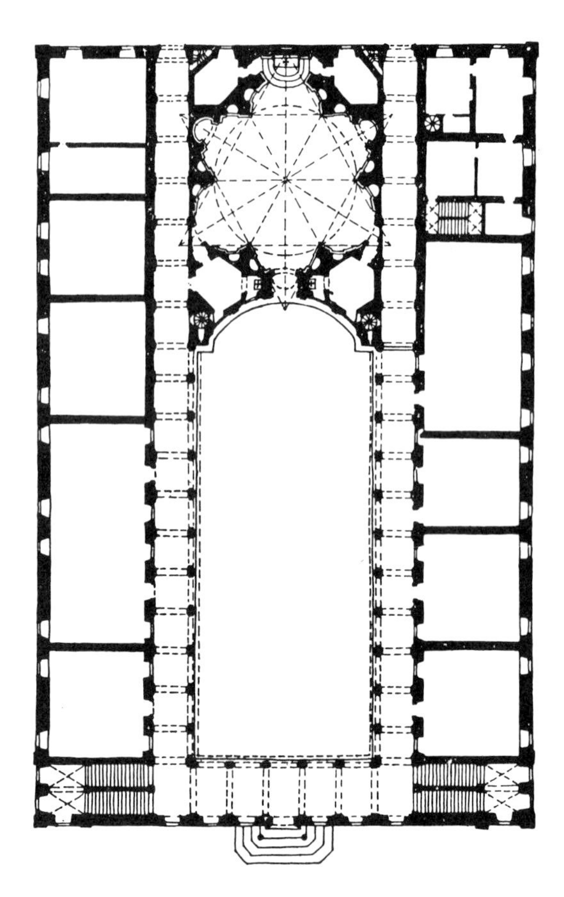

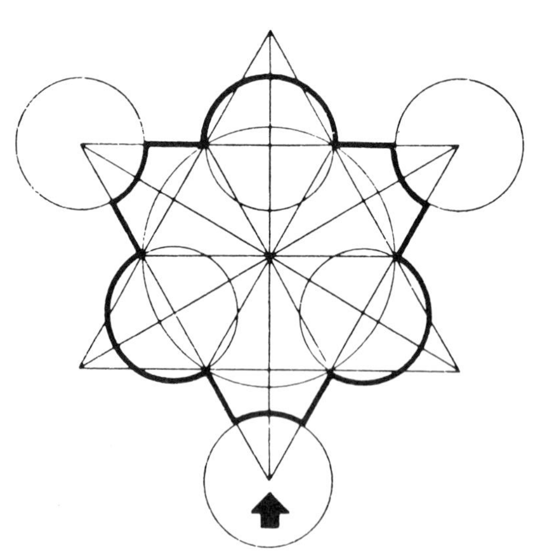

713–715 *General plan, geometrical schema and axial view of the courtyard of S. Ivo alla Sapienza, Rome, by Borromini*

this is developed in terms of elevation rather than plan, and according to a necessary law, inherent in the very organism. Borromini used this technique to reinforce the symmetry of the space around the vertical axis, hence the perspective nature of the general composition, but rejected the usual perspective hierarchy between the parts and the whole, and gave an ambiguity to the function of the architectural order, which serves only to state and rhythmically to mark the main figure of the organism, but not to give form to the articulations between the spatial elements of the empty space, and is fused with the

716 *The roof of S. Ivo*

717–719 *A detail from S. Ivo and two of Borromini's designs for the floor*

720 *S. Ivo, seen from the road behind the church*

other wall decorations, in relation to which it functions as a purely two-dimensional framework. He thus demonstrated the possibility of generalizing the traditional rules of composition, and of attaining the usual rationalization of spatial relations by other means, using other and more complex outlines. The work is an active demonstration of this thesis; the compositional law should not be too soon perceived in its single parts, but must instantly be realized in the building as a whole, to produce the 'marvellous' theorized about by men of letters; the anomalies of the plot are justified by the regularity of the solution.

The organic nature of the inner space has its counterpart in the independence between interior and exterior. S. Ivo, like many of Borromini's other organisms, derives from the superimposition of two different shells, one facing inner space and one facing outer space. The task, in both cases, of composing a complete and definitive spectacle, demands a high degree of disengagement between the two. In this case the church is drowned by the volume of the palazzo by Giacomo della Porta, and only the dome protrudes above the roof; for this reason Borromini preferred to shape it as an autonomous organism – a high drum with six equal lobes, topped by an extravagant lantern with a spiral finial – to be viewed frontally along the axis of the courtyard or obliquely from the square behind, above the horizontal cornice of the palazzo (Figs 715, 720).

The commission he received in 1646 for the restoration of S. Giovanni in Laterano (Fig. 721) put Borromini face to face with an illustrious theme, comparable to that of St Peter's which was occupying Bernini. But both the conditions of the work and the intentions of the designer were completely different; with S. Giovanni it was not a matter of gradually bringing to maturity a series of solutions, of fitting them into a long cycle of building activity, but of transforming the medieval church within an extremely limited space of time, because of the imminence of the holy year 1650; furthermore the coherence pursued by Borromini was not of a historical nature, and it was precisely the limited length of time available that enabled him to design a scheme straight off, a gigantic scenario, possibly transforming the festive adornment for the solemn occasion into a permanent architectural covering.[37] For Bernini's diachronic continuity Borromini substituted his own synchronic continuity; the occasion of a single day was contrasted with a procedure that was prolonged in time.

Innocent X's programme provided for the transformation of the original body with a nave and two pairs of aisles, retaining the old transept and much of the masonry. Borromini agreed to adapt his architecture to the original masonry shell, but not to confuse it with the already existing elements, as Bernini did in 1655 in S. Maria del Popolo; he preferred to renounce distributive invention rather than decorative continuity, and only unwillingly resigned himself to retaining the flat sixteenth-century ceiling. In these conditions the plan was limited to the choice of a new rhythmical element, which in the aisles included a pair of adjoining bays, and in the nave was extended to a complex wall motif. The complication of this element hindered a simultaneous understanding of the whole sequence, and made a successive understanding necessary; the observer first compares the parts that are different and complementary within the motif, and perceives the general rhythmic law only when, as he starts to move, he sees the same parts reappear, in the same order, in the following motif. Thus any consideration of the overall proportion of the space loses its importance, and all attention is concentrated on the rhythmic repetition.

In ideological terms Borromini's thesis was no different from that of Bernini; both accepted the permanent value of the classical ideal – hence of the reference to ancient models and correspondence of forms with

721 *Borromini's restoration of the basilica of S. Giovanni in Laterano, Rome*

geometric positions – and both wanted to broaden the current repertoire indefinitely, to translate the potential universality of the rules into reality. But for Bernini this range was to be formed over the course of time, through successive homogeneous contributions, and only by fitting into this process was it possible to broaden it further, while for Borromini it was always possible to put oneself outside this process and discover its alternatives through personal research. For Bernini the inexhaustibility of classicism was successive in nature, for Borromini it was simultaneous; the validity of the results was assured for Bernini by incorporation into a collective experience, for Borromini by a personal one. Bernini's position was no less demanding than that of his rival, and met with no fewer difficulties at a more inward level, since that faith in the universality of classicism was no longer a social reality, as in the sixteenth century; but Bernini, starting from the understanding of the course of modern classicism, by now two centuries old, understood the untimeliness of Borromini's rigour, while for Borromini, who had to prove the validity of his programme for the broadening of classicism on his own, rigour was a primary requirement: only by building other compositional models with his own efforts, as coherent as those arrived at after successive corrections in the course of time, did it become possible to present them as alternatives to the current ones. Borromini committed himself to this attempt with all the resources of his extraordinary talent; he studied the possible variants of all the traditional elements, and particularly the standardized ones, to the point of largely sacrificing their recognizability; he attempted a whole series of new symbolic associations; he supervised modes of executive procedure with exceptional severity, and concentrated on these to enrich further the range of effects available; he sought precedents to justify his innovations in peripheral sectors or those forgotten by tradition. This research was almost always expended on separate episodes, and did not hold good beyond a certain scale of dimension; furthermore, in his desire to obtain an absolute connection, he often ended by revealing some marginal but unsurmountable contradiction, such as those connected with black and white paving,[38] which betrayed the contradictory character of the initial thesis.

The reputations of the two great rivals throws another light on their initial disagreement. Their ideals were both in a certain sense out-of-date; they did not open a new cycle of experiments, based on the reaffirmation of the universality of classicism; rather they concluded the era in which this universality was valid as a functioning certainty. Bernini's work served as a model for the formation of a new, expanded tradition, which dominated much of Italian and European production, including both aristocratic and popular production; the freedom of his research was translated into a broader range of possible solutions and made it possible to set aside the dangerous problem of the limits of classicism with greater ease. Borromini's work, on the other hand, influenced aristocratic production, as far as his overall compositions were concerned – and from the second half of the seventeenth century they became the main examples for *avant-garde* European experiment, from Guarini to Neumann – whereas it influenced popular production in terms of details. These, which in Borromini's work were systematically subordinated to the whole, formed an impressive repertoire of geometrical and figurative inventions on their own account, based on a thorough knowledge of building techniques (in stone, marble, brick, stucco, plaster and iron), not only extremely varied but classifiable into a coherent system, as critical analysis later showed.[39] Borromini's mode of procedure did not authorize the detachment of this repertoire, which had to be considered as a by-product of the main research, but common experience carried out this operation not without cause; in fact the

722, 723 *A basin in the refectory of the Filippini, Rome and a detail from S. Ivo by Borromini*

extending of classicism, which Borromini attempted in vain in an ideological sense, was easily achieved in an empirical sense; from Brunelleschi onwards no artist had enriched the architectural repertoire with so many new individual solutions, developing the morphological potentialities of ordinary processes. In these inventions Borromini gave voice and formal dignity to an authentic popular experience, that of the builder's craftsmanship long relegated to the margins of architectural culture, and in this way, in contrast to his *avant-garde* programme, he encouraged a new popular building culture, which emerged only in details, while the general structures remained dominated by the culture of the ruling class.

The prestige of the Roman school was at its height towards the last third of the seventeenth century. From 1664 to 1665 Bernini was making his journey through France, certainly the most spectacular ceremony ever organized by a sovereign – who called himself the Sun King – in homage to an artist; in 1666 the French Académie des Beaux Arts set up the *prix de Rome*, its permanent representation in the city that was to be considered as the authentic source of international classicism from now on. But the inventive fervour of the Roman school died out in the last third of the century and new models of European art now came from the great cities of the north. What was left in Rome was a cultural prestige which remained unassailed up to the Romantic era and a building tradition operating with continuity at least until the first third of the eighteenth century, which gave a homogeneous and somehow definitive character to the city setting.

A host of architects, partly from the school of Bernini – Carlo Rainaldi (1611–91), Carlo Fontana (1634–1714), Mattia de' Rossi (1637–75), G. B. Contini (1641–1723) – worked without introducing any innovations comparable to the preceding ones, but managed to add the finishing touches to the urban form

724 *The Spada chapel in S. Girolamo della Carità, Rome, by Borromini*

in accordance with a common taste; in this period the city that had been shaken by the contributions of Sixtus V was settling down into an architectural balance which reflected the achievement of economic and social stability. The most significant works gave their character to some of the key points of the city: the completion of the twin churches at the heads of the trident of piazza del Popolo (Bernini and Rainaldi, 1661–78), the exterior apse of S. Maria Maggiore which determined the appearance of piazza Esquilino around Fontana's obelisk (Rainaldi, 1669–75), the layout of the harbour of Ripetta (Specchi, 1693–5), the square in front of S. Ignazio (Raguzzini, 1727–8), the flight of steps at Trinità dei Monti (Specchi and De Sanctis, 1721–5), the Trevi fountain (Salvi, 1732). Schemes for town houses and *ville suburbane* were also being carried out: Villa Borghese (1605), Villa Ludovisi (1621), Villa Sacchetti (1625), Villa Doria Pamphili (1644), were followed by Villa Albani (1732), Villa Lancellotti, Villa Massimo and Villa Chigi.

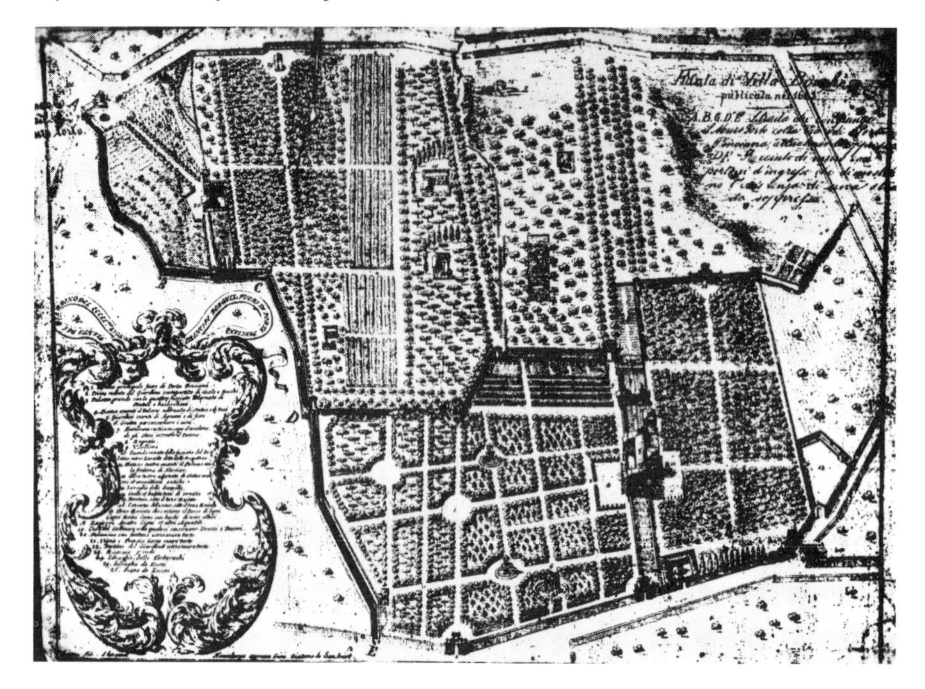

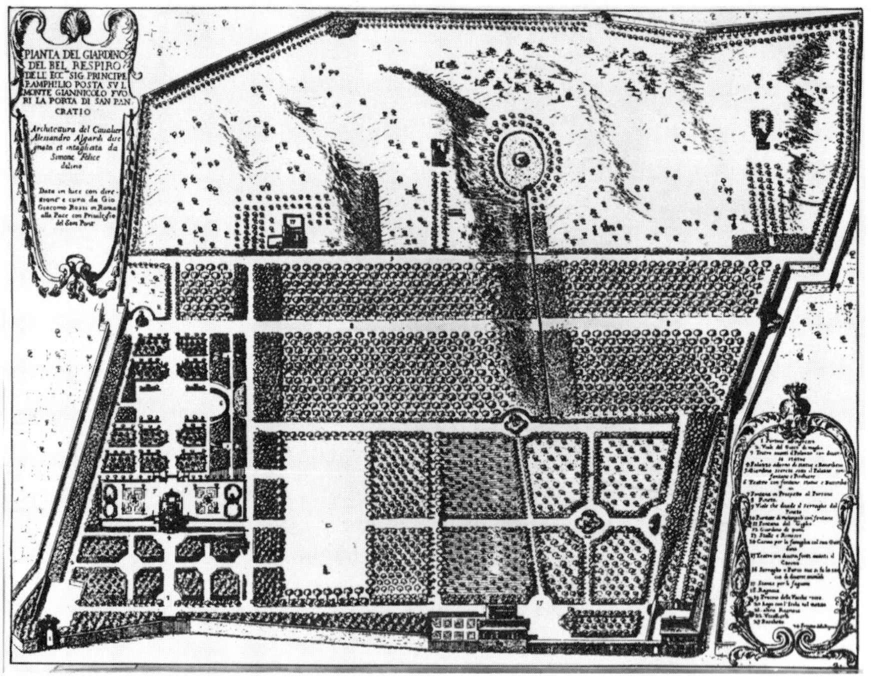

725, 726 *Plans of two seventeenth-century villas in Rome: Villa Borghese and Villa Doria Pamphili*

727 *View of Villa Doria Pamphili*

728 *Piazza Navona, Rome, seen from the fontana del Moro, looking north, before the square was closed to traffic*
729 *An entertainment in piazza Navona in 1648*

In this way, the belt of parks that concluded the expansion of the papal city towards the hills was completed, particularly in the eastern arc; this green belt, which separated the city not from other built-up areas but from the empty expanse of the surrounding countryside, marked the definitive border of the urban form and placed immediately beyond the margin of the built-up zone the tree-filled landscape which had now been completely eliminated within the city fabric. The plan by G. B. Nolli (1748) presents a vivid image of the city at the end of this cycle of transformations (Fig. 734).

The same process of arrangement took place in the small urban centres surrounding Rome, almost always isolated amid expanses of land that were static both visually and productively. Among the most important schemes were the street tridents of Albano and Genzano, the planned extensions for S. Martino al Cimino, S. Gregorio a Sassola (Figs 732–3), Roccagorga, the princely villas in the Castelli district: Villa Mondragone and Villa Torlonia at Frascati, Villa Barberini at Castelgandolfo and Villa Chigi at Ariccia.

The further transformations introduced into this urban and rural landscape – not until 1870 so as noticeably to change its character – were to have their causes and their models outside the Roman scene.

The alternatives of the European avant-garde

The innovating proposals of the Roman school, as we have noted, were important in terms of the legacy of classicism, and the more decisively they reaffirmed the universality of the classical repertoire, the more radical they were. The programmes of Bernini and Borromini coincided on this point, and the various experiments found a reason for unity, while they remained irreconcilable and unquestionable as personal choices.

The European experiments – influenced largely by the Roman ones – differed first according to whether and to what degree they sprang from a classical tradition already previously assimilated: for this reason they sometimes produced a vindication *of* classicism, against different previous traditions or against an incomplete assimilation of this same classical repertoire, sometimes a vindication *in* classicism, similar to the Roman one. Their common character remains the tendentiousness of choice, which makes the use of the word *avant-garde* plausible, conceived though it was for the advanced experiments in European artistic culture between the end of the nineteenth century and the beginning of the twentieth. Their result was not the establishment of a new unified movement, but the stabilization, from then on, of a range of alternative choices, which were to be co-ordinated by absolute

730, 731 *The Fontana della Barcaccia in piazza di Spagna, Rome*

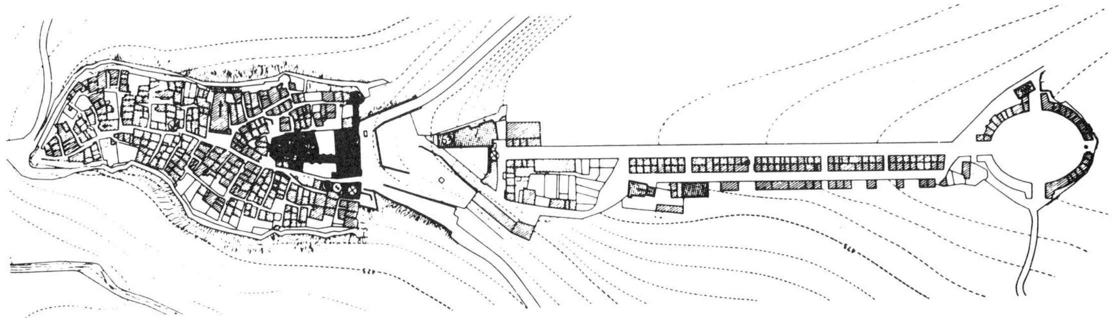

732, 733 *General view and plan of the seventeenth-century extension of S. Gregorio a Sassola near Rome*

734 *The street network of Rome in the plan by G. B. Nolli, 1748*

régimes on the political and organizational level in the last third of the seventeenth century.

In Spain the assimilation of Italian classicism took place in the reign of Philip II and coincided with the moment in which the official building repertoire widespread throughout the countries of the Counter-Reformation was formed, in its turn largely influenced by Spanish contributions; one need think only of the type of the Jesuit church, which if it also depended upon possibly predominant humanistic or ancient models, found an immediate echo in Spanish tradition, and was used in Spain longer than in any other country. Francisco Bautista, whom we have already mentioned and who used this typology, was born in 1594 and was therefore a contemporary of Pietro da Cortona, Bernini, Borromini and, in his own country, Velazquez and Zurbarán. Throughout the whole of the seventeenth century, as in Rome during the early years, there did not seem to be any relation between the novelties of the pictorial experiments and the conformism of the architectural ones. The tragic political conflicts of the age of Olivares, the splendour of the poetry of Tirso de Molina and Calderón, the range of human experiences, both courtly and popular, reflected in

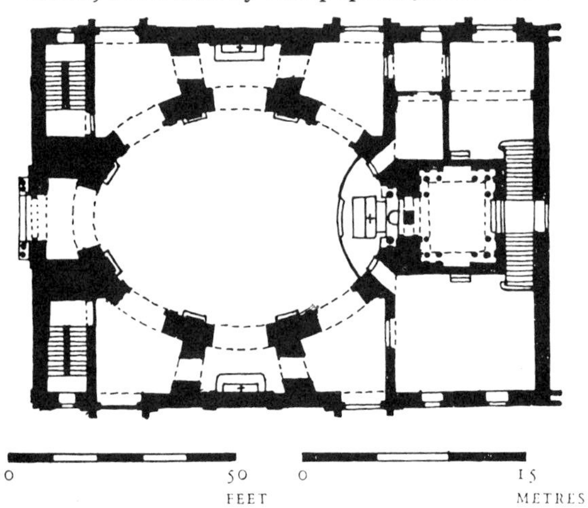

736 *Plan of the church of the Desamparados, Valencia*

735 *Chapel of S. Isidro, church of S. Andrès, Madrid*

the painting of Velazquez did not find a proportionate parallel in architecture, but only a sumptuous backdrop.

The first architectural innovations occurred around the middle of the century; in 1642 Pedro de la Torre built the chapel of S. Isidro adjoining the church of S. Andrès in Madrid (Fig. 735) where the low squared nave was reduced to a vestibule for the great domed presbytery, decorated with free-standing columns; in 1647 Diego Martinez Ponce de Urrana designed the church of the Desamparados in Valencia (Fig. 736), which has an oval plan inscribed in a rectangle and presented a typological invention frequently used, from now onwards, in the whole area of Spanish influence: the *camarín*, a richly decorated chapel enclosed and raised behind the presbytery, which served to approach the main altar with greater devotion; thus the liturgical space was doubled to become two spaces, communicating not spatially but only psychologically, through the thickness of the common altar, designed on two intentionally different scales. From the 1630s onwards the first classical *retablo*

737, 738 *Façade of S. Pablo, Valladolid and façade of S. Miguel de los Reyes, Valencia*

façades appeared in the Levant and in Andalusia – for instance that of S. Miguel de los Reyes at Valencia, begun in 1632 by Martin de Olinda (Fig. 738) – which took up a motif already developed in the late Middle Ages (Fig. 737) and established a significant correspondence between the external façade and the end portion of the inner space; neither has a perspective relationship with the organism of the church, but they emerge as autonomous objects, with their own spatial depth – the decorations are arranged on various superimposed planes – and were executed by groups of specialized craftsmen.

These innovations were developed in Spain and the American colonies from the second half of the seventeenth century. We are still in the field of the typological norm; architects invented some new types but did not dispute the principle of repetition which seemed inherent in Spanish artistic culture. An invention independent of typologies became possible only at the time of the Churriguera brothers, in the last decades of the century.

In Germany the course of architecture was altered by the Thirty Years' War (1618–48) which interrupted building production almost everywhere; thus as late as the second half of the seventeenth century an autonomous tradition based on the principles of classicism had still not come into being and the German princes still had regular recourse to Italian artists for their more demanding works. In Bavaria the Italian wife of the elector Ferdinand Maria, Henrietta Adelaide of Savoy (1652–76), tried unsuccessfully to summon Guarini, and from 1663 onwards was employing Agostino Barelli who began the church of the Theatines and the Nymphenburg palace in Munich. This was not a period of innovatory choices, but still one that tended to combine foreign styles, which in Germany was linked closely and directly with the international court style of absolut-

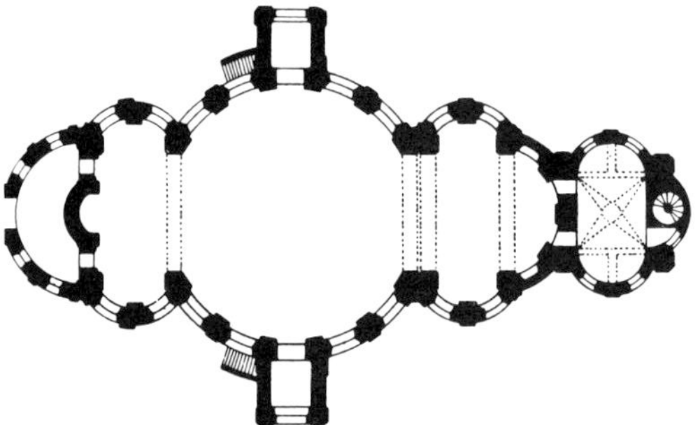

739, 740 *View and plan of the pilgrimage church of S. Maria Birnbaum near Aichach*

ism, from the late seventeenth century onwards. On the other hand an unsuspected liveliness of invention emerged at the level of popular production. In 1661, not far from the Bavarian capital, the builder Konstantin Pader organized the building of the pilgrimage church of S. Maria Birnbaum near Aichach, worked on by the peasants of the whole region. It is a composite organism, arranged around a dome and possibly inspired by the church of the abbey of Volders in the Tyrol, designed in 1620 by the amateur Ippolito Guarinoni. The interior is still incoherent; but the exterior – where the traditional stylistic connotations almost disappear and the volumes of the constructional elements are combined with astonishing skill – looks back to the last works of the late Gothic and forward to the developments of late German baroque (Figs 739–40). A little later the Dientzenhofer brothers met Guarini in Prague and grafted the contributions of the most up-to-date Italian culture on to local tradition. None the less the popular mould continued to condition the new tendencies in German architecture and we shall discuss this more fully later on.

In France the Renaissance repertoire was used for over a century in court production, though mainly as a system of details. The Italian influence continued in the second half of the sixteenth century, encouraged by the presence of Catherine de Médicis (queen from 1547 and regent from 1560), and produced a vast range of formal combinations, comparable to the linguistic blendings of the *Pléiade*. Du Bellay's manifesto came out in 1549, while de l'Orme was starting on the château of Anet, and Ronsard's literary companions were the contemporaries of de l'Orme and Lescot.

At the end of the century, and particularly from the reign of Henri IV (1598–1610), the tendency to classify the legacy of the Renaissance critically – in both a rational and a national sense – emerged; in our field it was further encouraged by the resumption of building production and the vast programme of public works. One could tentatively pursue the preceding comparison and establish a parallel between the reforming movement in art and the literary reform called for by Malherbe, but the comparison would need to be amended by two considerations.

In the first place the flexibility of the literary debate, in comparison with the artistic, established an increasingly marked time lag between the two orders of experiment. The contemporaries of Malherbe were the architects employed by Henri IV, Louis Métezeau (1562–1615) and Salomon de Brosse (1562–1626), versatile builders, accustomed to collective work, competent and stylistically easy-going, whereas Malherbe was already an isolated figure, polemical and intransigent; Malherbe admired the works of Henri IV at Fontainebleau, and described them in a famous quatrain:[40]

'Beaux et grands bâtiments d'éternelle structure
Superbes de matières, et d'ouvrages divers,
Où le plus digne roi qui soit en l'univers
Aux miracles de l'art fait céder la nature.'

But the admiration was purely rhetorical, and concerned only generically the jumble of buildings built one after the other within a century by François I, Charles IX and Henri IV: rather it established a future ideal, and evokes for us the unimpeachable composition of Vaux and of Versailles; literature was already engaged in its adventure with orderly reason.

In the second place, the force of Malherbe's polemic derived from the possibility of referring to common linguistic usage, of learning 'French in place Maubert', from the '*crocheteurs* of the Port-au-Foin'.[41] For architects there was no reference of this kind; there was nature – which in this case was an ideal set at the margins of sensible experience, definable precisely by leaving the usual representational conventions out of consideration – and classical antiquity, i.e. an ideal situated at the margins of human history. Neither of the two could be given in empirical form, and to make the repertoire of current forms tally with these models basically meant working within a given cultural tradition, rejecting certain conventions in favour of certain others. This operation – carried out in the following generation by Jacques Lemercier (1585–1654), Nicolas Poussin (1594–1666) and François Mansart (1598–1666) – was more superficial, and had less widely felt repercussions than its literary counterpart: the *querelles* which kept the world of letters in a perpetual state of agitation – linked to endless moral, scientific, social and political interests – arrived in the world of the arts muted, and already substantially resolved, for here these interests no longer had any hold.

In fact the new civilization that was being formed in France gave considerably less weight to visual elements than the Italian Renaissance had done. D'Alembert, who summed up the formation of modern classicism in 1750, outlined the relations between literature and the figurative arts as follows, reversing the approach that had grown up in Italy from the sixteenth to seventeenth centuries:[42]

'The fine arts are so closely linked to belles-lettres, that the very tendency to cultivate one also invites the perfecting of the other. . . .

But it must be admitted that the rebirth of painting and sculpture was far more rapid than that of poetry and music; and the reason is not hard to find. When the masterpieces of the ancients, in the various genres, began to be studied, those which had escaped the ravages of superstition and barbarity in large numbers immediately attracted the attention of the artists concerned. To imitate works by Praxiteles and Pheidias one had simply to do exactly as they had done, and an artist with talent had simply to observe attentively; so that Raphael and Michelangelo were very soon able to take their art to a peak of perfection which has not been surpassed since. In general, since the object of painting and sculpture falls rather within the domain of the senses, these arts could not fail to precede poetry, since the senses would inevitably be more immediately struck by the sensible and tangible beauties of the ancient statues, than the imagination would manage to grasp the more fleeting intellectual beauties of the ancient writers. Whence, when it began to discover them, the imitation of these same beauties, imperfect because of its servility and the foreign language in which it was expressed, could not but harm the progress of this same imagination. Let us imagine for a moment painters and sculptors deprived of the privilege of being able to use the same material used by the ancients: if they had, like the men of letters, lost time through the investigation and clumsy imitation of such material, rather than having recourse to another, suited to the imitation of the works they admired, they would undoubtedly have proceeded much more slowly and would still be engaged in the search for marble.'

This description – which does not correspond to the historical order of the facts – does express the hierarchy of cultural experience established during the same period.

Artistic beauty was considered as an affair for the senses, literary beauty as one for the intellect; this theoretical distinction concealed an institutional and social distinction, of which we shall talk at length later. The literary form raised many subtle questions about relation to contents, the limitations of language and so on, while artistic form was reduced to conformity, and therefore regarded as reproducible with absolute exactness, with the sole exception of the differences of material. The dualism between *res cogitans* and *res extensa* relegated the visual arts to the periphery of culture and assigned to them an illustrative, subordinate task.

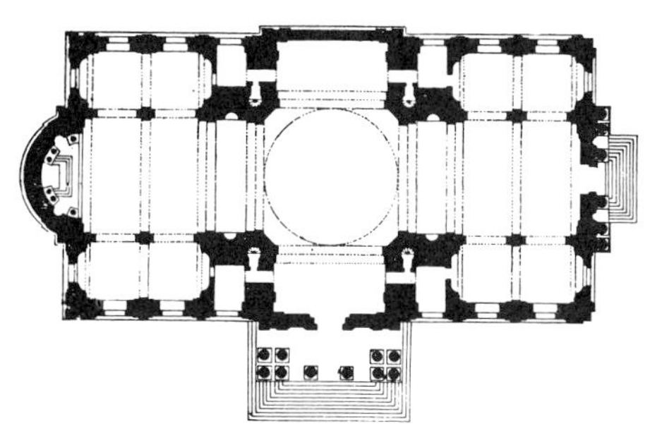

741, 742 *Church of the Sorbonne, Paris, by Lemercier*

The eighteenth-century clarity of this discourse is naturally foreign to the climate of the early seventeenth century; none the less the decisive choices, which made the development of French classicism possible, were made at this time; the relations of Lemercier, Poussin and Mansart with their contemporaries Corneille, Descartes and Pascal were already established in these terms.

Lemercier, a member of an already famous family of Parisian builders, was in Rome from 1607 until 1614, during the crucial years of the completion of St Peter's; but perhaps, as Blunt suggests, he was more interested in the academic and sedate style of the Sistine period – Fontana and della Porta – than in the typological innovations of Maderno; his master was probably Rosato Rosati, who in 1612 designed the church of S. Carlo ai Catinari which Lemercier imitated in the church of the Sorbonne (Figs 741–2). He was able to fuse the traditional eclecticism of early seventeenth-century French architecture with the rigour of the Roman style and this combination earned him great professional success; in 1624 he was commissioned by Louis XIII to build the extension of the Louvre courtyard and by Richelieu to build the Sorbonne (1626), his château in Indre-et-Loire (1631) and his town residence (from 1624).

This combination of logic and empiricism was even more fruitful in less monumentally demanding subjects. In 1623 the duke of Liancourt commissioned him to extend his Paris *hôtel* and here Lemercier laid down the prototype of this genre of town residence, incorporated into a continuous block, hence devoid of external regularity and based on a sequence of inner spaces – a courtyard with access for coaches, a pedestrian courtyard and a garden – each treated as an independent architectural setting; the architect's skill lay in the ingenious distribution of these spaces, without sacrificing either the distributional links or the symmetry of the single motifs. Like an expert director, the architect manoeuvred the architectural spectacle from the wings and his specific ability had to remain hidden (Fig. 743).

Mansart, who came of a more modest family and began his career as an assistant of de Brosse, achieved a more rigorous clarification of style without direct recourse to Italian models – which he probably never visited *in situ* – but with a more subtle process of direct

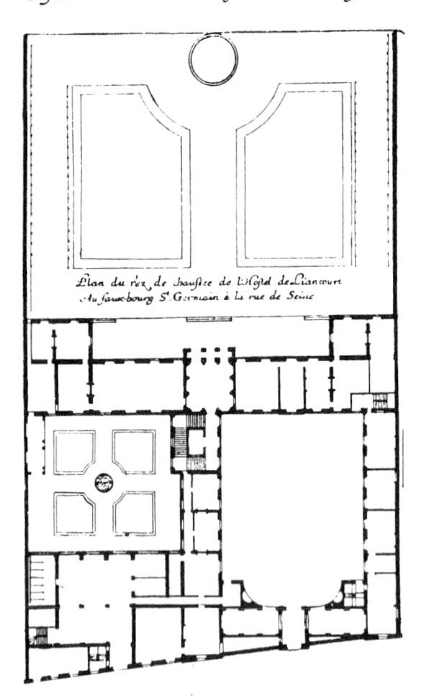

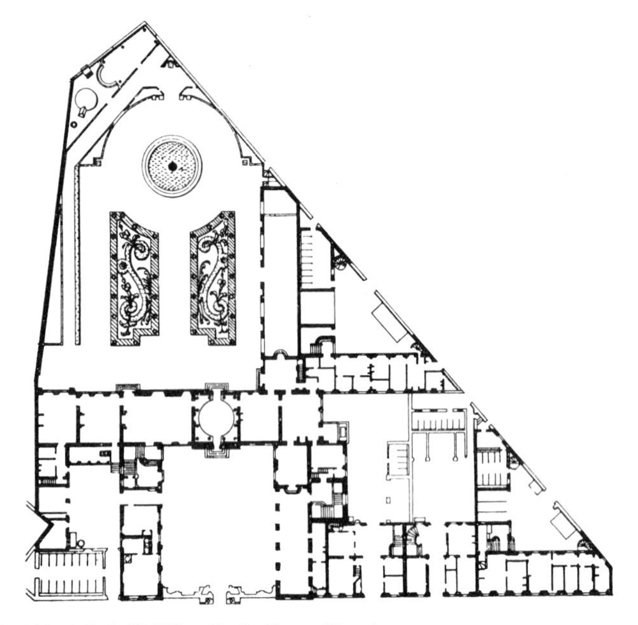

743, 744 *Plans of the Hôtel de Liancourt and the Hôtel de la Vrillière, Paris (from Blunt)*

and indirect criticism; this conscious detachment was all that was needed to obtain a perfectly judged organic quality, completely different from the Italian one hitherto used as an example. His exacting and professional classicism went well beyond that improvised by Lemercier with a divergence comparable to that which distinguished his respective contemporaries in painting, Poussin and Simon Vouet.

He began to work on his own in the 1620s, not for the court but for bourgeois clients who had become rich in the service of the state: Jean de Choisy (who commissioned him to build the château of Balleroy), Noël Brulart (who financed the church of the Visitation in Paris in 1632), Louis de la Vrillière (whose Paris *hôtel* Mansart designed in 1635, cleverly adapting the organism to a very irregular plot) (Fig. 744). In 1635, already famous, he entered into contact with court circles, and was commissioned to rebuild the château of Blois for Gaston d'Orléans; Anne of Austria asked him to design the Val-de-Grâce (from 1645 to 1646) (Figs 745–6) but shortly afterwards transferred the commission to Lemercier; later Colbert asked him for various designs, for the Louvre and St-Denis, but his hard, intransigent character lost him the favour of his clients, and when he died, in 1666, he had already been forgotten in favour of the new generation (Le Vau, Perrault and Le Nôtre).

The plan of the Val-de-Grâce and that of the chapel at Fresnes, probably contemporaneous, demonstrate the extent of François Mansart's cultural hinterland; the distributive point of departure was the Jesuit type with a nave without aisles and end dome; none the less the articulation of the walls was such that it eliminated the continuity of the masonry surfaces, as in the traditional Gothic structures used until the end of the sixteenth century, and the end with its three apses – one of which opened on to the convent choir – is reminiscent of Palladio's Redentore. The Hôtel de la Vrillière, designed in 1635, revealed Mansart's consummate skill in combining symmetry and asymmetry and in lowering the courtly tone without in any way compromising the correctness of the architectural apparatus.

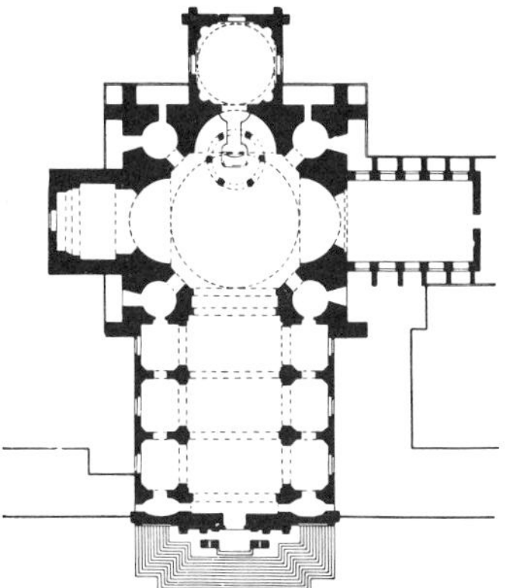

745, 746 *Church of Val-de-Grâce, Paris, by Lemercier and Mansart*

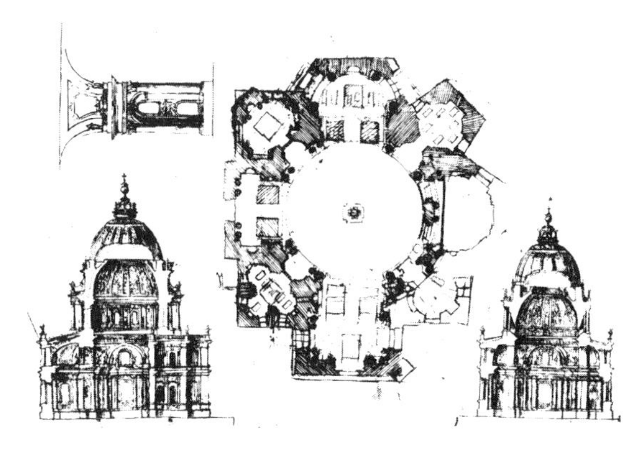

The château of Maisons-Laffitte (Figs 749–54), built from 1642 for René de Longueil, has been preserved with the complete décor as designed by the architect and gives a vivid impression of the synthesis of the arts as seen from this cultural viewpoint. The extremely simple composition – a rectangular C-shaped block framed by two lower wings – is subordinated to a long axial approach, which starts at the entrance on the front esplanade and continues into the gardens behind, thus making any movement of masses not appreciable along this main line quite pointless. The focus of the composition is the projection which marks the meeting-point between built-up volume and landscape axis, and is in fact repeated, with minimal variations, on both façades. This motif, considered according to the criteria of Italian classicism, appears confused and inorganic, because the architectural elements are not distributed in relation to the volumes

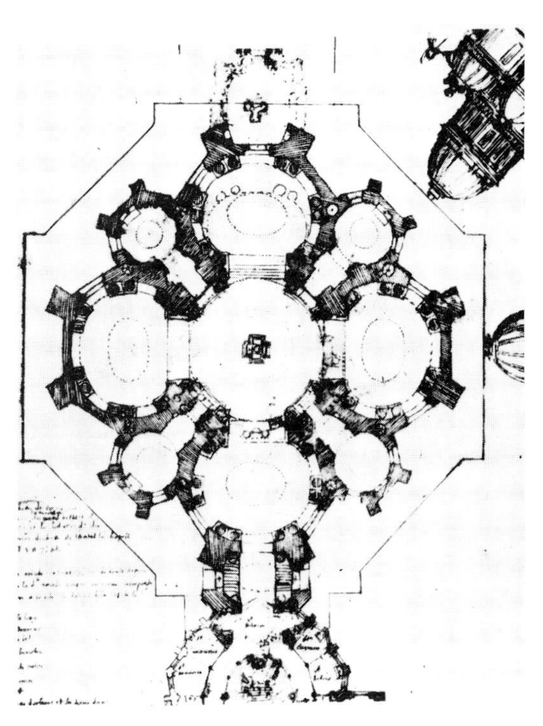

747, 748 *Sketches by Mansart for the royal chapel at St-Denis*

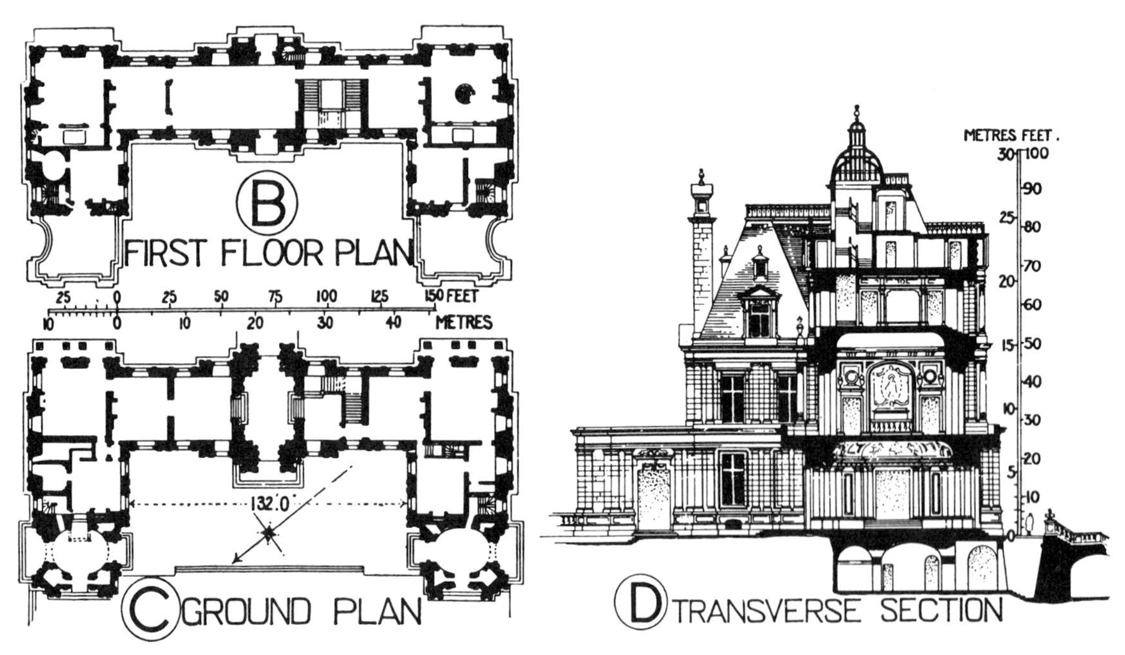

749–751 *Façade, plan and elevation of the château of Maisons-Laffitte*

752, 753 *The central motif of the façade and a detail of the interior of Maisons-Laffitte*

of the building, and appear to be dominated by a graphic logic, appreciable in the design rather than in the reality; but it is calculated in terms of the axis, i.e. it must be viewed as a two-dimensional composition from a considerable distance, and must emerge gradually as a three-dimensional one when it is examined from closer to; for this reason it is not a unitary volume, but a system of plastic elements whose chiaroscuro and projections are calculated to preserve the compositional coherence from the beginning to the end of the approach. The three superimposed orders are arranged on three different floors, with the furthest back protruding at the top to form the pediment and partly interpenetrating the pyramid-shaped roof; beneath this the two other orders stand a little further forward in full relief (with vases placed on the Ionic entablature) as does the further block protruding at the height of the lower order, causing the inner pair of twin columns to disappear. The orders therefore – impeccably proportioned according to the rules of superimposition – do not mark the articulations of the volumes, but constitute a general principle projected on the plane, the mainspring for the whole apparatus of the constructional and decorative elements, perfectly distanced and scaled: columns, pilasters, cornices, but also roofs, chimneys, door and window frames, balustrades, decorations in stone, wood and iron.

The same line of reasoning – more convincing, because of the greater importance of the views juxtaposed – is followed in the interior, for instance in the vestibule and staircase. The articulation of the spaces, elementary in its general lines, is worked out in terms of the plastic elements, which are

754 *Aerial view of Maisons-Laffitte*

presented in an orderly fashion, in the most favourable context, and remain 'clear and distinct' without being superimposed or merging into one another. Each category of decoration, though strictly subordinated to the general design, is present in its own right, and no undue trespassing of sculpture or painting into architecture is considered admissible, at the very moment when Bernini and the Roman artists were developing the opposite thesis; it is believed that Mansart himself designed much of the décor personally, but the means of assigning the various types of decoration to various specialists, hence of obtaining an indefinite perfecting of the architectural décor, was now at hand.

'Chaque ornement en sa place arrêté
Y semblait mis par la nécessité'

as Voltaire was later to write.[43]

Control of this apparatus on a large scale was still lacking; it eluded Mansart and entailed an executive organization still to be created. But the cultural instruments of the great political operation of Louis XIV and Colbert were already partly available.

In England the principle of stylistic fusion was one of the basic elements of the Elizabethan cultural climate, not only in architecture but in many other fields; it was the starting-point for the inventive freedom of the great writers, as for the designers of the great country houses. The building practice of the early seventeenth century saw the coming together of the tradition of the perpendicular Gothic, Flemish decoration drawn from the repertoire of Hieronymus Cock, and decoration from the Italian and French treatises which were circulating widely in England at the time. John Shute's treatise on the classical orders was published as early as 1563,[44] but in the fifty years that followed the orders were never used as instruments to rationalize compositions as a whole: planning remained a continuous process that could not be reduced to intellectual rules, committed to the skills and collective organization of the master builders, as in the Middle Ages.

Classicism came to England *ex abrupto*, under the form of an *avant-garde* discovery and choice, through the work of Inigo Jones (1573–1652), i.e. in circumstances that were absolutely novel. Jones was the oldest of the whole series of innovating architects considered in this chapter; he was born twelve years before Lemercier, the architect with whom, in Europe, he can most aptly be compared, and arrived in Italy at least five years earlier; as far as the English scene was concerned, it has been pointed out that Jones was only nine years younger than Shakespeare and the contemporary of some of the Elizabethan poets, for instance Donne and

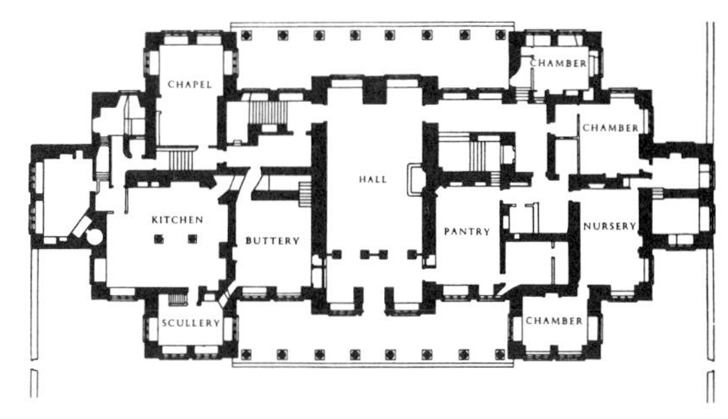

755, 756 *View and plan of Hardwick Hall, 1588*

Ben Jonson; his position *vis-à-vis* the other designers of his time is absolutely unique, not only because of a clash of tendencies (reminiscent of that of Rubens in Flanders and reproducing in reverse that of Caravaggio in Italy, both contemporaries of Jones) but even more because of a difference in professional position. He did not practise another artistic trade such as painting or sculpture, and he had not emerged from a building apprenticeship but was a designer, the first in England consciously to use design not as a craftsman's specialization, but as a universal instrument for the representation and selection of visible forms, in accordance with Italian tradition.[45]

In England the only practical activity where this skill found an application, not being linked to traditional productive activity, was in the design of stage scenery; in fact from 1605 Jones became stage designer at the court of James I, and made a considerable contribution to theatre life at court, one of the items of expense on which the new

757 *Scenery for a tragedy, by Inigo Jones, about 1630–40*

sovereign most eagerly lavished his money. The two instruments of Jones's new scenery were perspective and theatre machinery, derived from the Italian tradition; what concerns us is perspective, which made it possible to distribute the elements of the classical repertoire – architectural orders and so on – throughout an ordered spatial schema, at least in the fiction of the stage (Figs 757–8).

From 1613 to 1614 he guided a group of English nobles on a journey to Italy; from Germany the group went to Milan, Padua, Venice, Vicenza, then through Bologna, Florence and Siena to Rome and Naples; on their way back they went through Rome again, and then through Genoa, from where Jones went back to Venice; throughout his journey he carried a copy of Palladio's *Four Books* and used it as a guide to the study, primarily, of the ancient monuments; in Rome he obtained permission to organize excavations and discovered some ancient statues that he sent to England; in Venice he talked with Scamozzi, now an old man, and possibly learned from him to consider the experiments of modern Italian architecture according to the criteria of faithfulness to classical models.

The notes written by Jones in his Palladio are brief and strictly technical; his only theoretical declaration is contained in a book of sketches of 1615; he believed that 'all these composed ornaments the which proceed out of ye abundance of designers and wear brought in by Michill Angell and his followers' were not applicable to the main structures of buildings, but in 'gardens loggis stucco or ornaments of chimnies pieces'; 'outward ornaments oft [ought] to be sollid, propor-

758 *Country scenery by Inigo Jones for a play in 1638*

sionable according to the rulles, masculine and unaffected'.[46]

From 1615 to 1642 Jones held the post of surveyor of king's works; at this time he was still continuing his activities as a stage designer but transferred his organisms from stage to reality. The first important work, virtually the manifesto of the new English classicism, was the Queen's House in Greenwich (Figs 759–61), described by a gentleman in 1617 as having to be 'finished this summer, yt is saide to be some curious devise of Inigo Jones and will cost above four thousand pounds'.[47] It is a small symmetrical organism like the Palladian villas, enclosed in an impeccable architectural covering 'proportioned according to the rules' (but the regularity of the details contrasts with the singularity of the distribution; the house is cut into two by a road, and the two halves are joined by a bridge).

From 1619 to 1622 Jones built the Banqueting House at Whitehall (Figs 765–6), a first attempt to use the new style in a court building; the theoretical model was the Vitruvian basilica, already interpreted in his own time by Palladio, but modern functional requirements and Jones's reflective character produced a completely new result; classicism was considered as a method which restricted the procedure and not the final outcome of planning. Here, among other things, he also staged the court theatre performances, until in 1625, for fear of damaging the recent paintings by Rubens, he built a special wooden structure, the Masque House.

Between Charles I's ascent to the throne (1626) and the beginning of the Civil War

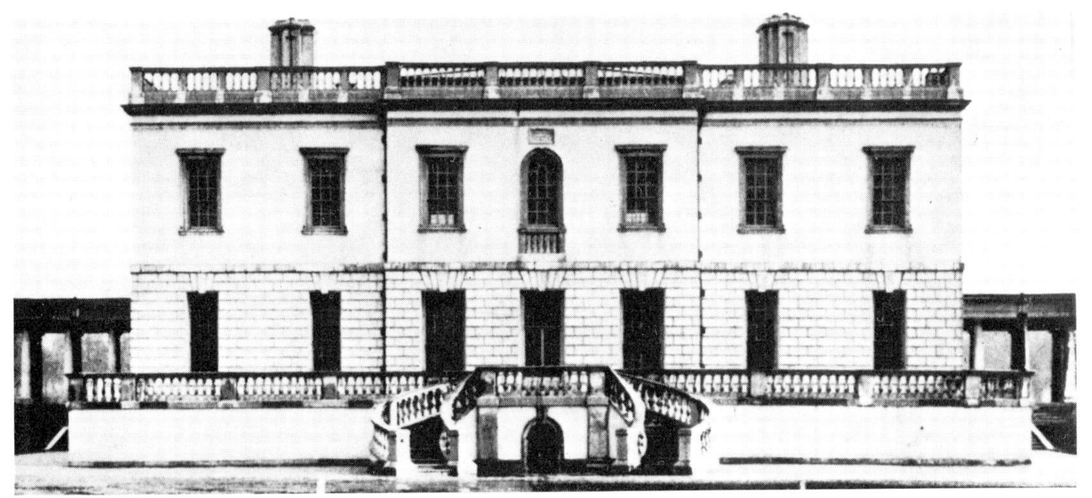

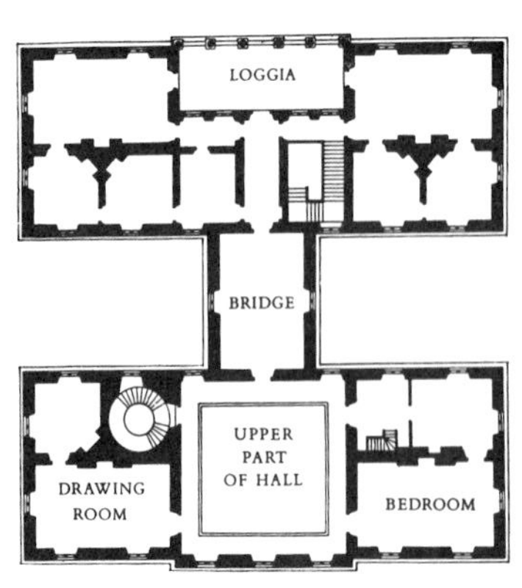

759–761 *Views and plan of the Queen's House, Greenwich, by Inigo Jones*

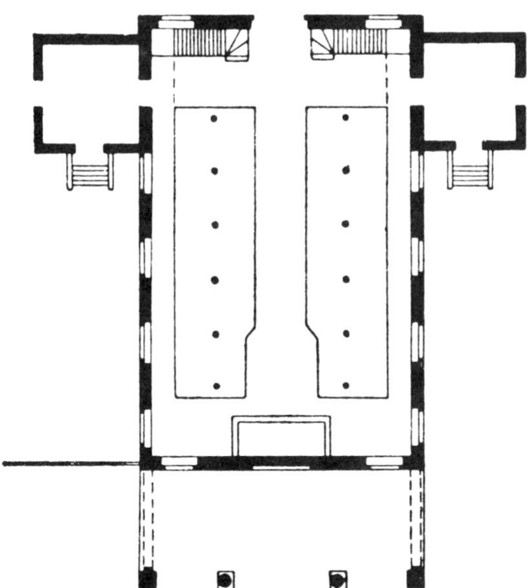

762, 763 *The piazza and church at Covent Garden by Inigo Jones*

764 *Lindsey House, Lincoln's Inn Fields, by Inigo Jones (from Campbell)*

(1642) Jones conceived his most important works: the new interior decoration for the Queen's House (1629), the piazza at Covent Garden (1631) (Figs 762–3) which we shall discuss later on, the restoration of St Paul's (1634) (Fig. 767) and the plans for a complete reconstruction of the Palace of Whitehall (1638), though here the whole organism –

765 *Plan and elevation of the Banqueting House, Whitehall, by Inigo Jones*

being impracticable in the technical and economic conditions of the England of Charles I – was resolved as a theoretical exercise in the antique style. In 1642 Jones left London and his official position was taken over by John Webb (1611–72), the closest of his collaborators; seven years later he died in Somerset House, where Cromwell was housing important state dignitaries.

Jones's artistic programme is characterized by two choices: that of ancient models, already widespread in Italy with all its numerous consequences, and – among the alternatives offered by Italian architectural culture – that of the Venetian classicism of Palladio and Scamozzi, in contrast to the Roman classicism of the post-Michelangelo period.

766 *Interior of the Banqueting House*

767 *The west front of St Paul's cathedral, London, as designed by Inigo Jones (from Campbell)*

The first choice had a clear ideological meaning; starting from the conditions of English architectural culture in the early seventeenth century, Jones rejected the classically inspired decorations that came to him at second or third hand through Italian, French or Flemish publications, and that formed a non-systematic repertoire; he went back to the sources, and in this way cut out every modern, political or religious meaning associated with these forms: the cultural model was ancient Rome, with its prestige as a supreme human example, as in Shakespeare, not Italian or Catholic Rome against which the nationalist and denominational polemic was being waged.

None the less in accepting the ancient models Jones came up against the methodological consequences already experienced in Italian culture: the standardization of the recurrent elements and the perspective organization of living space. In the England of the seventeenth century this methodology could no longer give rise to an intellectual advance comparable with the Italian one of two centuries before, but it was sufficient to move architectural experiment to a different mental level, and made itself felt as a universal instrument to order the various distributional and ceremonial needs of building production, as happened in France and other countries.

Jones's experience differed from the other European experiences in its unexpected and spectacular character; in England there existed a society sufficiently cultured to accept the ideal of classicism in an informed fashion, and hitherto sufficiently remote from the course of European artistic culture to become passionate about this ideal as a stirring novelty; for the first time classicism became an *avant-garde* option and even a sentimental myth, with curious pre-Romantic strands; we know for example that Jones explored and made measured drawings of the megalithic temple of Stonehenge, believing it to be a classical monument; his notes were used by Webb in 1655 when he published a book on the subject.[48]

The results of this experience were not comparable, either, in their finesse and cohesion, with those of contemporary French masters; its prevailing tone was a sort of spontaneous enthusiasm, not the professional gravity typical of Mansart and the French. But the rules that Mansart used as instruments for his rationalizing programme and which always ended up to some degree distorted, became for Jones an intellectual challenge and were accepted literally, with an earnestness that had long been unknown in the countries on the continent.

These circumstances explain the analogy between English classicism and Venetian classicism. Jones's inclination towards Palladio and Scamozzi was probably the result of a conscious selection from among the alternatives offered by Italian architectural practice; in the Venetian masters of the late sixteenth century – although they were operating in a different social and cultural context – Jones found both methodological clarity and first-hand reference to ancient models (and hence the minimizing of the 'modern' peculiarities referring to time and place) and the imaginative leaning towards a world of new forms. Palladian activity, as we have observed in the previous chapter, did not lead to a constant typology of general composition, but guaranteed an infinite variability of distributional solutions; hence its international appeal, in so far as the overall typology kept alive distinctive historical and geographical peculiarities. Jones continued this tendency with absolute unaffectedness, steering round the solid block of Tuscan and Roman experience, and firmly established the tone of Anglo-Saxon classicism which was to spread to both sides of the Atlantic.

The birth of the modern theatre

Between the end of the sixteenth century and the first half of the seventeenth the form of the modern theatre building emerged and assumed its permanent shape.[49]

This process was part of the research which we described earlier, and which was the immediate precedent of the *avant-garde* experiments of the early seventeenth century; it therefore registered not the personal inclinations of the innovating artists, but the average, common requirements, interpreted by the collective research of the previous generation. It was, however, influenced in a different way by the crisis in sensibility, and was closely bound up with the birth of the modern theatre which afforded the sensibility of the time one of its most important expressive and institutional outlets.

Neither the medieval nor the Renaissance theatre needed a permanent theatre building. Even in the fifteenth and sixteenth centuries

768 *The Roman theatre: illustration by Cesariano to the 1521 edition of Vitruvius*

dramatic action was an occasional ceremony presented either in the open air or indoors, in squares (Amsterdam, York, Angers and Mons), churches (Parma, Ferrara, Naples, Cologne, Nuremberg and Sterzing), in hospitals (Paris and Lisbon), in colleges (Oxford and Cambridge), in *scuole* (Venice and Florence) and, at Italian courts, in princely palaces; it was here that the need first arose to adapt certain architectural settings for theatrical performances, at first temporarily and later definitively: the first permanent European theatre was that set up in 1531 at the court of Ferrara.

The Italian court theatre posed a problem of décor, not of architecture; the architecture was that of the hall or garden, and the participation of the spectators in the dramatic action was ensured precisely by the simultaneous presence of spectators and actors in one single space, made such by the architectural setting.

Two distributive variants can, however, be distinguished:

1 The performance took place mainly in the centre of the empty space, where the actors spoke and where the seats of the most important spectators were placed, presented as an integral part of the performance; the tiers of steps for the spectators backed on to the two long walls or else on to three walls, leaving one of the short walls free for the raised platform; as in medieval theatres, this arrangement made two sets of action possible, one in the midst of the spectators and one isolated on the stage.

This distribution was adopted in the hall at Mantua in 1501, decorated with Mantegna's *Triumphs*, in the theatres set up by Vasari in Venice for the Compagnia della Calza (1542) and in Florence for Cosimo I in Palazzo Vecchio (1565), in the theatre by Buontalenti in the Uffizi (1585) and in the two theatres by Aleotti in the Sala Grande at Ferrara (1610–12).

2 The performance took place mainly on the platform and the whole public faced the stage; in this way a contrast was established between the space occupied by the spectators – who sat on a single flight of steps opposite the stage – and the stage occupied by the actors. Between the two areas was a free space (*piazza della scena*) which was used by both actors and public.

This was the mode of organization used in Ferrara for the marriage of Alfonso d'Este with Lucrezia Borgia (1501), the theatre by B. Genga in Urbino (1513), Raphael's theatre in Rome (1519) and Antonio da Sangallo's in Florence (1530).

The second variant lent itself to the tendency to imitate ancient models. The documents available were the texts of the classical dramas, the theoretical texts such as Aristotle's *Poetics*, Vitruvius' treatise and such ruins of the Roman theatres as still remained. Only the latter could give any precise idea of the ancient organisms, but until the middle of the sixteenth century, when Palladio made his measured drawings, artists preferred to substitute *de facto* observations by the most disparate conjectures taken from ancient texts, and particularly from the sibylline Vitruvian description; one need only compare the plates of the editions of Vitruvius published during the first half of the sixteenth century (Fig. 768) with those of the edition of Daniele Barbaro of 1556, which was based on Palladio's drawings.

The influence of these conjectures on the arrangement of modern theatres was at first fairly vague, suggesting the replacement of the straight tiers of steps by semi-circular ones; this innovation was adopted in the 1513 theatre by Rosselli and Peruzzi in Rome for the performance of the *Paliliae*, in Serlio's theatre at Vicenza of 1539 and duly noted in Serlio's treatise (Figs 773–4). The semicircular tier produced a flat bay in the centre, and this corresponded to the ancient orchestra and had no precise function in modern

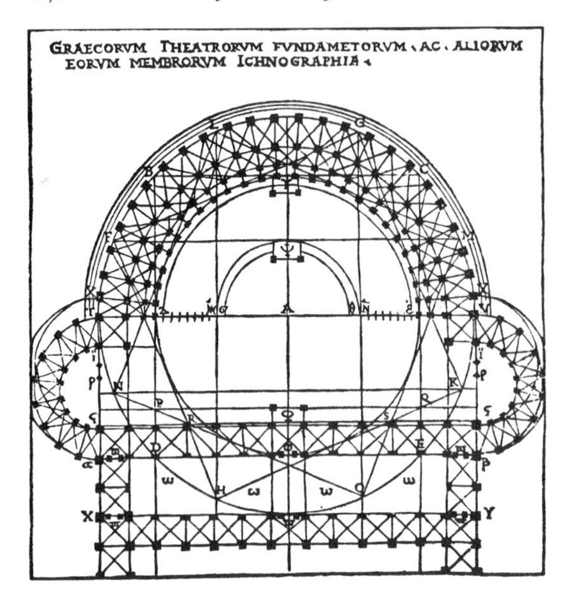

performances where it was always occupied by the spectators, not the actors.

The problem of the stage was somewhat more complicated. In most of the theatres of the first half of the sixteenth century the set was a temporary piece of equipment introduced into the architecture of the room; but the application of perspective to the arrangement of the scenery gave rise to a spatial antithesis between set and room, and ultimately made the old unity of the theatrical space untenable. The Renaissance set, even when interpreting ancient models – such as the three noted in Serlio's treatise – was not a

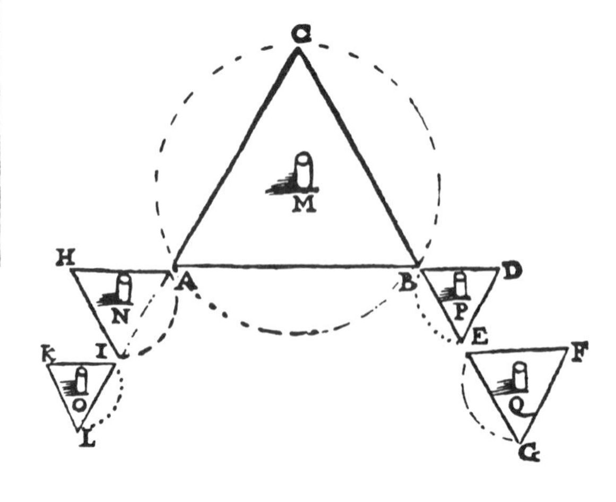

769, 770 *The Greek and Roman theatres, according to Cesariano*
771 *A comic set, after Serlio*
772 *Drawing of a set with the* periaktoi *by E. Danti, in his edition of Vignola's* Prospettiva, *1583*

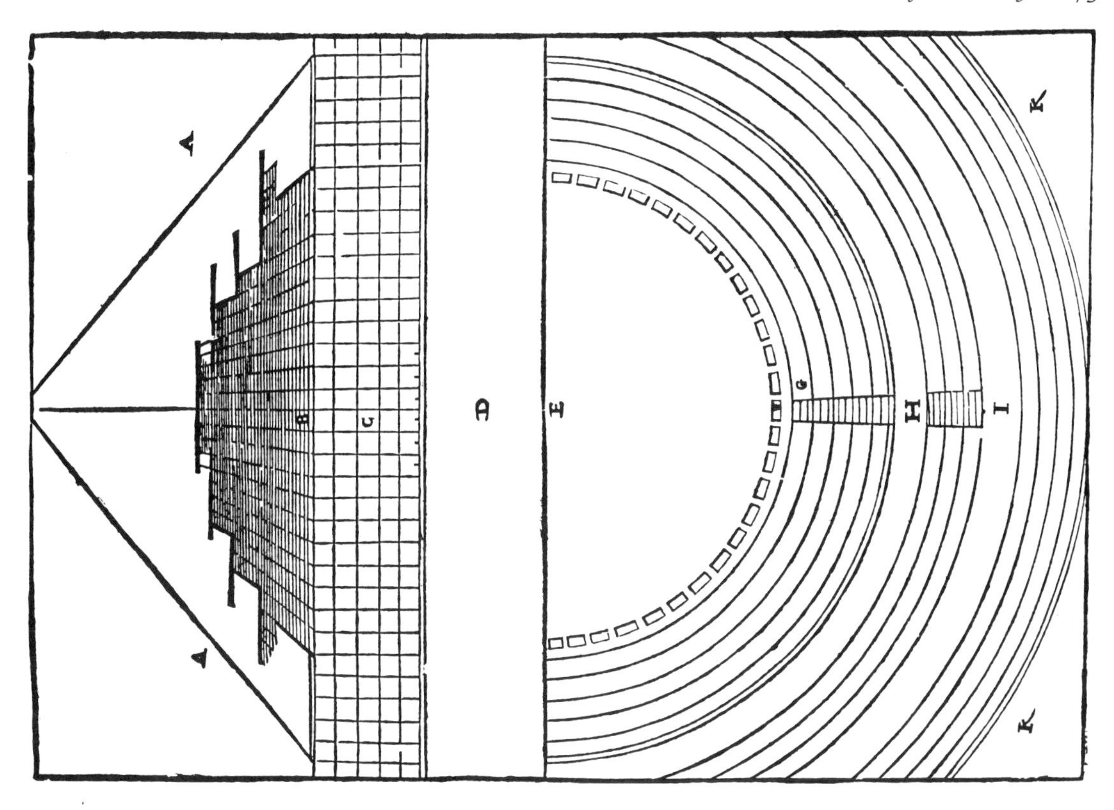

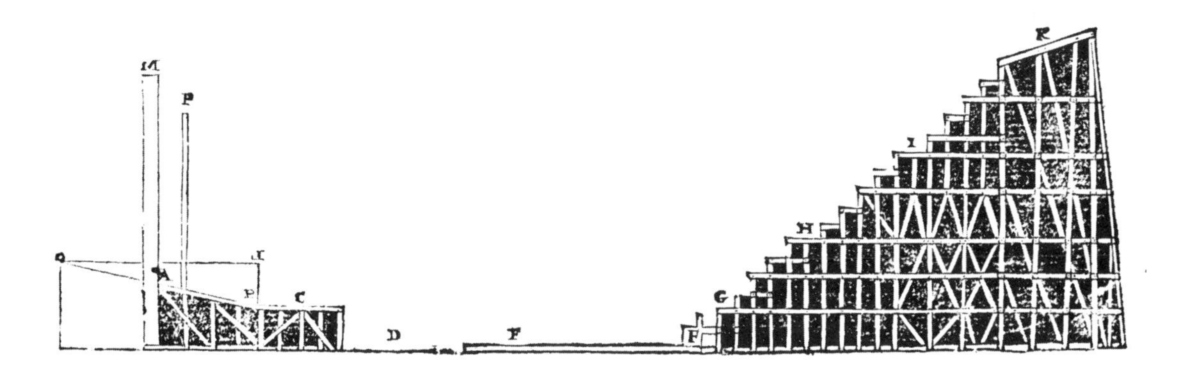

773, 774 *A modern theatrical diagram from Serlio's treatise*

775 *The* frons scaenae *according to Daniele Barbaro*

wall but an Albertian 'window', which represented a complete space: a city or scene from nature. From the middle of the sixteenth century the *prospetto scenico* appeared, a painted partition which helped to hide the increasingly cumbersome machinery and gave the perspective set a frontal framework, although it remained an element independent of the architecture of the room.

In Venetian circles of the second half of the sixteenth century an important attempt was made to co-ordinate these elements, and to realize – with the historical earnestness which distinguished local culture – a worthy modern equivalent of the ancient theatre.

Palladio was the protagonist of this singular endeavour; in 1556 he provided Barbaro with the drawings for the Vitruvian theatre and for the *frons scaenae* – which was interpreted precisely as the architectural realization of the *prospetto scenico* previously used; in 1565 he organized a temporary theatre in Venice for another Compagnia della Calza, and later designed a permanent theatre for the Accademia degli Olimpici in Vicenza, completed in 1585 by Scamozzi (Figs 776–7). This theatre included a semi-elliptical *cavea* topped by a colonnade and a rectangular stage enclosed by a splendid architectural set; the two architectural systems, ingeniously but only partly linked by certain recurrent motifs, were topped by a crowning element, as if they were under the open sky, i.e. they relegate the outer shell of the building into the background and hide the irregularity of the masonry perimeter from those in the theatre. The architectural set has five openings of diminishing width in place of the Vitruvian doors, beyond which we see another perspective scene by Scamozzi, representing seven city streets.

This architectural organism reveals the ambiguity of the theatrical programme of Palladio and his clients in the most significant way. Artists and men of letters, interpreting Vitruvius' directions concerning the *frons*

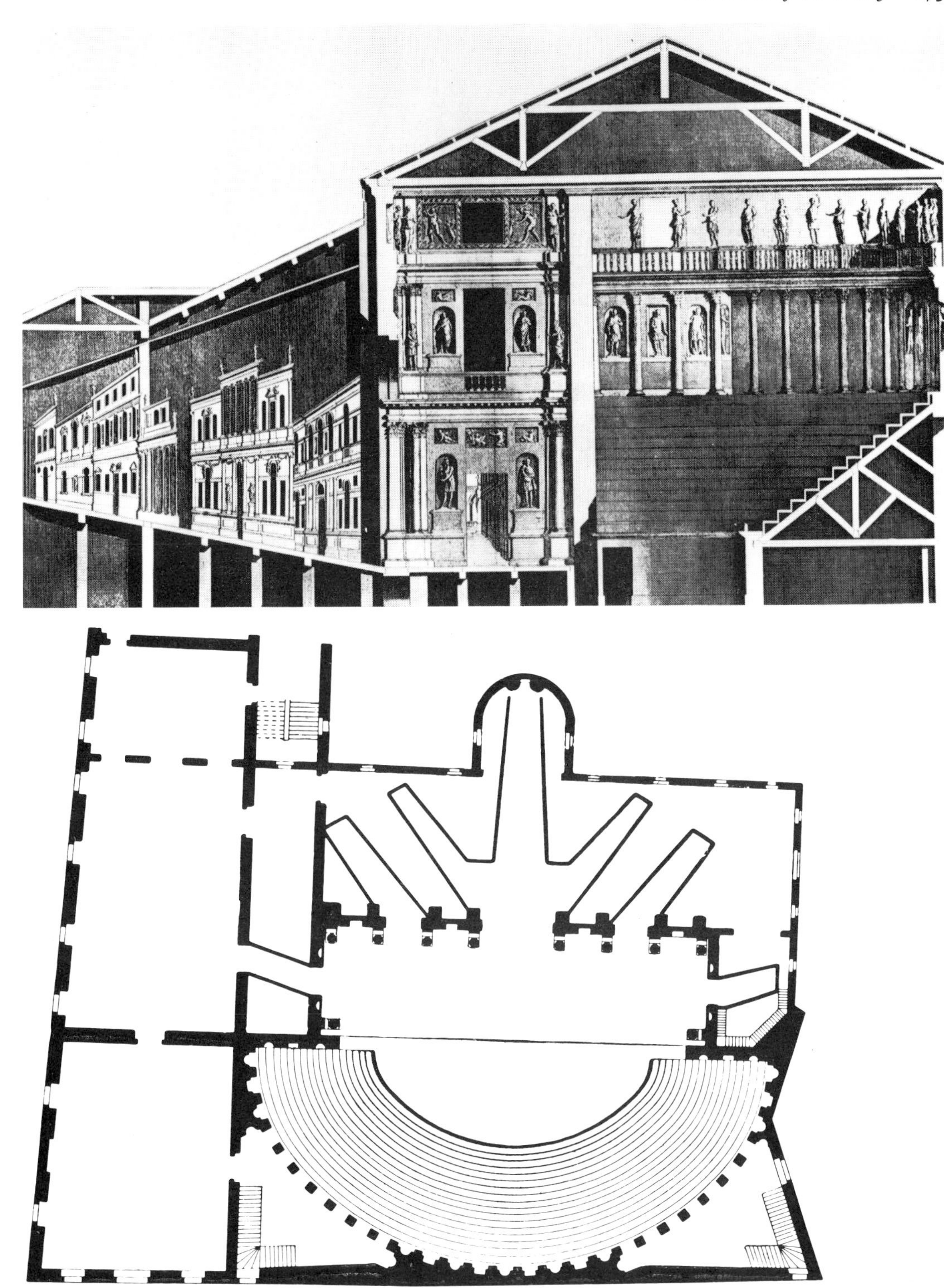

776, 777 *Palladio's Teatro Olimpico, Vicenza (from Bertotti-Scamozzi)*

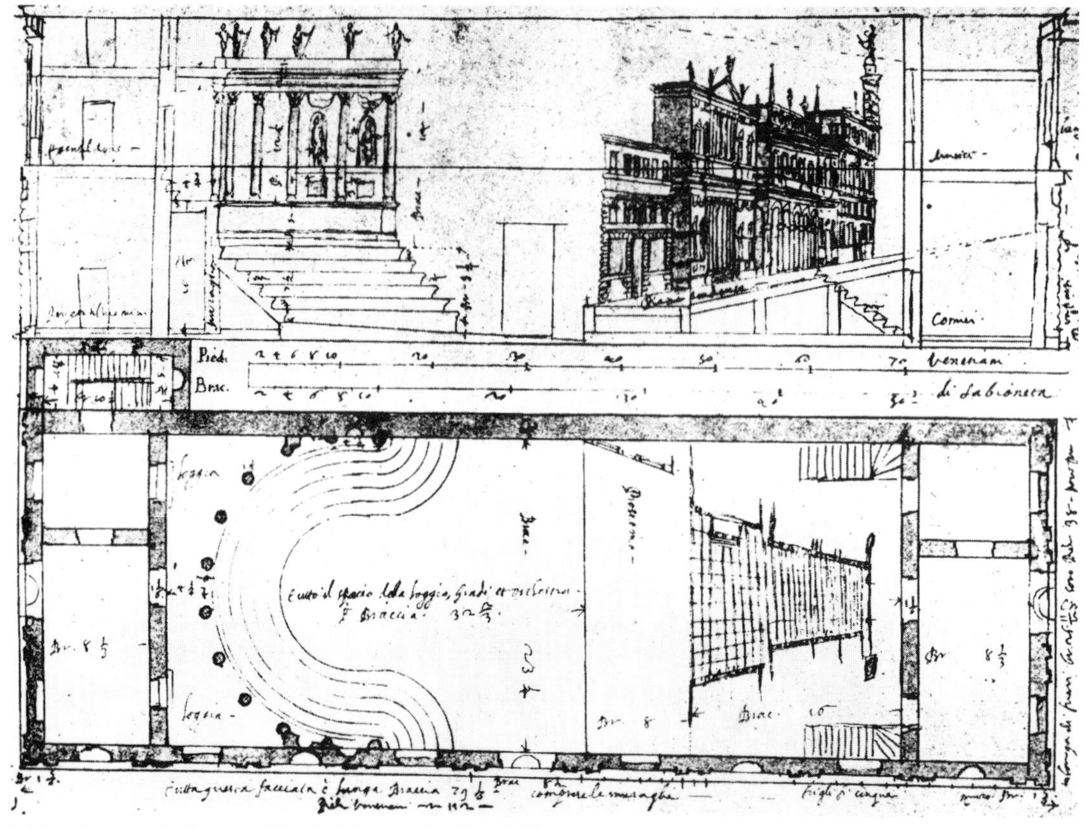

778 *Drawing by Scamozzi for the* Teatro all'antica, *Sabbioneta*

scaenae, never freed themselves from the modern concept of the set in depth, already implicit in the medieval mansions and rationalized in the sixteenth-century perspective set, hence from the idea that the *prospetto scenico* must somehow also involve the spaces behind; hence the complicated conjectures about apertures, *valvae mediae* and *hospitalia*, and about the porticoes situated behind the set.

This ambiguity was more than a technical uncertainty; in fact the *frons scaenae* was the boundary of a single space where actors and spectators were together, that is to say – in the case of the Roman theatre – the architectural transcription of the Greek landscape setting, where the drama took place under the eyes of the spectators; the unity of the theatrical setting was the guarantee of the specific character of the drama, which was not an action remembered, but realized in the presence of the spectators, in the same physical space as the one where the spectators were.

In the Italian Renaissance, this aspect was no longer a social reality but a cultural datum to be reconstructed through the critical study of texts and documents. The conflict between architectural set and perspective set concealed that between direct and indirect representation of the drama, and could be resolved only on theatrical grounds, i.e. according to the character of the drama to be performed. For this reason it persisted for as long as drama *all'antica* in Italy in the sixteenth century remained a literary reconstruction or a worldly ceremony, and did not become a new, genuine theatrical experience.

In Palladio's Teatro Olimpico the two types of set, i.e. the two potential characters of theatrical representation, were offered contemporaneously. It has been observed that the perspective scenery of Vicenza is simply the plastic translation of the views painted on the *periaktoi* placed by Barbaro behind the doors of the Vitruvian set. Perhaps Palladio had thought of placing so many *periaktoi* behind the openings, which would have had the three conventional perspective scenes painted on them, and the action would all have taken place in front of the architectural set; then the *periaktoi*, through the work of Scamozzi, were replaced by the three-dimensional and fixed perspective set, to facilitate the entrances of the actors, and it became possible for the actors to speak either in front of or behind the architectural set.

The Palladian theatre gave rise to a series of imitations, including the *Teatro all'antica* by Scamozzi in Sabbioneta (1588) (Figs 778–9), the theatre by Aleotti for the

779 *The* Teatro all'antica, *Sabbioneta*

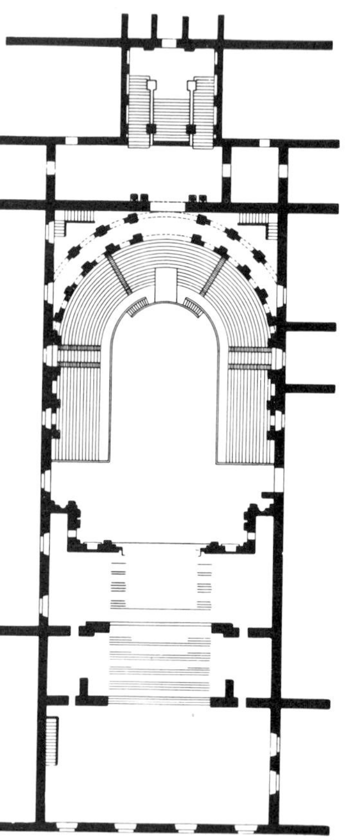

780–782 *Views of the auditorium and stage and plan of the Farnese theatre, Parma, by G. B. Aleotti*

Accademia degli Intrepidi in Ferrara (1605), the other theatre by Aleotti for Ranuccio I Farnese at Parma (1618) (Figs 780–2) and the one designed by Inigo Jones in the drawing kept at Worcester College, Oxford (1623).

The Farnese theatre is significant both for the layout of the tier of seats – semi-circular, lengthening out into a U – and for the structure of the architectural set which framed a single, very wide opening; the stage now went beyond the threshold of this opening and occupied the perspective space created amid the machinery which filled the spacious premises behind. In this, which may be considered as the last of the great court theatres of the Renaissance, the main characteristics of the theatre *all'antica* that was to develop and spread during the following century were already present.

In the late sixteenth century, together with the court theatres, the first public theatres or *stanze* were being built: the Teatro della Spelta at Modena (1539), the Teatro della Sala at Bologna (1547), the Teatro delle Saline at Genoa (c. 1550), the Sala delle Commedie at Reggio Emilia (1568) and the two theatres of S. Cassian in Venice described by Francesco Sansovino in 1581.[50] These halls, even when they reproduced the models of the court theatres, had to tackle the new problem of preventing the mingling of the public, of housing together different social classes of spectators; the Neapolitan *stanze* of the end of the sixteenth and early seventeenth centuries were organized with a ground floor and raised galleries, sometimes divided into boxes; these were a secondary addition for the moment, but later they were to become one of the basic elements of the *teatro all'italiana*.

In the other European countries the court theatre was always a temporary installation, while the public theatre was soon housed in permanent buildings, in no way dependent on court models, but answering the needs of an already fully formed dramatic tradition, outside the tutelage of the central power.

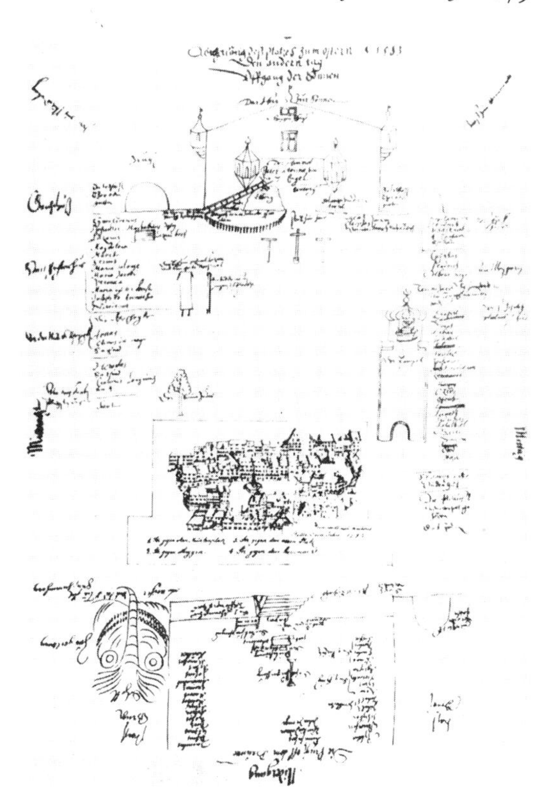

783 *Set for a performance in the square at Lucerne in 1597*

784 *Detail of the set for the* Passion *at Valenciennes in 1547*

The French *confréries*, the Flemish chambers of rhetoric, the English colleges, the German *Meistersinger* directed spectacles which were an integral part of urban life and which, through a series of approximations, arrived at a definitive type of building.

In Spain theatres were organized, at first temporarily, in the old courtyards (*corrales* or *patios*); after the middle of the sixteenth century they became permanent installations, retaining the original distribution. The square space of the courtyard was surrounded by one or two orders of balconies (*celosías*); one of the sides was occupied by the permanent stage (perspective and changeable scenery was introduced only at the end of the seventeenth century), and the side opposite by the section reserved for women (*cazuela*); in some cases there was a third order (*torrinha*), used as a gallery. The space was covered by a large awning, and was presented as a setting similar to the spaces of normal life – the courtyard was the typical structure of the town building fabric – where the dramatic action took place in the midst of the public and had the public itself looking out from the balconies as its backdrop. The first permanent theatres were opened in Seville – Corral de don Juan (1549), de las Ataranzas (1575), de doña Elvira (1579); then in Madrid – Corral de la Cruz (1579), del Principe (1583); in Valencia – Corral de l'Olivera (1584); and in Lisbon – Patio das Arcas (1594).

Elizabethan drama took place in a series of public theatres, which functioned in London from 1576 to 1642[51] and have all disappeared, so that their distribution has to be reconstructed – with some uncertainty – from documents and theatrical texts. The Elizabethan theatre, too, was originally an open yard, circular or polygonal in shape, on to which up to five tiers of galleries looked; a sector of these galleries was occupied by the tiring house, which included the storehouses, premises for the actors and, towards the yard, a chamber that could open up, topped by a gallery (tarass), which were used respectively

785 *A* corral *at Granada (from D'Amico)*

for scenes set in interiors or in high places; the tiring house stood behind a raised platform, protected by a canopy, which occupied the central part of the yard and which was where the main body of the action took place.

The wealthier public sat in the galleries or on the stage, the ordinary public in the ground-floor space, around the platform; the stage offered simultaneously three possible places for the dramatic action: the outer stage, which was normally used for exteriors, defined by only a few symbolic props, since the action took place in the same space as the spectators and could be seen, not only from the front, but also from the sides and even from behind; the inner stage, which was used to represent interiors, or secondary settings opening on to the outside (for instance Prospero's cave) and which was sometimes organized as a stage in the Italian fashion, with proscenium and curtain; and the upper stage, which was used to represent high places (the platform in front of the castle of Elsinor, or Juliet's balcony) and made it possible to carry on an action separate from or simultaneous with the main one.

This complex organization, which could be interpreted as a multiple medieval set unified and organized around a Renaissance axis of symmetry, was closely linked to the theatrical technique of the great Elizabethan writers, and made a vast scale of effects possible, from

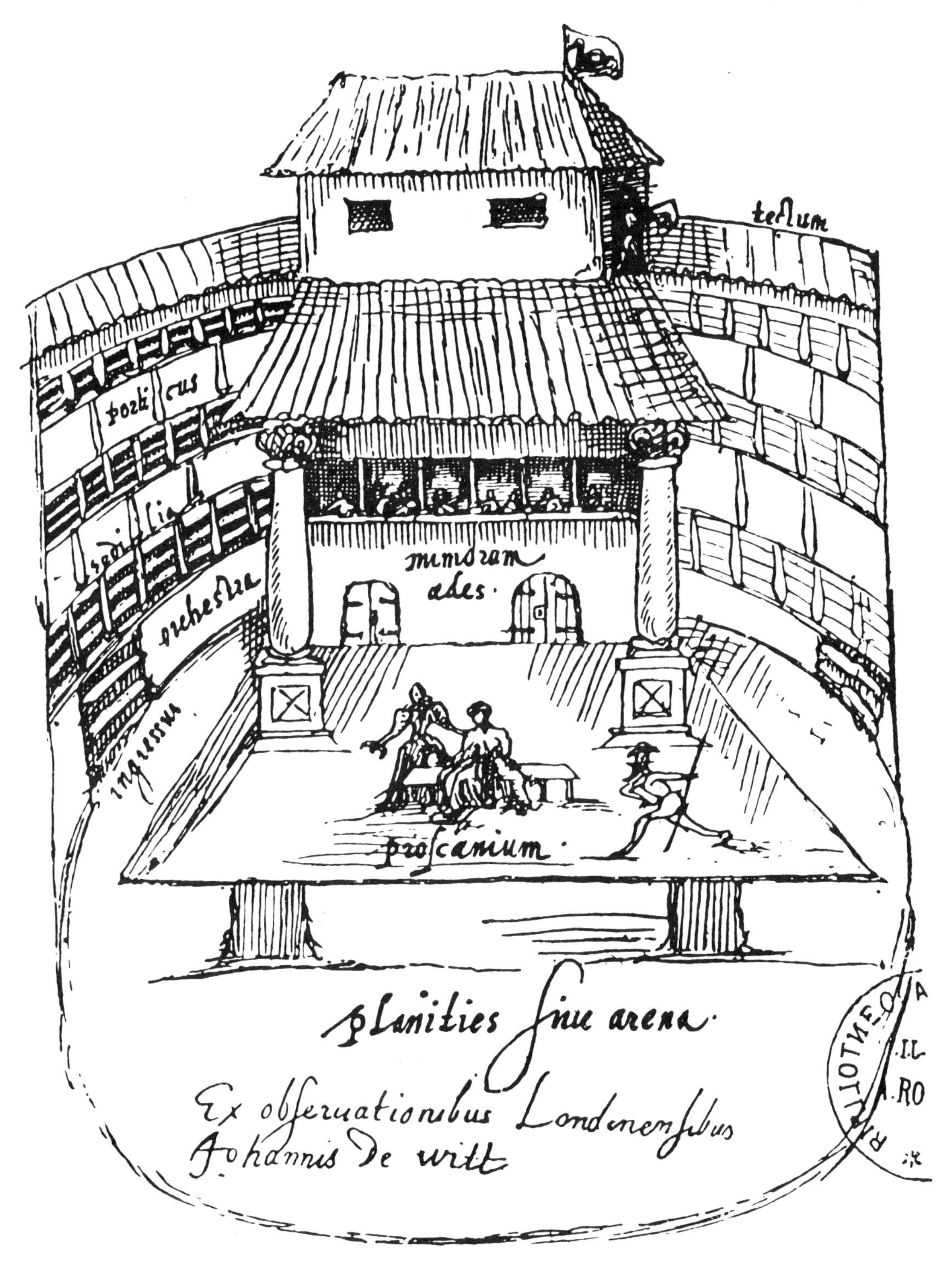

786 *Drawing by Johann de Witt, showing a Shakespearian theatre*

787 *View of London in the early seventeenth century showing two theatres in the foreground*

the full relief of the scenes on the platform to the perspective illusion of those that took place on the inner stage. The conflict between the two concepts of scenery, which led to an unstable compromise in Italy, together with the uncertainty of a theoretical interpretation of ancient models, here tended to broaden the repercussions of a new dramatic poetry which alone guaranteed the coherence of the theatrical spectacle, and helped to produce the specific tone of Shakespearian drama, poised between reality and illusion. The poet incorporated into the play the contemplation of the play itself (as in *Hamlet*, where he stages the play within a play) and sometimes intervened in person to comment upon and make explicit the theatrical fiction, as in the prologue to *Henry V*:

'O for a Muse of fire, that would ascend
The brightest heaven of invention,
A kingdom for a stage, princes to act,
And monarchs to behold the swelling
scene! . . .
But pardon, gentles all,
The flat unraisèd spirits that have dared
On this unworthy scaffold to bring forth
So great an object: can this cockpit hold
The vasty fields of France? or may we cram
Within this wooden O the very casques
That did affright the air at Agincourt?
O, pardon! since a crookèd figure may
Attest in little place a million;
And let us, ciphers to this great accompt,
On your imaginary forces work.'

For theatrical performances in France the existing rooms in hospitals, market *halles*, *jeux de paume* or noble residences were adapted. The first permanent public theatre in Paris (after 1550) was that of the Hôtel de Bourgogne which had a fixed stage running the whole length of a wall and an amphitheatre in front of it, completed by a row of stalls running along the other three walls. The first court theatres too – that of the Palais du Petit Bourbon (1629), and Lemercier's in the Palais Royal (1640) – had a distribution similar to this, though the latter also had a perspective set in the Italian fashion framed in the *prospetto scenico*. For a long time some important spectators – the *marquis* criticized by Molière – were allowed on to the stage at either side of the actors.

In the Low Countries the chambers of rhetoric performed in the open air or in the halls of public buildings: in Antwerp in the old Stock Exchange, in the Hague in the riding school. In 1638 the architect Jacob van Campen built the first permanent monumental theatre in Amsterdam, the Amsterdamsche Stadsscheuwburg for the Nederduytsche Academie; this had an elliptical plan with the main axis lengthways; half of the ellipse was occupied by a large fixed stage, the other half by the stalls, surrounded by two tiers of boxes and above these by yet another set of steps for the bourgeois public. This theatre was already an original invention, comparable to the most important works of European *avant-garde* culture.

The European theatres hitherto described depended more or less closely upon the concept of the fixed stage, hence upon the simultaneous presence of actors and spectators within a single space, and they followed the various national needs, architecturally incoherent but precise and vital, of modern dramatic poetry.

Italy saw the almost contemporaneous birth of a new type of spectacle – opera – and of a new type of building – the *teatro all'italiana* – closely linked to one another in their turn.

The idea of combining poetry and music in a new form of artistic performance was discussed about 1580 at the Camerata dei Bardi in Florence – frequented by Galileo Galilei, Piero Strozzi and Giulio Caccini – and developed theoretically by Galileo in his *Dialogo della musica antica e della moderna* (1581); in 1588 Ferdinand I summoned Emilio de' Cavalieri from Rome to become superintendent of court spectacles, and he organized the first sung actions on stage, though arousing disagreement among the Bardi group; in 1594 Corsi, Rinuccini and Peri composed a *Dafne* – performed privately between 1598 and 1600 – and in 1600 *Euridice*, performed in Palazzo Pitti for the wedding of Marie de Médicis with Henri IV of France. The following year Claudio Monteverdi was appointed *maestro di cappella* at Mantua; here his *Orfeo* was performed in 1607 and in 1608 his *Arianna*, with a libretto by Rinuccini. From then on opera found a place in all Italian and European courts.

The *recitar cantando* elaborated by the Florentines was born as yet another attempt to revive ancient drama; hence the criticisms of Cavalieri's spectacles 'which have nothing to do with the real and proper theatre music . . . since they do not obey the information that is to be found in ancient writers'.[52] Men of letters and musicians of the Bardi group had as their model the synthesis of words and music realized in Greek drama – of which they knew only the texts and literary descriptions – and aimed at creating a music which would combine with the meanings of words, hence 'a well-tempered course between the suspended and slow movements of song, and that of speech, rapid and hasty';[53] they rejected both music as an accompaniment to spoken words, and words as phonetic material for an independent musical construction, as in the traditional contrapuntal style.

But the results of this research altered the theoretical programme completely, i.e. they revealed the autonomy of the new musical expression and initiated the developments of modern music; thus in the theatrical field this experiment put an end to attempts to re-establish the basic scenic condition of all ancient and medieval theatre, i.e. the spatial coexistence of actors and spectators in a single setting (the Greek *plein air*, the architectural hollow of the Roman theatre, the urban space of the medieval or the private space of the sixteenth-century theatres). In fact music brought with it a participation in

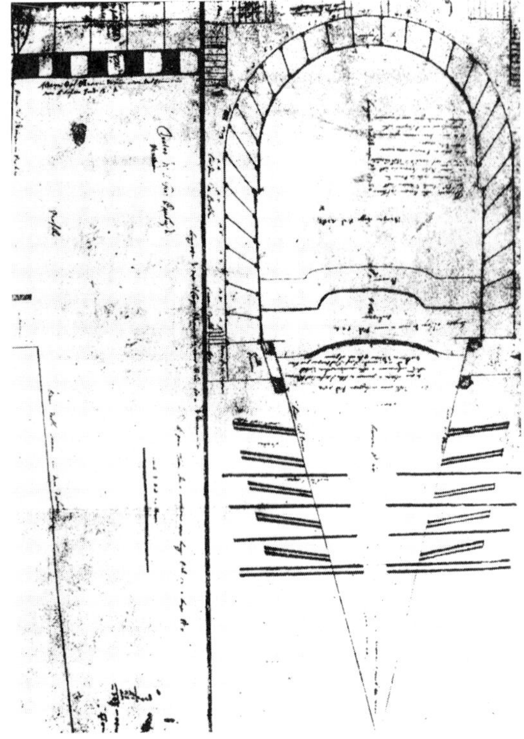

788 *The theatre of SS. Giovanni e Paolo, Venice, 1650*

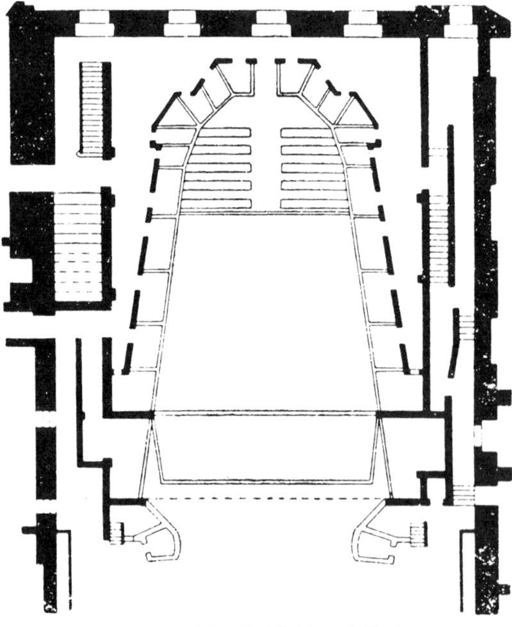

789 *The theatre of the Palais Royal, Paris*

the drama of a temporal nature which replaced the spatial participation and made the total absorption of the visual framework into the perspective set plausible; the action took place in the imaginary space of the stage, beyond the opening of the proscenium, and became present through the identification of its time with the inward time of those listening.

Just at this period, and in relation to this new form of spectacle, a new type of theatre was perfected, which was no longer a single space but the combination between the two spaces – auditorium and stage – communicating through the proscenium. There was no possibility of a common spatial dimension between these two; the auditorium was an architectural space, and when the curtain was closed it presented the assembled company with an image of itself arranged in a certain hierarchical order; the stage was a technical space, which when the curtain was open presented an illusory picture, similar to an animated painting; the spectator perceived his own real situation within the space of the auditorium, and the illusory situation in the space of the stage, separately.

The organization of the auditorium and that of the stage developed separately, based on different needs. That of the auditorium – relatively open in court theatres, where the spectators came by invitation and belonged to a homogeneous class – became rigid and constrained in public theatres, where different categories of spectators had to sit together and paid different prices. The first opera for a public audience was organized in 1637 in the Venetian theatre of S. Cassian, which had an auditorium with a flight of tiered seats; but in 1639 the Ferrara architect Alfonso Chenda, when refurbishing the Teatro della Sala at Bologna, built five tiers of boxes around the stalls which meant that space was put to good use and allowed the wealthier public to attend the spectacle more or less privately; this arrangement was adopted in 1641 in the Formagliari theatre in

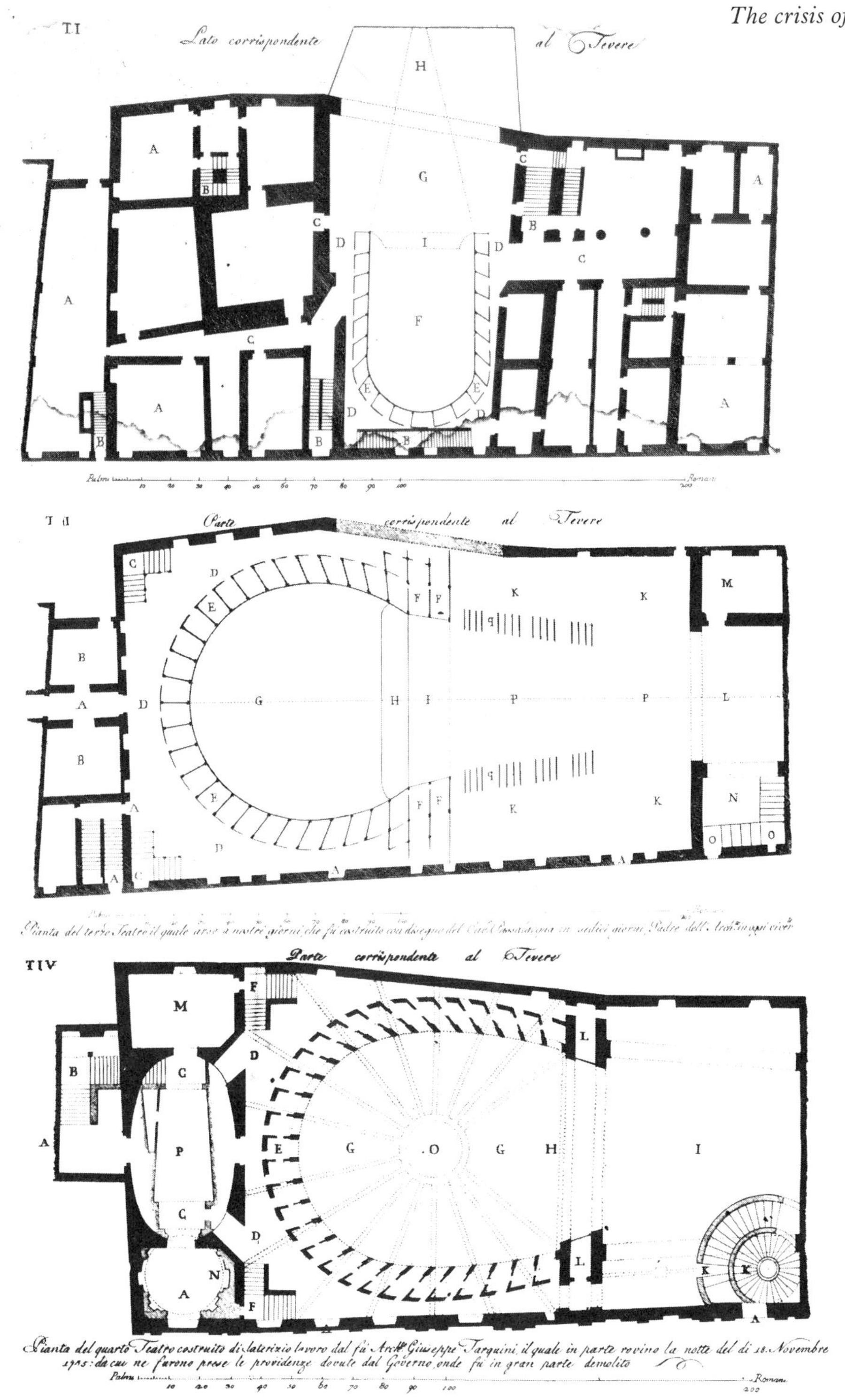

790–792 *The theatre of Tor di Nona, Rome, in three successive reconstructions (from F. Giorgi,* Descrizione del teatro di Tor di Nona, *Rome, 1795)*

793 *A theatrical set by G. B. Pannini at the Teatro Argentina, Rome, in 1747. Louvre, Paris*

Venice, in 1653 in the Falcone in Naples, in 1654 in the new theatre of SS. Giovanni e Paolo in Venice (Fig. 788), in 1656 in the Teatro degli Immobili in Florence and it became typical of almost all later theatres. Abroad too – along with the spread of musical drama – the main theatres were altered according to the same criteria or replaced by new buildings on the model of the Italian ones: in 1645 Jacopo Torelli arrived in Paris and refurbished the stage equipment of the theatres of the Petit Bourbon and Palais Royal; in 1659 Carlo Vigarani arrived there too, built the Salle des Machines at the Tuileries (1660), where Lully's operas were performed, and restored the hall of the Petit Bourbon (1673). In England, after the Restoration, theatrical life was dominated by the managers William Davenant, who followed the court into exile in Paris at the time of Torelli and in 1661 opened the new theatre in Lincoln's Inn Fields, and Tom Killigrew, who had been in Italy in 1635 and performed from 1662 onwards at Drury lane; after the fire of 1666 Wren built two new theatres in 1672 and 1674 for these companies; they retained some elements of the Elizabethan stage – the protruding proscenium (apron stage) and the galleries at the sides – and the elliptical plan already experimented with in Amsterdam in 1638. In Holland in 1665 Jan Vos replaced the architectural set of the

Stadsscheuwburg with a perspective set. In Germany the main courts built their opera houses after the Peace of Westphalia (Vienna and Munich in 1651, Halle in 1654, Dresden in 1667, Brunswick in 1680); the stage was imitated from Italian models, but the auditorium, destined for an invited public, was organized with tiers of seats or continuous galleries; the system of boxes was adopted later at Celle (1672) and Hanover (1689), in the new theatre at Brunswick (1680), and became the general rule, in Germany and in all Europe, in the eighteenth century.

Scene painting as a corollary of scientific perspective was now a complicated speciality, mainly through the work of the Italian professionals who were active in many European countries, but it was also cultivated, as a preparation for the extension of architecture, by some of the most important masters, Jones, Webb, Bernini and Juvara. The theatrical stage, together with landscaped gardens, was the space which could be dominated by perspective at will; here Torelli – like his contemporary Le Nôtre – could realize the whole gradation of the effects conceived in theory, from foreground to vanishing-point. Also for this reason the theatre was important as a cultural symbol at a time when perspective was no longer able to regulate the transformations of the inhabited landscape.

six

The *grand siècle*

Is it possible to describe the *grand siècle* through architecture? To what degree did the new rational classicism – with which we dealt in the last chapter, considering the relations between literary classicism and artistic classicism – transform the urban and rural setting of French society of the seventeenth century?

A first reply to these questions is contained in the beginning of *The Discourse on Method* where Descartes compares his programme to that of an architect, and explains the difference between planning a building and transforming a city.

Descartes was in Germany, 'shut up alone in a stove-heated room where I had complete leisure to occupy myself with my own thoughts':[1]

'One of the first considerations that occurred to me was that there is very often less perfection in works composed of several portions, and carried out by the hands of various masters, than in those on which one individual alone has worked. Thus we see that buildings planned and carried out by one architect alone are usually more beautiful and better proportioned than those which many have tried to put into order and improve, making use of old walls which were built with other ends in view. In the same way also, those ancient cities which, originally mere villages, have become in the process of time great towns, are usually badly constructed in comparison with those which are regularly laid out on a plan by a surveyor who is free to follow his own ideas. Even though, considering their buildings each one apart, there is often as much or more display of skill in the one case than in the other, the former have large buildings and small buildings indiscriminately placed together, thus rendering the streets crooked and irregular, so that it might be said that it was chance rather than the will of man guided by reason that led to such an arrangement. And if we consider that this happens despite the fact that from all time there have been certain officials who have had the special duty of looking after the buildings of private individuals in order that they may be public ornaments, we shall understand how difficult it is to bring about much that is satisfactory in operating only upon the works of others. . . .

It is true that we do not find that all the houses in a town are razed to the ground for the sole reason that the town is to be rebuilt in another fashion, with streets made more beautiful; but at the same time we see that many people cause their own houses to be knocked down in order to rebuild them, and that sometimes they are forced to do so where there is danger of the houses falling of themselves, and when the foundations are not secure. From such examples I argued to myself that there is no plausibility in the claim of any private individual to reform a state by altering everything, and by overturning it throughout, in order to set it right again. Nor is it likewise probable that the whole body of the Sciences, or the order of teaching established by the Schools, should be reformed. But as regards all the opinions which up to this time I had embraced, I thought I could not do better than endeavour once and for all to sweep them completely away, so that they might later on be replaced, either by others which were better, or by the same, when I had made them conform to the uniformity of a rational scheme. And I firmly believed that by this means I should succeed much better than if I had only built on old foundations, and relied on principles of which I allowed myself to be in youth persuaded without having inquired into their truth. For although in so doing I recognized various difficulties, these were at the same time not unsurmountable, nor comparable to those which are found in reformation of the most insignificant kind in matters which concern the public. In the case of great bodies it is so difficult a task to raise them again when they are once thrown down, or even to keep them in their places when they are thoroughly shaken; and their fall cannot be otherwise than very violent. Then as to any imperfection that they may possess (and the very diversity that is found between them is sufficient to tell us that these in many cases exist) custom has doubtless greatly mitigated them, while it has also helped us to avoid, or insensibly corrected a number against which mere foresight would have found it difficult to guard. And finally the imperfections are almost always more supportable than would be the process of removing them. . . .

This is the reason why I cannot in any way approve of those turbulent and unsuccessful spirits who, being called neither by birth nor fortune to the management of public affairs, never fail to have always in their minds some new reforms. And if I thought that in this treatise there was contained the smallest justification for this folly, I should be very sorry to allow it to be published. My design has never extended beyond trying to reform my own opinion and to build on a foundation which is entirely my own.'

This passage states with extreme clarity both the ambitions of the rationalist culture of the *grand siècle* and the limitations which that culture recognized and accepted in advance; even the circumspection of the author in presenting his discourse, to palliate the criticism of the time, was translated into a sort of self-criticism, and remained as basic features of Cartesian research, valid for most of the cultural phenomena up to the time of Louis XIV. The coexistence between culture and power was based on the interchange between rational order and traditional order, the one obtaining – roughly speaking – in the individual sphere, the other in the social, and this interchange functioned so long as intellectual research refrained from analysing it; when this limitation ceased, in the eighteenth century, research was directed precisely towards the structures of the *ancien régime*, and rationalist culture, passing into the hands of the classes excluded from the traditional political system (the 'turbulent and unsuccessful spirits who, being called neither by birth nor fortune to the management of public affairs, never fail to have in their minds some new reforms'), prepared that very 'sudden change' which Descartes was deploring.

794 *Plan of Paris in 1609*

A PARIS
VASSALLIEV DIT NICOLAY
Topographie et Ingenieur
De France
LA RIVIERE DE SEINE

For architecture the Cartesian limitation made itself felt above all on the town-planning scale. Literature and the figurative arts explored the inexhaustible field of individual feelings and cases, and rational analysis found its limit in the culture of *grandeur d'âme*, which was the psychological basis of absolute power. In the same way architecture drew upon a wide range of single buildings to elaborate upon them, and the selection of the distributional and constructional character had to be combined with the requirements of *grandeur* which increasingly distinguished court buildings from more modest ones; but beyond this scale the architect could not avoid encountering the problems of urban and regional organization, i.e. of the co-ordination between the settlements of all the social classes, and was not in a position to apply fully on this scale the criteria of perspective regularity used on the building scale. The Sun King, with his power rhetorically exaggerated by the praises of artists and writers, did not succeed in building a new city, or even in modifying very profoundly the organism of his capital, established in the late Middle Ages. Hence the double character of the new architectural classicism: it partly belonged to art (together with painting, sculpture, music and poetry) and helped, with homogeneous criteria, to form the décor of the setting within which the new ruling class moved, and it belonged partly to politics, and contributed to the management of the social structures which supported this setting, with a stupefying mixture of heterogeneous criteria and expedients; the work of Lebrun echoed that of Colbert.

But the formation of this cultural system must be examined chronologically, for at the end of the century it was to become the common model for all European countries.

The reign of Henri IV (1589–1610) saw the beginning of the organization of the administrative apparatus, on which monarchic absolutism was based. Sully became a member of the government in 1596, and the person mainly responsible for royal policy from 1598 onwards, when Henri IV's power was firmly established; as superintendent of finances Sully took a series of decisive measures: he lowered legal interest, authorized the free export of grain and wine, repressed the abuses and the autonomist tendencies of the civil servants, made possible France's economic revival and the reconstruction of the royal finances. Meanwhile he personally assumed responsibility for some of the main sectors of public life: in 1599 he was appointed superintendent of fortifications and grand master of artillery, in 1600 commander of the troops during the war in Savoy, in 1602 governor of the Bastille, in 1603 ambassador to James I of England. In the building field the post of superintendent of buildings was combined with that of superintendent of finances, and was given first of all to Nicolas de Harlay (1594–1600), then to Sully (1600–11); but the real *chef de service* was Jean de Fourcy, appointed *contrôleur des bâtiments* in 1594 and *surintendant*, after Sully, from 1611 to 1624; the *surintendant* and *contrôleur* were helped by an inspector general of buildings (Donon), an inspector general of gardens (Maisoncelles) and a treasurer. Furthermore, from 1597 onwards, Sully was grand commissioner of highways; Henry IV created the post of *grand voyer de France* for him and assigned him as lieutenants, from 1600, the *trésoriers de France*; his province included roads, canals and the planting of trees.

These measures established a solid link between the administrative and technical apparatus, and ensured civil servants the upper hand over planners. Fourcy intervened immediately to modify the privileges of the architects; in 1594, while Jacques II Androuet du Cerceau was engaged in designing the Louvre, he granted the same position to Louis Métezeau, with whom he had business connections; Androuet protested to the king, but the latter upheld Fourcy, and in 1599 he forbade architects 'to meddle in anything

795 *The* parvis *of Notre Dame, Paris, at the beginning of the seventeenth century (from Merian)*

concerning the post of *surintendant des bâtiments*'.[2] The old titles conferred upon the architects of the royal buildings gradually lost their monopolistic character and were turned into ordinary posts which could be granted to a number of people; the title of royal architect, for instance, belonged to Jacques II Androuet du Cerceau (1594–1614) and Salomon de Brosse (1614–15) but was held contemporaneously by Louis Métezeau (1594–1615) and later by his brother Clément II Métezeau.

The salaries of civil servants and architects are an eloquent index of their place in the social hierarchy. The *surintendant* and *contrôleur* received 6,000 *livres* a year, the inspectors general from 3,000 to 5,000 *livres*, the *grand voyer* 2,000 *livres*, while the royal architects under Henry IV received 800 *livres*; Clément Métezeau obtained 1,200 *livres* in 1618 and 2,400 in 1625, which was not much more than the pay of the designers (600 *livres* in 1618) and was sometimes halved in times of difficulty. In compensation they could work for other employers, leave their posts to their descendants and sometimes obtain a pension for relatives; Louis Métezeau's widow received a pension of 600 *livres*, later increased to 1,000. The salaries connected with professional work were, however, quite a different matter from the earnings of the great personages of court: during the same period Nicolas de l'Hôpital was receiving 120,000 *livres* a year, Count de Nogent 180,000, the highest army officers had incomes varying between 60,000 and 100,000 and became clients of the royal architects, little inferior to the sovereign in liberality and financial resources.[3]

Henri IV, for his part, was eager to encourage building work, and exhorted his subjects to do likewise; he declared himself 'a friend of buildings' and claimed, against anyone believing him to be mean, that he made three things willingly: 'war, love and buildings'.[4] Sully in his *Mémoires* calculated that, between 1594 and 1607, he had spent the following sums for the king:[5]

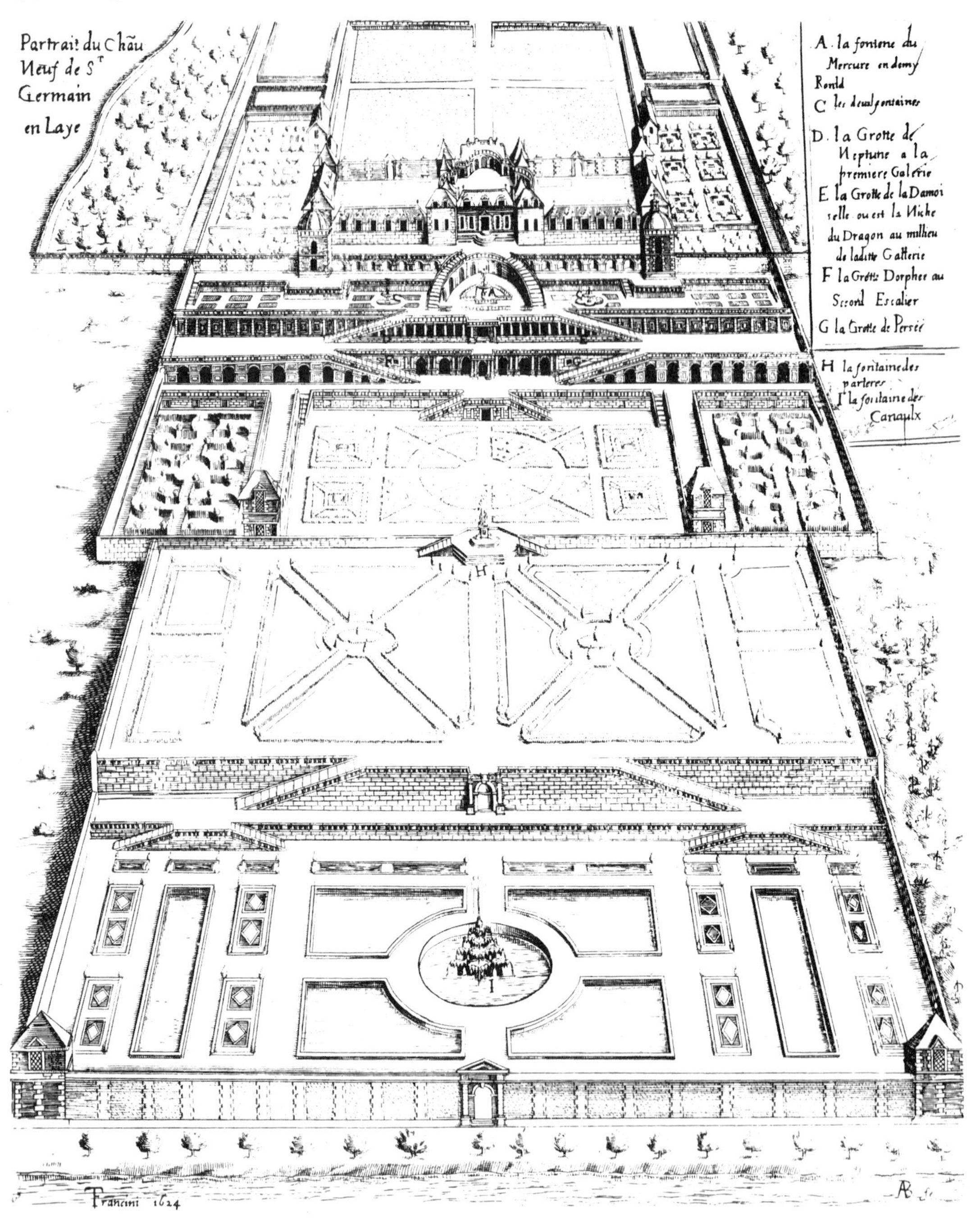

796 *The park of St-Germain-en-Laye in a print of 1624*

for palaces and churches	6,150,000 *livres*
for fortifications	5,785,000 *livres*
for bridges and roads	4,855,000 *livres*
for 'royal furnishings'	1,800,000 *livres*

The building policy of Henri IV and Sully also required the control of workmen's wages. In 1597 the corporative régime was extended to the whole of France (but in 1602 it was limited to the great cities and to a certain number of trades). Building workers were dependent on a *maître général des oeuvres de maçonnerie*, a post set up in 1595 (Guillaume Marchant, succeeded in 1604 by his son Louis). The traditional guilds were born once again to the advantage of absolutism and confirmed or introduced a series of restrictive rules concerning apprenticeship, charters, working hours and rates of pay: thus, while the price of building land and buildings was already increasing from 1599 onwards, wages remained unchanged until 1625, then tended to increase slowly and more certainly after the middle of the century. The profits from the rebuilding and the first phase of building development were totally appropriated by the capitalist class.

The corporative organization was controlled by a body of state civil servants, and their posts, like others, were saleable, so that their number increased rapidly; in 1645 a second *maître général* was introduced for structural work. The result of this was the anachronistic continuance of some medieval institutions; the guild of painters – which included, as in the past, artists and house painters – obtained confirmation of its privileges in 1582 and 1622; inter alia it could confiscate the equipment and materials of independent painters and sculptors.

Exceptions to this system applied to artists in the service of the king and the new manufactories promoted by the state to replace foreign luxury goods: those of leatherwork, glass and Pyrenean marble.

These measures were justified, to some degree, by the gravity of the economic crisis at the beginning of the reign of Henri IV; the effects of monetary inflation, reported by Jean Bodin to the Estates General in 1576, were added to the effects of civil war. In the building field the crisis was particularly violent; in Paris, besieged by Henri IV in 1589, 1590 and 1591, the suburbs of St-Germain, St-Antoine and the aqueducts had been destroyed; rents were reduced by a third in 1589, by half in 1590 and three-quarters in 1592, and tenants had permission not to pay without being prosecuted. The situation was normalized after Henri IV's entry into Paris in 1594, and building resumed its normal rhythm only in the early years of the seventeenth century. State intervention served first to solve this state of affairs, but then to create a framework of institutions which survived for a long time, and characterized the running of the *ancien régime* until 1789. The state functioned by controlling or itself running, through the new class of civil servants, certain economic or politically more important activities; building was one of these and it fell largely under the protection of the state which increasingly replaced local groups and bodies.

The works undertaken by Sully for Henri IV, during the short decade of his effective power, can be divided into three categories, which roughly correspond to the first three sections of the budget already quoted:

1 Works of fortification: here Sully enjoyed the greatest degree of freedom and did not encounter the resistance of peripheral bodies or civil servants. In fact the edict of May 1604 ('*Règlement que le roi veut que l'on observe pour les fortifications de chaque province du royaume*') laid down that the new works no longer depended upon the governors of the provinces or municipalities, but upon a body of inspectors and engineers; contract replaced the *corvée* system.

To put this law into action the first specialized body of royal engineers was formed. At this time French military technicians began to replace Italian ones; in 1594 Jean Errard published *La Fortification demonstrée et réduite en art*, and Jacques Perret in 1601 *L'Architecture et perspective des fortifications*; Errard was appointed chief engineer to the king, and laid out a chain of fortresses along the frontiers of France. In Paris Henri IV restored the walls of Charles V and began to build the extension to include the district of the Tuileries, already planned by Charles IX, but these works went ahead slowly and were to be proved useless in the middle of the century, when Louis XIV had the fortifications of Paris destroyed.

2 Roads, canals and land drainage, i.e. infrastructures on a regional scale: Sully acted as *grand voyer de France*, and often had to face the hostility of the provincial *voyers*, who did not accept the interference of the central power. He improved the road network, restored or had built a series of bridges, planned a network of navigable canals and in 1604 began the execution of the canal de Briare between the Seine and the Loire, drained the marshlands, ordered the conservation of the forests and planted the typical rows of elms along the main roads; city water supplies were procured by means of aqueducts of the traditional type, or by hoisting equipment, such as the pump in Paris on the Pont Neuf, known as the Samaritaine (1602).

Works in masonry, such as bridges, were the concern of builders: the Pont Neuf in Paris (1599–1607) was built by Guillaume Marchant, possibly under the supervision of Jacques II Androuet du Cerceau; the bridge over the Garonne at Toulouse, begun in 1544, was continued by Dominique Bachelier, Pierre Souffron (1597–1613) and finally Jacques Lemercier, who provided the definitive design in 1614.

For hydraulic works Sully turned to foreign specialists like Jean Lintlaer, the builder of the Samaritaine, and Humphrey Bradley, who in 1599 was appointed *maître des digues du royaume*.

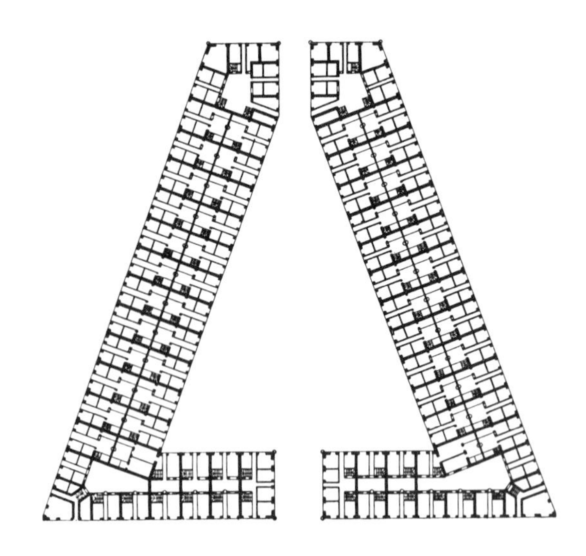

797 *Plan of place Dauphine, Paris (from Blunt)*

3 Buildings and the transformation of cities. The work on the royal châteaux at Fontainebleau, Vincennes, Monceaux-en-Brie, Verneuil and St-Germain-en-Laye belonged to the private sphere of the king and registered his personal preferences. For the most part it was the logical continuation of work carried out by his predecessors and did not introduce any great novelties; the only exception was the enlarging of his favourite residence of St-Germain-en-Laye which – possibly at the suggestion of the queen, Marie de Médicis – imitated the Italian model of terraced gardens opened up on a slope overlooking an extensive view. The palace, too, was built by Marchant, possibly to a plan by Métezeau. The garden sloping down to the Seine was realized by Claude Mollet, who claimed to have followed a plan by E. du Perac, the engraver who worked for a long time in Italy; Tommaso Francini came from Italy to deal with the hydraulic installations and was appointed *intendant des eaux* for all royal residences and founded a dynasty that was to be active for a long time in France (his descendants executed the fountains of Versailles for Louis XIV); the works, often

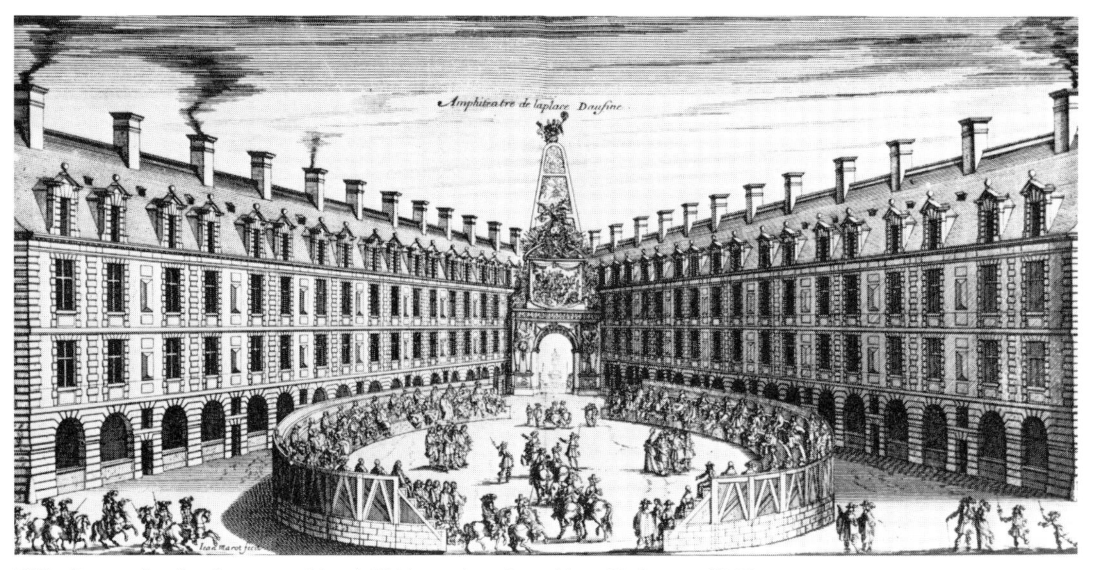

798 *Decoration for the entry of Louis XV into place Dauphine, 26 August 1660*

supervised by the king, went ahead rapidly and were completed by 1604.

Intervention in the cities, on the other hand, and particularly in Paris, amounted to a positive public programme, which rationally developed the possibilities afforded by the new administrative instruments, though it also registered the limitations of the previously established situations; it marked a turning-point in the slow transformation of the townscape of the capital.

In Paris city organization was particularly strong, and was usually in conflict with the court. The *maîtres généraux de maçonnerie* formed a dynasty unbroken since the time of François I; this position passed in 1544 from Pierre de Chambiges to his son-in-law Guillaume Guillain, then in 1582 to his son Pierre, in 1614 to his grandson Augustin I and in 1676 to the great-grandson Augustin II. In smaller towns the *maître maçon* usually performed the function of *voyer*, but in Paris their provinces were separate; Sully could therefore control the actions of the city functionaries in his capacity as *grand voyer*, and in 1603, to avoid direct conflicts, he

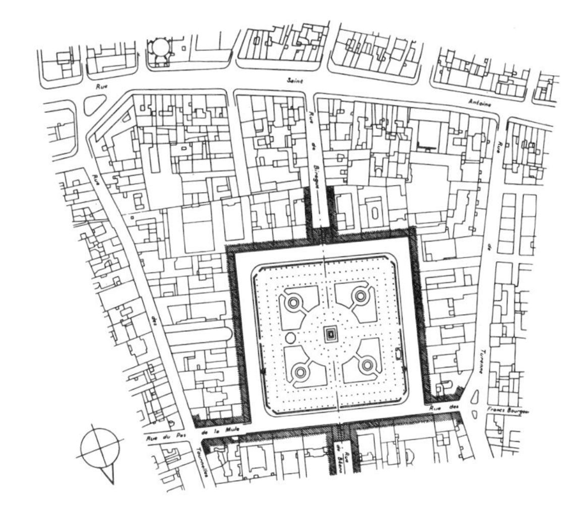

799 *Plan of place Royale (now place des Vosges), Paris (from Auzelle)*

800 *A tournament in place Royale in 1612*

acquired the post of *voyer* of Paris. In this position he had the power to see that the building regulations were observed (the edict of 1607 established that the *voyer* must set the alignment of new buildings and see that it had been respected by the completed buildings; if this were not the case, 'the ill-placed building shall be torn down'[6]) and to carry out the special works decided upon by the Council of State, i.e. the laying out of place Dauphine, place Royale and the enlargement of the Louvre.

Henri IV announced his proposal to '*embellir*' the city to the municipal authorities in a meeting of 11 March 1606.

The first scheme concerned the land adjoining the Pont Neuf, a bridge begun by Henri III in 1578, and situated at the western end of the Île de la Cité, to link the two new suburbs of St-Honoré and St-Germain. The original plan envisaged two rows of houses along the road bed, as on other Parisian bridges. Henri IV, who brought the work to completion between 1599 and 1606, did away with the houses and built a singular architectural complex on the island spanning the bridge: an equestrian statue at the vertex, and a triangular square, which gave a symmetrical form to the tip of the island and framed the statue against the background of the Louvre and Tuileries towards the river (Figs 797–8). The plan was realized from 1607 onwards, the land being ceded to the first *président du parlement*, de Harlay; the statue, commissioned from Giambologna, was cast in Florence by Pietro Tacca, and sent to its site in 1614. The author of the plan is unknown, but it is known that the division into plots was carried out by Fontaine and Marchant, the building work by François Petit (such activities were now the result of direct negotiation between client and contractor). On the left bank, along the axis of the new bridge, the rue Dauphine was begun in 1607, the first straight gash of demolition into the body of the medieval city; this road became the approach to the Palais du Luxembourg, which Marie de Médicis had built from 1611 onwards, and the houses running along it were to be all identical.

The second scheme – place Royale – was in the district of the Marais, on a site owned by the king where the decision to build a new symmetrical square had been made as early as 1563. The basic layout was traced in 1604, an almost exact square. Originally it was to have been bordered by buildings for a cloth manufactory, and one of these was built in the following year; in 1605 it was decided to build dwellings for the workers on the other three sides, but between 1606 and 1607 the block on the south side was built, formed of identical bourgeois dwellings and dominated in the centre by the *pavillon du roi*, which remained the property of the sovereign; it was then decided to demolish the manufactory and to repeat the same architectural motif on the other sides. The square was completed in 1612, when the tournament represented in Fig. 800 was held, and it functioned as a quiet aristocratic quarter, cut off from the traffic-bearing roads; the screen of buildings was broken only at one point, to let through the carriages which entered at a tangent on the north side; the other means of access were concealed beneath the arches of the porticoes. The central space was occupied by an enclosed esplanade, accessible only to the owners of the houses, and only in 1639, when Richelieu put the equestrian statue of Louis XIII there, did it become a public open space (Figs 799–800).

For this square, too, the names of the contractors are known (Jean Robelin for the *pavillon royal*) but not that of the designer; it is thought that it was Louis Métezeau, the brother of Clément who after 1610 designed the main square of Charleville, which we discussed in chapter 4. The architectural motif of the façades was extraordinarily dis-

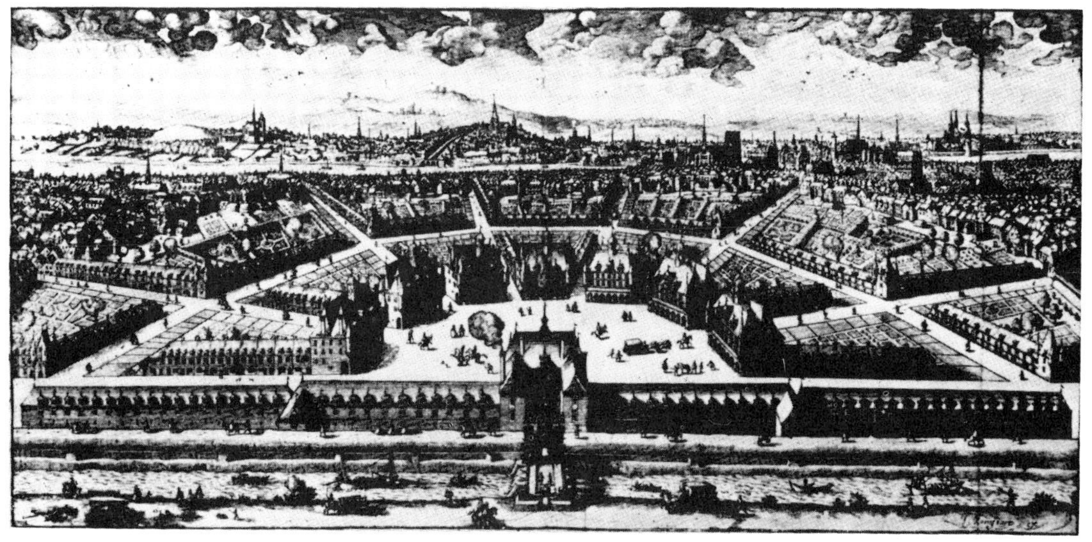

801 *View of the projected place de France, Paris*

802 *Panorama of Paris in 1615 (from Merian)*

FAVXBOVRGS DE PARIS AVEC LA DESCRIPTION DE SON ANTIQVITE
LA RIVIERE DE SEINE

803 *The façade of St-Etienne-du-Mont, Paris, 1610*

crete, as at Charleville, and meant that one could barely distinguish the various units; but the division of the properties was revealed by the roofs, since each house was covered by an independent hip roof. It was as though the architecture was a light veneer, indispensable but not predominant; the effect of the square derives from the direct visualizing of the town-planning operations, layout and division into plots.

In 1603 Henri IV designed a third semi-circular square – place de France – on the high ground near the Temple; but the processes of compulsory purchase dragged on until 1609 and the enterprise was broken off after the king's death (Fig. 801).

It should be noted that the three squares designed at this time had three regular forms, different and clearly recognizable: the triangle, the square and the semi-circle: the conception on the town-planning scale was in fact the decisive element, and the conception of the individual buildings was strictly subordinated to it.

But the most ambitious of Henri IV's building programmes – executed only very partially because of the shortage of time – concerned the Louvre. The old château and palace of the Tuileries, begun by Catherine de Médicis in 1564, had been abandoned and ruined since the time of the civil war; Henri IV had the two buildings restored, built the linking gallery to the south, on the banks of the Seine, and reorganized the gardens of the Tuileries; he also made plans to complete the *cour carrée* begun by Lescot, and to link the two palaces to the north as well, along the rue St-Honoré, demolishing the whole intermediate district, as Malherbe recounts in a letter to Reiresc in 1608; the first plan was completed by Louis XIII and Louis XIV, the second only by Napoleon III.

At the same time Sully was restoring the city's aqueducts; he took measures for streets to be cleaned, at first by contracting this service to private firms (Michel Gaultier in 1601, Raymond Vedel in 1608), then organizing it as a public service, financed with a tax on wine (1609); he had the sewers repaired and began covering in the gutters in the city; in 1606 and 1609 he arranged for the streets to be paved at the expense of the state. When Sully gave up his posts, in 1611, the continuity of the works was guaranteed by Fourcy in the superintendence of buildings, and by the lieutenants to the *grand voyer*; Sully, like Colbert and Haussmann, put into motion a mechanism that was collective and lasting.

Similar works of reconstruction and improvement were realized, at the same time, in other French cities. The rise in population necessitated the extension of Lille (1603), Aix-en-Provence (1605) and Rennes (1609); Lyon developed on the right bank of the Saône; in Rouen the gardens around the big houses of the old centre disappeared and were filled by new buildings. With letters patent authorizing the raising of local taxes, the king financed the construction of public buildings, such as the town hall in Toulon (1606) and the parliament in Rennes (1609). Like other civil servants of Henri IV, Sully was able to realize important building enterprises on his own account as well: the château of Rosny (1599), the improvements to the château of Sully (1602), the enlargement of the town of St-Amand (1605) and the

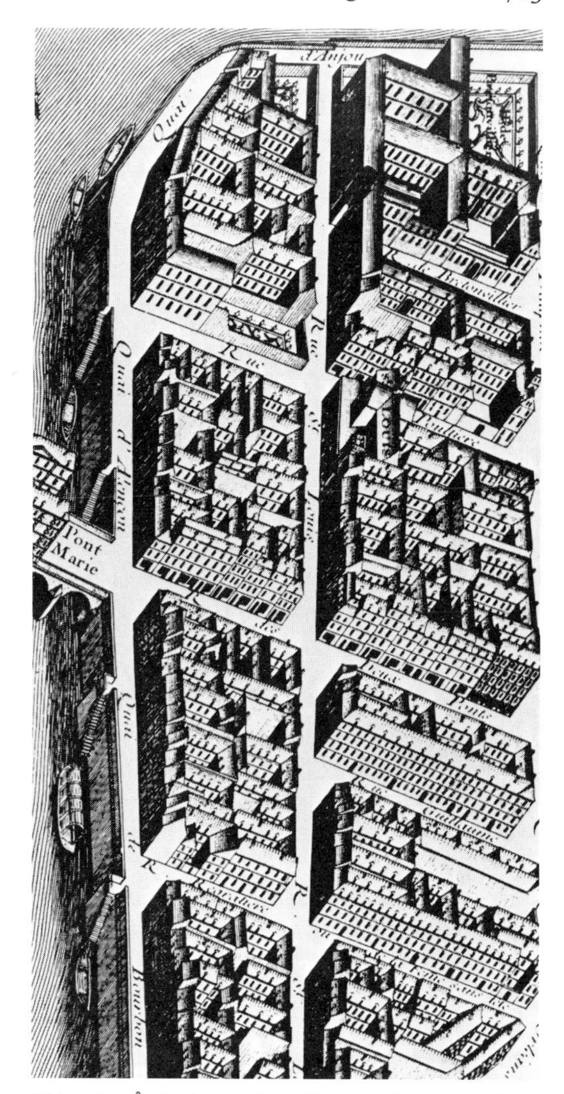

804 *The Île St-Louis, Paris (from the Turgot plan)*

building of the new city of Henrichemont (1608) which we have already discussed in chapter 4.

The author of the *Chasse du vieil grognard*, at the end of Henri IV's reign, described the new French countryside as follows:[7]

'At present we see our countryside enriched with superb edifices . . . and with bourgeois houses which are to be seen in quantity, built with admirable structures, roofed with slate, furnished with fountains and magnificent gardens well away from the courtyards where the peasants foregather, and we see the superb châteaux of the servants of the royal court, nobles and financiers, who in less than a year have upset a thousand rustic dwellings to make a new building.'

The decade of Henri IV was decisive in the formation of the building policy of the *ancien régime*; this was the moment of the formation of the organizational structure that made possible the *grands travaux* of Louis XIII, Louis XIV and Louis XV. At this period political, economic and administrative factors had the greatest weight, while technical contributions had not yet proportionately developed and figurative ones were at a minimum.

Between the murder of Henri IV (1610) and the beginning of the reign of Louis XIV (1661), the organization created by Henri IV continued to function but the balance of factors was altered. Under the rule of Marie de Médicis (1610–24) the effects of the economic stabilization produced by Sully continued, but the central power was weakened, and the initiative passed to private operators; this was the period of the great building speculators, of which we shall say more shortly. Under the rule of Richelieu (1624–43) and Mazarin (1643–61) the state's authority was strengthened, but France was engaged in external or civil wars, and the royal finances were frequently in a state of chaos, so that less building was undertaken; meanwhile the new French artistic culture – of which we spoke in chapter 5 – was emerging, as was the new scientific culture, which favoured technical progress. Thus Colbert, the second restorer of the French economy, had at his disposal a series of highly perfected instruments, which made possible the influential works of architecture and town-planning of the last decades of the seventeenth century.

Sully's economic policy caused the population of the cities to increase, and that of Paris first of all; between the last decade of the sixteenth century and 1637 its inhabitants increased from about 200,000 to 415,000. Real estate investments were made desirable by continuing inflation, and buildings afforded a higher income than agricultural land (from 4 to 6 per cent). The court encouraged building activity in every way, both to provide employment for workers and to put the enormous fortunes accumulated by the civil servants back into circulation.

These conditions encouraged building speculation, particularly in Paris.

In 1614 the engineer Christophe Marie – who rebuilt the Pont de Neuilly between 1608 and 1611 – was engaged in building a new bridge over the Seine upstream from the Île de la Cité, and received in exchange the authority to divide up the uninhabited islands existing on the river bed into building plots. In 1611 and 1614 Marie joined two wealthy functionaries of the military administration, Poulletier and Le Regrattier, and had legal proceedings brought against him by the canons of Notre Dame, who claimed possession of the islands. The royal council decided in 1616 that the king should acquire the sites, compensating the canons, and that the latter should retain their seigneurial right to the new district (this was the transition from the old feudal possession to the new right of landed ownership, which included the right to build). The bridge was opened to traffic in 1635, but in the meantime the new island, which took the name Île St-Louis, had been completely divided up into building plots (Fig. 804); during the next decade numerous luxury dwellings were built around the edges, mostly by Louis Le Vau. In 1643 Corneille was struck by the rapidity of this transformation, and wrote:[8]

'Paris semble à mes yeux un pays de roman;
J'y croyais ce matin voir une île enchantée
Je la laissai déserte et la trouve habitée.'

For the first time poetry was registering the surprise people felt at the gathering speed of urban changes; the form of the city was no longer the unchanging background to individual happenings, but a system that changed, in some places, at the same rate as human affairs.

On the left bank, opposite the Tuileries, lay the extensive property of queen Marguerite, the first wife of Henri IV, who died in 1615 leaving vast debts. The exploitation of this site was assigned in 1622 to a group of five financiers – de Garsanlan, de Vassan, Potier, Le Barbier and de Sandras – likewise high functionaries in the army and royal court. The plan for its division into plots also included a covered market, partly built between 1636 and 1643 and then demolished to make room in 1660 for the musketeers' barracks. The new district was connected to the right bank by a wooden bridge, built in 1631 by Le Barbier.

This district, like the previous one on the Île St-Louis, was organized on a grid plan similar to the sixteenth-century plans examined in chapter 4. The street network, in fact, was merely an instrument to give access to a series of plots, as regular as possible, and the architectural interest concerns the internal structure of the *hôtels*, with their courtyards and gardens, rather than the roads and squares.

In the old districts, too, many small alterations were transforming the old urban fabric.

In 1623 on the Île de la Cité, next to the Palais de Justice, the rue Neuve–St-Louis was begun, and in 1631 the rue Neuve–St-Anne, which completed the place Dauphine district. In the Marais, around the old centres of place Royale, the numerous *hôtels* which still characterize it were now being built; in 1610, covering an old sewer, the rue de Turenne was opened, and in 1626 some of the radial roads intended to branch off place de France were built, also to give access to the new bourgeois and noble houses. In the district of the Louvre, too, many *hôtels* were being built for court dignitaries, particularly on the sites made available by the demolition of the walls of Charles V and conceded for nothing by the king.

As usually happened, these speculative activities tipped the balance of building supply in favour of bourgeois or noblemen's houses, and produced an increase in the demand for popular housing; thus in the city the poor quarters became even denser, and suburbs began to grow up outside the city walls, particularly on the right bank. In 1638 Louis XIII issued a decree to 'repress the abuse of building, both in city and suburbs, in the places where hitherto buildings have been neither built nor planned, and in particular in the said suburbs, and beyond them in the sites which hitherto served for the cultivation of vegetables, salads and fruit necessary to feed the city'.[9] The ordinance absolutely prohibited building outside a certain perimeter, but it had no effect; as early as 1639 the archbishop of Paris established the parish of the Madeleine, and the king granted the Dominicans permission to build a convent at Charonne. A decree of 1644 instituted a fine on new buildings, proportionate with the surface occupied.

In this period the population of Paris rose

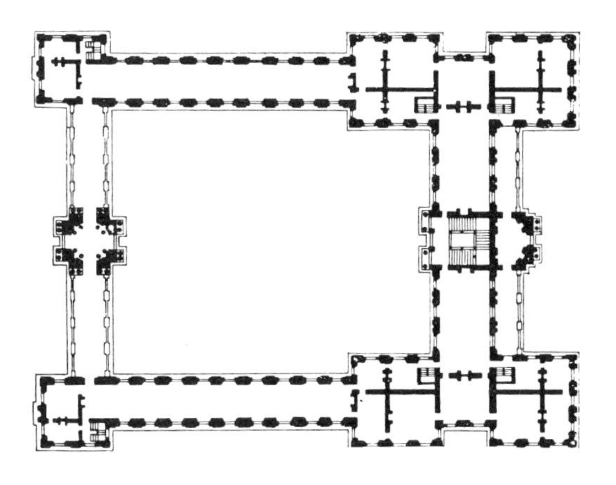

805 *Plan of the Palais du Luxembourg, Paris*

806 *The* cour carrée *of the Louvre, Paris*

above 400,000 inhabitants and the writers of the time, disconcerted by the extent of this urban agglomeration hitherto unknown in Europe, compared the French capital to the great cities of ancient times, though information as to its actual size and population were still very uncertain.

Jacques Gomboust, in 1652, began his description of Paris with these words:[10]

'This great and famous city is second only in age to the most famous in the world, which natural disasters, wars and fires have spared, making the comparison possible. Neither Rome, Constantinople, Naples, Venice, Lisbon, London, Vienna, Amsterdam, Antwerp nor all the other cities of Europe are equal to Paris in size, wealth, magnificence and population, not to mention excellence and diversity of all kinds of science and art, business and relations with the whole of the world; we may call her the queen of cities, since she is the capital city of a realm itself equally superior to others.'

The importance of the great city in the economic and cultural field was much greater than its numerical aspect; Paris was a reality distinct from the court – 'a miniature world', as Gomboust says – and when the court was held elsewhere, in Versailles, the city remained its opposite pole. If power was concentrated at court, Paris represented public opinion. But this multiform community, linked to the fortunes of the country and at the same time refractory to the logic of power, remained spatially elusive; the town-planning layout was still medieval, weakened in its fundamental structures and strained by an excessive load of buildings and people, yet not basically renewed. The precariousness of the urban balance concealed and at the same time worsened the contradictions of the political and social balance.

Political power, after the death of Henri IV, was neither forceful enough nor indeed equipped to master this organism as it grew from year to year.

Marie de Médicis decided to take up residence some way from the centre of the city; in 1611, with this end in mind, she acquired the Hôtel de Luxembourg, then other surrounding properties, and planned to build a new palace in their place, similar to that of the grand dukes of Tuscany where she had grown up. Louis Métezeau was commissioned to go to Florence to make measured drawings of Palazzo Pitti, and Salomon de Brosse, the queen's architect from 1608, was to prepare the designs; the building was begun in 1615, suspended after the murder of Concini in 1617, and completed from 1620 to 1627, at enormous expense (750,000 *livres* up to 1622) (Fig. 805). In building this work de Brosse was making his own personal speculation, and appears as

807 *The courtyard of the Palais Royal, Paris, on the basis of the Palais Cardinal de Richelieu*

both architect and contractor and as stone-supplier; in fact he gave rise to some scandal and was dismissed as contractor, but remained in his position as designer; the best artists of the time, including Rubens, were commissioned for the decorations.

A second undertaking by Marie de Médicis, more important for its future consequences, concerned the *promenades* outside the city limits. In 1599 the Mail had been opened in Paris, an avenue for the public to walk in to the east of the city; similar avenues existed in Blois and Tours. The queen had laid out the green area between the Champs-Élysées and the Seine, on the model of the Cascine in Florence, and opened a new avenue, called Cours-la-Reine, which prolonged the space of the city beyond the ring of fortifications under construction; the enclosed city of the Middle Ages and sixteenth century was about to be transformed into the open city of Louis XIV, where the peripheral *boulevards* replaced the fortifications.

Louis XIII liked to live outside the court environment; in 1623 he had a small château built at Versailles, and had on several occasions continued the work begun by Henri IV at Fontainebleau. But meanwhile Richelieu persuaded him to resume work on the Louvre; on 5 January 1624 the king ordered the suspension of all initiatives within the perimeter concerned, and on 14 April he issued a call for tenders. The design was by the new leader of French classicism, Lemercier, while the de Brosse and du Cerceau families appear as contractors (Fig. 806).

Between 1624 and 1643 Lemercier realized most of the great *cour carrée*, doubling the size of Lescot's building. In 1638 the charge of superintendent of buildings passed from Henri de Fourcy, son of Jean, to Sublet de Noyers, who had even greater ambitions for the work; Poussin was summoned from Rome for the decoration of the Grande Galérie, but he stayed only from 1641 to 1642, being unused to the restricting Parisian type of organization.

Richelieu competed with the king in displaying his power through monumental buildings; his personal income was between 1,000,000 and 3,000,000 *livres* which enabled him in effect to maintain a court. In the country he acquired and enlarged the châteaux of Rueil (1621), Limours (1623), and Bois-le-Vicomte (1628), always in a measure proportionate to his increasing political importance. In Paris in 1627 he received the old Hôtel de Luxembourg as a gift from the queen, but from 1624 he began to acquire a series of properties near the porte St-Honoré, between the Louvre and the old circle of walls, then between this and the new one traced by Henri IV. Here Richelieu realized at the same time a new palace – designed by Lemercier – and a new district. The negotiations for the acquisition of sites were long and hindered by the complex ramifications of landed, economic and political interests. Richelieu used a singular combination of public and private instruments: in 1631 he procured for himself the general management of the new fortifications, and in 1633 he conceded the execution of the works to a secondary figure – Charles Frogier – who acted on behalf of Le Barbier, the lotter of queen Marguerite's *hôtel*; he, as was usual, committed himself to executing the work, to compensate the owners and divide up the surrounding sites, with the exemption of those needed by the Cardinal for the palace and garden. Richelieu, the king and their dependants, including Clément Métezeau, Vouet and Lully, took part in this operation as financiers; the du Cerceau and de Brosse were involved as contractors.

The building of the Palais Cardinal de Richelieu followed the course of these transactions; the organism includes two courtyards and a garden, aligned along a main axis; it was completed by a library, chapel and theatre, opened in 1641; along one side ran a series of plots for small *hôtels*, conceded by Richelieu to Le Barbier and with permission, in some cases, to use the garden. Richelieu flattered himself that he was an architect, as well as a dramatic writer, but here with greater reason, because he alone was in simultaneous control of the administrative, economic and technical aspects of the undertaking. Sauval described the palace, a few years afterwards, with these words:[11]

'If it is said that its plan is the most irregular in Paris and the whole kingdom . . . this irregularity, after all, derives only from the fact that we have seen [it] extend and grow with the fortune and hopes of the prime minister. Lemercier, the best and most solid architect of our time, has conducted the building of this great and magnificent palace, or rather Lemercier, in the execution of this palace, merely followed the intention of Cardinal Richelieu, since the latter publicly claimed that he was its sole architect.'

Lemercier had to reconcile the restrictions of the terrain with the demands of monumental dignity; his skill lay in concealing the irregularity that lay behind the façade and in producing an architectural framework as simple and regular as possible. In 1636, twelve years after work had begun, the building was complete and Richelieu presented it to the king; his heirs were to be the *concierges* of the palace and housed in a lateral building. This *coup de théâtre* completed the effect of the great architectural operation; in the passage already quoted, Corneille registered the admiration and surprise felt at the rapidity of the change:[12]

'*Toute une ville entière, avec pompe bâtie*
Semble d'un vieux fossé par miracle sortie.'

808 *Aerial view of the town of Richelieu*

At the same time, from 1624 onwards, the Cardinal began work on the transformation of his family estate at Richelieu: he extended the château, laid out the surrounding park, and in 1631 decided to build a new town alongside the château.

The instruments of this realization were still the feudal ones of royal permission – in 1633 he obtained the privilege of 'building a walled town, with the permission to establish markets and fairs benefiting from the same prerogatives as the towns of Niort and Fontenay-le-Comte'[13] – and of fiscal exemption for the new buildings. The financing of the roads and walls was dealt with by the state administration. Work was proceeding well in 1638, when St Vincent de Paul visited the infirmary organized by his order, and in 1640, when Richelieu decided to found an academy, a college and printing press there. But after the death of the Cardinal, in 1642, part of the population abandoned the town; La Fontaine, who was writing in 1663, pointed out the contrast between the architectural apparatus and the mediocrity of the social life:[14]

'Ce sont des bâtiments fort hauts
Leur aspect vous plairait sans fauts
Les dedans ont quelques défauts
Le plus grand, c'est que manquent d'hôtes.'

In Richelieu, too, the Cardinal made use of Jacques Lemercier, who designed the architecture of the château and general plan of the town, but assigned the actual supervision of the work to his brothers, Pierre and Nicolas,

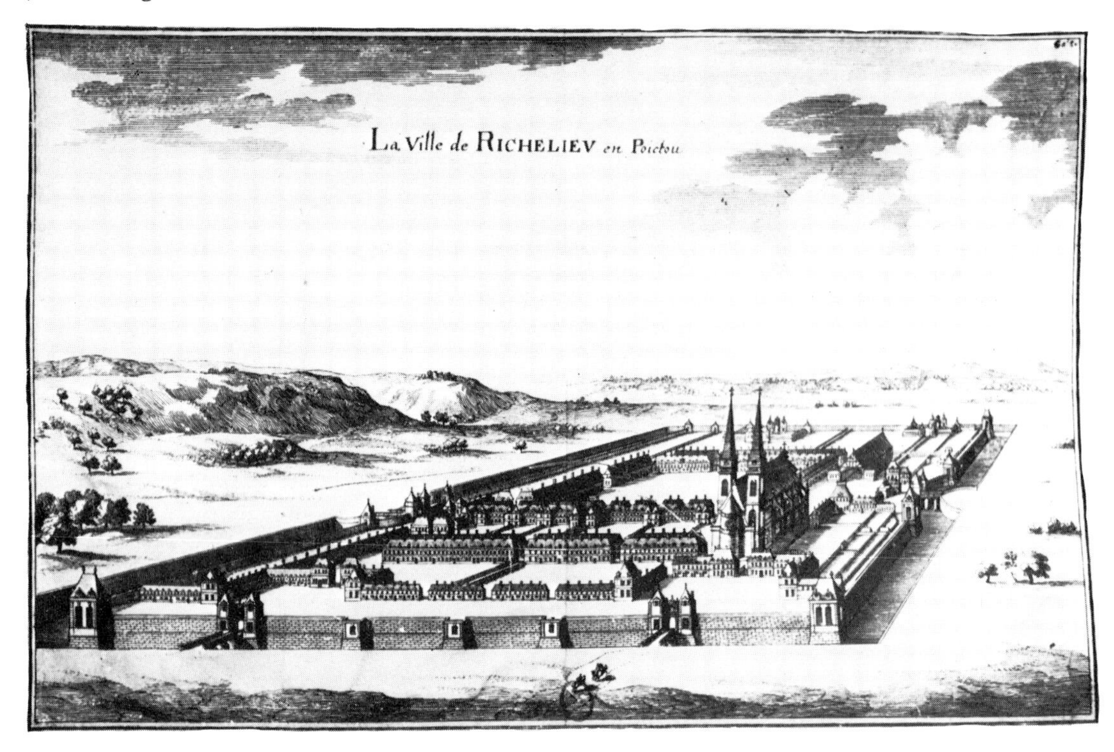

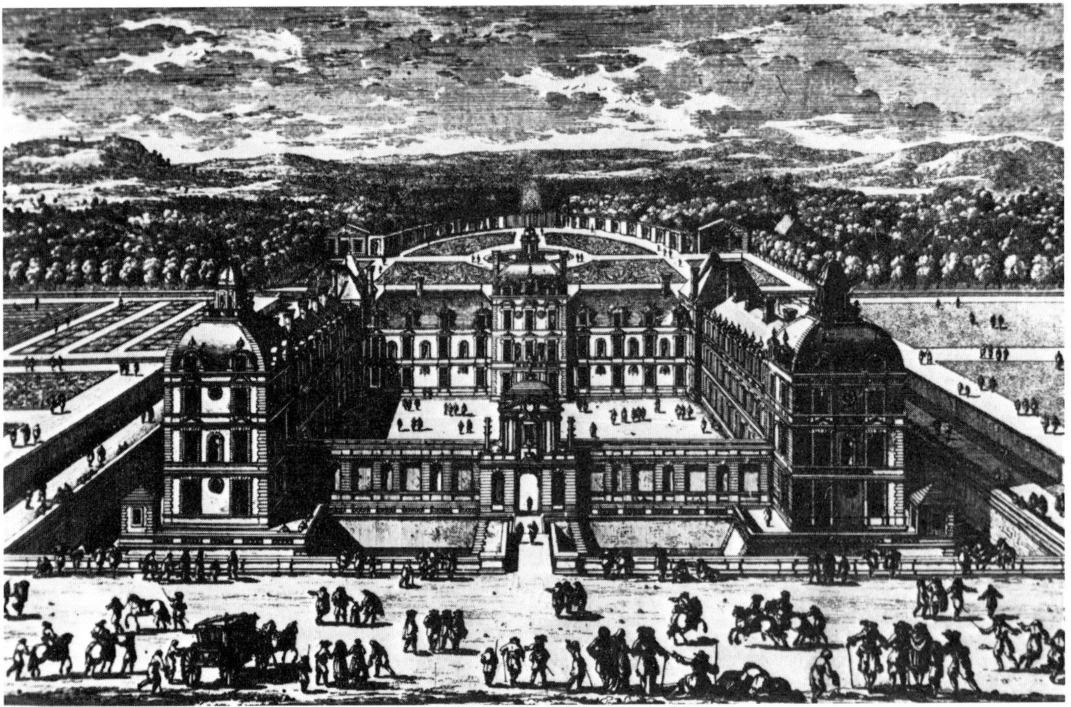

809, 810 *View of Richelieu and its château (from Perelle)*

811 *Aerial view of the main street of Richelieu*

and left the design of the town's buildings to other masters of lesser prestige. The château, as usual, was organized in terms of the two axial views from the entrance and from the park; the town developed along the axis of one of the transversal avenues of the park, and has a grid plan, articulated as at Charleville so as to produce a central square and three secondary ones. The houses of the *grande rue*, designed by Jean Barbet, were all identical; the pattern of the façades is very simple, but its repetition throughout the whole length of the road delighted contemporary writers, who praised the 'symmetry' of the ensemble almost with identical words.[15]

The architectural problem was to grade the decorative details from the aristocratic tone of the château to the bourgeois tone of the town houses, and the operative cycle reflected this gradation exactly. In its general composition the city acted as a frame and perspective preparation for the château, not unlike the tree-filled spaces of the park; for this reason the main element was not the square or any of the town's buildings, but the axial road, treated similarly to one of the avenues. Thus La Fontaine's irony hits home: Richelieu is an empty stage, and Tallemont rightly called it a 'town of cards'.[16]

The cycle of works undertaken by Richelieu and Louis XIII was interrupted suddenly by the death of the two protagonists, between 1642 and 1643. What remains is a series of ambitious architectural pieces, but mutually independent and not linked by any overall design. The new requirements of regularity and monumental propriety remained as occasional trappings and had not yet been translated into a new approach to organisms. Furthermore these works, though designed and decorated by some of the best artists of the time, did not express the best of contemporary artistic culture. A partial but extremely significant antagonism was emerging between power and culture – in the artistic as in the literary and scientific fields; important clients were not in a position to make use of the more original experiments, and these were organized in an individual way, outside and sometimes in opposition to the control of the official apparatus. The case of Poussin, widely acclaimed but permanently exiled in Rome, was similar to the cases of Corneille, Descartes and Pascal; in architecture too – where these conflicts, as we have already observed, were less strong – the most brilliant artist of the time, François Mansart, never attained a professional position comparable to those of his less gifted rivals, Lemercier and Le Vau.

The important cultural experiments which were proliferating during Richelieu's period of government should rather be considered as points of departure for the subsequent cultural synthesis, attained at the time of Colbert. In 1624 the first writings of Gassendi appeared; in 1629 Corneille had his first play performed and in 1637 achieved a resounding success with *Le Cid*; in 1635 Richelieu founded the Académie in France, and the new institution began its career by criticizing the work of the young dramatic writer, already triumphantly accepted by the public; from 1635 onwards François Mansart, almost forty years old, obtained his first court commissions; in 1637 Descartes' *Geometry* and *The Discourse on Method* appeared; between 1640 and 1642, as we have said, Poussin returned to Paris; in 1642 Pascal constructed his calculating machine; in 1643 Molière made his theatrical début.

The experiences altered the terms of the cultural debate; it is necessary for us to point out some of the important consequences for the future in the field of architecture:

1 The 'methodical doubt' of the new theoretical thought did not halt when faced with the commonplaces of artistic culture. The main concern of scientists, philosophers and moralists was no longer the world of visible appearances, but that of reasoning and feeling: the system of the universe and the human heart; none the less rational analysis was applied occasionally to artistic concepts, and they were discussed with an independence of judgment which has no parallel from the sixteenth century onwards. At the beginning of this chapter we quoted a well-known discourse on architecture by Descartes. Pascal wrote this surprising definition of symmetry, one of the key concepts of classicism: 'Symmetry in what we see at a glance. Based on the fact that there is no reason to do otherwise.'[17]

In another of his *Pensées* Pascal tried to translate artistic experiment totally into terms of usage:[18]

'There is a certain model of attractiveness and beauty consisting in a certain relation between our nature, weak or strong as it may be, and the thing which pleases us. Everything that conforms to this pattern attracts us, be it a house, a song, a speech, verse, prose, a woman, birds, rivers, trees, clothes etc. Everything which does not conform to this model is displeasing to people of good taste. And as there is an exact relation between a song and a house based on this good model, because both resemble a single model, though each in its own way, there is in the same way an exact relation between things based on bad models. It is not that there is only one bad model, because there are innumerable, but every bad sonnet, for example, whatever false model it is based on, is exactly like a woman dressed according to that model. Nothing gives a better idea of the absurdity of a bad sonnet than to consider and then to imagine a woman or house conforming to that model.'

The social implication of these judgments was minimal for the moment; but in the following generation they were to produce the arguments of Blondel, Félibien, Charles Perrault and the rational classicism of the late seventeenth century.

2 The development of scientific research influenced building technique. Progress in geometry found an immediate application in the methods of representing three-dimensional objects on the plane; and therefore in perspective, and in calculations for stone-cutting.

After the treatise by Salomon de Caus – *Perspective des ombres et des miroirs*, 1612 – numerous publications of a theoretical character appeared – the *Optiques* of père Mersenne, published posthumously in 1651, the *Perspective curieuse* by père Nicéron, written before 1642 and printed in 1663 – or of a technical character, like the manuals of Aleaume[19] and père du Breuil.[20] The essay by Gérard Desargues[21] presented a contrasting viewpoint, based on the theory of conic sections with which the young Pascal was also concerning himself at that time.[22]

Desargues was also interested in stone-cutting; in 1643, together with the traditional theses of père Derand,[23] an essay of his appeared edited by A. Bosse, which aimed to 'study this matter thoroughly, and reduce it to a universal art of mathematics'.[24] In 1640 Sublet de Noyers commended the workers of the Louvre to apply these rules; Desargues himself, after 1644, designed some staircases of a new type and possibly collaborated with Lemercier on the building of the Sorbonne.

Progress in other fields of building technique was slower. In 1615 and 1644 de Caus published his treatises on mechanics[25] and hydraulics;[26] at this time the technology of pumps was being refined, making it possible to utilize new supplies of water; Pierre Vernier was improving topographical instruments, and in 1631 published the description of the level that bears his name.[27]

3 The new figurative experiments rendered out of date the traditional typological repertoire on which the most important building and town-planning undertakings had hitherto been based. Collectively accepted standards, as we have seen, were replaced by a plurality of hypotheses and individual options. Apart from architecture and the figurative arts, a large number of new or newly fashionable social phenomena were affected by the change in taste: the theatre, religious and civil ceremonies, increasingly complex forms of public and private life. As Hautecoeur[28] says, these phenomena in their turn had an influence on the formation of the *grand goût* in architecture and the major arts.

Changes in manners were considerable, particularly during the government of Mazarin (1643–61); the queen mother, Anne of Austria, was used to the pomp of the Spanish court; Mazarin had been the assistant of Cardinal Barberini, knew the sophisticated Roman artistic scene and cultivated a series of contacts with Italy. These two continued and carried to extremes Richelieu's passion for extravagance: Sauval wrote that Mazarin 'had despoiled the whole world of its riches and curiosities, of its finest furnishings and curiosities, finest books, rarest manuscripts, most illustrious paintings and statues'.[29] His fortune, after his death, was estimated at 40,000,000 *livres*.

Mazarin introduced the Italian theatre to Paris; in 1645 Jacopo Torelli staged the *Finta Pazza* at the Petit Bourbon and in 1647 *Orfeo* at the Palais Royal, amazing the spectators with his scene changes; Corneille and the musician Assoucy wrote *Andromeda* for the queen, performed in 1650 at the Palais Royal, and the writer spoke with irony of the visual apparatus, which 'prevents one from paying attention to what the actors are saying'.[30] From 1659 to 1662, as we have seen, Vigarani was constructing the Salle des Machines at the Tuileries.

This period saw the formation of the style of great public ceremonies: royal ceremonies

– such as the coronation of Louis XIV at Rheims in 1654, and his entrance into Paris in 1660 – funerals, religious festivals, fireworks; in 1660 père Mersenne published a treatise on fireworks,[31] and in 1686 a treatise on funerals.

The Theatines, invited to Paris in 1644 by Mazarin, opened the church of Ste-Anne-la-Royale in 1648, where they organized the magnificent theatrical masses criticized by La Bruyère.[32] In his will the Cardinal bequeathed them a sum to build a new church; the design was by Guarini, and building work, begun in 1662, was interrupted in 1669; it seems however that Guarini's invention produced in Paris only a momentary curiosity (Fig. 812).

The décor required by these ceremonies entailed the building of temporary architecture, which in many cases anticipated later tendencies. The gap between imagination and reality was bridged by perspective illusion, and the geometrical research mentioned earlier found here another field of application.

The artists who developed the new tendencies of taste on the scale of building and landscaping were Louis II Le Vau (1612–70), André Le Nôtre (1613–1700) and Charles Lebrun (1619–90).

Le Vau came from a family of builders. Louis I, *grand voyer* and inspector general of buildings, had two sons, Louis II and François, and introduced them at an early age to the world of building works and speculation. Louis II started his career by building a series of buildings on the Île St-Louis: the Hôtel Lambert (1640), (Fig. 814), the Hôtel Hesselin (1642), and later the Hôtel Lauzun (1656); the Le Vau family acted on the island as the intermediaries of Poulletier, and acquired for themselves a large number of sites and houses. Around the middle of the century Louis II became the favourite architect of the great financiers: he designed the château of Raincy for Bordier, the château of Meudon for Servien, the château of Vincennes for

812 *Guarini's design for the church of Ste-Anne-la-Royale, Paris*

Mazarin and from 1656 to 1660 the château of Vaux-le-Vicomte for the extremely rich superintendent of finances, Fouquet; in 1655 he was appointed architect of the Louvre and Tuileries in the place of Lemercier, and in 1664 he completed the closing in of the *cour carrée*.

Vaux-le-Vicomte was in many ways the most important work built before Louis XIV came to power. Here, together with Le Vau, the designer of gardens Le Nôtre and the

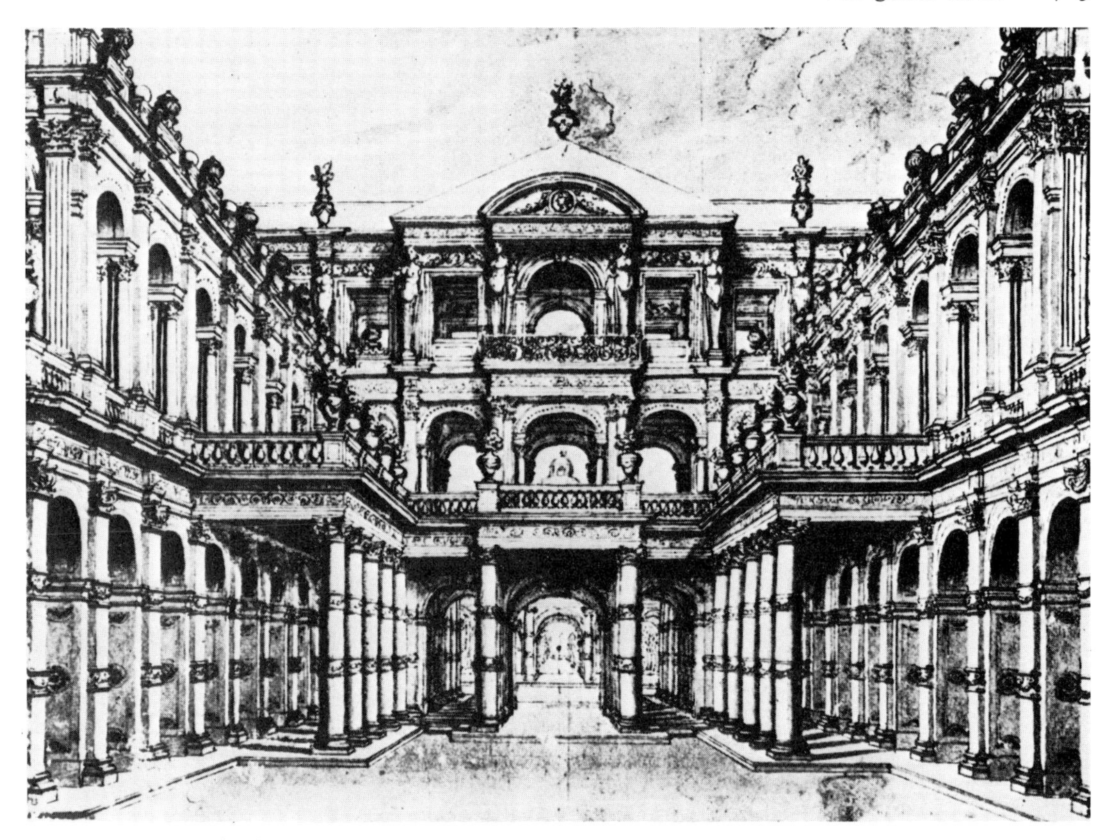

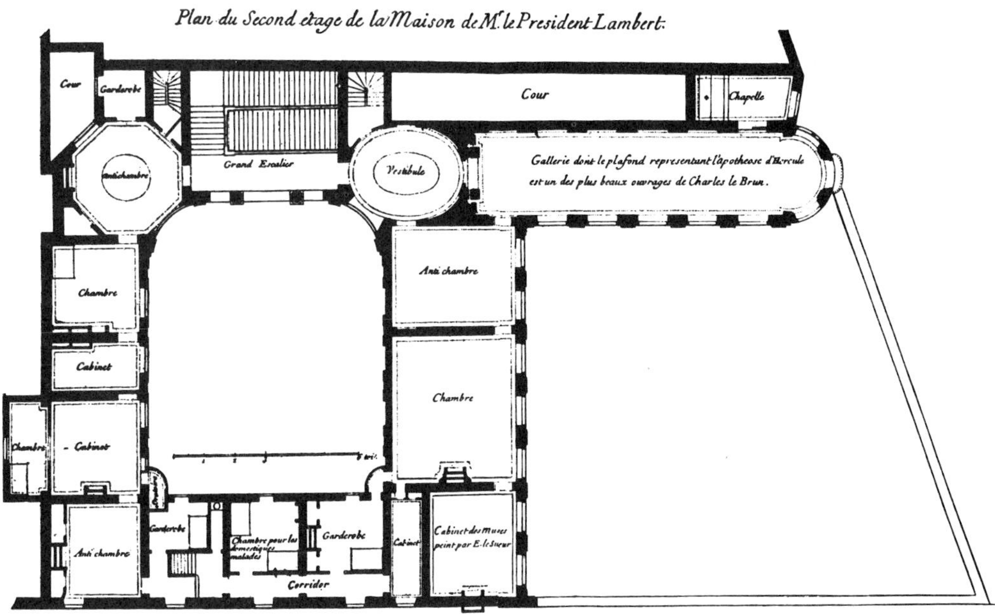

813 *Set by Torelli for* Il trionfo della continenza
814 *Plan of the Hôtel Lambert, Paris*

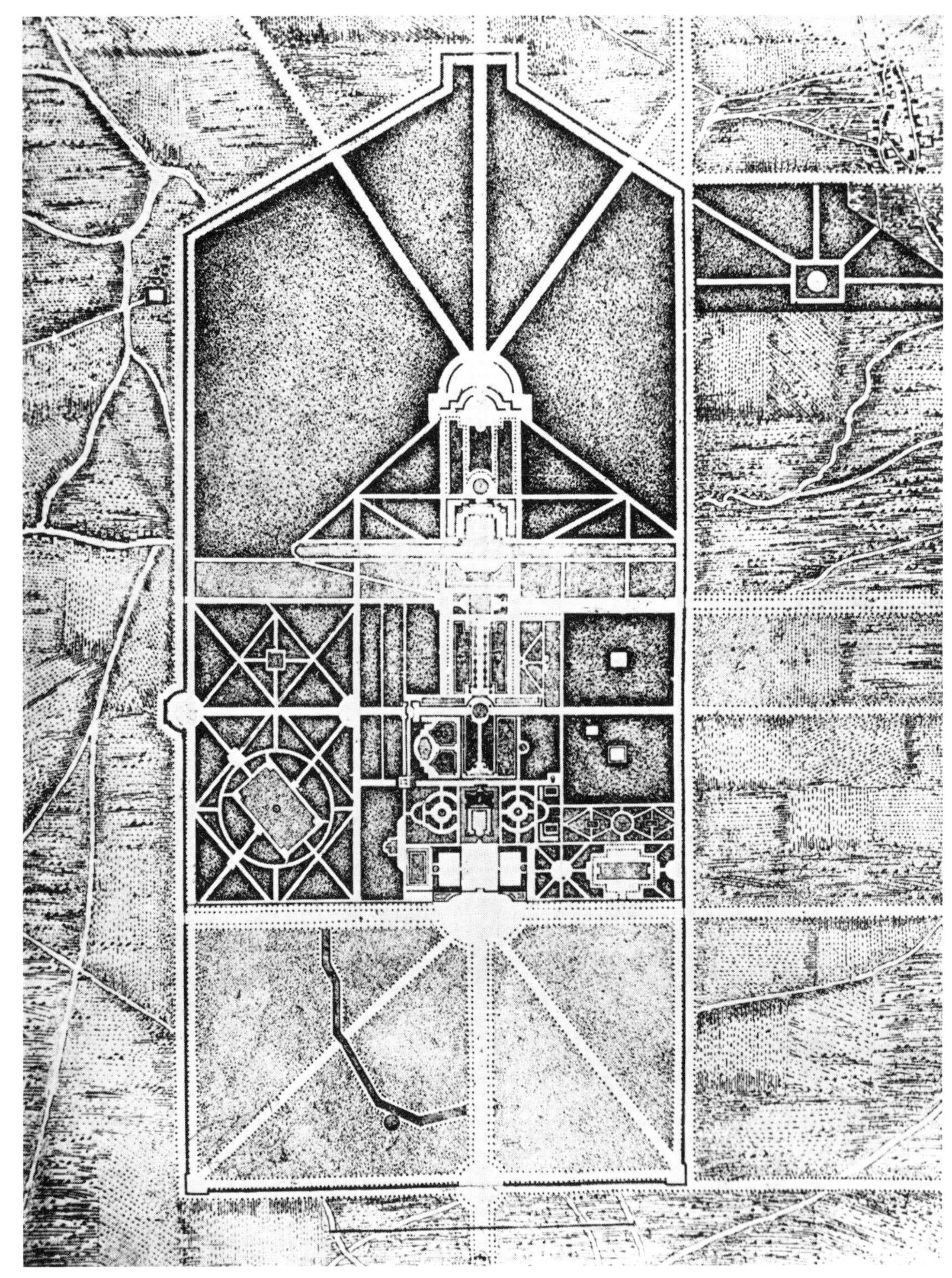

815 *Plan of the park, Vaux-le-Vicomte. Bibliothèque Nationale, Paris*

816 *The château and park at Vaux, from the entrance*

decorator Lebrun worked on a large-scale project for the first time. Their collaboration marked the beginning of a new cycle of experiments: the 'magnificent manner', cultivated individually by Poussin in his painter's studio, became a methodology for the organization of collective work, and could be applied to the creation of an entire landscape, from the basic shaping of the terrain to the final decorative details (Figs 815–18).

Le Nôtre and Lebrun had studied together in the *atelier* of Simon Vouet: Le Nôtre inherited the post of gardener at the Tuileries from his father in 1637, and acquired considerable competence, which in 1656 earned him the title of *contrôleur général des bâtiments du roi*. Lebrun settled in Rome from 1642 to 1646, and was influenced by the example of Poussin; when he went back to Paris, he designed the décor for the gallery of the Hôtel Lambert (1646) and some rooms in the Hôtel de la Rivière (1653). From 1656 onwards they were summoned to Vaux, together with Le Vau, and had to co-ordinate the activities of an army of executors; all three revealed a marked ability for running collective work, and a full appreciation of the possibilities and fundamental limits of this procedure. The individual refinement typical of Mansart or Poussin remained an unattainable model; but the refinement of the individual parts was sacrificed to the coherence of the ensemble. The whole composition, from the large to the small scale, was dominated by the same spirit of clarity and measure, and the various objects – landscape,

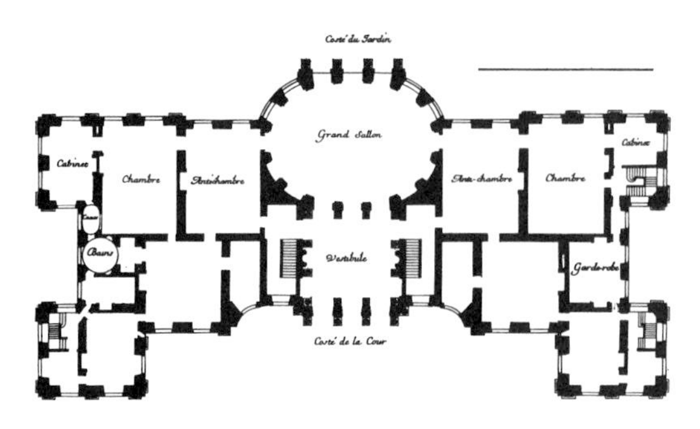

817, 818 *View of the park and plan of the château, Vaux*

trees, pools, buildings, sculptures, paintings and furnishings – formed a continuous gradation, designed and executed with common criteria.

Let us examine the elements of this gradation. Le Nôtre's garden was not only the cornice, but also the dominant structure of the great complex. The château rises on an elevated platform, opened in the middle of the woods, and marks the border between two unequal spaces, treated in a different way. The first, towards the entrance, is regularized by a series of low buildings which surround a vast courtyard; here all the services are concentrated and isolated. The second, reserved for the seigneurs, stretches away over a valley that slopes down longitudinally and transversally; the architectural garden, to be looked at as a foreground, lies along the slope from the château to the bottom of the valley, and is dominated by a symmetrical avenue, along the axis of the building; but the side features – flowerbeds, pools, fountains and groups of trees – are differentiated so as to make up for the transversal slope, and realize a gradual transition from symmetry to asymmetry. The rectangular basin half-way down the slope and the canal dug out at the bottom of the slope – originally a small river – open up two perspectives perpendicular to the main approach and point to the second orographic axis of the ground with their different backdrops. The slope opposite the valley, beyond the canal, serves to conclude the perspective of the main avenue and to give material form to the vanishing-point; in fact a second system of avenues and terraces, simpler and more restricted, leads to a terrace with a grotto and fountain, whose great jet functions as a point at infinity for the perspective picture, and as the pivot of a fan of avenues running into the forest. The terrace of the grotto in its turn functions as a *point de vue* for an inverse perspective, whose vanishing-point is the château surrounded by its terraces.

The figurative models used by Le Nôtre had already been used by the landscape gardeners of the first half of the century – the dynasty of the Mollets, who laid out the parks of St-Germain, Fontainebleau, Monceaux – and were described in the treatise by André Mollet published a few years earlier:[33]

'Of all the things needed for the laying out of a garden, the first is to be able to plant a great avenue of two or three rows of elms or limes, which must be traced perpendicular to the front façade of the house; at the beginning of it a great semi-circle or square should be made. Then in front of the back part of the house flowerbeds should be created *en broderie*, easily visible from the windows, with no intervening trees, hedges or other high things that could prevent the eye from travelling through space. After these flowerbeds will come the lawns, groves, avenues, high and low hedges in their right places, arranged in such a way that most of these avenues shall have as a backdrop some statue or fountain centre, and at the ends of these avenues lovely perspectives on canvas shall be placed, so that they can be removed from the inclemencies of the weather if so desired.'

The painted backdrops were direct imitations of stage scenery, and indicated the desire to create the infinitely vanishing perspectives conceived by Torelli in gardens, as on the stage. But Le Nôtre's aim was different: to attempt the physical representation of the infinite, rather than the figurative representation: in other words, to control a whole portion of countryside, from foreground to background, according to the criteria of regularity and symmetry. He used avenues, flowerbeds, terraces, pools and fountains to this end, but organized them in a calculated system which interpreted the geographical situation of the place, and aimed at the total rationalization of the landscape, including the background at infinity.

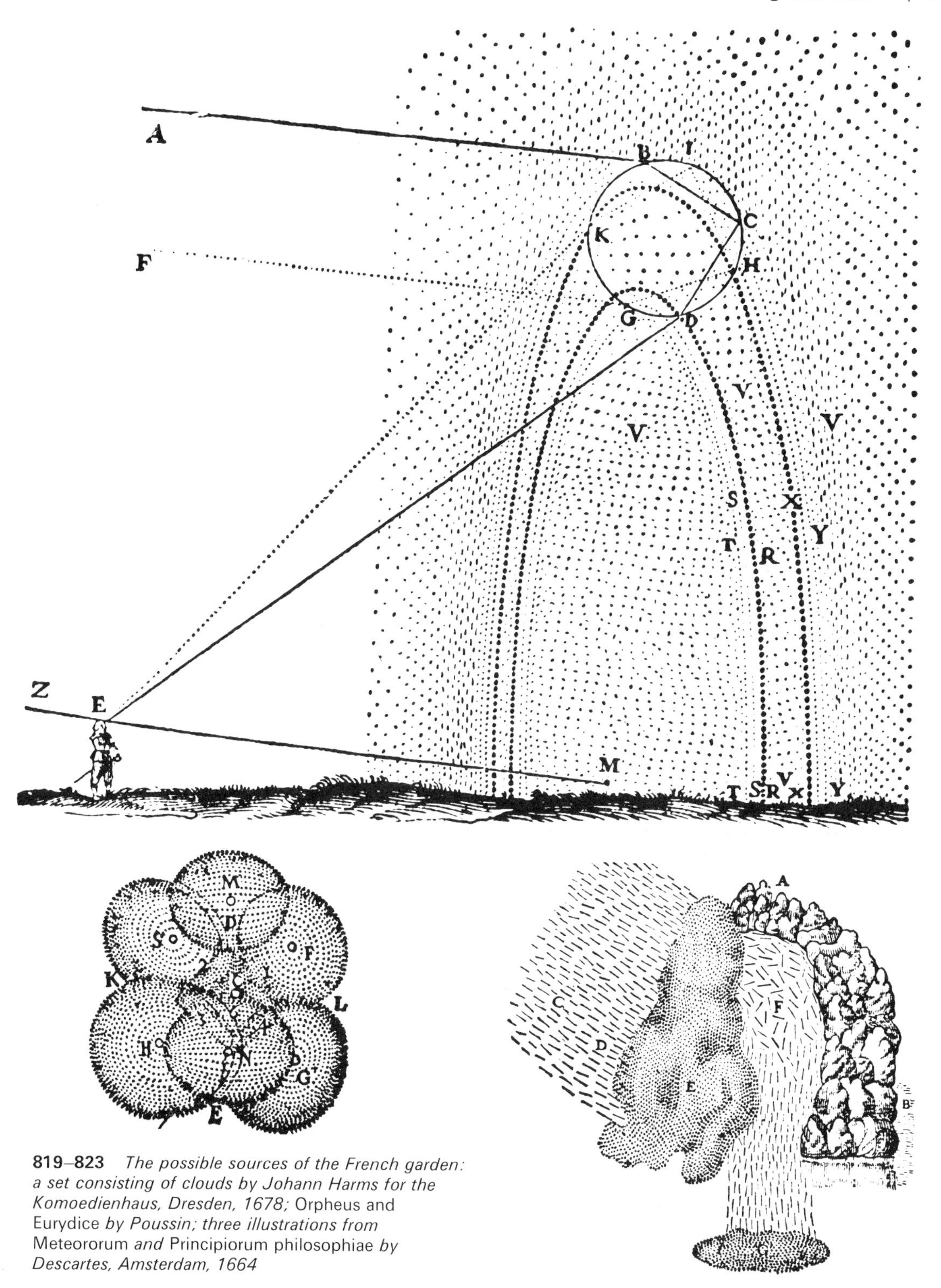

819–823 *The possible sources of the French garden: a set consisting of clouds by Johann Harms for the Komoedienhaus, Dresden, 1678;* Orpheus and Eurydice *by Poussin; three illustrations from* Meteororum *and* Principiorum philosophiae *by Descartes, Amsterdam, 1664*

This attempt broke away from both the experience of the Italian and European Renaissance up to the end of the seventeenth century, and from the tradition of the 'Italian garden'.

In the architecture of the fifteenth and sixteenth centuries in Italy what concerned the designers was to achieve the symbolic representation of the perspective infinite, which was achieved by making the vanishing-point of an axis of symmetry coincide with a curved structure: the apse for a longitudinal axis, the dome for a vertical one. Only Bramante, in his courageous research into the extreme possibilities of classicism, encountered for a moment – in the courtyard of the Belvedere – the problem of the physical representation of the infinite, i.e. the laying out of a space so big that the more distant structures counted, by approximation, as the background at infinity of the perspective whole.

The Italian gardens of the sixteenth and seventeenth centuries, too, were organized according to the principle of limited views. The garden remained linked to the house in that its dimensions were comparable with those of the house; the architecturally defined views did not in practice exceed 200 metres, and the whole garden, as a regular and measurable architectural object, was introduced into the irregular and non-measurable landscape, contrasting with or gradually merging into it. For this reason in many cases high places were preferred, where a natural panorama of infinite distance could be enjoyed, in contrast to the artificial and limited panorama of the architecture and garden.

But the 'French garden' conceived by Le Nôtre eliminated this antithesis; for this reason it occupied preferably not an open height but a hollow, and established a continuous gradation from nearby objects to distant ones, from views measured in hundreds of metres to those measured in thousands; at Vaux the two main perspective axes – that joining château to grotto and the length of the transversal canal – measure about 1,200 metres, and the whole park measures about three kilometres by one and a half.

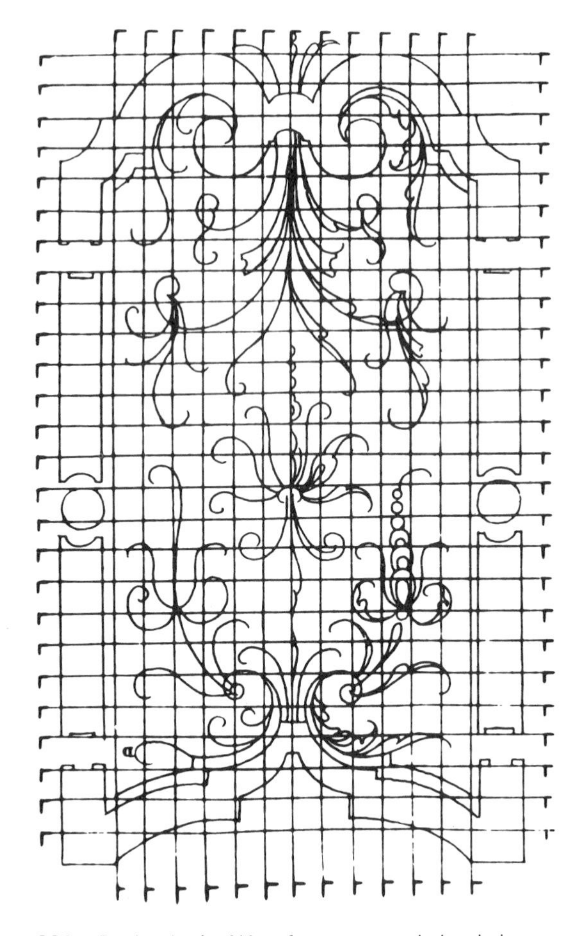

824 *Design by Le Nôtre for a* parterre de broderie

The work of Le Nôtre introduced the first important qualitative leap in the history of French classicism; it opened up a field of new experiments, and created a spatial organism fitted to the operative means of the prevailing social and economic systems, as well as to the ideals of the visual culture of the time. If the sovereigns and capitalists of the seventeenth century were not in a position to realize a new city, i.e. to order men and their houses in accordance with the criteria of the *grand goût*, they could at least mould the elements of the natural landscape and have their way with rivers, hills, trees and fountains.

This new spatial approach inevitably threatened architectural composition; in fact the weak point in the continuity of the layout of Vaux was Le Vau's architecture, which was one of the two perspective poles in Le Nôtre's park.

Le Vau tried to force the tone; he gave the château a lively plan, with curved outlines combined with straight ones, emphasized the articulation of the volumes by means of a striking roof, which reproduced the fitting together of the various *corps de logis*, and increased the importance of the secondary plastic elements. But these effects were lost in the great surrounding spaces and, seen from a long distance, diminished the mass of the château; in the façade facing the garden the designer introduced an oval room protruding outwards on the exterior – as in the most daring compositions by Borromini and Pietro da Cortona – and with a domed roof. Here, where one of the vanishing-points of the general scheme took on concrete form, Le Vau adopted the old symbol of the perspective infinite, the dome; from a distance this cannot be perceived as volume, and does not enter into a plastic relationship with the open spaces, like the dome of St Peter's with Bernini's piazza, but is only a point of light, not unlike the jet of water from the fountain which is facing it.

In the decorative details, on the other hand, Lebrun's direction was as precise and consistent as Le Nôtre's of the garden. He had the cartoons of the statues executed by Poussin in Rome, and co-ordinated the work of the sculptors – Anguier, Poissant, Lespagnandelle – who worked on them *in situ*; he designed the interior décor in gilded wood or stucco, the cartoons for the hangings woven in Fouquet's factories at Maincy, and did some of the paintings himself; he chose the furniture, the household goods, and introduced glass, mirrors and painted canvases alongside the traditional materials.

From the building scale downwards, the executive perfection and taste for smooth and shining materials made it possible to obtain a wide gradation of effects down to the smallest details. The decorations, rich though they are, are always clear and uncluttered; the decorative details, spaced out so as not to be confused with one another, were presented in a calculated order, from the vestibules where architectural décor predominated to the private apartments where architecture was overshadowed by the figurative decorations of the covering surfaces (Figs 825–7).

The opening of Vaux, on 17 August 1661, was described by La Fontaine, poet of the Fouquet household. Fouquet entertained the king, queen, Mlle de la Vallière and the whole court; the evening included a dinner prepared by Vatel, the performance of a ballet by Molière, staged by Lebrun to music by Lully, and a fireworks display in the park. Three weeks later Colbert had Fouquet arrested, confiscated his goods and transferred the artists of Vaux to the service of the king. The team created by Fouquet thus became part of the far vaster organization conceived and created by Colbert for the new sovereign Louis XIV.

The young king, as is well known, began his reign (1661–1715) by declaring that he did not want to appoint a prime minister, but wished to govern on his own; this did not mean that the king did without collaborators, indeed he made use of a ruling group of the first order and an even more numerous body of civil servants, but he committed himself to discussing with them regularly all the details of the administration, and devoted himself earnestly to the 'trade of king'; architecture was one of his favourite subjects, and as time passed he acquired an almost professional competence, which enabled him to deal directly with his architects on all matters.

From 1661 Jean-Baptiste Colbert (1619–83) was the administrator of Mazarin's legacy, and was therefore well acquainted

825–827 *Interiors of the château of Vaux and a design by Lebrun for the dome*

with the various aspects of state affairs. After the fall of Fouquet the post of superintendent of finances was abolished, and its powers passed to the royal council, dominated by Colbert – from 1661 with the title of intendant, and from 1665 of controller general; through his control of finances, like Sully, he did in fact direct the policy of the first twenty years of Louis XIV's reign.

A cold and persevering character – Mme de Sévigné called him 'le Nord' – with an enormous capacity for work, Colbert set himself the task of rationalizing the administrative and financial mechanism of the state: the disorder created by the administrations of Richelieu and Mazarin was measured by the fact that, of a total fiscal burden of 85,000,000, the treasury received only 31,000,000. Colbert, while retaining the system of indirect taxation, harshly repressed the main abuses, and by 1667 he had already managed to double revenue and reduce the public debt to an acceptable level.

At the same time Colbert was promoting the country's economic development. He saw clearly, with his Cartesian temperament, that the power of the government was a consequence of national prosperity; at the same time he considered wealth as a fixed datum, and prosperity as a phenomenon of concentration, not of development. Here Colbert's technical and artistic programme fitted into

828 *Louis XIV (engraving by Gaille)*

his general economic design; he wanted to make good all the productive and organizational deficiencies of France, to concentrate along her borders all the trades and industries on which the prosperity of other nations was based, particularly those of luxury goods; technical and artistic modernization were two necessary conditions for this attempt and acquired a strictly political value. This explains, among other things, Colbert's broadmindedness in his work of cultural advancement: like Molière, he did not hesitate to poach on other people's preserves; in 1661 he commandeered Fouquet's whole team, in 1665 he summoned Bernini from Rome, in 1666 he had four of Venice's master glassmakers come illegally from Murano.

To realize his programme Colbert, like Sully, did not hesitate to assume direct responsibility for the sectors he considered most important and delicate; in 1664 he was appointed superintendent of buildings, in 1669 minister of royal palaces as well as of the navy and colonies, in 1672 protector of the academy of architecture. He aimed to subordinate foreign policy to his economic policy as well, but here – where his personal authority ceased – he found himself confronted by other equally authoritative civil servants: the diplomat de Lionne, the minister of war Le Tellier and his son, the marquis de Louvois.

Colbert's rational policy thus came up against the policy of force inherent in absolute power, and was finally engulfed by it, after the war with Holland and Peace of Nijmegen in 1678; in 1683 Colbert died and the political leadership passed to Louvois, who also inherited, from 1683 to 1691, the position of superintendent of buildings; this conflict, as we shall see, had its repercussions in the affairs of architecture.

We must now consider Colbert's policy in the field of building and town-planning point by point, distinguishing three groups of activities:

1 The reform of the instruments of public control

After the fall of Sublet de Noyers, the post of superintendent of buildings was occupied by mediocre and corrupt functionaries: Le Camus, from 1643 to 1656, and Ratabon from 1656 to 1664. Colbert, who held this post from 1664 to 1683, also held the titles of superintendent of the châteaux of Fontainebleau and Monceaux, from which he drew a total income of 21,000 *livres*.

He had working under him:

(a) *managerial officials*, i.e. the controller general (Le Nôtre, who received 5,000 *livres*), the three intendants (4,500 *livres*) and treasurer (2,800 *livres*). To these were added an official historian – André Félibien (1619–95), with a salary of 1,200 *livres* – and a designer, Israel Silvestre (1621–91), with a salary of 400 *livres*.

(b) *external officials*, i.e. the first architect of the king (Le Vau, with a salary of 6,000 *livres*), the royal architects – who in 1664 were François Mansart (1,000 *livres*), Pierre Le Muet (1,000 *livres*) and François d'Orbay (600 *livres*) – the first painter of the king (Lebrun, with 8,800 *livres*), the painters, sculptors and other technical specialists of all sectors of building (it should be remembered that at this time Molière was receiving a salary of 1,000 *livres* and Racine 800).

(c) *the commis*, i.e. executive officials. From 1663 to 1678 Colbert had as *premier commis* Charles Perrault (1628–1703) who, together with his brother Claude, played a most important part in Colbert's policy.

This small group of people took on an enormous quantity of work, in every corner of France, and made every effort to bring it all together into a common programme. In this sector, too, as in the whole administrative machine organized by Colbert, it would be superfluous to point out the infinite difficulties which faced a centralized control and the infinite occasions of failure. 'On the contrary what is astonishing is that with so few men, such limited powers of coercion, and so few agents in the field, a scheme of this magnitude could ever have been conceived, formulated and even sometimes successfully carried out.'[34]

Colbert studied all possible means to improve the efficiency of the administration, repressed personal abuses, in 1665 attempted to suppress the selling of government posts, improved the procedure for awarding contracts (but the king decided against his desire to extend to civil works the system of allocation to the lowest tender, used in military works, which led to the disadvantages complained about by Perrault and Vauban),[35] and sometimes had work sites supervised by police and the army. Here, too, as in the other branches of the administration, Colbert instituted a regular budget, which revealed the extent of the sums destined for royal buildings; the annual budget, which in 1664 was about 3,000,000 *livres*, rose in 1671 to 7,000,000, sank to 3,000,000 during the Dutch war, rose again to 8,000,000 after the Peace of Nijmegen and reached the record figure of 16,000,000 in 1685; after 1689, and until the end of the reign, it settled at between 2,000,000 and 3,000,000. Altogether Louis XIV spent over 200,000,000 *livres* on his buildings, almost half of it on Versailles; sums of money judged enormous by contemporaries. But one must bear in mind that the expenses of war in a single year – for instance 1689 or 1701 – rose to as much as 100,000,000 *livres*, i.e. more than the entire sum spent in fifty years on Versailles.

The functions of the *grand voyer*, abolished in 1621, were attributed in 1645 to the three treasurers and a varying number of royal engineers – eleven at the end of the reign of Louis XIV – but Colbert reserved the supervision of the various activities (roadworks, bridges, canals, plantations) for his intendants, and firmly reduced the independence of civil servants or peripheral bodies.

To discipline productive activities, and particularly those connected with architecture and the applied arts, Colbert used and further complicated the system of guilds; from 1672 to 1691 the number of Parisian guilds increased from 60 to 129. The state appointed the masters, prescribed the materials and the methods of working them, appointed inspectors and controllers, guaranteed the quality of the products with special trade marks, guaranteed price levels with customs tariffs and partly ensured the sale of luxury products, in that the annual acquisitions of the court amounted to 800,000 *livres*.

Furthermore Colbert organized a series of state industries, the royal manufactories: these included the glassworks of St-Gobain, the tapestry works at Beauvais, the carpet-workshop of the Savonnerie, the crown furniture workshop at Les Gobelins; this last, founded in 1663 and run by Lebrun, was able to produce a vast range of household goods – furniture, hangings, textiles – and hence completely to furnish the interiors of the new royal buildings: the factory (which employed up to 1,800 workers) had a school added to it in 1667.

Some royal manufactories, situated out of Paris, were organized as small towns, e.g. the mirror factory at Tour-la-Ville, near Cherbourg (1666) and the cloth factory at Villeneuvette (1667).

The same total discipline was introduced, with some circumspection, into the world of artists and men of letters. In France there was already the academy of literature, founded in 1635 by Richelieu, and the academy of painting and sculpture founded by Mazarin in 1651. Colbert had to move with more discretion in his dealings with men of letters: in 1662 he set up the academy of inscriptions, and appointed the architect Claude Perrault one of the founder members, together with poets and scholars. The Petite Académie counted among its members Racine – who had obtained his first success in 1667 with *Andromaque* – and Boileau, who became the quasi-official controller of literary production, but without the authoritarian and organizational instruments Lebrun had at his disposal. In the artistic field Colbert's intervention was much heavier; in 1663 he named Lebrun director of the academy of painting and sculpture; in 1666 he founded the Académie de France in Rome, and made the apprenticeship of French artists in the capital of classicism official with the institution of the *prix de Rome*;[36] also in 1666 he founded the academy of sciences, in 1669 the academy of music and in 1671 the academy of architecture.

The latter served to provide a framework for both the committee of experts annexed to the superintendence of buildings (composed in 1664 of Le Vau, Lebrun and François Mansart) and the body of royal architects; in fact the decree of 1676 reserved this title to members of the royal academy of architecture. The first members were nominated by the king: the president François Blondel (1618–86), then Bruand, Gittard, Le Pautre, Le Vau, Mignard, d'Orbay, and the secretary Félibien; they received an attendance counter of eleven *livres* per session, a salary of 500 *livres* (1,000 for d'Orbay, responsible for the designs of the buildings) and had to give up acting as contractors. Thus the separation between art and trade was sanctioned, and the figure of the master builder, who had guaranteed the continuity of the French architectural tradition since the Middle Ages, disappeared.

Despite this, the academy treated all the aesthetic, technical, administrative and legal aspects of architecture on the new intellectual level; it organized a proper school which replaced the old-fashioned apprenticeship; it functioned as a superior building council; it inspected work sites, cellars and workrooms to check that processes were being carried out correctly and it acted as a court for building disputes.

According to the cultural tradition of the time, the doctrine of the academy could be regarded as established only when it was expressed in literary form; for this reason, following the artistic literature of the preceding decades,[37] the academy published or promoted a series of works, where the whole matter was codified with extraordinary seriousness.[38]

The academicians applied to architecture the Cartesian approach of methodical doubt, and reconstructed the foundations of planning, using reason or *bon sens*: reason, experience, the authority of Vitruvius and the classics (which, however, could be continually contested, where it went against the first two requirements). They re-expounded the Renaissance theories of musical proportions, specifying them in the rigorous language of the new scientific culture, though they preferred to avoid over-contrived proportions: d'Aviler[39] proposed the simplification of the proportions of the orders (seven modules for the Tuscan, eight for the Doric, nine for the Ionic and ten for the Corinthian; every order must be divided into nineteen parts, four for the pedestal, twelve for the column and three for the entablature; the composite order was considered with diffidence and was not advised). The academy cultivated the idea of laying down rules 'to arrive at a unique and perfect beauty, which could be followed by all operators and would be accessible to all the public',[40] but continually put off their definition; it was particularly chary of individual judgments, and accepted the authority of the masters for their value as a collective norm. Blondel wrote:[41]

> 'I myself, since in a continual state of self-doubt, feel more reassured by conforming to the reasonings and practice of the great masters ancient and modern, leaving the delight in the singularity of their opinions to others who have, with the force of their genius, risen above the common level.'

Comparison between the value of the ancient and modern masters also greatly interested the academicians, at the time of the *querelle des anciens et des modernes*. Blondel,

829 Vision of St Paul *by Poussin. Louvre, Paris*

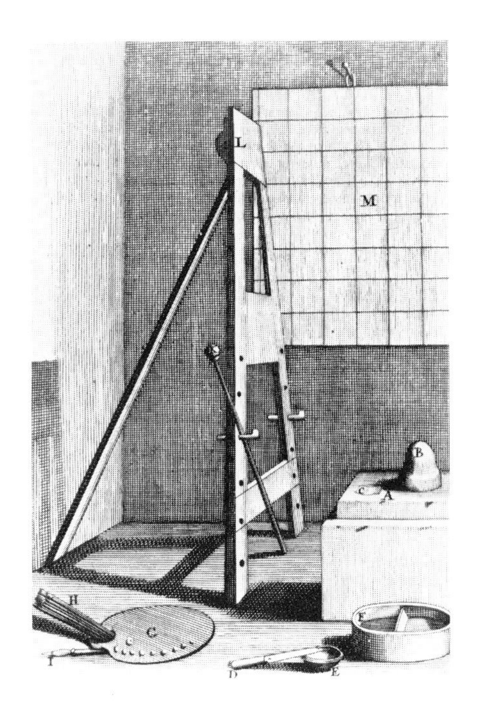

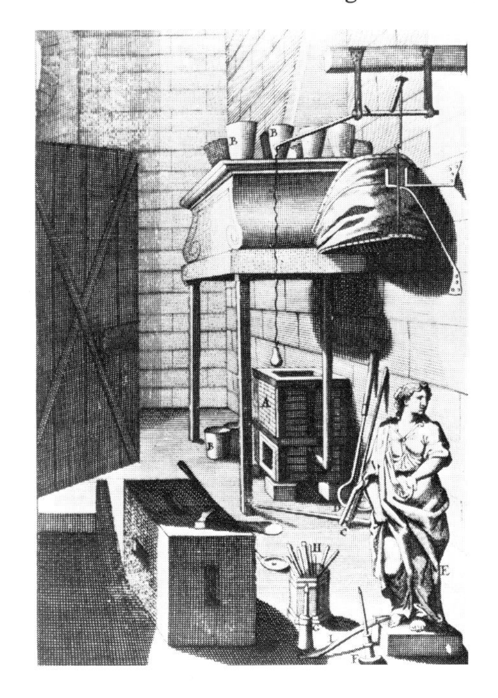

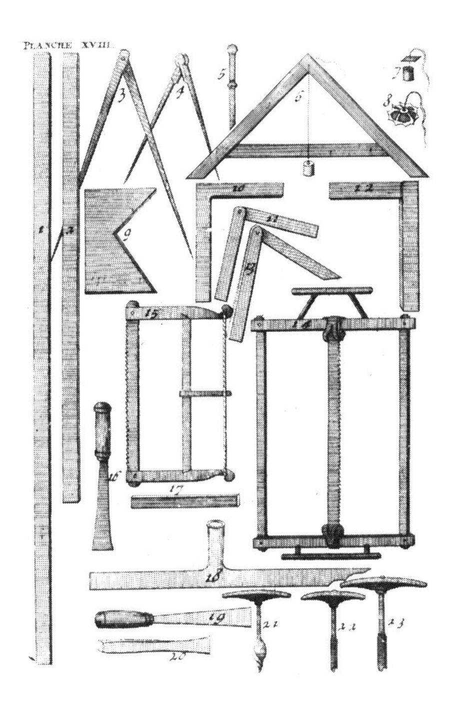

830–833 *Four plates from* Des Principes de l'architecture, de la sculpture, de la peinture et des autres arts *by Félibien. Painting, sculpture, the* oeuvrages de rocaille *and the carpenter's instruments*

834 *Portrait of Lebrun, first painter of the king, by Largillière. Louvre, Paris*

like Boileau, defended the ancients; Claude Perrault, like Fontenelle, defended the moderns. Nor was it mere chance that the last two were also members of the academy of sciences, and saw in the *esprit de géométrie* the particular character of modern culture.

2 *The infrastructures*

Colbert's economic policy required above all an improvement in the means of communications: roads and canals. Colbert judged the old royal roads, 45 feet wide, insufficient and classified them in two categories, to which he assigned the width of 68 feet (20 metres) and 60 feet (18 metres); but these roads, though spacious and straight, were not equally well maintained, because of the lack of a rational system of paving and because of the irregularity of their upkeep, organized from place to place according to the *corvée* system.

Together with the road system Colbert also improved the network of navigable canals (the 'running roads' as Pascal wrote). In 1664 the tax-collector Pierre Paul Riquet (1604–80) was authorized to build the canal du Midi, to link the Garonne to the Aude, i.e. the Atlantic to the Mediterranean; the work, 240 kilometres long and with 120 locks, was completed in 1681.

To assist the development of the French navy Colbert was particularly attentive to the laying out of the ports; here his technical collaborator was Louis Nicolas de Clerville (1610–78), already commissary general of fortifications under Mazarin, but a specialist in hydraulic constructions.

Rochefort, the first French port on the Atlantic coast, was founded in 1665 at the mouth of the Charente, in the place chosen by a royal commission on which Blondel also served. At first only the working portion was built: the naval shipyard, rope-factory, and cannon foundry. In 1669, the king founded the new town, and the plans were prepared, including the monumental one that Lavedan attributes to François Le Vau; but the definitive plan, designed by de Clerville, was based on a simple grid plan layout, in accordance with sixteenth-century tradition (Fig. 835).

Brest, a mere Breton village, was chosen in 1666 as a naval base in anticipation of the war with England; the town grew gradually, and was officially laid out about 1695 by Vauban, who designed the extension plan and built the ring of fortifications (Figs 836–7).

Lorient was founded in 1666 as a trading base for the East and West India Companies; the town developed slowly because of the crisis in the Company, and took shape only in 1736, after the success of Law's new Compagnie des Indes.

Sète, at the mouth of the canal du Midi on the Mediterranean side, was founded in 1666 by de Clerville, and remained a small coastal centre, which did not really develop until the nineteenth century.

In 1664, at the mouth of the Garonne, Colbert completed the building of the lighthouse of Cardouan, the first important modern building of this kind, about 50 metres high; four lighthousemen, supplied with provisions every six months, kept a wood fire burning permanently at its top.

Military constructions were only partly subject to Colbert's planning. But in this sector a body of specialists and a scientific organization was formed for the first time, which took in virtually the whole field of engineering. Furthermore the successor of de Clerville as 'commissary general of fortifications', Sébastien Le Prestre de Vauban (1633–1707), was by far the most intelligent engineer of the *grand siècle*; he created the figure of the modern engineer and achieved a fuller understanding than anyone else of the real cultural responsibilities underlying architecture.

Vauban became *ingénieur du roi* in 1655, and after the peace of 1657 began to study methods of fortification with rational criteria. Colbert and Louvois soon put his talent to

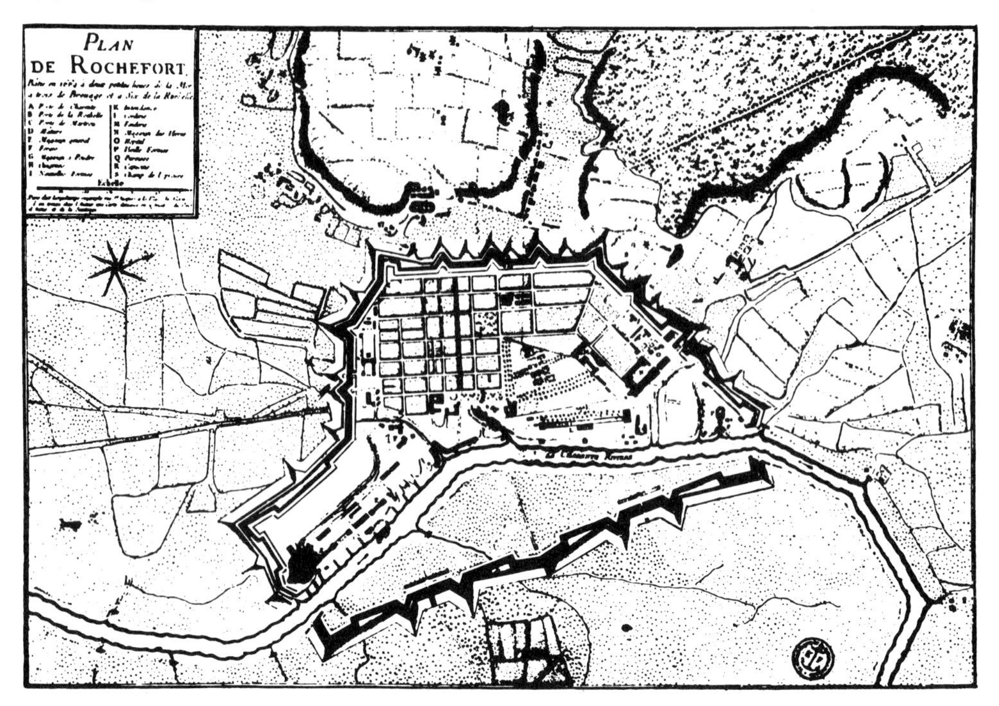

835 *Plan of Rochefort (from Lavedan)*

836 *View of the* plan relief *of Brest. Musée des Invalides, Paris*

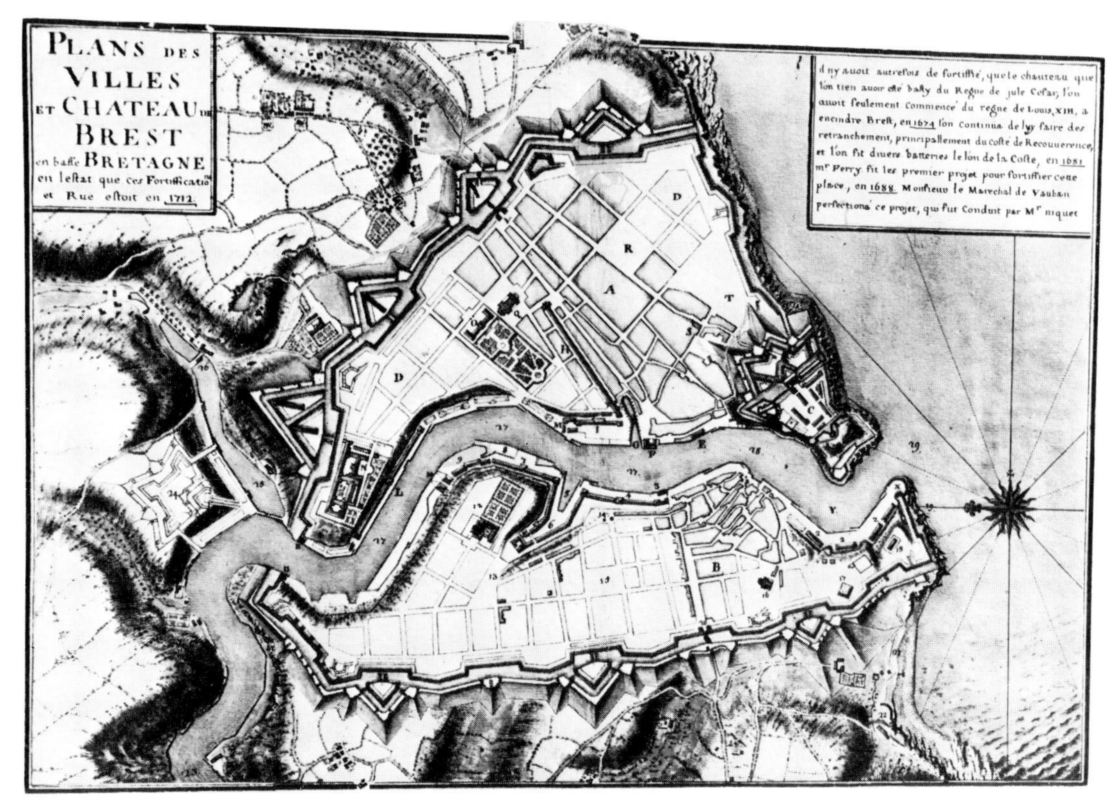

837 *Plan of Brest in 1712, with Vauban's extension*

good use; in 1666 Colbert made him director of works in his department and Vauban began to produce the models of the main fortresses, still preserved at the Invalides; in 1669 Louvois invited him to write his first theoretical work on the conduct of sieges.[42]

During the war with Holland Vauban successfully directed the sieges of Nijmegen, Maastricht and Besançon; on this occasion, in 1672, he proposed that military engineers should be grouped together into a special service, the Corps du Génie. In 1716 the Corps des Ponts et Chaussées was formed on this model, i.e. the organization of civil engineers.

After the Peace of Nijmegen Vauban became commissary general in the place of de Clerville, organized a continuous system of fortresses along the French borders and gradually improved his system of bulwarks; in many cases the works of fortification entailed a general town-planning scheme, for the extension of an existing city (Lille in 1682, Brest in 1695) or for the foundation of a new one (Huningue, Sarrelouis and Longwy in 1679; Montlouis in 1681; Montdauphin in 1692; Neufbrisach, which is regarded as his masterpiece, in 1698). Vauban eliminated the geometrical symbols, which derived from the humanistic myth of the ideal city, and studied the most reasonable combinations between the polygonal perimeters and the internal grid plan layout (Figs 836–42). In many cases he designed the buildings and architectural accessories, in a simple style and with absolute technical correctness.

His competence extended to all aspects of the art of war – he invented the *bayonet à*

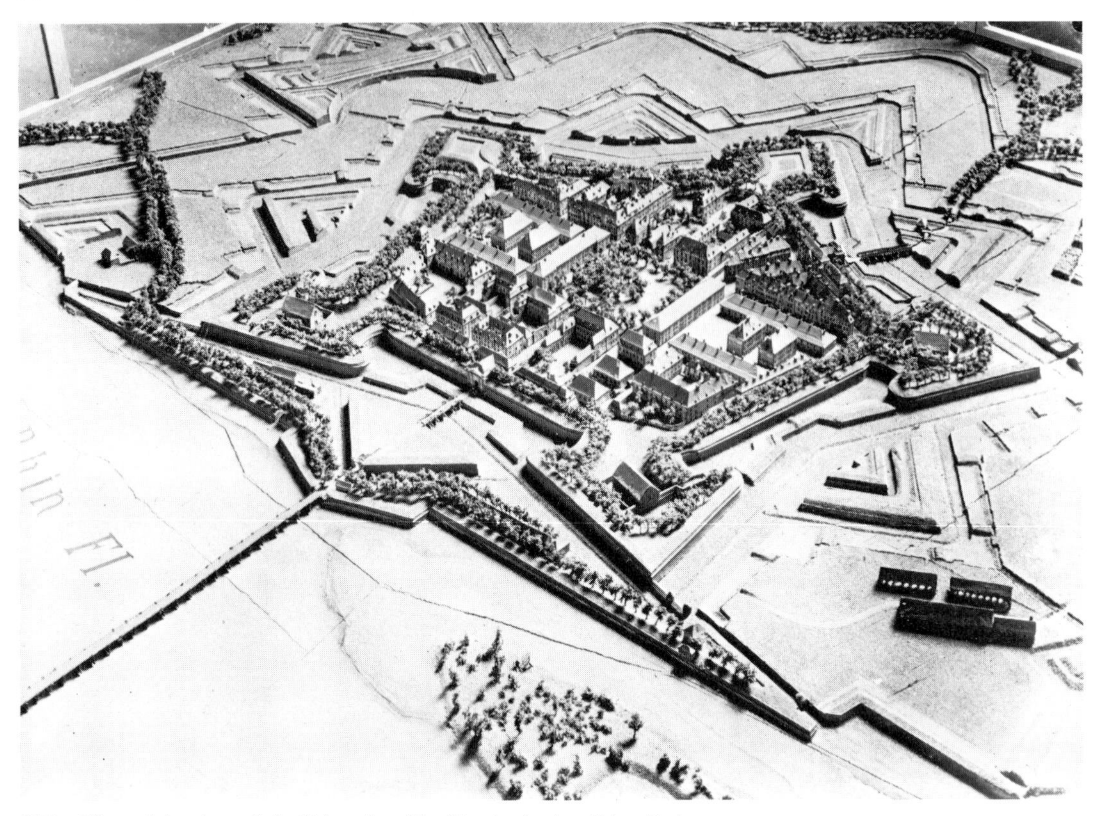

838 *View of the* plan relief *of Montdauphin. Musée des Invalides, Paris*

douille, organized a series of experiments on explosives, on which he wrote a treatise[43] – and of civil engineering; he left a *Traité de l'art de construction* and a collection of *Maximes bonnes à observer par tous ceux qui font bastir*, where scientific rigour was accompanied by a human sympathy for the inhabitant, still unknown at this period (one of the maxims says: 'consider in so far as is possible the fireplaces and bed, so that a person lying on his side may see the fire').[44] For Vauban the sum total of the experiences formed a single discipline, the *génie* (engineering):[45]

'Engineering is a métier beyond our forces; it embraces too many things for a man to be able to exercise it to a supreme degree of perfection. I have a good enough opinion of myself to believe myself one of the most gifted of the company, capable of instructing the best among us, but despite this, when I examine myself, I see myself to be merely half an engineer, after forty years of intense application and great experience. The glory belongs solely to Him who has vouchsafed me my life to date.'

He understood well that scientific investigation required specialization sector by sector; in his personal refusal to accept these limitations Vauban was not modern, and his example had no issue. But he was the only one of the great figures of his time who was thoroughly acquainted with all the aspects of planning, the rules of the technical or artistic

839 *View of the* plan relief *of Strasburg. Musée des Invalides, Paris*

proceedings and the precariousness of their administrative, economic and social supports; for this reason he reflected on their interrelationships and when necessary pronounced severe moral judgments, already in the style of the *philosophes* of the next century.

3 *Urban schemes*

Starting from his economic programme, Colbert attempted to concentrate the building activities of the state on the great cities and above all on Paris. He wrote in his instructions to his son: 'Paris, being the capital of the realm and the dwelling place of kings, sets the whole of the rest of the kingdom in motion, and it is here that all businesses have their beginnings.'

Unsuccessfully, Colbert opposed the king's tendency, which was a preference for Versailles or one of the other country residences, and which meant that as long a period of time as several years could go by without his going to the Louvre; in a famous letter of 1663 he dared to reproach king Louis: Versailles was made for entertainment, Paris for glory, and the king 'was in the hands of two men – Le Vau and Le Nôtre – who knew him almost exclusively at Versailles, i.e. in pleasure and entertainment, and knew nothing of his love for glory'.[46]

But Colbert's argument was ill-chosen. At Versailles, apart from pleasure, the king found the satisfaction of a grandiose setting

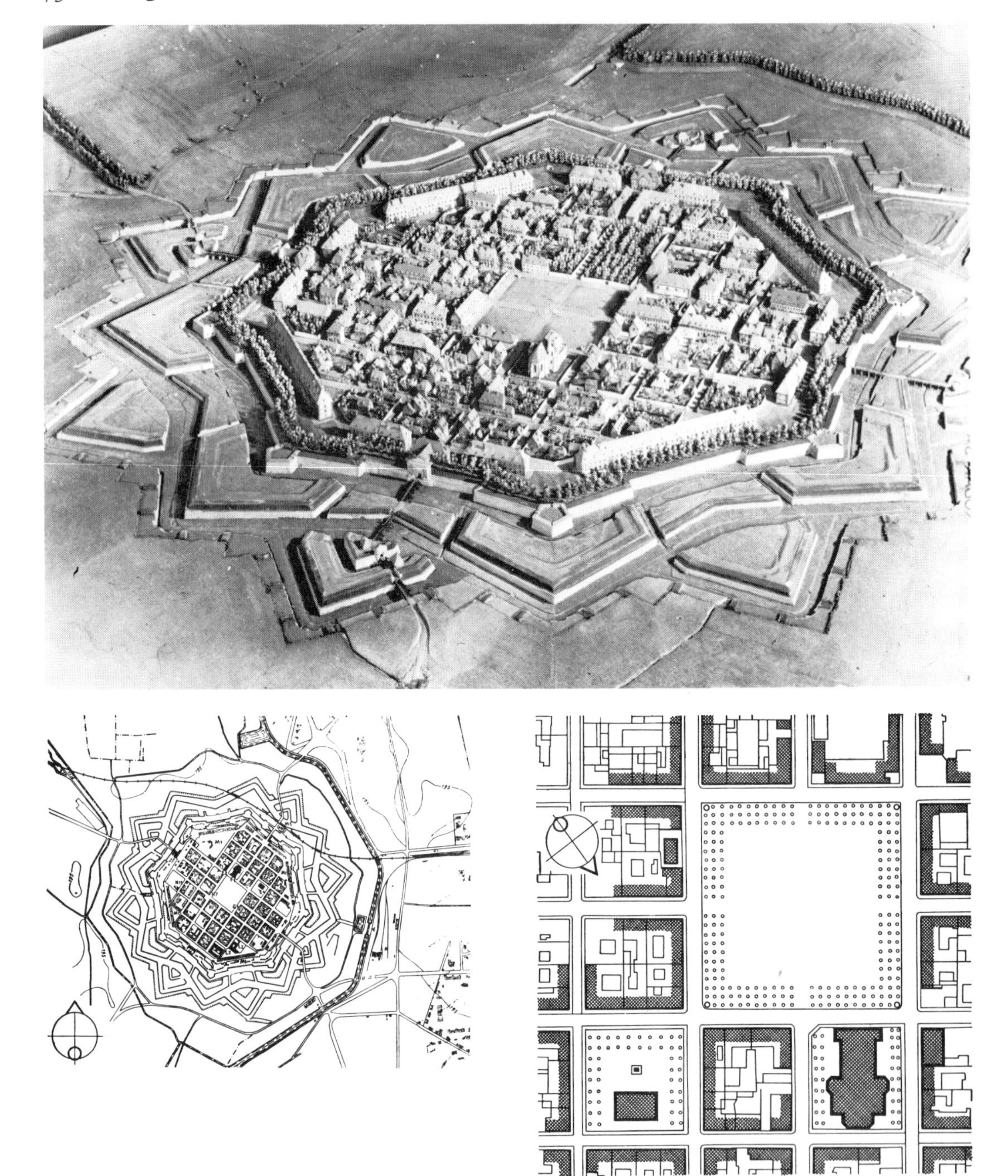

840–842 *The fortified town and central square of Neufbrisach (*plan relief *at the Musée des Invalides, plans from Auzelle)*

843 *Gate of the fortress at Montdauphin, by Vauban*

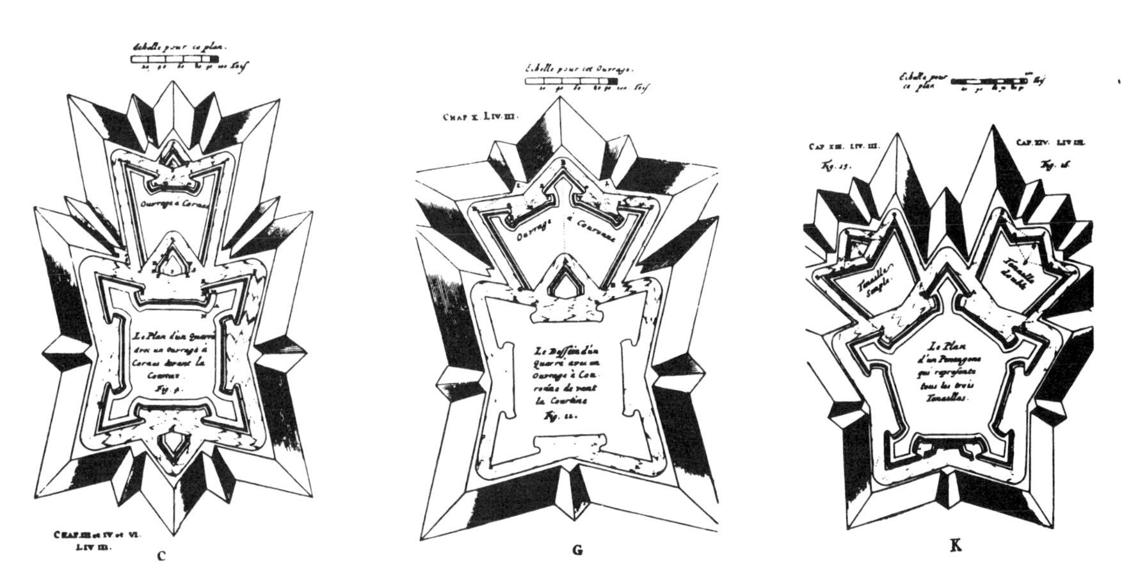

844 *Theoretical types of fortification from Vauban,* Manière de fortifier, *Amsterdam, 1689*

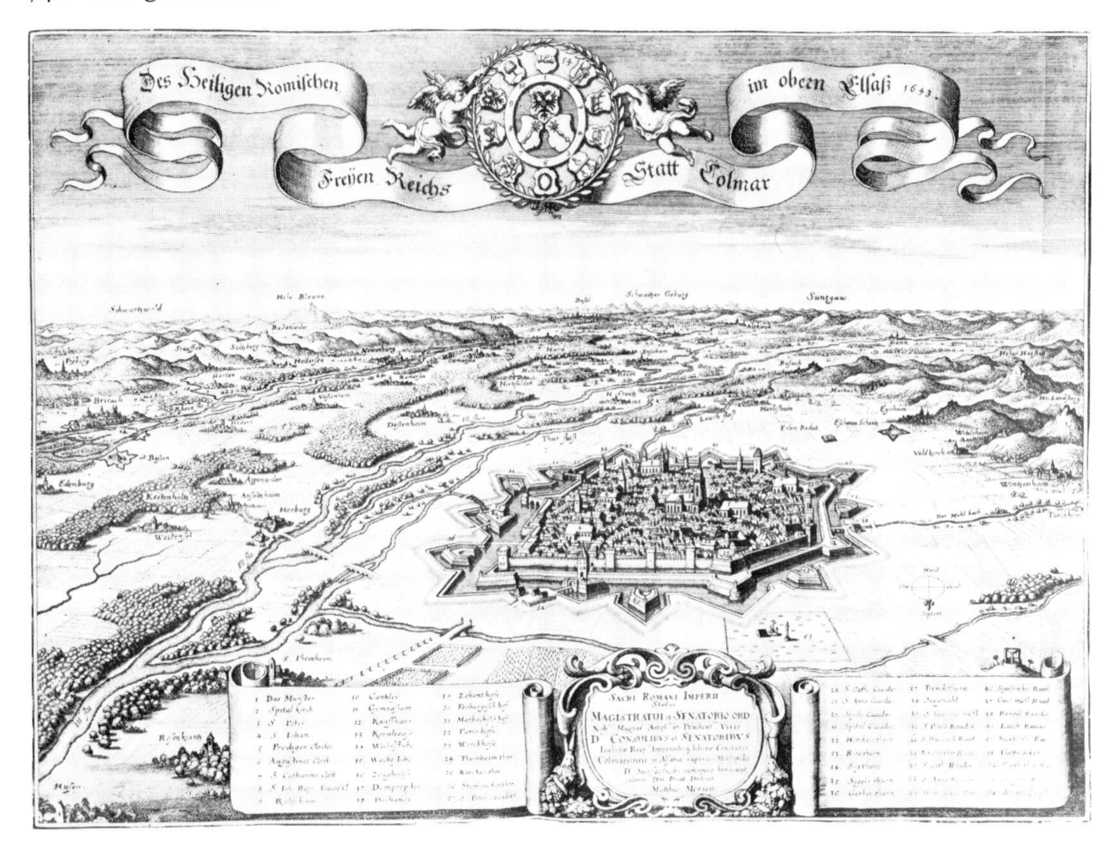

and also, after 1677, the physical space for the complicated bureaucratic mechanism of government, while in Paris he had to reckon with a ready-made city, difficult to change. The architectural results proved Louis XIV right; the creation of a new urban landscape, which was not possible in Paris, in the midst of the restrictions of the medieval organism, became possible on the unencumbered terrain of Versailles. The demands of greatness clashed with those of economy; the main contradiction of absolutism emerged in the field of town-planning too.

The two programmes, that of Colbert for Paris and that of Louis XIV for Versailles, developed in a parallel fashion and were connected in many ways, politically, economically and stylistically. Each has frequently been examined on its own account, down to the smallest details; we shall here attempt a simultaneous exposition of the two, to point out their common characteristics, which are more significant in a general account.

Up to 1664 – i.e. under Ratabon's superintendence – Le Vau continued work on the Louvre, on the hospital of the Salpêtrière, and after 1662 on the Collège des Quatre Nations. Meanwhile Le Vau, Le Nôtre and Lebrun began laying out the château of Versailles. Louis XIII's building remained almost intact, but was incorporated into a new general scheme, between a large entrance space surrounded by service buildings and a vast garden with a series of sloping terraces, as at Vaux. Three radiating avenues started from the entrance gates, leading to St-Cloud, Sèvres and Sceaux, i.e. linking the château to the other centres of the west suburbs of Paris; similarly from the end of the garden – just beyond the present-day bassin d'Apollon,

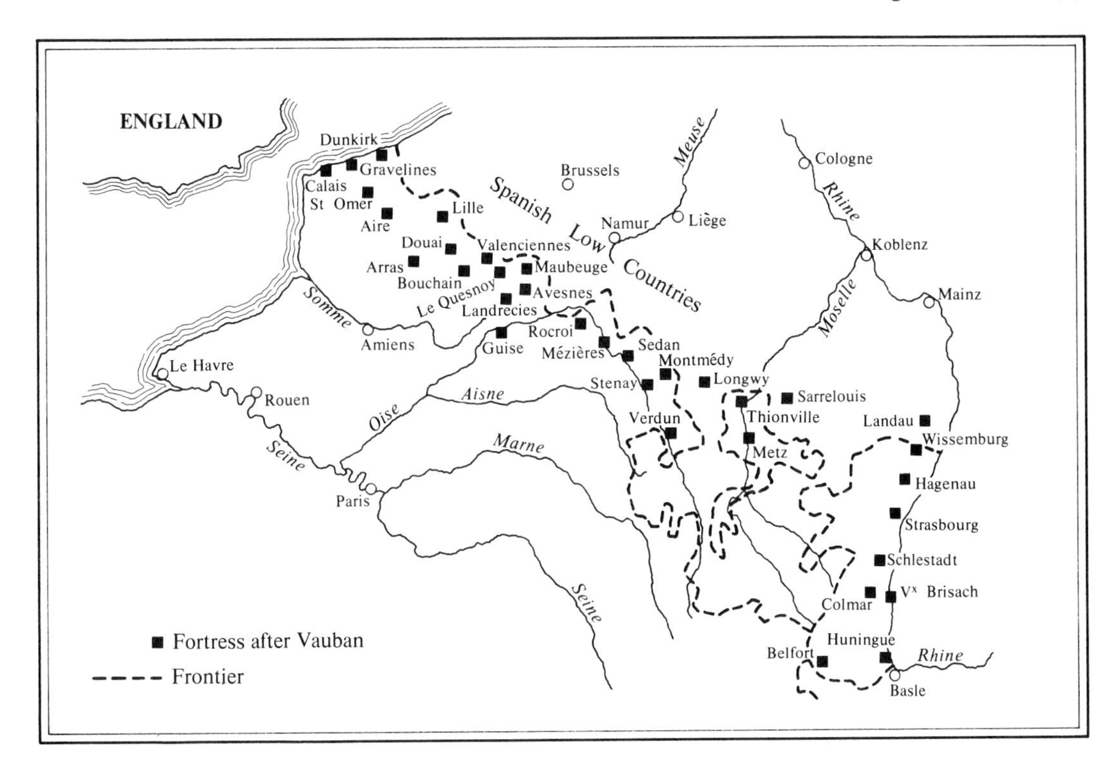

845 *The fortified town of Colmar in 1663 (from Merian)*
846 *The chain of fortified towns constructed along the French frontier by Vauban after 1678 (from Croizet)*

i.e. about half a kilometre away from the château – there started another radiating series of five avenues running into the park. With significant indifference, this scheme put buildings and park on a level, and virtually annulled the bulk of the château in a grandiose town-planning design; the terraced garden measures half a square kilometre, the three entrance avenues are from 70 to 90 metres long, and the great space in front of the gates covers almost six hectares (Figs 847–8).

It seems certain that the designer of such an organism would be the gardener Le Nôtre, as Lavedan[47] supposes, rather than the architect Le Vau, as Brinkmann believes.[48] Town-planning design as it is understood today – i.e. a methodology for activity on a large scale, specifically different from that of the building scale – first appears, at the time of the Sun King, in the form of landscape design. The relationship of Le Nôtre with other artists working on Versailles – Le Vau, Claude Perrault, Lebrun – was already that of co-ordinating town-planner with sectorial specialists; current institutions did not permit the clear development of this relationship, indeed Le Nôtre, as a gardener, figured as responsible for a specialized sector and one subordinated to architecture. Probably in fact he avoided this conventional hierarchy by means of his post of controller general of buildings and his broad technical competence, as well as by the decisive importance of his spatial conceptions; his reserved character helped him to avoid clashes with official architects, but clients valued his judgment on strictly architectural questions as well, and Louis XIV sometimes took him as arbiter in controversies with other collaborators. He appears today, together with Vauban, as the main protagonist of the new French architectural civilization; as in the technical field Vauban redefined the methodology of the process of planning – hence the relation with scientific research and political programming – so Le Nôtre established the specific theme of the next cycle of experiments, i.e. the leap from the traditional scale of planning to a new scale, which physically represents the infinite dimension of perspective, and which realized the only worthwhile example of the Cartesian order assumed by science to exist beneath the chaotic appearance of the natural universe, but unattainable through technical expertise in every other part of the artificial universe (La Bruyère adopts the description of the park of Chantilly[49] to introduce a consideration of the cosmic order). This transition was prepared by a long series of figurative experiments and scientific elaborations during the course of the seventeenth century. Le Nôtre seems to have been uninterested in the theories of the scientists, but interested in landscape painting; we know that he bought pictures by Poussin (Fig. 820), and Claude Lorrain and that he collected Chinese porcelain. His artistic education was completely orthodox, but he grasped an unexplored possibility in the traditional precepts of perspective and symmetry and dropped the tacit dimensional limitations within which these precepts had hitherto been applied; he thus laid down a premise indispensable not only for the new tasks of building design, according to new quantities involved, but also to the further developments of the figurative arts: to the architecture of Hardouin-Mansart and Soufflot, but also to painting, from Watteau to Constable.

In the twenty years from 1664 to 1683 artists found themselves obliged to address themselves to Colbert, and he became co-ordinator of all official architectural undertakings.

When he took over Ratabon's position, he immediately tackled the obvious problems of the capital with his usual efficiency, but committed himself fully to the hierarchy of traditional values and recognized authorities. For him the main problem – at least at this point – was the completion of the Louvre, and to resolve it he needed an architect of renown; thus, while he commissioned Le Nôtre to redesign the Tuileries gardens and to plan the avenues of the adjacent open spaces, he sent his emissary to Rome to make contact with the most illustrious architects of the moment, Pietro da Cortona, Rainaldi, Candiani and Bernini. Bernini was clearly the most distinguished, and from 1664 to 1665 he prepared two plans which were criticized by both Colbert and his secretary Charles Perrault; at this point Colbert decided to have Bernini come to Paris, and organized the journey of the old master in the summer of 1665 with positively regal magnificence.

From his very first plans Bernini aimed to eliminate the solid character of the quadrilateral, where the architectural decoration, as in the royal squares, rue St-Honoré and the beginning of the Pont Neuf, was a wall motif independent of the shape of the volumes. To dominate this mass architecturally, according to his training, meant establishing an equivalence and a continuation of scale between the volumes and the plastic decorative details, therefore to articulate the overall volume (which measured about 150 metres a side) into minor episodes; to do this, on the inside Bernini restricted and enlivened the courtyard by backing a double order of loggias on to the existing building, and on the outside he modelled the projection so as to obtain a sequence of unequal blocks, and applied the giant order in both cases, i.e. a larger-scale finish nearer to that of the whole. In successive versions Bernini varied the form of the elements, but retained these proportionate features, firmly rejecting the criticism of the French architects; furthermore he made provisions for the creation of a free space around the palace by demolishing

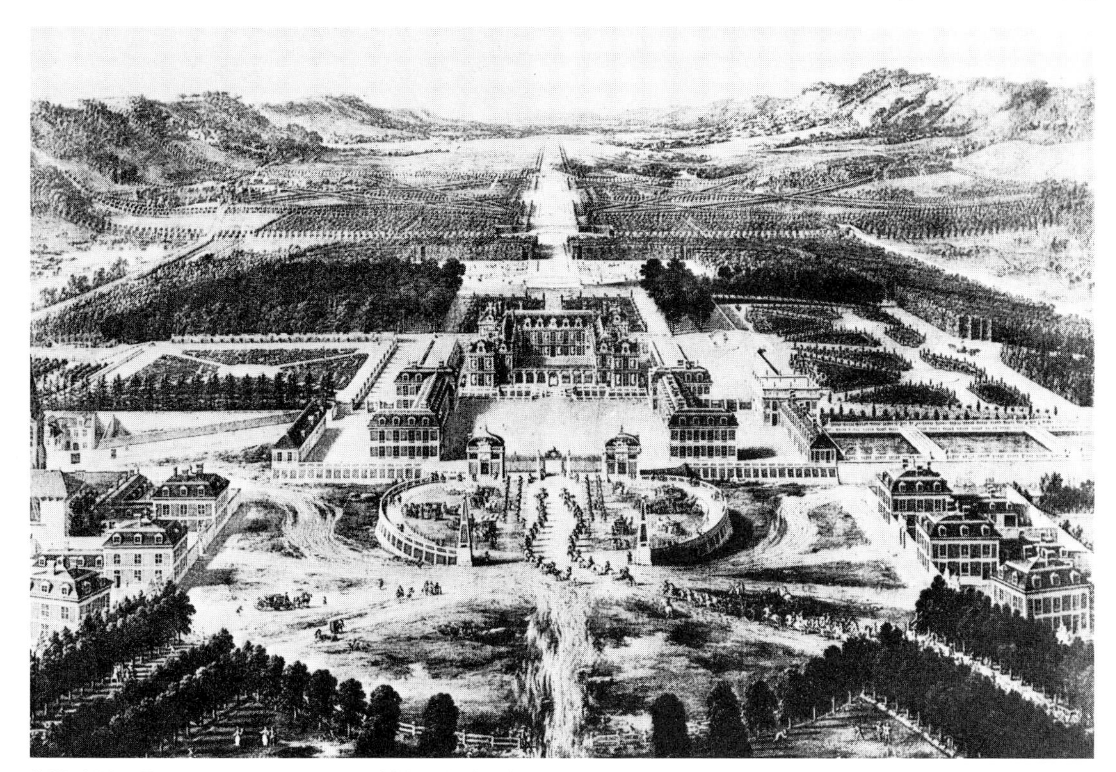

847, 848 *The park at Versailles in 1666: painting by Patel and engraving by La Pointe*

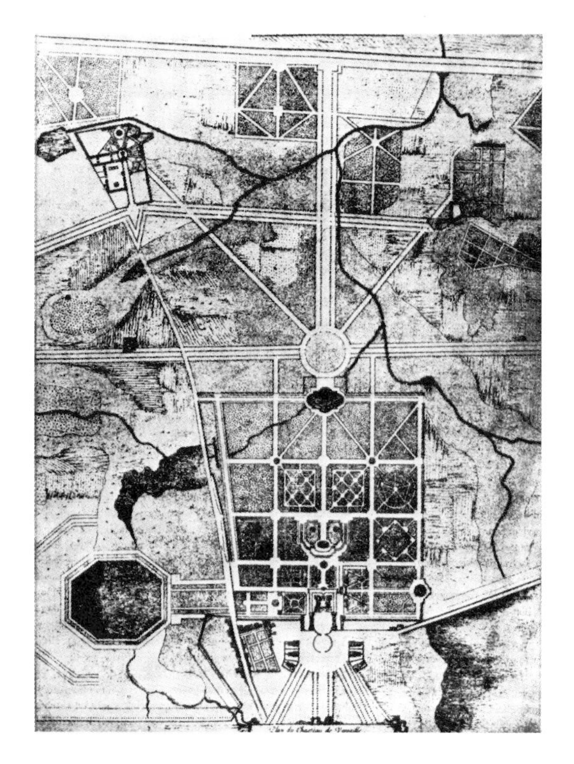

the whole district lying between the Seine, rue St-Honoré and the beginning of the Pont Neuf, and organizing a square in front of the building, roughly the size of its own bulk, as at St Peter's, decorated with loggias and foundations (Figs 850–1).

The objections that Bernini met with in Paris were of two kinds: those of Colbert, who was not used to such independence in the interpretation of the distributive programme, and those of the French artists, who were working out a completely different spatial approach: the disengagement of the decorative details from the mass of the building, so as to attribute to both a simple regular form, and so as to bear comparison with the infinite vistas of the new landscape schemes.

It is interesting to see that Bernini criticized the French, and the French criticized Bernini almost with the same words: faulty proportions and lack of grandiosity.[50] Each understood something different by these phrases: Bernini's 'proportion' was the humanistic notion of the commensurability of visual forms, the French one was the Cartesian notion of discretionary choice over a continuity that was infinitely divisible; Bernini's 'grandiosity', though contrasting with the building fabric of Paris, was linked to a traditional urban scale already in fact bypassed in the preceding experiments by Le Vau and Le Nôtre. The great square to be opened in front of the Louvre, which rightly alarmed Colbert because of its economic and legal cost, was none the less an empty space still comparable with the surrounding full volumes and, like the square at St Peter's, determined views which did not go much beyond the already mentioned limit of 200 metres.

In the autumn of 1665 the king laid the first stone of Bernini's palace, and sent the master back to Rome. But Colbert hesitated to proceed with the work: the palace seemed too grand economically, and not grand enough stylistically; in 1667, after having written to Bernini that the king had decided not to use his design, he handed over the work to a committee that included Le Vau, Lebrun and Claude Perrault (1613–88), Charles's elder brother.

Since the first two were deeply involved elsewhere, Perrault was mainly responsible for the executive solution;[51] since it had been decided to retain the already completed courtyard, the problem was reduced to designing the external façades, of which only two, the south and east ones, looked on to existing open spaces (the Seine) or projected ones (the square in front). For the latter Perrault adopted Bernini's giant order, but eliminated the casuistry of the projection and gave the order, rationally, the solidity of a real colonnade detached from the wall. The uniform motif of coupled columns is just broken in the centre by the pediment and different spacing of the shafts, on the sides of

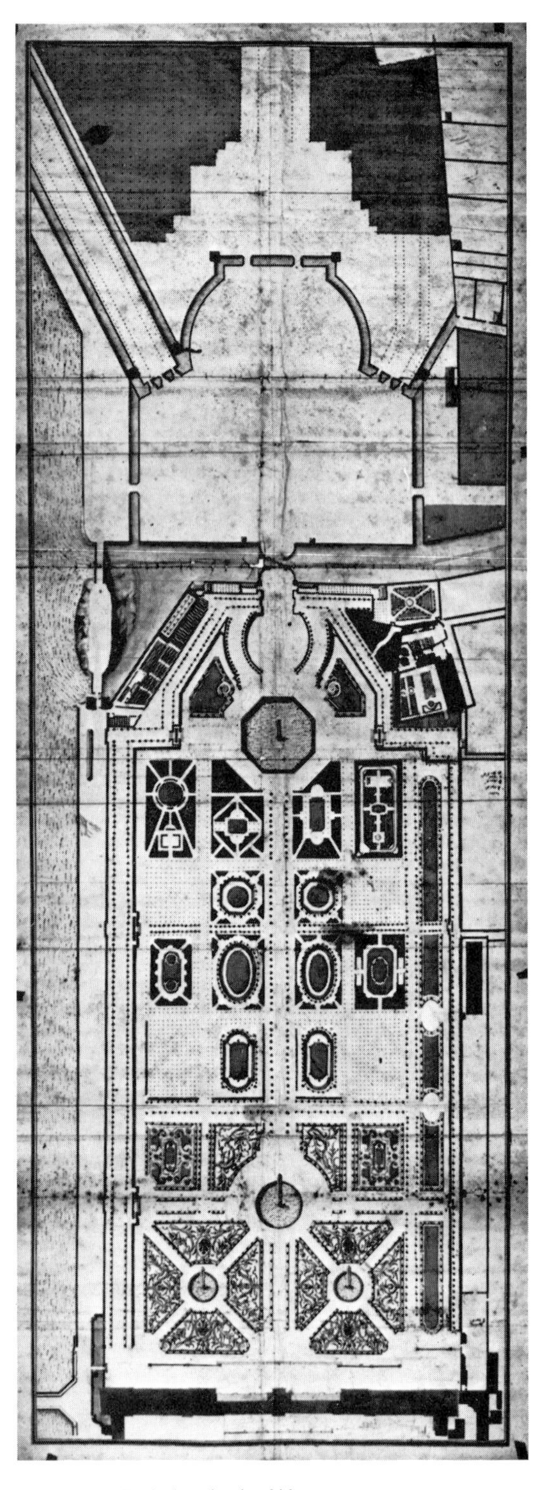

849 *The Tuileries, by Le Nôtre*

the two solid blocks. On the southern façade the columns become pilasters, and frame the decorative motifs of Lescot's *corps de logis*.

This solution did not produce a new organism, like that envisaged by Bernini, but an intelligent adaptation to the topographical limitations and actual possibilities of action; it resolved the corner view from the river and the Île de la Cité – similar to that of the old Louvre – and presented the new palace as an elementary volume, ideally linked to the scale of the great peripheral schemes. Its organization was immediately comprehensible, in accordance with the Vitruvian norms and those of court propriety; the execution was carried out with a scientific spirit, almost with virtuosity; the elements protruding from the colonnade were held together by an elaborate iron structure, the rain water from the roofs was carried off towards the interior by lead pipes.

Theoretically, Colbert did not renounce the *grand dessein* of linking Louvre and Tuileries in a single organism; in 1667 he forbade any new building within the relevant perimeter, and in 1668 commissioned Perrault to study the plan; he, with his archaeological imagination, envisaged a series of great courtyards and even an amphitheatre that could be transformed to stage sea battles. Colbert naturally felt somewhat hesitant given the vastness of the undertaking, until in 1677 Louis XIV decided to abandon the Louvre and suspend all work on it.

While Perrault was organizing work on the Louvre, Le Vau and Lebrun were working with Le Nôtre at Versailles to enlarge the royal residence further. From 1668 to 1671 Le Nôtre was modifying the park: beyond

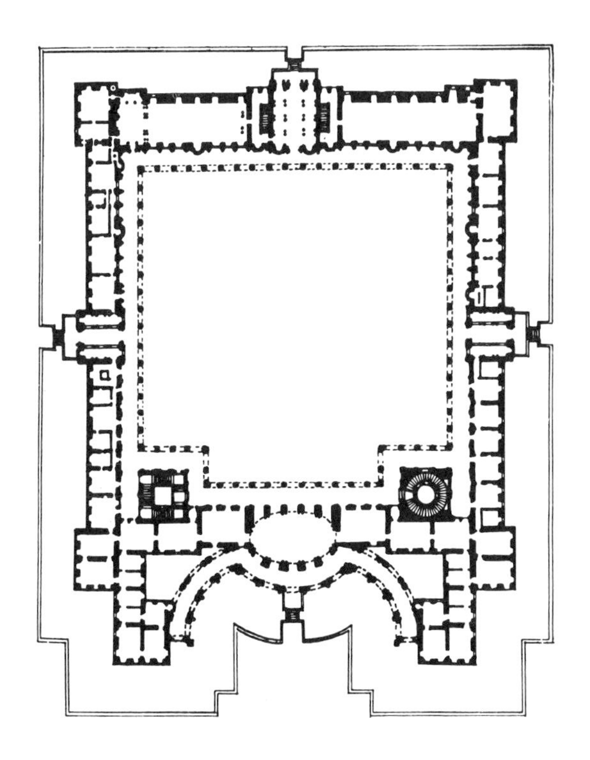

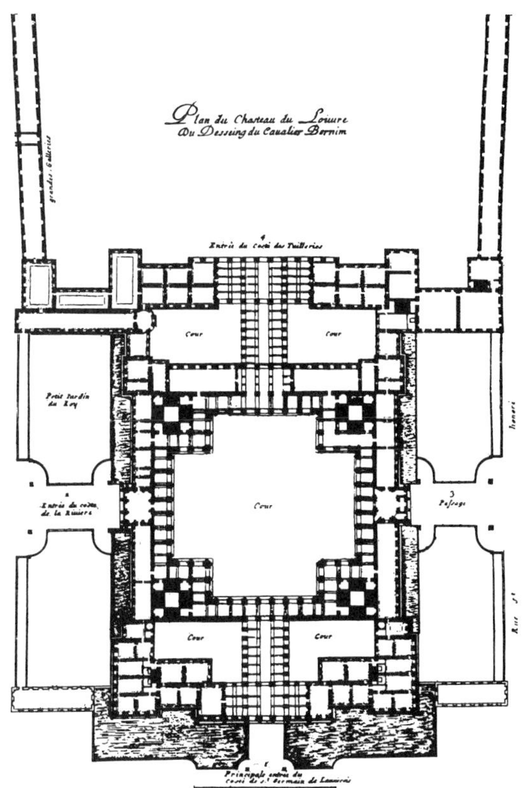

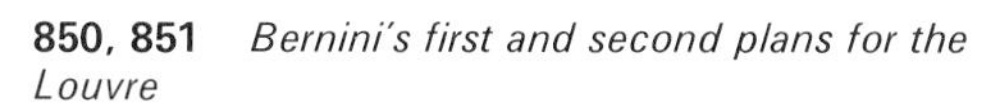
850, 851 *Bernini's first and second plans for the Louvre*

the sequence of sloping *parterres*, in place of the middle avenue, he had the *grand canal* dug in the form of a cross, which did create a couple of orthogonal Cartesian axes through the tree-filled landscape and brought out the symmetry of the main architectural complex; the longitudinal arm was over one and a half kilometres long, and the transversal one about a kilometre; thus the main axis starting from the château has its perspective end on the heights beyond the canal, about three kilometres away, where Le Nôtre organized a new star of ten radiating avenues; as usual, this symbolized the vanishing-point of the architectural system, where the plurality of vistas of the landscape universe began again.

The previous terraced park thus became the introduction to the new park laid out in the woody hollow – which was called the *petit parc*, because it occupied only a portion of the enclosed ground belonging to the king – and it linked the building scale of the château to the geographical scale of the surrounding layout. Le Nôtre also modified the decoration of the *parterres*, so that they should be in tune with the new backdrop; he largely replaced the *broderies* with ornamental pools, and used the jets of water to introduce a hint at the third dimension into the great expanse of space.

This whole composition was contained in a slight hollow, and the architectural views coincided with the more distant ones permitted by the nature of the land. Le Nôtre had to modify and strain the natural setting: the hill on which the château stood had to be artificially enlarged to extend the *parterres* as much as he wanted; the marshy land of the valley was drained, by lowering the water table and raising the water needed for the fountains by means of wells; the vegetation of the woods was changed, other species were planted. The park was peopled with sculptures, automatons, curiosities of all sorts; in the maze there were representations, with self-propelled figures, of the fables of La Fontaine, published in 1668. Thus, all in all, the park of Versailles was a grandiose

852 *The east façade of the Louvre*
853, 854 *Bernini's equestrian statue of Louis XIV (altered by Girardon) and the maquette in Villa Borghese, Rome*

demonstration of the sway of art over nature. 'The gardens of Versailles', wrote Blondel in 1752, 'are limited on all sides, and are gloomy for those who are not lovers of the fine arts. All the treasures they enclose present the eye rather with the power of the human spirit than the simplicity of nature.'[52]

The mass of the château had to be enlarged to bear comparison with the new dimension of the park. Le Vau and Perrault, with their orderly mentalities, suggested the demolition of the old building of Louis XIII and its replacement by a new organism; but the king and Colbert decided to retain it, and Le Vau designed a new U-shaped *corps de logis* which enclosed the old one on three sides, and therefore realized a new monumental block towards the park (Fig. 859) leaving the old courtyard standing on the entrance side, now to be sumptuously decorated.

Le Vau's new organism was a compact block, quite different from the loosely articulated ensemble of Vaux; only the terrace, which cut deeply into the volume from the first floor upwards, produced a summary articulation of volumes, calculated to be seen from a distance. The architectural facing was influenced by Bernini's plans for the Louvre: a massive basement, an order of free columns or engaged pilasters, and an attic topped by a balustrade, with a series of statues; none the less the main order was made to coincide, rationalistically, only with the *piano nobile*. Seen from the park the château still acted as a datum point, but acquired a chromatic value proportionate to the length of the axis.

The internal decoration was co-ordinated by Lebrun, designed by his team of assistants – Coypel, Blanchard, Houasse, La Fosse, Jouvenet – and executed by the Gobelins workshops. The richness of the materials and the delicacy of the treatment persisted in every detail; the figurative representation made use of the whole tradition of classicism amassed so far, and followed a complex and detailed symbolic programme, conceived and carried out with a breadth and thoroughness hitherto unknown in the secular sphere. All mythology connected directly or indirectly with the image of the sun was utilized to glorify the person of the Sun King to the point of paradox (Figs 862–4).

While the west part was being transformed into a grandiose scenario, the east part, divided up by the three avenues of Le Nôtre, was growing into a new town. In 1671 the king put out an edict offering for sale the sites included within the triangular sectors between the avenues, with the usual exemptions; in this way the residences of those connected with the court, and the public buildings needed by the new district grew up around regular streets and squares. But the town still remained a secondary part of the scheme, dominated by the park and created in terms of a single person.

Versailles was the spatial support, the visible and durable expression of the etiquette which regulated the movements of the court of Louis XIV: the château and park were the stable features of the scenario which, on festive occasions, the king's artists had to vary and enrich in so many different ways: stability produced respect for power, variability produced wonder at power.

The park, which was seen along the main axes of symmetry as a solemn and permanent spectacle, was also a sequence of special spectacles, produced in a fixed order following a pre-established course. An ordinance of 1672 proclaimed:[53]

'The king desires that the fountains shall always work in the following order when His Majesty arrives at Versailles; and when he does not wish it, he will let it be known. When His Majesty arrives by the *route de l'étang*, the *maître fontainier* shall have care to put water:

in the Pyramid
in the *allée d'eau*
in the Dragon

and shall gauge all so carefully that these fountains shall reach their perfection when

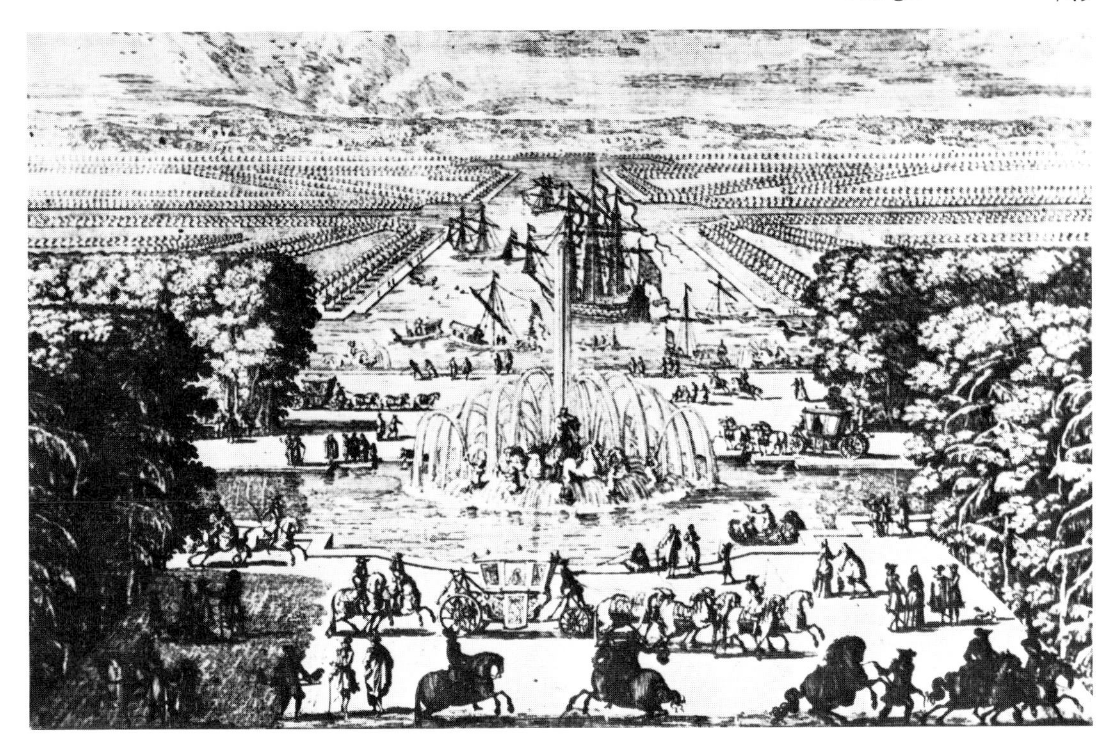

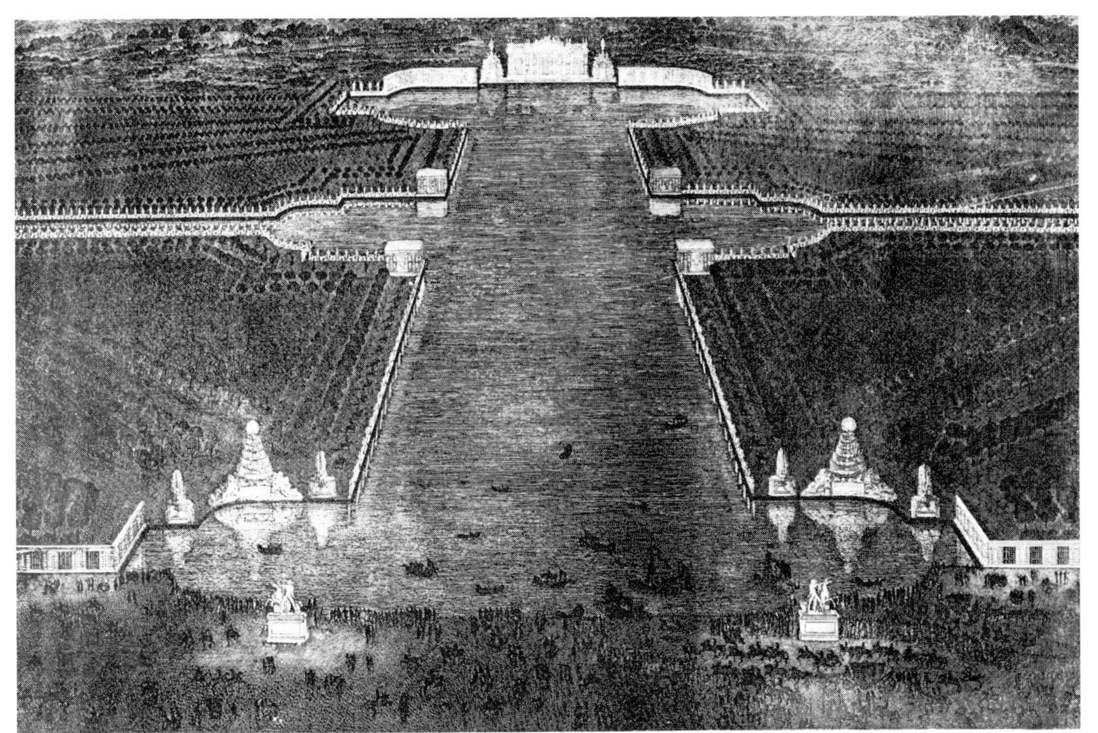

855, 856 *The* grand canal *at Versailles by day (Langlois) and by night (Le Pautre)*

857 *The Bassin de Latone at Versailles and the beginning of the* grand canal

His Majesty shall be at the *point de vue* at the end of the road. From whichever side His Majesty may come, He desires that the fountains of the courtyard, the Terrace and Siren shall start to function on his arrival. . . . Since the fountains of the Pavillon cannot function except by turning off the Pyramid, the fountain-worker in charge of these two fountains shall take care not to stop the Pyramid until His Majesty has entered into the small avenue . . . of the Pavillon, and cannot see the Pyramid, and immediately he shall let the water into the Pavillon, so that it shall be functioning before His Majesty can see it. When His Majesty is no longer in the *petit parc*, all shall be shut off. When His Majesty shall be on the canal, the fountain of Apollo shall be still functioning, but the jets at the feet of the horses shall be stopped until His Majesty re-enters the *petit parc*. The king desires that all that has been said concerning his person should be observed for persons of regard who may enter the park and whom His Majesty shall have ordered to be shown the fountains.'

Many writers have stressed the political and social importance of these ceremonies, from the time of Louis XIV onwards. This was not gratuitous display, it was a necessary part of the system of power on which absolute monarchy was based; but for those very reasons the expanse of Versailles could not become a city, and had to remain an empty stage for the king. 'There are more statues in the garden of his palace than citizens in a great city', Montesquieu has the Persian Usbek say, at the end of the reign of the Sun King.[54]

858 *One of the decorative vases around the Bassin de Latone*

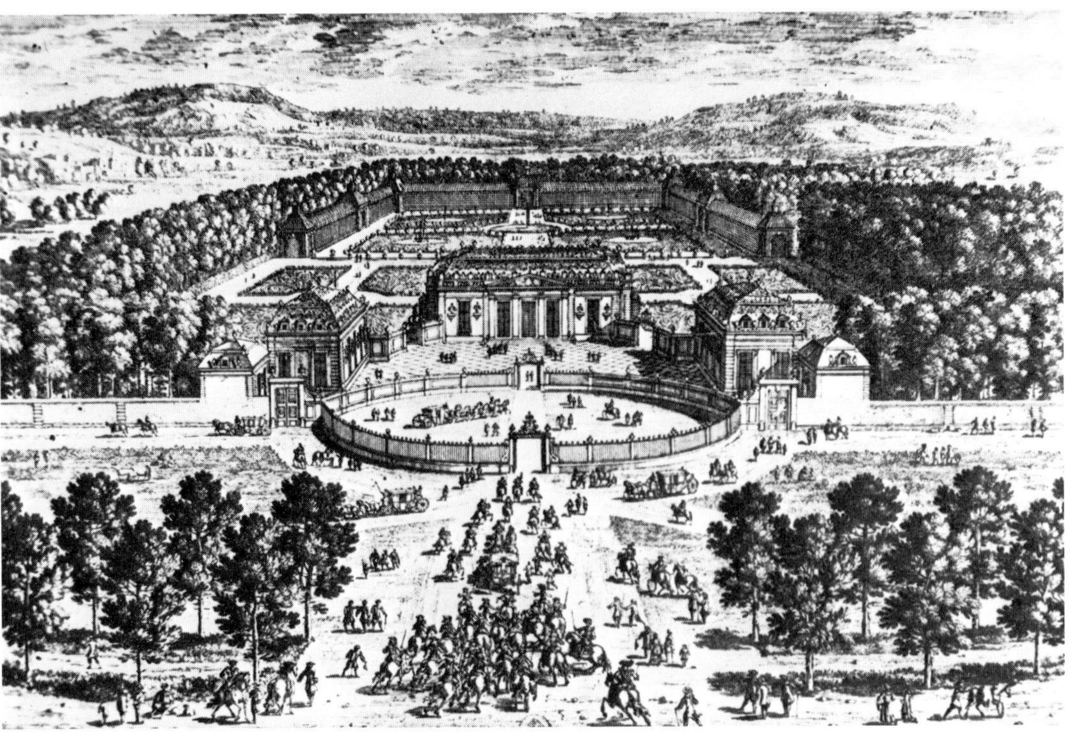

859, 860 *The new château of Versailles and the Trianon de Porcelaine by Le Vau (Perelle)*
861 *Detail of the ceiling of the Salle de Mercure, Versailles*

862–864 *Figure from Descartes'* Meteororum*; image of the sun on one of the piers of the outer wall of the Hôtel des Invalides and on a leaf of the door of the Salle de Vénus at Versailles*

Versailles was the great landscape novelty of the late seventeenth century; the literature of the time, attentive to every original phenomenon, commented on this new reality in all its aspects, not forgetting the negative ones; Mme de Sévigné admired the richness of the new apartments, but wrote to Bussy-Rabutin in 1678[55] describing the 'carts full of corpses' which came out of the work-sites every night; he, in reply, wrote:

'Kings can, by dint of money, give to the earth a shape different from its natural one, but the quality of the air and water is not in their power. It would be a singular misfortune if after having spent one hundred million, Versailles were to become uninhabitable.'

The observation on the unhealthiness of the air and water – which recurs as a positive obsession in the correspondence of the time – was a commonplace; the mortality on the sites implies quite different combinations of causes. The acuteness of the remark lies in its pointing out that architectural activities take place on the level of the geographical setting, even if current moralism led the author to point out the ultimate limits of this new power.

The creator of Versailles, Le Nôtre, was now at the height of his fame; his annual income was about 30,000 *livres*. The main persons at court had recourse to his skill; he laid out the park of St-Cloud for the duke of Orléans, the château of Chantilly for Le Grand Condé (Fig. 865), the château of Sceaux for Colbert, the château of Meudon for Louvois and that of Clagny for Mme de Montespan. The king 'lent' his gardener to other European sovereigns: in 1662 to Charles II of England, in 1683 to the queen of Sweden, in 1698 again to William III of England. In 1679 Le Nôtre made a journey to Italy, to visit the most famous gardens, and on his return declared: 'The Italians have no gardens which approach ours, they are absolutely ignorant of the art of gardening';[56] a haughty judgment, but fully founded, because the *jardins à la française* were a new spatial experiment, imitated henceforward throughout Europe and rich in consequences for the future.

After Versailles the reversal of the traditional hierarchy between park and architecture was a *fait accompli*, and made itself felt well beyond the field of country residences. We have already said that the programme of Louis XIV for Versailles was the political, organizational and figurative alternative to Colbert's programme for Paris; we must now remark that the works of Colbert in Paris, particularly from 1670 onwards, moved from the centre to the outskirts, from the scale of architecture to that of landscape, and produced a transformation of the city different from that conceived in the previous decade, but no less significant; the structural model for this transformation was provided in fact by Versailles.

To make sense of the comparison between the two experiments, one must consider the infinitely more complex operative cycle which Colbert had to use in the capital.

He had above all to establish a relationship with the city magistracy and had the good fortune to find two efficient collaborators in these circles: the *prévôt des marchands* Le Pelletier (in office from 1668 to 1676) and his special architect, François Blondel, who later became the first director of the academy of architecture: most of the technical officials of the city, such as François Villedo, Michel Mollet and Jean Beausire, were also Colbert's subordinates as members of the superintendence. Furthermore in 1666 Colbert set up a council of police which was to control both public order and the physical organization of the city and in 1667 he appointed a *lieutenant général* of police: Nicolas de la Reynie (1625–1709) held this post until 1697 and was the person really responsible for Paris town-planning. Thus the administrative solution from which Haussmann profited two centuries later was already in existence.

The council of police immediately embarked on intensive activity in the old city: in 1666 it organized the cleansing and public lighting of the streets, in 1667 it fixed a height limit for buildings and forbade projections on to public spaces, in 1668 it required owners to install latrines in every house and laid down rules for the cleansing of drains. From 1666 onwards it studied means to increase the water supply, granted permits for building other pumps along the Seine, and other aqueducts; in 1671 it ordered the building of fifteen more public fountains, some of a monumental character, in addition to the twenty-two existing ones. The banks of the river were laid out with *quais* and the hitherto non-existent embankments. Some new roads were traced, some old ones widened and straightened, such as the rue de la Ferronnerie where in 1669 a uniform architectural motif to be repeated throughout its length was established.

But the most important measures were those concerning the new outskirts. The city, which now had about 600,000 inhabitants, had already extended well beyond the limits fixed by Louis XIII, and the circle of the fortifications, though recently completed around the district of the Louvre, had lost all military significance. In 1672 Colbert fixed a new boundary beyond which it was forbidden to build (corresponding roughly to the local customs barrier of the *fermiers généraux*, built by Louis XVI in 1785–7) but abandoned the idea of fortifying the capital and began to transform the old enclosed city into an open one. From 1670 to 1676 he had the fortifications of the right bank destroyed, and laid out a tree-lined avenue in their place, 18 toises wide,[57] 'for the greater propriety of the city and to serve as a walking place for the inhabitants';[58] he planned a similar ring of avenues around the built-up area of the left bank, but here, not being able to utilize a strip of land already publicly owned, he was not in a position to start on the works (this ring was to be carried out gradually during the course of the eighteenth century). In this way the *grands boulevards* came into existence: not a series of isolated trunks, like the walks of the first half of the seventeenth century, but a new network surrounding the previous one traced in the Middle Ages and giving access to the urbanized countryside around the city. Outside the ring of the *boulevards* Colbert laid out a series of roads, of which, however, only one was connected directly with the ring: the *patte d'oie* designed in 1665 by Le Nôtre on the axis of the Tuileries gardens, formed of the old Cours-la-Reine on the banks of the Seine, by the great middle portion of the Champs-Élysées (which led to a group of radiating roads laid out by Le Nôtre in 1670 – the present Rond Point – and later to a second group laid out in 1724 at the top of the Chaillot hill, the present Étoile) and by a third symmetrical road in the direction of Faubourg St-Honoré which was left unfinished.

The other tree-lined radial roads, on the right bank, were the avenue St-Denis, the avenue de Meaux (which was the beginning of the road to Germany) and the avenue de Vincennes, conceived as a monumental entrance to the city from the west; in view of the already considerable development of the suburbs beyond the old walls, these axes stopped respectively at La Chappelle, La Villette and Charonne (where the place du Trône was laid out). In 1679 Colbert planned an extension of the avenue de Vincennes as far as the porte St-Antoine, and also thought of joining the two monumental roads running out towards east and west, with a large road through the old city on the axis of the Louvre. Similarly on the left bank the two roads running in from the south were laid out, i.e. the *grandes routes* of Fontainebleau and Orléans; also from 1670 to 1676 the hospital of the Invalides was built opposite the Champs-Élysées (Libéral Bruant, 1635–97) and a new series of radiating avenues extending outward towards the countryside was organized behind the building.

865 *View of the park at Chantilly laid out by Le Nôtre (Perelle)*

This system of green zones – formed of the corridors of tree-lined avenues, of the tree-filled areas of forest and the enclosed spaces of the parks – was peopled not only by châteaux and large isolated buildings – hospitals, convents, etc. – but also by a series of monumental objects: gates or triumphal arches, designed by Blondel and Perrault. Large numbers of noblemen's houses grew up around these focal points, surrounded by gardens; Boileau described it as a 'land of Cockaigne' reserved for the rich, who 'found themselves in the country without having to leave the town'.[59]

These enterprises were co-ordinated, from a certain point onwards, into a positive town-planning scheme, extended to the whole city and conceived as an extrapolation of the actual situation. An edict of 1676 summed up all the work in progress, and continued:[60]

'Having decided to ensure that works which may be carried out in the city in future should be regulated according to a precise plan, we have ordained that an exact plan of the city should be carried out, marking not only those works executed according to our orders, but also those we intend should be continued and completed.'

The plan, executed by Bullet and Blondel, was kept up to date until the first decades of the eighteenth century; in it one sees the belt of avenues on the left bank, the projected isolation of the Louvre and a series of lesser works.

A famous note among Colbert's papers offers a vivid summary of his town-planning policy: 'Endless rows of trees everywhere. Triumphal arch for the conquests of the earth. Observatory for the heavens. Pyramid. Difficulties of execution.'[61]

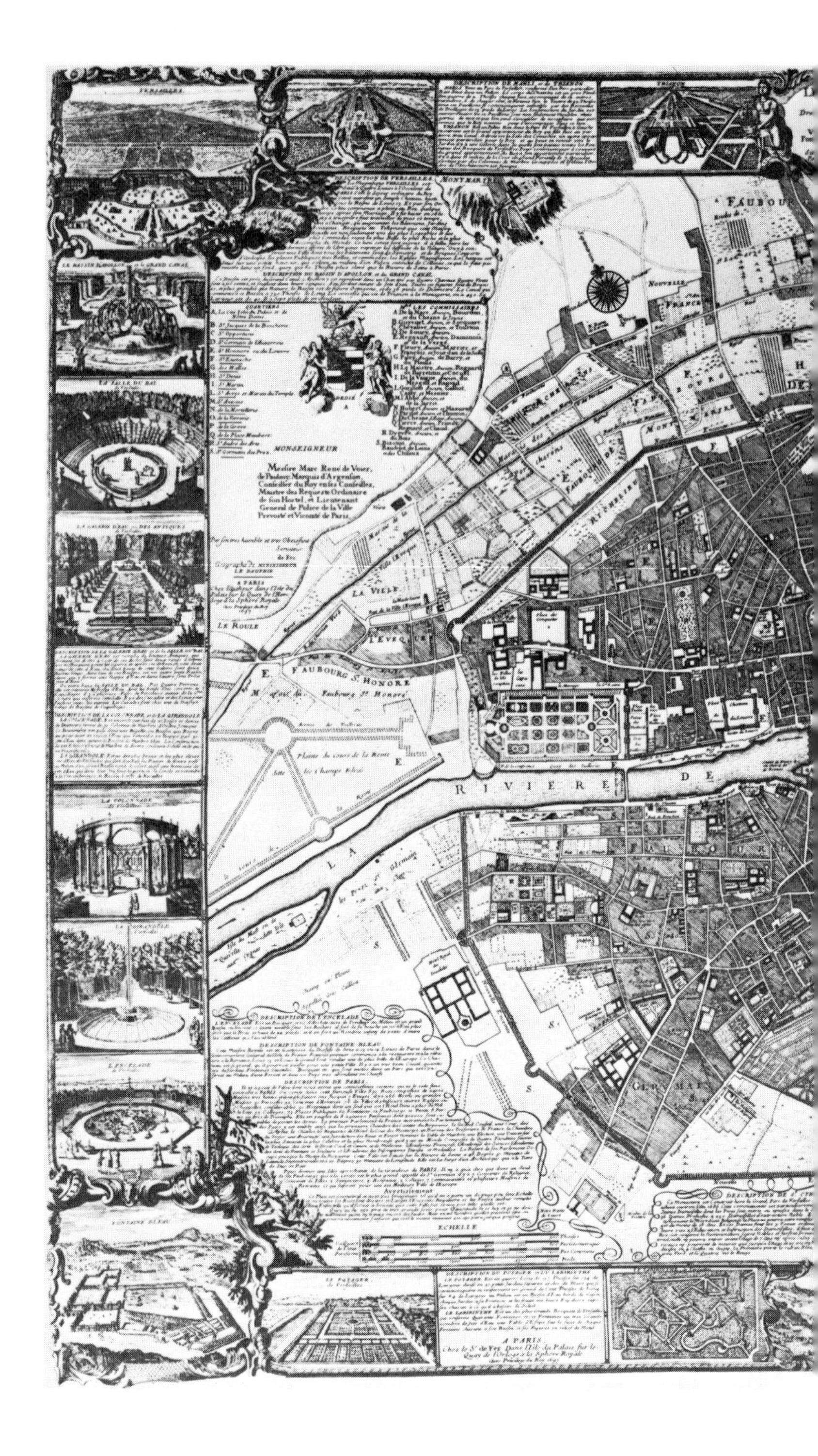

866 *Plan of Paris in 1697, showing the complete ringing by the* boulevards

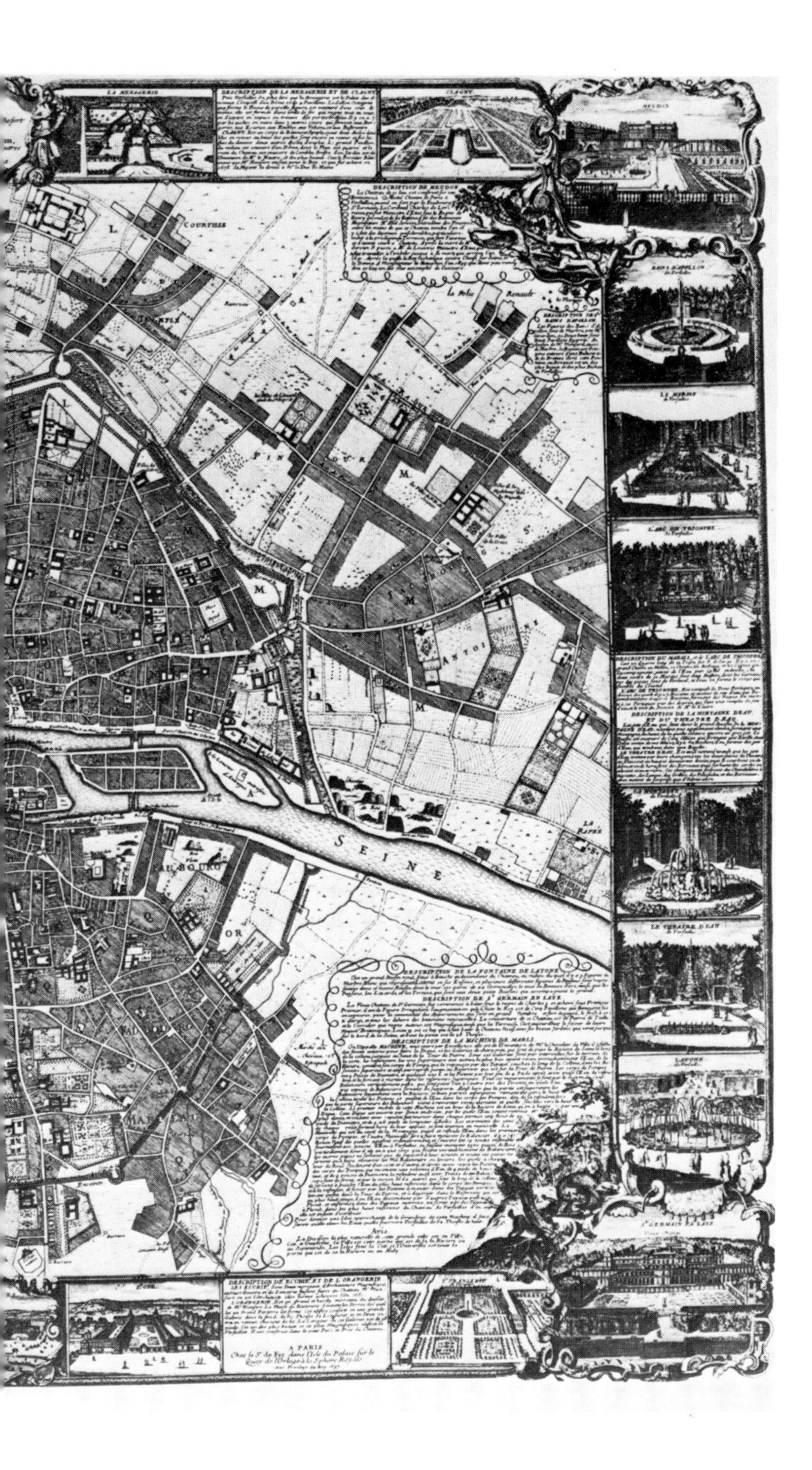
LA MENAGERIE
CLAGNY
MEUDON
DESCRIPTION DE MEUDON
S E I N E
DESCRIPTION DE LA FONTAINE DE LATONE
DESCRIPTION DE S.T GERMAIN EN LAYE
DESCRIPTION DE LA MACHINE DE MARLI
A PARIS

867 *The entrance to the Hôtel des Invalides*

868 *The courtyard of the Hôtel des Invalides*

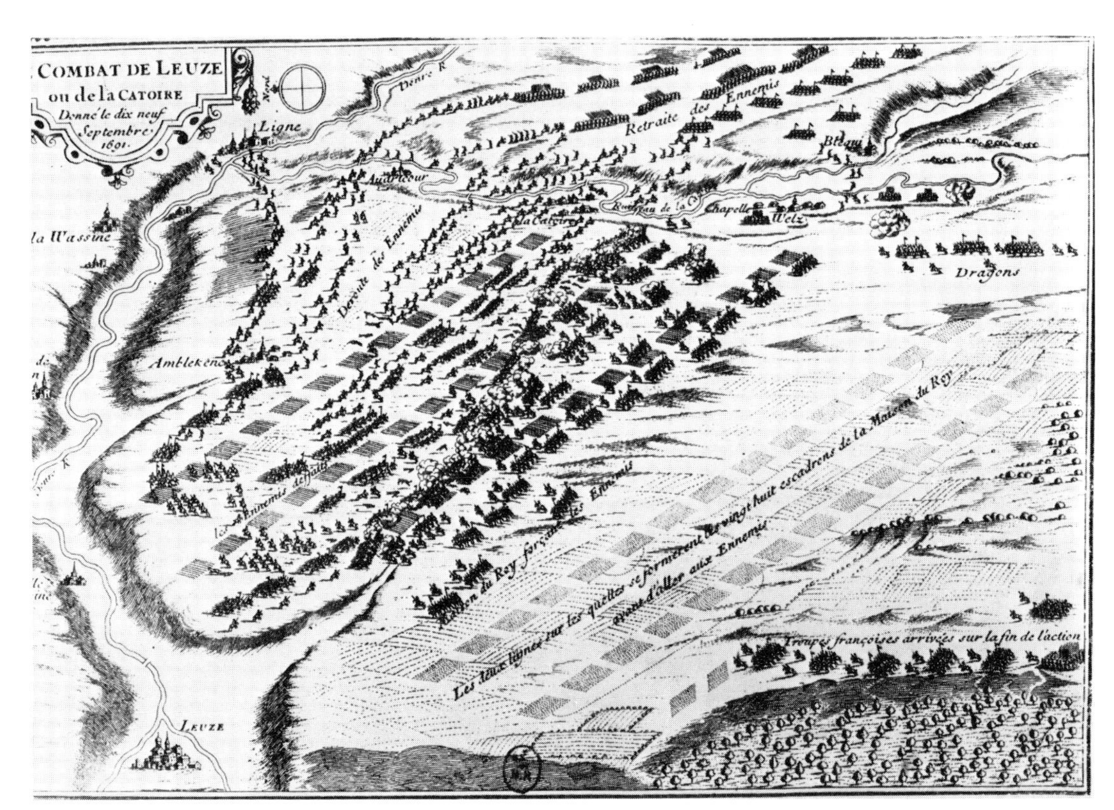

869 *The battle of Leuze, 19 September 1691*

Trees, monuments and executive difficulties; the earthly order compared with the heavenly one, but continually related to the concrete means of execution, to real obstacles, frequently financial but also economic, legal, social and moral.

As yet there was no theoretical awareness of these obstacles, and indeed there was not to be for a long time to come. Colbert recognized them and tackled them on empirical grounds; most of his contemporaries, and even his later critics, were unaware of them or considered them in a context unconnected with building or town-planning. Voltaire, for example, wrote in 1741:[62]

'If Louis XIV had spent on Paris a fifth of what he lavished on Versailles to violate nature, Paris would be as beautiful throughout as it is between the Tuileries and Palais Royal, and would have become the most magnificent city in the World.'

Colbert would have smiled at so unlikely a financial hope; furthermore, together with the costs, he would have considered the other infinite difficulties, superable only with patience and minute attention to detail. His great claim to merit was his very everyday empiricism, 'the study of details' and the 'diligent attention to the slightest needs of the state' that La Bruyère judged an 'essential part of good government',[63] and which are certainly an essential part of urban planning; another great planner, Haussmann, affirmed two centuries later: 'secondary matters may not be overlooked'.[64] It is extraordinary to see Colbert finding the time to concern himself with endless small problems: while he was working on the *grand dessein* for the Louvre, he had swans sent from Denmark to populate an island on the Seine, and when they escaped to Normandy he wrote to the intendant of Rouen to catch them and send them back to Paris.[65] This meticulous industry was simply a recurrent battle, dogged and even dramatic, against a combination of adverse circumstances. The programme of imposing a geometrical and monumental order on a city and region previously urbanized according to completely different criteria, was limited from the outset by the modest size and sporadic nature of subsequent transformations, and became almost unrealizable because of the lack of any official public control on the forces that produced these transformations. The encouragement given to the production of luxury goods – i.e. the economic policy on which the protection of the arts was based – was largely thwarted by economic stagnation, and functioned only if the state, through the acquisitions of the court, also ensured to some degree that the goods produced would be absorbed. More generally, the policy of development came up against the economic and demographic recession that more recent studies have discerned, and the policy of rationalization of the state, undertaken through the means of absolutism, was made impossible by the irrational structure of absolute power.

The character of the urbanization achieved by Colbert around Paris, consisting essentially of green zones and monumental key points – the network of avenues leading to the perspective focuses of old and new monuments, extended into the surrounding countryside and were organized as landscape scenery around the *parterres* and mirrors of water of the suburban parks – was the combined outcome of the new methods of perspective control conceived by Le Nôtre and of the old obstacles to a rational development of urban planning, which Colbert did not manage to remove. Looking at a map of the Parisian *banlieue* at the end of Louis XIV's reign (Figs 870–1) one can clearly see two superimposed fabrics: the dense, irregular and well-knit fabric of the medieval city, from which roads radiated directly to the other surrounding centres, and the sparse, broken but geometrically precise fabric of the new schemes, which coagulated in the great nodal point of Versailles and lesser points of St-Cloud, St-Germain-en-Laye, Marly,

Meudon, Sceaux and Vincennes. The second fabric anticipated the future outskirts (which in fact incorporate a large part of its layout, transforming avenues into city streets, as can be seen in Fig. 873) but was not yet an alternative to the first fabric, which continued to perform the vital functions of the city's life.

As the administrative work begun by Richelieu, Mazarin and Colbert, in untoward circumstances and with limited means, was to be concluded only by bourgeois governments, after the great revolution, so the new city dreamed of by Colbert and his artists for the glory of Louis XIV was to be realized only two centuries later, for the glory and safety of Napoleon III: the monumental perspectives which Colbert opened into the countryside among the trees, Haussmann could open up right in the heart of the city amid the houses; the planners, however, were no longer Le Nôtre, Le Vau or Mansart, but the engineers and academicians of the Second Empire and Third Republic.

Colbert's nineteen years of power prepared the way for the seventeen years of power of Haussmann; the two men had many points in common – energy, meticulousness, patience, approval of commonplaces, sense of propriety – and there is a surprising administrative continuity between the two experiments, which none the less highlights the enormous political, ideological and cultural differences. The perfect visual regularity of the classic *ordonnances* of Paris and Versailles, accepted henceforth as sovereign models of propriety throughout the European world, was the precarious result of a stormy struggle against circumstances; in the nineteenth century this very regularity – distorted and vulgarized by two centuries of wear – became the conventional stylistic veneer of an administrative action at last coherent and secure.

In the next chapter we shall look at the long series of European schemes modelled on those of Paris; we must now consider some schemes promoted by Colbert in the smaller towns in France and the colonies.

The preferences of the controller general went to coastal towns, for economic reasons already described. In Marseilles, as in Paris, the old fortifications to the east of the city were destroyed, and a tree-lined avenue 40 metres wide was created in their place; in the neighbouring zone a new district with straight streets, large blocks and well-spaced buildings alternating with gardens was built, but was surrounded by a new circle of walls; the man behind this programme was the intendant Nicolas Arnoul, and the main designer was the sculptor Pierre Puget (1622–94); the plans were prepared between 1667 and 1670, their execution being very slow because of resistance on the part of the municipality. In Toulon and Brest, in the last decades of the century, Vauban laid out the new districts in the shelter of his fortifications. In these cases the works of defence hindered the kind of urban schemes which tended to become integrated with the countryside; the open city of Paris remained a unique organism in the France of the seventeenth century.

In the colonies of North America the population was extremely low, and proper towns were not needed so much as strongholds like Quebec, founded in 1608, and Montreal, founded in 1641. Colbert gave Quebec the title of city in 1663, but it was only in the eighteenth century that a small built-up centre formed there (Figs 874–5).

In the Antilles, on the other hand, Colbert built an important town, Fort-de-France, the capital of Martinique. The West India Company, set up in 1664, incorporated the island into its territory, with the two forts of St-Pierre and Fort-de-France, founded in 1635 and 1638; the company went bankrupt in 1675, but at the same time the island's prosperity began, and it became one of the most important centres of sugar-cane growing. In 1666 Colbert sent François Blondel

870 *Plan of Paris and its suburbs in 1731*

ET SES ENVIRONS.
PARTIE DE LA PLAINE DE ST DENIS
Grande Route
Avenue de Vincennes
Plaine de Bercy
Plaine d'Ivry

871 *Diagram showing the built-up areas around Paris in the middle of the eighteenth century. Fine lines: roads of medieval origin; darker lines: sixteenth- and seventeenth-century roads; dense dots: parks; scattered dots: woods.*

1 Maisons-Laffitte 2 St-Germain-en-Laye 3 Marly 4 Versailles 5 Clagny 6 St-Cloud 7 Bois de Boulogne 8 Meudon 9 Sceaux 10 Vincennes 11 Livry 12 St-Maur 13 Gros Bois

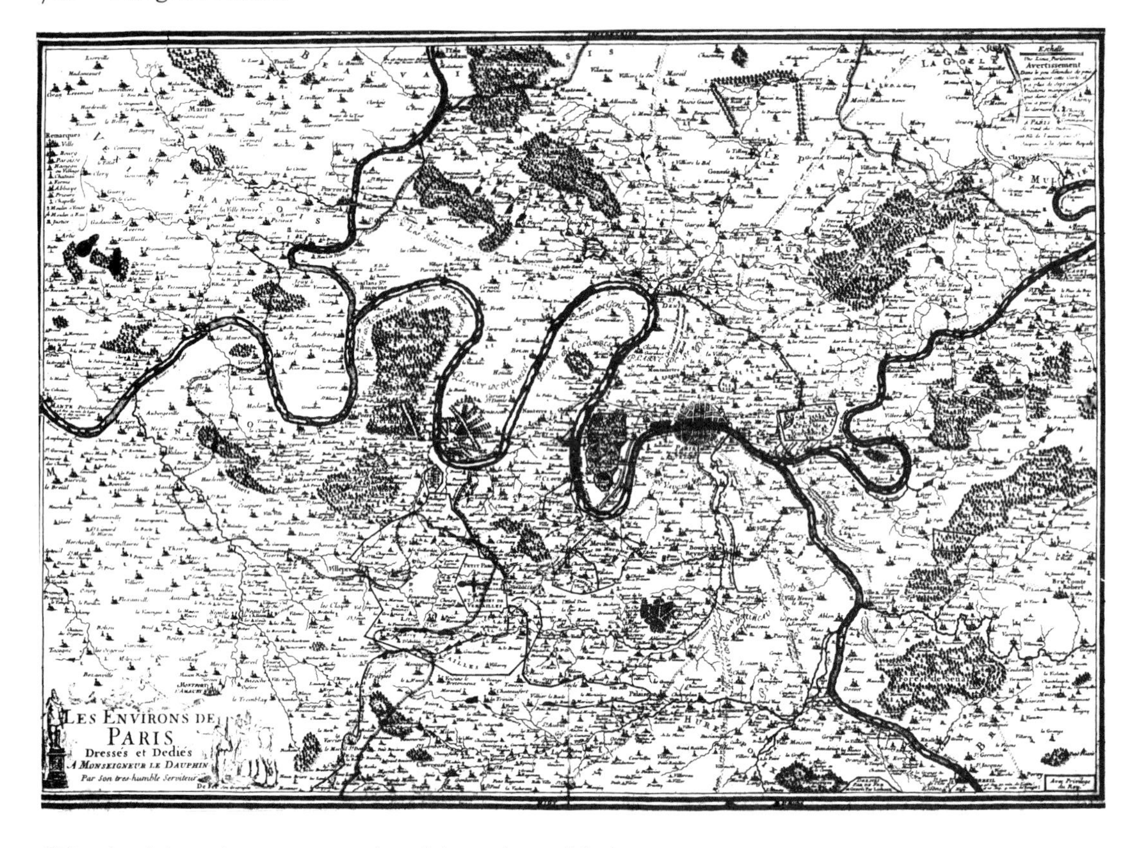

872 *An eighteenth-century engraving of the environs of Paris*
873 *The current street network of Paris, incorporating the green routes and parks of the* ancien régime

there to study possibilities for settlement, then chose Fort-de-France as capital and in 1668 had a plan of the city drawn up, which was approved in 1671.[66] The terrain was a marshy plain, which needed to be drained with a network of canals, and the street network of the city reproduced the grid system of the drainage works; this layout subsequently functioned like that of the Spanish American cities, and controlled successive expansions, from 1693 onwards.

Colbert's death in 1683 and the revocation of the edict of Nantes in 1685 marked a turning-point in French policy which had immediate repercussions on architecture. Money spent on buildings was still inversely proportionate to money spent on military matters; for this reason it is necessary to distinguish the periods of peace, in which Louis XIV could devote large sums to building and town-planning work – the decade from the Peace of Nijmegen (1678) to the beginning of the war against the second coalition (1689), and to a lesser extent the five years from Ryswick (1697) to the beginning of the Spanish Succession (1701) – from the periods of war in which work-sites were shut down or were proceeding more slowly. In political terms there is a distinction between the period of aggressive imperialism, until 1689, and the period of withdrawal before the enemy coalition, from 1689 to 1714; or, after the 'time of action' (1661–79), the 'time of scorn' (1679–89) and the 'time of trial' (1689–1715).[67] This distinction is paralleled, in architecture, by the period of the great

monumental plans and the period of finishing touches and minor undertakings; concern for prestige grew together with the exaltation of the personal power of the king, but the ability to carry out important town-planning transformations lessened, because the organizational direction guaranteed by Colbert until 1683 was now lacking.

The post of superintendent of buildings was occupied by Louvois (1683–91), by Colbert's cousin Colbert de Villacerf (1691–9) and lastly by Hardouin-Mansart (1691–1708); then it was abolished, and replaced by a department of building. But from 1675 onwards the real management of architectural works passed into the hands of the young and brilliant Jules Hardouin (1646–1708), great-nephew of François Mansart and bearer of the same name after 1668.

Hardouin-Mansart, son of a royal painter, worked on the work-site at Versailles as a young man, and in 1675, at the advice of Le Nôtre, was chosen by the king to design Mme de Montespan's new residence at Clagny, near Versailles; in the same year king Louis authorized him to attend academy sessions, and in 1677 – when he decided to remove all government officials to Versailles – he commissioned the young architect to design the third extension of the château. This was the beginning of the most spectacular professional career of modern times: Hardouin-Mansart was appointed first architect to the king, designed and realized, without difficulty, an extraordinary number of buildings and town-planning schemes, became rich and noble; he was the first architect again to obtain the post of superintendent of buildings, i.e. the management of the great public works, hitherto held by politicians, starting from Sully, and entered, on equal terms, into the privileged sphere of wielders of power; in 1699 his position gained him an annual income of about 60,000 *livres*.

Admired unreservedly in his own day, he was keenly criticized subsequently, from Saint-Simon[68] to Viollet-le-Duc.[69] His success was attributed to an exceptional capacity to organize others and even reduced to 'a gigantic case of charlatanry and imposture'.[70]

Saint-Simon tells how Hardouin-Mansart designed in close collaboration with Louis XIV and attributed the desired decisions to the king, flattering his vanity.[71] Many designs and writings by Hardouin-Mansart annotated point-by-point by king Louis have in fact been preserved (Fig. 877). But Hardouin-Mansart probably exercised this same capacity for dialogue with all the members of his circle, seizing the problems to be resolved and the cultural instruments available to this end. Even if he limited himself to co-ordinating the work of his collaborators, he thus obtained a series of results that were to be unattainable henceforward through individual endeavour; he understood that this was the last way left open to impersonate the figure of the great Renaissance artist, already on the point of being dismembered by rational criticism.

The first important work by Hardouin-Mansart, the extension of Versailles, was also the most successful. Versailles became for him what St Peter's had been for Bernini half a century earlier: the work of a whole lifetime, worked upon and perfected on a number of occasions with a deep sense of history, without interrupting the continuity of previous contributions.

To transport the governmental apparatus to Versailles meant tripling the size of the building, transforming a pleasure palace into a work place, or rather extending the order and etiquette which already regulated the king's day to the whole community of officials, fusing and identifying the public and private features of the French court. This was the moment of the Peace of Nijmegen (1678); king Louis could direct the sums hitherto employed on the war with Holland to the new works, and was at the peak of his political fortunes; Versailles must become the visual expression of his new prestige.

Hardouin-Mansart decided to add to Le Vau's block:

1 Two wings running breadthways, which would contain the working premises, the theatre and chapel, rationally distributed around a series of secondary courtyards; the area of the two wings was the same, though the inner distribution was different.

2 Two wings running depthways, which contained premises for services and which framed a large new entrance square, occupying a part of the space formed by the convergence of the three avenues.

The new organism, seen from the park, presented a grandiose continuous façade about 600 metres long and bent forward in a Ω shape in the centre, to embrace the original nucleus (Fig. 882). Hardouin-Mansart eliminated every further complication of volume; he filled in the middle terrace – using its place for the new state rooms – and repeated Le Vau's motif along the whole façade, with the groups of twin columns protruding, at varying intervals, from the stone facing. These external modifications were judged 'disastrous',[72] because they destroyed the original proportion between the order and volumes of the building, and indeed, from a short distance, compromised the plastic balance of the façade, but this indifference to the traditional rules of composition was largely compensated for by the importance of the effects in terms of landscape. When the observer moves away far enough no longer to see the relief of the decorative details, the

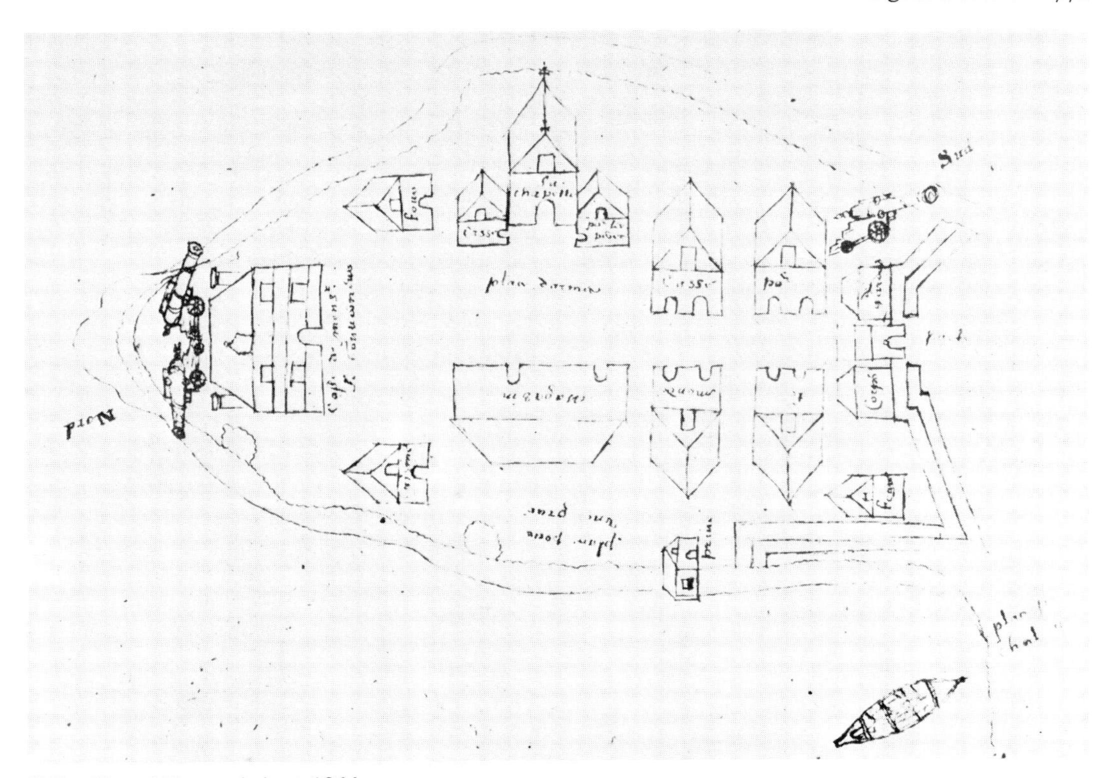

874 *Plan of Montreal about 1644*

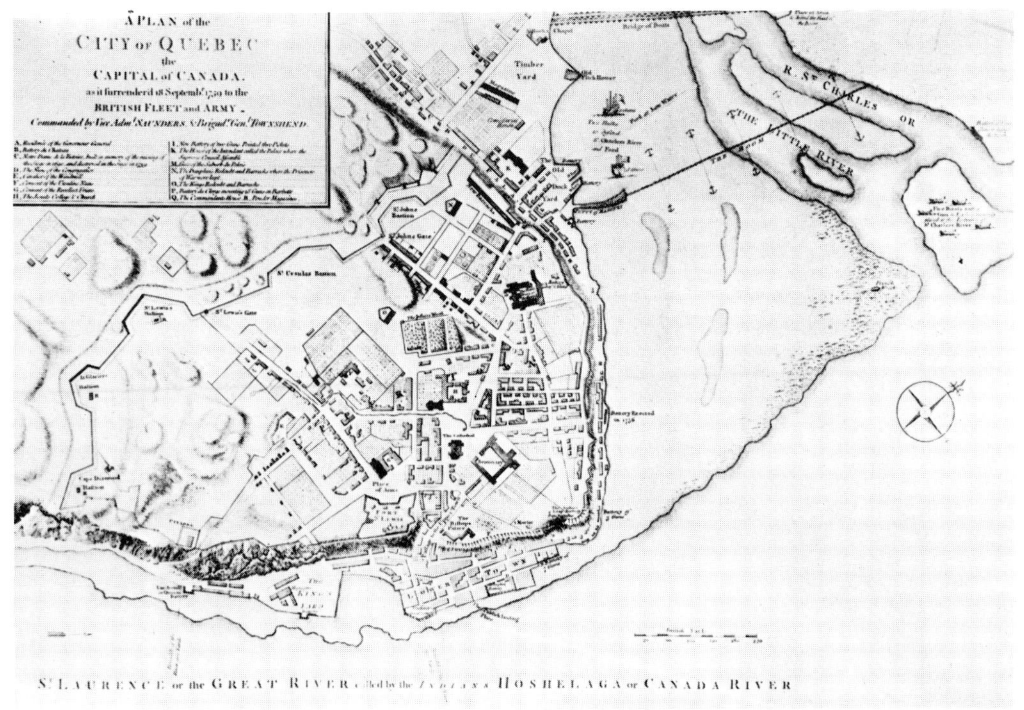

875 *Plan of Quebec in 1759 (from Reps)*

great façade appears as a compact volume which limits the horizon of the park, and its inflexion, intentionally elementary, becomes a piece of moulding on the scale of landscape, perceptible even from a great distance. The central salient still indicates the point of origin of the main perspective axis, but the entire building, which occupies half a kilometre of the horizon, is no longer a punctiform creation: it is now a barrier which receives and returns the pressure of the concave space of the park. For the first time court building assumed the spatial scale and value of the great utilitarian structures – bridges, dykes and aqueducts – and could bear comparison to the empty spaces calculated by Le Nôtre. It could be that the architect picked up a cue from the great designer of gardens; in any case he grasped the dimensions imposed by Le Nôtre and replied to the challenge with the traditional means of architecture.

The view from the entrance is equally interesting. Already Le Vau had had the idea of presenting the courtyard of Louis XIII's château as the backdrop to a larger courtyard created in front of it. Hardouin-Mansart's new organism further complicated this effect, and presented three U-shaped motifs contained one in the other, ranged over the slope of the hill as though over the rising floor of a stage. This arrangement – seen from in front from the middle avenue or from a three-quarter view from the side ones – functioned in fact as a theatrical backdrop, and caused the last *corps de logis* containing the private apartments of the king, as everyone knew, to recede indefinitely. The royal residence was presented to the eyes of the profane as the vanishing-point of the urban scene, at the end of the rectilinear perspective two kilometres long (Figs 884–5, 889).

The strong projection of the two end wings also made it possible to close in the outer expanse of space architecturally; from 1679 to 1686 Hardouin-Mansart built the stables which occupied the two acute angles between the two avenues, and realized a space in the shape of an equilateral triangle in front of the château, surrounded by two- or three-storey buildings, a space which was roughly equivalent to the overall dimensions of the built-up volumes (the side of the triangle measures almost half a kilometre). The other service buildings could be placed behind this architectural enclosure, without disturbing the symmetry, and they included the Grand Commun built from 1682 to 1684 to house the 1,500 persons connected with the kitchens.

Inside Hardouin-Mansart modified the distribution and furnishing of many rooms, and created a new group of reception rooms at the centre of the west façade: the Salon de la Guerre and the Salon de la Paix, linked by the Galérie des Glaces.

The decoration of these rooms – and particularly of the Galérie, over 70 metres long – was a new, sensational *tour de force* by Lebrun and his specialists. The symmetrical open arches in the two long sides of the Galérie were filled, on the outer wall, by the windows which looked out over the park near the main axis calculated by Le Nôtre and, on the inside wall, by the mirrors produced by the royal manufactories: an unheard-of luxury when one realizes that at that time the production of a square metre of mirror took 5,000 workman-hours. For the first time mirrors played an important part in the architectural composition, both because they gave the illusion of doubling the lesser dimension of the room, like paintings or Renaissance reliefs in perspective, and corrected the unusual relation between length and breadth, and because they reflected and accentuated the presence of the outside view. But the actual masonry casing – just slightly differentiated by the varying spacing of the windows, as a result of the external architectural motif – was almost annulled by a dazzling assembly of decorations in the most varied materials: the white, green and purplish marble of the walls, the stuccoes of the ceiling, the gilt bronze of the capitals and

876, 877 *Portrait of Hardouin-Mansart by Coysevox and a memorandum of 1696 written by Hardouin-Mansart, with comments by Louis XIV*

bases, the glasswork and mirrors with their frames of chased bronze, the objects in silver and *vermeil*, the velvet chairs, the porphyry vases with the orange trees, the two great carpets specially woven in the Savonnerie. The painted panels of the ceiling did not represent the usual mythical allegories, but the actual happenings of the reign of Louis XIV: the king governing alone, order re-established in the finances, the people assisted in famine, duels abolished, the navy newly strengthened, the fine arts patronized, ambassadors sent all over the world. Colbert added to the official instructions for the painters the 'prudent restriction . . . not to include anything not in accord with the truth, nor anything too offensive to foreign powers';[73] painting even registers the nuances of high politics. This spectacular décor unfolds in full view of the panorama and refers continually back to the great landscape spectacle, laid out in the area outside.

Hardouin-Mansart carried out numerous alterations in the park, all tending to increase the architectural basis of the avenues established by Le Nôtre.

The transversal axis of the higher esplanade, in front of the château, was emphasized by a series of new schemes, to the north – where the *allée d'eau* was prolonged and adorned with new sculptures – and more particularly to the south, where the difference in level of the ground which surrounded the *parterre du midi* was resolved from 1681 to 1686 with the building of the Orangerie and the two great staircases. This axis, too, had an

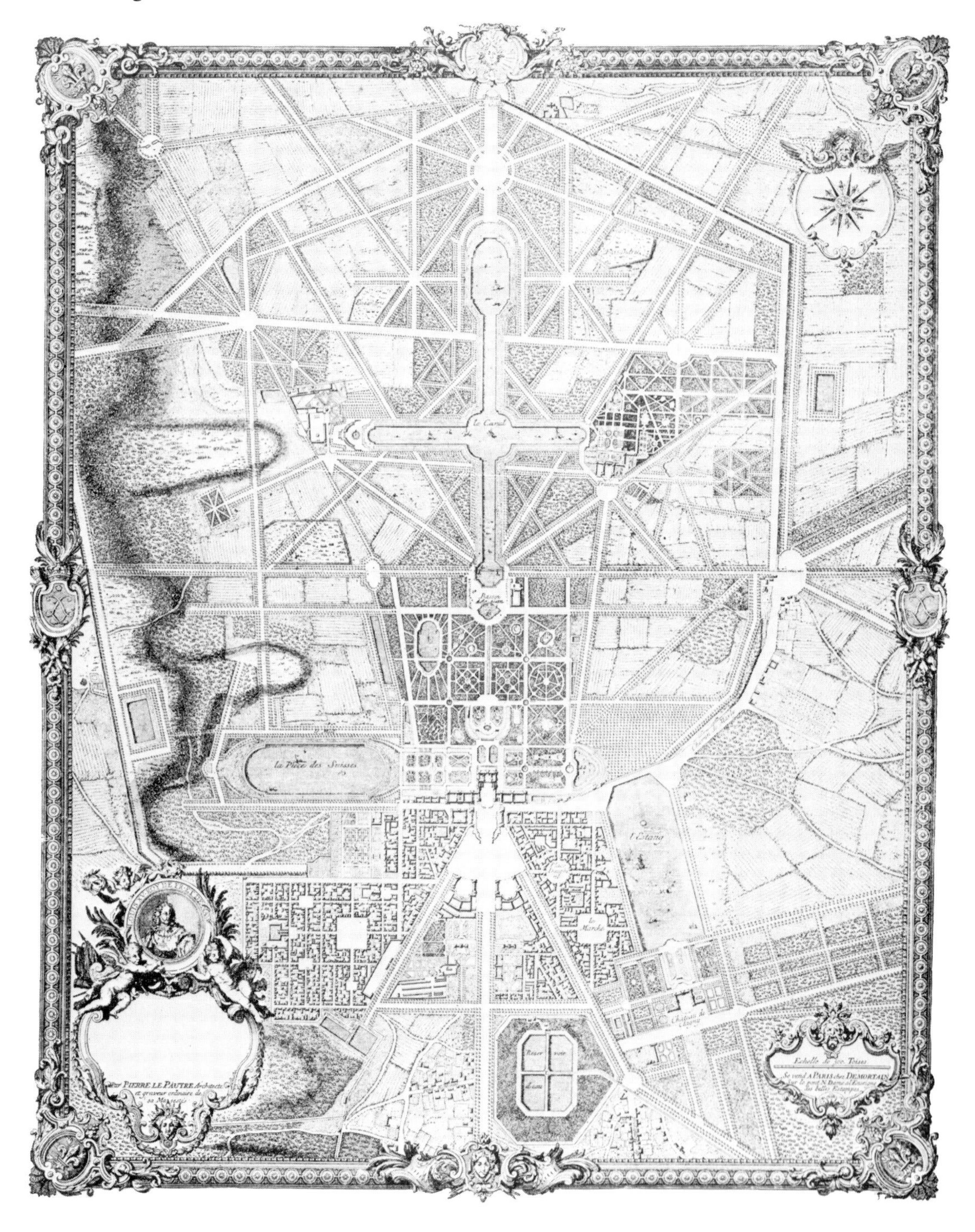

878 *Versailles at the end of the reign of Louis XIV (Le Pautre's plan)*

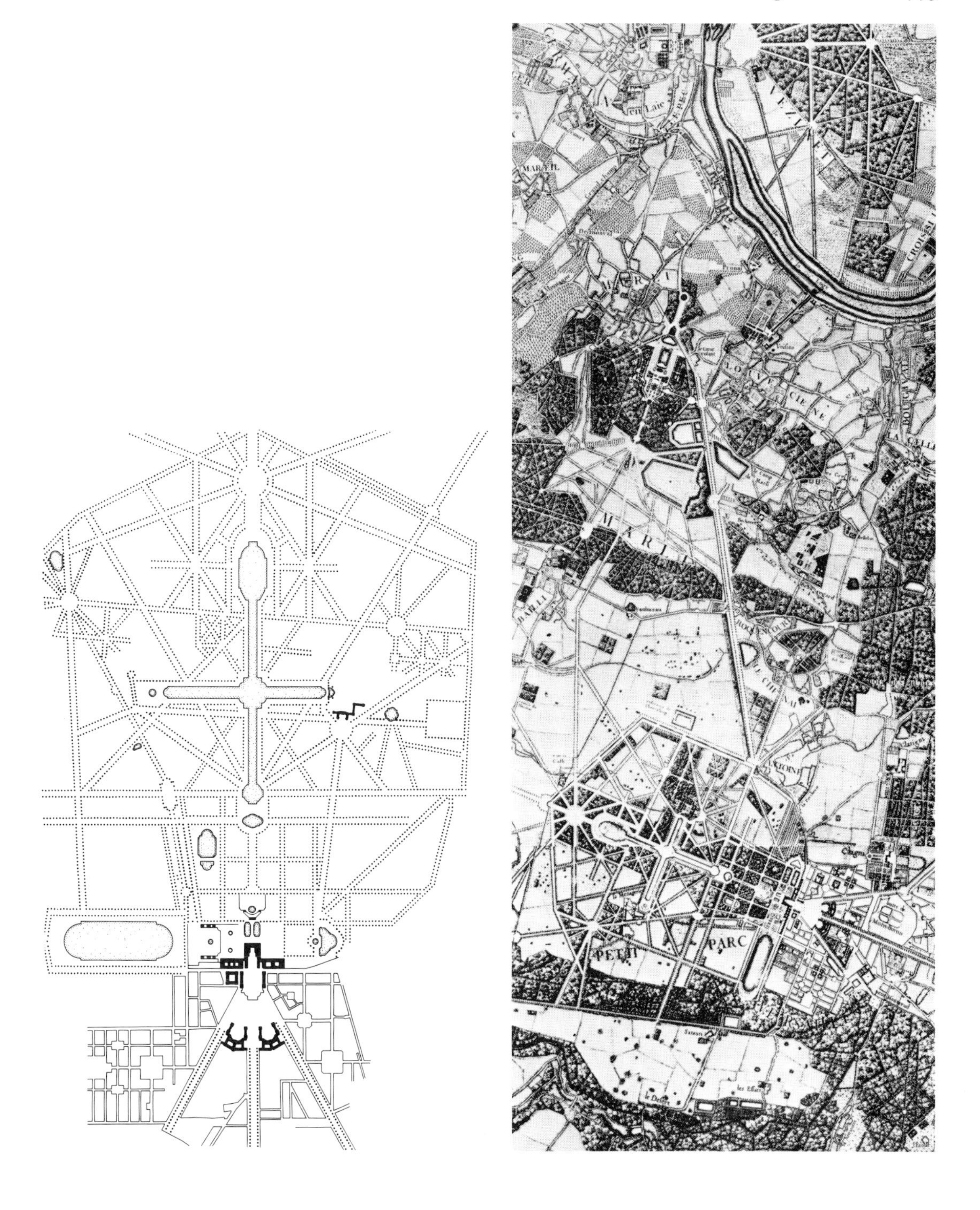

879 *Plan of the complex at Versailles; buildings of the château and Grand Trianon shown in black*
880 *The three royal parks: (from top to bottom) St-Germain-en-Laye, Marly and Versailles*

881 *View of the terrace of Versailles in front of Hardouin-Mansart's façade*

infinite perspective backdrop, i.e. the pool dug out by Swiss soldiers at the same time, which measured about 200 by 700 metres; the whole view, from the centre of the façade of the château, is over a kilometre long.

From 1685 to 1698, in one of the small woods along the main axis of the park, Hardouin-Mansart built the most famous of his ornamental schemes, the colonnade which defines a circular space with purely architectural means, columns, arches and buttresses, though whittled away to the limit compatible with stability.

From 1687 to 1688, at the northern end of the *grand canal*, Hardouin-Mansart built the Trianon in the place of a pavilion of Le Vau's: a small independent one-storey residence, deep in the woods. The garden laid out by Le Nôtre was fitted into one of the compartments of the *petit parc* and was traced on an intentionally smaller scale; the lightness of the architectural and sculptural decoration and the respect for the natural elements looked forward to the new course to be taken by the art of garden design in the eighteenth century. The portico at the centre of the west façade reproduced the spatial situation of the Galérie des Glaces: an elongated, airy space, open on to a landscape background which formed its fourth wall (Fig. 890).

The digging of the basin by the Swiss soldiers also helped to drain the surrounding land, and made it possible to enlarge the city of Versailles in the region to the south of the three avenues. The king's architect traced the road network, outlined plots that were to be built upon with uniform façades towards the roads and main squares, and designed the public buildings, including the parish church, always respecting the hierarchy between city and château.

Not far from Versailles the king had Hardouin-Mansart build a new separate residence at Marly (1679–86); here the external layout was absolutely dominant, and instead of a compact building there was a series of small solid pavilions – one for the king (Fig. 892) and twelve for guests – set around a large pool. A straight tree-lined avenue joined Marly to the park of Versailles, and established the visual unity between the two organisms with the means typical of landscape planning.

The work-site of Versailles in the 1680s was the largest ever organized in Europe from the time of the Romans onwards; in 1684 22,000 men and 6,000 horses were working on it, and in 1685 more than 35,000 men.[74] This gigantic undertaking proceeded with an astonishing mixture of prodigality and mean-

882, 883 *The new façade by Hardouin-Mansart*

884 *The main entrance of Versailles*

ness: from 1679 to 1688 the budget of the superintendence was more than 80,000,000 *livres*, but the carpentry of the Galérie des Glaces was done with salvaged timber, the discarded curtaining from Versailles was used for the apartments of the grand Dauphin at Meudon and the damasks from Meudon were used to drape the boats on the *grand canal* at Versailles.

Equally impressive and eventful works were organized to increase the flow of water to the fountains. From 1675 to 1682 the famous machine was built at Marly, which made the water of the Seine go up a hill about 160 metres high, and was described by contemporaries as a 'forest of wood and iron', so noisy that it could be heard many kilometres away (Fig. 893); a part of the water was diverted to Versailles in 1685. From 1680 onwards Thomas Gobert built the aqueduct in the uplands of Saclay, using the new pipes of pig-iron produced in the French factories. From 1684 to 1688 work began on a new aqueduct to carry the waters of the Eure to Versailles; the mathematician La Hire calculated the differences in level, Vauban prepared the plan and directed the work, employing 22,000 soldiers and 8,000 workmen, Hardouin-Mansart designed the enormous aqueduct over the valley of Maintenon, almost five kilometres long and seventy high, but work was interrupted when war broke out again, and the troops had to return to the front; the arches of the first order, as impressive as Roman ruins, remained to dominate the countryside.

From 1682 the court of Louis XIV was installed in the great work-site of Versailles,

885, 886 *Two views of the entrance*

887 *The Galérie des Glaces at Versailles*

'among the white-washers';[75] it consisted of 100,000 persons. The combination of work and play, of magnificence and meanness, produced a disconcerting atmosphere, of which we have numerous contrasting descriptions:[76]

'The rigours of an etiquette of Spanish formality [a historian of our time has written] did not prevent serious overcrowding in which, from time to time, the royal family was all but submerged; access to the monarch was at the same time easy and very difficult; while after a few days corridors and galleries became so deep in refuse that king and court were compelled to go and seek a change of air at Marly or elsewhere. Bontemps, Louis's personal valet, never succeeded in ridding the château of rogues and loose women. The flower of the nobility was lodged in conditions of squalor under the roof. The time was spent alternatively in gaming, entertainments and in prayer. . . . All Europe knew that this artificial capital was the scene of all major decisions and already dreamed of imitating it.'

The architecture of Hardouin-Mansart was the calculated, severe, slightly detached backdrop for this tumultuous show; the disorder of the functions was concealed by the uniform covering of the façades, small everyday incidents were lost in the succession of galleries or the boundless spaces of the park. The actual architecture safeguarded the

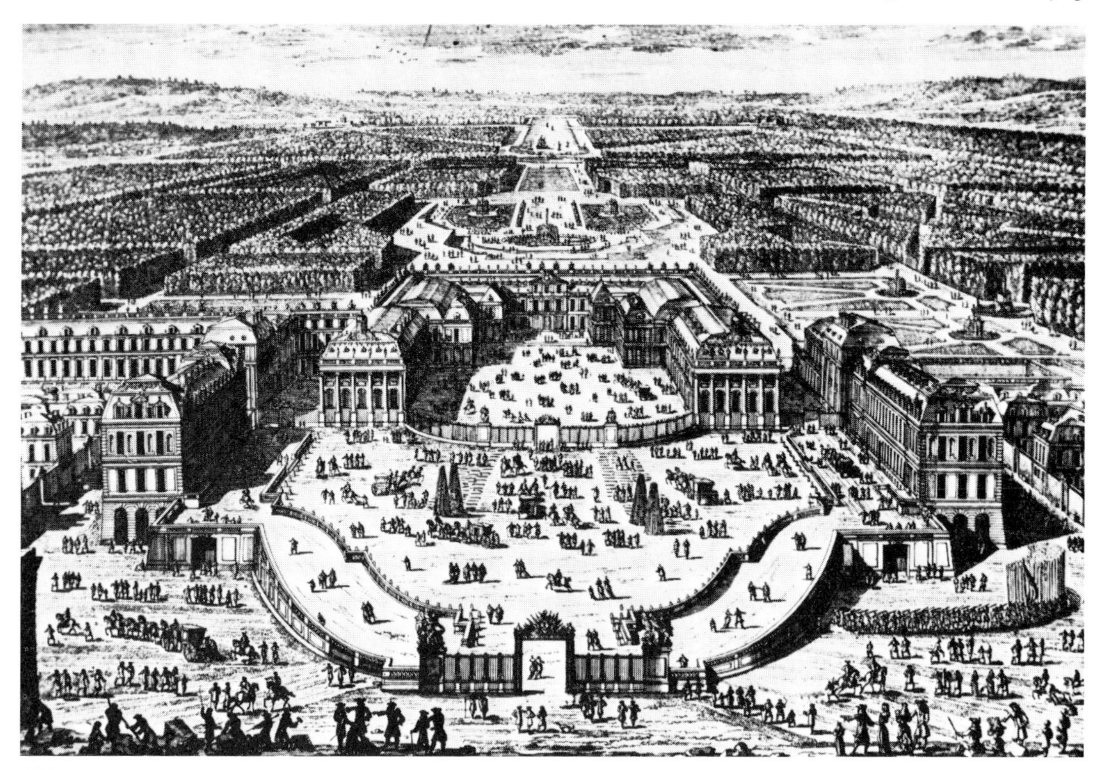

888 *(left) The Salon de la Guerre*
889 *View of Versailles in 1688 (Langlois)*

conventional idea of regality and prestige, and could now be separated from present circumstances and transmitted to future ages.

While working on Versailles, Hardouin-Mansart carried out a series of activities in Paris and other French cities, which would be covered by the modern term 'town design'; these were architectural schemes which did not go beyond the conventional building scale and did not transform the organism of the city, but were fitted in as independent episodes; while in Versailles he adhered to the landscape scale already defined by Le Nôtre, in Paris and the other centres he adapted himself to the building scale fixed in the course of previous transformations, from Henri IV to Colbert.

The two royal squares of Paris – place des Victoires and place Vendôme – were born of a combination of speculative and commemorative motives. The first was embarked upon by the Maréchal de France La Feuillade, who acquired a number of sites in the district near the Palais Royal and set out to build a square, with an equestrian statue of Louis XIV, redividing up the plots and selling adjacent sites; in 1685 the municipality contributed to this enterprise by commissioning Hardouin-Mansart to design the plan; in 1686 Hardouin-Mansart began work on what was felt to be the most important part of the complex, i.e. the statue, but the houses were merely marked out, and were completed slowly during the following decades. Possibly at the suggestion of the academy Hardouin-Mansart chose a round perimeter, regularizing the

890 *The portico of the Grand Trianon*
891 *The Grand Trianon (engraving by Perelle)*
892 *The pavillon du roi at Marly (plan by F. Blondel)*

mouths of existing streets as much as possible, and established a uniform design for the façades of the houses (Fig. 896).

The second has a more complicated history: in 1685, after the death of Colbert, Hardouin-Mansart and Louvois persuaded the king himself to undertake the building of another square, and the architect drew the king's attention to a zone upstream from the Tuileries, where he had acquired some sites in 1682. Hardouin-Mansart designed a rectangular square, open on one side towards rue St-Honoré. The work was allotted in 1686 to Marcel Gabriel, a relative of the architect, but was broken off almost immediately because of the resumption of war; in 1698, after the peace of Ryswick, Hardouin-Mansart worked on a new form of square, rectangular with bevelled corners, to increase the extension of the edge area to be built along; the king built the façades at his own expense, and in 1699 – in the middle of this architectural shell behind which there was no building – the statue of the king was begun. The sites were acquired by a group of financiers, among whom Hardouin-Mansart figures once again, alongside two of his relatives; a famous epigram observes that the statue of Louis XIII is found amidst persons of quality, that of Henri IV near the houses of the people, and that of Louis XIV in the midst of financiers (Figs 897–9).[77]

The third important work by Hardouin-Mansart in Paris, eminently a 'prestige' work, was the domed building joined to the hospital of the Invalides (1680–1706). The church

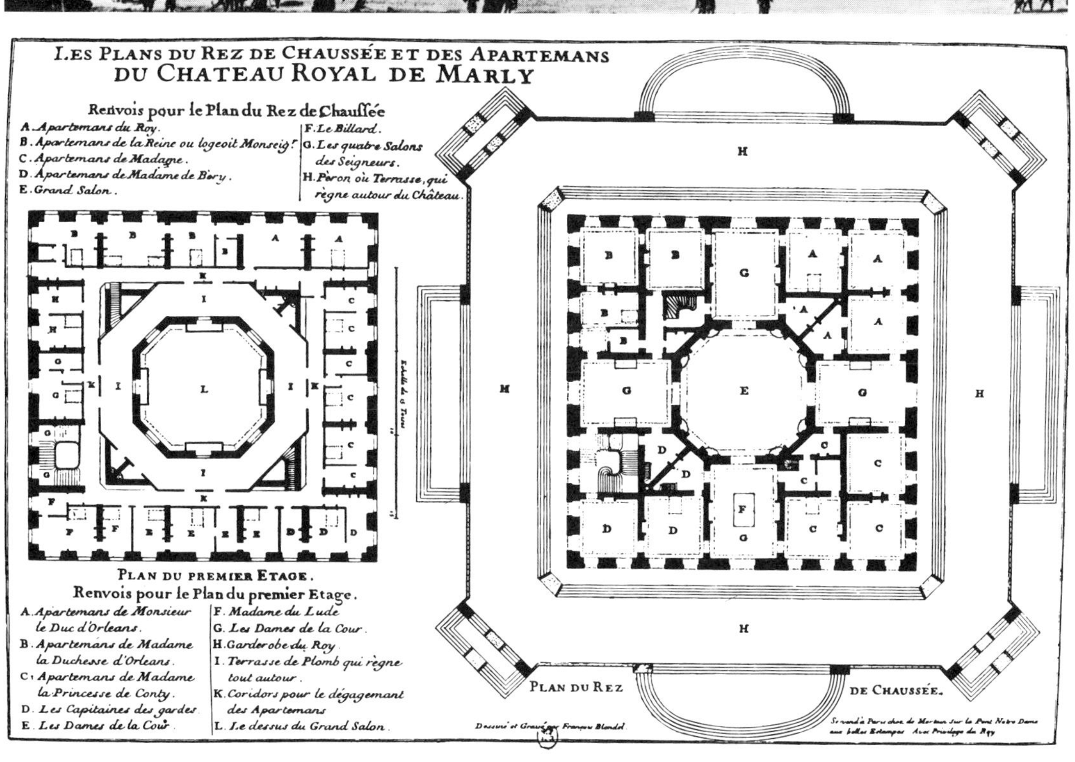
LES PLANS DU REZ DE CHAUSSÉE ET DES APARTEMANS
DU CHATEAU ROYAL DE MARLY
Renvois pour le Plan du Rez de Chaussée
A. Apartemans du Roy.
B. Apartemans de la Reine ou logeoit Monseig.r
C. Apartemans de Madagne.
D. Apartemans de Madame de Bery.
E. Grand Salon.
F. Le Billard.
G. Les quatre Salons des Seigneurs.
H. Péron ou Terrasse, qui règne autour du Château.
PLAN DU PREMIER ETAGE.
Renvois pour le Plan du premier Etage.
A. Apartemans de Monsieur le Duc d'Orleans.
B. Apartemans de Madame la Duchesse d'Orleans.
C. Apartemans de Madame la Princesse de Conty.
D. Les Capitaines des gardes.
E. Les Dames de la Cour.
F. Madame du Lude.
G. Les Dames de la Cour.
H. Garderobe du Roy.
I. Terrasse de Plomb qui règne tout autour.
K. Coridors pour le dégagemant des Apartemans.
L. Le dessus du Grand Salon.
PLAN DU REZ
DE CHAUSSÉE.

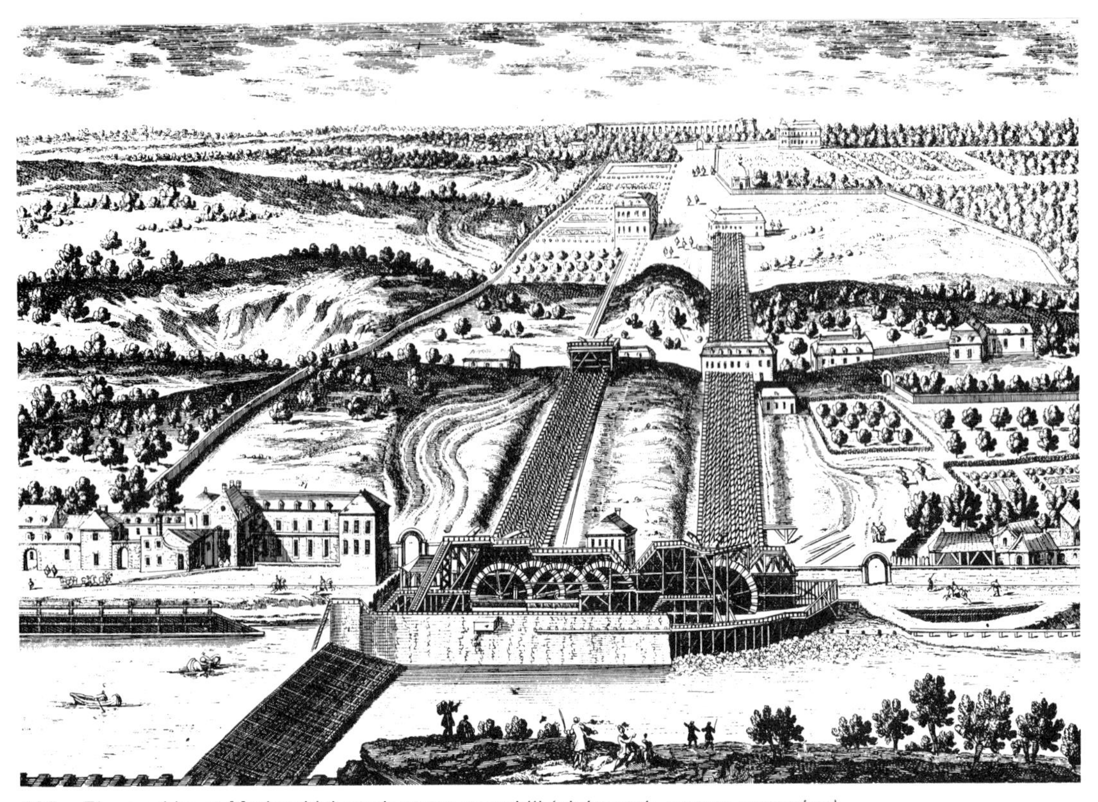

893 *The machine at Marly which made water go uphill (eighteenth-century engraving)*

already built by Bruand was a structure with a nave and two aisles, reserved for soldiers; the new church added by Hardouin-Mansart was a grandiose organism on a central plan, which acted as a parish church for the neighbourhood (a single altar, visible from both sides, served both parts as in traditional convents) and which with its extremely high dome dominated both the horizontal block of the building and the expanse of open space from the south.

The dome is an ingenious double structure, calculated in terms of a double effect, internal and external: the first drum, whose buttresses are decorated with double columns as at St Peter's, lights the inner space with its windows and supports a first stone ceiling; the second drum, supported by upturned corbels, has another order of windows, and gives light to the space between the first and a second masonry dome, which acts as a background to the previous one; a third dome in wood covered with lead covers the whole complex, and heightens the external profile further.

Outside, the well-known problem of linking dome and façade arises, as in Michelangelo's and Maderno's St Peter's. Hardouin-Mansart resolves it by minimizing the three-dimensional detachment between the two structures; the dome rises immediately behind the elaborate frontal composition of the façade, and is linked to it by subtle graphic parallels: its total width corresponds to that of the projection with the columns; the axial buttress is done away with and the drum has a double spacing, which has the same width as the central motif of the façade, crowned

894, 895 *The cypher branded on the furniture at Versailles and the back of a piece of furniture with its inventory number*

by the tympanum. It is obvious that this composition loses its balance if seen from three-quarters on (Figs 903–4); in fact the architect calculated it as backdrop to an indefinite axial approach, i.e. to a country avenue, not to a square in the midst of the fabric of a city. He also planned to frame the church between two quarter-circle porticoed wings, accentuating the similarity with Bernini's scheme in St Peter's square. But the very substitution of the quarter-circles for the semi-circles shows that the spatial character is completely different: the ensemble organized by Hardouin-Mansart was a backdrop to be seen, not a space to be entered, and the range of effects that concerned the architect was the one that would be obtained by moving along the axis, not along the arc of the square (Fig. 905).

The church of the Invalides was built slowly, with innumerable difficulties, and completed only after a period of thirty years. Most work in the provinces had the same fate and only the town hall in Arles, designed in 1675, was completed in 1684; the royal square in Dijon, designed in 1686, the triumphal arch in Tours (1687) and the Lyon town hall (1700) met with many difficulties and were built later.

Hardouin-Mansart had a group of first-class collaborators: his cousin Jacques IV Gabriel (1667–1742), C. A. D'Aviler (1653–1700), Robert de Cotte (1656–1735), Pierre Le Pautre (1600–1744), the young G. G. Boffrand (1667–1754), and he was able to maintain a constantly high artistic and technical standard despite the great number of his commissions; in many cases, indeed, technical precision seems to have been the main quality on which he concentrated for the characterization of his organisms; for example in the Orangerie at Versailles and in the famous vaulted hall in the town hall in Arles, a masterpiece of seventeenth-century stereotomy (Figs 908–9). He also supplied the designs for certain technical works: the already mentioned aqueduct at Maintenon (1684; Fig. 907), the Pont Royal in Paris (1685), the canal between the Seine and Marne (1690), the bridge at Moulins (1704). In these cases he prepared general plans in accordance with the advice of specialists (the

896 *Place des Victoires, Paris*
Opposite
897–899 *Place Vendôme, Paris: present plan (from Auzelle) and comparison of two plans of Hardouin-Mansart of 1685 and 1698 (from Lavedan)*

versatile Vauban for Maintenon; the Belgian engineer François Romain (1648–1735), for the Pont Royal – he did the foundations with the new caisson technique and later became the first director of the Corps des Ponts et Chaussées); then he handed over the elaboration of the executive plans to contractors (for the Pont Royal his cousin Jacques Gabriel). Adapting himself to this routine, Hardouin-Mansart had the intelligence to reduce stylistic extras to a minimum, so as to be able to introduce the inevitable variations in measurements without difficulty at the executive stage.

In the last years of the reign of Louis XIV building activity was reduced because of the almost continuous wars and because of the austerity introduced at court by Mme de Maintenon, who was already criticizing the monumentality and regularity of royal residences in a bourgeois spirit, and who complained that she would have to 'die in symmetry'.[78]

While the 'difficulties of execution' considered by Colbert were growing to such an extent as to compromise the execution of programmes, the cultural approach to the problems of architecture was also changing. Over the period 1690–1715 most of the protagonists of the *grand siècle* had died: Lebrun in 1690, Puget in 1694, La Fontaine in 1695, Racine in 1699, Le Nôtre in 1700, Charles Perrault in 1703, Bossuet in 1704, Vauban in 1707, Hardouin-Mansart in 1708, Boileau in 1711; and meanwhile, before the end of the reign of Louis XIV, another series

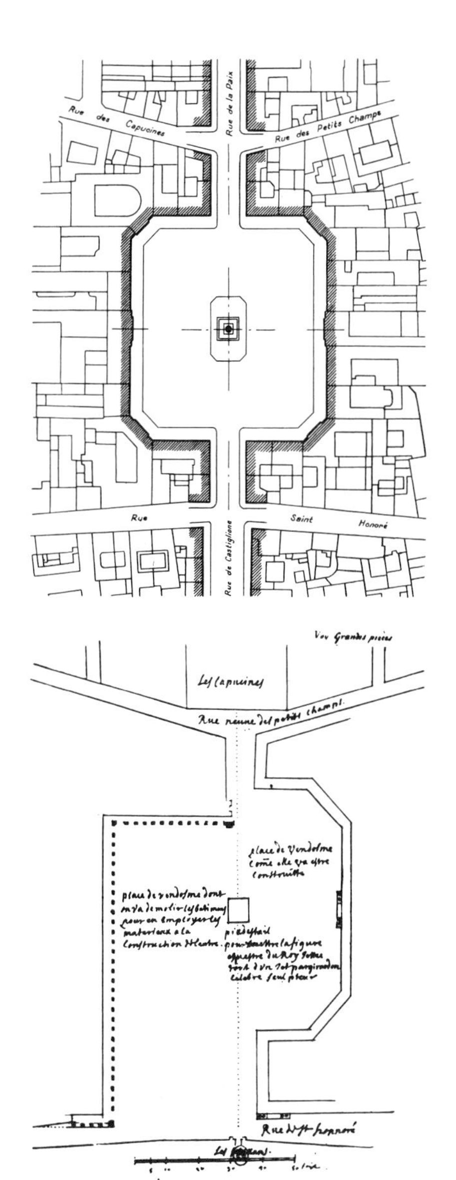

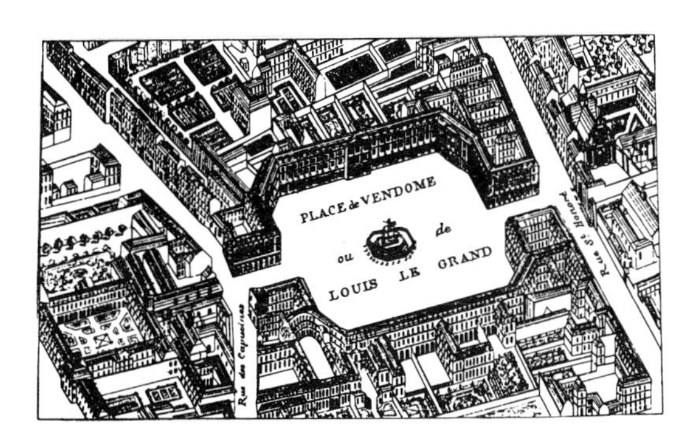

of completely new experiments was beginning: in 1702 Watteau arrived in Paris, and won the *prix de Rome*; from 1708 to 1713 Montesquieu was frequenting the Sorbonne; from 1702 onwards Saint-Simon returned to Versailles and turned his implacable intelligence to observing the society of the Sun King, which he was to describe in his *Mémoires*. 'Modern' classicism, which had been the ideal aim of the past generation, now appeared as a *fait accompli*, both in letters and in the arts, and La Bruyère was concerned to point out the parallelism of the two results:[79]

'We have had to do to style what we have done to architecture. We have entirely abandoned the Gothic manner; we brought back the Doric, Ionic and Corinthian orders, that which had been seen only in the ruins of ancient Greek and Roman became modern, and is now displayed in our porticoes and peristyles. In the same way, in our writings we can only reach perfection and, if possible, surpass the ancients, by imitating them.

How many centuries elapsed before men, in the arts and sciences, were able to return to the taste of antiquity and, at long last, became simple and natural once more.

A man has been nurtured on the ancients and the ablest modern writers, he has squeezed them to extract all he can from them to fill out his own works, and when at last he becomes an author and thinks he can stand on his own feet, he turns against them and abuses them, like those children who, having grown robust and strong by sucking good milk, beat their nurses.'

In 1688, when La Bruyère's work came out, the topic of the day was precisely the *querelle* between ancients and moderns, alluded to in the passage quoted. All the intellectuals of the time took up positions in this debate, where Boileau remained alone obstinately to defend the primacy of the ancients: in 1687 Charles Perrault, one of the defenders of the moderns, read to the

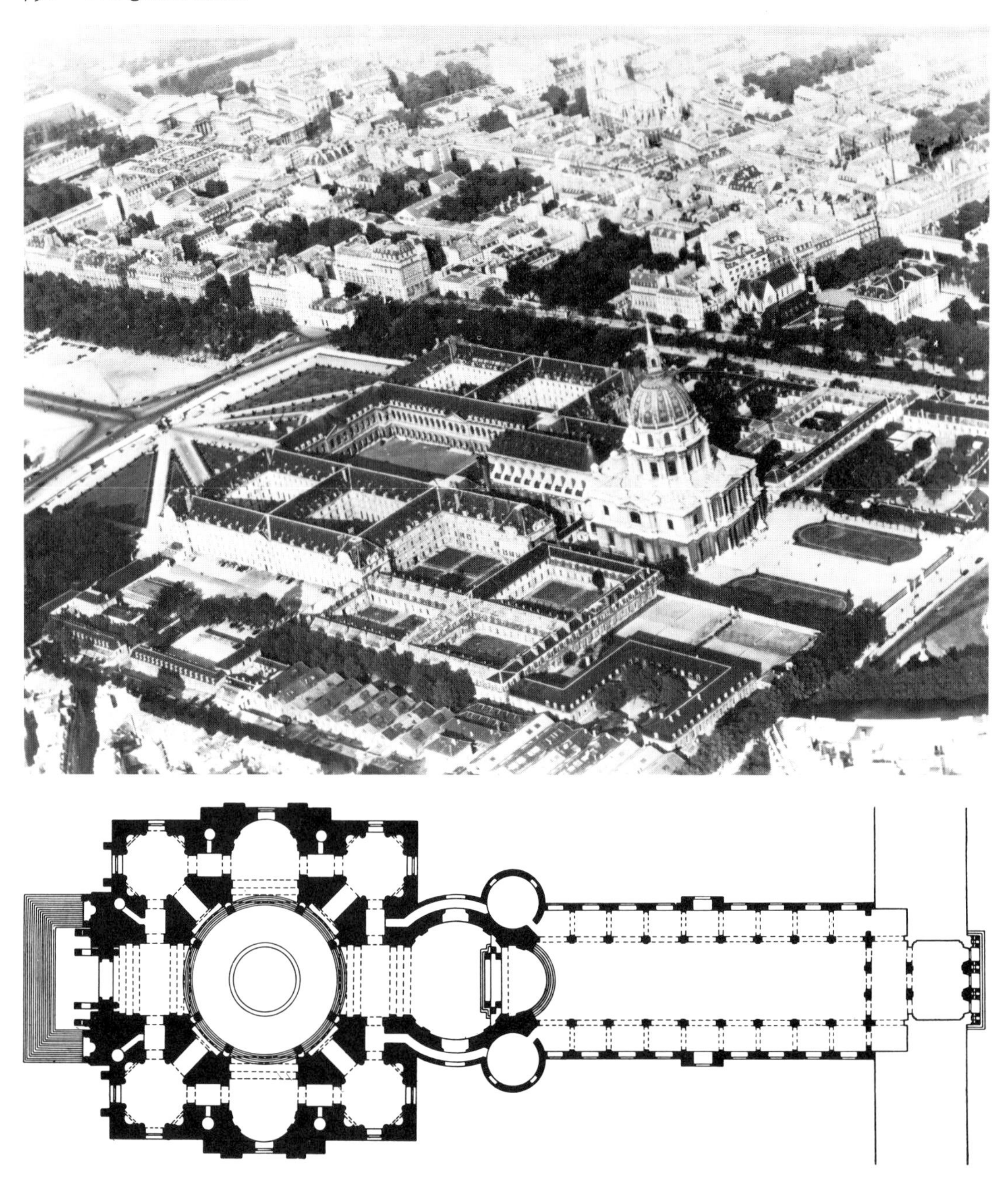

900, 901 *Hardouin-Mansart's church at the Hôtel des Invalides: aerial view and plan*
902 *The space between the two domes of the Invalides*

903 *Frontal view of the Invalides*

904 *Three-quarter view of the Invalides*

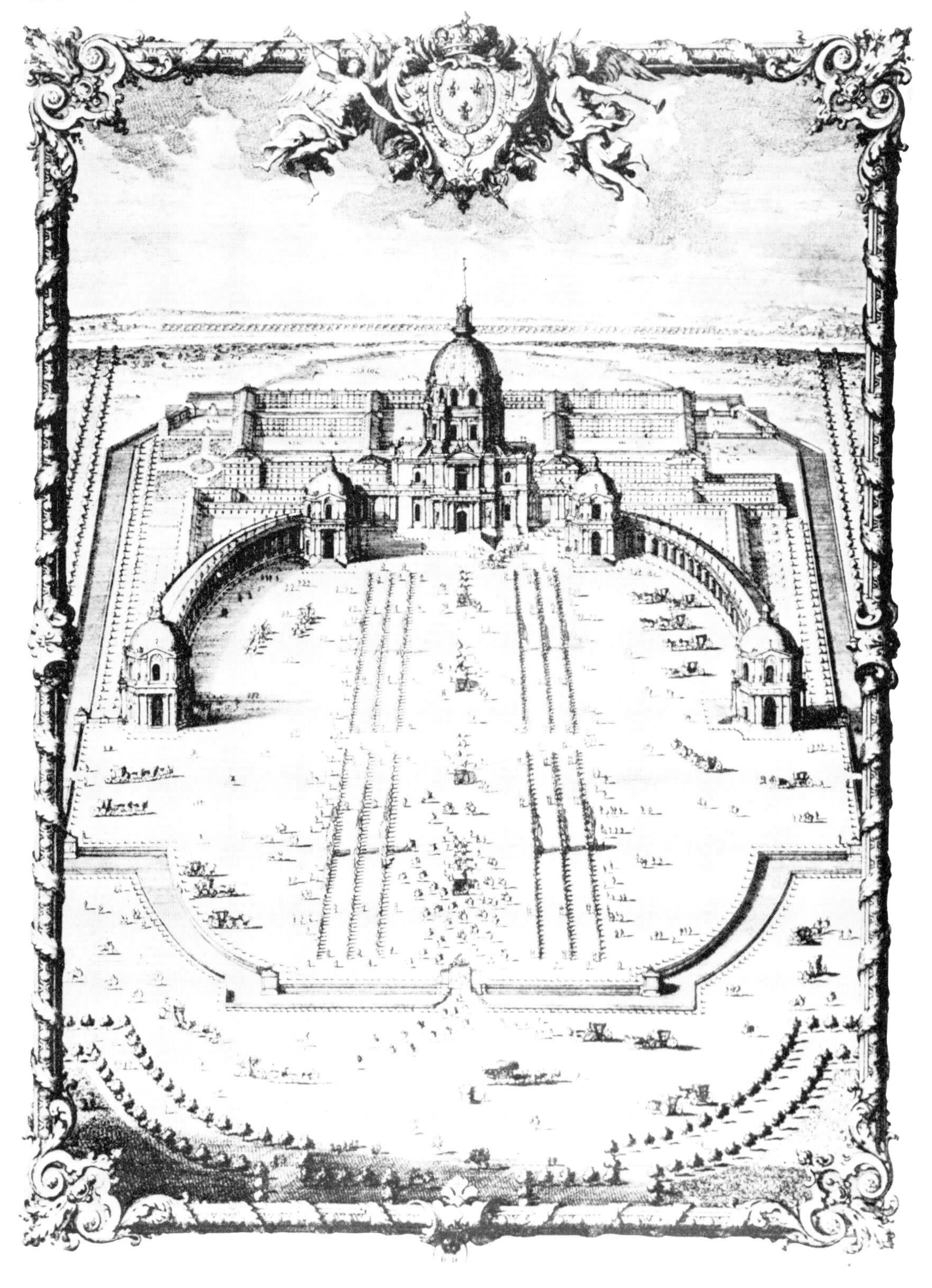

905 *(left) Hardouin-Mansart's plan for the place des Invalides*
906 *A road running into place Royale, Dijon*

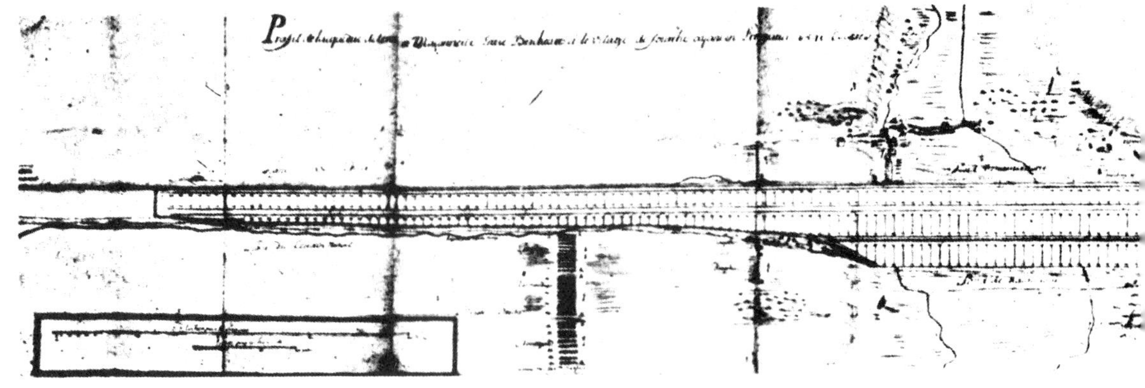

907 *Hardouin-Mansart's design for an aqueduct at Maintenon*

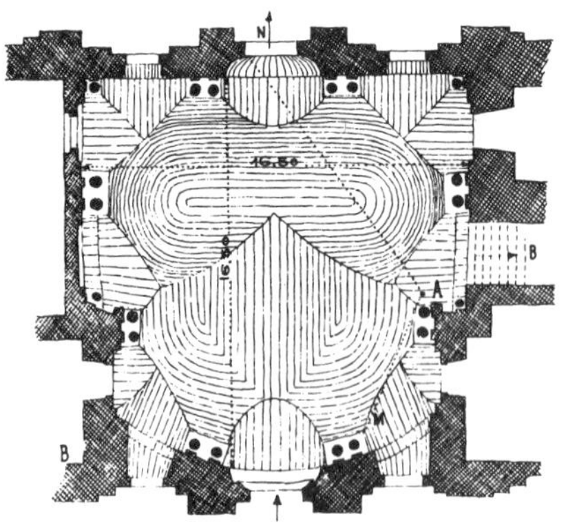

908, 909 *The vestibule of the town hall at Arles: interior view and plan*

academy his poem *Le Siècle de Louis le Grand*, where exaltation of the present is put at the service of political loyalism. A similar debate took place in the academy of painting between *poussinistes* and *rubénistes*, at the academy of architecture between Blondel – who defended the universal value of aesthetic rules – and Claude Perrault, who considered that beauty was founded on habit.[80]

In architecture the conflict was blunted from the start by the fact that there was no plausible alternative to the classical repertoire, and discussion was always over some specific element (coupled columns, the giant order, the *ordre français* proposed by Lebrun and applied in the Galérie des Glaces, decorative decisions), to be considered within or without this repertoire. But some general characters of the *querelle*, and some aggressive theses of the 'moderns', left a lasting mark in our field too.

Among the first was certainly the retrospective spirit, the habit of weighing up the present to compare it with the past and of standing aside from one's own time in order to judge it coolly. Literary culture, precisely while claiming primacy over artistic culture,[81] invaded the domain of the arts and affected the range of production and of the use of artistic products with its judgments. Litera-

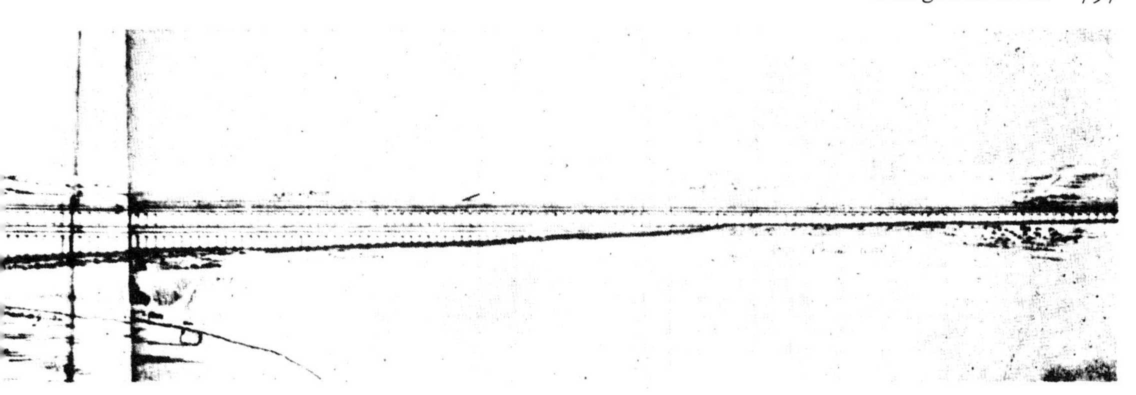

ture, too, like the arts, was broadly involved in the operation of political centralization carried out during the reign of Louis XIV, and helped to exalt the new prestige of the monarchy, but adherence to this programme was continually balanced by a lucid moralism; a writer like La Bruyère, who sincerely admired the great king, ended his extremely perceptive description of the splendours of the court with this reflection:[82]

'A healthy spirit draws from court life a taste for solitude and retreat.'

Literature kept a radical critical discourse alive, something that was still lacking in the field of art, and ultimately influenced artistic experience, destroying the certainty of the rhetorical process; the logic of propriety, etiquette, didactic hedonism and hedonistic didacticism was ultimately judged by the logic of reason and human dignity.

Among the theses of the 'moderns' that should be noted was the extension of the scientific spirit into fields traditionally reserved for the humanistic spirit, and also the idea of progress.

The older men like Boileau and Huet took the part of poetry, and lamented its passing.[83] Of the exponents of the new generation, Fontenelle wrote:[84]

'The geometrical spirit is not so attached to geometry as not to be able to be detached from it, and applied to other sciences. A work of politics, of ethics, of criticism and possibly even of eloquence, if compiled by the hand of a geometrician, will gain in beauty, because in any case all the sciences are the same. The order, clarity, precision and exactitude which have been prevailing in good texts for some time could well have their ultimate origin in this geometrical spirit which is spreading ever further.'

In Furetière's *Dictionnaire*, under *lettres*, we read this definition: 'The real belles-lettres are physics, geometry and the exact sciences.'[85]

Interchange of terminology between the various fields is frequent; in Fontenelle's *Entretiens sur la pluralité des mondes* (1686), a scientist explains modern astronomy to a lady as they walk in a park, and asks for her attention to 'follow the plot of the system and appreciate its beauty'.[86]

Some decades later Houdar de la Motte compared prose with poetry, turned a scene from Racine's *Mithridate* into prose to prove the point, and translated Homer eliminating the parts regarded as defective;

910 Harlequin and Columbine *by Watteau. Wallace Collection, London*

the new aesthetic ideal was not the 'impetuous style' of Pindar still defended by Boileau,[87] but an 'even and sustained harmony'[88] (the same formula with which one could characterize the work of Hardouin-Mansart and his pupils, *vis-à-vis* the previous tradition).

La Bruyère, who was only a reflective witness to this debate, certainly expressed a common conviction when he wrote:[89]

'There is in art a point of perfection, just as there is in nature a point of excellence or of ripeness. The man who feels it and loves it has perfect taste; the man who does not feel it, and who loves what falls short of it or is in excess of it, has defective taste. So there is good taste and bad taste, and we are justified in arguing about our tastes.'

This attitude justifies the thesis of progress, not only for the sciences but also for the arts. Perrault[90] observed that 'the general order of nature' is always the same, and human capacities do not change during the course of history; but what does change is the legacy of knowledge, and if the arts must appeal to the heart, the heart, too, is increasingly well understood. Therefore the moderns do not possess a greater genius, but greater abundance of precepts, and are in a position to achieve better results.

Perrault – who as Colbert's secretary had first-hand experience of the formation of the new cultural synthesis, being at the motive centre of the political and administrative action – wanted to contrast the past with the present, not the uncertain future:[91]

'I own that I consider myself fortunate to know the happiness we enjoy; it is a great pleasure to survey all the past ages in which I see the birth and progress of all things, but nothing which has not received a new increase and lustre in our own times. Our age has, in some sort, arrived at the summit of perfection. And since for some years the rate of progress is much slower and appears almost insensible – as the days seem to cease to lengthen when the solstice is near – it is pleasant to think that there are not many things for which we need envy future generations.'

Fontenelle – who was thirty years younger, and who considered the new already established classicism from the outside – looked instead to the future, where he expected to find a rapid and continual progress of all the sciences. The modern idea of progress was thus formulated; it is true that this analysis was not yet applied to social and political mechanisms, but 'every science develops after other preliminary sciences and not before'[92] and 'strongly established things cannot be attacked except by degrees'.[93]

The terms of the figurative tradition, as we have observed many times, prevented these discussions from being extended to our field as they should have been; all in all, the visual arts, and architecture in particular, formed a less exposed island, where the '*crise de la conscience européenne*' of which Hazard[94] spoke revealed itself only partially, and where evasion and rhetorical persuasion were still possible.

But there was another path still open for the dismantling of the traditional synthesis: the exploration of the contrast between the rationality of methods – technique, formal rules – and the irrationality of the economic and administrative processes, on which the work of the engineers and architects was based.

The specialist in a position to see this relationship clearly was Vauban. He extended his interests beyond the scope of technical matters, and realized that the responsibility of technical work could not be divided up according to the fields of a traditional classification of human interests, but would have to embrace all the processes which contributed to the actual operation sector by sector; for this reason he analysed the structural condition of his work with equal professional commitment and rigour of method, brought to light the economic, social and political obstacles that lay behind it and managed to lift the 'veil of government' as Cardinal de Retz wrote.[95] In 1686 he prepared a report for the sovereign on the revocation of the edict of Nantes, and dared to write to the Sun King, before Fénelon, that 'kings are indeed masters of their subjects' lives and goods, but never of their opinions, because men's inmost feelings are beyond their power';[96] in 1698 he prepared the *Projet d'une dixième royale*, an objective and technically precise examination of the economic conditions of the kingdom (the intendents' investigations lasted from 1697 to 1700 and allowed Vauban himself to lay the basis for the first exact census of the French population), but also an eloquent summary of his personal experience:[97]

'The wandering life I have led for above forty years has given me opportunities of seeing and observing, often and in different manners, the most part of the provinces of this Kingdom; and . . . the poverty of the people having often moved my compassion, has put me upon an Enquiry into the causes of it. . . . It is evident that that Evil is carried to so great a height, that if it is not speedily remedied, the poorest sort of people will be plunged into such extreme misery, that it will be impossible for them ever to recover; the high roads in the country and the streets of our cities and towns being already crowded with beggars, whom mere hunger and cold have drove from their houses . . . in these late times, near a tenth part of the people are actually reduced to beggary; of the other nine parts, not five of them are in a position to give alms to that tenth, by reason of the miserable condition they are reduced to, and the small pittance that is left them. Of the four other parts of the people, three are in hard circumstances, by reason of their great debts; and I should not be much out of the way if I averred that, great and small together, there are not ten thousand of them whose circumstances are easy.'

This description, and Perrault's poem on the century of Louis le Grand – written at ten years' distance one from the other by two persons both involved in the history of architecture, though at the two extremes of the range of skills utilized by the ruling class – showed the two faces of the same reality. Perrault represented the rule, Vauban the exception; all the same it is interesting to note that a radical critique of the division of responsibility established three centuries earlier in Italian humanistic circles should first have come precisely from those with technical experience.

Vauban, like the fine planner he was, described the state of affairs in order to present an alternative programme: a new system of uniform taxes for all classes which anticipated the arguments discussed at the Estates General of 1789 with singular precision. His book was published in 1708, and prohibited by order of the king; soon afterwards Vauban died, it was said, of disappointment at this conflict.

The various discussions we have mentioned still did not touch the core of architectural classicism – i.e. the permanent validity of a language derived from ancient models – but they did considerably modify its position in society. Just while the ruling class was making a grandiose effort to put classicism at the service of absolutism, i.e. to utilize the unconditional value of its rules to reinforce the unquestionable authority of the new political leadership, the old social basis of classicism was being destroyed, which was a hierarchy of a traditional type, strengthened by time and history. Just as the old pyramid of rights and duties was weakened by the growth of the new power of the state, so the old use of classicism as a sign of recognized authority was replaced by its new use, as an instrument of technical rationalization and

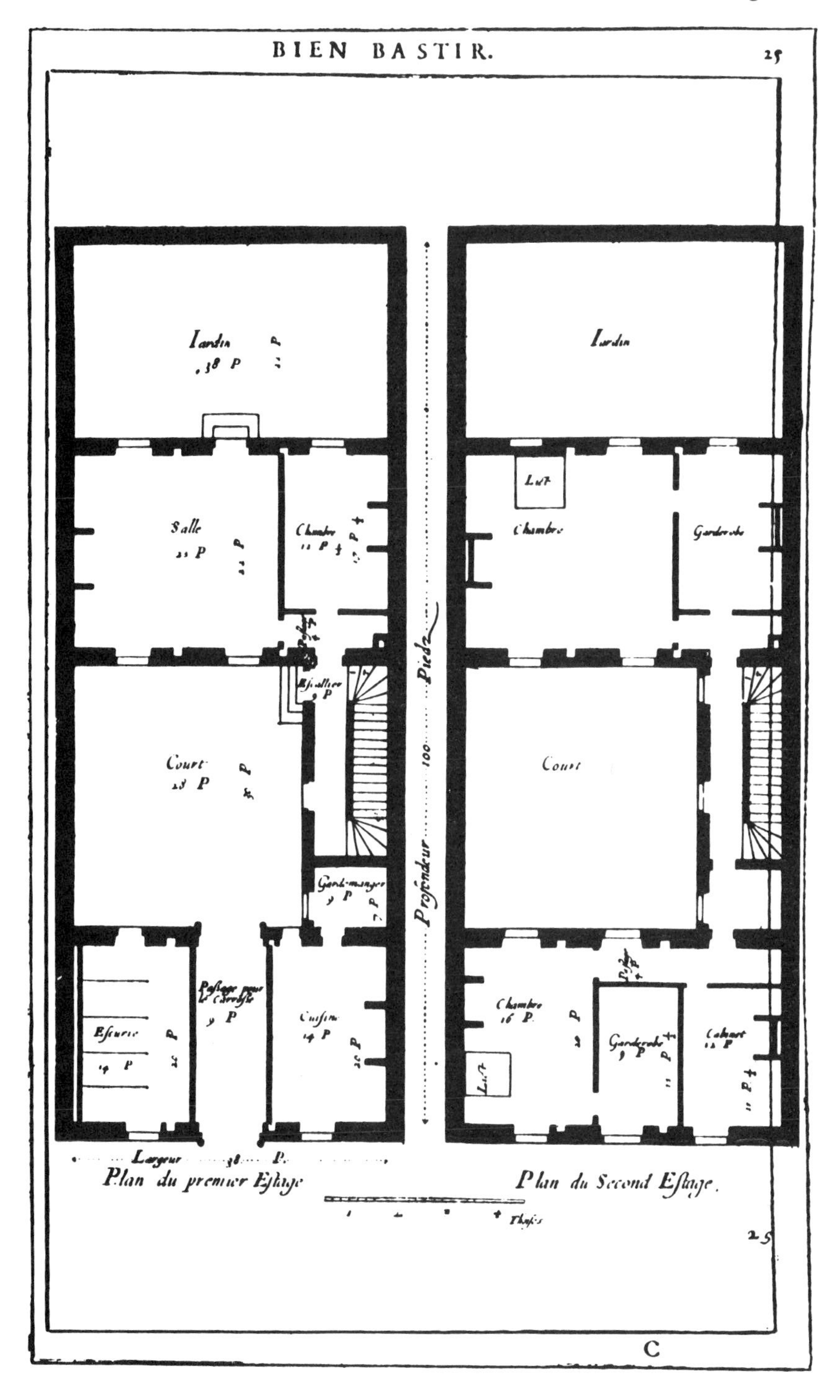

911 *A bourgeois town house, from P. Le Muet,* Manière de bien bastir pour toutes sortes de personnes *(1623), 1663 edition*

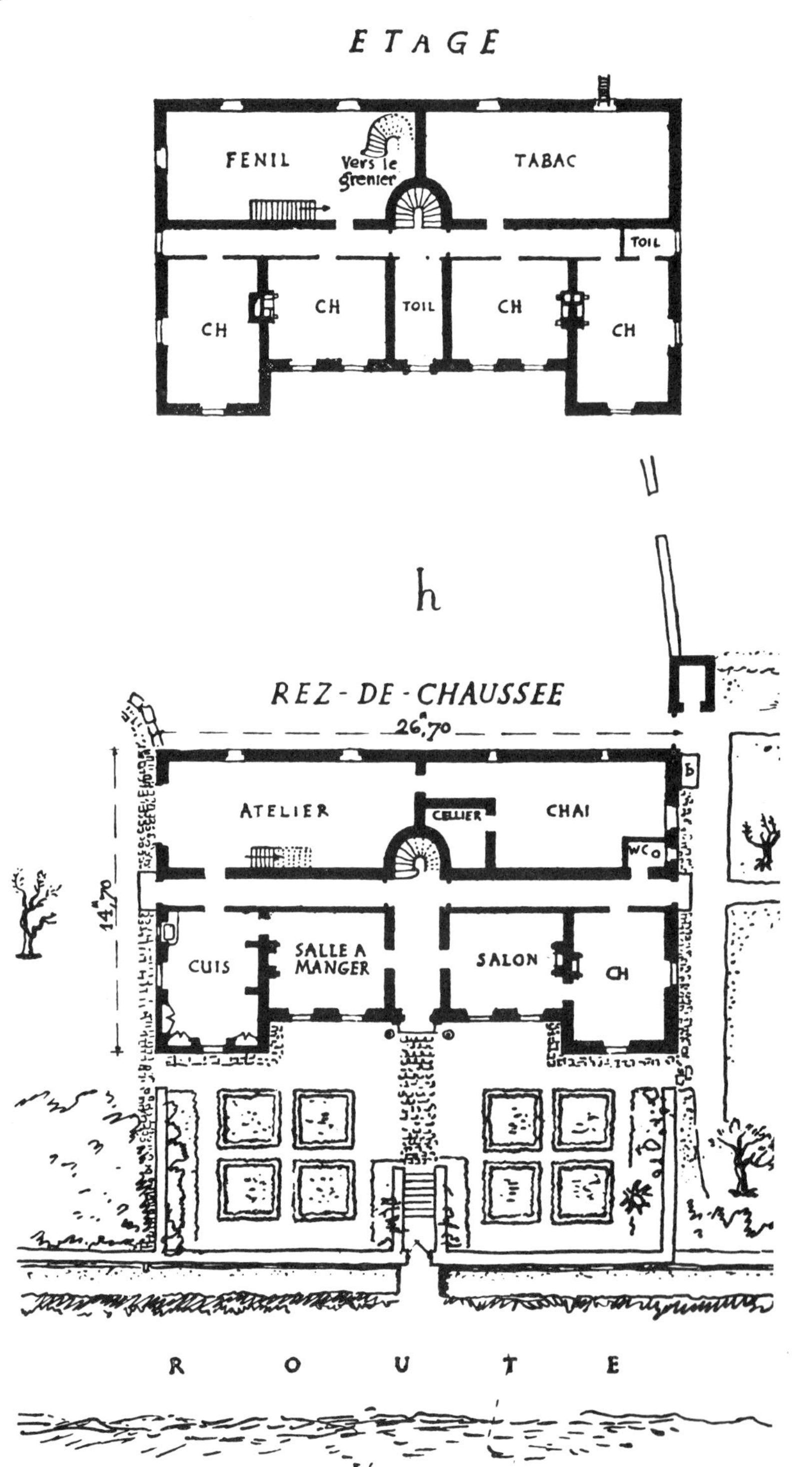

912 *An eighteenth-century French country building (Jouy-le-Comte, Seine-et-Oise)*

conventional subordination.

The ultimate result of this transformation was therefore the detachment of classicism from constituted authority: the repertoire of French classicism, elaborated during the *grand siècle*, became the recognized model for all the absolutist governments of Europe, but was also available to the bourgeoisie either as a symbol of social promotion, or as an expression of the new rigorous rationalism and as the particular philosophy of the Third Estate in the ascendant.

Until the last third of the seventeenth century the elaboration of the new classicism was largely restricted to court building and increased the gap between this and popular building; in the last third, and especially after the experience of Hardouin-Mansart, court classicism became so simplified as to influence ordinary production once again; thus the detachment between monuments and ordinary buildings began to diminish, and the simple models of rationalized classicism – the square, the circle, solid volumes, the uniform and infinite rhythmic divisions – spread throughout all town and country production, except for the most humble, which escaped the control of the cultured classes and continued to reproduce medieval models.

In the next chapter we shall try to give an overall account of European classicism, from the seventeenth century to the first half of the eighteenth, and the general picture will emerge from the superimposition of two outlines: that of court culture and that of bourgeois culture, in many cases closely linked and largely coinciding in formal results, but distinct and sometimes conflicting in inspiration and aims.

In Europe, from about 1650, the forms elaborated in France in the *grand siècle* were the inevitable models for the arts, literature and manners in both court and bourgeois culture. Even the older models, classical and Italian, were to be received from now on through the filter of the French. The very possibility of applying them in political and social circumstances different from the ones in which they were first conceived, made it possible to estimate their resolutive value. The praise of the fruits of absolutism was therefore fully justified, as it was written in the eighteenth century by the theorist of the new tolerant and bourgeois society:[98]

'One can say with certainty that, from the last years of cardinal Richelieu to those following the death of Louis XIV, a general revolution took place in our arts, in our spirit, in our manners and in our government, which shall be an eternal mark of glory for our country. Furthermore this happy influx has not been limited to France, but has extended to England, arousing the sense of emulation which that lively and daring nation needed, it has transplanted good taste to Germany, the sciences to Russia and has even re-animated the languishing Italy, so that all Europe owes a debt to the court of Louis XIV for its urbane manners and sociable spirit.'

913 *A supper at the Hofburg, Vienna, at the time of Joseph I*

seven

Court classicism and bourgeois classicism in the growth of the modern city

Even a summary account of the urban changes in Europe and the European colonies, from about 1600 to 1750, forces one to consider once again the problem of the relationship between architecture and power.

In the sixteenth century, when classicism was still an *avant-garde* cultural hypothesis, we distinguished between experiments promoted by political power and by economic power, i.e. the two very restricted classes which dominated Renaissance society.

In the seventeenth century things changed. We have considered the exemplary case of France, where the links of classicism with political absolutism and economic mercantilism were particularly clear; but the structures of political power and economic power no longer coincided with the predominance of a restricted and relatively homogeneous group: they depended on an organizational combination, in which various social classes took part: the court, the nobility, the clergy and the financiers, but also the new bureaucratic apparatus, the new guilds, the artists, the scholars in their academies, and so on. The ruling classes were still a privileged minority, and the lower classes still a minority excluded from these discussions on culture and power; none the less no class on its own was in a position to manage the resources of the new productive cycle, and to present itself as the bearer of an exclusive technical or aesthetic hypothesis. The theses of Renaissance scientific and artistic culture were in fact an essential part of the organizational struggle on which modern states were based, and though they were used as an instrument of power they gradually lost the distinctive marks of classicism, and acquired a generic, neutral character, which made them utilizable by the new classes in the ascendant.

All this favoured a progressive detachment of cultural problems from social and political ones and this was registered, in an inverse sense, by investigation into social history:[1]

'While a new, cosmopolitan culture was beginning to polish manners and the arts and literature to an even surface, at the economic and social level, and in the organization of wealth and force differences grew greater than ever before.'

This is not the place to discuss the social, economic and political differences between states and classes, we need simply observe that these differences were clearly observable in the architecture of the beginning of the seventeenth century, while they emerged less easily and less clearly from the end of the seventeenth century onwards. This detach-

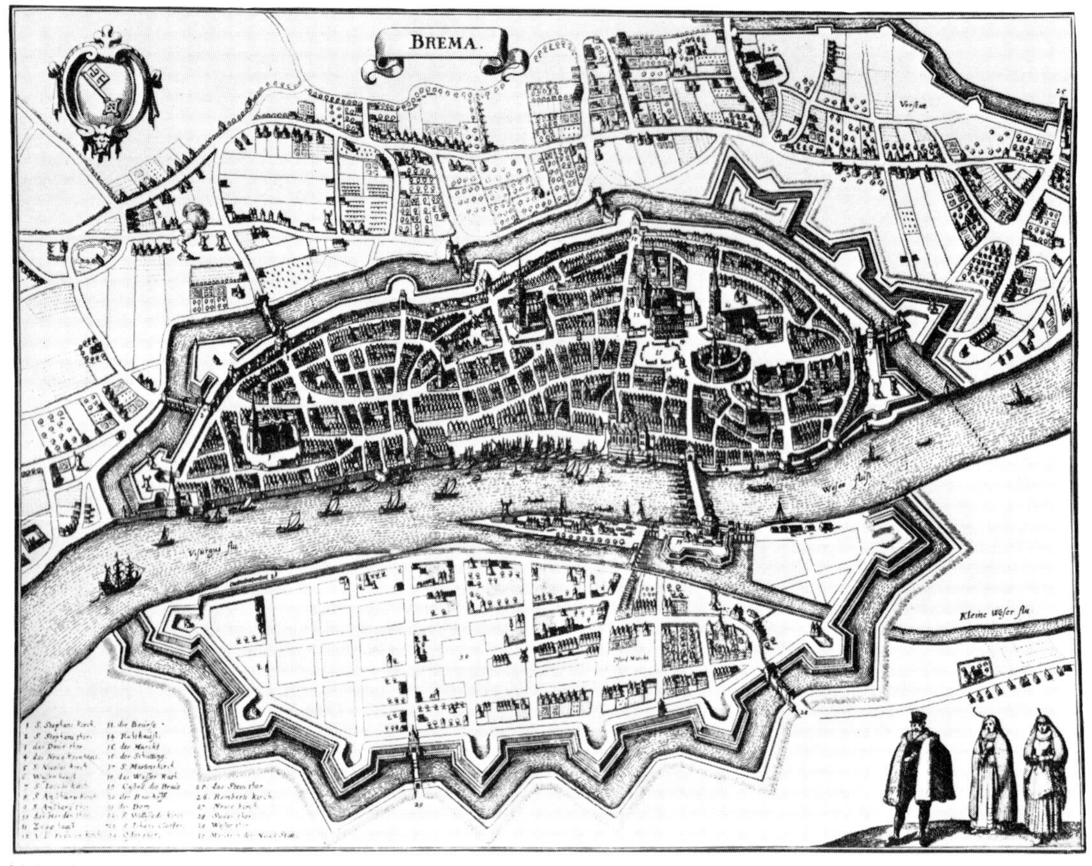

914 *Plan of Bremen in 1653 with the sixteenth-century addition (from Merian)*

ment of architecture from the vital interests of society finally caused the disintegration of the original cultural system from which it started, and announced the crisis of architectural classicism as early as the beginning of the eighteenth century, and in some cases even earlier.

What we need to do is to trace – beneath the continuity of concrete experiments – this point of rupture in cultural discussion, which puts an end to our historical account, even if classicism continued broadly to influence building and town-planning at least throughout the nineteenth century.

The absolutism of the early seventeenth century

The building and town-planning undertakings promoted by the European governments of the first half of the seventeenth century – if one excludes Italy and Holland – were very similar to those of Henri IV in France, which we discussed in chapter 6.

Town plans were based on sixteenth-century grid plan patterns and in some cases on the radiocentric one, but as a theoretical notion not realized in the execution; building activity started from elementary geometrical layouts – for instance piazzas from the square

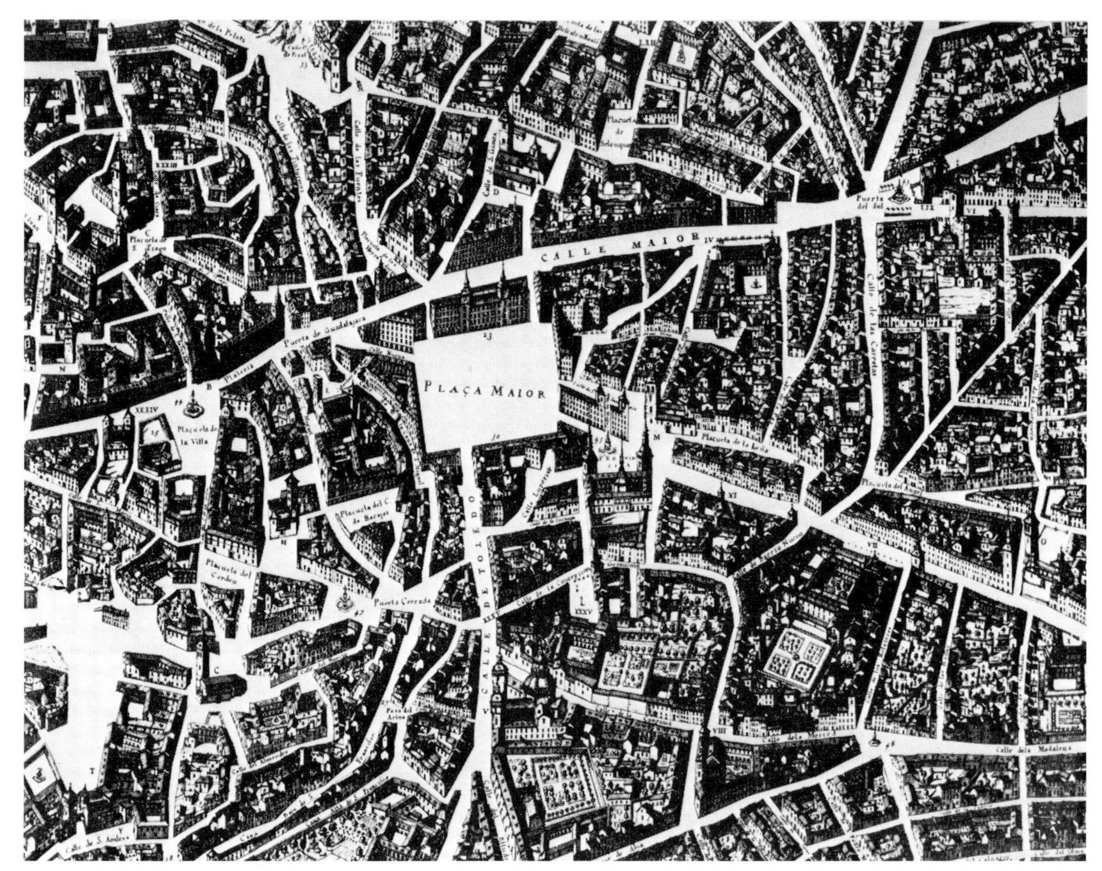

915 *The* plaza mayor *of Madrid in a plan of 1656*

or rectangle – and their architectural clothing was summary, conventional, i.e. it added a superficial stylistic patina to the blocks created by the operations of street layout and division into plots, without affecting the articulation of the volumes.

These undertakings, in fact, derived from dealings between clients and builders, on the basis of figurative models already acquired; architects did not intervene at this stage, but only later regarding decorative finish.

The royal squares of Henri IV (1604 and 1606) and the ducal square in Charleville (1610) were echoed by the *plaza mayor* in Madrid, laid out in 1617; here, too, the screen of building was unbroken, and the adjacent streets entered the square through the porticoes; the houses had uniform façades, very simple in design, a stone portico, a solid screen of three storeys in brick and a mansard roof, as in the French prototypes; the design was by Juan de Mora (1586–1646 or 1648) (Fig. 915).

In other Spanish cities – as in Toledo in 1605 – the *plaza mayor* was built or rebuilt in a regular shape; but the utilitarian American models rather than European court models tended to be used.

916 *Plan of the city of Madrid in 1683*

MATRITVM VRBS REGIA
CAMINO DE ALCALA
CALLE DE ALCALA
PRADO
GRANDE
CAMPO DE

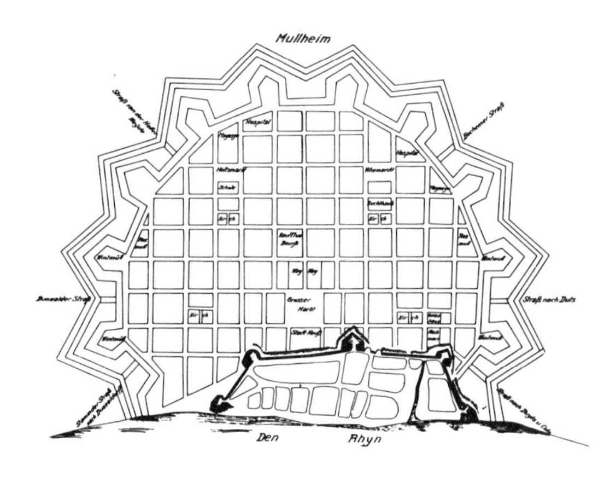

917 *Model of the fortified town of Charleroi in the seventeenth century. Hôtel des Invalides, Paris*
918 *Plan of the fortified town of Mulheim, founded in 1612 opposite Cologne*

The reconstruction of Lerma, begun in 1604 by the duke don Francisco, the all-powerful favourite of Philip III, was a special case; the architect Francisco de Mora (c. 1546–1610) introduced a series of monumental architectural episodes into the old organism – *plaza mayor*, ducal palace, religious houses – perfectly balanced among themselves, though out of proportion with the small provincial town.

The founding or planned extension of whole cities was an exceptional operation in Europe. We have considered the group of fortified towns built along both sides of the Franco-imperial frontier between the end of the sixteenth century and beginning of the seventeenth, and those realized by Vauban at the time of Louis XIV (to which should be added the important fortress of Charleroi, founded in 1666 on a radiocentric plan) (Fig. 917); apart from these, in France, there were Richelieu (1631) and Rochefort (1665), in Ireland, Londonderry (1613), in Italy the first extension of Turin (1620), in Germany the extension of Bremen (1623), of Hamburg and Stuttgart; all were based on the Renaissance grid plan interrupted by one or more regular squares with closed corners (Figs 914, 918).

But in the Scandinavian countries the seventeenth century was the main period of urbanization; here the sovereigns of Sweden and Denmark founded a large number of towns, utilizing models already elaborated by European architectural culture and the technical experience of Flemish engineers, the only ones then equipped to direct works of this scope.

Christian IV of Denmark, who reigned from 1588 to 1648, first employed Hans Steenwinkel (d. 1601) of Antwerp as chief architect; from 1598 onwards Steenwinkel built the arsenal of Copenhagen – a rectangular block which surrounded the dock – about 1600 he laid out the new ring of fortifications around the capital, and at the same time the new town of Christianopel in Skäne: a grid plan organism distorted so as to adapt to a narrow peninsula, surrounded by walls and bastions (Fig. 919).

After that Christian IV built a series of new towns in the outlying provinces of his state: Christianstad in Skäne (designed by the Dutchman Jean Semp, 1614) (Fig. 920); Bredsted in Schleswig-Holstein (also by Jean Semp, 1616) and Glückstadt (planned in 1616 by the Frenchman Pacheval, a pupil of the military engineers of Henri IV, Perret and Errard) (Fig. 921); in Norway, annexed to Denmark in 1623, Christiania (the new capital, rebuilt after the fire of 1624; Fig. 922) and Christiansand (designed in 1641 by the Dutchman H. J. Schiort).

In 1617 Jean Semp supplied two plans for the new district of Christianhavn in Copenhagen, on the island beyond the port-canal.

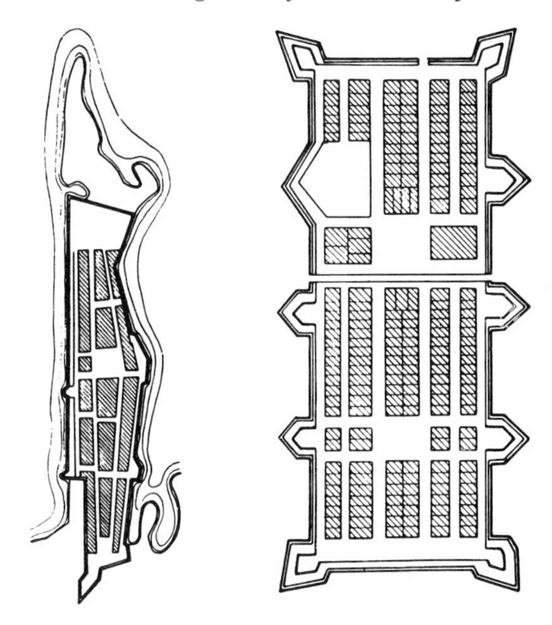

919, 920 *Plans of cities founded by Christian IV: Christianopel and Christianstad*

921 *Plan of Glückstadt in 1628*

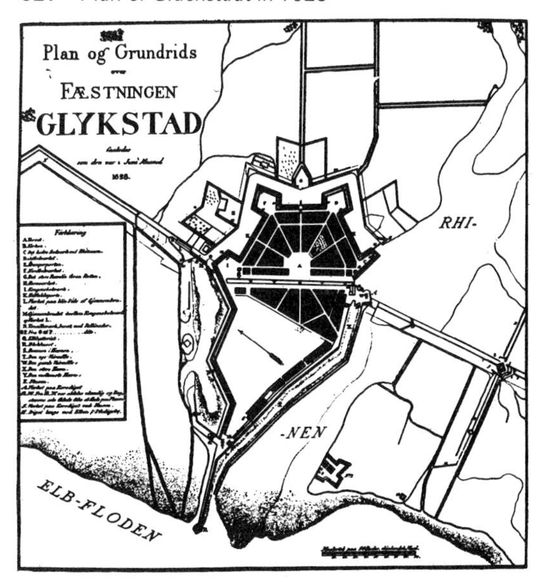

Meanwhile the problem of urbanizing the free zone between the medieval city and fortifications of 1600 arose: in the first decades of the century the king built the district of Nye Skipperboder for the sailors of the fleet, on a

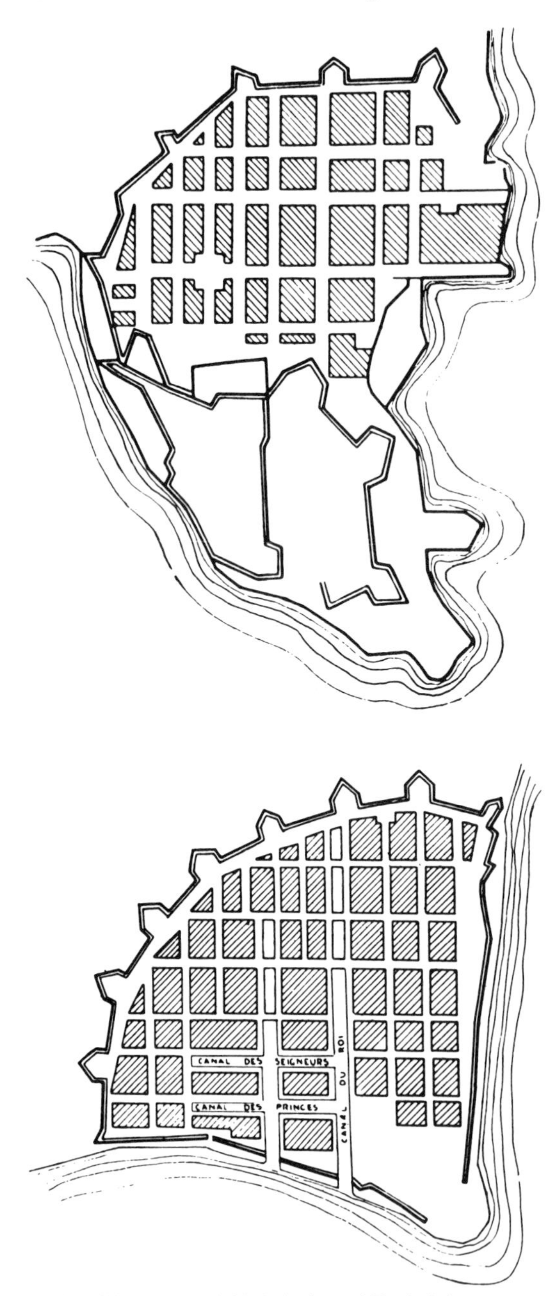

922, 923 *Plans of Christiania and Fredericia, founded by Christian IV*

site adjacent to the old nucleus and the arsenal; then in 1629 he commissioned Richard Douchette to design a plan for the whole district – a radiating series of sixteen streets which ran into an octagonal square (Fig. 925); then in 1631 he realized the other district of Nyboder for sailors and harbour-workers in accordance with this scheme, formed of parallel terraces of houses inscribed in three of the trapezoid plots (Figs 924, 926).

But the extension of this design to the whole city remained problematical, and finally it was found preferable to fall back on a grid plan system, fitting the already completed district into its mesh. Christian's successor, Frederick III (1648–70) concluded these undertakings in 1649 by approving the new general plan of Copenhagen and from 1648 onwards by building the two new cities envisaged by Christian IV for Jutland, the trading centre of Frederikssund and the fortress of Fredericia (Fig. 923).

In Sweden urbanization began under Charles IX (1550–1611), then intensified under Gustavus Adolphus (1611–32) and in the period of regency until the beginning of the reign of Christina (1644). The cities, classified either as harbours or inland, made it possible to concentrate economic exchanges and to submit them to state regulations; with this in mind the rulers promoted the extension of existing urban centres – Jonköping in 1612, Uppsala in 1643 – and founded a large number of new ones, including Mariestad (1600), Göteborg (1604, enlarged in 1620), Boras (1632; Fig. 928), Helsingfors (1639). The old capital, Stockholm, stood on an island and could not be extended like the other cities but from 1640 onwards the two adjacent peninsulas were built up, Norrmalm and Södermalm, according to a common plan and with roads of uniform width (Fig. 927). From 1643 onwards artists trained according to European court taste began to circulate at the court of Christina; they included Nikodemus Tessin the Elder (1615–81), who in 1650 designed the plan for the new city of Gäule, and Jean de la Vallée, who designed a new monumental scheme for Norrmalm in 1650.

The designs for the Scandinavian cities made disconcertingly arbitrary use of numerous heterogeneous models: the medieval grid plan (Christianopel, Christianstad, Helsingfors), the Renaissance grid plan, more regular and subordinated to one axis of perspective or more (Christiania, Christiansand, the second plan for Christianhavn, Fredericia, Jonköping, Uppsala, Göteborg), in some cases an undifferentiated grid plan that could be extended indefinitely like those of the American cities (Boras) or, for military or prestige reasons, the radiocentric scheme (Glückstadt, the first plan for Christianhavn, the 1629 plan for Copenhagen).

This last scheme was accepted for execution only at Glückstadt, which was an isolated fortress; in the other cases it remained on paper, and was replaced by a grid plan scheme more or less differentiated

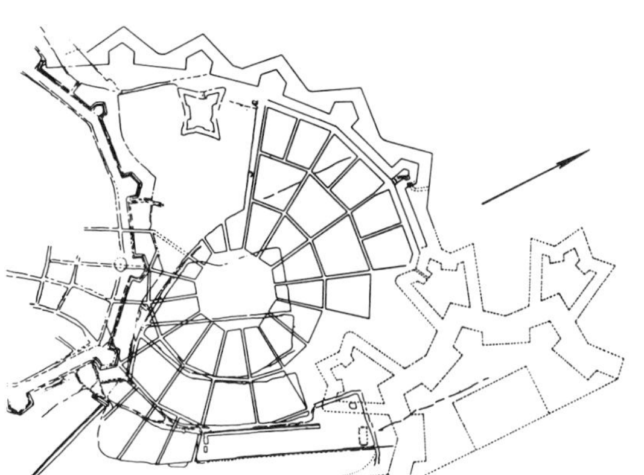

924 *View of the Nyboder district in Copenhagen*
925, 926 *Diagram of Douchette's plan for Copenhagen, 1629 and plan of the built-up area of Copenhagen in 1650*

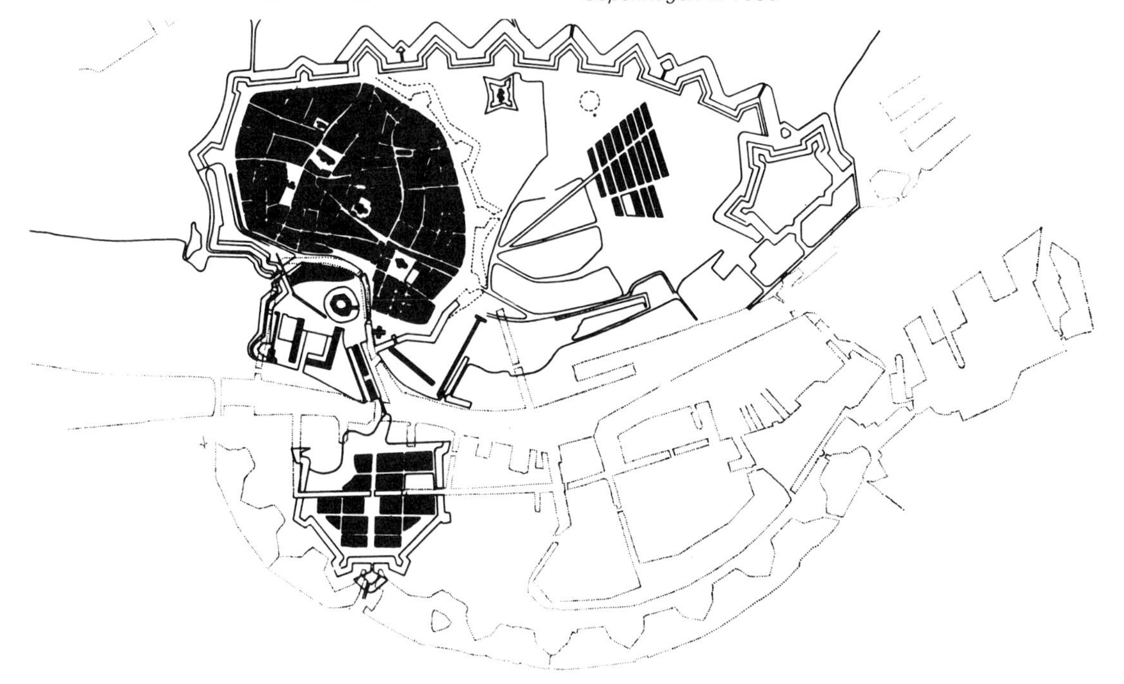

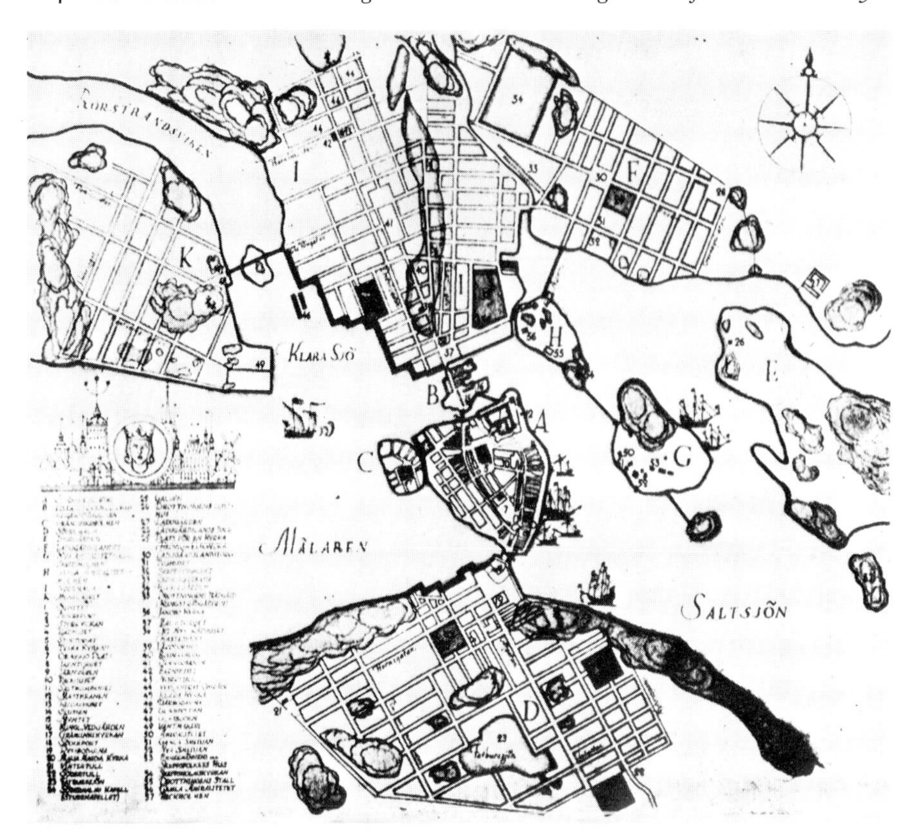

927 *Plan of Stockholm in 1650*

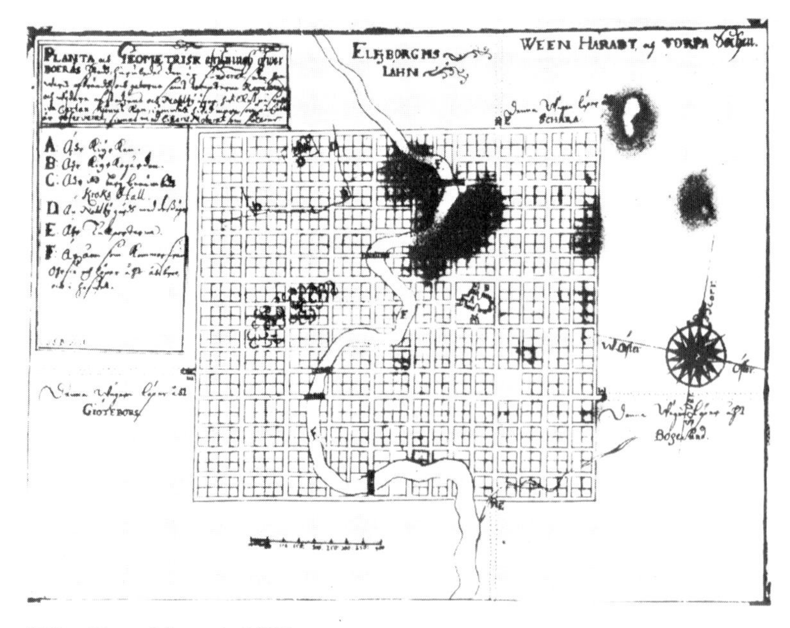

928 *Plan of Boras in 1682*

according to the degree necessary for adaptation to the characteristics of the terrain (1649 plan for Copenhagen). The grid plan, or the combination of various grid plan motifs, was also utilized to urbanize very irregular sites, such as the suburbs of Stockholm.

The Scandinavian cities of the early seventeenth century depended upon a precise political-economic programme, and made few concessions to monumental demands, like the cities of the American colonies a century before. Furthermore this cycle of planned operations was not as broad and systematic as the previous one, and took place while architectural culture no longer had exclusive faith in a certain system of visual models, indeed it took into consideration a wide range of different hypotheses, as was explained in chapter 5. For this reason these operations did not follow a uniform standard, but remained to some degree independent one from another.

A weakening factor, common to all the European experiments mentioned so far, was dependence upon the contradictions of absolute power which, while it was asserting itself as the superior, unquestionable authority, no longer had adequate means to control the economic and social processes, including the transformation of urban organisms. The plans of the new cities, in Italy, France, England and Scandinavia, were intentionally schematic hypotheses of development, which took no account of the moments and methods of realization; a glaring lack of co-ordination existed between town-planning and building-planning, because of which town-planning schemes remained inoperative and were only implemented after long delays, or not at all, since in the interim they had been outmoded by new functional needs or new stylistic tendencies. The street systems envisaged in the 1629 and 1649 plans for Copenhagen, in the 1620 plan for Göteborg and in those of 1640 for Stockholm posed the problem of a new urban dimension in the abstract, but remained two-dimensional plans, which were not translated into new spatial organisms; they were quantitative extrapolations, formulated on the basis of an architectural culture which did not yet possess the instruments to control the new spatial dimensions qualitatively.

The Dutch exception

'Holland [wrote Luzzatto], a small confederation of seven provincial states, whose policy was inspired by the mercantile, marine and industrial bourgeoisie of a few main cities, can be considered as the last great representative, in western Europe, of the city economy, understood in the broadest sense of the word: of an economy, that is, which could extend its field of action to a world market, while its base, centre and ruling criteria still continued to be exclusively those of the city.'[2]

In the political, economic and cultural history of Europe the Dutch Republic was therefore 'the exception and not the rule'.[3] Her economic well-being emerged in the ambit of the medieval pre-mercantilist economic system, grew triumphantly in competition with the great mercantilist powers and contributed to the birth of a world finance market, which threatened the mercantilism of the nation states; thus Holland became the cradle of the new post-mercantilist economic ideas, and in fact 'by-passed mercantilism' as Huizinga says.[4] Her trade was not restrained by official controls – with the exception of the colonial one, managed by the East and West India Companies – and her industry developed in accordance with the old guild system, untouched by the new state corporativism of other European countries. The political régime retained a series of municipal and Burgundian institutions, and made use of the medieval concept of freedom as a special privilege, but developed a balance of powers which anticipated the political tendencies of the Enlightenment and the eighteenth-

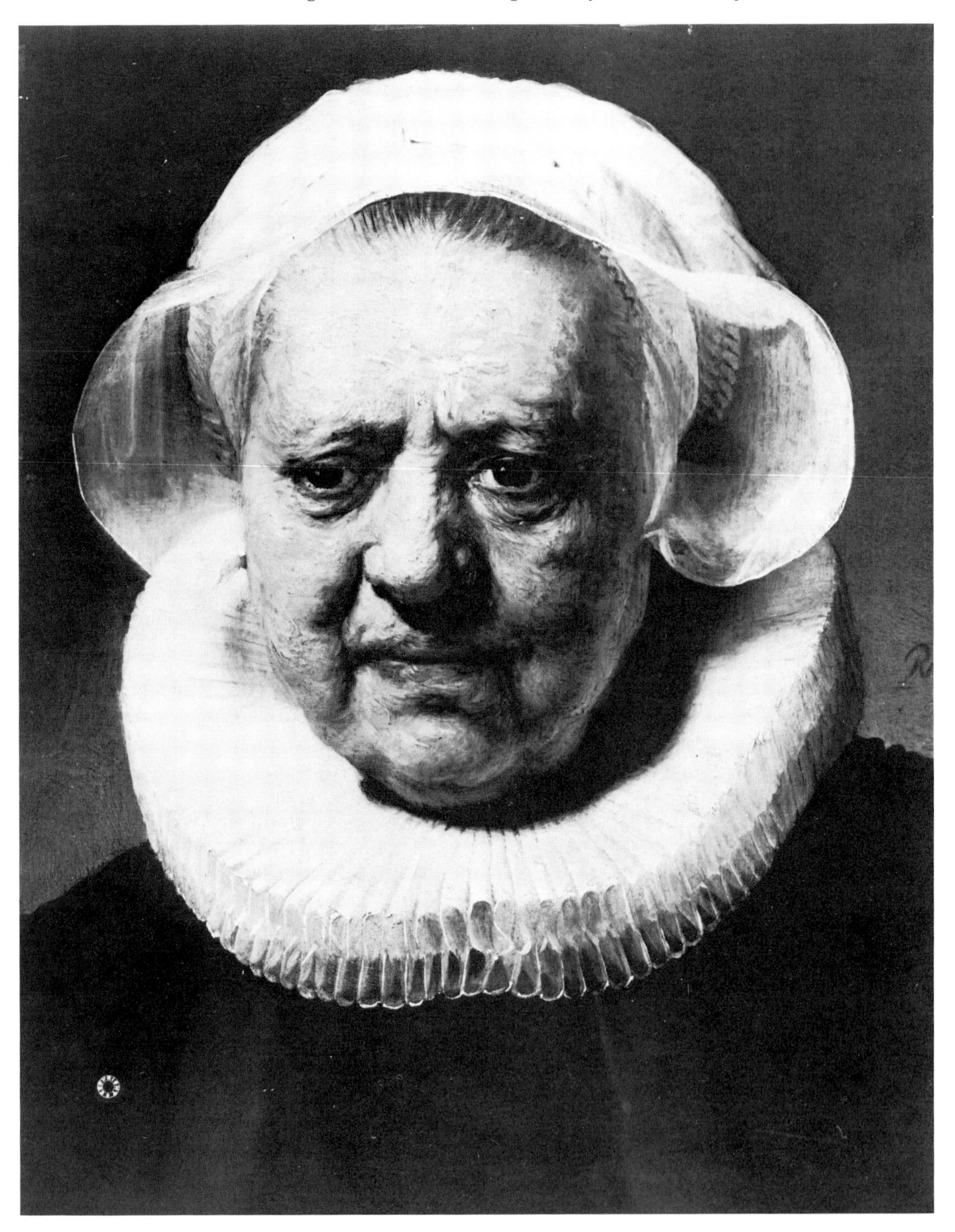

929 Portrait of an old woman *by Rembrandt. National Gallery, London*

century idea of freedom as a common right. Dutch art and literature long escaped the levelling effects of European classicism and transmitted other equally decisive influences to the modern mind; during the seventeenth century, Amsterdam, where Rembrandt, Huygens, Vondel and Spinoza were working contemporaneously with De Witt, harboured the main European writers and thinkers who were in difficulties with their own governments, from Descartes (1629–49) to Locke (1683–9).

The singularity of the Dutch experience was fully confirmed in the field of architecture and town-planning.

At the end of the seventeenth century half of the Dutch population lived in towns: an absolutely extraordinary fact in Europe, where the nation most advanced economically, England, still had 77 per cent of her population engaged in agriculture.[5] The growth of the Dutch cities – exceptional in extent and speed – was none the less effected with continuing respect for the character of the medieval centres, and with methods only partly different from the traditional ones. Clients, planners and executors successfully preserved the main characteristics of old town-planning praxis: the efficiency of public control, the capacity to create new urban forms independent of regular geometrical figures, the closeness of town-planning and building-planning, the co-ordination in space not here cut off from co-ordination in time; at the same time they were by no means prejudiced against the technical and figurative improvements dependent on the new scientific mentality and the new visual education. Developing these heterogeneous principles simultaneously, they created a series of urban settings that were extremely original, that proved significant even after the crisis of monumental European planning, and contributed to the growth of a new town-planning civilization, bourgeois and anti-monumental. Thus the republic – together with mercantilism and absolutism – missed out on the conventional European *grand goût*; it managed to batten the medieval tradition directly on to eighteenth-century experience, to develop its own local heritage to a cosmopolitan level.

The revolt against Spanish rule began in 1566, and the independence of the new state was recognized in 1609. During this period Holland's economy and town-planning system was already fully developed, even before the political system was formed; indeed the rebellion was born to preserve an already mainly crystallized civil reality from the levelling influence of the Spanish state and Catholic church.

In our field we must bear in mind that not only the city, but even the land around it was a man-made creation; the marshy plains around the mouths of the great rivers – the Rhine, Scheldt and Meuse – changed shape and size over the centuries; these transformations were corrected by a series of interventions by man, which became more efficacious with the progress of engineering and received an extraordinary boost in the second half of the sixteenth century, after the disastrous floodings of the first half (1508, 1509, 1514, 1516 and 1532).

Between 1540 and 1565 over 35,000 hectares were reclaimed and some inland basins began to be dried out: the Dergmeer, the Kerkmeer, the Kromwater, the Weidgreb, the Rietgreb and the Egmondermeer. The main figure in this new phase was the dyke-builder Andries Vierlingh, who gained European fame and wrote the *Tractaat van dickagie* about 1578.

The war against Spain does not seem to have retarded, but rather to have intensified these works of draining and shoring up the coastline and river banks. The city merchants willingly invested their money in works of reclamation, which procured new agricultural land, and William the Silent assisted the undertaking in every way possible. The windmill, perfected in the previous century, became the main instrument for the raising

930 *Aerial view of Nieuwveen*

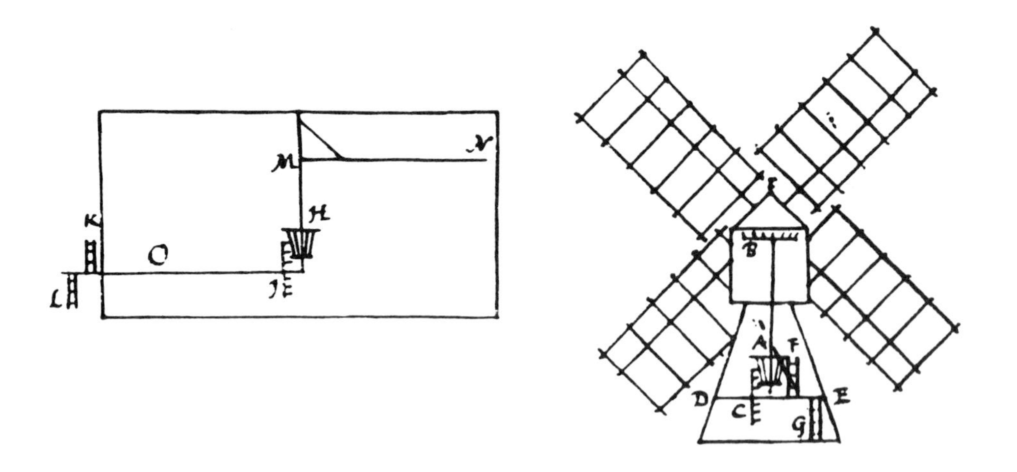

931 *Sketch by Stevin for a drainage mill (patent of 28 November 1589)*
932 *Aerial view of Nieuwerkerk aan de Jissel*

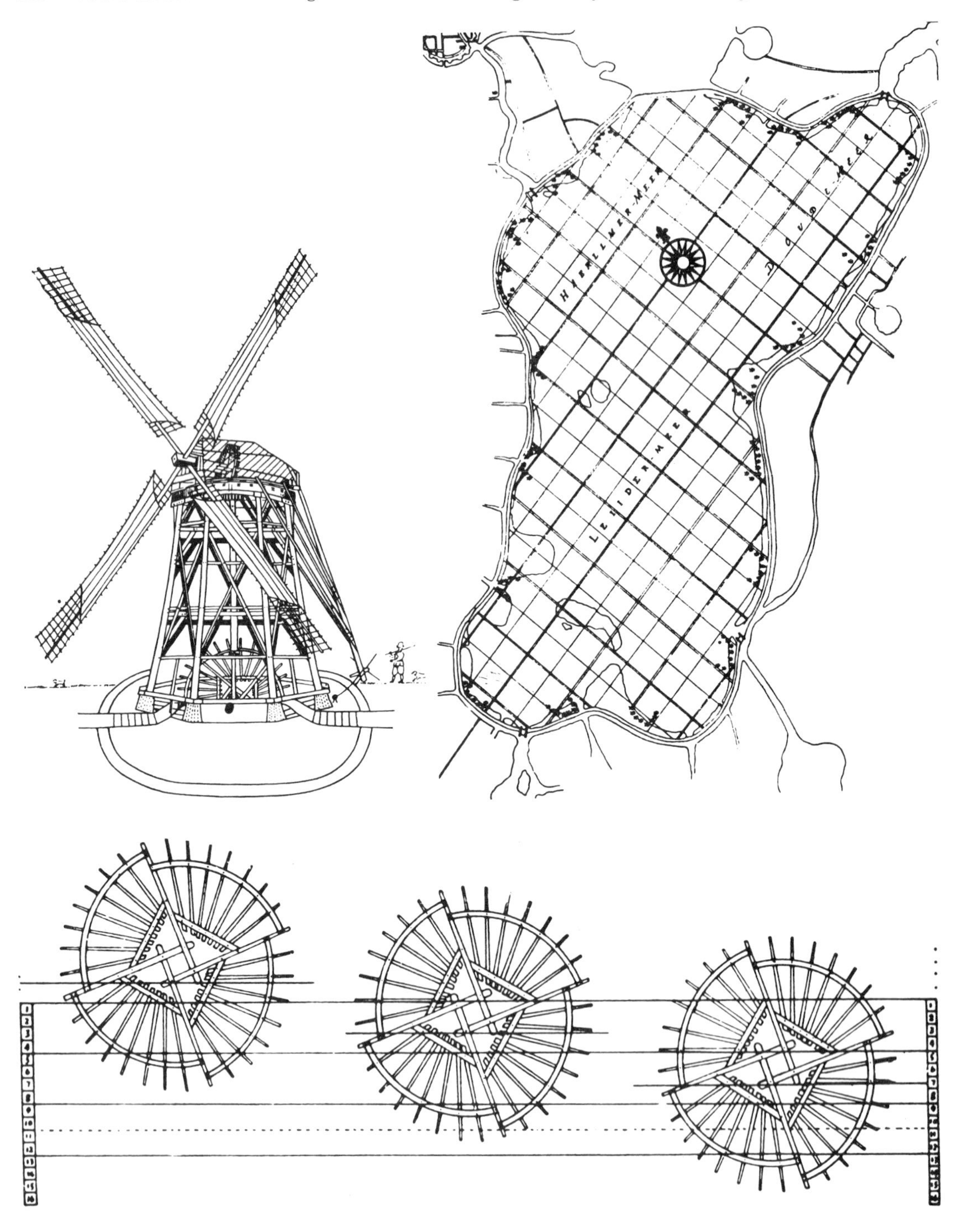

933–935 *Drawings by Leeghwater: mill for the Beemster* polder; *drainage plan for Haarlemmermeer; system of drainage with wheels*

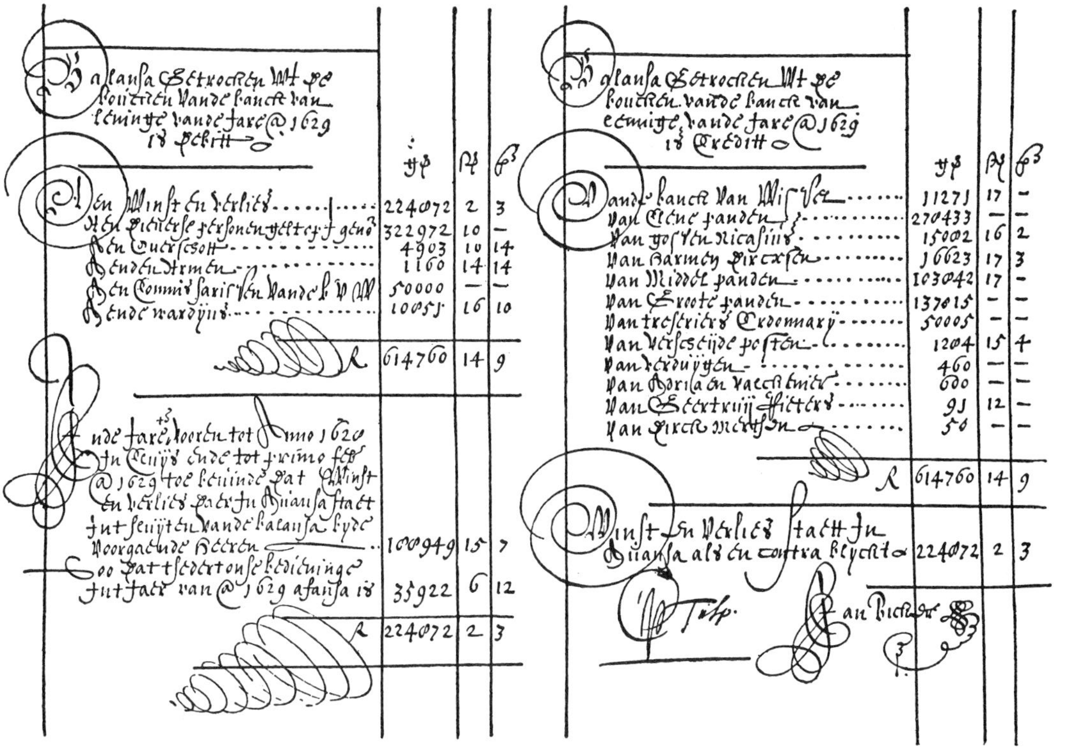

936 *The accounts of a Dutch bank in 1629*

of water: from 1560 to 1700 the Estates General granted 102 patents for drainage windmills. Many Dutch specialists worked on the reclamation of marshy ground in Europe and even in America, such as Martins at Mexico City towards the end of the sixteenth century and Vermuyden in England after 1630.

Together with the generals, the men of government, navigators and publicists who safeguarded the existence and prosperity of the United Provinces (Maurice of Nassau, Jan van Oldenbarneveldt, Jan Pieterzoon Coen and Hugo Grotius), scientists such as Simon Stevin (1548–1620) and builders such as Lieven de Key (1565–1627), Hendrik de Keyser (1565–1621), Jan Leeghwater (1575–1650) and Hendrik Staets also made their contribution to the urban and rural landscape.

The term 'builders', in the traditional medieval sense, still aptly described their professional character: they were specialists who had grown up in the atmosphere of the city building guilds, linked stably not to a certain category of products, but to a certain subject – masonry work – and to a certain executive procedure. Retaining this character they acquired the scientific methods of planning and formal standards elaborated by Italian culture without effort, and were in a position to design utilitarian works (bridges, dykes, fortifications), architectural works (ordinary houses, monumental buildings) and general schemes on an urban or regional scale (projects for towns, plans for drainage).

The mathematician Simon Stevin was the most important theoretician in the field of hydraulic works – in 1584, 1588 and 1589 he obtained three of the main patents for the building of windmills – and of military

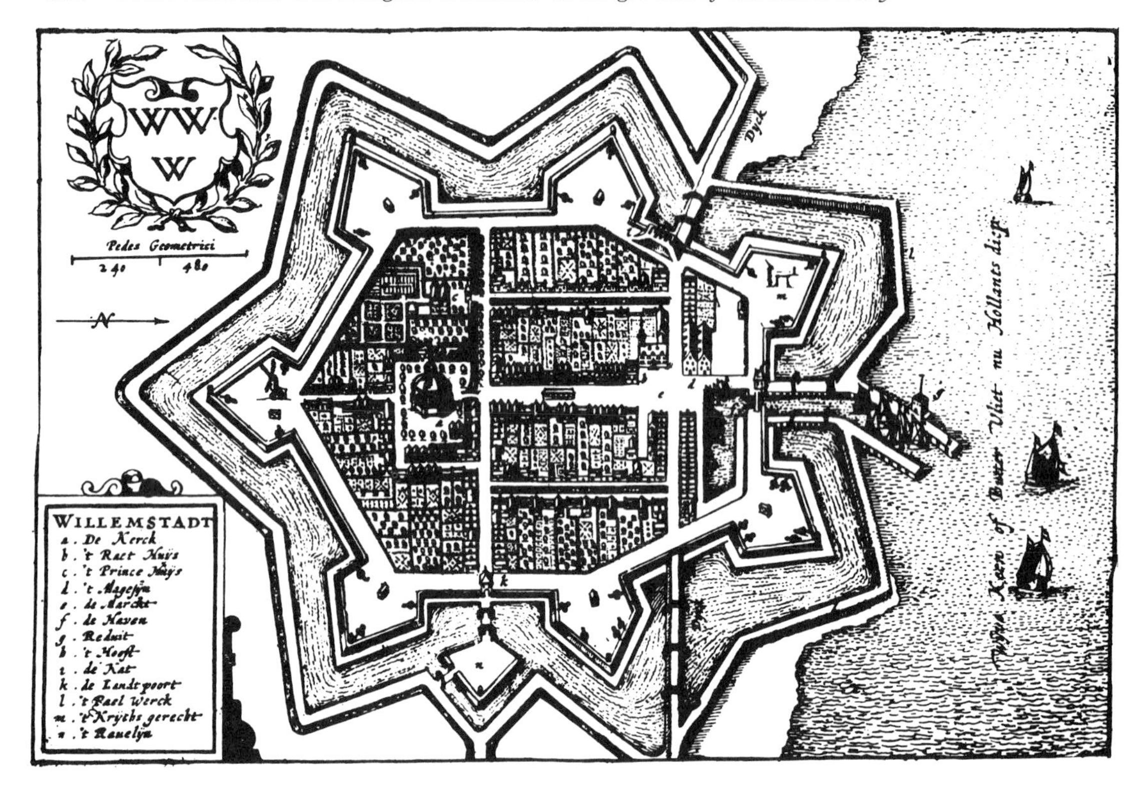

works; he invented the system of fortification known as 'old Dutch', a system tried out with success by his contemporary Adriaen Anthoniszoon during the war against the Spaniards, and used to build both new fortresses (Willemstadt, 1583; Coerworden, 1597; Figs 937–8) and the walls of the main cities (Leiden, Alkmaar, Zutphen, Deventer, the second last defensive circle of Amsterdam in 1593); he wrote the treatises *Van de molens* (1586) and *Sterctenbouwing* (1594) which remained the classic texts in the field of hydraulics and military art until the middle of the seventeenth century.

Jan Leeghwater was the man responsible for most of the reclamation work in the first half of the seventeenth century: the Zijpe in 1599, the Wogmer in 1608, the Beemster in 1612, the Purmer in 1622, the Wormer in 1626, the Heer Hugoward in 1631, the Schermer in 1635; it has been calculated that from 1590 to 1640 80,000 hectares were

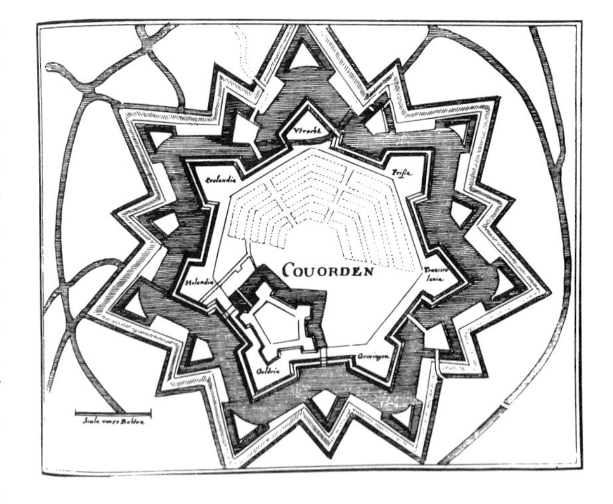

937, 938 *Plan of Willemstadt in 1632 and plan of Coerworden in 1659 (from Merian)*

939, 940 *Aerial view of Naarden and detail of the ramparts*

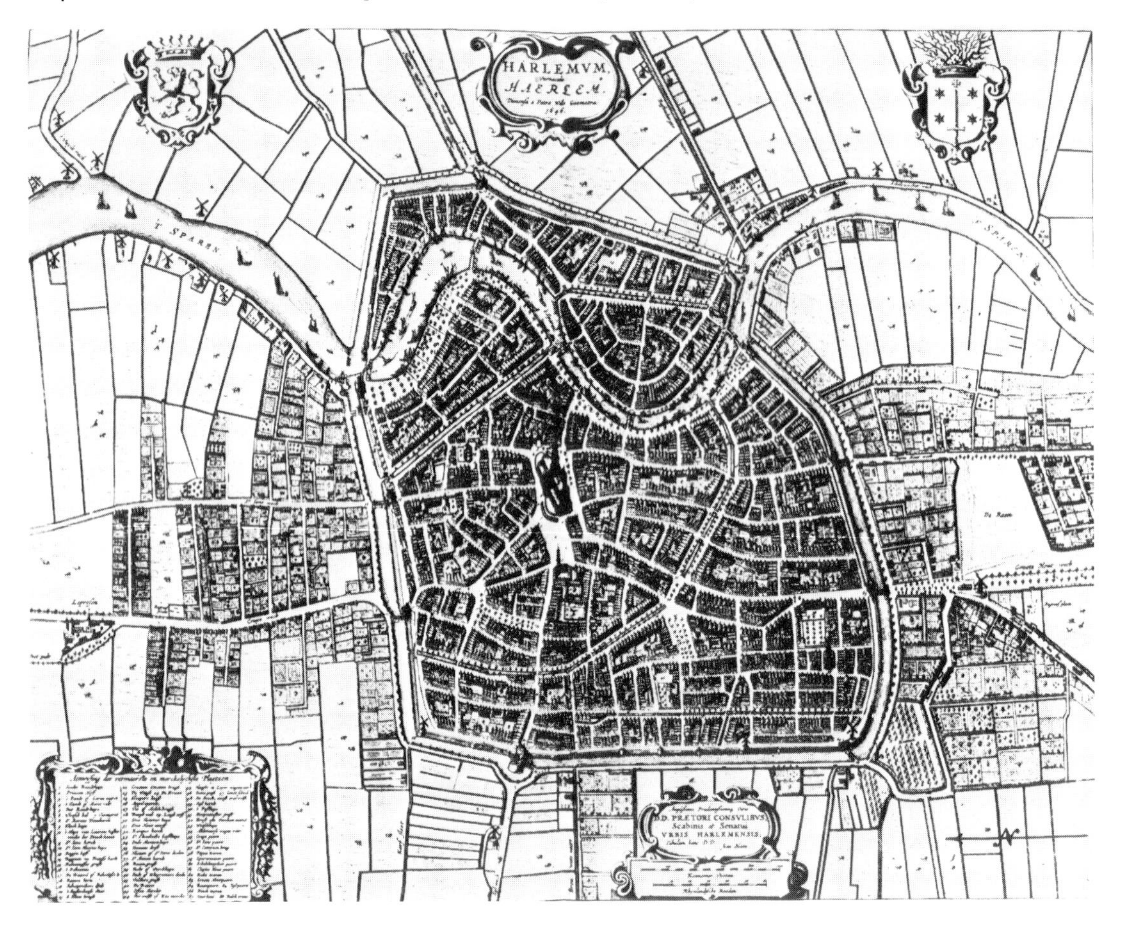

reclaimed, and a further 45,000 in the following century. Leeghwater also planned the draining of the largest inland water in Holland, the Haarlemmermeer, by the installation of 160 windmills (an undertaking that was to be completed only in 1852); meanwhile he was also active in the architectural field, and built a series of elegant *Raadhuises* in the villages of northern Holland.

Lieven de Key, chief architect of the city of Haarlem, was the co-ordinator of the first large town-planning undertaking after the formation of the new independent state: the scheme for a vast area of the city, bombarded during the siege of 1572–3 and then destroyed by fire in 1576. The administration assigned this task to the Stadsfabryk, administered by de Key, which was both a technical office and a planning authority and which had considerable financial means at its disposal: first a detailed map of the city was made with the exact locations of buildings remaining or destroyed (published by Tomas Tomaszoon in 1578), then the plan of reconstruction was prepared, which almost completely renewed the network of roads, of canals, and the dividing up of the sites; the weavers' houses and workshops were grouped around a long straight canal (Raamgracht and Voldersgracht), which gave access to two elongated rows of plots (Fig. 941). The plan was accurately executed in the following fifty years; de Key designed some of the more important buildings: the new headquarters of

941 *Plan of Haarlem in 1646 (the rebuilt part is at the bottom)*
942, 943 *The central square of Haarlem and a road with terrace houses for the elderly by L. de Key*

944 *Aerial view of the main square at Delft*
945 *Plan of Amsterdam in 1544 (cat. d'Ailly, no. 30)*

the butchers' guild (1602), a series of terrace houses for elderly people (1610) (Fig. 943), the tower of the Nieuwe Kerk (1613) and a large number of private dwellings. He and his contemporary de Keyser – who worked in Amsterdam, as we shall see – defined the type of seventeenth-century Dutch brick house, with its large windows, stepped pediments and the classically inspired decorations popularized by de Vries.

Staets and de Keyser were responsible for the most grandiose urban scheme designed and implemented in Holland – or indeed in Europe – in the seventeenth century: the extension of Amsterdam.

As early as the first half of the sixteenth century Amsterdam was an important trading city. The map by Cornelis Antoniszoon (Fig. 945) shows the city when it had about 40,000 inhabitants; the two banks of the Amstel and the dyke that blocks its water halfway down its course through the city (the

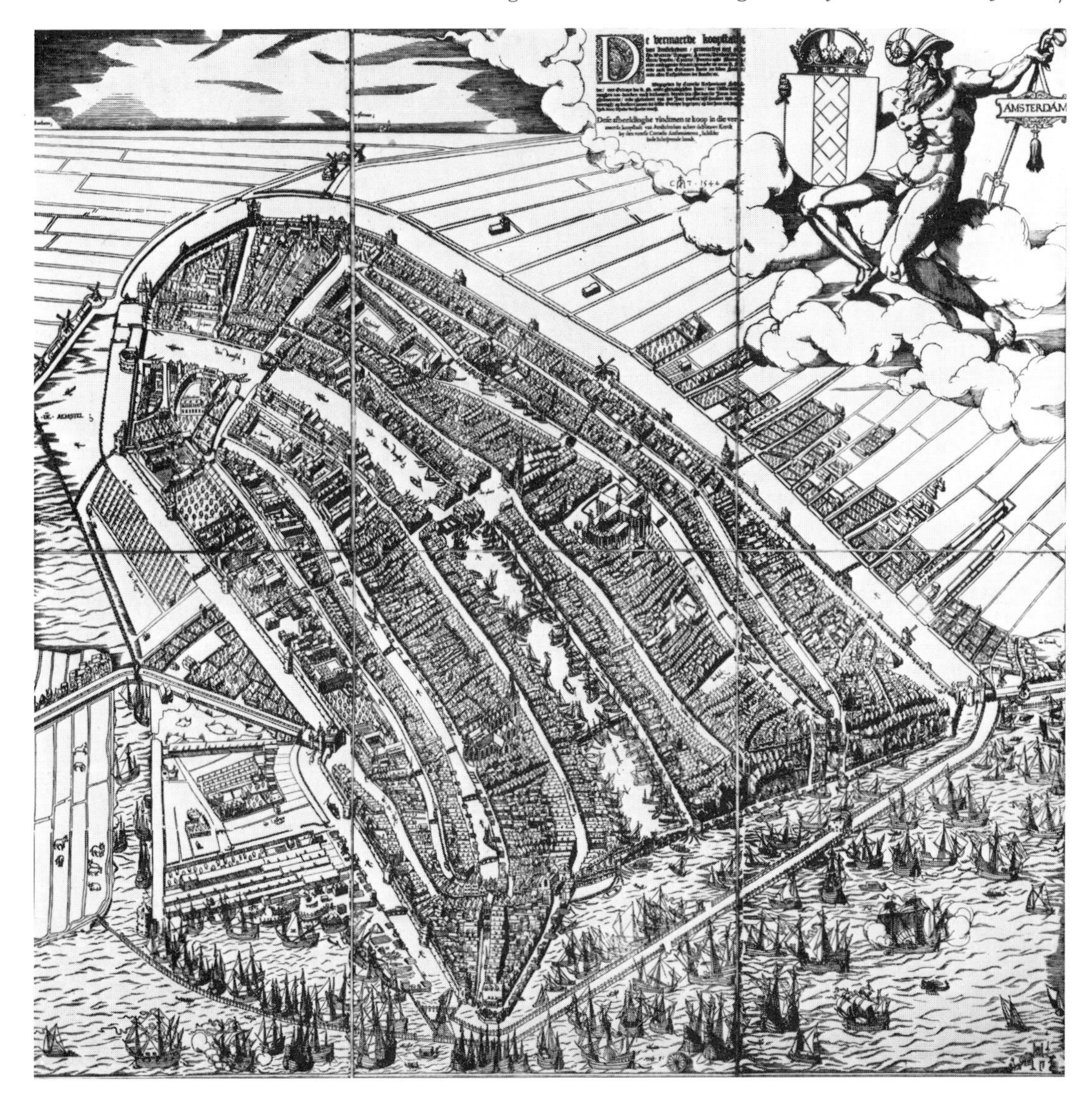

Dam, still the heart of the city even today) formed the original nucleus, surrounded by other lesser canals, the 1481 walls and the large defensive moat.

In 1578 the troops of William the Silent occupied the city and drove out the old administration which had remained faithful to Spain; seven years later Antwerp fell definitively into the hands of the Spaniards, and the Dutch, masters of the sea, kept up a blockade at the mouth of the Scheldt, which made the great Flemish port unusable. This was the start of the amazing growth of Amsterdam which replaced Antwerp as centre of world trade, housed a part of the industrial population which had fled from the southern provinces and actually controlled the policy of the Estates General until 1618, through the work of its advocate van Oldenbarneveldt.

The organism contained within the fifteenth-century walls was not able to cope with the continually growing population; in

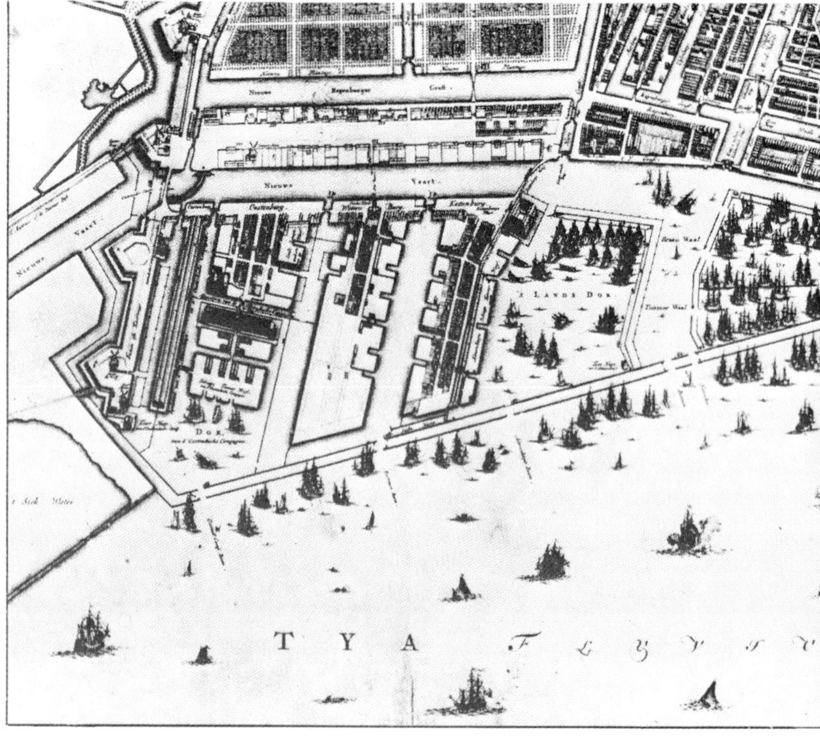

946 *Plan of Amsterdam in 1732 (cat. d'Ailly, no. 266)*

DAM
NAMEN
HET Y.

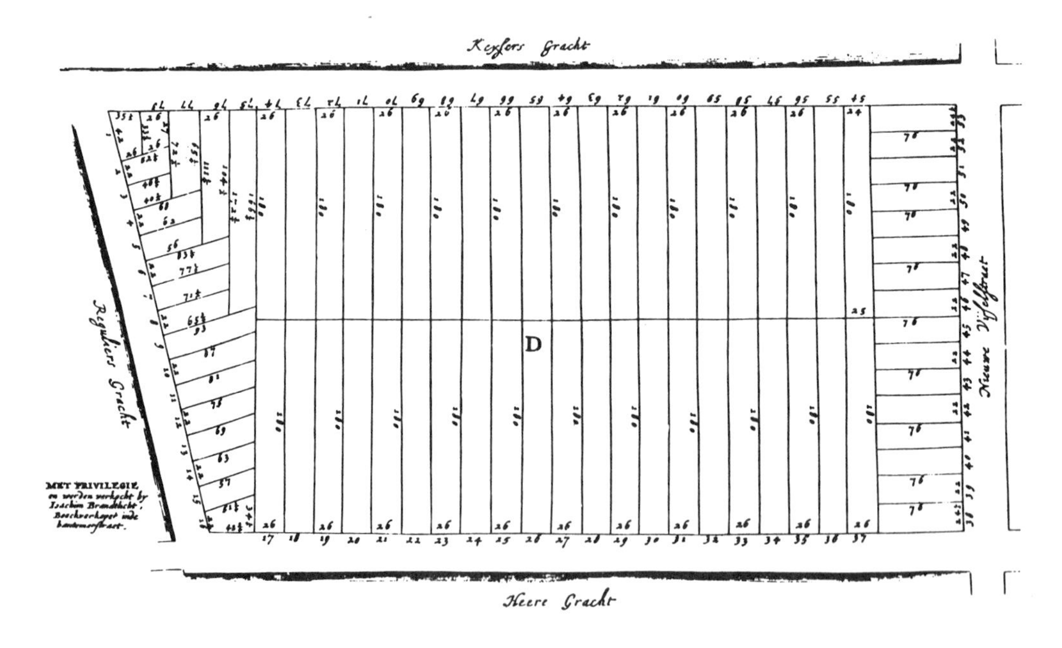

947, 948 *Aerial view of the centre of Amsterdam and plan of the building plots on a block between the main canals, 1612*

the last decades of the sixteenth century the old peripheral moat (Singel, Kloveniersburgwal and Geldersekade) was incorporated into the city as an internal canal, and the naval shipyard was built along the eastern margin: from 1593 all the elements were enclosed within a new semi-circle of fortified walls, agreed upon with Maurice of Nassau and built according to Stevin's rules.

But at the same time the administration was preparing plans for a further grandiose extension of the city: the overall plan was drawn up by Staets towards the end of the sixteenth century, passed in 1607, and made definitive in 1609 by the central government, which authorized the compulsory purchase of the necessary sites. The plan was to dig three canals concentric with the 1593 fortifications, beginning from the western edge of the city and proceeding, over a series of operations, to the eastern part, where a public park (the Plantage) was envisaged, and an extension of the naval dockyard.

This plan was executed completely during the course of the seventeenth century. The series of three canals was created in the western sector by 1625 (as we see in the great map produced by Balthasar Floriszoon); it was continued as far as the Amstel by 1663, and as far as the eastern sector by the end of the century. The first circle of walls of over six kilometres which closed the city in within a semi-circle, already completed by the mid-sixteenth century, was subsequently modified according to the 'new Dutch' system invented by Menno van Coehorn (1641–1704), the rival of Vauban. At the same period, the population of the city was rising from 50,000 inhabitants in 1612 to 125,000 in 1632 and to about 200,000 in the second half of the century.

The plan of Amsterdam stands out among all the town-planning experiments of the seventeenth century for the exceptional character of its design and execution (Figs 946–53).

The three semi-circular canals – Heerengracht, Keisergracht and Prinsengracht – have a fixed width of 25 metres, and include four lanes of about 6 metres each for medium-sized ships, one for each direction and two for mooring. Loading quays of 11 metres wide ran along the canals, planted with two rows of elms; building plots included between the two canals had an overall depth of 102 metres, and there was a compulsory free space of at least 48 metres between the back façades of the houses, i.e. a double row of gardens each 24 metres long.

The three seventeenth-century canals, at the moment of maximum development, were respectively three and a half, four and four and a half kilometres long. While the sixteenth-century canal immediately next to them on the inside, Singel, describes an irregular curve, they themselves were traced in a broken arc, so as to make building plots more regular; the individual stretches of the arc have lengths varying from half a kilometre to a kilometre or more, and are therefore comparable, as far as their ground measurements are concerned, to the canals traced by Le Nôtre half a century later (Vaux, Sceaux, Chantilly, the two arms of the canal at Versailles). But here there was no question of perspective settings, to be looked along; the elms were not flanking but filling the space and, together with the rigging of the ships, they broke up the sweeping views along the axes of the canals; no building was treated in a special way simply because it happened to correspond to those axes, and furthermore the houses aligned on the two banks were not uniform scenery subordinated to a general image, but each was composed symmetrically on its own account with its own individuality, and required an axial view from a limited distance which corresponded to the transversal section of the canal (less than 50 metres, as in medieval squares; Figs 951–2). The sum total of the scene, i.e. the canal with its series of houses, was to be appreciated not as a single prospect, but as a rhythmic sequence; this is confirmed by the innumerable con-

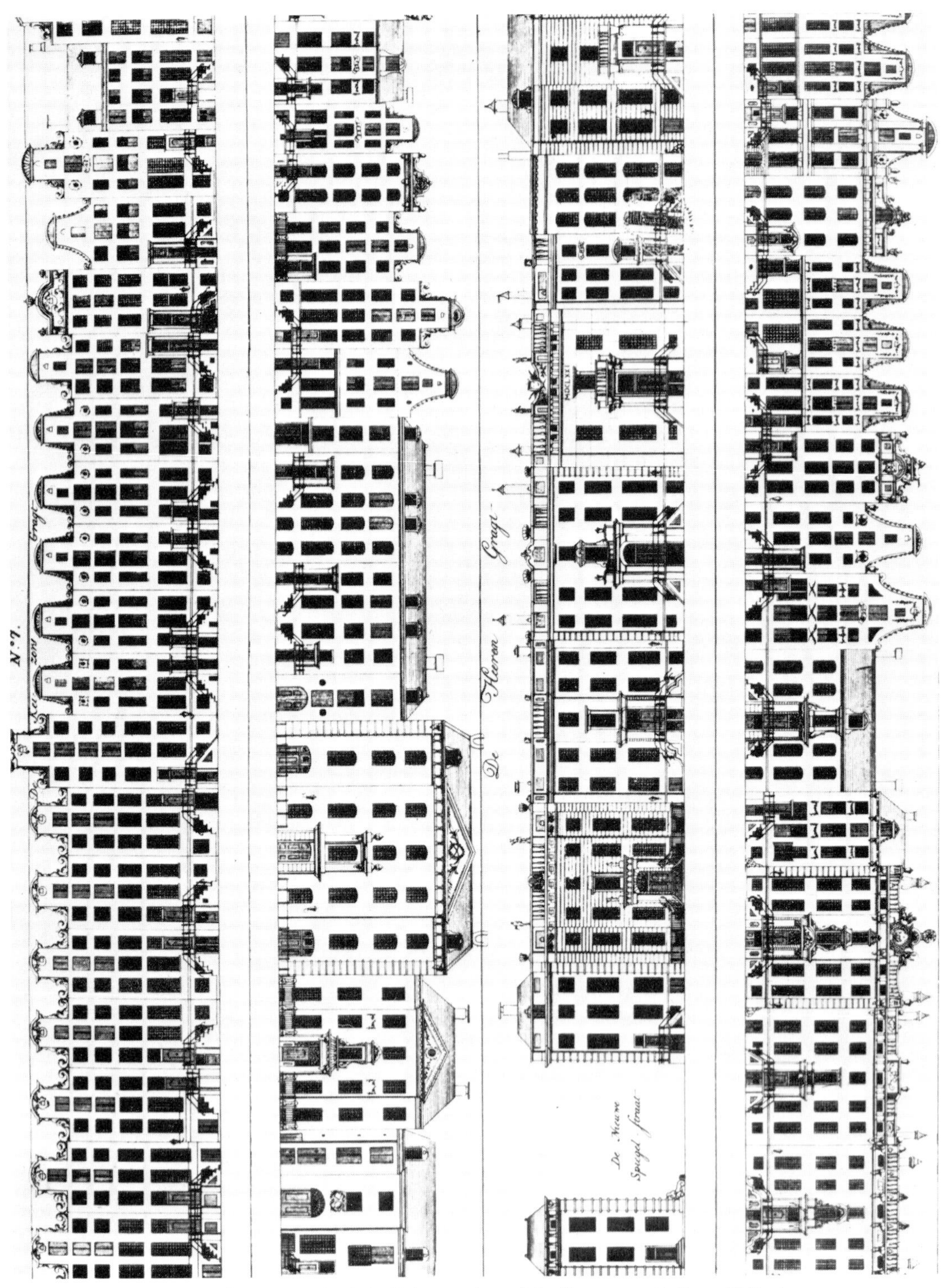

949 *Façades of houses along a stretch of the Keisergracht and the Heerengracht (from Philips)*

950 *A canal in Amsterdam, painted by H. P. Schouten, c. 1770*

temporary graphic representations – paintings and engravings – which portray certain stretches of canal from below (for instance from the parapets of the bridges), almost always in three-quarter view, or from above, axonometrically projected, the general view of the city with the houses aligned in endless rows (Fig. 953). The canals were not empty spaces to be seen as background, but spaces for life to be carried on in, to move over and enjoy as a foreground; the extent of the whole could be discovered by moving around and synthesizing so many successive visual pictures, of which the engravings from below, often published in series, offered an anthology, and the axonometrical view a general recapitulation.

These spaces – which provided about twenty-five kilometres of quays for the loading and unloading of merchandise, i.e. an essential instrument of the city's economic life – also formed a fantastic architectural route, which could reasonably be compared, even just as a visual experience, to Versailles. While Le Nôtre was designing and excavating the pools in the park of king Louis, the citizens of Amsterdam were finishing building the second section of Staets' plan, up to the point where the three canals meet the Amstel. When Le Nôtre's trees were barely planted, and were not sufficient to define the great spaces of the ornamental basins, the canals of Amsterdam were already edged with houses and piles of merchandise. Over the former, as though across a stage, the king and court moved on pleasure boats or gondo-

951, 952 *Buildings along one of the great 25-metre canals of Amsterdam, seen from the opposite bank*

las presented by the Venetian republic; along the second sailed four thousand ships from the seas the world over, loaded with riches sufficient to buy the Sun King's palace many times over.

The modes of execution were equally singular and unlike those of the other European countries. The 1607 plan was promptly implemented, with more or less continuous work and without serious interruption. The implementation was not dependent upon the desires of a prince – which might either wane (Henri IV) or persist (Louis XIV) – but upon a collective interest that was stable in time, and a permanent administrative mechanism. It was not a doubtful expense, but a productive investment; a calculated relation existed between cost and result, and its financing was ensured through the formulation of the plan.

The planning authority had the means to control all the factors involved: it compulsorily purchased the sites, carried out public works, restricted private building with regulations, had recourse to a repertoire fully accepted both by the town-planning coordinators and the designers of buildings. Some of the regulations had already been laid down previously and were linked to medieval legislation; the most important was the ordinance of 1565, which remained in force until the beginning of the nineteenth century: this stated that the municipal inspectors must examine and approve the foundations of the building, before work began on the main superstructures; that every building unit must have its own latrine; that the street paving carried out by the authorities must be paid for by the owners of the houses fronting on to it, in

proportion to their frontage. Other directions were formulated during the course of events, for instance the ordinance of 1663 which listed a series of unwholesome or noisy activities, to be excluded from residential areas.

The municipality built the amenities and public buildings at its own expense and was in a position to set aside and promptly spend sums no less vast than those boasted of by Louis XIV; each of the twenty-two bastions of the outer wall cost 500,000 florins, and the new town hall by van Campen cost almost 8,000,000. In 1662 the annual expenditure for public works reached 1,500,000 florins, but was greatly reduced during the wars with France.

This procedure had its weak points: the compulsory purchase of sites was decided by the municipal bodies, which included the richest citizens who had often acquired the sites to be purchased in advance, and fixed disproportionately high compensations. Furthermore the community did not control the indirect effects of the operation, i.e. the increase in value of sites adjacent to those compulsorily purchased; thus to the outside of the Prinsengracht, in the western sector, was a zone included within the fortifications but which had remained in the hands of private individuals, where a speculative district grew up from 1620 onwards: the Jordaan, destined for the lower-class population and formed of a series of eleven parallel canals; thus the social hierarchy was revealed and confirmed by the hierarchy of urban settlement. These facts anticipated some drawbacks typical of the bourgeois city; but for this very reason they introduced into the seventeenth-century scene the range of prob-

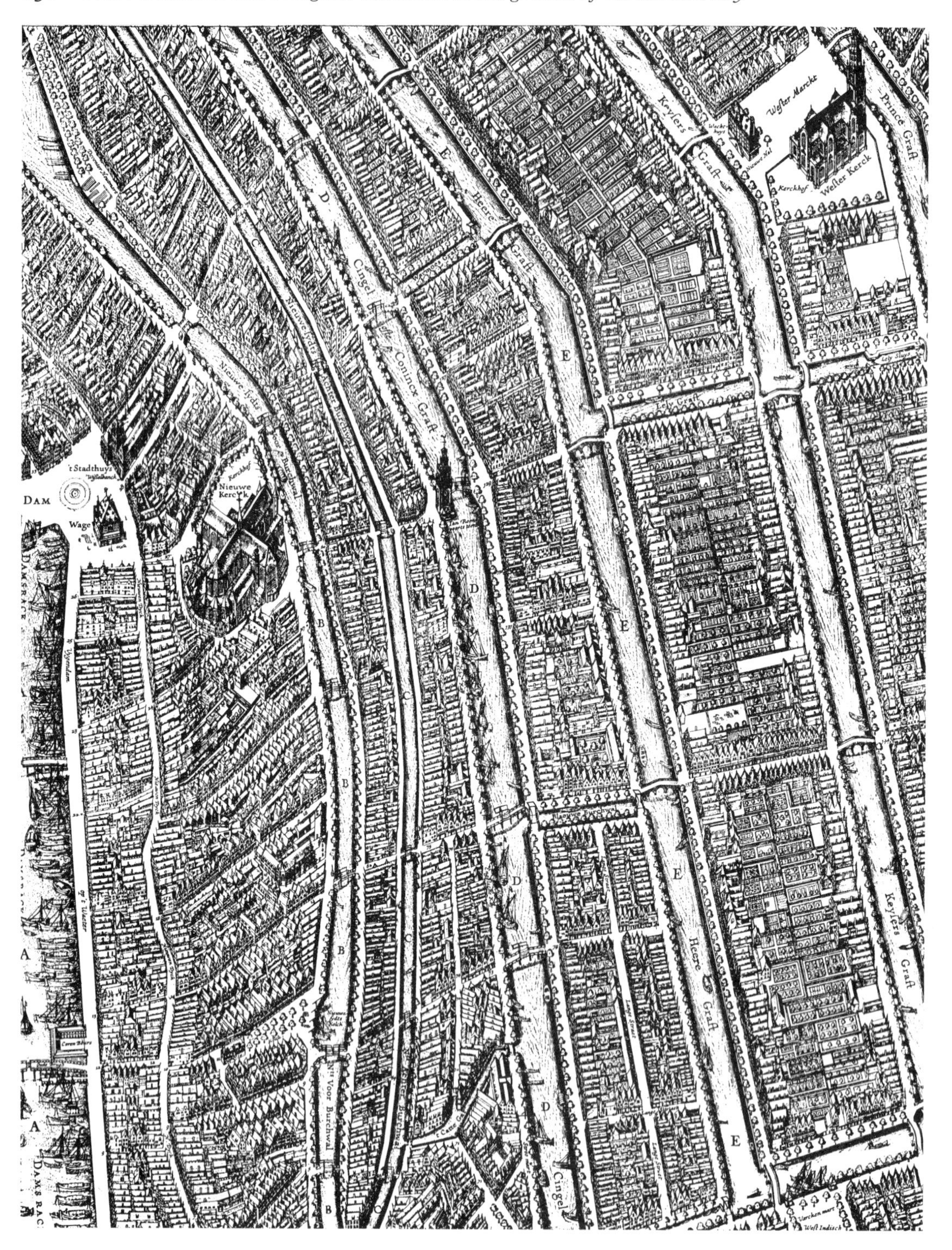

953 *Detail of the 1625 plan of Amsterdam (cat. d'Ailly, no. 117) between the Dam and the new canals.*

lems that belonged to a later and technically more advanced phase of urban development.

Amsterdam remained a unique case, because no other Dutch centre after the Middle Ages experienced a comparable period of growth. Several others implemented less conspicuous developments, though no less organic: Leiden in 1610, 1644 and 1659, Haarlem in 1671. In these cases the new districts remained peripheral additions and did not basically modify the organism of the city established in the Middle Ages; the further developments of the modern outskirts have in many cases annulled the seventeenth-century patterns; canals have been filled in and old houses replaced by others of a different character. More important was the town-planning activity in the colonies, where, together with many others, the Dutch founded three cities destined to figure among the great metropolises of the modern world: Batavia in 1619 (Fig. 954), New Amsterdam (later called New York by the English conquerors) in 1625, and Cape Town in 1652. Since these were trading ports, inhabited only by the European colonizers, the planners unhesitatingly repeated the standards of the mother country: the network of canals to drain the building land and facilitate the distribution of goods to the doors of the buildings, perpendicular plots with the unbroken terrace of houses in front and gardens behind, organic shapes, independent of any abstract geometrical rule. Climate and geographical conditions were not always favourable to the functioning of this arrangement: in Batavia the canals were infested with crocodiles, and the stagnant waters made conditions intolerable for health, so that the city was rebuilt on another site in the nineteenth century. New York and Cape Town, too, could grow only by abandoning the original procedure and adopting the uniform grid plan. The models of Dutch planning, perfect in their own setting and their own dimensions, could be neither exported nor turned into general models.

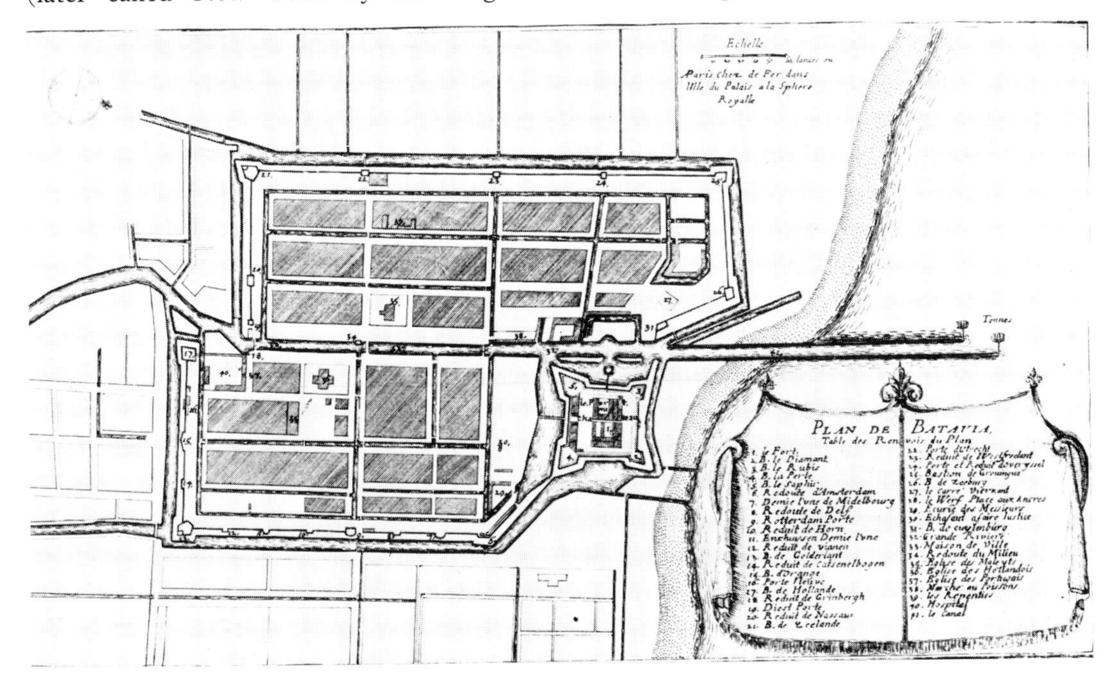

954 *Plan of Batavia in the Dutch East Indies, 1700*

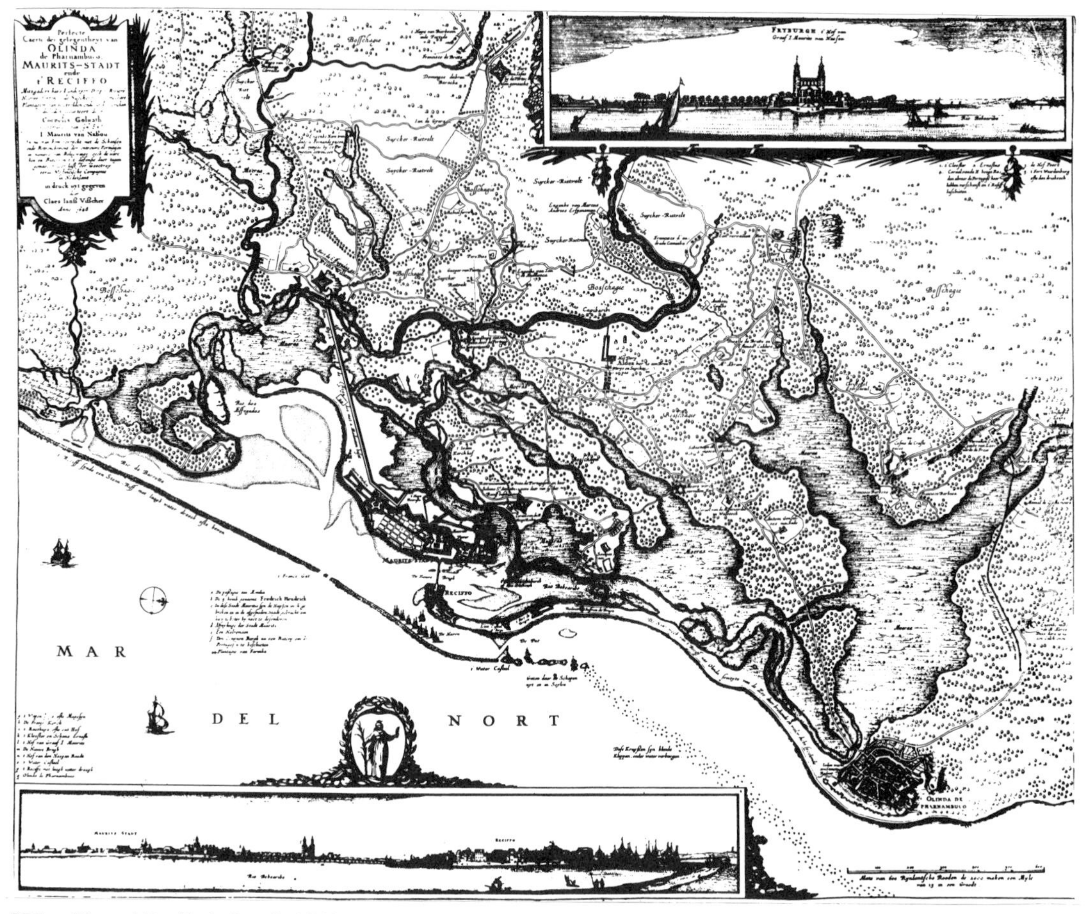

955 *Plan of Recife in Brazil, 1648*

The transition from town-planning to building-planning has still to be considered. In Amsterdam the protagonist of the first phase of expansion, in the first decades of the seventeenth century, was Hendrik de Keyser, chief architect of the city from 1591 to 1621; he designed a large number of private houses and the main public buildings: the Zuidkerk (1606), Stock Exchange (1608), Westerkerk (1620) (Figs 956–8), still on the basis of building types sanctioned by tradition. His buildings thus fit remarkably naturally into the urban fabric, without any untoward emphasis; only the church towers, tall and elegantly worked, function as landmarks and give vertical balance to the horizontal series of terrace houses. His successors, and particularly Daniel Stalpaert (1615–76), continued his work coherently, both by supervising the execution of the urban plan and by generally guaranteeing the continuity of building production; variations of formal fashions scarcely weaken the spectacular unity of the architectural fabric of the city.

The wealth of the city was still not expressed in terms of extravagance and monumentality; the Venetian patrician Tommaso Contarini, visiting Amsterdam at the beginning of the seventeenth century, instinctively compared this style of life with the old

956 *The Amsterdam Stock Exchange, in a print by Fouquet*

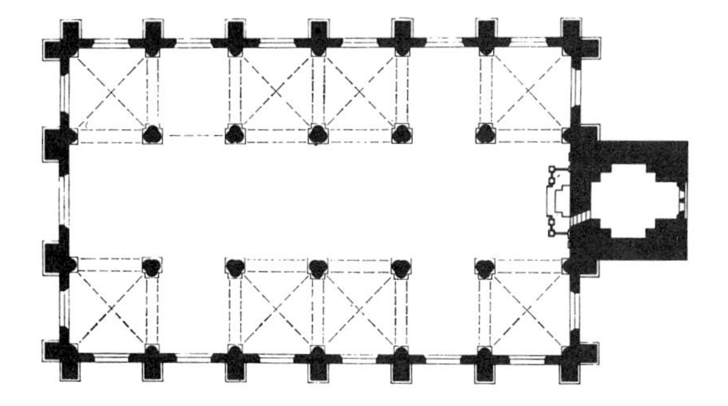

957, 958 *Plan and interior of the Westerkerk by de Keyser (from Fouquet)*

style of his own city, and noted the contrast with the prodigality that reigned in Venice:[6]

'[The inhabitants of Amsterdam] abound in riches and comforts in such moderation that one sees neither display nor extraordinary pomp, since all retain the true mediocrity of a modest fortune both at home and abroad, without one seeing either ornament or silverware or tableware or seats of silk, just as one used not to see them in this city either in the time of our ancestors.'

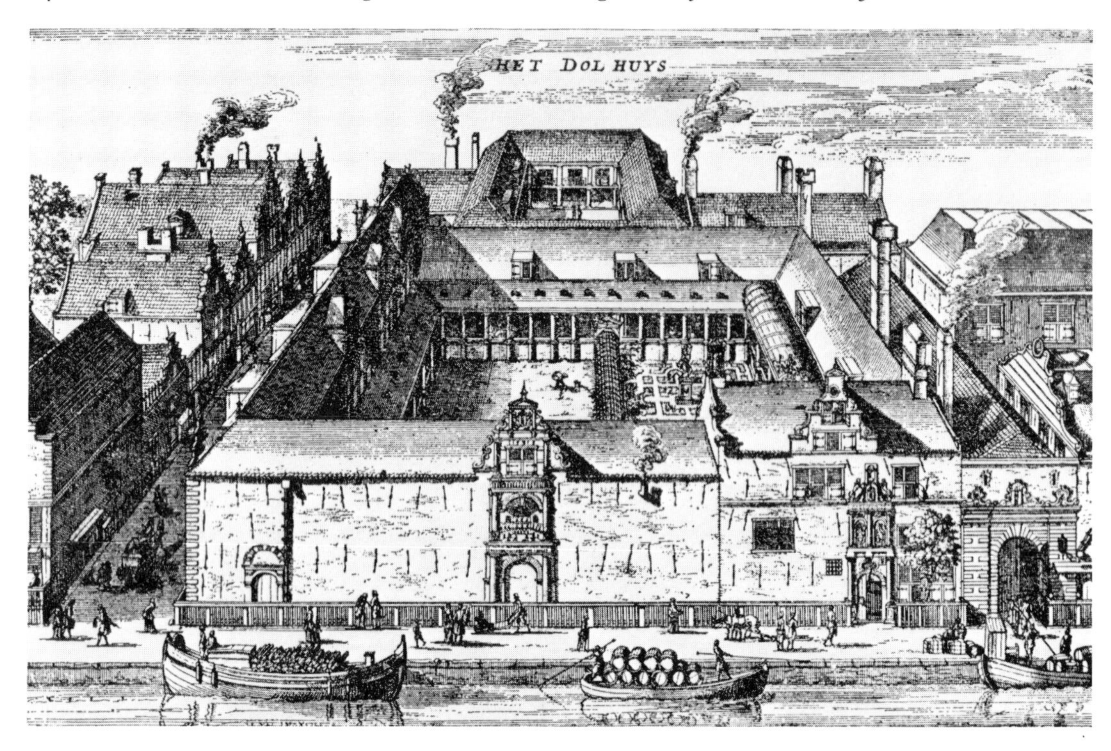

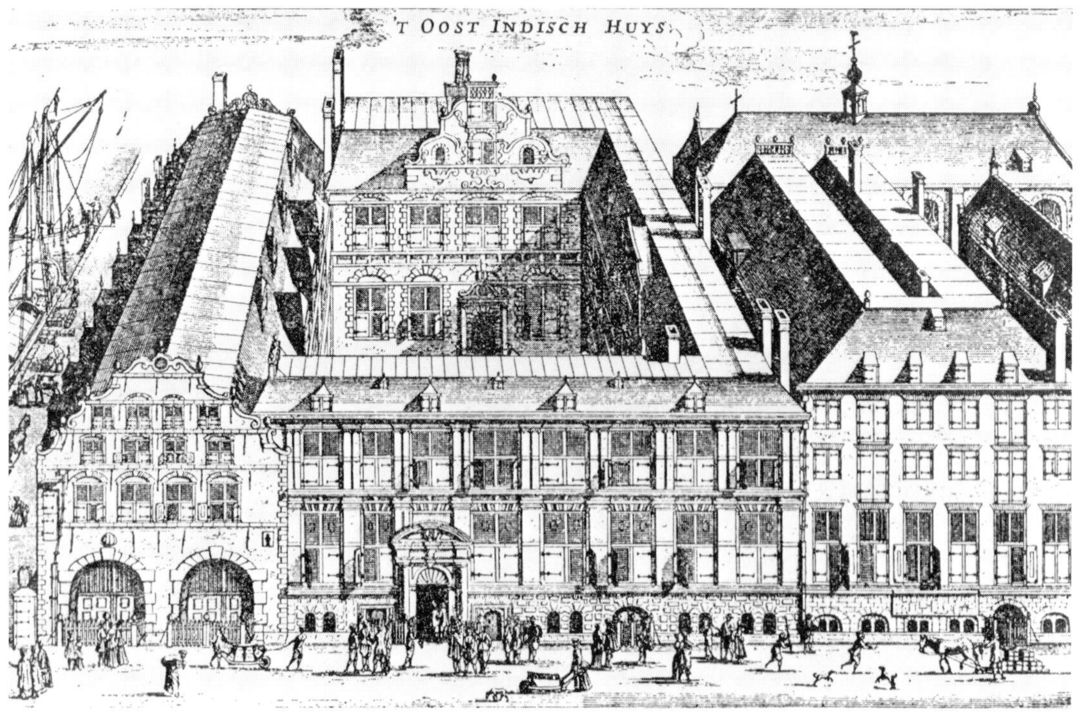

959, 960 *The Dolhuis (wine store) and the Oost-Indisch Huys, Amsterdam, in 1663*

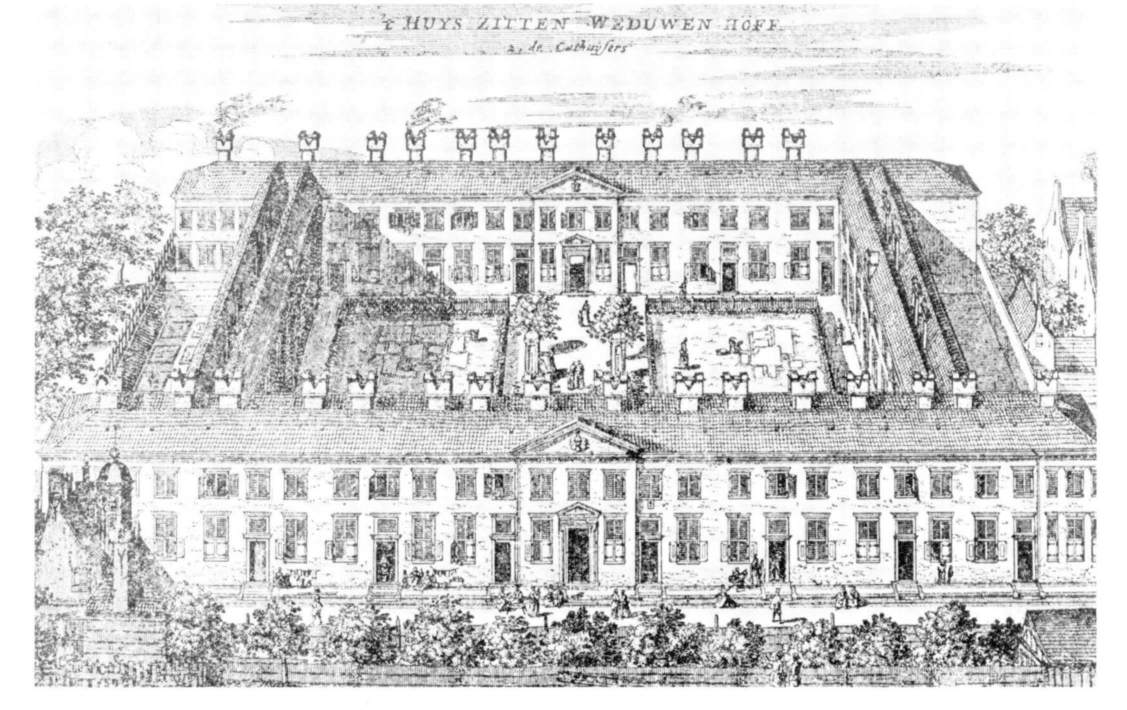

961, 962 *The Burgerweeshuis (boarding school) and the Huiszitten-Weduwenhof (widows' home), Amsterdam, in 1663*

963, 964 *Exterior view and plan of the Mauritshuis, the Hague, by J. van Campen*

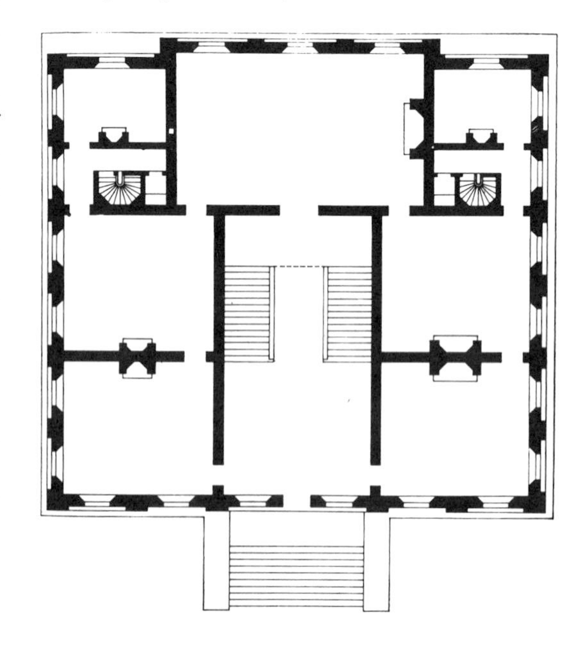

From the 1630s onwards the solidity of the traditional repertoire was undermined, here as in other European capitals, because of the spread of *avant-garde* activity, which questioned the very uniformity of the consistent styles. In Holland a new generation of planners arose who were trained not in practical building but in painting: Paulus Moreelse (1571–1638), later Jacob van Campen (1595–1637), Salomon de Bray (1597–1664) and Pieter Post (1608–69). These last, contemporaries of François Mansart, Bernini and the great Dutch and European classical painters, adopted the vocabulary of orthodox classicism and used it to create a series of new building organisms, conceived as exceptions in the normal fabric of the town.

In 1627 de Bray became chief architect of Haarlem in the place of de Key; he provided the city with a series of new monumental works (e.g. the Zijlpoort, 1627) and in 1661

965, 966 *Exterior view and plan of the Amsterdam town hall, now the royal palace, by J. van Campen*

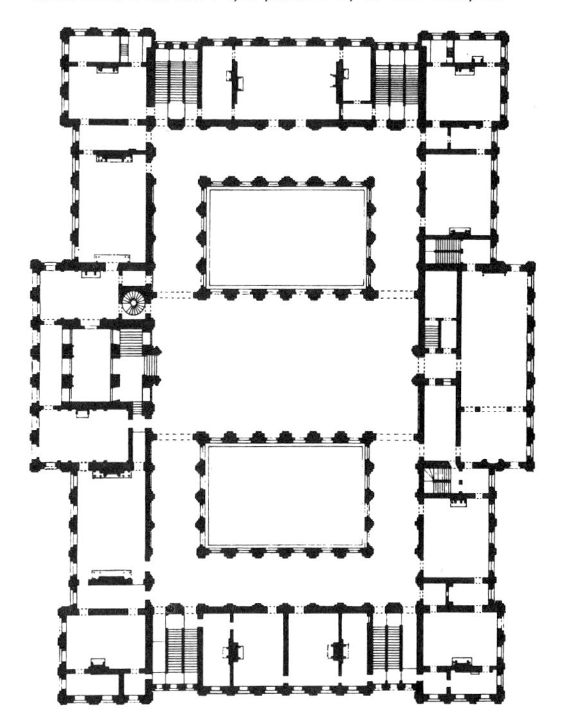

drew up the plan for the extension of the city, which was made definitive in 1671.

In 1633 van Campen, court architect of the house of Orange, designed the first residence in the style of international classicism, the Mauritshuis in the Hague (Figs 963–4) and in 1640 the palace for the *stadhouder* Frederik Hendrik; in Amsterdam in 1638 the Stadsscheuwburg, which we have already mentioned, and in 1648 the great town hall (Figs 965–6); and in Haarlem in 1645 the Nieuwe Kerk, on a central plan. These buildings had an extraordinary success with the intellectual class, precisely because they represented a new world, fondly described in literary contrast with everyday experience, like the exotic costumes of the figures of Rembrandt or the rocky landscapes, with waterfalls, painted by Ruisdael. Vondel wrote a poem to celebrate the town hall at Amsterdam and Constantijn Huygens praised

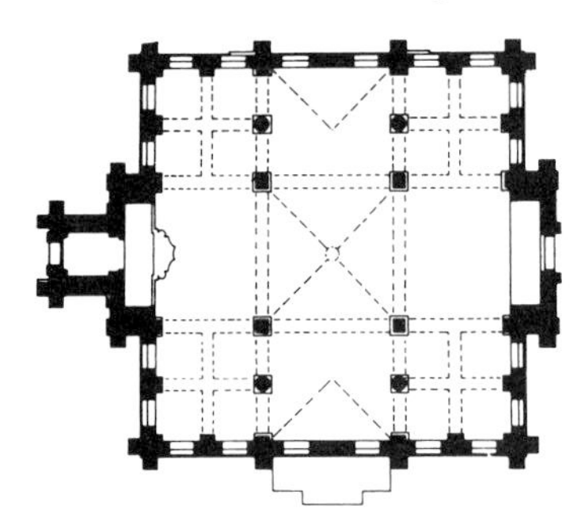

967 *Plan of the Nieuwe Kerk, Haarlem*

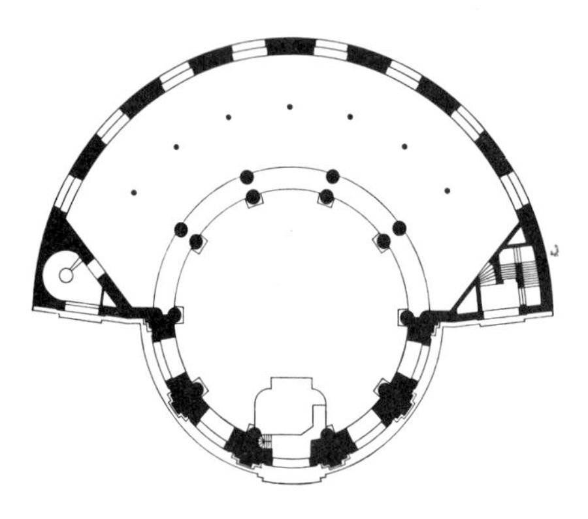

968 *Plan of the Nieuwe Lutherse Kerk, Amsterdam*

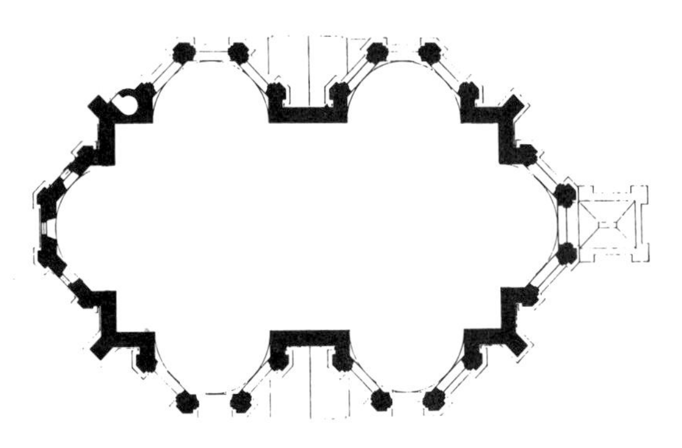

969 *Plan of the Nieuwe Kerk, the Hague*

the architect with these words:[7]

'Van Campen, dien de eer voor eeuwich toe sal hooren
Van't blinde Nederlands mis-bouwende gesicht,
De vuyle Gotsche schel te hebben afgelicht.'

But the most important novelty lay not in the stylistic variations, but in the distributive experiment that they made possible. The town hall of Amsterdam is important not for its mediocre classically-inspired façade, but for the enormous vaulted hall occupying the full height of the building amid the multi-storey *corps de logis*; the Nieuwe Kerk of Haarlem, an organism based on an inscribed cross, took its place in a new range of religious building types independent of the traditional ones, together with the Marekerk of Leiden (by Arent van's-Gravesande, 1639; an octagonal plan), the Nieuwe Lutherse Kerk of Amsterdam (by Adrien Dortsman, 1668: a fan) and the Nieuwe Kerk of the Hague (by Pieter Noorwits, 1649; two interlinked four-lobed spaces) (Figs 967–9).

Post, who succeeded van Campen as court architect, synthesized the classical elements with the traditional ones; also in 1643 he provided a plan for the extension of Haarlem, which was never implemented because of the war with England.

One of the pupils of van Campen, Philip Vingboms (1608–78), also a painter and architect, built a series of monumental houses on the canals of Amsterdam, where the steep roofs, instead of being clearly revealed on the façade, were concealed by classical cornices or pediments, and traditional decorations were replaced by the canonic ones.

The relationship between architecture and figurative painting – the latter considered as a formal apprenticeship for the latter, in accordance with Renaissance custom – was a minor and short-lived episode; but the relationship between architecture and landscape painting must be considered, because it is a constant feature of Dutch artistic culture.

970 Landscape with dunes, *by Philips Koninck, 1664. Boymans museum, Rotterdam*

The painter of landscapes had nothing to do with architects: he worked in a separate field, which did not lend itself to personal eclecticism, indeed tended towards rigid specialization. Not only were there separate groups of painters of country landscapes – van Goyen, Cuyp, Dujardin, Ruisdael, van de Velde, Hobbema – and of town views – van der Heyden, Berckheyde – but even painters who limited themselves to reproducing certain particular subjects: in the first group, van de Cappelle and Bakhuyzen painted only sea pieces, van der Neer winter landscapes, Potter countrysides with herds, Wouwerman landscapes with horses; in the second group, Saenredam and Emanuel de Witte painted only church interiors. The conceptual origin of these specializations was similar to that of the master builders we have already mentioned: they were connected to the objective subject matter, not the subjective form of the work. Furthermore these 'capillary researches'[8] which explored all the aspects of the visible world with a craftsman's patience and with impeccable technical mastery, helped ordinary people to perceive urban and architectural scenes as unified, organized realities; the architectural images were always presented as backdrops to everyday life, not as self-sufficient perspective spectacles.

In this way the sense of the organic nature of the urban scene, inherited from medieval culture, was retained in the new perspective culture and transmitted to the culture of late classicism, naturalistic and critically aware.

The prosperity attained and the alterations already introduced into the urban and rural landscape caused the functioning of the Dutch economy to change at the end of the seventeenth century; building operations, made necessary by productive and commercial needs, became a type of investment which largely replaced the ones usual in trade and industry. In 1673 William Temple described the 'new city' of Amsterdam with admiration, and observed: 'the extent is so spacious, and the buildings of so much greater beauty and cost than the old, that it must have employed a vast proportion of that stock which in this city was before wholly turned into trade'.[9]

Dutch ships and fortifications repelled the assault of the armies of Louis XIV, and Dutch merchants successfully resisted Colbert's economic strategy. None the less the Dutch monopoly of sea trade had to come to terms with the growing power of England, and was not expanding, but aiming to conserve what it had.

Though prosperity continued, the intellectual fervour which had sustained the previous phase of expansion was fading out in the new mood of satisfied conservation. By the Peace of Nijmegen the main figures of the 'golden age' were already dead: van Campen as early as 1657, Rembrandt and Post in 1669, de Witt in 1672, Vermeer in 1675, de Ruyter and Stalpaert in 1676, Spinoza in 1677, Vondel in 1679.

The political and cultural synthesis attained after the wars of independence, though it successfully preserved an internal balance and was to be long-lasting, could no longer bear comparison with the new European developments; it was linked to a dimension of civil life and intellectual experiment that had already been virtually superseded in other countries. From this period and throughout the eighteenth century the economy, and the power and culture, of Holland coexisted with other realities, and dealt with the transformations arising from them; some of the values elaborated in the Dutch experiment – the republican ideal, religious tolerance, the new forms of commercial and financial organization, hydraulic techniques, the feeling for man-made landscape, a new visual experience of forms under light and a new series of scientific experiments on the natural world – became the common heritage of European culture, but tended rather to be developed in other countries, under other forms of civic life.

The presence and prosperity of the Dutch republic, from the last decades of the sixteenth century onwards, proved that the dominant characteristics of European culture and political life – the centralization of power, religious intolerance, conformism and obsequiousness to authority – were neither exclusive nor inevitable; they were the proof, as Huizinga says, that the spirit of the age 'was not here, as elsewhere, embodied in absolutism'.[10]

The political constitution based on municipal autonomy, the specialization of painting according to content and the planned development of the city still belonged to the medieval tradition, and revealed that this tradition did contain a useful margin that could still be utilized for new experiments in the age of scientific research and critical thought.

When the theoretical bases of classicism and authoritarian institutions began to be threatened throughout Europe, the Dutch experiment became a valuable point of reference; later, in the century of the Enlightenment, it kept alive an awareness of the need for *rapport* between progress and tradition, though even this moved into second place *vis-à-vis* the revolutionary tasks that were now imminent.

The spread of the *grand goût*

The experience of French classicism, of which we talked in chapter 6, influenced architecture in all European countries from the reign of Louis XIV onwards, and particularly court architecture. This hegemony was indisputable in the artistic as well as the literary field; it was noted with satisfaction by the French and with a variety of reactions, both positive and negative, by writers of other countries.

There are, however, two levels of this phenomenon to be distinguished in every situation. There was the imitation of already established forms – the obvious aspect, and easier to observe – and there was the repercussion of the critical debate on modern classicism, which emerged in France the moment the initial point of balance had been passed, i.e. about 1680. The two components combined, at various times, in different ways; sometimes formal imitations prevailed, in that the importing of classical models *per se* represented an absolute novelty, and the canonic forms acquired a special certainty, which was lasting (for instance in the Russia of Peter the Great); in other cases the novelty was not the formal repertoire, but the new reflected character of the modern classicism, and the example of France intensified an already existing and lively discussion, i.e. hastened the disintegration of historical classicism (in the Catholic countries, and also particularly in England).

The combined effects of these two processes, which took place on various levels, made themselves felt over a long period; the classical forms codified in France during the *grand siècle* continued to be used throughout the world – on their own, or as an alternative to other systems of forms – at least until the end of the nineteenth century; discussion of the validity of classicism, though basically resolved by the middle of the eighteenth century, was continually taken up again almost until our own day, and ceased entirely only when the movement of modern architecture began.

It is not our purpose to describe the enormous multitude of experiments which still use, or which presuppose, the theoretical validity of classical models. We shall follow their succession up to the point where the continuity of the historical process begun in the fifteenth century ceases, i.e. when modern classicism ceases to be considered as a manifestation of historical classicism. At this point the biography of classicism – which is the object of this book – is substantially concluded, and there begins the biography of neoclassicism, or rather that of eclecticism, since the neoclassical tendency soon emerged as one of the possible alternatives for utilizing the whole repertoire of architectural forms of the past.

The classifications of these experiments is difficult; it is possible to group them together according to countries – but in this case the international dimension is lost, and it was one of the most important features of this architectural cycle – or according to levels: court architecture and bourgeois architecture, experimental and routine, but these distinctions tend to be made more rigid than the truth warrants, and they ignore the interaction between one level and another, which was one more salient characteristic of our period.

We shall take an in-between path, distinguishing three geographical groups – continental Europe, England and the colonies overseas – and selecting from each either individual experiments or successions of experiments, as is most suitable.

Continental Europe

In France, as we have said, the architectural undertakings of the *grand siècle* were of two kinds: the transformation of an already important urban organism (Paris) and the creation of a new one (Versailles). The first proved impossible as a transformation of the already urbanized nucleus and as a fundamental alteration of the original pattern, and resolved itself into the formation of a new periphery; the second succeeded in so far as the new organism was not a city made of houses, but a park made of trees, *parterres* and ornamental pools.

In the rest of Europe, too, the undertakings of absolutism can be classified in the same way, because they depended on the same mechanisms and because they directly imitated the French experience (the most original part of which, the contribution by Le Nôtre, was codified by Jean-Baptiste Le Blond (1679–1710) in the treatise *Théorie et pratique du jardinage*, which appeared anonymously in the first half of the eighteenth century as a basic text on the art of gardening). They differed among themselves with the diversity of local circumstances: in some cases authoritarian intervention was weaker in relation to the size of the pre-existing settlement, and produced only single schemes (buildings, avenues, etc.) not co-ordinated into any overall plan; in other cases the intervention outweighed a much weaker pre-existing fabric, and produced a more coherent urban plan, or indeed a new settlement completely governed by the regularity of a plan.

In the Spanish world the first alternative was more usual: the large towns that had grown up in the sixteenth and seventeenth centuries, and had been impoverished by the decline of the late seventeenth century, could only partially be laid out and modernized in the eighteenth.

Madrid already had over 200,000 inhabitants in the sixteenth century, but it remained a great disordered village; the calle Mayor and *plaza mayor* built from the late sixteenth century to the early seventeenth, stand out in successive plans as the only regular features in an irregular city fabric. A programme of further transformation was promoted after 1715 by the new Bourbon dynasty and was carried out by Francisco Antonio Salcedo y Aguirre, *corregidor* of Madrid from 1715 to 1729; the main works were the puente de Toledo, the paseo de la Virgen del Puerto, the improvements to the aqueducts and the fountains. Philip V, grandson of the Sun King, also wanted to create his own Versailles in the mountainous landscape of Castille; he had a plan prepared for the rebuilding of Aranjuez (begun by Herrera in the late sixteenth century and destroyed in 1667), then he laid out the gardens of La Granja near Segovia (1719–23). In 1734 a fire ruined the old castle of Madrid, and the king commissioned a new palace from the famous Juvara, who died two years later and designated his pupil B. B. Sacchetti as his successor; work began in 1738 and carried on over a long period of time. The residence of Aranjuez, too, destroyed by a fire in 1748, was rebuilt by Ferdinand VI in accordance with a plan by Santiago Bonavia, who included an impressive park and a town of 20,000 inhabitants at the service of the court, as at Versailles (Fig. 971). Each of these works remained subordinated to the older fabric; the country residences, some considerable way from Madrid, did not influence its periphery and remained exceptional and isolated episodes.

The later cycle of works by Charles III (1759–88) was more organic. In Madrid the whole circuit of the city was affected by the new *paseos*, that of la Florida to the north, that of las Delicias to the south and especially that of the Prado, completed by the Observatory, the botanic garden and the museum (the west side being occupied by the royal palace); in the outlying region various new agricultural and industrial centres were founded, planned with the criteria of enlightened despotism.

This same Charles of Bourbon was king of Naples from 1734 to 1759. It was a long time since Spanish rule had promoted planned interventions in the populous cities of southern Italy and the islands (if one excepts the reconstruction of the Sicilian cities after the earthquake of 1693, on the spot as with Catania and Augusta or on a new site as with Avola, Granmichele and Noto); the new king, on the other hand, did have an ambitious programme of transformations in accordance with European examples, particularly for the capital, Naples, which in 1742 had as many as 294,000 inhabitants but had grown up on a

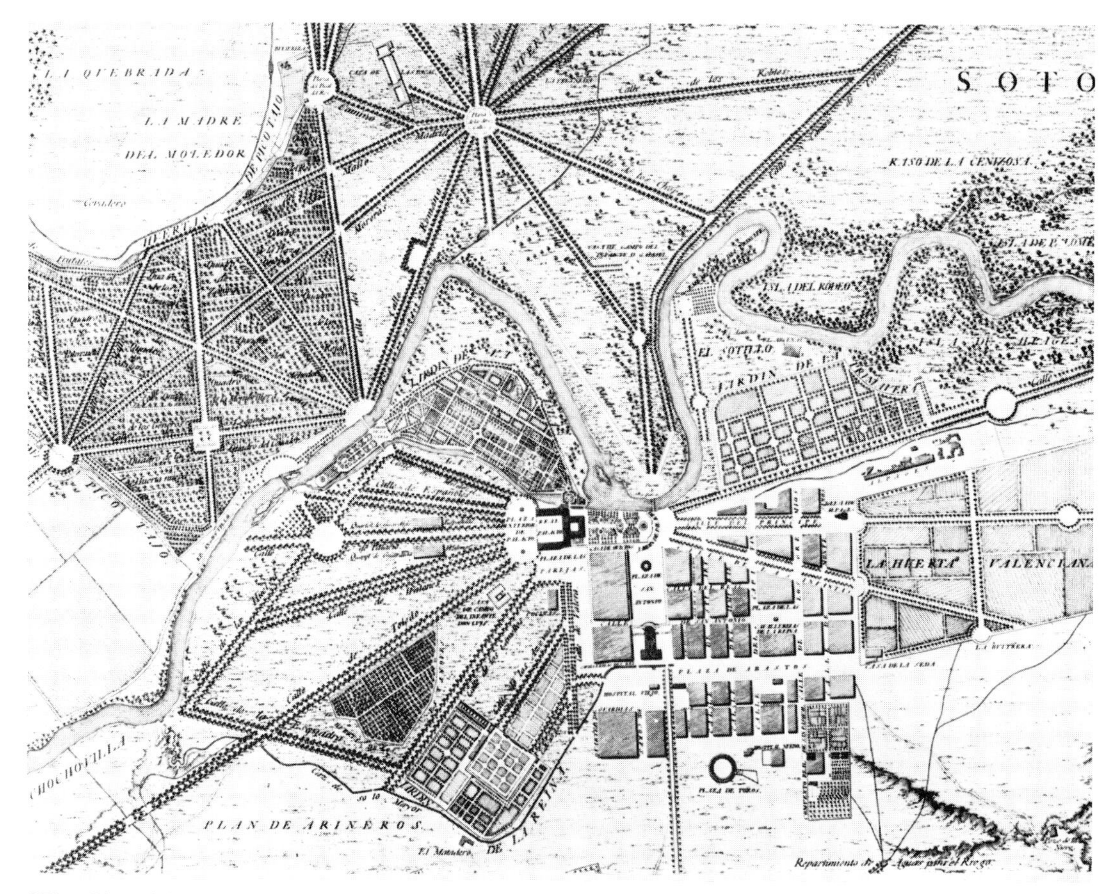

971 *Plan of the park and city of Aranjuez, near Madrid, in 1775*

basis that had remained almost unchanged since the time of Toledo. In the city Charles III modernized the port (1739–45) and put up some public buildings, such as the Tribunale della Salute all'Immacolatella; outside the walls he built the suburban roads: the Marinella, running towards the village of Loreto; the coast road to Mergellina, and the via Foria, where the immense Albergo dei Poveri was built from 1751, designed by Fuga: a hostel for 8,000 persons, which was to have a frontage over 600 metres long.

In the territory behind, from 1743, Charles built the villa of Capodimonte (where the Farnese collection inherited from his mother was housed in 1759) and from 1752 the great villa of Caserta; the first was designed by G. A. Medrano, the second by the famous Vanvitelli, emulating the greatest royal residences of Europe (the main axis of the park which extends over the hill is three kilometres long, as at Versailles; Fig. 972). These great enterprises of the Enlightenment dominate the scenery of city and countryside but, because of their vastly different proportions, did not correct the disorder that had now inevitably supervened.

Turin now stood out among the Italian capitals already laid out in the previous centuries, by virtue of the alterations made to it in connection with the increased importance of the house of Savoy. This capital of the dukes of Savoy, which was based on a reticular Roman pattern, was extended for

972 *Aerial view of the palace and park of Caserta*

the first time in 1620, under Carlo Emanuele I, to a plan by the ducal architect Carlo di Castellamonte, as already mentioned among the experiments of the early seventeenth century (Fig. 975). In the fifty years that followed, the population of Turin rose from 25,000 to 40,000, and in 1673, at the end of the reign of Carlo Emanuele II, the architect Amedeo di Castellamonte, son of the previous architect, planned a second extension (Fig. 976), which took the *zona di comando* – i.e. the complex of the ducal palace, cathedral and castle, hitherto situated in a corner – to the centre of the new urban organism; into the focal points of this plan Guarino Guarini (1624–83) fitted his amazing architectural inventions: the church of S. Lorenzo (designed about 1666), the cappella della Sindone

(1668; Fig. 979) and the Palazzo Carignano (1680). In 1714 Juvara (1676–1736) built the third extension for Vittorio Amedeo II (Fig. 977), at the other end of the Roman nucleus. The pattern of the new districts was based on those of the Roman grid plan; the three operations were linked by an obvious continuity, and it was in their details that they registered the changes in taste of the hundred years that separated them. Only the doubling of piazza Castello – which became a great square of about 200 metres a side, occupied in the centre by the old fortress (Fig. 978) – and the oblique layout of via di Po, which also converges upon the castle, make allusions to the radiocentric symmetry and grandiose dimensions of the Parisian models. In via di Po and piazza Carlina it was decided that the houses 'were all to be of a uniform height, and with the prescribed porticoes and ornaments'.[11] Because of its strategic position Turin could not become an open city, and

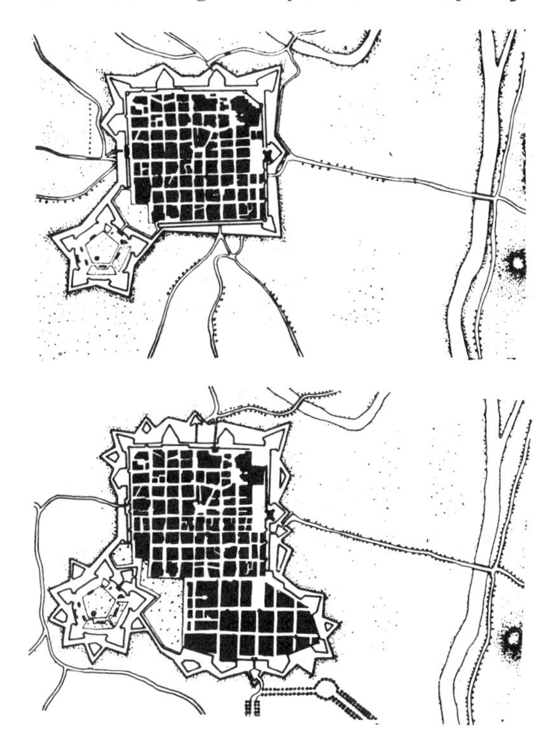

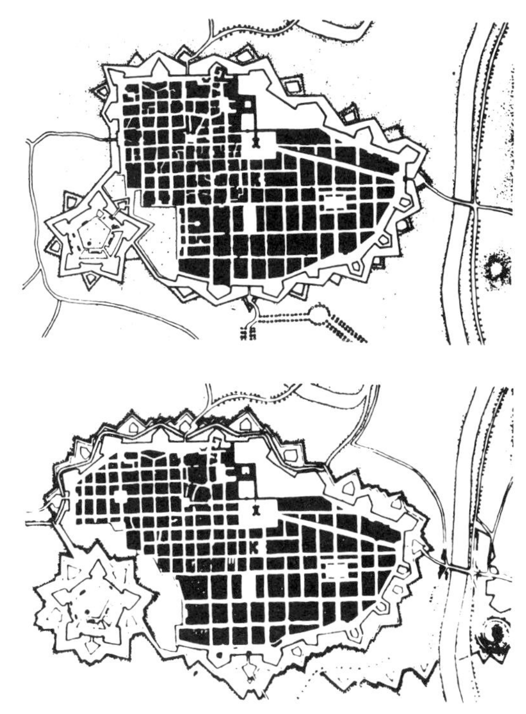

973 *View of via Garibaldi, Turin*
974–977 *Plans of Turin: the Roman city; the first extension, 1620; the second, 1673; and the third, 1714*

978 *Aerial view of piazza Castello, Turin*

until the nineteenth century it remained one of the most important fortified cities in Europe, dominated by the citadel and surrounded by an impressive ring of bastions, enlarged at various stages to make room for successive expansions. Any functional and visual contact between city and countryside was therefore out of the question, and the landscape schemes implemented by Juvara for Vittorio Amedeo II – the basilica of Superga, 1718 and the hunting lodge of Stupinigi, 1729 – were episodes isolated in the countryside, not likely to form a new out-of-town fabric linked to the city (Figs 983–6).

In Protestant Europe the new operations were smoothly fitted in among those described in the first section. Copenhagen, as we have seen, developed within the perimeter of the walls of Christian IV, and the town-plan of the new city – a grid plan, like those of most of the Danish cities of the early seventeenth century – was approved by Frederick II in 1649. From the second half of the seventeenth century French artists appeared at the Danish court. Christian V laid out Nytory Square, at the boundary between the old city and the new, and here in 1688 Lamoureux placed the equestrian statue of the king: after the fire of 1728 Frederick IV had the royal palace rebuilt, as well as many other buildings of the old centre; in 1748 Frederick V founded the academy of fine arts, and commissioned its teachers to carry out a vast programme of

979 *Piazza Castello, Turin, with the royal palace. To the left is the church of S. Lorenzo and the cappella della Sindone by Guarini*

980, 981 *Views of via del Carmine and via di Po, Turin*

982 *Plan of Turin in the eighteenth century*

Contrada di Po
Porta di Po
Piazza Carlina

983 *The hunting lodge of Stupinigi, near Turin*

transformations, which gave the Danish capital a modern appearance. Nikolai Eigtved (1701–54), director of the architectural department from 1751 to 1754, traced the octagonal Amalienborg square and surrounding district, modifying the design of the 1649 plan (Figs 988–9); the Frenchman Nicolas-Henri Jardin (1720–99), who succeeded to his position, built the great domed church on the axis of the square, and in 1764 the sculptor Sally, director of the figurative arts department, made the statue of the king in the centre of the octagon. The new district was completed by a hospital and a botanical gardens.

Stockholm in the middle of the seventeenth century was already a modern city; alongside the medieval nucleus, on the island, the two suburbs of Norrmalm and Södermalm were growing up, on a grid plan pattern. Nikodemus Tessin the Younger (1654–1728) – educated in Italy and in contact with the court of Louis XIV – began to direct work on the royal palace in 1690, and proposed a plan for the monumental reconstruction of the city centre, known from a drawing of 1712 (Fig. 990); it was a monumental sequence formed of the royal palace, Parliament and a regular square with a large domed church. But apart from the reconstruction of the royal palace, Tessin's plan remained inoperative; only at the end of the eighteenth century, under Gustavus III, was the square realized, based on another plan.

984 *Aerial view of Stupinigi and its park*

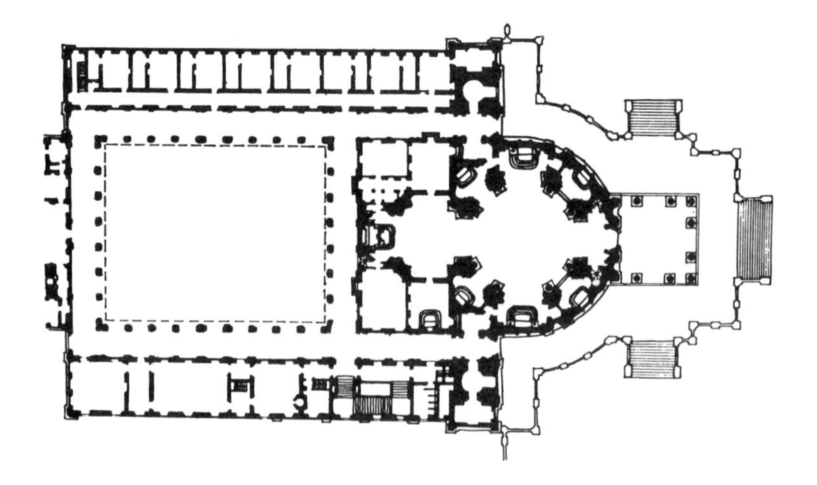

985, 986 *View and plan of the basilica of Superga*

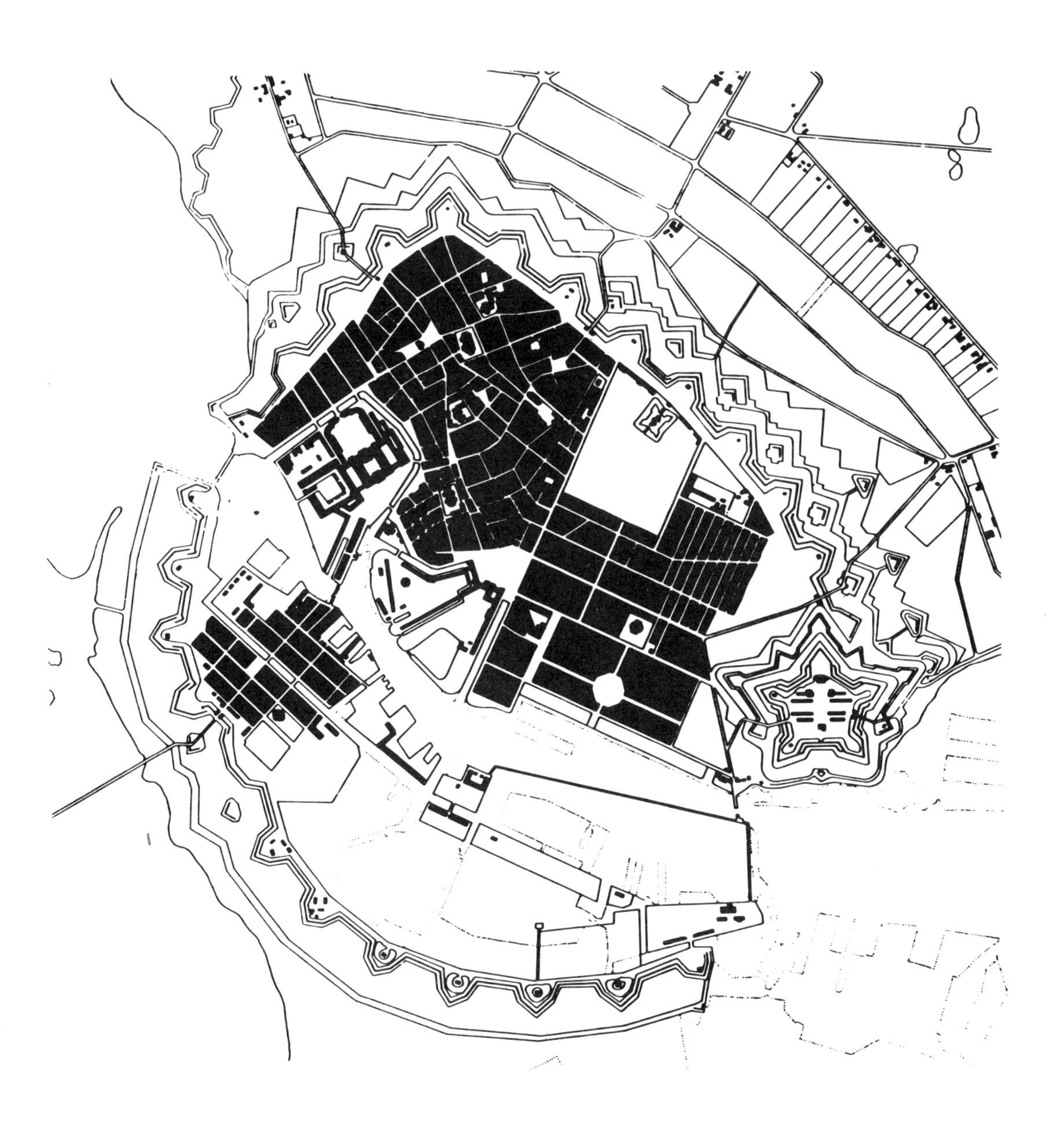

987 *Plan of the built-up area of Copenhagen in 1750*

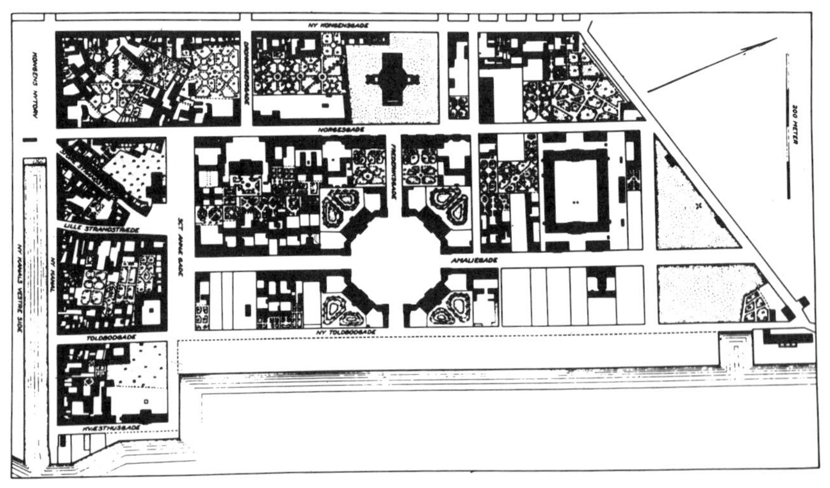

988, 989 *View of the Amalienborg square and the Amalienborg district of Copenhagen*

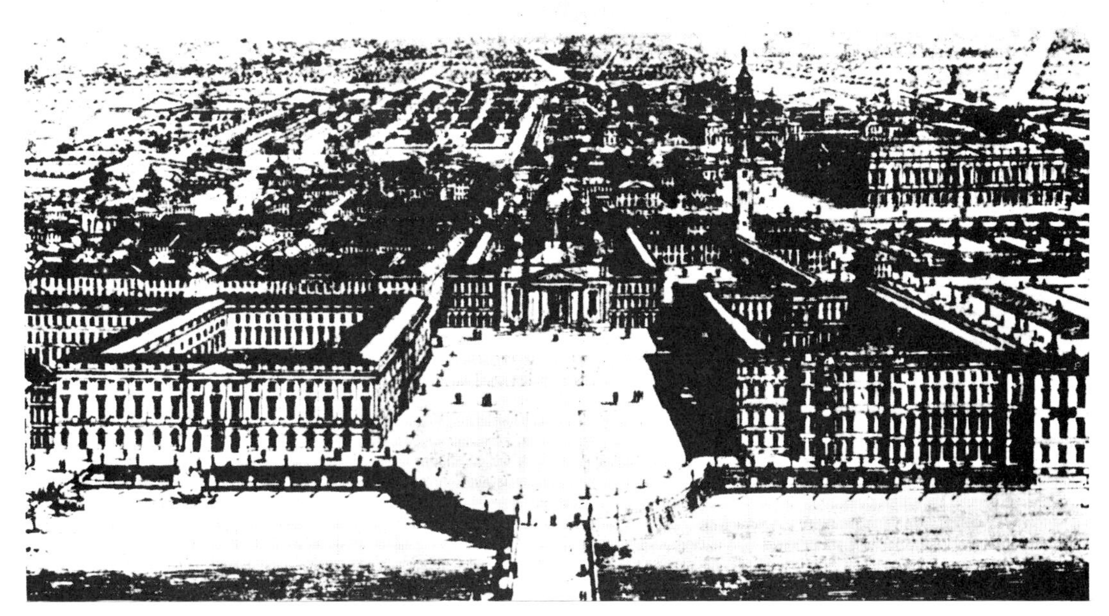

990 *Design by Tessin the Younger for the royal palace and square, Stockholm*

Gardening *à la française* was widespread in Scandinavia as early as the middle of the seventeenth century, while André Mollet was at the court of queen Christina of Sweden; his treatise of 1751 was published in Stockholm and dedicated to the queen. Between 1760 and 1770 Hedwig Leonora, wife of Charles IX, had the Swedish royal parks of Jakobsdal and Drottningholm laid out (the latter was subsequently transformed in the second half of the eighteenth century by Louisa Ulrica, sister of Frederick the Great). Dahlberg's collection of engravings of Swedish castles, published in 1735, shows a series of images that conform closely to the French model. In Denmark Frederick IV built the residence of Fredericksberg (1707) and that of Fredensborg on the occasion of the peace with Sweden.

One of the most important of the German capitals was Vienna, where the imperial dynasty of the Hapsburgs settled after the battle of Kahlenberg (1683) and soon afterwards embarked on a series of impressive works to transform it from a fortified frontier town into a modern metropolis. The suburbs around the fortified city had been largely destroyed during the last siege. A commission presided over by prince Eugene of Savoy, the victorious general, laid down the necessary provisions for the future security of the city; a strip of about half a kilometre wide, the Glacis, was to be left free around the old city and was later laid out as gardens; in 1704 a second fortified circle was drawn around the suburbs, the Linienwall which was transformed between 1718 and 1724 into a regular bastioned circle; around this another controlled zone was laid out, 200 metres wide. Meanwhile the suburbs were being rebuilt at a great rate between the two fortified rings, with no overall plan and following the lines of the old in-running roads (Fig. 992). Here the court dignitaries, including prince Eu-

991 *View of Vienna in 1656 (from Merian)*

gene, built their splendid private residences: the Belvedere (from 1693), the Schwarzenberg palace (1715) and the Liechtenstein palace. On the land between the Donaukanal and the Danube prince Eugene also built the Schloss Hof which, in 1736, together with the Belvedere, became the property of the emperor; the park of the Prater was laid out on the axis of this castle. Fischer von Erlach (1656–1723), architect of Joseph I from 1690 to 1711 and of Charles VI from 1712 to 1723, punctuated the city with monuments intended to express imperial dignity, whose dimensions, grandeur and complexity of formal reference were intentionally remote from those of princely and bourgeois buildings: the Karlskirche of 1716 (Figs 1062–3), the library (1716), the Hofburg (1718), the castle of Schönbrunn designed in 1690 in grandiose dimensions not inferior to those of Versailles; the castle was to stand on the top of a hill, overlooking a vast composition of *parterres* and avenues. But for its actual execution the artist had to fall back upon a more modest plan; the castle stood near a road that went to Vienna, and looked on to a slight upward slope, at the top of which there was to be an open pavilion (later built by Hohenburg in 1775, and called the Gloriette); the garden was laid out in the reign of Maria Theresa (1740–80) by the Dutch designer Steckhoven (Figs 996–1000).

Many other German cities were capitals of one or other of the numerous states into which the old imperial kingdom was divided, some of considerable size even during the Middle Ages, some small or indeed minute. It was in the latter that absolutism was able to work the most coherent transformations, and sometimes to create new organisms, also planned with absolute regularity.

Let us look first at the towns based on traditional plans: Munich, Stuttgart, Hanover and the other bishoprics on the Rhine, where the most important additions were the suburban parks on the edges of the cities. About 1670 the duke Ernst Johann Friedrich

992 *Plan of the eighteenth-century street network of Vienna and Schönbrunn. The tree-lined avenues are shown in black*

993 *Plan of Vienna in 1832*

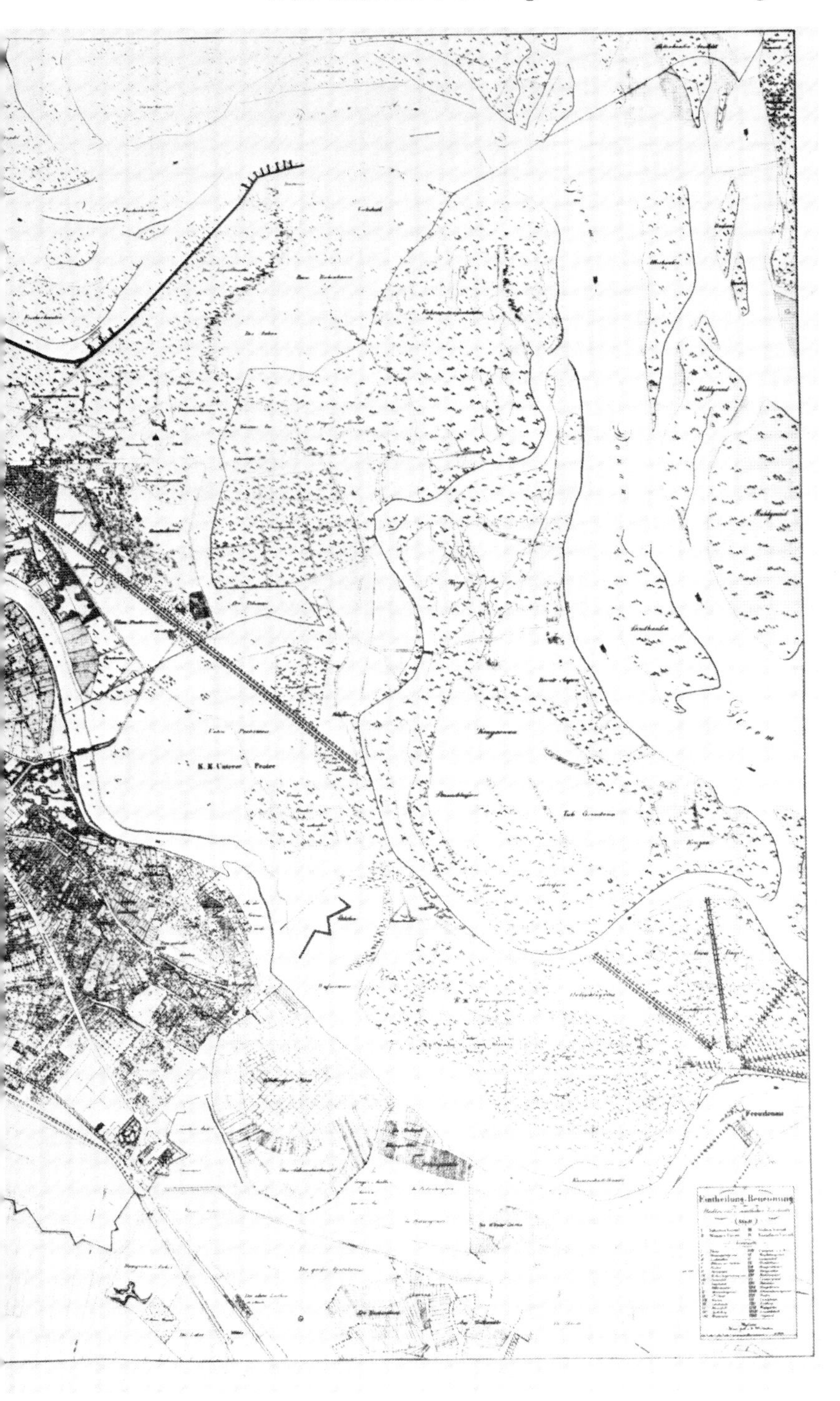
K. K. Unterer Prater
Freudenau

994 *The terrace of the Belvedere with Vienna in the distance, as shown by Schutz*

of Hanover engaged a pupil of Le Nôtre, Charbonnier, to lay out the park of Herrenhausen, while he commissioned the Italian Quirini to build the castle. Max Emanuel of Bavaria, who lived in exile in Paris from 1704 to 1715, took François Girard to Munich, where he completely re-elaborated the two seventeenth-century parks of Nymphenburg and Schlessheim, subordinating their symmetry to an axial canal. Nymphenburg – which became the Bavarian Versailles (Figs 1003–5) – also had a *pavillon à l'indien*, the Pagodenburg, reminiscent of the *Trianon de Porcelaine* by Le Vau, and a neo-Gothic retreat, built about 1725–8. For the archbishop of Cologne, a relative of the dukes of Bavaria, Girard designed the park of Brühl, likewise well-provided with canals and with a Chinese pavilion, known as the '*maison sans gêne*'. In 1715 Ludwig IV of Württemberg

995 *The terrace of the Belvedere today*

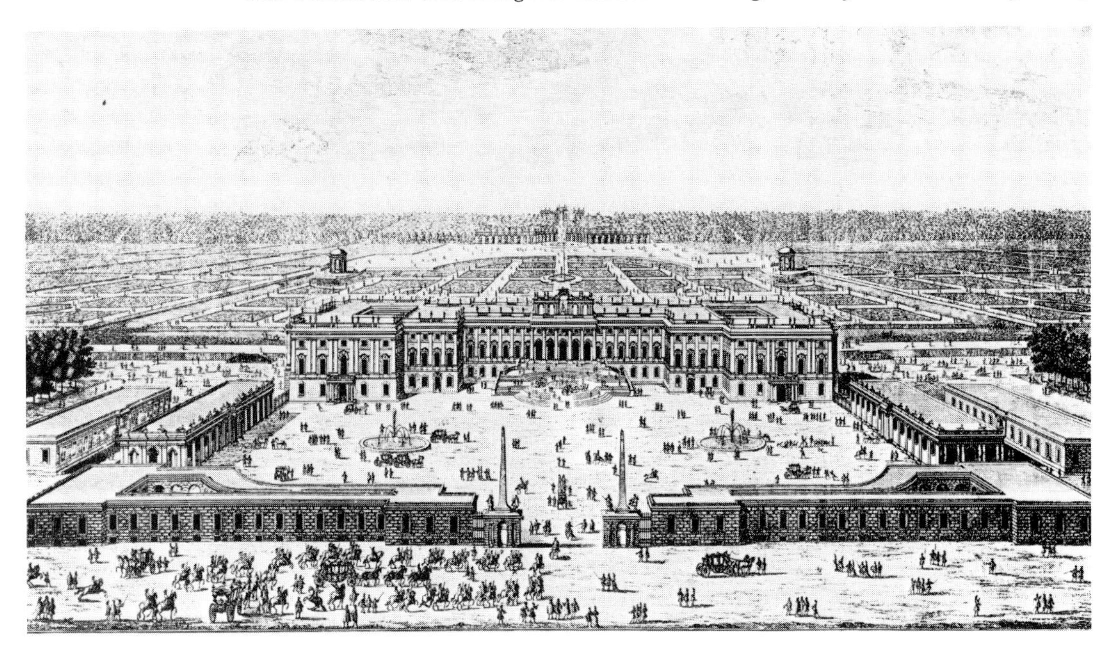

996, 997 *Plans by Fischer von Erlach for the park of Schönbrunn, near Vienna*

998–1000 *Views of the park and castle of Schönbrunn and general plan (from Gothein)*

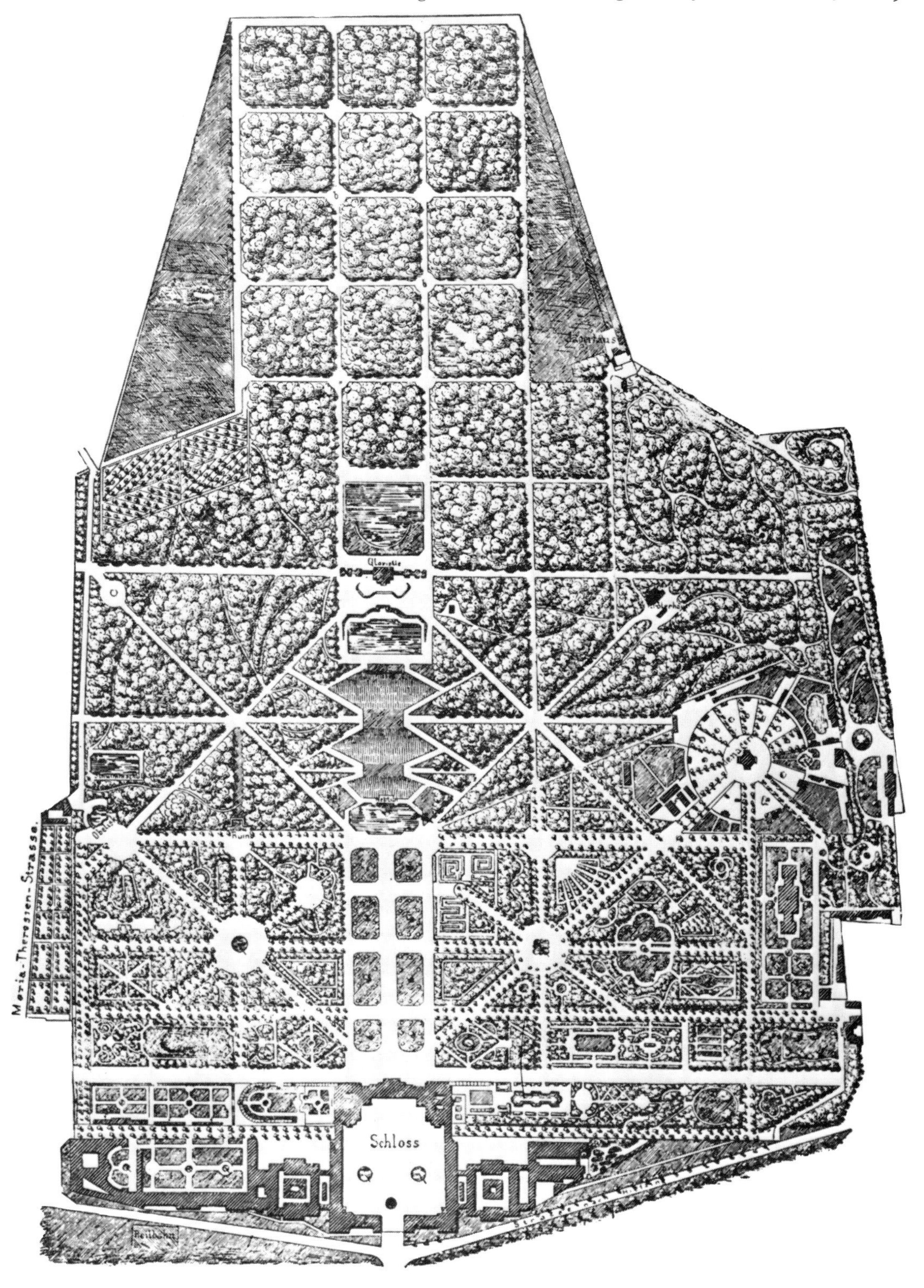
Maria-Theresien-Strasse
Schloss

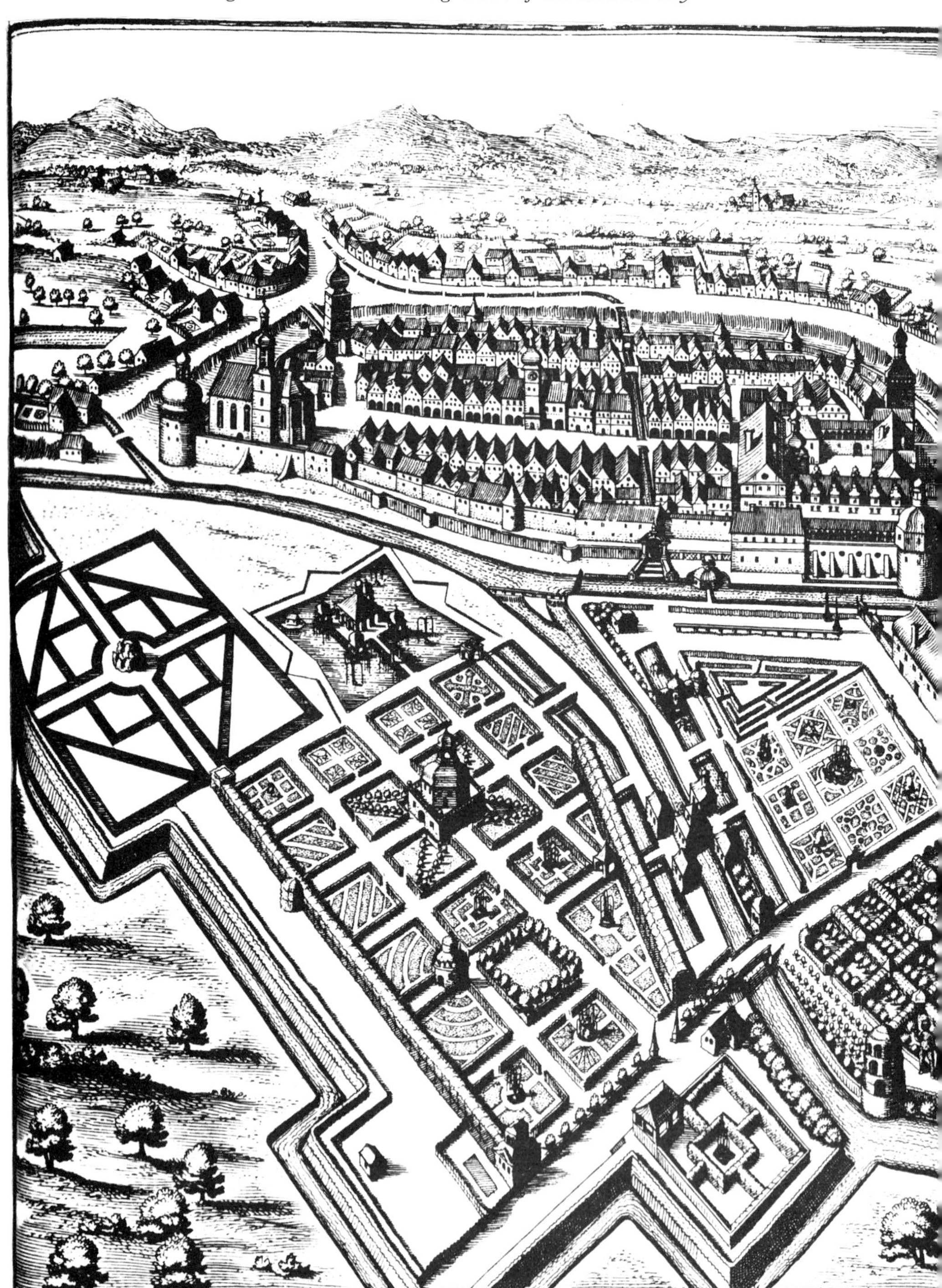

1001 *Schlaccowerdt, a small German city with princely residence and its garden (from Merian, 1650)*

PROSPECT des Dürchleüch
tigen Hochgebornen Fürsten
und Herren Herrn Julij Hein-
rici Hertzogen zü Sachsen
Engern und Westphalen, Re-
sident Schlosses Statt und
Erbaweten Lustgartens zü
Schlaccowerdt.

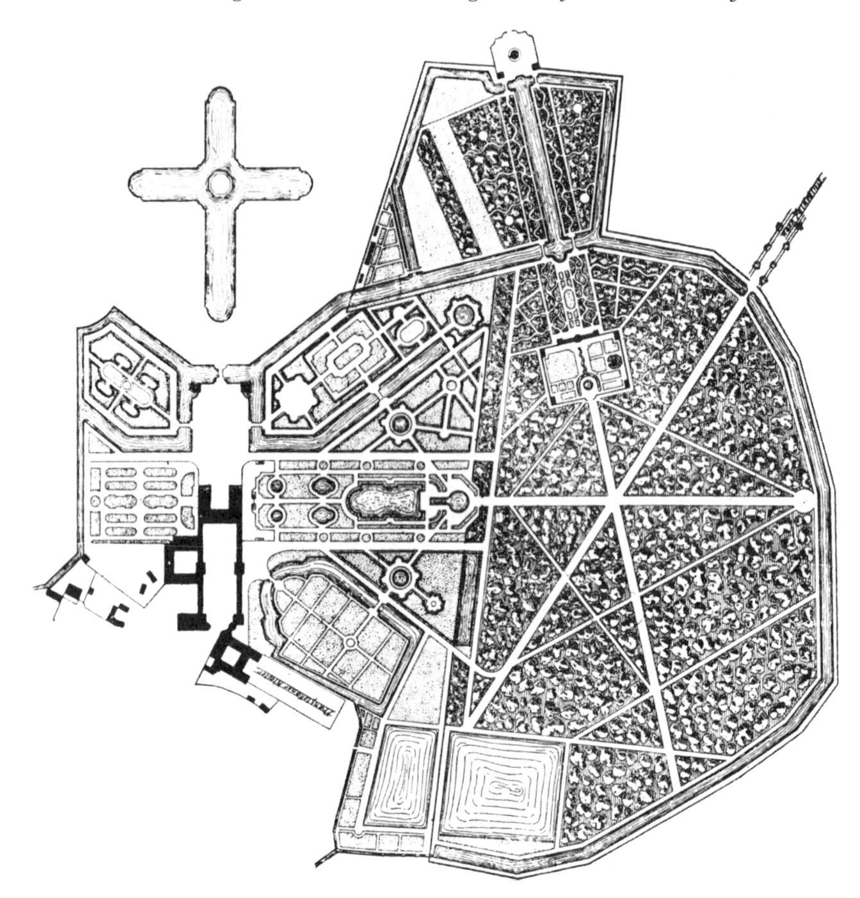

1002 *Plan of the park of Brühl (from Gothein)*

built the palace of Ludwigsburg, near Stuttgart, ingeniously laid out in a hollow in such a way that the castle occupied the lowest position (Figs 1007–8); the designer was Giuseppe Frisoni, an Italian educated in France.

Among the ecclesiastical princes, particularly active in this field, were the members of the Schönbörn family: Lothar Franz, archbishop of Bamberg from 1693 and of Mainz from 1695, built the parks of Marquandsburg and Pommersfelden near Bamberg, La Favorite on the banks of the Rhine near Mainz, and added to his private castle of Gaibach, set halfway up a hillside. Another branch of the family had a large residence near the river Ems, in the purest French style; Damian Hugo, bishop of Speyer, commissioned Balthasar Neumann (1687–1753) to design the park, then in 1728 to complete the interior of his residence of Bruchsal.

In other capitals the urban schemes and parks were fused in a more unitary manner.

Berlin, the capital of Prussia, was formed in the middle of the seventeenth century of two small towns – Berlin and Cölln – one on each side of the Spree; the Elector's palace was situated near Cölln, with a garden on the banks of the river (Fig. 1009). In 1640 Frederick William I came into power and began the expansion of the city, whose population rose from 10,000 to 60,000 between 1650 and 1710. In 1647 the Grand

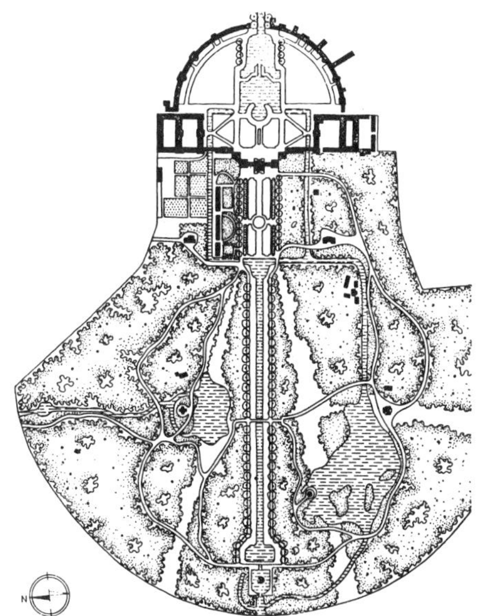

1003–1005 *The park of Nymphenburg, near Munich*

1006 *Plan of Munich and Nymphenburg in 1826*

Schwabing
Bogenhausen
Haidhausen
Ramersdorf
in der Lohe
Obergiesing

1007, 1008 *Two views, taken in opposite directions along the principal axis of the park of Ludwigsburg, near Stuttgart*

Elector opened up an avenue running directly westwards from the palace – the future Unter den Linden – and organized the new districts along the axis: Friedrichswerder (1662), Dorotheenstadt (1674), Friedrichstadt (1688), on a broad grid plan similar to the Scandinavian one. The nucleus of the city – Berlin, Cölln and Friedrichswerder – was enclosed by a ring of fortified walls, built from 1658 to 1685 by the Dutch engineer J. G. Memhardt; the other two districts constituted a 'modern' and planned expansion, the *Vorstadt*, but other suburbs grew up unplanned around the edges of the city. His successor Ferdinand I

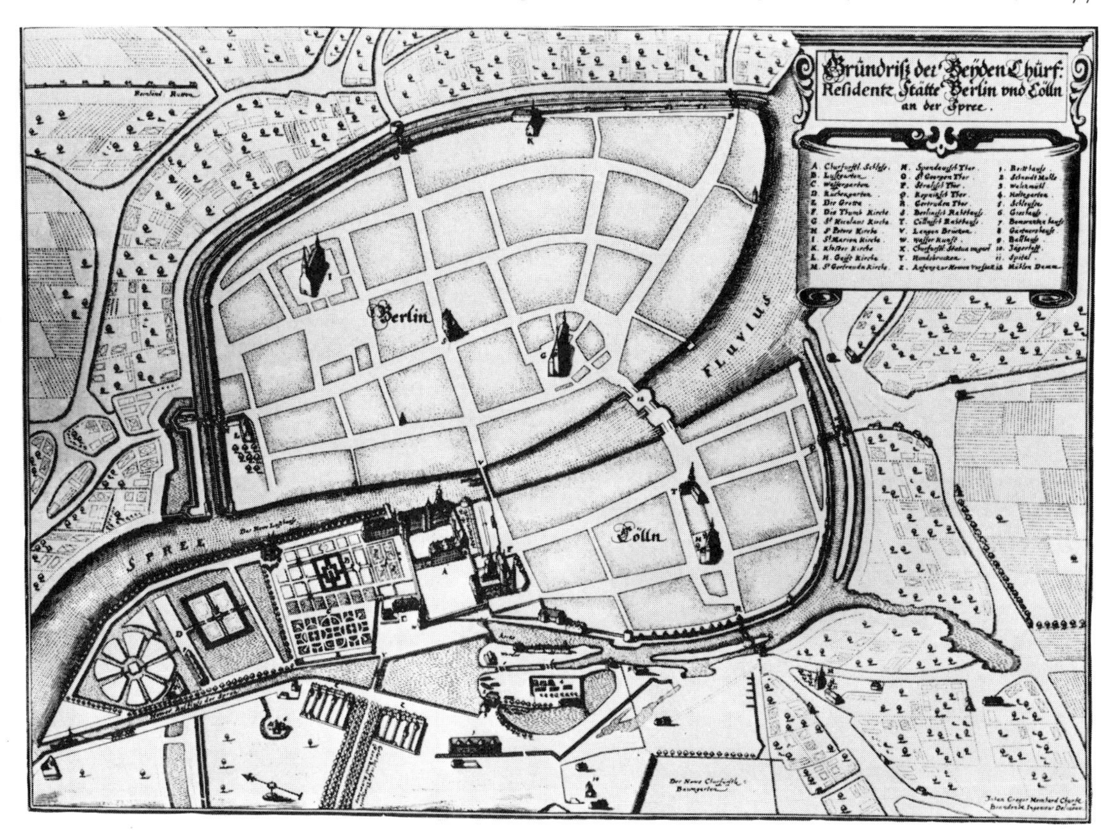

(1688–1713, king of Prussia from 1701) unified the five nuclei and surrounded the agglomeration with a new series of walls, which served mainly as a customs barrier to protect city industries; after the revocation of the edict of Nantes many French Protestants settled in Berlin – around 1700 they accounted for about a quarter of the population – and made a considerable contribution to the life of the city. From 1721 onwards Friedrichstadt was extended by means of a series of diagonal streets and open spaces of regular shapes, square, octagonal and circular. Andreas Schlüter (1662–1714), sculptor and royal architect, while working on the royal palace and Zeughaus, designed a monumental square at the point of juncture between the palace and the old city, which was never to be built. After the coronation of Frederick II

1009 *Plan of Berlin and Cölln in 1652 (from Merian)*
1010 *Plan of the eighteenth-century additions to Berlin (from Gutkind)*

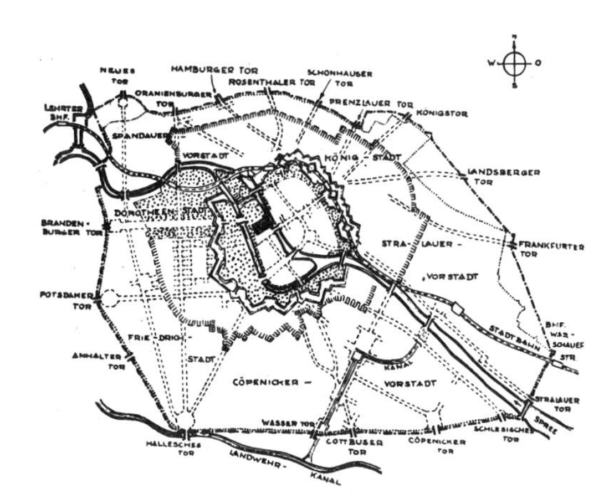

(1740) the city continued to develop with ever-increasing rapidity; in 1756, on the eve of the Seven Years' War, it had 100,000 inhabitants, in 1786, at the death of the king, it had over 150,000. Frederick II usually resided in Potsdam in his castle, which we shall discuss later, and encouraged the development of the capital with forcible operations unparalleled in Europe, which broadly fixed the features of its building structure well into the future. These operations were of two types: barracks, and collective multi-storey houses, built by the state. The barracks made up a considerable part of the city organism, in that the garrison, between the end of the Seven Years' War and the death of Frederick, rose from 20,000 to 36,000 men, i.e. one-fifth of the residential population. The collective houses were not unlike the barracks: the state built the load-bearing walls and roofs, in accordance with uniform models, and put them at the disposal of private individuals; hence the name *Immediatbauten*. In this way the king artificially achieved an urban development as yet unattainable by private enterprise, and obviated the shortage of accommodation and price rises for some time; but he established a style which was to remain constant for a long time and which was to become obsessive in the city in the nineteenth century. In the *Vorstadt* Frederick II began the building of a new complex of monumental buildings: the Opera, built by Knobelsdorff, a new royal palace and the academy of sciences; Algarotti, in a letter to the architect in 1743, saw here the realization in building of the king's own cultural idea – power which protects the arts and sciences – and suggested a name for it that already reflected the new neoclassical spirit, the 'Forum of Frederick'.[12] This composition, too, was formed of the juxtaposition of homogeneous unarticulated blocks around a square, and received its definitive form only at the end of the nineteenth century.

Near Berlin Frederick I built the parks of Oranienburg and Charlottenburg, and profited from the abundance of water in the soil of Brandenburg to adorn his gardens with exceptionally extensive lakes and canals (though he always insisted upon the great parade grounds for military exercises in front of his castles); Frederick II inherited his taste for gardens from his mother – who from 1725 lived in her villa on the Spree, called Mon Bijou – and in 1744, soon after his coronation, began to build the park of Sans-Souci near Potsdam, for which he himself drew the first designs. The royal architect George Knobelsdorff (1699–1753) directed the execution of the works, combining the geometrical standards of the French garden with the naturalistic ones that had just become fashionable in England (Figs 1011–14).

Dresden, the capital of Saxony, was severely damaged by fire in 1685; successive rulers – Augustus the Strong from 1694 to 1733, Augustus II from 1733 to 1763 – had it rebuilt in accordance with new criteria which combined the rationality of the regulations against further fires with the sweeping spirit of the great green spaces, daringly incorporated into the heart of the city, on the two banks of the Elbe. Caspar von Klengel (1630–91) traced the plan for the complete reconstruction of the older part of the city on the right bank of the Elbe; this became the *Neue Königstadt*, with the extremely broad and straight *Hauptstrasse* leading on to the bridge. On the left bank the medieval *Altstadt* was retained, but the space towards the river was cleared, around the castle, for the Zwinger by Matthaeus Daniel Pöppelmann (1662–1736) – a garden enclosed by a fantastical architectural screen, completed between 1709 and 1718 (Fig. 1015) – then in 1722 the Frauenkirche by Georg Bähr (1666–1738), in 1736 the Hofkirche by Gaetano Chiaveri (1689–1770). Pöppelmann and his collaborators – R. Leplat, Z. Longuelune, J. C. Knöffel, J. H. Schwarze – realized a large number of palazzi and parks for the court (the Japanese palazzo (1727–33) which

1011 *View of the park of Charlottenburg, near Berlin*

1012, 1013 *Views of the castle and park of Charlottenburg*
1014 *Plan of the park of Sans-Souci, near Potsdam*

1015 *The Zwinger, Dresden, after restoration*

commands the symmetrical design of the western part of the Königstadt, the 'great gardens' on the outskirts), and for the noble families. From 1721 to 1724 Leplat laid out the Grünes Gewölbe to house the sovereign's jewel collection.

Outside the city the Elbe, transformed into a monumental water course, ran through the parks of Pillnitz (1720), Gross Sedlitz (1723) and Ubigau (1724). In this way the elements artificially linked in the natural countryside coexisted within an exceptional balance, only partly disturbed by the later development of the city.

Kassel, capital of the landgrave of Assia-Nassau, included an older nucleus (the *Altstadt*) on the left bank of the Fulda and a suburb on the right bank (the *Unterneustadt*); the castle is at the south-west corner of the *Altstadt* and communicates with the park of the Orangerie, between two branches of the river (Fig. 1020).

The extension was the work of the French Protestants, expelled in 1685 after the revocation of the edict of Nantes; they brought to Germany a contribution of men, capital and ideas which, as we have said, influenced the development of Berlin and elsewhere also produced some new planned settlements where the exiles continued to live together: the new towns of Erlangen (1686) and Karlshafen (1699), the extension of Anspach (1685), of Crefeld (on three separate occas-

ions, in 1698, 1711 and 1739) and that of Kassel (1688). Here they received a section of land from the landgrave Charles to the west of the *Altstadt*, where they built a grid plan town on a plan by Paul du Ry, the *Oberneustadt*; this same du Ry, who had already worked for William of Orange at Maastricht, laid out the castle and adjoining gardens for the sovereign (Fig. 1021).

For some decades the new addition remained isolated outside the walls; when these were destroyed a link-up was effected by means of a great rectangular space, the Friedrichsplatz, and later with a second circular space, the Königsplatz, designed by nephew of Paul's, Louis du Ry, who in 1748 was working in Paris under J.-F. Blondel. The whole organism was enclosed by a new circle of walls in 1781 (Fig. 1022).

From 1700 to 1717 the park of Wilhelmshöhe was built on a hill near Kassel, to a plan

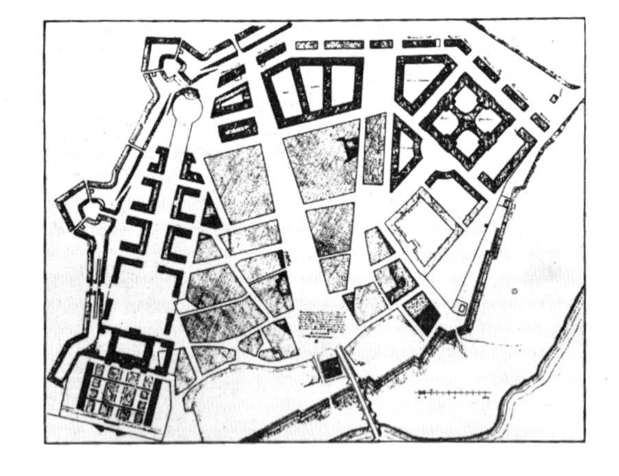

1016 *A view of the 'great gardens' of Dresden in 1719*
1017 *Plan of the* Neue Königstadt *of Dresden in the eighteenth century*

1018, 1019 *Two views of Dresden painted by B. Bellotto*

by the Italian G. F. Guernieri: a sloping axial composition of terraces, flights of steps and waterfalls, which culminates in a copy of the 'Farnese Hercules'. Another park in the French style, Wilhalmsthal, designed by F. de Cuvilliés, was laid out in 1745.

Würzburg was an old bourgeois town dominated by the castle of Marienberg, the Residenz of the Prince Bishop (Fig. 1024). Johann Philip Franz von Schönbörn, elected in 1719, decided to move his capital from the castle to the town, and in 1722 appointed a building committee to carry out the necessary transformations; here the dominant personality was Balthasar Neumann, a captain in the military engineers, educated at the imperial court of Vienna.

The busy, non-military organism of Würzburg was naturally much more difficult to transform than the military organism of Mannheim. The first step to be taken was to choose an unoccupied site at the edge of the medieval built-up area for the bishop's new Residenz; a large square separated the palace from the town, and the gardens, as at Mannheim, abutted on to the fortified perimeter. The plan was worked out with the assistance of the main German architects of the time, Johann Dientzenhofer (1665–1726), Maximilian von Welsch (1671–1745) and Lucas Hildebrandt (1688–1751), but Neumann became the co-ordinator of their contributions; in 1723 in Paris he put the finishing touches to the plans that had already been prepared, after consultation with Boffrand

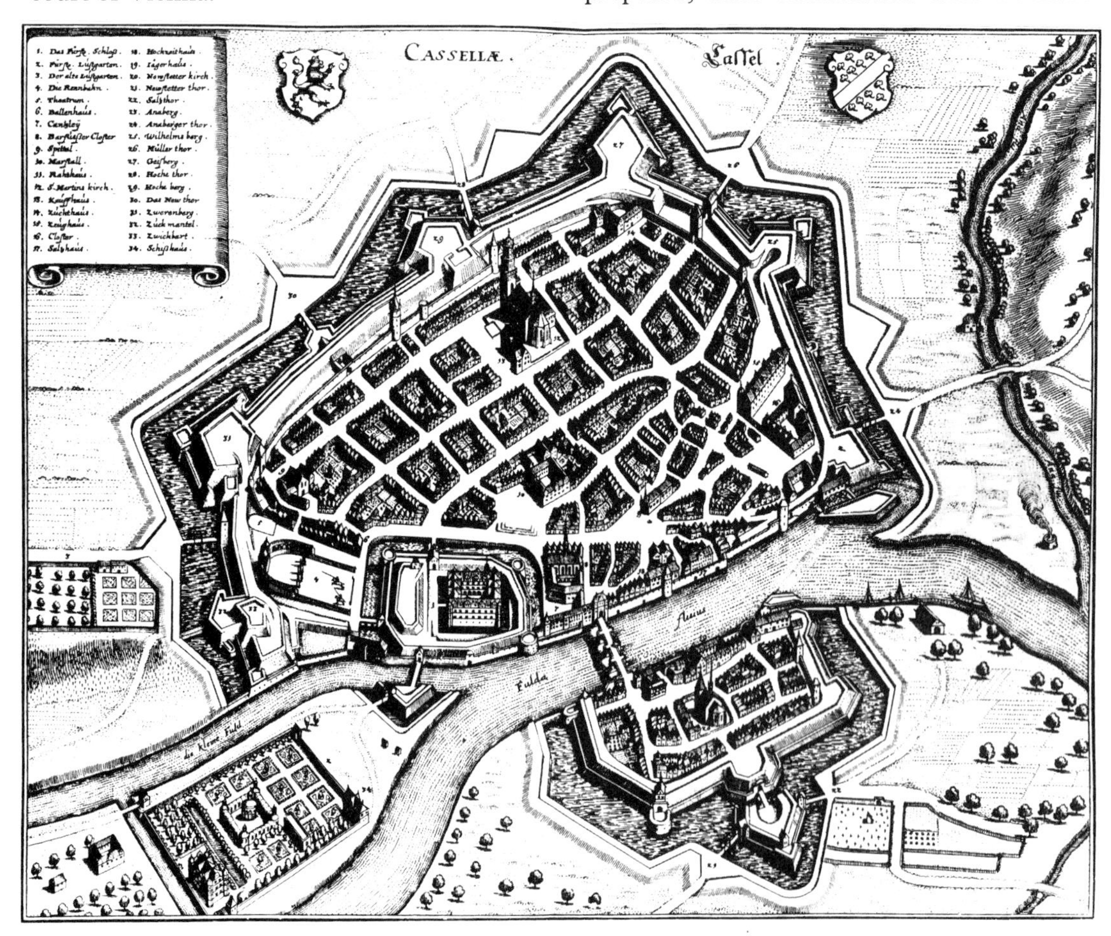

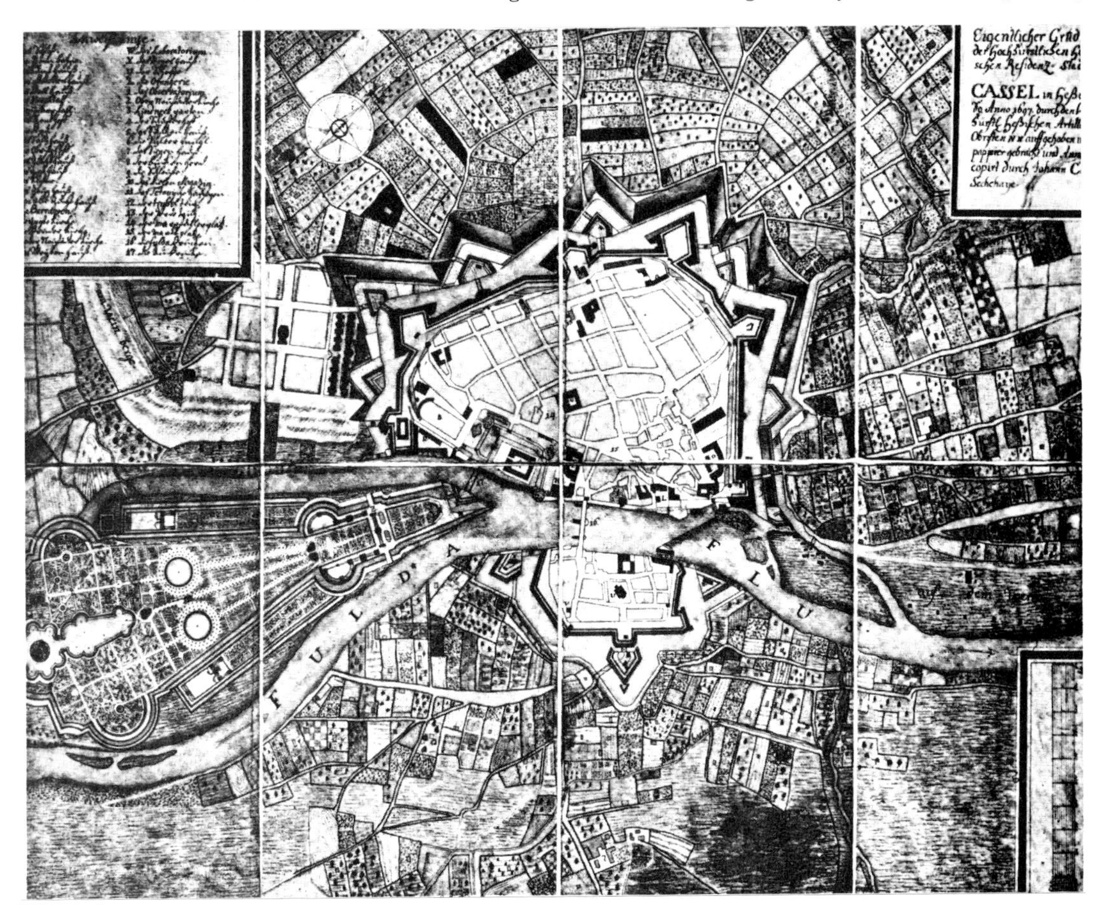

1020 *(left) Plan of Kassel in the middle of the seventeenth century (from Merian)*
1021 *Plan of Kassel in 1717*
1022 *The squares linking Kassel and the* Oberneustadt, *1786*

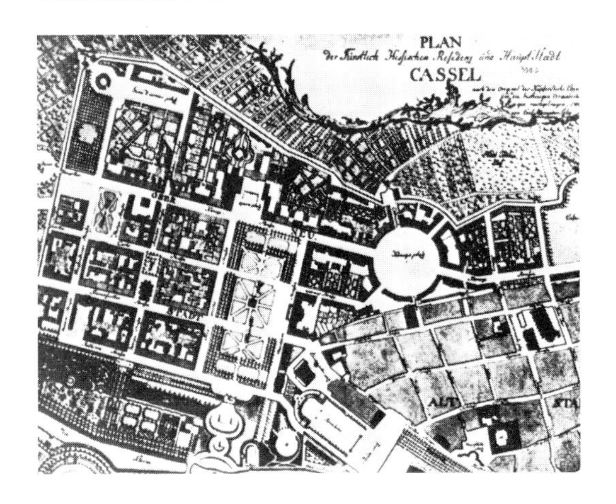

and Robert de Cotte, and in 1729, when Johann Philip Franz was succeeded by his cousin Friedrich Karl, Neumann was appointed chief architect of the palace and town.

The transformation of the town was completed, in its essentials, from then onwards until the death of the new prince, in 1746; Neumann built the bishop's palace, with its amazing interior frescoed by Tiepolo (Figs 1027–33), designed the gardens (1730) and the chapel of the Nikolausberg (1747), had out an encircling *boulevard* along the walls, moved the market place, laid down the regulations for private building – which included the respecting of road alignments and the abolition of projections – and directed the building of the roads, bridges and aqueduct. The programme also provided for the

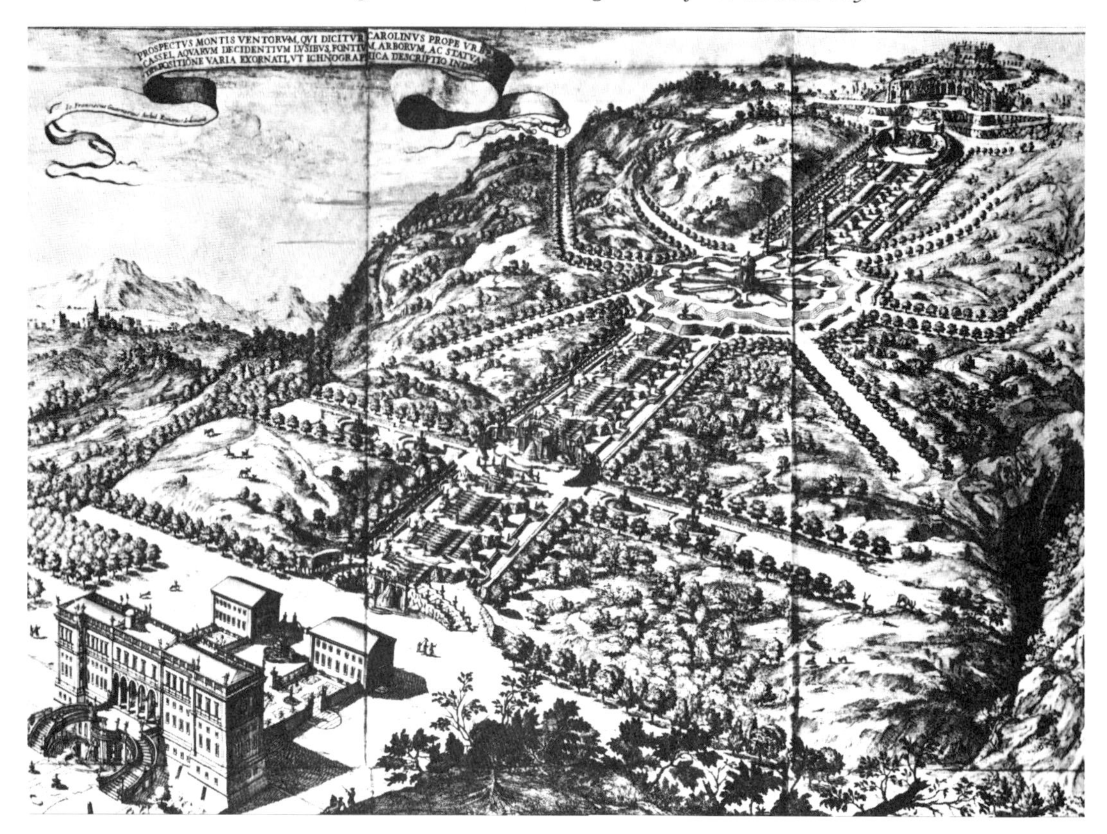

building of a commercial storehouse and a public garden.

The organic quality of the medieval plan and the hilly nature of the ground prevented the use of a geometrical layout on a large scale, but for this reason too Würzburg emerged as the most unified of all the German *Residenzstädte*, where the arbitrary nature of the eighteenth-century activities was balanced by the logic and historic nature of the older settlement.

In short, in two cases the new capital was an organism designed *ex novo*, and could have a completely regular shape, that is to say be completely subordinated to the Residenz which occupied the main perspective focal point.

Mannheim, founded in 1607 as a fortress at the meeting of the Rhine and the Neckar, was

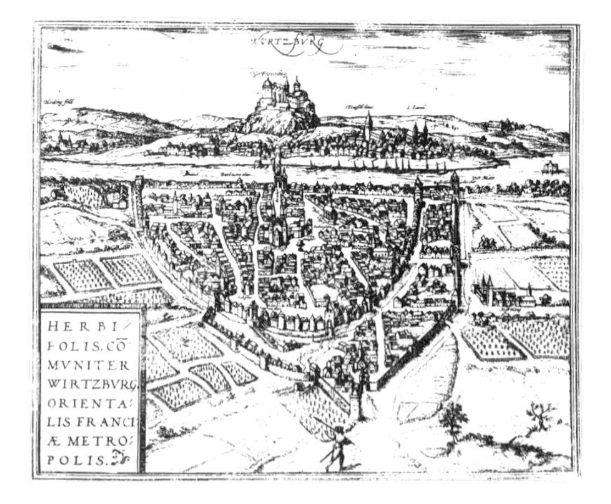

1023 *View of the park of Wilhelmshöhe*
1024 *Plan of Würzburg in the sixteenth century*
Opposite
1025 *Portrait of B. Neumann, from Tiepolo's frescoes in the bishop's palace at Würzburg*
1026 *Plan of Würzburg in the eighteenth century*

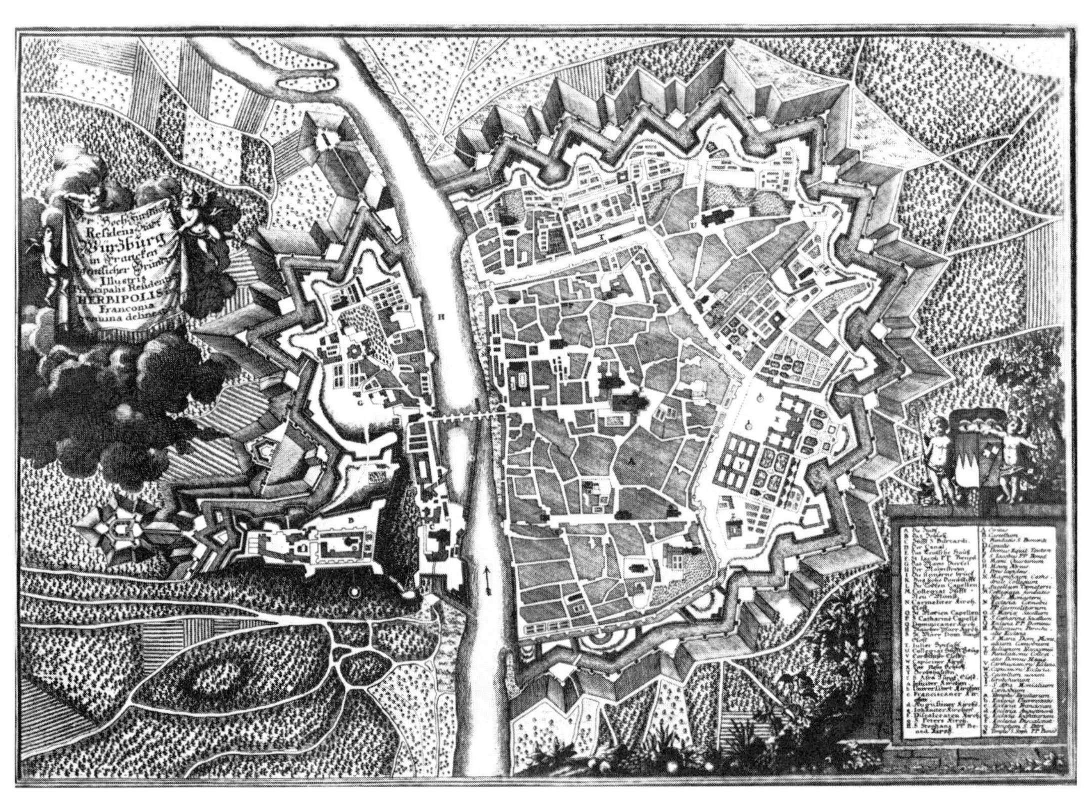
Illustris
HERBIPOLIS
Franconia

1027, 1028 *Views of the bishop's palace at Würzburg*

1029, 1030 *Two views of the main staircase in the bishop's palace*

originally an organism not dissimilar to the military towns of the late sixteenth century which we discussed in chapter 4; the ten-sided fortified perimeter included a built-up area on a grid plan, but the internal area was largely occupied by an enormous seven-sided citadel (Fig. 1036). During the war between Louis XIV and the second coalition the town was largely destroyed, and after the Peace of Ryswick, in 1699, the Elector Palatine decided to rebuild it as his Residenz, instead of Heidelberg; he had the princely palace sited on the area of the original citadel – an elongated block, with a façade half a kilometre long looking in the direction of the town – and the *Oberstadt*, or residential district for the nobles and courtiers, on the strip of land in front of it:.a grid divided up by seven roads perpendicular to the façade and ten parallel ones. To the right and left the grid was extended so as to fill the polygon of the fortifications, and made up the *Unterstadt*, where the ordinary burghers lived.

The street network – probably traced on that of 1607 – is just barely differentiated by the wider section of the road on the axis of the palace (Breitstrasse, sixteen metres wide) and the middle road running crosswise (Planken) which is actually an elongated square, with two rows of trees; the parade ground and market place were created along the Breitstrasse in the place of two blocks. Each set of houses was distinguished by a combination of letters – from A to K to the west of the Breitstrasse and from L to U to the left, starting from the palace – and of numbers, from one to seven starting from the axial road and moving outwards. The eighteenth-century capital thus maintained the schematic layout of the seventeenth-century military town, but this now became a sort of *parterre* built in front of the façade of the palace. The grid plan – used in America as a rhythmical device, infinitely extensible, and tried out repeatedly in the English colonies at precisely this time – here remained an enclosed perspective design, and in fact had no influence

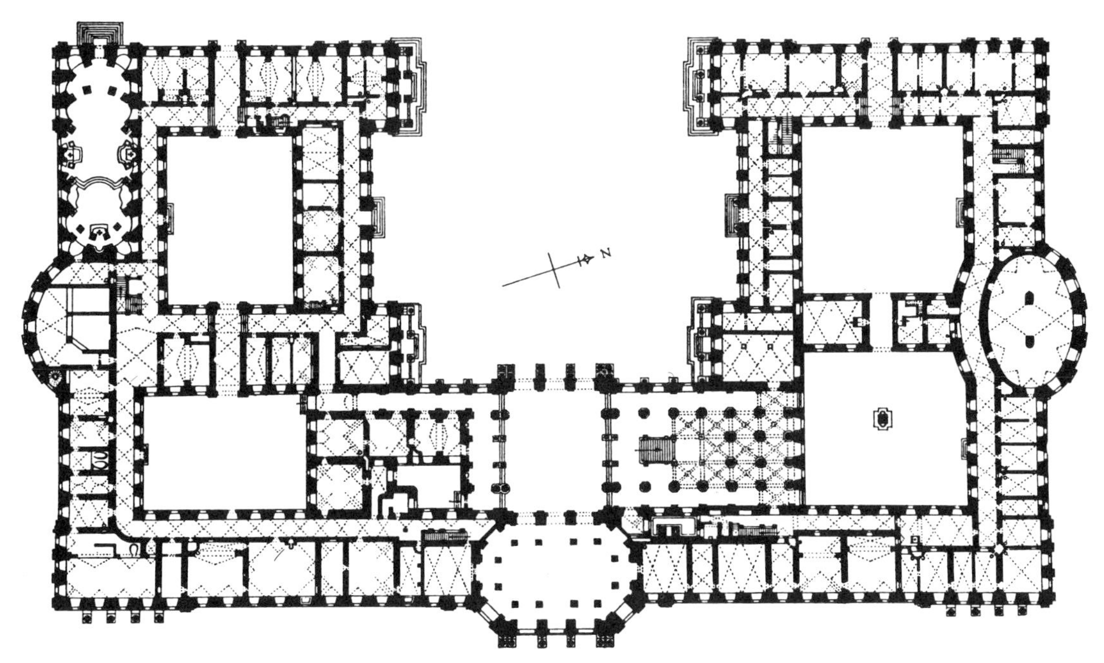

1031 *(left) The bishop's palace seen from the park*
1032, 1033 *View of the park and plan of the bishop's palace*

1034 *Würzburg in 1723, engraving by B. Neumann*

S.R.I. Principi ac Domino

1035 *The Kaisersaal in the bishop's palace, with frescoes by Tiepolo*
1036 *Plan of Mannheim in 1645 (from Merian)*
1037 *View of Mannheim in 1758*

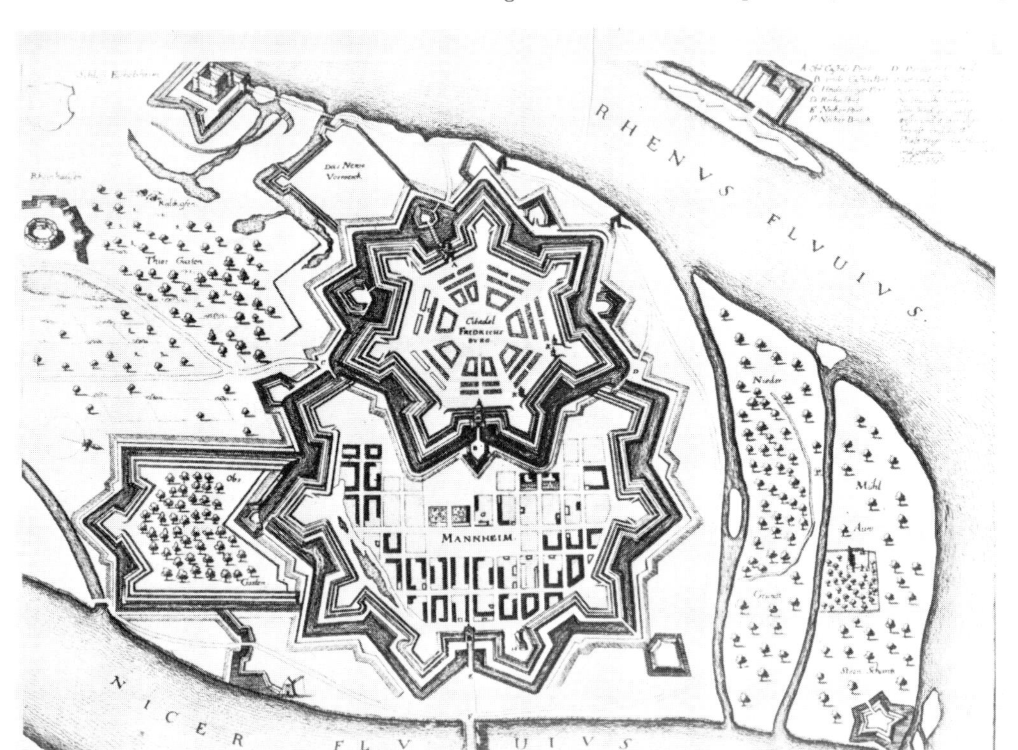
RHENVS FLVVIVS.
Citadel FRIDRICHS BVRG
MANNHEIM
NICER FLVVIVS
Thier Garten
Nieder
Mühl
Obs
Garten

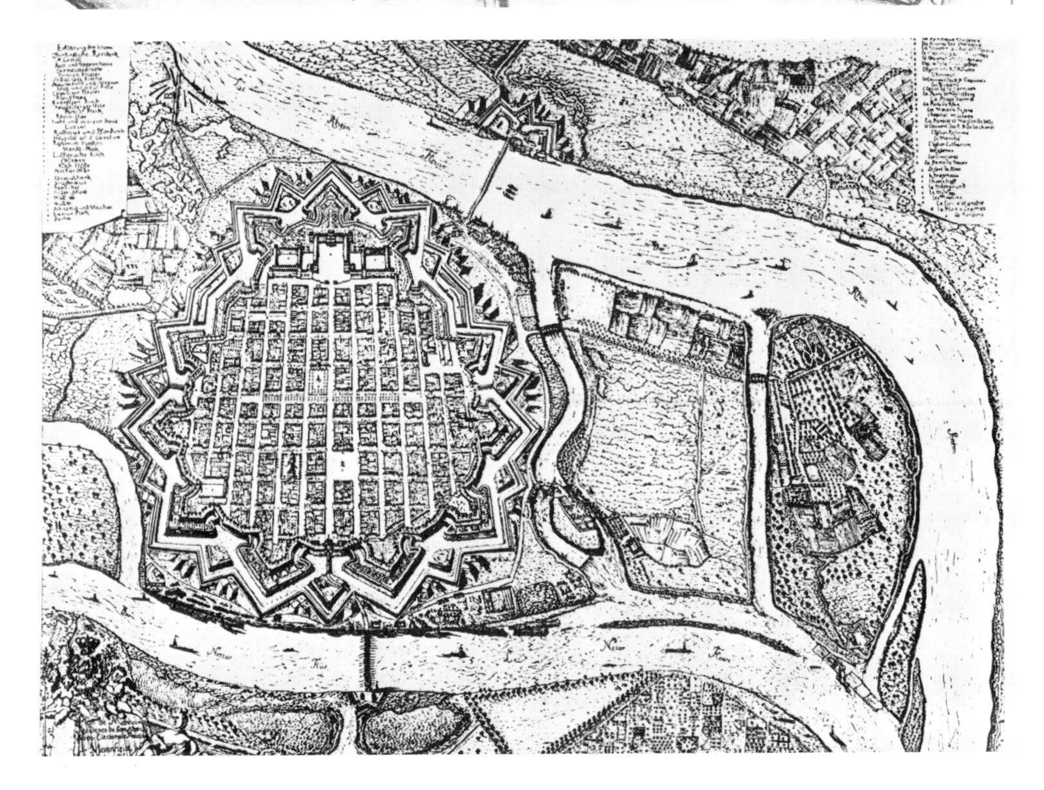

1038 *The eighteenth-century street system of Mannheim shown against the present system*

on the later development of the town, after the demolition of the walls in the late eighteenth century (Fig. 1038).

Karlsruhe was the new capital founded by the margrave Karl Wilhelm of Durlach in 1715, in the middle of a forest on the banks of the Rhine. The geometrical layout chosen for both the palace and the town was not the grid plan – the urban structure par excellence – but the *étoile*, i.e. the structure most typical of seventeenth-century parks. In this case the tower of the palace marked the centre of the figure, and thirty-two roads converged upon it; nine of them, running southwards, formed the street network of the residential area, and were run through by a chord which functioned – and still functions today – as a commercial cross-piece (Fig. 1045); the other twenty-three ran indefinitely into the forest

1039 *The central part of the façade of the princely palace, Mannheim*

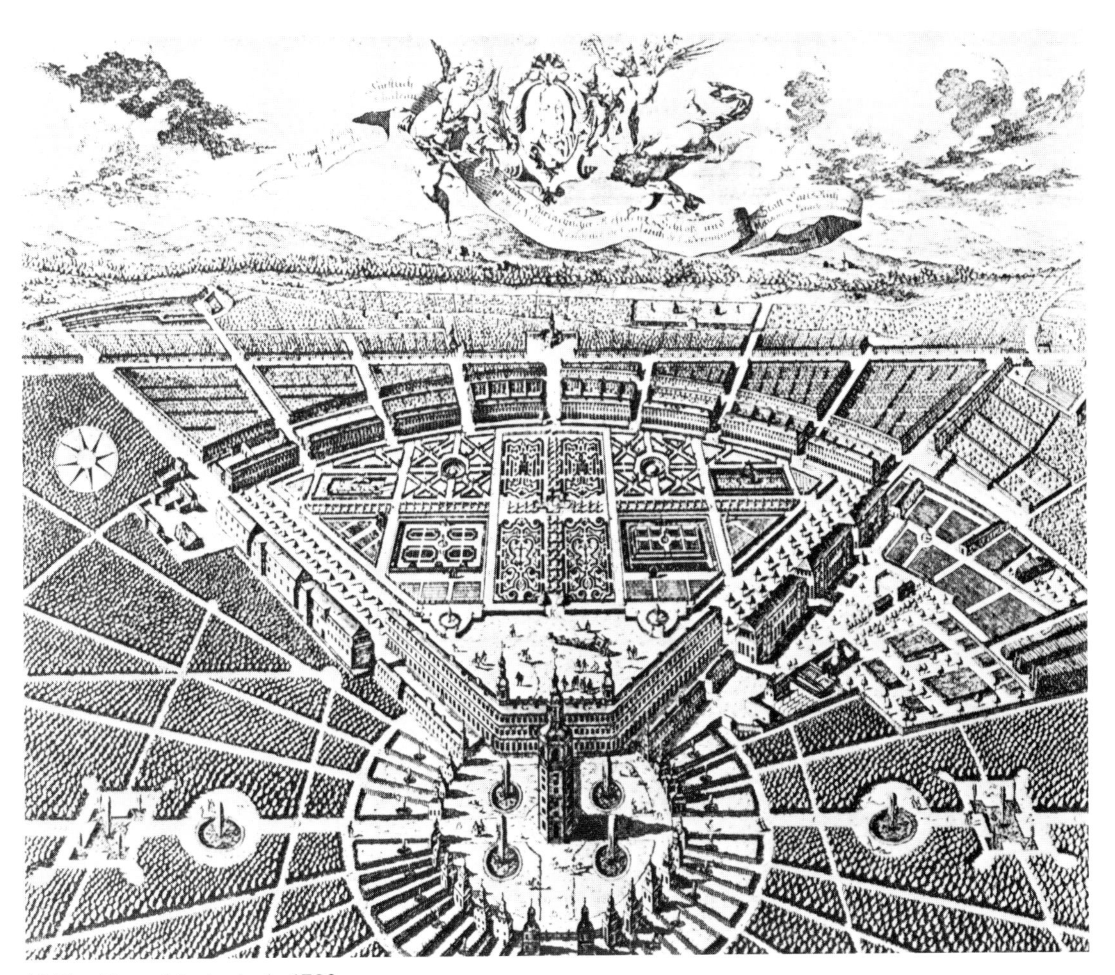

1040 *View of Karlsruhe in 1739*

Kurtzer Begriff
aller derer
Freyheiten/ PRIVILEGIEN,
und
Sonderbahrer Begnadigungen/
Wormit
Der Durchleuchtigste Fürst und Herr/
HERR
CARL,
Marggraff zu Baden und Hochberg/ Land-Graff zu Sausenberg/ Graff zu Sponheim und Eberstein/ Herr zu Rötelen/ Badenweiler/ Lahr und Mahlberg rc. Der Röm. Kayserl. und Königl. Cathol. Mayest. wie auch des Löbl. Schwäbischen Crayses bestellter respective General-Feld-Marschall und General-Feld-Zeugmeister/ auch Obrister über ein Keyserl. Regiment zu Fuß rc.
Die Jenige/ welche hinkünfftig bey und neben
Dero Neu-Erbauenden Lust-Hauß
Carols-Ruhe
Mit Anbauung Neuer Behausungen rc.
Sich niderlassen werden/
anzusehen gedencket.

Gedruckt zu Durlach/ durch Theodor Hechten.

1041 *Licence of the margrave Karl Wilhelm for the founding of Karlsruhe*

1042, 1043 *Views of the palace of Karlsruhe*

1044 *The eighteenth-century street system of Karlsruhe shown against the present system*

towards the north, and joined the network of the perspective approaches of the park.

All the roads in the built-up area, as at Mannheim, had the noble residence as their backdrop; it was bent round *à patte de poule* and enclosed a section of a circle laid out as a *parterre*; the houses which looked on to this space, along the arc of circumference, all had identical façades.

At Karlsruhe the assimilation of the city into the park was more complete and coherent than in any other city of the time; the houses were only a particular piece of furnishing for the great perspective space centred on the princely palace. The city proper was therefore strongly affected by it (all the angles of entry of the streets, and all their lengths, were different, determined solely by the demands

1045 *An early twentieth-century view of the Kaiserstrasse, Karlsruhe*

of the design of the ground plan; for this reason the radiating design, though by its nature extensible indefinitely, was abandoned as soon as the city began to grow beyond a certain limit) (Fig. 1044); but precisely because of its immobile spatial coherence, which excluded all change, the design of Karlsruhe was admired more than any other in its own time and was imitated in various small German towns: Neustrelitz in Mecklenburg (1724) and the other Karlsruhe in Silesia (1743).

St Petersburg, the new capital of Russia, was founded by Peter the Great with a similar aim, but its political importance, its geographical situation and the ups and downs of its actual execution make it a special case,

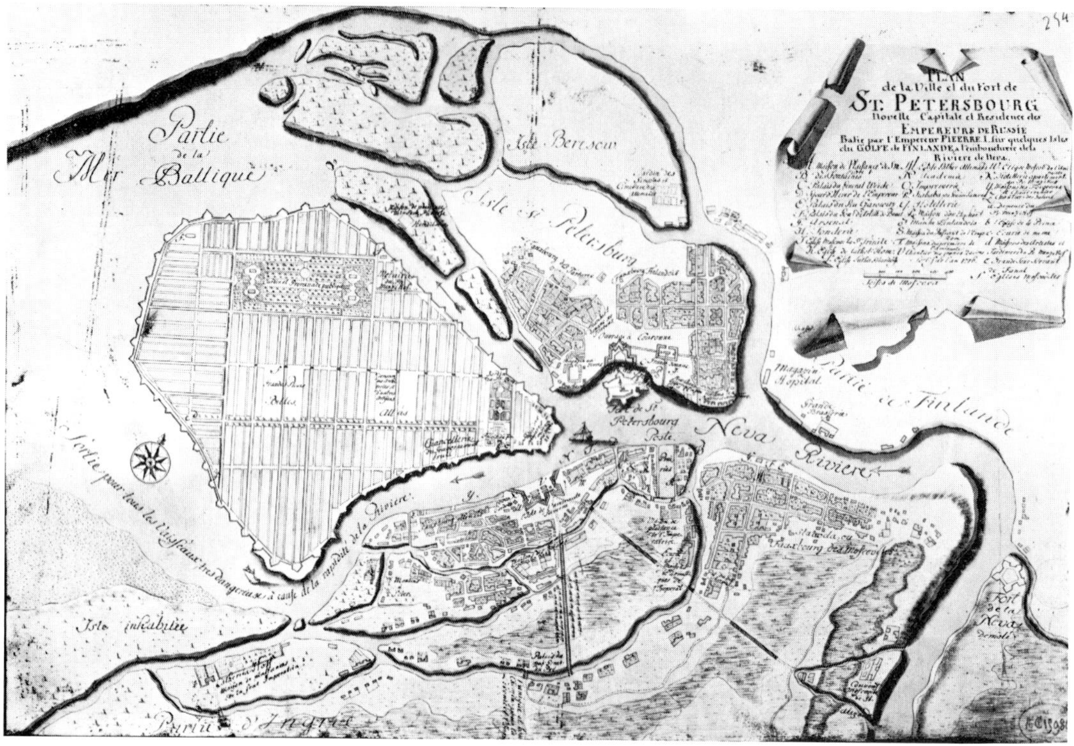

1046 *Plan of St Petersburg at the beginning of the eighteenth century*

different from the small planned capitals of the Rhenish principalities.

Peter I came to power in 1689, when he was still very young, took a long journey through Europe from 1697 to 1698, and immediately afterwards introduced a series of administrative, technical and moral reforms to bring Russia into line with the modern world. At the same time he waged a series of wars against the Turks and Swedes for access to the Black Sea (conquest of Azov, 1696) and the Baltic (conquest of the mouth of the Neva, 1700). The decision to found a new city here – taken on 29 June 1703 – was part of the programme to bring Russia closer to the west and to safeguard her new maritime frontiers.

The estuary of the Neva included two large islands: on the first stood the fortress of St Peter and St Paul, while the second was leased to Peter's favourite, Menshikov; the palace of the Tsar, the Admiralty, the naval shipyards and the cathedral were built on the mainland, opposite the fortress. The designer of the main buildings was the Italian Domenico Trezzini (1670–1734). The climate, nature of the terrain and distance from older built-up centres made work initially very difficult, and the Tsar had to resort to coercion: all the court dignitaries were obliged to build themselves houses in the new city, and 100,000 prisoners or convicts supplied the manpower.

For the first ten years the city remained a fortified outpost without any overall plan. In 1712 it became the new state capital, in the place of Moscow, and the Tsar confronted the problem of planning its further development; in 1713 he had Schlüter come from Berlin, but he died the following year before having produced a plan; in 1716 he sent for Le Blond from Paris, appointed him royal architect and commissioned him to prepare

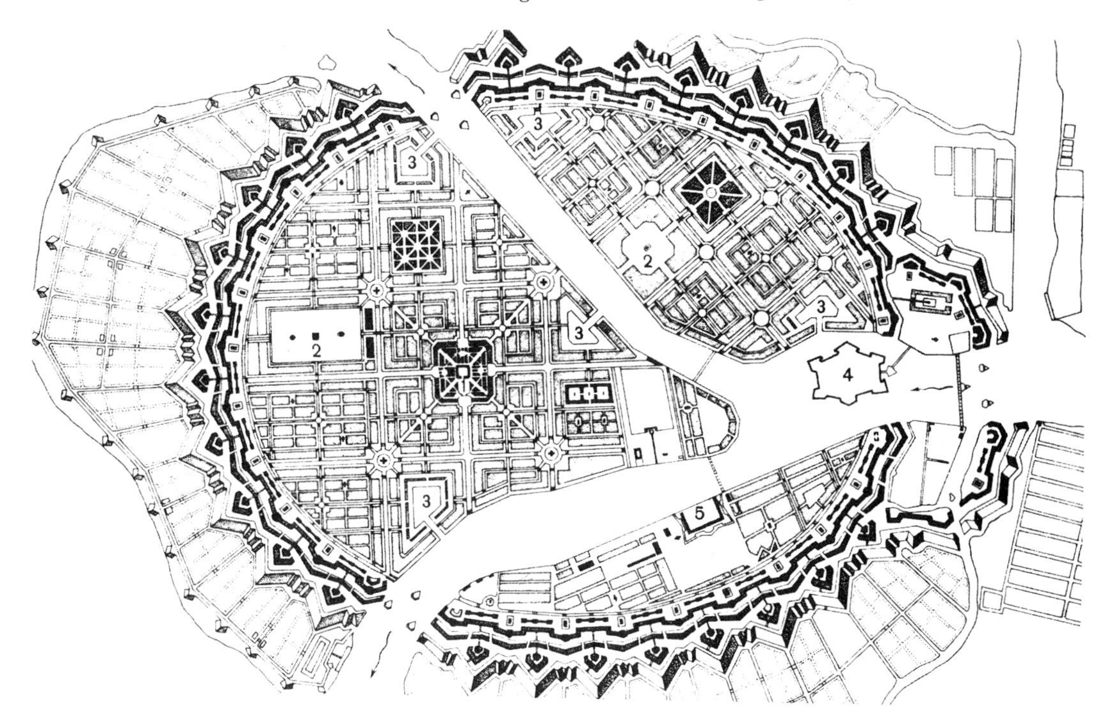

1047 *Le Blond's plan for St Petersburg, 1716*

the general scheme of the city. Le Blond presented a report on the 'irregular and poor composition practised in the buildings of St Petersburg' and a design, accompanied by a second explicative report, which was immediately approved by the monarch.

Le Blond's plan (Fig. 1047) fixed a fortified oval perimeter, which took in the two islands and a small part of the left bank of the river; each of the three zones was urbanized according to a geometric design with large square meshes, enlivened with squares of various shapes and diagonal roads, though orientated in different ways. Together with the street network, there was also to be a network of canals, as in the Dutch cities visited by the Tsar; there were different districts for each of the great families who were to populate the city, with a church, a market accessible by water, a school and a ground for military exercises; noisy industrial activities were concentrated on the outskirts, and hospitals, the cemetery and slaughterhouses were situated outside the city.

Despite these detailed measures, the plan was extremely contrived: 'a plan for a garden, applied to a city,' as Lavedan says.[13] Furthermore the insecure organization of the state prevented the faithful execution of such a plan, which modified the situation of ownership and, in some cases, altered the already existing buildings. Thus after the death of Le Blond in 1719 and that of Peter the Great in 1723 the city still had no general plan.

Over the following decades the form of the city was defined by a series of partial decisions; about 1730 Eropkin, Zemtsov and Korobov laid out the three radiating roads which converged on the Admiralty tower – Ascension Prospect, Admiralty Prospect and Nevsky Prospect – around which the fabric of the city on the left bank of the river was

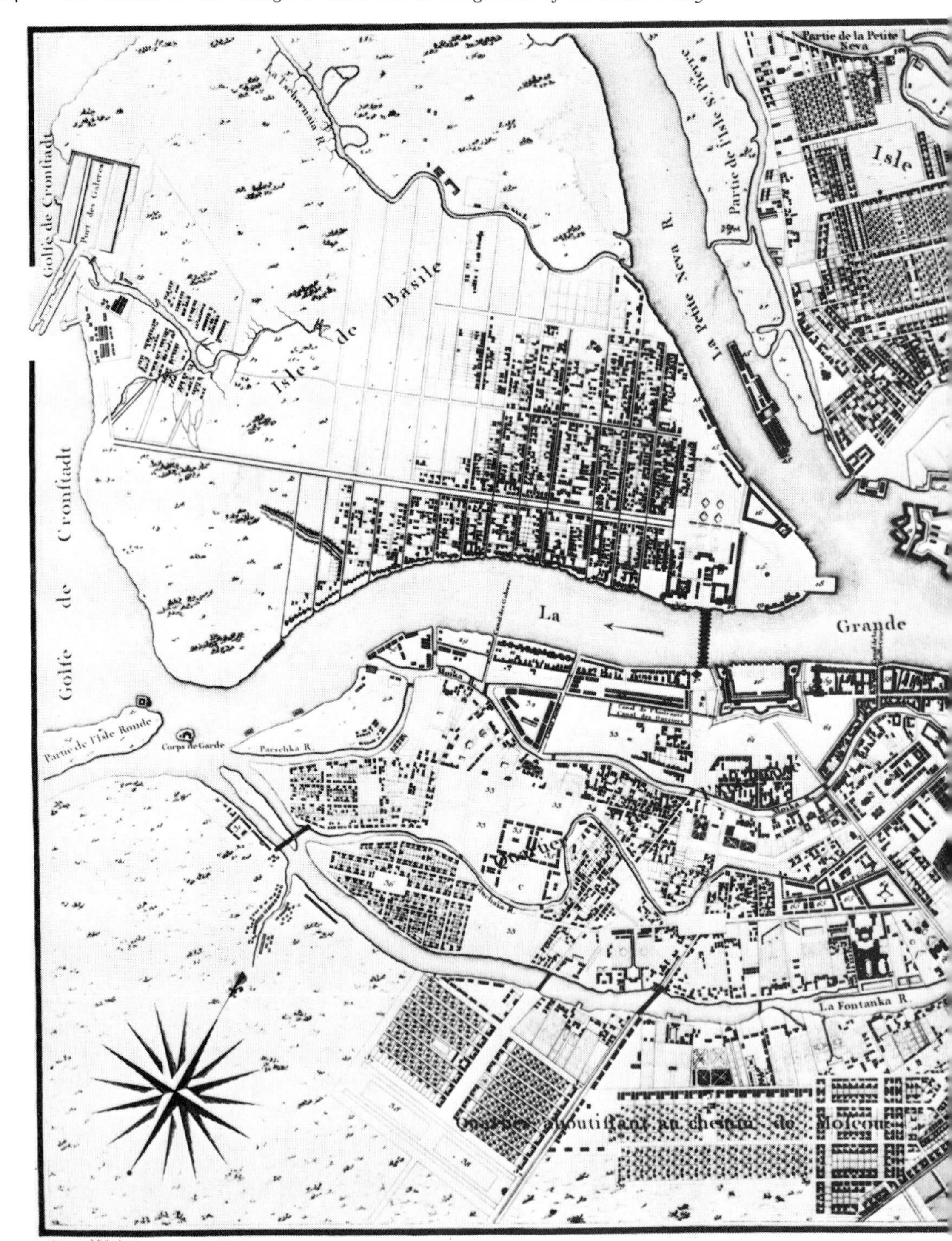

1048 *Plan of St Petersburg in 1753*

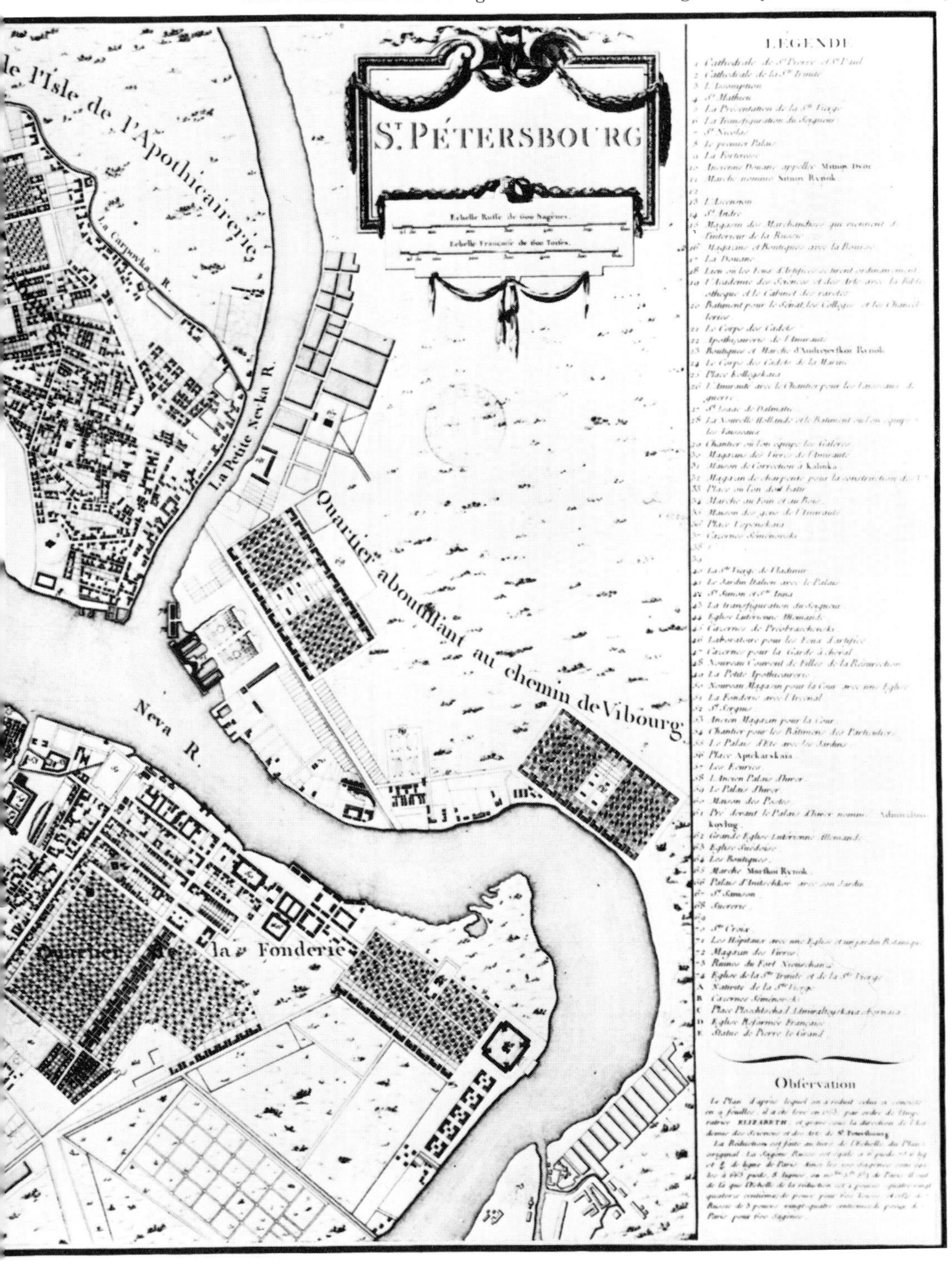

S.T PÉTERSBOURG
LEGENDE
le l'Isle de l'Apothicairerie
La Carpovka R.
La Petite Nevka R.
Quartier aboutissant au chemin de Vibourg
Neva R.
la Fonderie
Observation

1049, 1050 *Views of St Petersburg: the façade of the Winter Palace overlooking the Neva, and the buildings of the imperial colleges*

1051 *The Exchange and merchants' storehouse on the little Neva, St Petersburg*

organized; Menshikov's island remained divided up, as originally, into a series of rectangular plots. The parks of Strelna, Peterhof, Tsarskoe Selo and Oranienbaum were planted around the city.

Elizabeth (1741–62) employed as royal architect Bartolomeo Rastrelli (1700–71), an Italian trained in France, who built a series of monumental buildings: the Smolny convent (1748), Voronkov Palace (1749), Stroganov Palace (1752) and Winter Palace (1754). The situation of the city in the middle of the century is documented in the great plan executed at the imperial academy of arts and sciences (1753; Fig. 1048).

In 1763 Catherine II organized a competition for the 'beautification' of the city; an exhibition of the plans was to be held, presented anonymously, and the competitors were to be allowed to criticize the plans exhibited.[14] The judging committee thus gathered together a large number of proposals and observations, on the basis of which it prepared *ex officio* a new general plan; this was the new basis for the scheme of the late eighteenth and early nineteenth centuries which were to give the city its definitive monumental aspect (Figs 1049–51).

The dozen or so capital cities we have discussed – though chosen from among those where the recent building and town-planning developments were most coherent – demonstrate once again the precariousness of the intervention of absolute power in urban organisms: the coherence of the results depended upon an exceptional rigidity of control (the most orderly towns were those where two militaristic dynasties were in command, the house of Savoy and the Hohenzollern) or upon the small size of the centre, which could thus be more easily

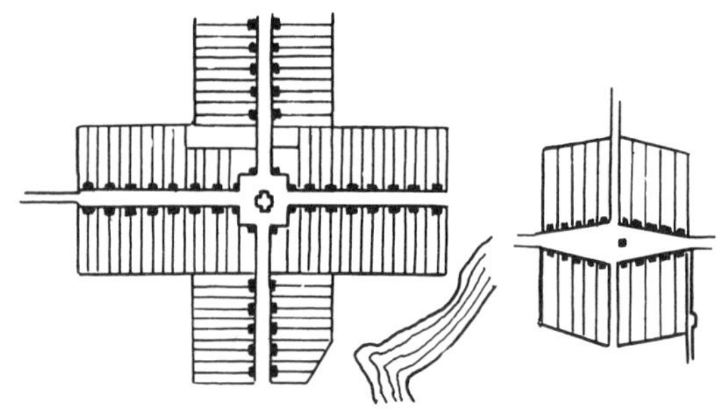

1052 *Plans of the Prussian towns of Gosen and Müggelheim*

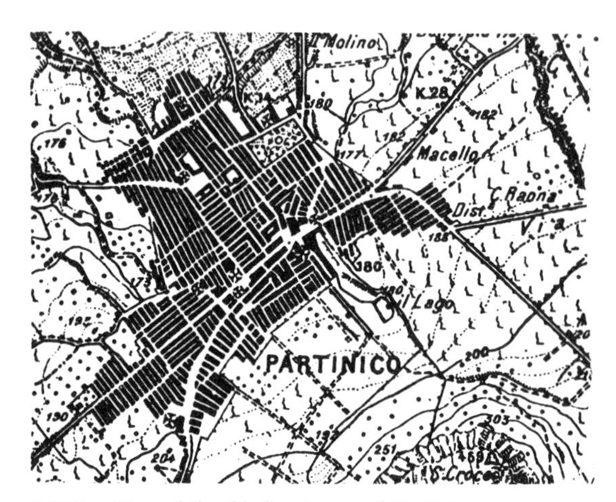

1053 *Plan of the Sicilian town of Partinico*

subordinated to organization around large spaces of parkland. The antagonism between power and city – which in all other cases made it desirable to set the princely residences some distance from the urban organisms – was only suppressed, not overcome.

Outside the capitals absolute power found few other opportunities for organized intervention, and the margin of arbitrariness inherent in its methods almost always prevented a successful interpretation of local needs (see the plans for the new Sicilian towns, Avola and Granmichele, which imposed the radiating forms of Renaissance tradition upon a humble fabric of peasant dwellings). Agricultural settlement was a current problem only at the extremities of Europe: in western Sicily, where, around the end of the seventeenth century and the beginning of the eighteenth, a series of large peasant townships – Partinico, Cinisi, Balestrate, Pachino and many others – designed indifferently by means of a grid of elongated or square lots, were built by *latifundisti*; in the plain of Brandenburg, where in the middle of the eighteenth century Frederick II founded a number of small townships, organized in a linear fashion along a road (Müggelheim), a pair of intersecting roads (Gosen) or on a grid plan around a square (Kietz); later in Spain, in 1767, Charles III decreed that the Sierra Morena should be populated with German and Flemish settlers, and had some small towns built to regular plans – La Carolina, La Carlota, Las Navas de Tolosa, La Luisiana; in Russia Elizabeth and more particularly Catherine II built townships and also important towns, for instance Tula and the enormous Yekaterinoslav (work upon which went ahead with great haste from 1784 to 1787 for the meeting of the empress with the Hapsburg emperor Joseph II, and was broken off soon afterwards).

Planned from above, the concentration of industrial activities in certain specialized centres produced the formation of rigidly ordered new urban organisms: in France we have already mentioned Tour-la-Ville and Villeneuvette, founded by Colbert; later we find Nuevo Batzán in Spain, a small mining town designed in 1709 by José Benito Churriguera (1665–1725) for the banker Juan de Goyeneche, freely adapting the usual grid plan to the nature of the terrain; Jorgetown in Minorca, a naval base founded by the English in 1711, which was possibly the prototype of the other eighteenth-century Spanish naval bases, El Ferrol (1752), Barceloneta (1755) and San Carlos (1776), all made up of long terrace blocks side by side. Only the perspective garden on its own was a model realizable everywhere without difficulties and

1054, 1055 *Aerial view and plan of Granmichele*

in fact it gave rise to a homogeneous praxis, which went beyond the geographical limits so far considered and was superimposed upon other traditions still operating: in England, as we shall see, and in Holland, where the taste for the enclosed Renaissance garden persisted, codified in the manual of Van der Groen,[15] and sometimes embellished by natural curiosities as was Riat's garden.[16] But when William of Orange married Mary Stuart, the influence of the French *grand goût* arrived from England: the royal couple had the parks of Het Loo and Honslaerdyk made near the Hague, and of Heemstede near Utrecht which, since they were on absolutely

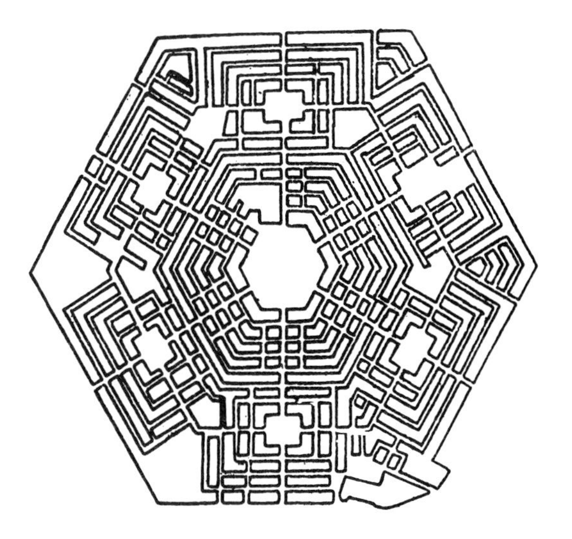

flat ground, did not offer the overall views typical of the great French and German parks, but became sequences of limited and enclosed spaces, not unlike the traditional ones, and only organized into great symmetrical compositions in terms of their ground plan (Fig. 1058).

Even the emperor of China commissioned two Jesuit missionaries, Michel Benoit and Giuseppe Castiglione, to lay out a small European garden in the park of the winter palace with mazes, fountains and *jeux d'eau*, called 'Hsieh ch'i ch'u' (harmonious, strange and pleasing) (Figs 1056–7).

The visual, functional and social organic quality that could not be achieved in the cities was made up for by the purely visual organic quality of the parks, and the open spaces, on the whole, had more effect on urban and out-of-town structures than the building schemes themselves.

The artists who took part in these undertakings on a large scale – chosen, as we have seen, from an international range, on the basis of their prestige or the prestige of the trend to which they belonged – had to combine the personal experiment in which they were involved with the requirements, almost always generic and uninspiring, of their clients.

This problem derived from the fact that building and town-planning types – i.e. the universally accepted models, which formed the natural common ground between client and designers – had become problematical after about 1630. *Avant-garde* artists were in a position to offer the ruling classes a range of different formal solutions, justified on the basis of a biased reasoning, stylistic, figurative or symbolic; in this way an uncertainty entered into the relationship, a margin of objection or of misunderstanding, whose outcome was open conflict, or more frequently the submission of the artist to the choices and caprices of the client.

There are several phases to be distinguished in this process. The generation of Bernini and François Mansart (both born in 1598), of Pietro da Cortona (1596) and Borromini (1599), contemporaries of the great masters of painting, Poussin (1594), Velazquez (1599) and Rembrandt (1606), pursued a universal and exclusive programme of regeneration, though they looked in different degrees towards past and future, and they pursued this programme with equal coherence on every scale of design.

This general attitude to creation continued roughly until the end of the seventeenth century. In Italy the last two masters capable of leading the European debate, and also in fact active in the international field, were Guarini (born in 1624) and Juvara (born in 1676). Guarini, engaged in his geometrical

1056, 1057 *Two views of the European garden of the Summer Palace of the emperor of China (from Gothein)*

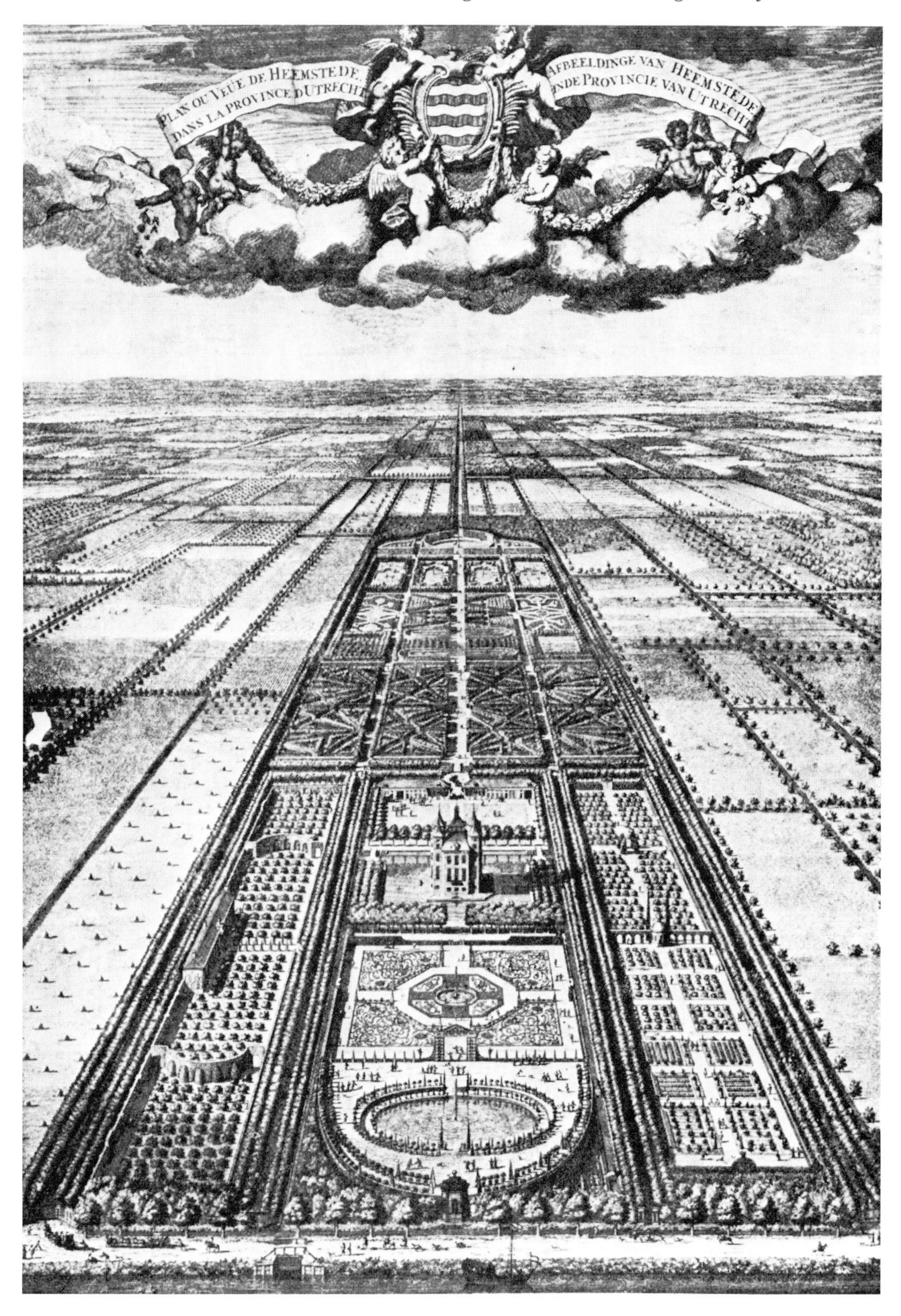

1058 *View of the park of Heemstede, near Utrecht*

and mathematical research into the possible variants of the traditional symmetrical structures, worked in Turin from 1666 to 1680, as we have seen, but in 1662 he was in Paris where he provided the designs for Ste-Anne-la-Royale, in 1679 he designed the church of St Mary of Altötting, in Prague, and at some unspecified period travelled through Spain and Portugal, where he designed the church of S. Maria de la Divina Providencia in Lisbon. Juvara, though active in Turin from 1714 onwards, went to Portugal in 1719, to London and Paris in 1720, and to Madrid in 1735 where he died the following year; necessarily, he partly accepted the court models of international classicism, but continued Bernini's experiment with a freedom of his own, even in larger organisms, such as Stupinigi and the palazzi in Madrid and Lisbon.

In Germany this programme remained current for architects born before Juvara: Fischer von Erlach (born in 1656), Schlüter (1662), Pöppelmann (1662), Bähr (1666), Hildebrandt (1668), who took part in the urban transformations already mentioned, the Dientzenhofer (Georg, 1643–89; Christoph, 1655–1722; Johann, 1665–1726), Jakob Prandtauer (1660–1726), Franz Beer (1660–1726). All these, who began working before the end of the century, designed or aspired to design, with this same creative commitment, simple isolated organisms – the chapel of Waldsassen, by Georg Dientzenhofer, 1685; St Lawrence at Gabel, by Hildebrandt, 1699; the Frauenkirche at Dresden, by Bähr, 1722 – or large articulated complexes, such as Melk (Prandtauer, 1702), the Zwinger (Pöppelmann, 1711), Weingarten (Beer, 1715), Göttweig (Hildebrandt, 1718). Fischer von Erlach consciously aspired to a synthesis of ancient classicism and the different variants of modern classicism, and also tried to combine all the illustrious elements of the past, remote and immediate, in a single composition, such as the Karlskirche of Vienna (1716; Figs 1062–3); his collection of engravings, *Entwurf einer historischen Architektur in Abbildung unterschiedener berühmten Gebäuden des Altertums under fremder Völker* (1705, published in 1751) was the last single 'theatre' of universal architecture, and at the same time a precursor of the eclectic collections of future historicism (Figs 1064–6).

Meanwhile the spread of the *grand goût*, and the acceptance, at least at court level, of the new conventional models elaborated in France – the town residence with the enclosed courtyard, or expanded into a horseshoe shape around an open one, the *villa suburbana* with symmetrical wings or detached pavilions, linked to *parterres* and the landscaped garden; the royal square, with a geometrical plan and uniform façades; the monumental domed church; the rhythmic and indefinite composition for great utilitarian buildings and urban organisms – did not interrupt the host of local experiments, but polarized them. From now on the work of formal invention

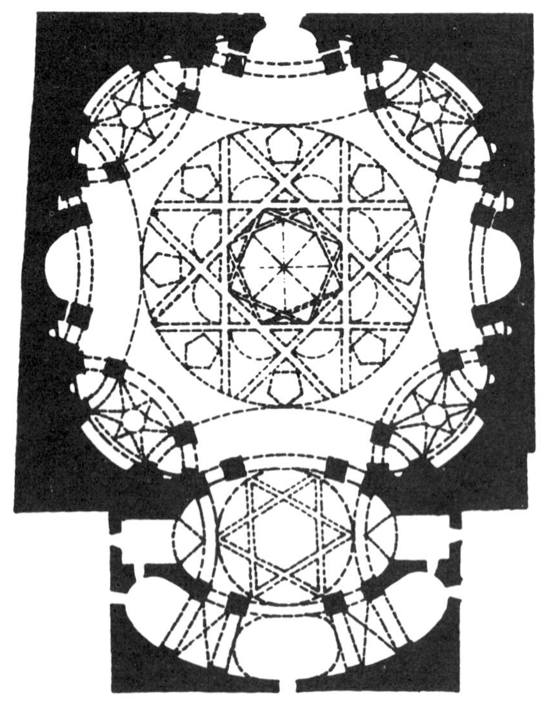

1059, 1060 *Plan of S. Lorenzo, Turin and view of the cupola by Guarini*

1061 *Design for a stage set by F. Juvara, 1728. Museo civico, Turin*

tended to be staggered over several levels: the large scale and mass production, where conventional models remained largely obligatory; the medium scale and the creation of special organisms, either isolated or incorporated into already existing ones, where personal experiment could be carried out under cover of the restraints of repetition or functional subordination, and had an ample margin of choice from among the possible variations of the usual building types; and the small scale, i.e. the creation of decorative details and furnishings, where there was almost unlimited freedom.

These were the conditions under which the artists of the following generation worked, born in the last fifteen years of the century: Dominikus Zimmermann (1685–1766), Kos-

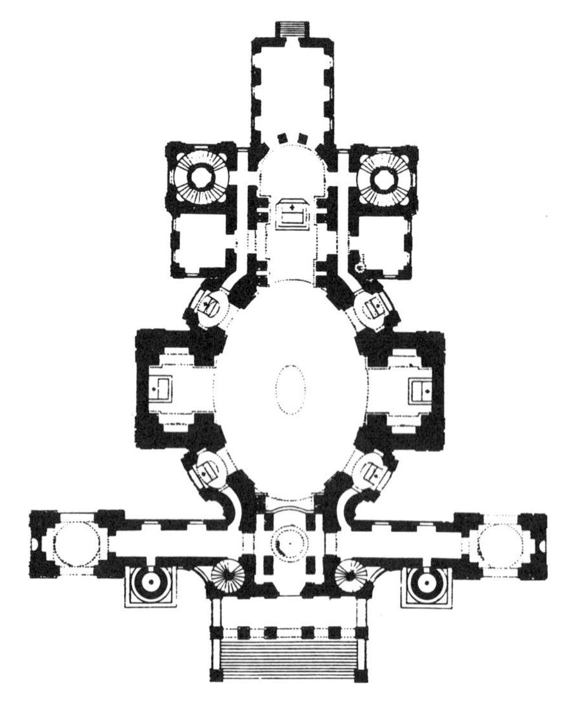

mas Damian Asam (1686–1739), Balthasar Neumann (1687–1753), Kilian Ignaz Dientzenhofer (1689–1751), Johann Michael Fischer (1692–1766), Egid Quirin Asam (1692–1750). Of these only Neumann was involved in the great urban operations of the time, as we have seen, and concerned himself eclectically with bridges, roads, gardens, fortifications and building projects on a large and small scale; but the degree of his involvement, from one category of work to another, is significant: the engineering works were designed according to strict technical and stereotyped criteria; the larger works of

1062, 1063 *Plan and view of the Karlskirche, Vienna*

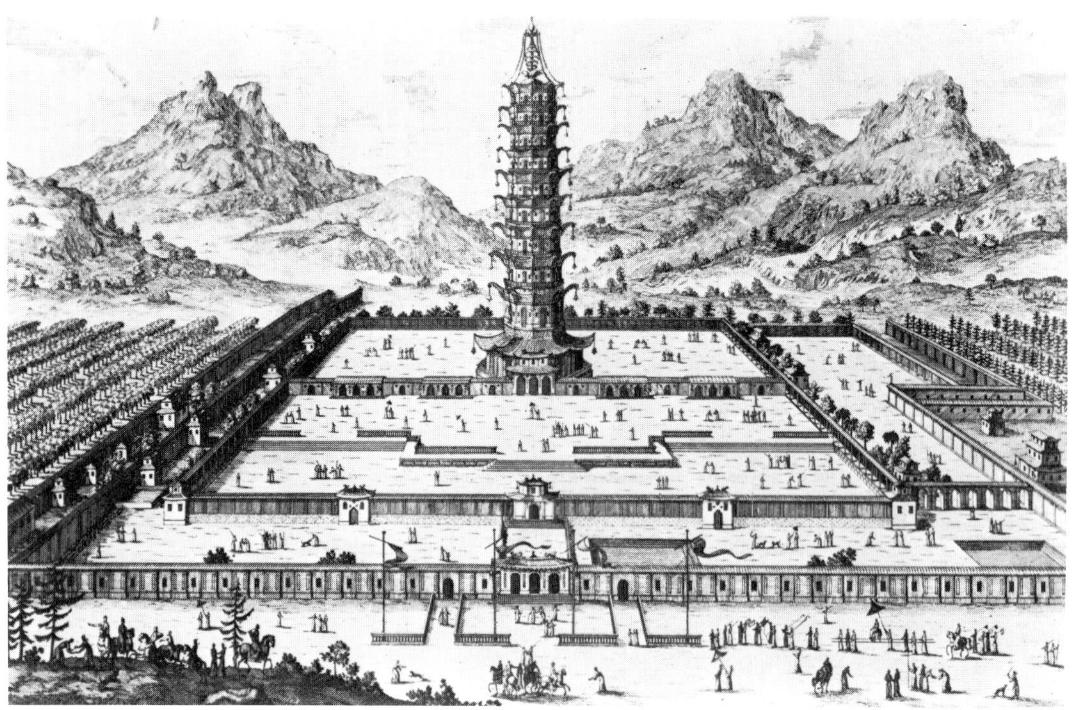

1064, 1065 *Two illustrations from Fischer von Erlach's collection: the temple of Zeus at Olympia and the temple of Nanking*

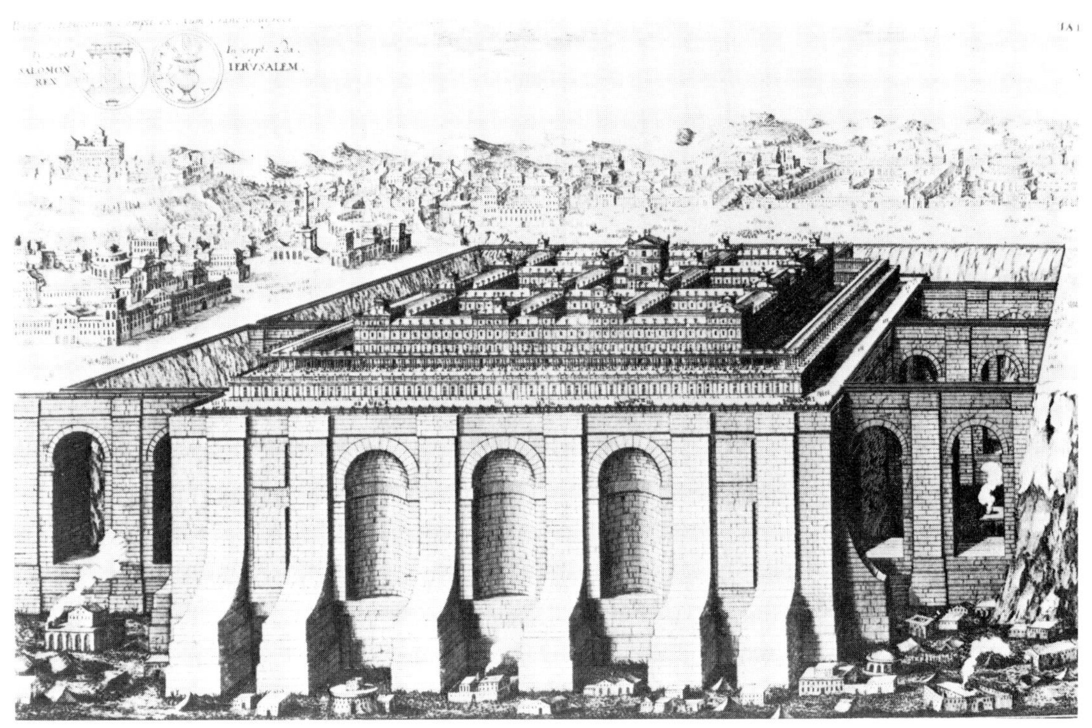

1066 *An illustration from Fischer von Erlach's collection: the temple of Solomon*

1067–1069 *Plans of the chapel of Waldsassen, St Lawrence at Gabel and the Frauenkirche at Dresden*

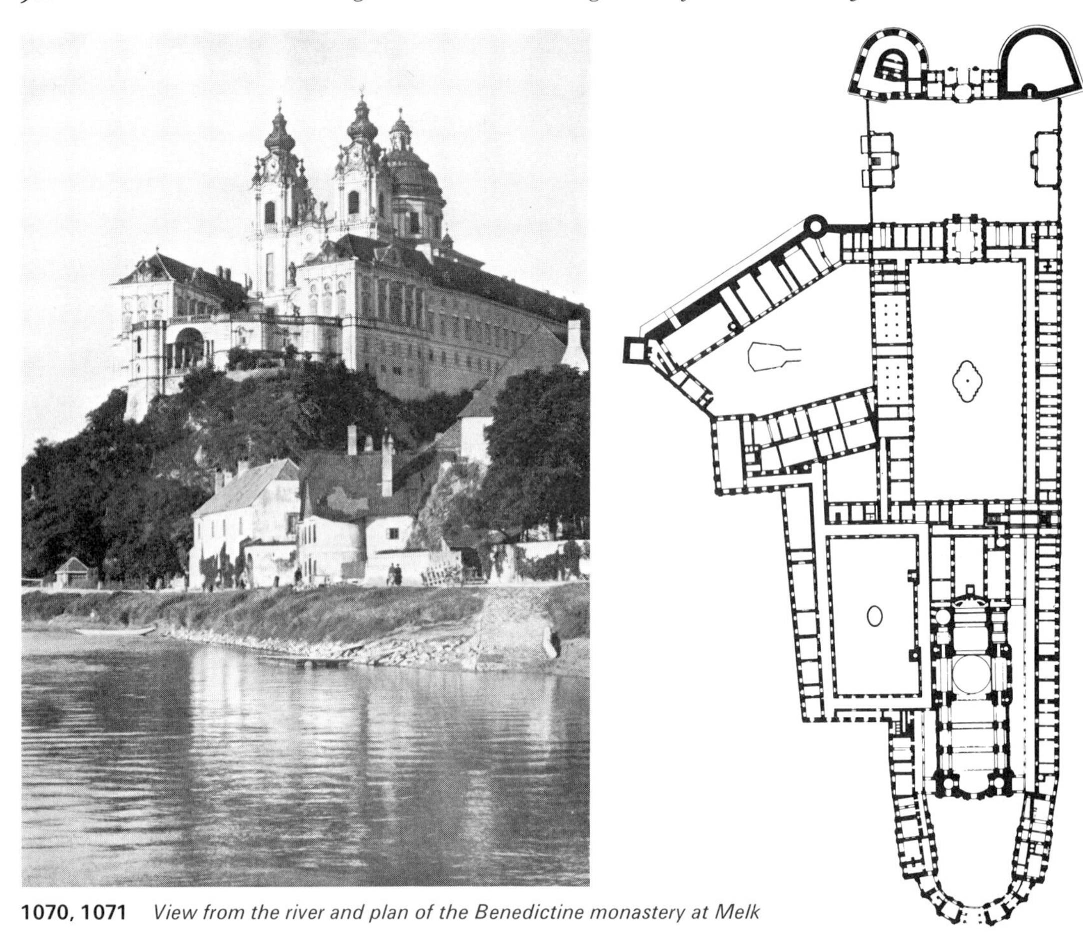

1070, 1071 *View from the river and plan of the Benedictine monastery at Melk*

architecture, such as the princely palaces and gardens, followed the most widespread court models, i.e. respected the elementary patterns of composition, symmetry and hierarchy; the smaller works of architecture, such as the chapel of the Nikolausberg, and some elements of the larger works – the great staircase in the palace of Bruchsal, the main staircase, the main rooms and the chapel in the palace of Würzburg – were freely invented as individual organisms where the hierarchy between architecture and decoration was no longer distinguishable.

The other masters mentioned worked in a more restricted field; they were in fact (the phrase is not unintentional) specialists in special buildings, not monumental in the court sense, and not repeatable *en masse*; they worked in close contact with specialists in building decoration, particularly workers in stucco: Johann Zimmermann (1680–1758), Joseph Anton (1696–1770) and Johann Michael Feichmayr (1709–72). Their most successful works were certain pilgrimage churches and some private or abbey churches, usually in small centres or in the open country, which were suitable subjects for pure fantasy, which had to produce an impression rather than serve a function: Steinhausen (1728) and Wies (1754) by the Zimmermann brothers; St John Nepomuk in Munich (1733) by the Asam brothers; Vierzehnheiligen (1743), Neresheim (1747) and the chapel of the Nikolausberg (1747) by

1072 *The Benedictine monastery at Weingarten in an engraving of 1723*

1073 *The ceiling of the church at Diessen by Fischer*

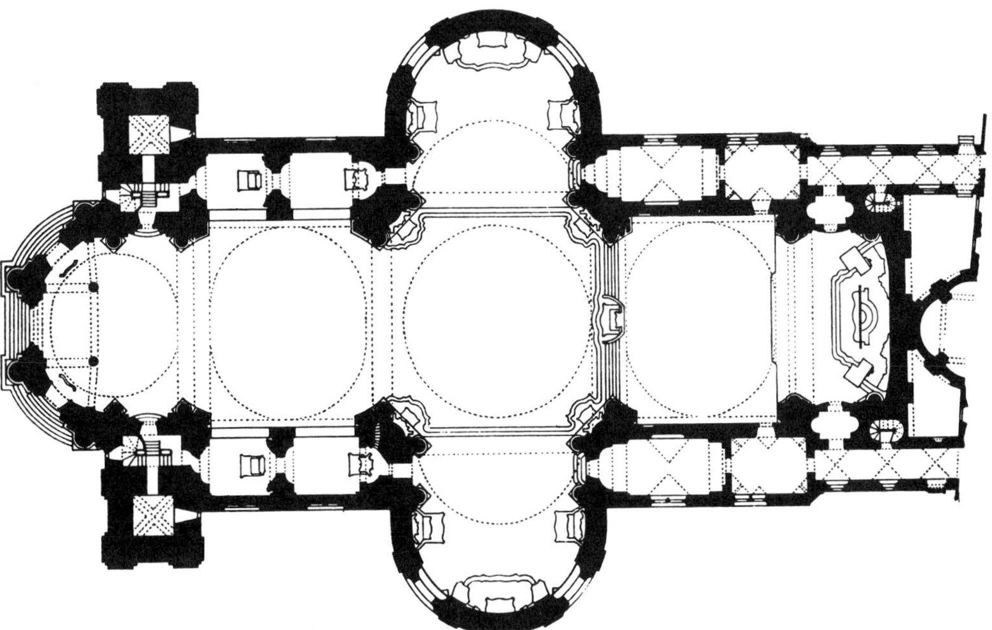

1074, 1075 *Interior and plan of the abbey church of Ottobeuren by Fischer*

Neumann; Diessen (1732), Ottobeuren (1737), Rott-am-Inn (1759) by Fischer.

These buildings (Figs 1073–85) were designed from the interior outwards; the exterior seems merely to be a 'wrong side', almost always of lesser importance and originality (for example, the complex organism of Vierzehnheiligen is dissembled within a much more simple covering, which reproduced the volumes of a traditional cruciform organism; in other cases – the Wies, the chapel of the Nikolausberg – the base is an unadorned wall, and only the form of the roof reveals in part the articulation of the inner ceiling). Only when one has crossed the threshold does the organism suddenly reveal itself as a spectacle of the imagination, though it actually surrounds the spectator and engages his physical dimension, besides his contemplative attention. Primary architectural elements – columns, cornices, arches, doors and windows – and secondary ones – altars, pulpits, organs, singers' galleries and paintings – were given equal status and mingled in an absolute visual continuity, which impressed the ordinary spectator with the richness of its forms and range of colour. But the architect, like an expert musician, regulated the dazzling complexity of his effects by means of a concise intellectual mechanism (usually with a geometrical device formed from the intersection of elementary solid figures); he produced qualities through a free and dextrous combination of quantities. The educated spectator understood this generative structure, and followed through the chain of transient combinations, until he discovered the stable elements and unvarying rules of combination. This style, as Pevsner says, 'asks for an exact understanding – which is a job for the expert: architects' architecture, as the fugue is musicians' music'.[17]

The freedom of these designers, serene and unlimited in a field hedged around with restrictive laws, is comparable to that of the contemporary musicians: Bach and Handel, both born in 1685; these churches and palaces were the original places of performance for their works, and even today they are the ideal settings, acoustically and optically, for the works of these composers. Here, too, effects of timbre and of composition, popular features and those appreciated only by specialists, were fused for the last time in a perfect, though ephemeral unity. The designers' dexterity of combination was perfectly matched by the manual ability of the executors; the intellectual virtuosity, perceptible in the whole, found a parallel in the physical virtuosity of the refinements: the *stucco lustro*, the gilding, pictures and frescoes, the ornaments in gilded or painted wood.

The illustrious works we have quoted thus became the prototypes for a vast, extraordinarily compact lesser production; in the

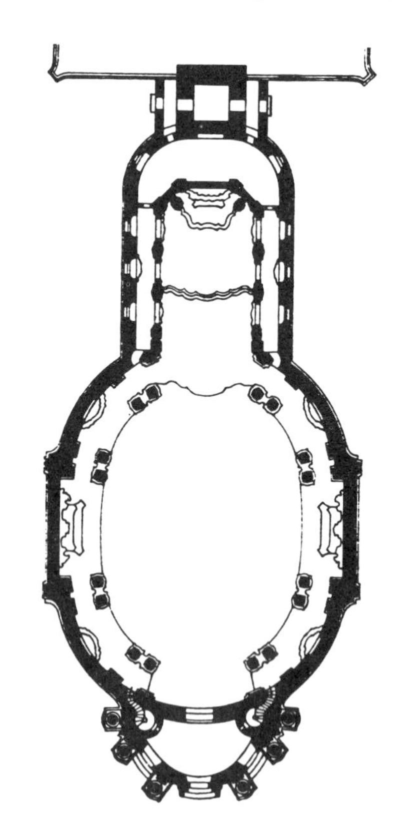

1076–1079 *(overleaf) Plan, exterior and two interior views of the Wies church by the Zimmermann brothers*

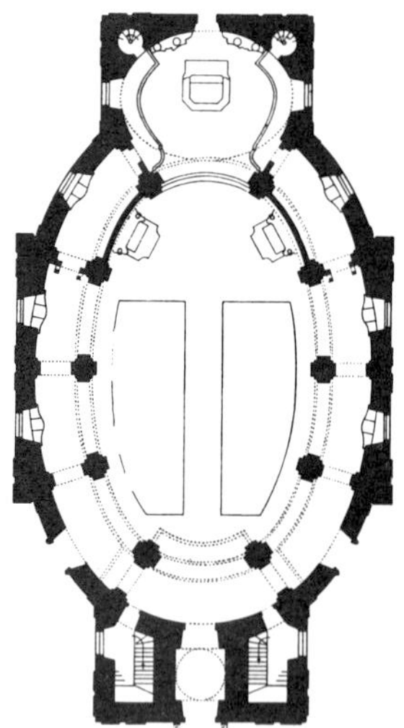

1080, 1081 *Interior and plan of the Steinhausen church by the Zimmermann brothers*

1082–1084 *The church of the Vierzehnheiligen by B. Neumann*

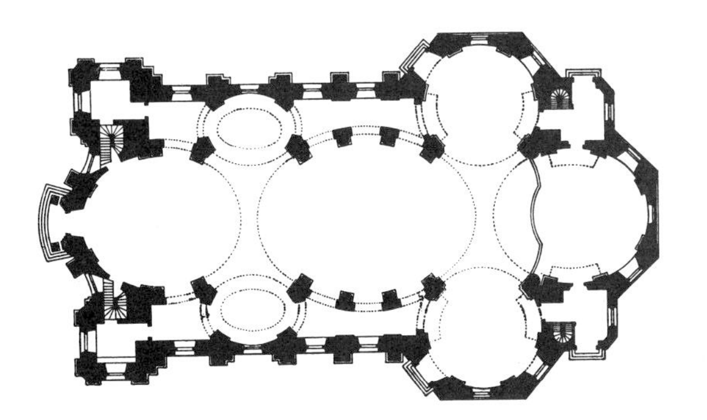

1085 *(left) Interior of the church of St John Nepomuk, Munich, by the Asam brothers*
1086, 1087 *The parish church of Oberammergau*

valleys of Austria, Bohemia, Bavaria and both sides of the Alps small agricultural and industrial communities built a series of churches, homogeneous in style and infinitely varied in individual solutions (Figs 1086–8); the design of the decorative details, as was natural, became predominant over the creation of the actual organisms, but did not impair the balance of these works beyond a certain point; and in their entirety they constitute one of the richest European artistic heritages, henceforward an integral part of custom and landscape.

The experience of the last German generation, born in the last years of the seventeenth century, is comparable to that of contemporary Roman architects – Giuseppe Sardi, 1680–1753; Filippo Raguzzini, c. 1680–1771; Gabriele Valvassori, 1683–1761 – and with the Spanish 'delirious fools'[18] – Pedro de Ribera (c. 1683–1742) and Narciso Tomé (c. 1690–1742). There was a difference between them and the previous generation – noticeable even in the executive continuity of some families of builders: for instance between Kilian Ignaz Dientzenhofer and his father Christoph, or between Alberto Churriguera (1676–c. 1750) and his older brothers José Benito (1665–1725) and Joaquín (1674–1724) – not adequately expressed by the general terms such as 'baroque' and 'rococo'. This difference involves not so much general tendency as professional position; José Benito Churriguera, though ousted from official activity to the advantage of his contemporary Teodoro Ardemáns (1664–1726), who became the royal architect in 1702, had the opportunity of designing on a vast scale for the banker Juan de Goyeneche, who commissioned him to design the town of Nuevo Batzán, which we have already mentioned; Alberto, considered the most brilliant of the three brothers, after having designed the famous *plaza mayor* at Salamanca (Fig. 1089), had to exercise his talent on the details of the cathedrals of Valladolid and Salamanca, and in some small churches, while Juvara, Sacchetti and Ventura Rodriguez were controlling the great royal building sites in the line that went from court classicism to neoclassicism.

The Italian architects we have mentioned, though educated in and sensitive to European tendencies, played a secondary part in the modification of the townscape. What counted in the eyes of foreigners making the grand tour in Italy were the glories of the past (in fact the landscape painters, Pannini in Rome and Canaletto in Venice – both born in 1697 – perpetuated the already well-established historical aspect of the great Renaissance centres, seen in retrospective images); what

1088, 1090 *(right)* *The parish church of Riva in Valsesia*

1089 *The* plaza mayor, *Salamanca, by A. Churriguera*

later transformed these urban organisms, even if only in part, was the addition of monumental buildings by the classical architects belonging to the following generation, Alessandro Galilei (1691–1736), Ferdinando Fuga (1699–1781), Luigi Vanvitelli (1700–73).

The nature of the 'rococo' is particularly characteristic in the sphere of court activity in France and northern Europe. The masters of this *art nouveau*, which according to Blondel had been invented in France in the first fifty years of the eighteenth century,[19] were the architects Gilles Marie Oppenordt (1672–1742), Nicolas Pineau (1684–1754), Juste Aurèle Meissonnier (1695–1750), François de Cuvilliés (1695–1768) and the painters Antoine Watteau (1684–1721) and François Boucher (1703–70); the distinction between the specializations, in this case, was fairly uncertain, in that both found a common working field in the decoration of interiors, starting from the repertoire of Pierre Le Pautre (1660–1744); they themselves spread the new decorative style in Europe, together with the planners of the great buildings and gardens: Pineau together with Le Blond at St Petersburg from 1716, Oppenordt at La Granja in 1720, Watteau in London in 1719, Cuvilliés in Munich in 1728; Boucher's

1091 *The church of Valinotto, 1738, by B. Vittone, from* Istruzioni elementari

1092, 1093 *The* transparente *by Tomé in Toledo cathedral*

cartoons for tapestries were reproduced for the king of Sweden, the king of Naples and even for the emperor of China.

Their activity did not characterize a period, and was not antithetical to the classical tendency on the same level, but produced a historical result of the greatest importance: it disengaged the style of decorations and objects of applied art from that of architectural works and organisms on a town-planning scale. Even though there was evident interaction between them, the various genres of design evolved separately, and the fact that they were out of phase contributed more than any single figurative tendency to the disintegration of the unity of the classical style.

England

When Charles II became king of England, in 1660, he gave the post of surveyor general of works to one of his noble supporters, Sir John Denham, an amateur poet and artist; but the real arbiter in the field of building, in the early years of the Restoration, was the treasurer Hugh May (1622–84), who during Cromwell's Protectorate had been in Holland with the duke of Buckingham. He brought the new Dutch classicism of van Campen and Post to England, built a series of residences for the noble persons of the court and established a lasting stylistic and building tradition.

The two first royal buildings were the new gallery of Somerset House, built in 1661 according to a design left by Inigo Jones, and the palace of Greenwich, begun by Webb in 1662; both of which declared the desire to re-establish the continuity of the court tradition broken at the fall of Charles I.

But the mobility of cultural interest, characteristic of this period of English history, encouraged many developments, one of the most important of which was the movement of men of science – as well as

1094 *A door in the bishop's palace, Würzburg*

1095 *An interior at Versailles in Louis XV style*

artists like Jones and Webb, and men of letters like Denham – in the direction of architecture.

Gresham College, in London, provided the initial setting for this encounter. Here, since 1640, at the instigation of Theodore Haak, a group of physicists, astronomers and doctors had formed itself, including Jonathan Goddard and John Wilkins; from 1646 Robert Boyle attended these meetings: then, for political reasons, most of these men moved to Oxford – Wilkins in 1649, Goddard in 1651, Boyle in 1653 – and met in Boyle's house. At the time of the Restoration, the group returned to London, and on 28 November – in the mood of reconciliation which characterized the beginning of the government of Charles II and Clarendon – met at Gresham College to discuss the formation of a scientific society acknowledged by the king. Those present were Wren – holder of the chair of astronomy at Gresham from 1657 and at Trinity College Oxford from 1658 – Lord Brouncker, Moray, Neile, Wilkins, Goddard, Petty, Balle and Hill, who prepared a list of another thirty members; Moray took it upon himself to obtain the royal approval, and the association – called the Royal Society for Improving Natural Knowledge by Experiments – was officially recognized between 1662 and 1663. The society nominated Lord Brouncker as president, Oldenburg (and in 1672 Evelyn) as secretary and Hooke, Boyle's assistant, as curator of experiments; as its motto it chose a phrase from Horace, *nullius in verba*, and began to publish the *Philosophical Transactions* in 1664; Newton joined it as a member in 1671, and became president in 1703.

At least three of these men, John Evelyn (1620–1706), Christopher Wren (1632–1723) and Robert Hooke (1635–1703), played an important part in the field of architecture.

Evelyn, a rich landowner and friend of the collector Lord Arundel, travelled in France, Holland and Italy during the civil war, and stayed in Rome from 1644 to 1645 with his contemporary Roger Pratt; in 1651 he returned to England and devoted himself to his main passion, gardening; in 1664 he published the English translation of the book by Fréart de Chambray *A Parallel of the Ancient Architecture with the Modern*, with a glossary of technical terms similar to those of scientific terms compiled at the same time by other members of the Royal Society. His diary, begun in 1640, bore witness to his boundless interest in the spectacle of art and nature, and contained, among innumerable other accounts, a series of descriptions of the main European gardens (Villa d'Este at Tivoli, Palazzo Doria at Genoa, Boboli, Pratolino, the Quirinale, the Bois de Boulogne, the Luxembourg).

Wren, son of a rector, studied science at Oxford, was interested in astronomy – he helped to establish the link between the discoveries of Kepler and Newton's system – but also in numerous practical matters: meteorological instruments, waterworks, etching processes, improvements in naval construction. In 1661 he turned down the offer to direct some harbour work in Tangier, and in 1663 presented the Royal Society with the model of his first building, the theatre to be built at Oxford for archbishop Sheldon, which imitated the structure and decoration of the theatre of Marcellus, described in Serlio's treatise; Wren replaced the semicircular layout with a polygonal one, so as not to have to distort the single bays of the outer walls, and resolved the problems of the decorative apparatus with a somewhat mechanical skill. In the summer of 1665 he went to Paris, where he met Mansart, Le Vau and Bernini, visited the royal châteaux around the city, and possibly the cities of Holland; at his return he was consulted, together with Evelyn, Pratt and May, in connection with the restoration of the Gothic cathedral of St Paul's, and suggested rebuilding the crossing of the two arms with a great dome, in the place of the unsafe medieval tower.

Hooke, born of a modest family, served an

apprenticeship as a portrait-painter in Lely's studio, studied at Westminster school and then at Oxford, where he entered the scientific circle already mentioned; he became Boyle's assistant and helped him to construct the *machina Boyleana*, then, while he was the curator of experiments for the Royal Society, was used by Wren, because of his extraordinary graphic ability, as collaborator in his works of architecture. Hooke's scientific interests – in optics, mechanics, statics – and his capacity for discovering practical applications of new techniques (microscope, barometer, anchor escapement and spring balance in watches) turned out to be important in the field of engineering and architectural composition; his personal contribution, in the works nominally attributed to Wren, still remains to be fully assessed.

These men were available to demonstrate their abilities after the great fire of 1666 which destroyed a very large part of the city of London.

About a week after the end of the fire, 13 September, the king issued a proclamation announcing that the city was to be rebuilt in stone and brick, with wider roads and according to a new plan. The task of preparing the reconstruction – i.e. of making the detailed survey of the properties to be redistributed, and of elaborating new standards – was given to three representatives of the king (Wren, Pratt and May) and three representatives of the city (Hooke, Edward Jerman and Peter Mills; these last two, a carpenter and bricklayer coming from the old professional organization, were the planners favoured by the city guilds and magistrates).

On 11 and 13 September Wren and Evelyn presented the king with two plans for the reconstruction of the city (Figs 1097–9), possibly already prepared and discussed before the fire; both were based on a *grand dessein* of a continental type, i.e. on a combination of series of roads converging upon the main buildings (cathedral and stock exchange); Evelyn's plan was summary and rigidly formal like the plan of a garden, Wren's thorough, reasonable and adroitly adapted to the surrounding organism. A few days later other plans were presented to the authorities and to public opinion: two more by Evelyn, more elaborate than the first, one by captain Valentin Knight (who envisaged twelve main streets perpendicular to the river and twenty-four minor ones, parallel to the bank, but neither straight nor geometrically traced) (Fig. 1100), one by Robert Hooke (who suggested a grid with square meshes, distorted only to link up with the Strand and surrounding fabric, spared by the fire); later Richard Newcourt proposed a more complicated grid plan where every section constituted a parish.

The eight plans fully represented the state of English town-planning culture in the first years of the Restoration. Only Evelyn and Wren seemed aware of the new European monumental taste, Knight based himself on Dutch models, Hooke and Newcourt upon the sixteenth-century grid plan, already widely applied in America and Scandinavia, and indeed they are often quoted as possible sources for the plans of the towns founded in the English overseas colonies from the end of the seventeenth century onwards.

But the implementation of the new plan – independently of its design – met with insurmountable difficulties. Even the survey of the sites and the ascertaining of ownership seemed impossible because of the difficulty of moving the rubble and the absence of a great many property owners; compulsory purchase and property rearrangement seemed even more impracticable because of a series of legal, economic and political obstacles. The English monarchy did not possess the proven town-planning instruments of Dutch administration, nor the money and arbitrary power of Louis XIV.

As early as November the idea of a new plan was put aside; the reconstruction of the city was thus restricted to these provisions:

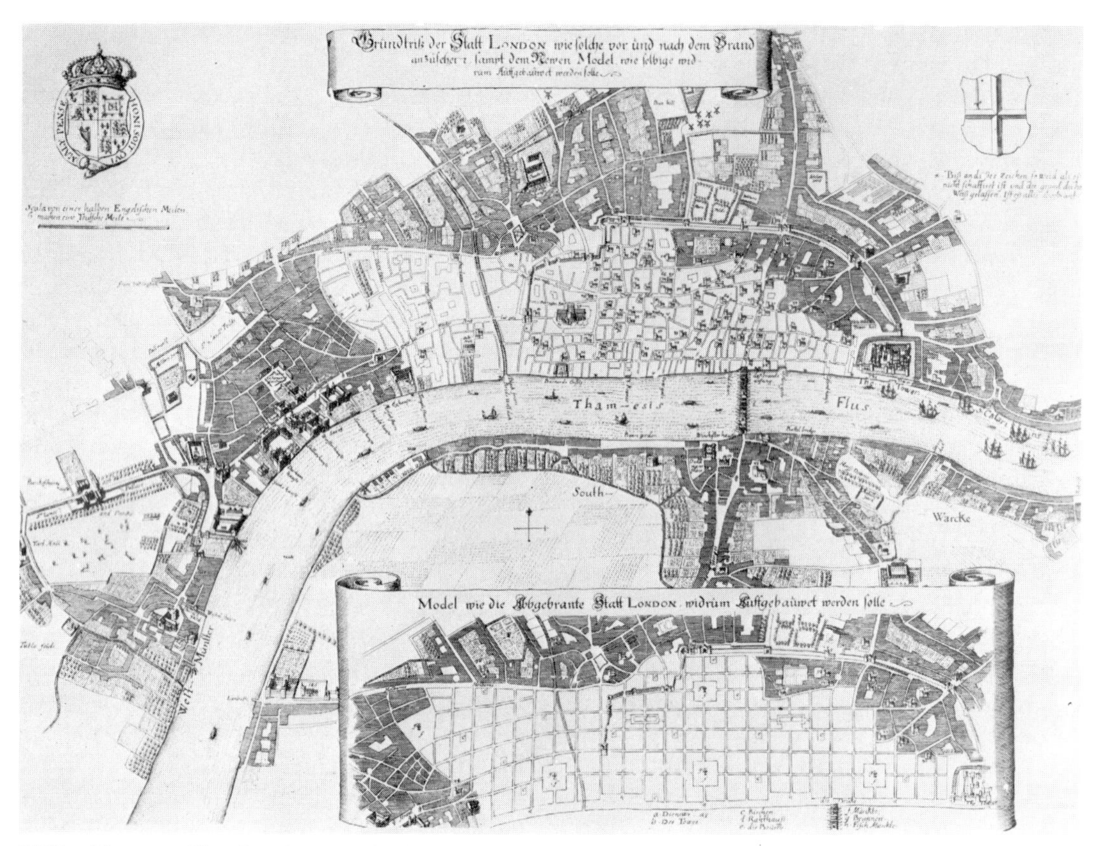

1096 *The area of London destroyed by fire in 1666 and Hooke's plan for rebuilding*
1097, 1098 *Evelyn's first two plans for rebuilding*

1 The broadening of roads; given the character of the medieval division into plots, with deep and narrow parcels, this operation could be carried out without damage, indeed with positive advantage to the old owners. In October the six committee members distinguished four categories of streets, with the following widths: 70 feet, 50–42 feet, 30–25 feet and 16 feet (subsequently slightly reduced).

2 Hydraulic works: the canalization of the river Fleet, the improvement of sewers and the embankment (designed but not carried out) along the Thames.

3 Building regulations, which fixed not only the constructional features but also the distributive types of the new houses; three

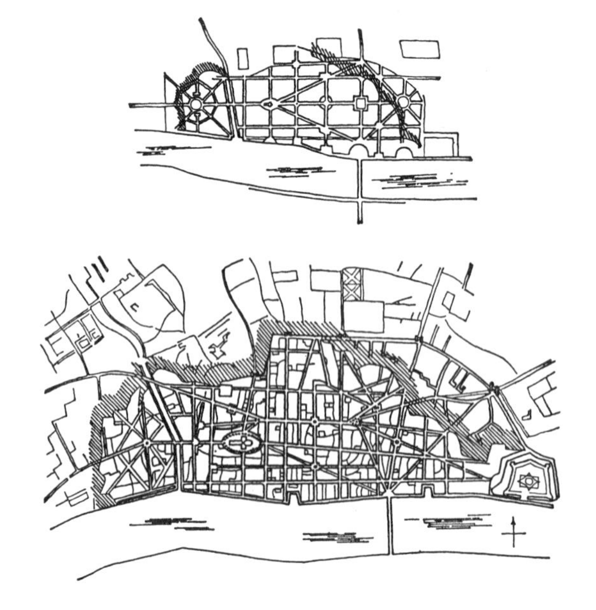

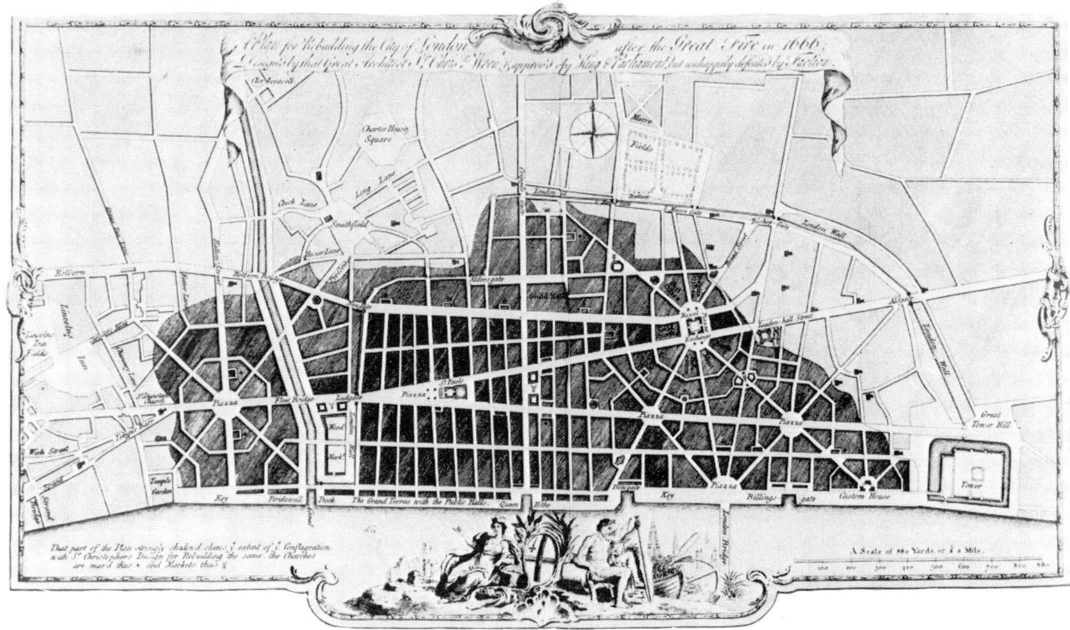

1099 *Wren's plan for rebuilding*

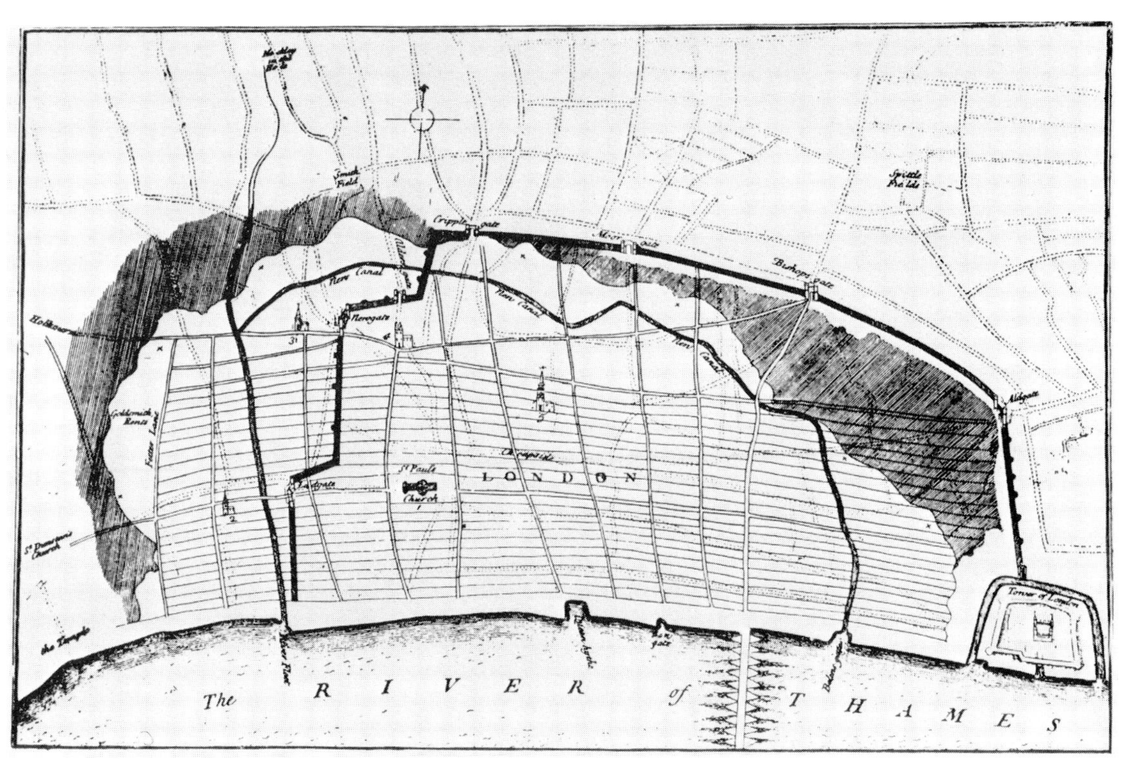

1100 *Knight's plan for rebuilding*

1101 *Portrait of Wren engraved by W. Holl*

sorts of ordinary houses were envisaged, of two, three and four storeys according to the width of the road (Fig. 1102), and a monumental type, freer, for the dwellings of the rich. These regulations remained in force until the present century, and influenced building not only in London, but throughout the country.

4 The reconstruction of public buildings: the Royal Exchange – designed by Jerman – the Halls of the City Companies and the churches, which were Wren's province, with the collaboration of Hooke, Oliver and Mills (later replaced by Edward Woodroffe).

The Act for Rebuilding the City of London, ratified in 1667, summarized all these provisions and authorized a tax on the goods going into the port of London to finance the works; a second more complete law was passed in 1670.

From this moment on Wren was almost completely absorbed in works of architecture; the law of 1670 reduced the number of parishes from 87 to 51, but each needed a new church; furthermore there was the problem of rebuilding St Paul's cathedral in a modern form.

The 51 parish churches (Figs 1103–16) designed by Wren in name; were the result of a complex collective operation. These churches, as has been noted many times, were very different one from the other, and also from St Paul's cathedral; they were stylistically careless, with evident irregularities; they appeared to be improvised at random, rather than elaborated with care and by degrees. In many cases Wren certainly gave a free hand to his collaborators, whose standards were lower or who, like Hooke, were completely devoid of a sense of formal elegance; he himself, as designer or as organizer of other people's works, made a distinction between the noble theme of the cathedral and the more everyday themes of the churches. His procedure in this case consisted in establishing a fairly extensive range of distributive types – derived from Dutch examples, from the pages of treatises, from a personal interpretation of the Vitruvian basilica, or arrived at by freely intermingling these points of inspiration; in adapting them to the various sites which were often irregular and restricted by the surrounding houses; and in resolving the individual decorative problems on another scale, episodically and almost with indifference.

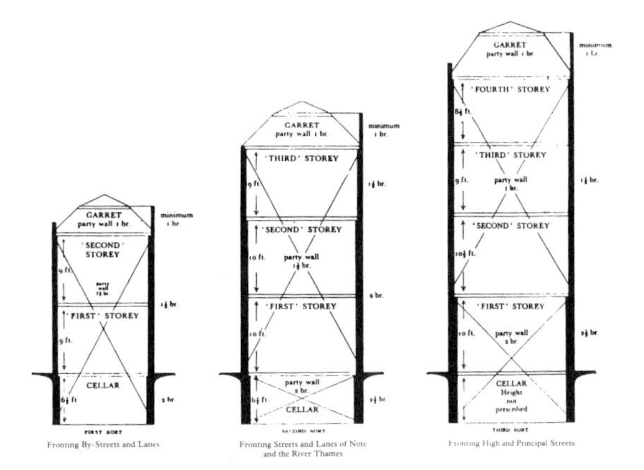

1102 *Building types laid down by the 1667 Act for Rebuilding the City of London*

The limited dimensions of the churches were compensated for in many cases by a tall and distinctive spire; here, too, starting from well-known Flemish models, Wren and his colleagues invented the most bizarre *pastiches* of classical decorations, and mingled structural elements – arches, columns, cornices, tympana, domes, pyramids – with secondary ones – obelisks, consoles, candelabra – without any concern for hierarchy; thus some of these spires, composed exclusively of classical elements, acquired a character very similar to the traditional Gothic one.

In St Paul's the problem was different. The great church had to dominate the view of London like the old one, and had to become the monument *par excellence*, i.e. visibly to represent, even in its most minor subtleties, the hierarchy of values on which the power of the state was based.

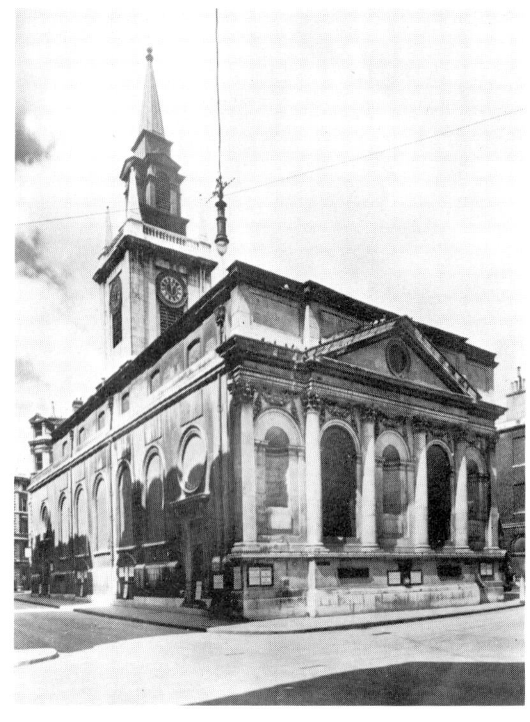

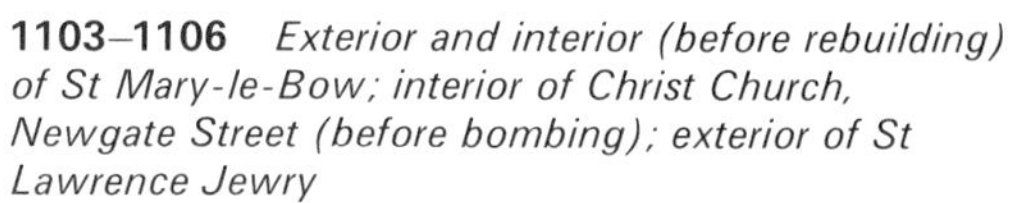

1103–1106 *Exterior and interior (before rebuilding) of St Mary-le-Bow; interior of Christ Church, Newgate Street (before bombing); exterior of St Lawrence Jewry*
1107–1112 *Plans of St Mildred, Bread street; St Benet Fink; St Anne and St Agnes; St James Garlickhythe; St Swithin, Cannon street; St Antholin*
1113 *(opposite)* *St Bride's*

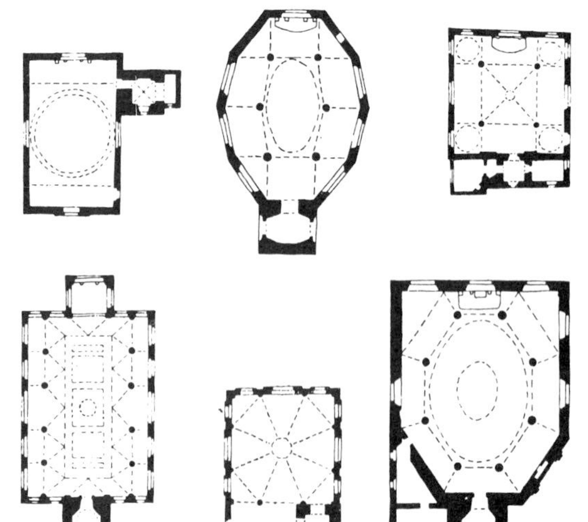

1114 *Interior (before reorganization) of St Bride's*

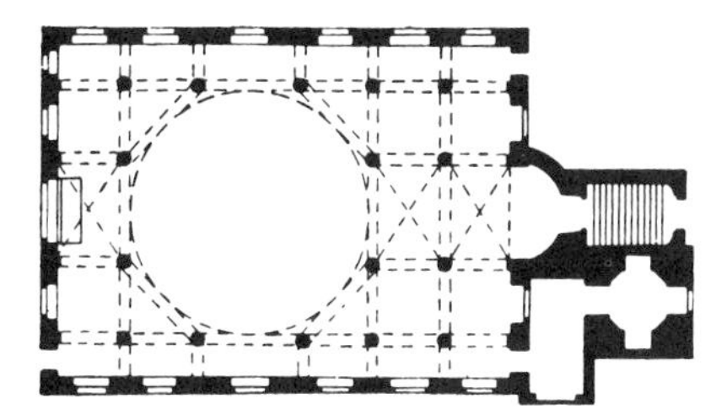

1115, 1116 *Interior and plan of St Stephen Walbrook*

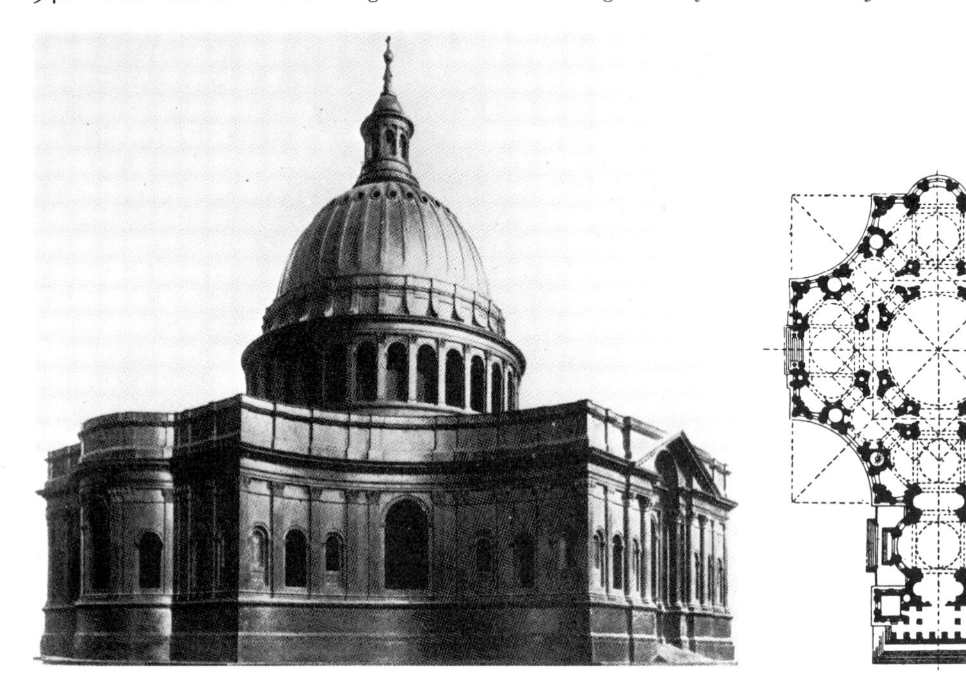

1117, 1118 *Model and plan of Wren's 1673 plan for St Paul's cathedral*

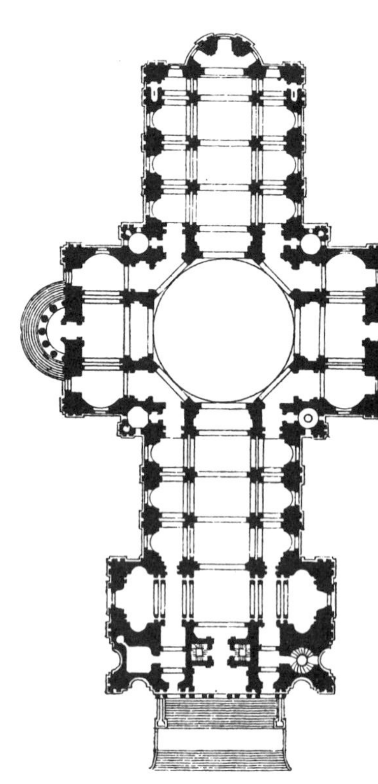

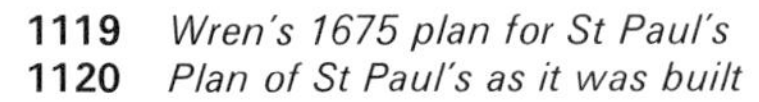

1119 *Wren's 1675 plan for St Paul's*
1120 *Plan of St Paul's as it was built*

1121 *St Paul's cathedral among the buildings of the City*

The available models for a large monumental church were the Italian and French: St Peter's and the royal chapel just designed by Mansart for St-Denis; they had a double character, classical, i.e. universally acceptable, and Catholic, i.e. politically and religiously controversial; this distinction, at that time, was far more serious than it had been at the time of Inigo Jones. The power representing Catholic imperialism was no longer distant, ailing Spain, but the nearby and aggressive France of Louis XIV. While Wren was preparing the designs for St Paul's, the ministry of the 'Cabal' was in power and Charles II was signing the secret treaty of Dover; the Francophile tendency was a component of the English political game, and the enforced restoration of Catholicism a by no means remote possibility.

Wren, with his detached spirit, was far from eager to have his own personal choice involved in this conflict: the relation between art and ideology did not concern artists – as had been the case in the sixteenth century and as was to be the case again, in different terms, in the eighteenth – but established authority. However, with his extraordinary social sensitivity, Wren registered the fluctuations of the argument in responsible circles; he had to reconcile the traditional idea of a 'cathedral' and the modern idea of a domed 'temple', the need to fit it smoothly into the organism of the city and to dominate it with a recapitulatory form, the opportunity of using the symbols of classicism to underpin authority and the need to avoid an exotic qualification of these symbols, retaining a reference, however slight, to medieval English typologies.

The evolution of the plan for St Paul's is much more informative than the single chosen solution. At first the idea was to retain part of the Gothic structure still standing; in 1668 a new collapse made complete demolition preferable, and the building of a completely new building, 'handsome and noble, and suitable to all the Ends of it and to the reputation of the City, and the Nation'.[20] Wren prepared a first plan, which consisted of the coupling of a great rectangular choir and a domed vestibule; this was approved in 1670 but appeared old-fashioned and not sufficiently organic a few years later. Wren then conceived a large symmetrical composition, with either equal or unequal arms, dominated by a central dome, and in 1673 a wooden model was built, which was criticized as being too different from the traditional ecclesiastical type and too theoretical (Figs 1117–18). The next project, of 1675, went to the opposite extreme: it adopted a traditional cruciform plan, laid out starting from the eight piers of the dome, it abandoned the external giant order and concealed the hemispheric volume of the dome, but enlarged the lantern so as to transform it into a second slighter dome, which supported a tall timber spire; this was the transcription into classical forms of a Gothic organism (Fig. 1119). From here, through successive variants, Wren arrived at the definitive version: he altered the position of the eight piers, designed an outer covering with two superimposed orders, abandoned the spire and progressively raised the profile of the dome, which was once more the dominant feature of the building, commensurate with the city panorama rather than the organism below (Figs 1120–5).

The form of the dome, hemispherical and surrounded by a colonnade, may derive from the Bramante dome reproduced in Serlio's treatise, and perhaps even more from the classical image that an Englishman of the seventeenth century might have read into the sixteenth-century design. But Wren wanted

1122 *Interior view of St Paul's*

to develop this silhouette vertically, to the maximum degree allowed by the compactness of the form and the stability of the supporting structures. For this reason the internal drum, with its pilastered decoration which repeats the motif of the peristyle, was distorted into a truncated cone; the internal dome, in accordance with Mansart's idea repeated later by Hardouin-Mansart at Les Invalides, ended in an open *oculus*; the lantern was supported by a second conical dome, lit from the openings in the attic, and the external silhouette was created with a third wooden dome, covered with lead. Every fourth intercolumniation, in the peristyle surrounding the drum, was walled in to give greater stability to the whole, but in such a way as scarcely to interrupt the uniform rhythm of the supports.

This complicated structure, which pro-

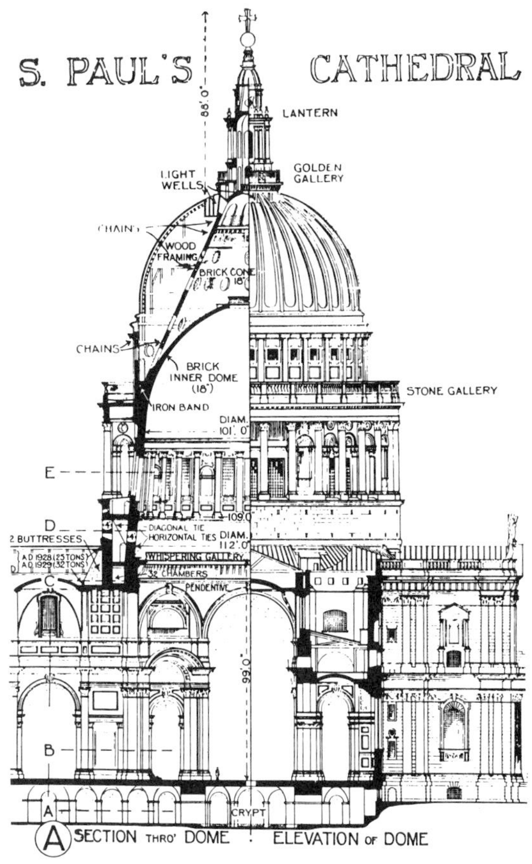

1123–1125 *Section and details of St Paul's*

duced a sensational perspective effect inside but which, on the outside, appeared as a simple 'reposeful' shell,[21] praised almost without exception by English historians up to the present time, was the result of an extremely skilful compromise. The perfection of this work is completely different from the perfection of a work by Bernini, based on the three-dimensional development of a plastic organism, or of a French classical work, based on the balanced organization of a portion of infinite space, but still on the unity of invention and the continuity of the visual organization; here unity and continuity are deliberately sacrificed: the balance is obtained by correcting one motif with another, shrewdly judging the contrasts and adroitly combining a large number of heterogeneous parts.

Wren was a man of science, and many attempts have been made to draw parallels between his architecture and his scientific experiments. In a more restricted sense, his scientific education revealed itself in the ingeniousness of the static organism; none the less even this aspect of his work must be specified carefully. At Oxford Wren certainly knew John Wallis, the mathematician who studied the theory of the load of beams and who calculated the structure drawn in Serlio's treatise; Hooke concerned himself with these problems personally, and formulated one of the laws on the elasticity of solid bodies. But it does not appear that either of them applied this knowledge to the practice of architecture; Wren, like all the other planners of his time, used structural schemes and measures already tried by experiment and improved their

1126 *Detail of Chelsea Hospital*
1127 *Greenwich Hospital*

functioning intuitively, with relevant corrections.

In fact his scientific education did not amount to a generic mental habit, applicable to any order of ideas, as it was conceived from the eighteenth century onwards, but as an apprenticeship strictly linked to physical studies. In this sense he was not a scientist, but a mathematician and physicist, and did not claim to apply the scientific method to architecture; his previous activity in the field of science produced rather, in architecture, the attitude of a dilettante, which persisted throughout his long career and which did not conflict at all with his seriousness, competence and intellectual rigour. It emerged in his indifference for the different formal systems, in his liking for variants, in his ability to explore the whole range of possible solutions to a problem.

1128 *Wren's addition to Hampton Court Palace*

In this way Wren's work still belonged fully to the sphere of seventeenth-century rhetoric; for him, too, architecture remained an 'adulatory art', as a very different artist, Guarino Guarini,[22] wrote in his own time, and architectural choices remained questions of propriety, measure. His scientific mentality helped him to move through this world of choices, with a coolness and detachment as yet unknown, i.e. it revealed, very early on, the political nature of the new European classicism. His deliberate adherence to the political, social and cultural reality of England, not only to the superficial and temporary characteristics but also to deeper ones, which were to last, explains his success and uninterrupted prestige: Wren interpreted the moment of the Restoration, but also several new aspects of English society, at a juncture when crucial institutional decisions

1129 *Fountain Court, Hampton Court Palace, by Wren*

1130 *View of Wren's building at Hampton Court Palace from the south-east*

were about to be made. Wren worked in seclusion, did not seem to take part in the conflicts of his times, and the site of St Paul's remained in action before and after the 1689 revolution; none the less the tone of his architecture, its rigour that was not without elasticity, its preference for human and practical values over theoretical ones, were in accord with the discussions of the men of letters and politicians who set the tone for the liberal and bourgeois culture of the new parliamentary state.

Wren remained in the post of surveyor general of the royal works under three sovereigns – Charles II, James II and William and Mary. For Charles II he designed Chelsea Hospital in 1681 and Winchester Palace in 1683 and for William and Mary he designed part of Hampton Court Palace from 1689 to 1698, and in 1695 Greenwich Hospital (Figs 1126–30).

The basic models, here too, were French: Les Invalides for hospitals, the Louvre and Versailles, naturally, for royal palaces; all organisms based on the mutual independence of layout of the volumes and the decorative parameter. This distinction enabled Wren to retain the block-like volumes, the broad articulations on a landscape scale, but to vary suitably the architectural texture, adopting the traditional coupling of walls in brick and finishing touches in stone, Dutch in origin, and to obtain a singular character of intimacy and accessibility, even in a court building like Hampton Court.

A royal palace required a garden laid on the same axes of symmetry. Here, too, French models were paramount, but came up against an English tradition already in existence, very different from the continental one, based on an interest in the natural elements – grass, trees and water – and on the creation of an immediate contact with the landscape.

In the reign of Elizabeth the Tradescant family moved from Holland to England, and introduced the taste for the botanic garden; John Tradescant senior, gardener to Lord Salisbury and Charles I, travelled through Europe and imported large consignments of flower bulbs from Holland; John junior was sent by his father to America in 1677, and introduced many new varieties of flower into England, for instance the red columbine, phlox and aster. Interest in gardens was widespread among the wealthy classes; James I was interested in botany; Bacon wrote an essay 'Of Gardens', attributing more importance to flowers and plants than to building schemes; Evelyn, as we have seen, visited the most important gardens of Europe comparing them to each other with the competence of an expert.

In 1658 André and Gabriel Mollet, the sons of Claude who had been Le Nôtre's master, settled in England, and from 1661 to 1666 were in the pay of Charles II as gardeners. At this time the king was laying out the gardens of Whitehall, Hampton Court, St

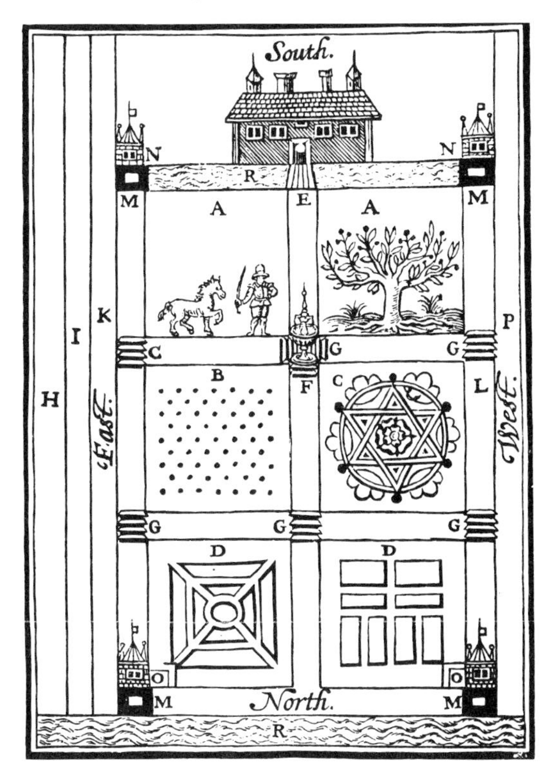

1131 *Plan of an English garden, 1618*

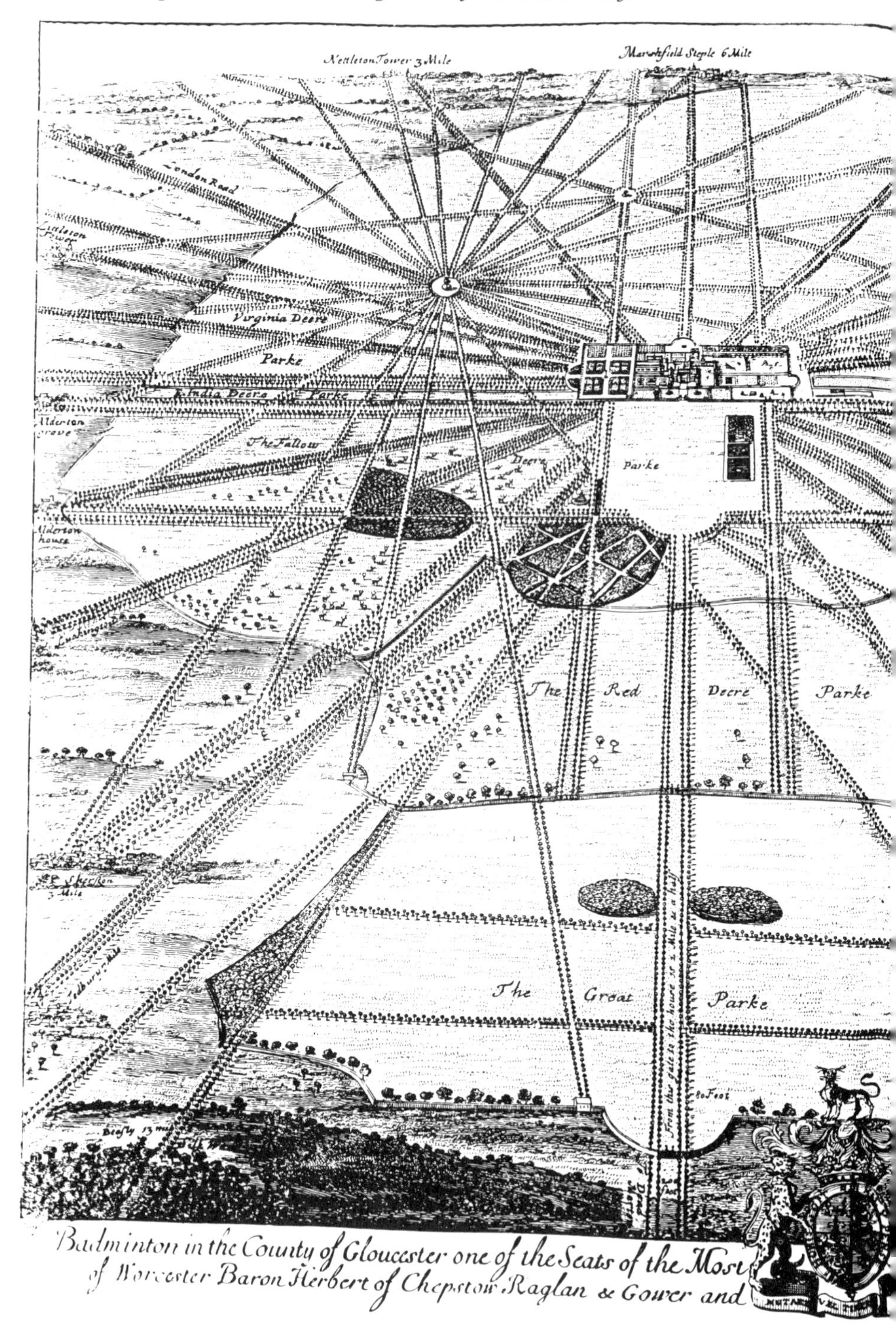

1132 *View of the park at Badminton in 1714 (from Knyff and Kip)*

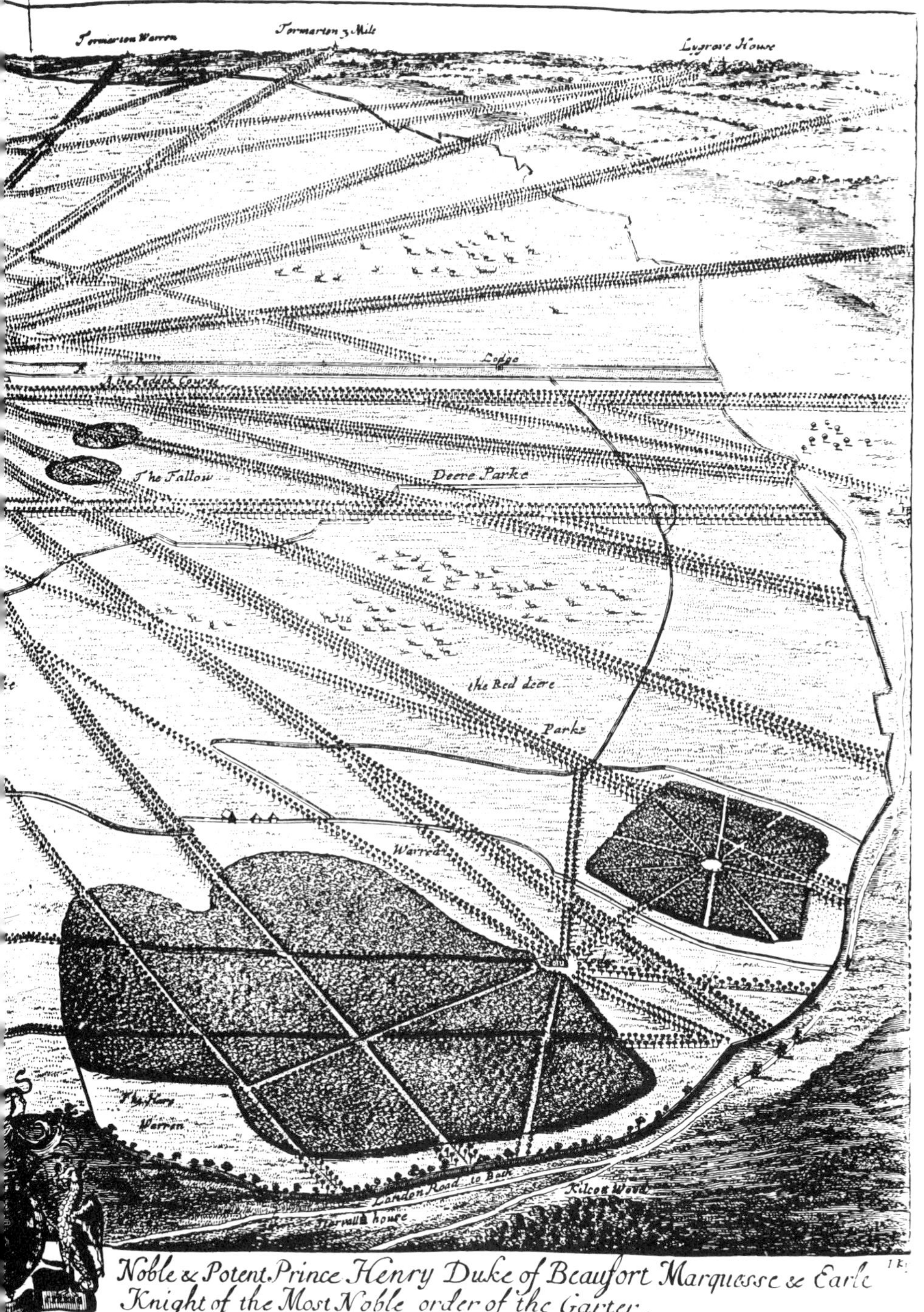
Lygrove House
Lodge
The Fallow
Deere Parke
the Red deere
Parke
Warren
Kilcot Wood
Noble & Potent Prince Henry Duke of Beaufort Marquesse & Earle
Knight of the Most Noble order of the Garter.

James's and Greenwich, and in 1662 he asked Hugues de Lionne if he could send Le Nôtre to London; it is not known for certain if Louis XIV's great gardener did personally come to London, but he certainly influenced Charles II's schemes either directly or through the Mollet brothers, and for Greenwich he supplied an autograph plan.[23]

These contributions were accepted with interest, but with a critical spirit: in 1665 John Rea published a treatise, *Ceres, Flora and Pomona*, where he said that a 'choice collection of living beauties, rare plants, flowers and fruits, are indeed the wealth, glory and delight of a garden',[24] that is to say, he intentionally reversed the continental rule according to which 'things which are built are superior to those which are planted'; in his diary Pepys tells of a walk with May in the park at Whitehall, during which he affirmed the superiority of English gardens, as places to walk among the beauties of nature.

In 1666, at the death of the Mollet brothers, the direction of the royal gardens went to John Rose who had studied in France; he founded the school of the English 'formal garden', though he also continued with his botanical studies, grew the pineapple in England, and wrote a treatise on vines and fruit trees. Two of Rose's pupils, George London (d. 1714) and Henry Wise (1635–1738), laid out for William and Mary the new gardens of Hampton Court linked to Wren's plan, with great radiating avenues but also with a very dense wood – which was known as the Wilderness – in a secluded corner.

Many landowners laid out their country parks in the French court style: the duke of Beaufort created Badminton, in Gloucestershire (1682) (Fig. 1132), the duke of Devonshire transformed the Renaissance garden of Chatsworth in Derbyshire (1685), Thomas Coke built Melbourne Hall in Derbyshire (1704). The great English parks of this period are illustrated in the Dutch publication by Leonard Knyff and Jan Kip, *Le Nouveau Théâtre de la Grande Bretagne* (1714).

In 1699 William Talman (1650–1719), the architect of Chatsworth, designed a sort of Trianon in the gardens of Hampton Court for William, and closely imitated the now illustrious models of Hardouin-Mansart; he occupied the post of comptroller of the royal works from 1689 to 1702 when he was replaced by Vanbrugh. But at this point English architecture took on a new lease of life, in the lively intellectual climate of the early eighteenth century.

Wren – who lived until 1723 and retained the position of surveyor general for fifty years, almost until his death – remained master and arbiter of English architecture during this period too; the most important architects of the new generation, Nicholas Hawksmoor (1661–1736), John Vanbrugh (1664–1726) and Thomas Archer (1668–1743), used his experience as a starting-point, and for a long time Hawksmoor worked in his service. But the process of critical revision and conversion of architectural choices into practical, moral and social terms – which in Wren's work was checked by a still seventeenth-century feeling of propriety, of hierarchical prudence – was sharply accelerated among his younger pupils; their activity has been assessed in many contrasting ways: in manuals it is known as 'English baroque', while Emil Kaufmann saw in it the negation of the organic quality of the baroque and the early anticipation of the 'revolutionary' architects of the end of the century.

A correct assessment must necessarily avoid such ambiguous terminology, and consider this architectural period in the context of the new English culture emerging at the beginning of the eighteenth century. Hawksmoor, Vanbrugh and Archer were contemporaries of Swift and Arbuthnot (both born in 1667), Shaftesbury (1671), Addison and Steele (1672); Vanbrugh, the most gifted as an artist, also wrote plays, was a militant Whig and one of the most notable members of the Kit-Cat Club; in their turn politicians and writers, particularly Swift and later Pope,

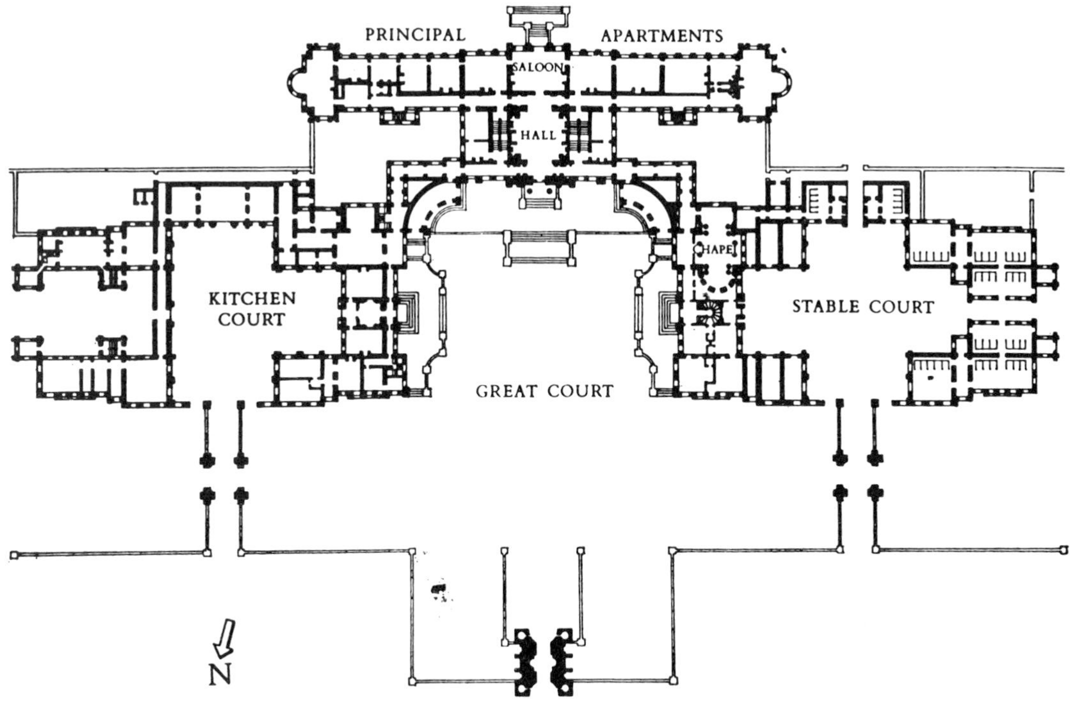

1133, 1134 *View and plan of Castle Howard, Yorkshire*

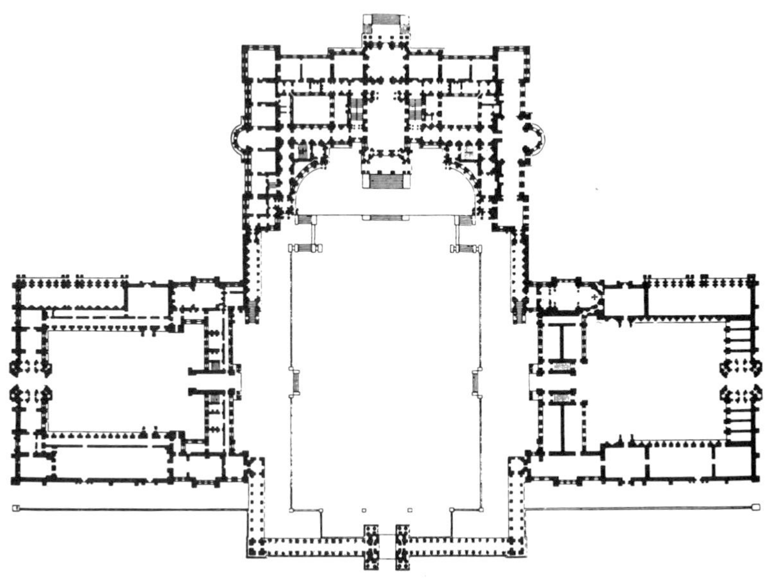

1135, 1136 *(opposite) Two views of Blenheim Palace, seat of the dukes of Marlborough*
1137, 1138 *The Long Gallery at Blenheim and plan of the palace*

1139 *Detail of the exterior of Blenheim: the entrance*

1140 *Seaton Delaval by Vanbrugh*

discussed architecture with passion and expertise. Contacts with Europe were ever more numerous, particularly after 1714 when Hanover was linked to the English crown, and they were no longer unilateral. Among the intellectuals who emigrated to England after the revocation of the edict of Nantes, Boyer published his *Dictionnaire royal* (1702) and translated Addison; de Maizeaux was involved in all the literary controversies of the time; Coste became a member of the Royal Society, translated Shaftesbury, Newton and Locke, guided many English nobles on their grand tour of Europe. Meanwhile from 1697 Höchstetter published the *Oratio de utilitate peregrinationis anglicanae* in Tübingen; Voltaire was in London from 1726 to 1729 and established the inverse practice of the journey to England for European intellectuals; Handel settled in England in 1710. Vanbrugh was a prisoner in France from 1690, Archer may have paid a personal visit to the works of Italian baroque artists by whom he was inspired; Alessandro Galilei, in his turn, spent five years of his youth in England (1714–19), at the time of the most important works of Vanbrugh and Hawksmoor.

Hawksmoor and Vanbrugh worked together as designers from 1699 to 1726, the first after a long apprenticeship, the second after a sudden conversion from his previous political and literary interests, 'without thought or lecture' as Swift observed.[25] Vanbrugh, who figured in the forefront because of his livelier temperament, came to fame in 1701, when he designed the country

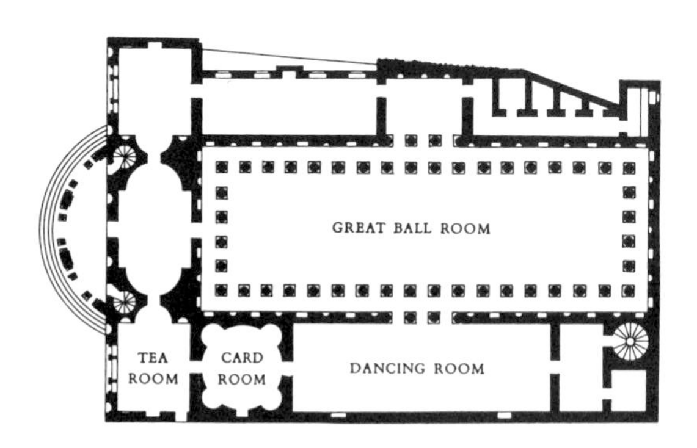

1141, 1142 *View and plan of the Assembly Rooms, York*

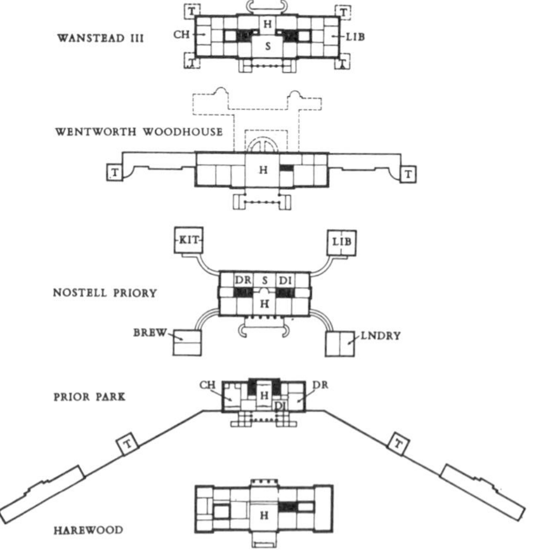

1143 *Some plans of English Palladian villas (from Summerson)*

1144, 1145 *View and plan of Lord Burlington's Chiswick House*

house of Castle Howard (Figs 1133–4) for the earl of Carlisle, and in 1702 obtained the post of comptroller of royal buildings, i.e. lieutenant of the septuagenarian Wren. In 1704 he was chosen by the duke of Marlborough to design the great palace of Blenheim, the largest-scale work of the English eighteenth century (Figs 1135–9).

In these two country houses the inevitable model, i.e. the blocks articulated in Ω shapes as in Versailles, was transformed by the breaking up of the compact volume and the considerable prominence of the plastic decorative details, which further fragmented the

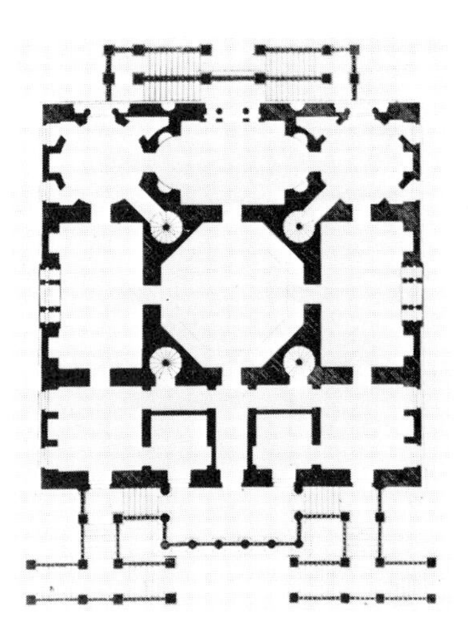

1146, 1147 *Tom Tower, Oxford and one of the campanili of St Paul's*

general composition. The result was an extremely complex spatial counterpoint, fantastical and cold at the same time, where Wren's aggregation of mutually contrasting elements was carried to an extreme.

In certain minor buildings – Goose-pie House, Whitehall (1699), the country houses built at the end of his career, Grimsthorpe (1722) and Seaton Delaval (1720) (Fig. 1140) – this monumental eloquence faded and a punctilious juxtaposition of disparate elements remained, intentionally fragmentary.

Hawksmoor, who had worked with Wren on the City churches, built other singular religious buildings in and around the City – Christ Church, Spitalfields, 1714; St George in the East, 1715; St Mary Woolnoth, 1716 – where the assembling of the classical elements became virtually an experiment in the extreme conditions of compositional balance; after the death of his partner, he completed the building of Blenheim and built the round mausoleum in the park of Castle Howard (1729), isolated as an elementary symbol of architecture amid the green of the trees and of the fields.

The tension always present in these works, resolved as coolness, restraint or exuberant animation, was the visual sign of a moment when architectural composition was no longer an exclusive and authoritarian rite, but a subject of continual controversy, which ricocheted from one sector of the cultural debate to another. Hawksmoor wrote in 1732 of the mausoleum of Castle Howard: 'I hope that Mr. Pope will not set his satire upon us for it.'[26] The great change was not the succeeding of one formal tendency by another, but the loss of naturalness and faith in a mode of composition. It was therefore understandable that the outcome of this experiment should not be any permanent attitude but a swing in debate that continued during the eighteenth century, the breadth of its oscillations progressively increasing.

In 1715 Colen Campbell published the

first book of *Vitruvius Britannicus*, illustrating the buildings of the previous decades, but criticizing, in the introduction, the excessive freedom of contemporary architects, with whom he contrasted Palladio and Inigo Jones. In the same year Giacomo Leoni translated Palladio's treatise into English once again, and Alberti's in 1726. Lord Burlington (1694–1756) financed the publication of William Kent's *Designs of Inigo Jones* (1727) and Robert Castel's *Villas of the Ancients* (1728) and had a collection of drawings by Palladio printed under the Italian title *Fabbriche antiche*. In 1728 Robert Morris wrote *An Essay in Defence of Ancient Architecture*.

Campbell and Lord Burlington were the promoters of the neo-Palladian movement. Between 1715 and 1720 Campbell built Wanstead House in Essex, which became the prototype of a series of medium-sized country houses built in the first half of the eighteenth century; in 1717 Lord Burlington commissioned Campbell to build his London house, and in 1719, returning from a journey to Italy, he brought with him the designer William Kent (1685–1748) who became his collaborator in his later works of architecture: Tottenham Park (1721), Chiswick House (1725) (Figs 1144–5) and the Assembly Rooms at York (1730) (Figs 1141–2). The stylistic problem of the 'return to Palladio' was linked to the social problem of transferring to domestic and ordinary building – i.e. to the residences of the now more numerous wealthy classes and the public buildings necessary for the richer and more varied social life – the classical propriety of the great monuments built in the early eighteenth century. Campbell dedicated one design of *Vitruvius Britannicus* to Robert Walpole, where he wished to indicate the method of 'introducing the *Temple* beauties in a private Building'.[27] But the Palladian solution, like every particular stylistic formula, was neither unique nor exclusive, and broadened the debate without settling it.

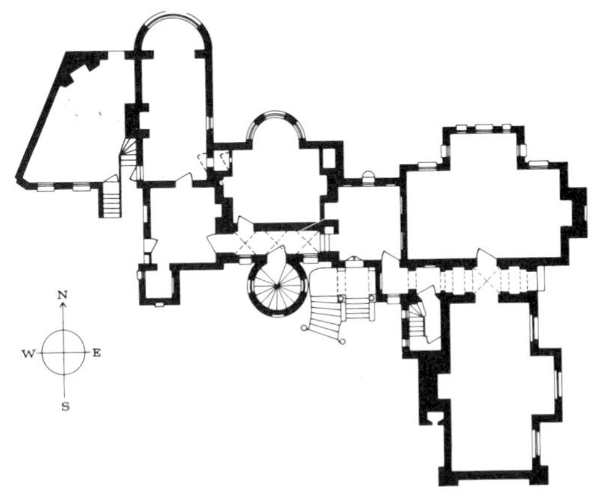

1148, 1149 *View and plan of Vanbrugh's house at Blackheath*

No purpose would be served here by describing the further ups and downs of the *avant-garde* tendencies. But three consequences of this debate should, however, be noted, because they were of crucial importance for European artistic culture:

1 The abandonment of the classical repertoire as an exclusive code of architectural composition, and the resumption – even if sporadic – of the medieval repertoire.

In 1681 Wren designed Tom Tower in Christ Church, Oxford (Fig. 1146) and adopted the Gothic style 'to agree with the Founder's [Wolsey's] work'. At Oxford – as in many other places in England and the continent – buildings had been constructed in the Gothic tradition throughout the seventeenth century, but Wren was not following this tradition: he used the Gothic as a deliberate choice, selected certain of its stylistic elements (pointed two-light windows, pinnacles, ogival buttresses) and combined them in an ordered composition of undoubtedly classical taste. This choice – the first known of this kind – remained as a fortuitous episode in his work, yet it had an extraordinary methodological significance; Wren found it acceptable that the actual elements – i.e. the unvarying structures of classical composition – could be altered as the subject required.

From then on the administration of public works had occasion to design a series of Gothic organisms: some towers for London churches, such as St Mary Aldermary (Dickinson, 1702), and St Michael, Cornhill (Hawksmoor, 1721); Hawksmoor built the west towers of Westminster Abbey and completed All Souls in Oxford in Gothic style.

Vanbrugh was interested in the Gothic in a completely new way, as an exciting image of an alien exotic past; he unsuccessfully proposed to retain the ruins of a medieval castle in the park at Blenheim, and in 1717 built a romantic building in brick for himself at Blackheath, almost devoid of stylistic connotations, but clearly inspired by the modes of the remote past (Figs 1148–9). In the same year Pope published *Eloïsa to Abelard*, where he showed his appreciation of medieval settings with a very similar sensibility:[28]

'These moss-grown domes with spiry turrets crowned,
Where awful arches make a noonday night,
And the dim windows shed a solemn light.'

In the 1730s William Kent found the right formula to interpret the medieval artistic repertoire and make it accessible to a vast public; in 1732, at the advice of Robert

1150 *A garden seat from P. Decker,* Gothic Architecture Decorated, *1759*
1151 *Lacock Abbey, Wiltshire, by Sanderson Miller*

Walpole, he built the wall of the courtyard which faces the Tudor Hall at Hampton Court in the Gothic style, in 1738 and 1742 he realized the new screens in Westminster Hall and Gloucester cathedral. He selected the elements which could be regarded as similar to the classical ones – columns, entablatures, arches, though of a special shape – and could therefore be composed in roughly the same way and made acceptable by accentuating their delicacy. This style had a rapid success and its grammar was formulated in 1742 by Batty Langley (1696–1751).[29]

The new generation of amateurs was deeply interested in these experiments. Sanderson Miller (1717–80), a squire with a taste for architecture, designed a series of Gothic

1152–1154 *Two rooms and a view of Strawberry Hill, Twickenham*

residences for his friends, of which the most important was Lacock Abbey, built in 1753 for John Ivory Talbot (Fig. 1151). In 1749 his contemporary Horace Walpole (1717–97) began to build his house, Strawberry Hill; the 'carcase' was by a professional architect, William Robinson (1720–75), and the interior decoration by a group of non-professional architect friends of Walpole's, including Richard Bentley (1708–82) and John Chute (1701–76); for the first time they set themselves the problem of faithfully imitating Gothic models with absolute precision, like contemporary archaeologists confirming the classical repertoire by studying and classifying its sources. The house was extended on several occasions until 1777 and acquired an irregular appearance, possibly fortuitous at the start, but pregnant with consequences for the future developments in taste; it became famous for the very reasons conceived by the owner, as a setting suited to producing a historical, retrospective emotion (Figs 1152–4).

The vogue for the Gothic style was not an independent tendency, but a consequence of certain more general attitudes. At first the curiosity about medieval forms was one of the manifestations of a universal curiosity about exotic forms: small Gothic buildings found a place, throughout Europe, in the furnishing of parks, beside Chinese pagodas and Indian pavilions. Later the exact imitation of the original models was connected with the new, scientific archaeological spirit which spread about the middle of the eighteenth century, as we shall see. But the Gothic revival contained an intellectual challenge different from that of the exotic style; it caused people to look back in time, rather than far in space, and to imitate a series of buildings to be found in all European countries, built at a time preceding the spread of classicism. Now this period was no longer considered as an obscure age, old history devoid of meaning, but as a different civilization, which had its rules that did not correspond to modern ones.

This change of perspective had repercussions on the use of the classical forms, which could no longer be considered privileged and superhistorical; they were the forms typical of another period, or indeed of the present, and had a *de facto* primacy in the sphere of taste (so much so that they influenced the use of other forms, like the Gothic), not a *de jure* primacy in the sphere of intellectual values. Thus the hierarchy of factors established in the Renaissance was reversed: taste was the fixed factor, stylistic forms the variable element.

2 The abandoning of geometrical composition and symmetry in the field of the garden schemes which for half a century had functioned as the favoured landscape setting for building schemes.

Generally the Cartesian simplicity of the French models was lost in the first half of the eighteenth century, just as scene painting based on axial perspective was complicated, at the same time, by the introduction of the oblique view. But the rule that representable space could be reduced to a combination of lines and geometrical surfaces still remained at the basis of the representation.

In England, as we have said, the idea of the 'formal garden' in the French style was introduced soon after the Restoration, and was found frequently in the early eighteenth century. But from the first it had been the butt of various objections, because of the unnatural distortion it introduced among the natural elements of the landscape; these were intensified at the beginning of the century, and led to a positive rejection of the traditional models.

In 1685 William Temple, the owner of Moor Park, contrasted the regular European gardens with the irregular Chinese ones which 'could be more beautiful than any other'.[30]

'Among us, the beauty of building and planting is placed chiefly in some certain proportions, symmetries or uniformities;

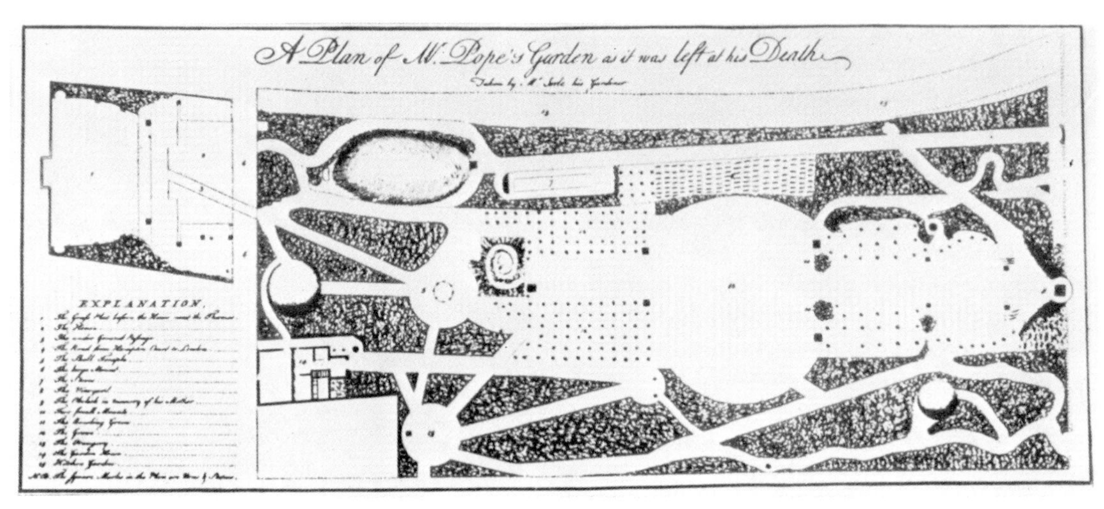

1155 *The garden at Twickenham designed by Pope in 1719*

our walks and trees ranged so as to answer one another, and at exact distances. The Chinese scorn this way of planting . . . their greatest reach of imagination is employed in contriving figures where the beauty shall be great, and strike the eye, but without any order or disposition of parts that shall be commonly or easily observed.'

He believed, however, that this method of composition could not commonly be adopted, 'because where regularity and symmetry dominate, it is difficult to make great and remarkable errors'.

In 1709 Shaftesbury declared his 'extravagant love' of wild nature:[31]

'where neither art, nor the Conceit or Caprice of man has spoiled their genuine order, by breaking in upon that primitive state. Even the rude rocks, the mossy caverns, the irregular unwrought grottoes, and broken falls of water, with all the horrid Graces of the Wilderness itself, as representing nature more, will be the more engaging, and appear with a magnificence beyond the formal mockery of princely gardens.'

Addison, in two essays published in the *Spectator* of 1712, compared the natural countryside and the countryside cultivated by man and expounded a more conciliatory point of view, suggesting an agreement between nature and art; in the practical field he blamed the habit of regularizing the forms of trees:[32]

'Trees are made to look like ninepins, like spheres, or like pyramids; we find the traces of scissors on every bush and on every plant. I do not know whether I am singular in my opinion, but for my own part, I would rather look upon a tree in all its abundance and diffusions of boughs and branches, than when it is cut and turned into a mathematical figure, and cannot but fancy an orchard in flower looked infinitely more delightful than all the little labyrinths of the most finished *parterre*.'

In 1713 Pope, in a mood of quite different irony, published in the *Spectator* a grotesque list of plants cultivated by a fashion-conscious gardener:[33]

'Adam and Eve in yew; Adam a little shattered by the fall of a tree of knowledge in the great storm, Eve and the serpent very flourishing.
The tower of Babel, not yet finished.
St. George in box; his arm scarce long

enough, but will be in condition to strike the dragon by next April.
A green dragon of the same, with a tail of ground ivy for the present.
N.B. These two not to be sold separately.
Edward the Black Prince in cypress.
A lauristine bear in blossom, with a juniper hunter in berrie.
A pair of giants, stunted, to be sold cheap.
A queen Elizabeth in phylyraea a little inclining to the green sickness, but full of growth.
Another queen Elizabeth in myrtle, which was very forward, but miscarried by being too near a ravine.
An old maid of honour in wormwood. A topping Ben Jonson in laurel.
Divers eminent modern poets in bays, somewhat blighted, to be disposed of, a pennyworth.
A quickset hog, shot up into a porcupine, by being forgot a week in rainy weather.
A lavender pig with sage growing in his belly.
Noah's ark in holly, standing on the mount; the ribes a little damaged for want of water.
A pair of maidenheads in fir, in great forwardness.'

In 1719 Pope settled in a house in Twickenham, and personally laid out a small garden, eliminating all geometrical schemes and setting himself out to copy 'Nature Unadorned' (Fig. 1155). The description of this garden and its beauties occurs many times in his works. This was the epoch of poetic accounts of landscapes; in 1712 Pope wrote the poem on the forest of Windsor, and from 1726 to 1730 Thomson was writing *The Seasons*; in 1732 Spence began to write his *Polymetis*, where he insisted on the relationship between poetry and painting (but the new appreciation of the natural landscape, which began in poetry and spread to gardening about the 1720s, spread to painting only in the 1740s, when the masters of the new

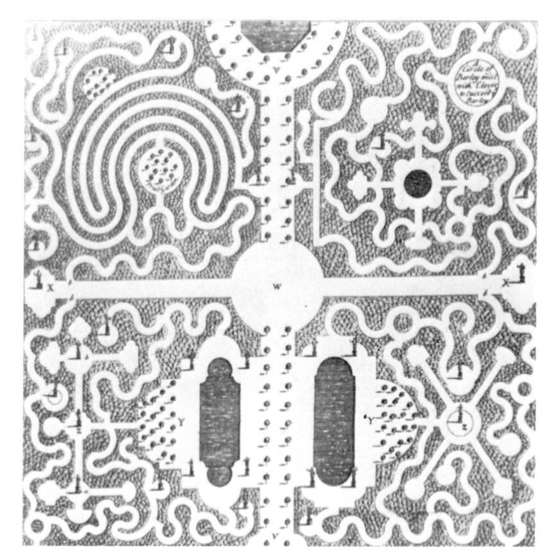

1156 *An illustration from Batty Langley,* New Principles of Gardening, *1726*

English landscape school, Wilson and Gainsborough, began their careers; Spence, too, was an amateur gardener, and considered gardening as a branch of painting).

This attitude was transmitted by amateurs to professionals in the art of gardening. In 1726 Batty Langley published his *New Principles of Gardening* and proposed, in the place of the traditional rectilinear layouts, a series of somewhat artificial curves (Fig. 1156). Charles Bridgeman was the first specialist to react against the formal gardens of London and Wise; he retained the main framework with straight avenues, but eliminated geometry in secondary matters and superimposed upon the first, a second system of curved paths, amid lakes and irregular clumps of woodland. William Kent, who laid out the gardens at Chiswick House[34] for Lord Burlington in 1729 and in 1738, at the death of Wise, became the most respected designer of gardens, made this 'transitional style' his own; he used his training as a painter, his knowledge of French landscape painting (Poussin, Claude Lorrain) and Italian landscape painting (Salvator Rosa) and was praised as the true initiator of the English landscape garden; he carried out some alterations to Blenheim Park, planted by Wise, and also Stowe Park laid out earlier in the century by Bridgeman for Viscount Cobham.

But the decisive moment of transition – i.e. the elimination of all axial plan, and the fusion of irregular elements into an autonomous composition – came towards the middle of the century with the work of Lancelot Brown (1715–83), an assistant gardener who worked at Stowe for Kent; his training was technical, not figurative, and enabled him both to assess accurately the course of formal procedure from project to execution, and also to eliminate the residual visual habits inherited from tradition. The great step – the abolition of symmetry and the representation of infinite space, without the mediation of perspective – was completed, a little more than three centuries after the invention of perspective (Figs 1157–8).

Brown, nicknamed 'Capability' because of his propensity to see the 'capabilities' of his clients' estates, had an enormous success in the second half of the century. He completed over a hundred works, was active at Warwick

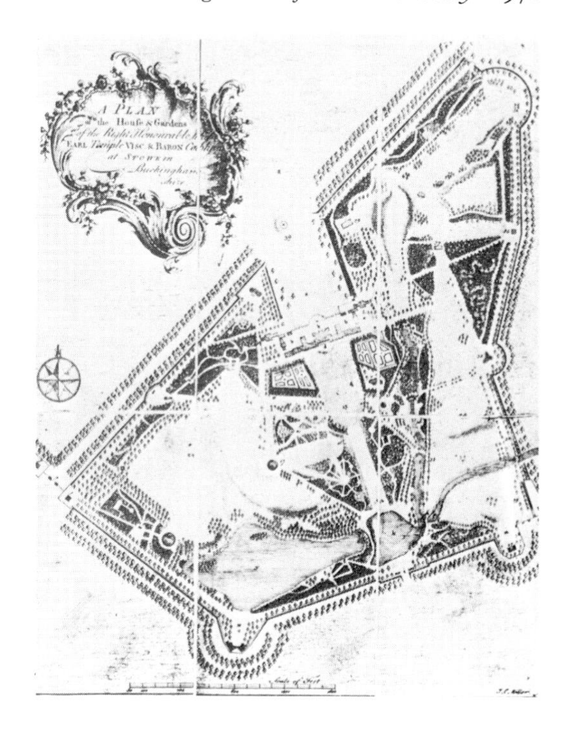

1157, 1158 *The garden at Stowe planned by Kent (1773 print) and that actually laid out by Capability Brown*

1159, 1160 *Two views of the park at Stourhead, with buildings placed 'naturally' in a countryside setting*

Castle, Chatsworth and Blenheim, and it is said that he had declined a work in Ireland saying that he had not yet finished laying out England. His respect for nature was of a stylistic order, not objective: to create his gardens he, too, like Le Nôtre, had to 'force' nature, to flatten hills, to dig out valleys and river beds, to alter the existing vegetation; the result was equally artificial, but extremely different in spatial character; it was a question of a narrative continuity, linked to the main approaches but devoid of *points de vue* and prearranged trajectories. Architecture no longer intervened in the overall layout, and its appearance as an isolated object – the main building, a pavilion or a bridge – acquired a completely new intensity (Figs 1159–60, 1163–5).

This setting was the most precise realization of the aesthetic ideals widespread around the middle of the eighteenth century. In 1745 Hogarth traced the serpentine line which later, in the *Analysis of Beauty* (1753) was defined as the 'line of beauty'; Burke accepted this tendency and developed it in a famous essay of 1756.[35] Shenstone – the poet who spent much of his fortune on laying out his garden, Leasowes – wrote *Random Thoughts on the Art of Gardening*, published after his death in 1764. Horace Walpole told the story of modern English gardening in the essay *The History of Modern Taste in Gardening*.

At the same time Gray, noting a conviction that was widespread, wrote:[36]

'The only proof of our original talent in matter of pleasure is our skill in gardening and the laying out of grounds. And this is no small honour to us, since neither Italy nor France has ever had the least notion of it, nor yet do the least comprehend when they see it. It is very certain, we copied nothing from them, nor had anything but nature for our model. (It is not forty years since) the art was born among us; and it is sure that there is nothing in Europe like it.'

After the middle of the century the reaction against the formal garden spread from England to the continent. Criticism of the regularity of traditional gardens, registered at first by men of letters such as Voltaire,[37] was repeated for the first time at a specialized level by the abbé Laugier;[38] in 1747 a missionary, père Attiret, published an account of Chinese gardens (translated into English in 1752) and lent weight to the opinion that English gardens were an imitation of Oriental ones; between 1770 and 1787 a large publication came out, *Le Jardin anglo-chinois*, which reproduced the most important English gardens and more than a hundred original drawings of Chinese ones, some of which had been sent directly by the emperor to the king of France. William Chambers, on the other

1161 *Plan of the English garden at Ermenonville*

hand, who had spent some time in China as a young man, compared the two, and in 1772 wrote the *Dissertation on Oriental Gardening* where he criticized the empty appearance of English landscape gardens and suggested further adorning the garden with artificial elements; from 1754 to 1763 he himself furnished the gardens of Kew with a series of ornamental buildings in various styles.

In France the idea of the naturalistic garden was appropriated, with great originality, by Rousseau. His most popular book, the *Nouvelle Eloïse* of 1761 (seventy-two French and foreign editions by the end of the eighteenth century) contains the description of an ideal garden;[39] in 1766 his last patron, the marquis of Girardin, began to lay out the garden of Ermenonville in accordance with Rousseau's criteria, and it was here that Rousseau was to have his tomb, on an island planted with poplars. In the last quarter of the century the English garden was fashionable all over Europe; in 1774 Louis XV had the park of the Petit Trianon laid out in this style by the Englishman Richard, in 1780 Philip of Orléans had the Parc Monceau laid out in Paris, between 1769 and 1773 the duke of Anhalt had the park of Wörlitz laid out at Dessau, and Goethe laid out the park of Weimar for prince Charles Augustus in 1775.

Goethe himself, describing the park at

1162 *Rousseau's tomb in the park at Ermenonville*

Dessau in 1778, was extraordinarily perceptive in grasping the new character of this open, undirected landscape, in contrast to the enclosed, perspective-orientated character of the formal French and Italian gardens:[40]

'The sight of a hill does not spur one on to walk towards a specific goal; one continues walking without wondering where one is or where one is going.'

In this field European Romanticism saw one of its main experiences and heaped eighteenth-century models with new ideological meanings, meanings which may arouse echoes even today.

3 The detachment of compositional experiment on a building scale from that on a town-planning scale, and the stabilization of the classical models as permanent elements of the urban scene.

The acceleration of compositional experiment, which we noted from the beginning of the eighteenth century onwards, could not fail to interrupt the continuity of planning from small- to large-scale. Castle Howard and Blenheim were the last great compositions where architecture presumed to embrace the whole visual horizon of the spectator; the smaller and more freely planned buildings that made up *avant-garde* production in the following decades emerged as

1163–1165 *Architecture in the natural setting of the garden: Nymphenburg, Castle Howard and Wilton House*

isolated objects, locked in their own law of composition and largely unconcerned with the surrounding scene. Many of them were very suitably set in contrasting surroundings: for instance the Palladian villas of Chiswick and Stourhead, inexorably symmetrical, were set in naturalistic parks laid out by Kent and Brown.

This experience could not be utilized in the layout of new urban spaces. Thus, parallel to this *avant-garde* production, a conventional production emerged, in connection with the units of building that could not be isolated as single organisms, but which were to be rhythmically associated so as to form a continuous fabric of blocks, roads and squares.

The architects who designed the buildings of the first type – town and country houses and churches – did not normally design buildings of the second type, i.e. terrace houses and urban complexes. These were largely the work of architect-builders, and in many cases architect-speculators, who bought the sites, built at their own expense and then resold or leased out the houses. The first of these, soon after the fire of London, was Nicholas Barbon (who died in 1698) who built Essex street (1682) and Red Lion square (1686); he used mainly standard plans, and the houses still standing are identical down to the last detail, though not co-ordinated into a general composition.

The building types varied, registering, with some delay, the oscillations of *avant-garde* tendencies; at first the Dutch models introduced and interpreted by May were followed religiously, until a neo-Palladian movement brought the models of Inigo Jones to light again, producing the houses on Covent Garden square, Great Queen street and Lincoln's Inn fields; but the display of over-ostentatious decoration became simpler with time, and a typology almost devoid of stylistic connotations emerged, ennobled by the delicacy of the proportions and the constructional precision ('Georgian', as it is called in the handbooks).

Town-planning types, on the other hand, did not vary, being those universally popularized in the second half of the seventeenth century: grid plan division into plots, usually in long blocks as in Holland, square or rectangular spaces with streets running in at the corners.

The main town-planning activity of the eighteenth century was realized with these criteria, i.e. in the district of London lying outside the confines of the city. The fabric of the houses and uniform streets, punctuated with the fine churches of Archer, Hawksmoor and Gibbs, was frequently broken up by squares, laid out by the great landowners on their suburban estates: Bloomsbury (1661) (Fig. 1166), Grosvenor square (1695, completed in 1725–30) (Fig. 1167), Cavendish square (1717), Berkeley square (1730), Bedford square (1775), Russell square (1800). In some cases – as in the north block of Grosvenor square, built by Shepherd in 1730 – the architect has tried to compose a series of façades as a single Palladian villa, with a central portico; but normally the rhythmic succession of many identical organisms was left undisguised, and guaranteed the continuity of the urban landscape whatever its extent.

In the course of the eighteenth century these outskirts of old London grew vastly, and indeed became the main body of the new city. Their character largely determined the character of the great metropolis, the largest city in Europe, which had 1,000,000 inhabitants by the end of the century; already in 1726 Defoe considered it a 'monstrous city' and was amazed to see that it no longer had a 'circumvallation';[41] in fact London was no longer a traditional city, that could be perceived as a visual unity, it was now a sequence of small independent elements, or elements grouped together in open rhythmic compositions, which now covered a whole region, further than the eye could see. The dome of St Paul's dominated the panorama of the old city and the towers of the abbey

1166 *Aerial view of Bloomsbury*

1167 *Aerial view of Grosvenor square*

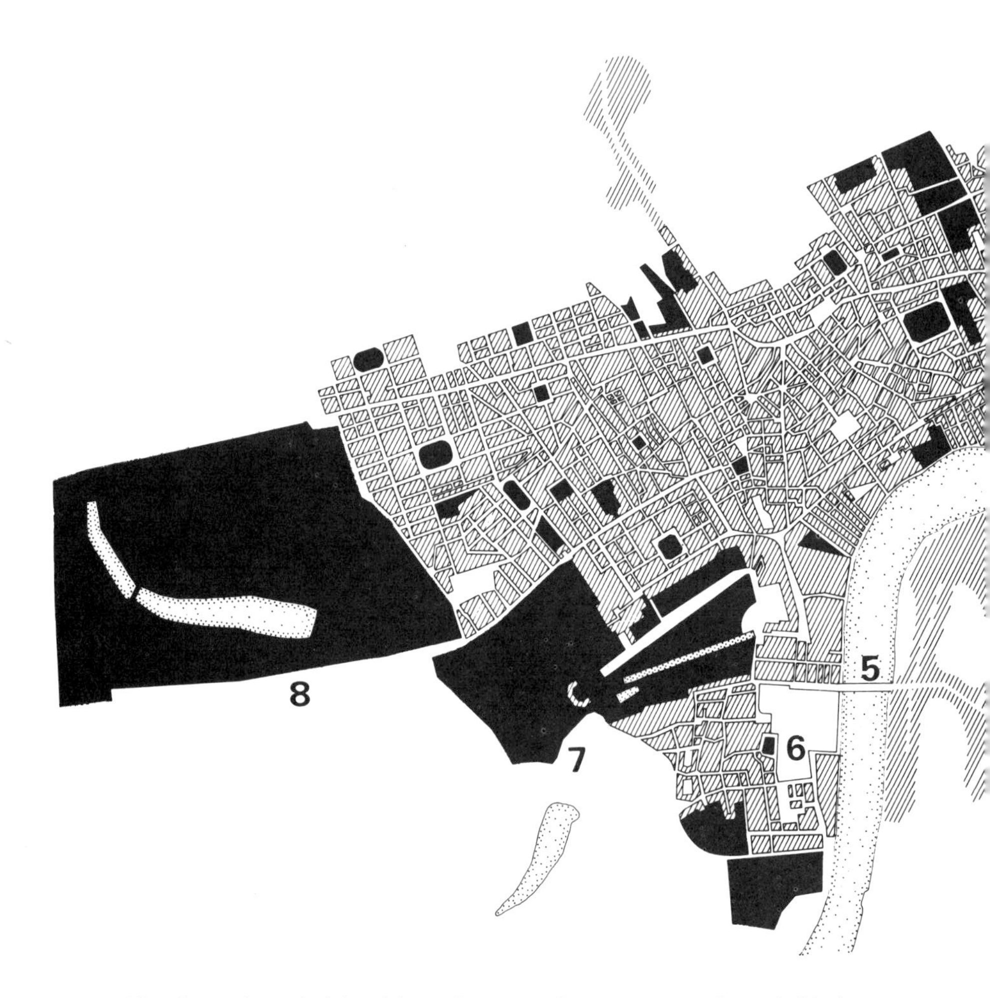

1168 *Plan of the outskirts of London at the end of the eighteenth century. Green zones are shown in black.*
1 The City 2 The Tower of London 3 London bridge 4 Blackfriars bridge 5 Westminster bridge
6 Westminster 7 St James's Park 8 Hyde Park

1
2
3

1169 *View of London by Canaletto. British Museum, London*

soared above the district of Westminster; these two views could be painted by Canaletto – who was in London from 1745 to 1755 – in traditional stylistic terms (Fig. 1169). But the fabric of the surrounding districts was not distinguished by any monument or complex of monuments; or if it were, it would be by the empty spaces that break up the compact building fabric, and which became the new centres of social life, equipped as meeting places both in the open and under cover (for instance the Rotunda at Ranelagh gardens, built in 1741). London bridge was no longer the obligatory passage across the Thames; upstream, Westminster bridge was opened in 1751, and Blackfriars in 1760, while downstream the ships collected in the port, with their forest of masts, and docks and warehouses multiplied. The Thames was the only space where one could gain a simultaneous view of the organism of the great city; looking east from Westminster lay the view later described by Wordsworth:[42]

'Ships, towers, domes, theatres and temples lie
Open unto the fields and to the sky,
All bright and glittering in the smokeless air.'

But entering the city one could no longer get this impression; what struck the eighteenth-century observers was the enormous quantity of traffic, sung of in epic manner by John Gay:[43]

'Who can recount the coach's various harms,
The legs disjointed and the broken arms?'

Anyone who managed to gaze through the traffic at the backdrop of buildings saw the scenes described so acutely by Heine, a century later than Defoe: 'hovels' instead of 'great palaces'; 'but it was precisely this uniformity and their incalculable number that left so magnificent an impression'.[44]

The urban standards spread, after about 1725, to other English cities. In 1727 John Wood (1704–54) moved from London to Bath – the spa which from 1725 onwards was the meeting place of the best English society – and began his charmed activities as planner-contractor. In 1725 he began to build Queen

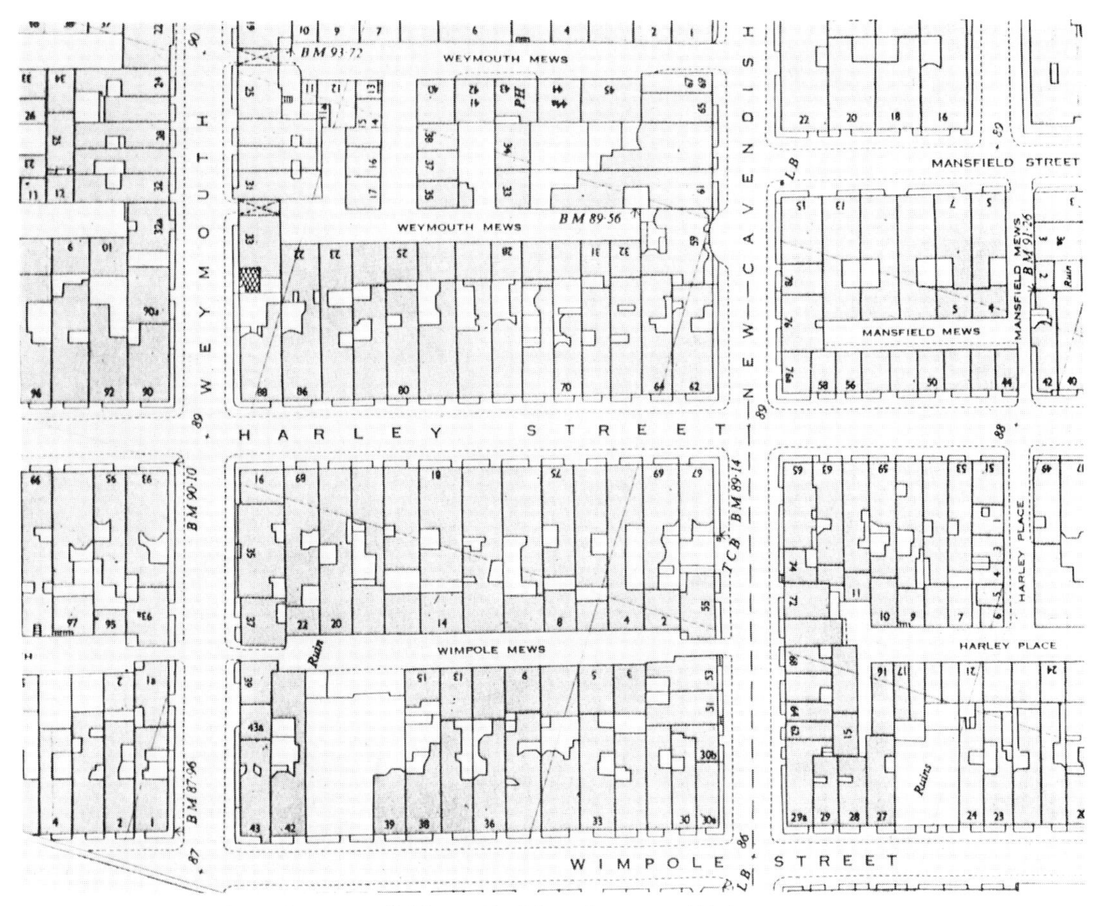

1170 *Part of the eighteenth-century divisions of building plots around Harley street*

square (Fig. 1174) and in 1753 the Circus (Figs 1178–80), linked to Queen square by a street with uniform façades, Gay street; the circular form, now making its first appearance in England, may have derived from the place des Victoires by Hardouin-Mansart, but was treated rather as an *étoile* in the manner of Le Nôtre, i.e. as a meeting-place for roads, with entries at 120° rather than 90°. Wood was a cultured artist, wrote a quasi-philosophical treatise,[45] and in Queen square he wanted to articulate the façade with a fake projection in the neo-Palladian style. But the logic of his building operations forced him to turn, in the Circus, to a uniformly rhythmic composition. His son John Wood the Younger (dead by 1782) completed the Circus in 1764, and in 1767 began to build, to the west of the Circus, Brook street and Royal Crescent, a semi-elliptical terrace of houses, freely overlooking the view of the wooded valley (Figs 1176–7). The invention of the crescent had a great success: it was repeated at Buxton in 1779, in Bath in 1788 and 1794, Brighton in 1798, and became one of the typical models of urban building in the early nineteenth century.

The town-planning typology defined in the first two-thirds of the eighteenth century could also be utilized for a large-scale composition like the extension of Edinburgh, decided upon in 1763. A lake to the north of the city was drained for this purpose, and in 1767 a competition was organized for the

1171, 1172 *Bath as laid out by John Wood the Elder and John Wood the Younger. 1 Queen square 2 The Circus 3 The Assembly Rooms 4 Royal Crescent*

general layout which was won by the local architect James Craig (d. 1795); he designed a district on a regular grid plan interrupted by two great squares and surrounded by vast gardens; to the south, too – where another of the city's architects, James Brown, created George square in 1766 – Craig put forward another plan of extension, but it was never implemented.

The district to the north, determined by Craig only as far as street layout was concerned, was realized in the second half of the eighteenth century; one of the two squares, Charlotte square, was designed by Robert

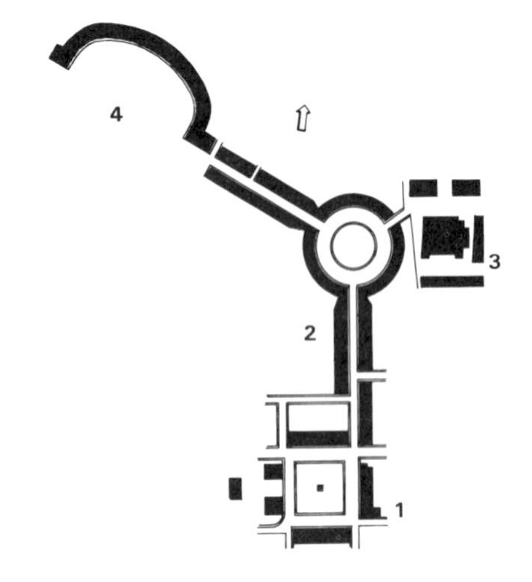

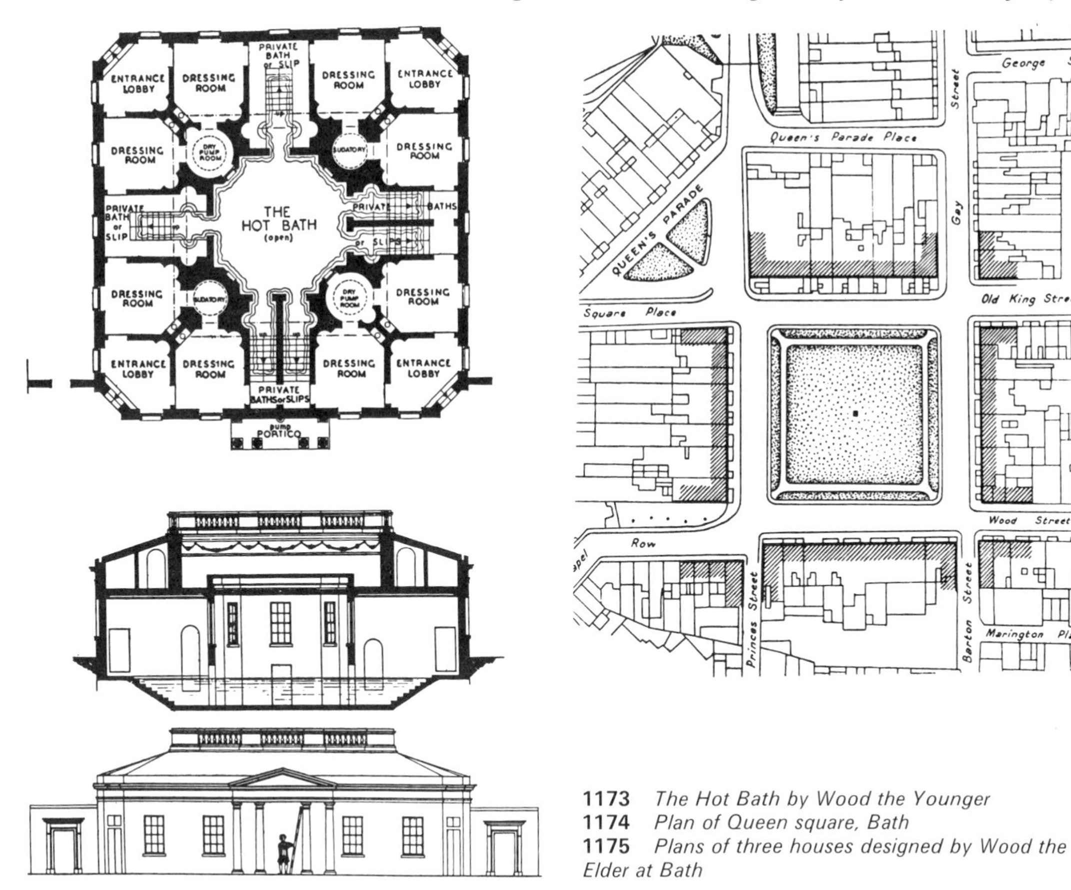

1173 *The Hot Bath by Wood the Younger*
1174 *Plan of Queen square, Bath*
1175 *Plans of three houses designed by Wood the Elder at Bath*

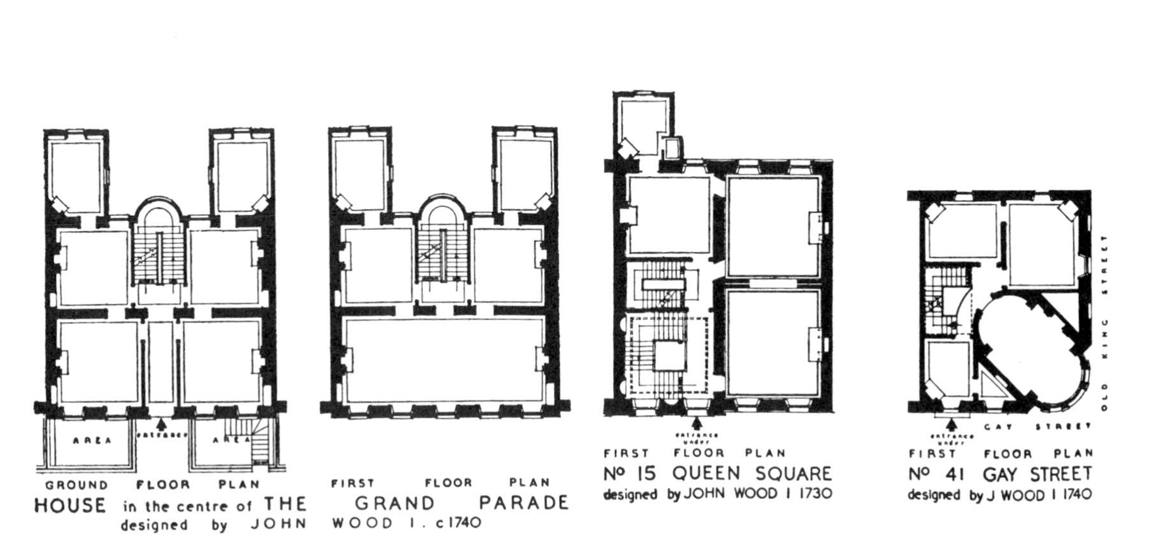

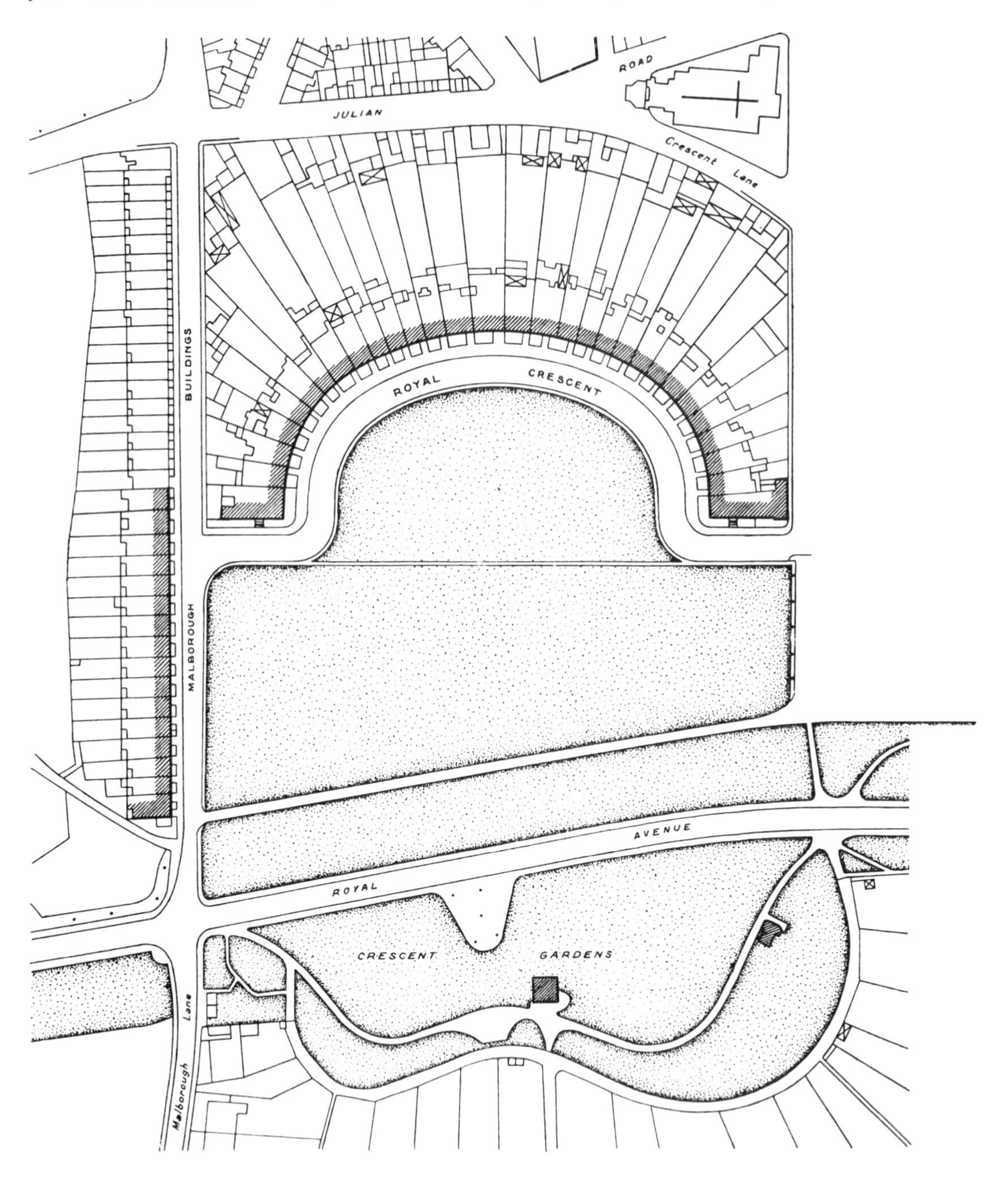

1176 *Plan of Royal Crescent*
1177 *Aerial view of Royal Crescent*

1178 *Aerial view of the Circus*

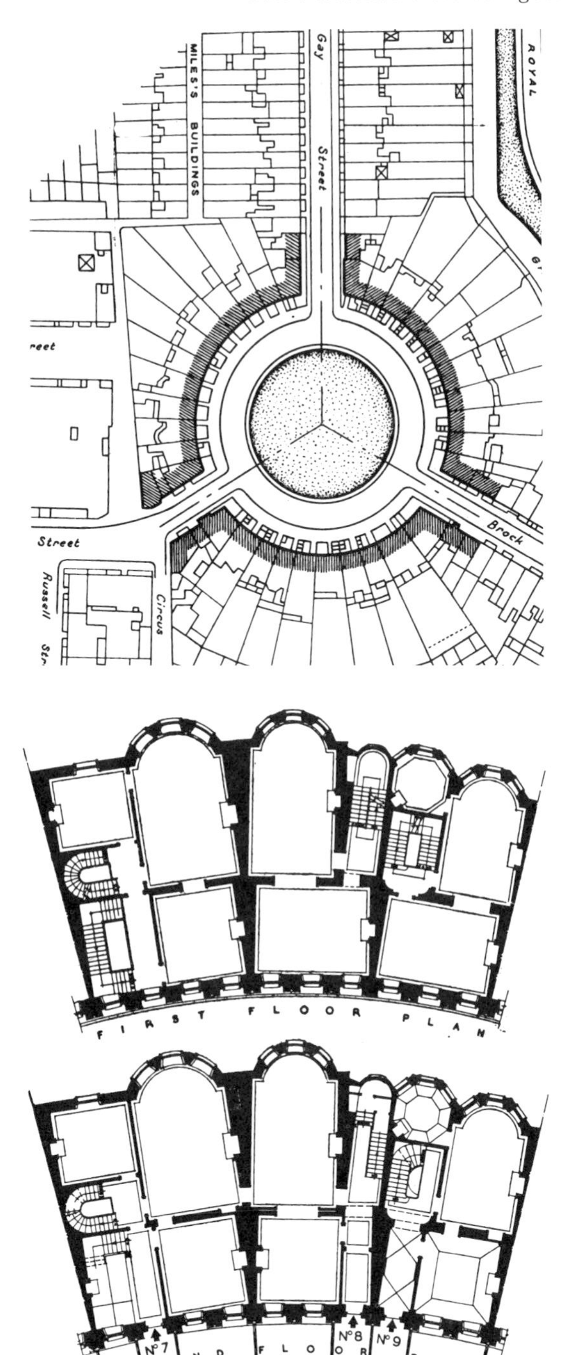

1179, 1180 *Plans of the Circus and a group of houses in it*

Adam in 1791. At the end of the century the surrounding sites, too, began to be urbanized, and here, in the 1820s, Scots architects realized a splendid series of squares, circuses and crescents in the style of the Woods (Figs 1181–2).

The dates, as is already clear, have a different meaning in this field from the one they have in architectural composition. The range of town-planning models, based on elementary geometrical forms and the rhythmic repetition of single elements, lingered on, and was transformed much more slowly than the building repertoire. Stylistic alternatives had no direct effect on these activities, but undermined the spontaneity of everyday models, and transformed choices into conventions accepted out of habit or discipline. The elegance of the Georgian schemes in London, Bath and Edinburgh should not deceive one: it was a carefully considered elegance, which in fact was gradually worn down and became, without any sudden transformation, the 'urban décor' of the nineteenth century, the property of middle-of-the-road bourgeois convention.

The three processes we have illustrated potentially repudiated the most important theses of the Renaissance system. The resumption of the Gothic repertoire denied the universal value and immutability of the standardized elements taken from classical antiquity; the naturalistic English garden repudiated geometrical mediation in the representation of space, and extended to the large scale that rejection of symmetry hitherto experimented only on the small scale of *rocaille* ornament; the separation of town planning from building planning repudiated the universal significance of the morphological choices, hence the vertical continuity of architectural culture. These three negations acted separately, and were not such as to produce an overall alternative; but they were enough to destroy the cultural unity of classicism and they created a void which for a long time was to remain unfilled.

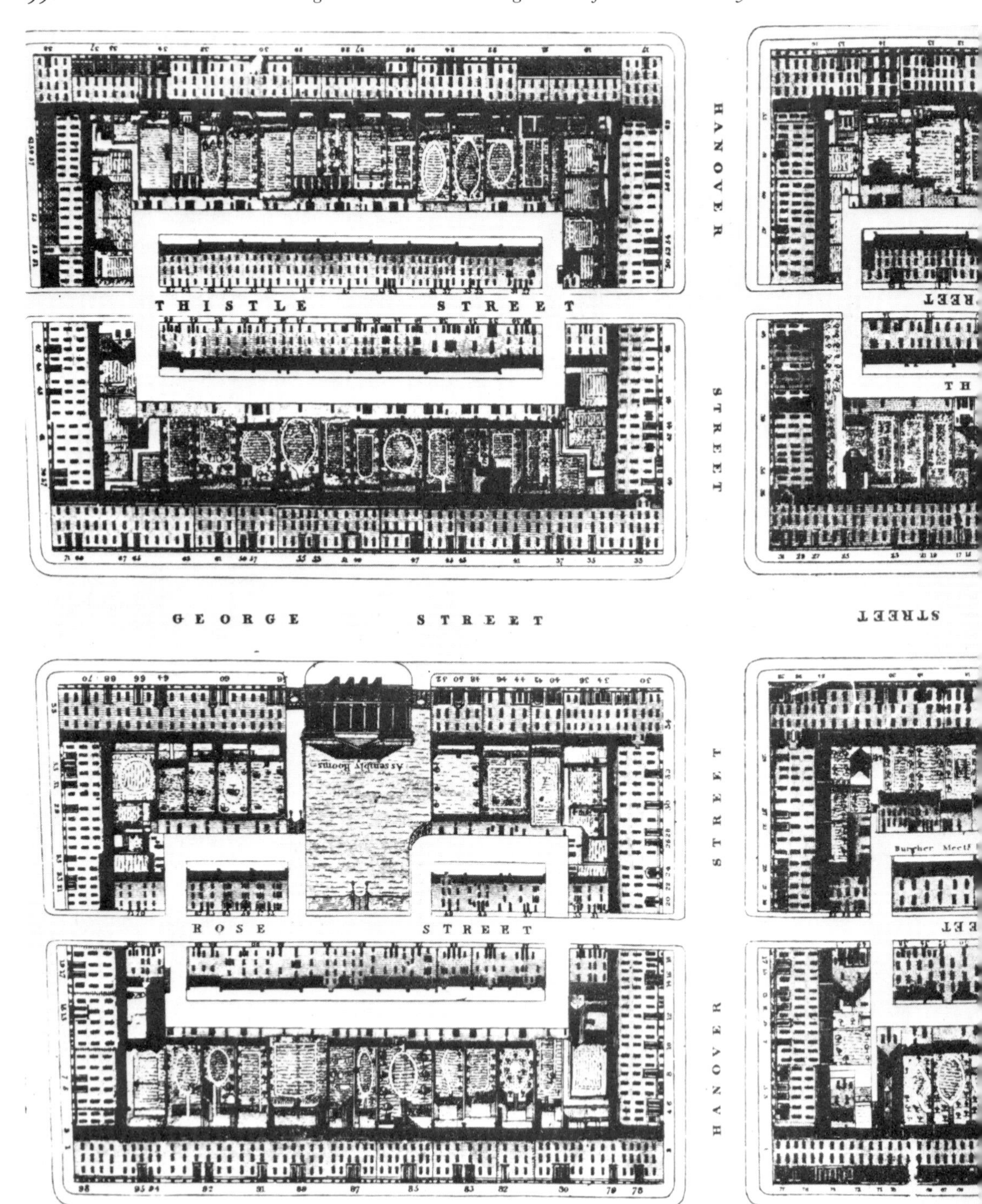

1181 *A part of Craig's district of Edinburgh, as it was built*

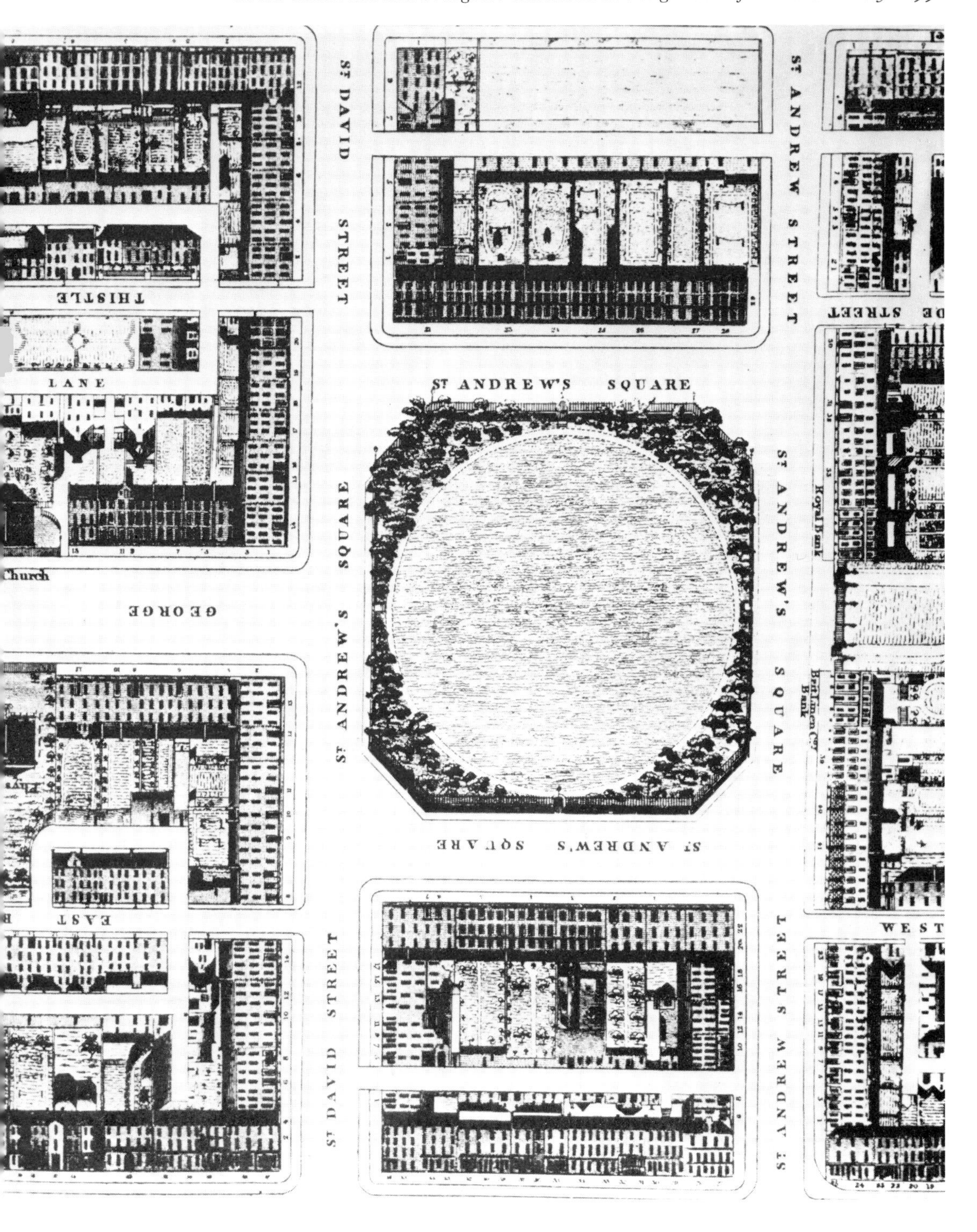
ST DAVID STREET
ST ANDREW STREET
THISTLE
STREET
LANE
ST ANDREW'S SQUARE
Royal Bank
British Linen Coy Bank
Church
GEORGE
EAST
WEST

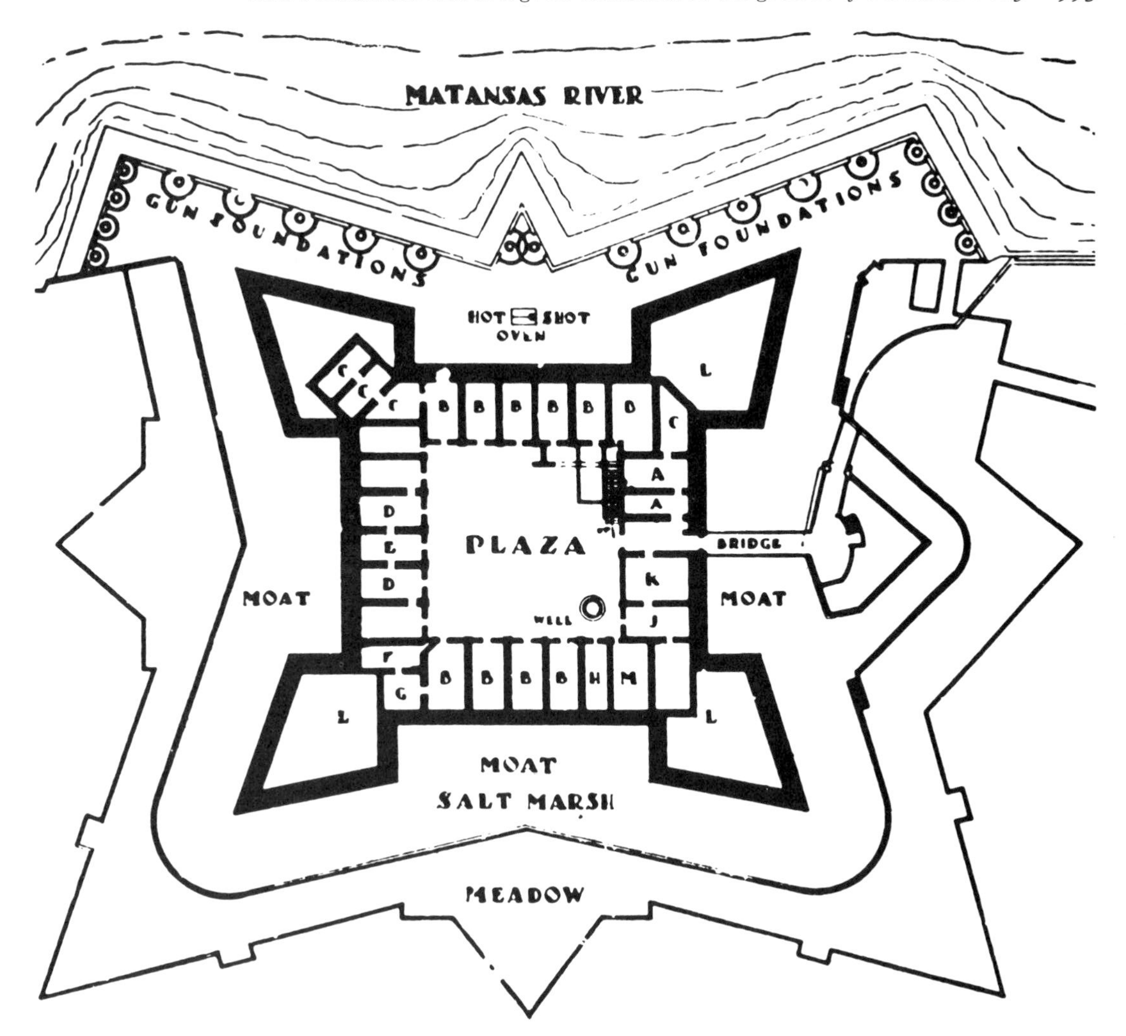

1182 *(left) Model of Edinburgh in cast iron, 1820, showing the eighteenth-century additions*
1183 *The fort of St Mark at St Augustine, Florida, showing the troops' quarters (B) and services*

The overseas colonies

In the Spanish colonies the inventive phase of urban colonization ended soon after the middle of the sixteenth century. The 1573 laws of Philip II marked the conclusion of the process, and its transformation into bureaucratic praxis.

The building of new cities continued, throughout the seventeenth and eighteenth centuries, around the borders of the empire. To the north the Spaniards founded San Antonio de Bejar in Texas (1718), Pensacola in Florida (after 1754) and Galvaez in Louisiana (1778); an expedition sent to California in 1769 founded some missions (San Diego, San Luis Rey), some fortified garrisons (San Diego in 1769, Monterey in 1770, San Francisco in 1776 and Santa Barbara in 1782) and later two *pueblos*, i.e. residential towns destined for expansion: San José in 1777 and Los Angeles in 1781.

The Governor of Lower California, Filippo de Neve, gave these instructions for the founding of Los Angeles:[46]

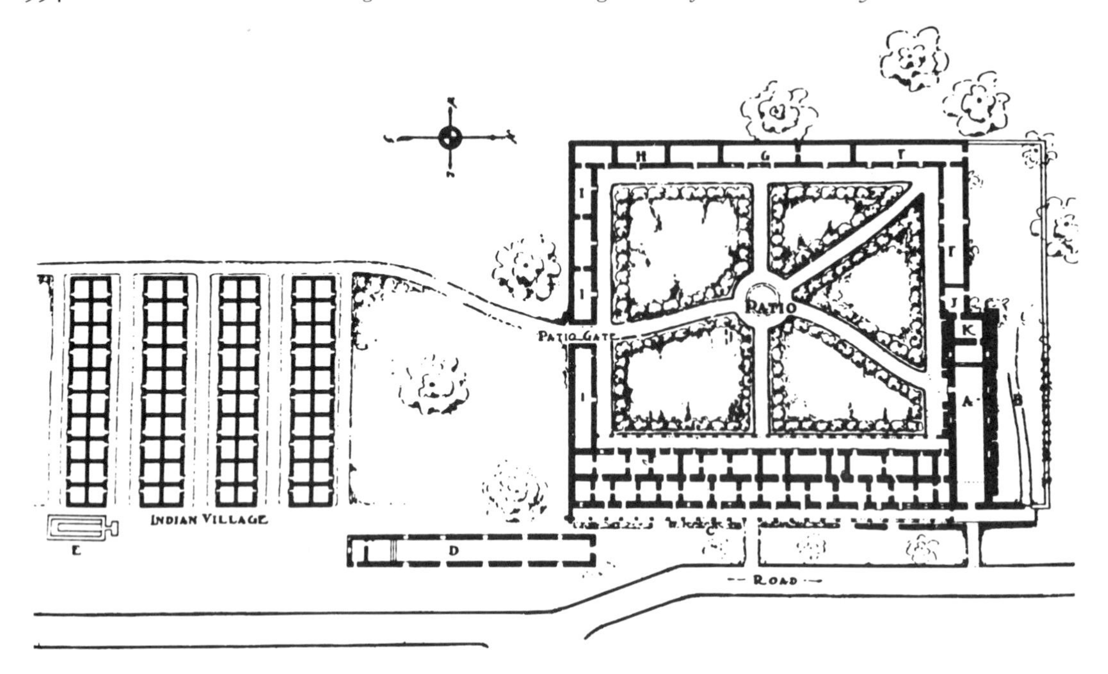

1184 *A Californian mission: A church B cemetery C priests' living quarters*
1185 *The* reduccion *at Candelaria, in an eighteenth-century print*

'The site where the pueblo is to be established shall be marked out, on land slightly elevated, exposed to the north and south winds. Measures shall be taken to avoid the dangers of floods; the most immediate vicinity to the river shall be preferred, taking care that from the pueblo the whole or greatest portion of the planting lands shall be seen. The plaza ought to be two hundred feet wide by three hundred feet long, from said plaza four main streets shall extend, two on each side, and besides these two other streets shall run by each corner. . . . For the purpose of building there shall be marked out as many building lots as there may be agricultural plots susceptible of irrigation. Also, a tract of land six hundred feet wide between the planting lands and the pueblo shall be left vacant. Every building lot shall measure sixty feet wide by one hundred and twenty long. . . . The front of the plaza looking towards the east shall be reserved to erect at the proper time the church and government buildings and other public offices, and the adjoining lots shall be allotted to settlers.'

Two centuries later the directions of the law of 1573 were still in force; this persistence, however, reveals the decay of Spanish–American colonial culture, and its detachment, now irrevocable, from European affairs.

A creative experiment in town-planning – though on a minor scale, and distorted by exceptional circumstances – took place at the other end of the continent, in the *reducciones* founded by the Jesuits in Paraguay between the end of the sixteenth and the beginning of the eighteenth century. *Reduccion* was the legal term used in the sixteenth century to indicate the new indigenous settlements, backed by the religious orders; the Jesuits, who arrived in South America in 1568 and in Asunción in 1575, took upon themselves the task of Christianizing the Indians of the inland forests, and although they started later

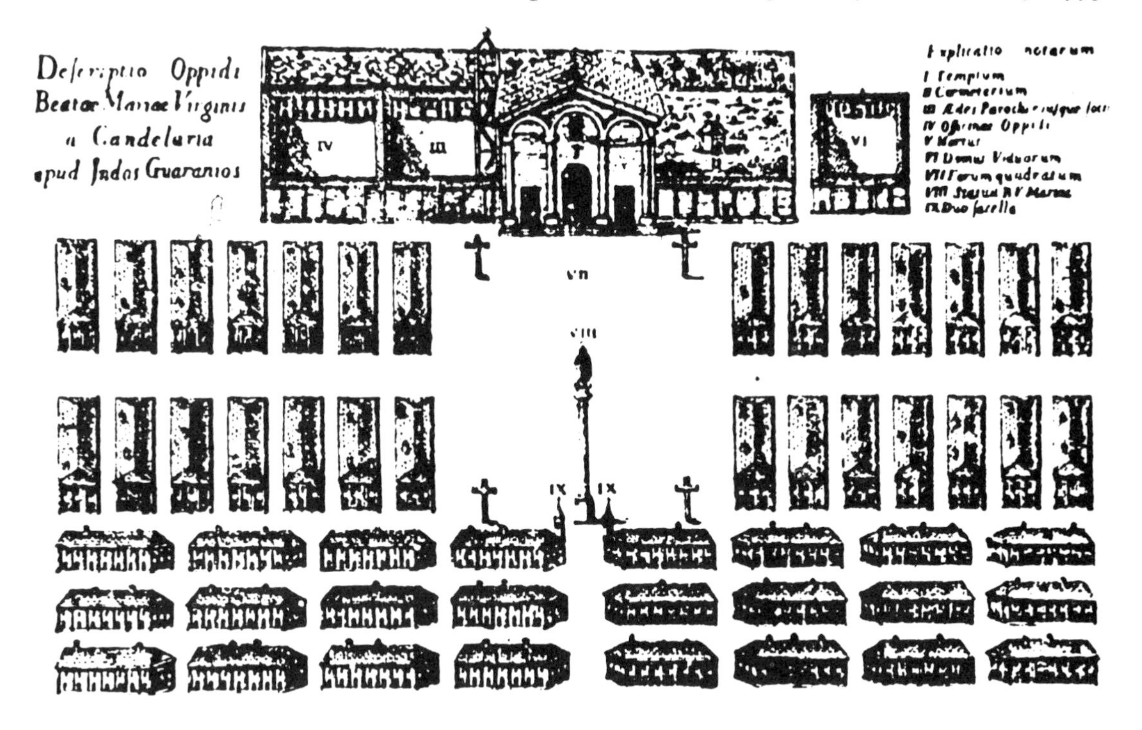

in relation to the other traditional orders, the Franciscans and Dominicans, they were animated by a Utopian impetus which still strongly reflected the cultural climate of the early sixteenth century.

In 1581 padre Bolanos founded the first *reduccion* for three hundred Indians, in the district of Guayrá; in 1607, the Society recognized the autonomous region of Paraguay, and the first provincial father, Diego de Torres, organized three expeditions to the hinterland, which founded a large number of *reducciones*: San Ignacio Guazù in 1609. San Ignacio Minì and Loreto in 1610, Itapuá in 1615, Yapeyú, San Nicolás and Santa Maria la Mayor in 1626, Candelaria in 1627, la Cruz in 1628, San Javier in 1629, Trinidad and San Carlos in 1631, Santo Tomé, San Cosme y Damián and San Miguel in 1632, Santa Ana, Aposteles and San José in 1633, Mártires de Japón in 1639. The placenames mingled Indian words and the names of saints old and new: a cultural universe that had to be fully represented in this corner of the world. From 1612 to 1618 the *reducciones* were subjected to assaults of the Paulist slave traders; the missionaries armed the Indians, led them on long transfer journeys through the forests, and ultimately defeated their adversaries in battle.

In 1647 the *reducciones* contained about 30,000 Indians; in the second half of the century the settlements multiplied undisturbed (Jesús in 1685, San Luis in 1687, San Borja and San Lorenzo in 1690, San Juan Bautista in 1697, Santa Rosa de Lima in 1698); at the beginning of the eighteenth century they had 90,000 inhabitants, and in 1732, at their peak, 140,000 inhabitants. But from 1700 onwards the *reducciones* were involved in European political conflicts; the Spaniards utilized the natives to wage war on the Portuguese, and in 1750 signed a treaty, yielding the Portuguese a part of the territory of the *reducciones*, in exchange for the region of Sacramento; the Jesuits refused to obey a coalition of Spaniards and Portuguese, and the Portuguese, disappointed at not having found the imaginary treasures of the Jesuits, abandoned this territory in 1761. In 1768 the Jesuits were expelled from the colonies and the *reducciones*, where they were replaced by the Franciscans; finally in 1816–17 the Portuguese occupied Paraguay and destroyed most of the *reducciones*.

The first villages were founded in accordance with the instructions of de Torres in 1609, which repeated the Spanish laws of 1573 on a smaller scale. The cultural basis of the operation was the same: the *guaraní* Indians belonged to the *guaycurú* culture, now studied by anthropologists, and it is legitimate to imagine that their village was organized like the present-day one, described by Lévi-Strauss: on a circular plan, divided diametrically by the men's house and formed of two contrasting groups; the social life of the natives was inseparable from this physical organization, and the substitution of the grid plan for the traditional circle took away from the Indians the topographical references necessary to their habits, leaving them in a cultural vacuum which could easily be filled by new religious and social ideas.

In the Jesuit *reducciones* which were absolutely isolated from the rest of the world, this substitution could be total; thus it has been claimed that the *reducciones* 'had as their sole origin none other than the application of the rules and spiritual exercises of St. Ignatius' and corresponded to the organization of Jesuit colleges.[47] As far as the physical organism was concerned, the *reducciones* differed from the towns founded in the sixteenth century by their smaller size and the limited anticipation of growth; in normal cases the population varied from 1,000 to 5,000 inhabitants. Thus the central square, which in sixteenth-century cities was a special feature introduced into the network, here became the basic element that determined the character of the whole settlement. It was usually a square open space, 150 metres wide; along one side stood the managerial buildings, i.e. in this order, the cemetery, the church, a first courtyard with the sacristy, the Jesuits' living quarters, the college, refectory and a second courtyard with the workshops, printing-works and arsenal. Along the other sides, in parallel rows, were the natives' houses; each family occupied a square room, ventilated on the two sides and topped by a garret; the two façades of each terrace were screened by porches. Between the houses stood the offices of the elected native authorities (one of the characteristic features of these communities), the widows' residences, the hospital, young children's school,

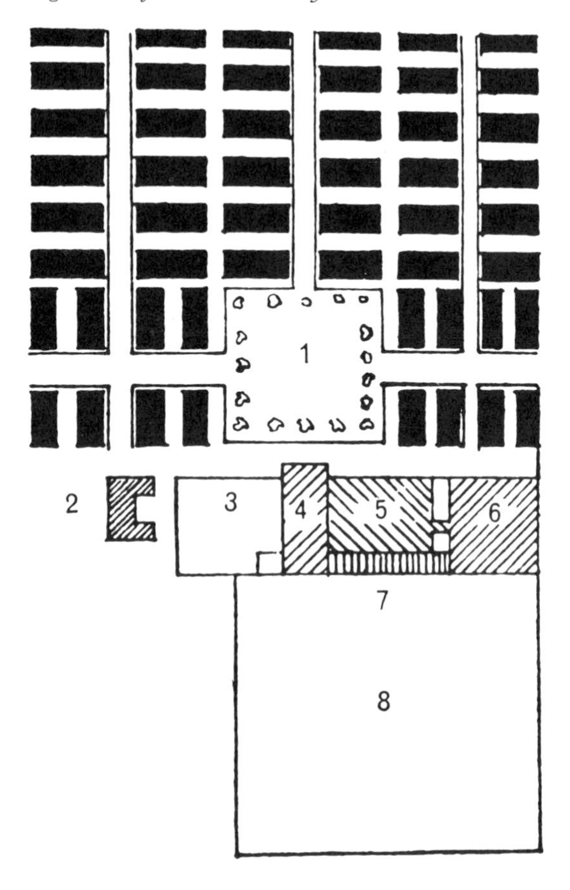

1186 *Plan of a typical Jesuit* reduccion *: 1 square 2 hospital 3 cemetery 4 church 5 school 6 widows' house 7 Jesuits' living quarters 8 garden*

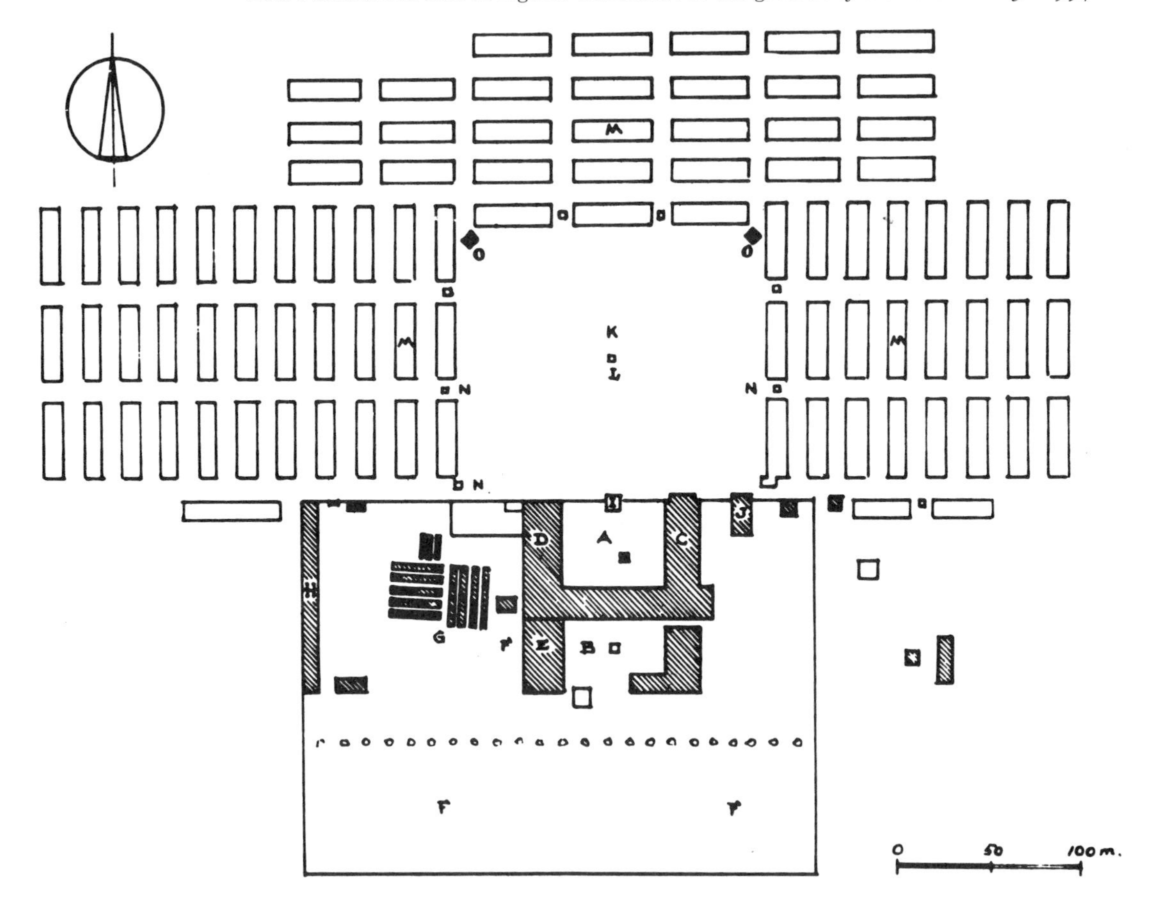

1187 *Plan of the* reduccion *of San José de Chiquitos in Bolivia: A college B* patio *C church D Jesuits' living quarters E refectory F kitchen garden G drying-rooms H laboratories I tower J funerary chapel K great cross L square M natives' houses N crosses O chapels*

storehouses, the prison and, as far away as possible, the hostel for visitors.

The three main roads that emerged along the axis of the square ran into the forest, to the three shrines dedicated to the patron saint, St Mark, and the Madonna. The basic square was always orientated according to the points of the compass (Figs 1185–7).

The churches had wooden frames subsequently filled in with walls of brick, and were covered inside with painted canvasses, and sometimes outside with stone carvings.

The sanitary arrangements were particularly carefully considered; the village usually stood on sloping ground, with two intercommunicating water basins upstream canalized in the direction of the *reduccion*; public latrines were accommodated behind the church. The cemetery separate from the church was an innovation which was to be introduced into Europe only at the end of the eighteenth century, and Muratori, who wrote a description of these missions in 1743,[48] compared this practice favourably with the European one.

In the eighteenth century the Jesuit *reducciones* were widely discussed by philosophers and moralists; Montesquieu judged them positively,[49] Voltaire mentioned them facetiously in *Candide*[50] and criticized them

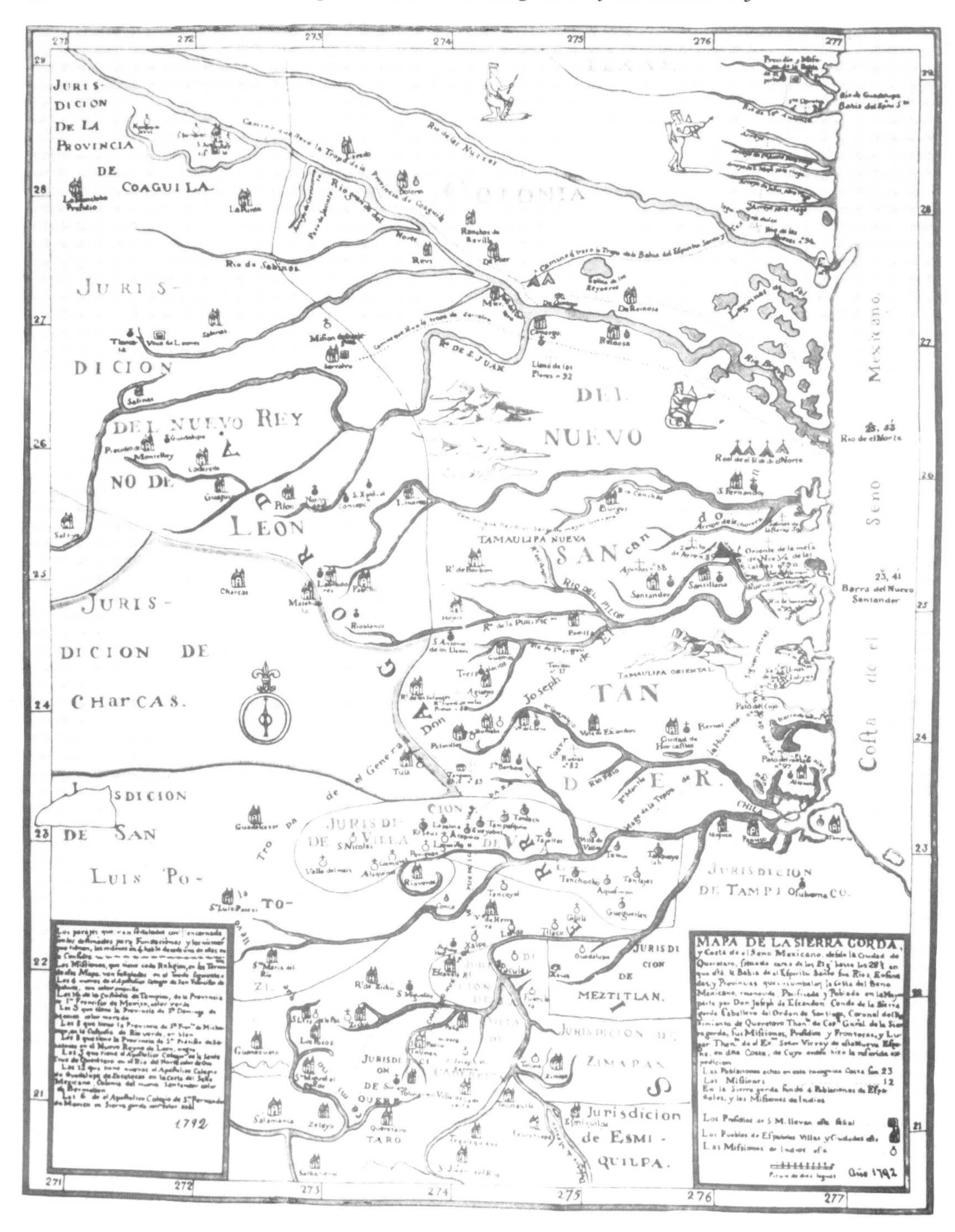

1188 *Map of 1792 showing Spanish possessions in Mexico*

1189 *Mexico and its lagoon in an eighteenth-century print*

more seriously in *Essai sur les Mœurs des nations*. The joint ownership of goods and political-religious administrations were sometimes judged as anticipations of a future rational state, sometimes as survivals of medieval despotism. But the most unusual characteristic, which the culture of the Enlightenment was not in a position to register, was the artificiality of these settlements, maintained by the presence of a few hundred missionaries and destined to disappear into nothingness the moment the Jesuits were driven away. The notion of the ideal city found its last foothold in the depths of the Paraguayan forest; henceforward it was an idea from the past, which could be kept alive only in exceptional circumstances, and could not be incorporated into the new economic and political universe.

In the rest of the Spanish colonial empire, when the phase of colonization was over, and the growth of the new cities also largely over, the moment had come for the planning of individual buildings.

Of the sixteenth-century cities only the two vice-regal capitals, Mexico and Lima, grew and altered to any considerable degree. In Mexico City Garcia Bravo's grid plan still dominated the layout of the seventeenth- and eighteenth-century city, but the surrounding region was drained from the last years of the seventeenth century, by Flemish engineers, and a suburban district grew up around it: to the west, the park of Alameda was created in the district of Chapultepec, a few suburbs grew up to the south and east, while, detached from the city, the district around the shrine of Guadalupe grew up. Within the old

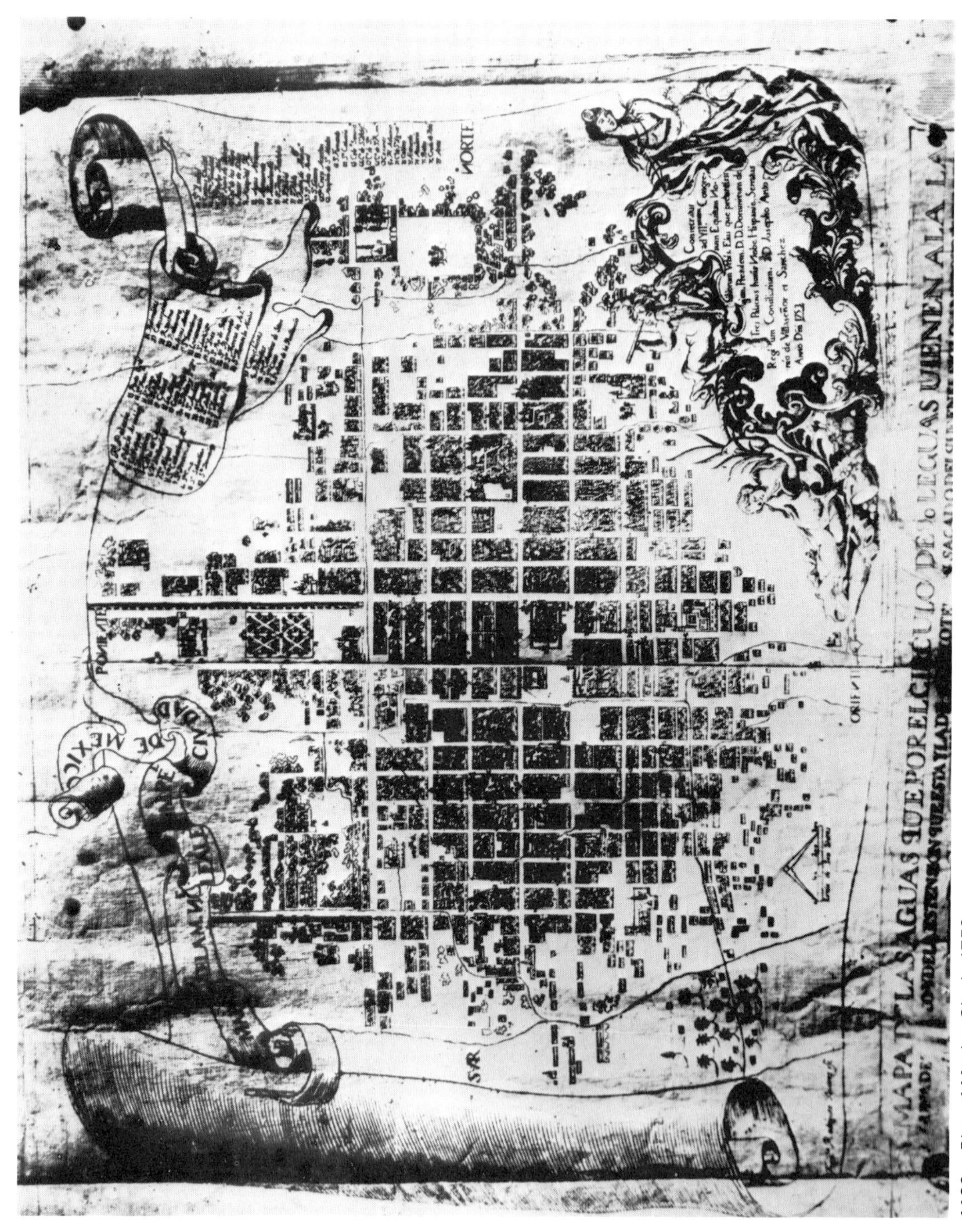

1190 *Plan of Mexico City in 1753*

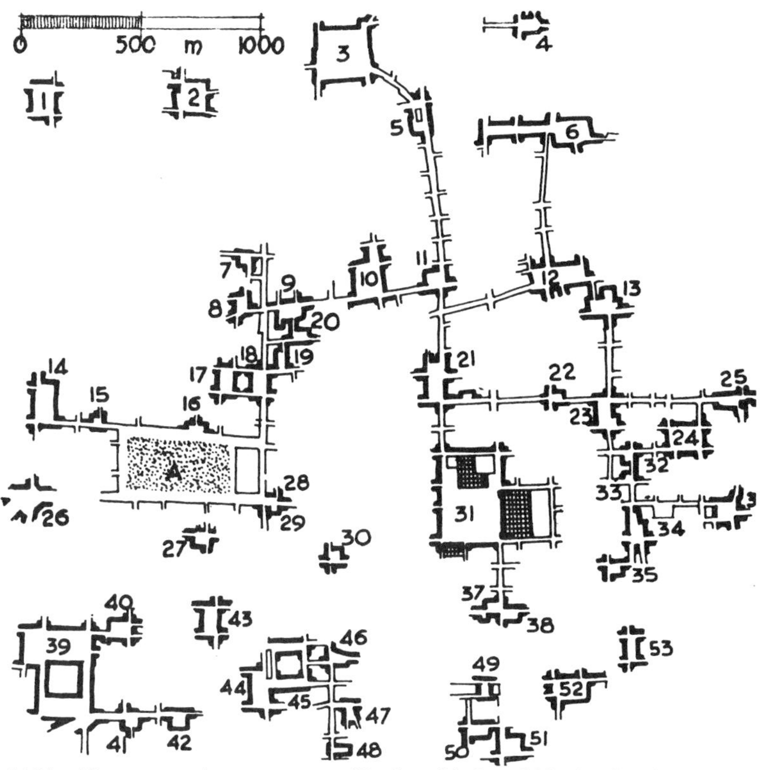

1191 *The system of squares opened in the grid plan of Mexico City from the seventeenth to the eighteenth century. A: Alameda; 31: Zócalo*

1192 *Plan of Lima in 1685*

1193 *An eighteenth-century block in Puebla*

1194 *The roofing of an eighteenth-century church in Oaxaca*

organism the grid plan was losing its undifferentiated character with the formation of a series of secondary squares (Fig. 1191). Other conspicuous spaces in addition to the public ones were the courtyards of some large religious buildings: the school of las Vizcainas (Pedro Bueno, 1734) and the college of San Ildefonso (Cristóbal de Escobar y Llamas, c. 1740). The setting of the Zócalo was completed in 1749, with the building of the Sagrario attached to the cathedral (Lorenzo Rodríguez). The seventeenth- and eighteenth-century buildings, in black and reddish volcanic stone, gave the townscape a particular compactness, and repeated a number of common peculiarities, including the window contained within an H-shaped frame going from one stringcourse to the other (Fig. 1193).

Late seventeenth- and eighteenth-century plans of Lima show an elongated city running along the banks of the river, only the central part of which followed the original grid plan lines. An irregular circle of fortifications limited the city organism, but left extensive green spaces within the city, particularly to the west (Fig. 1192). The architectural layout of the Peruvian capital is much less important than that of Mexico; none the less an autonomous style was formed in the middle of the seventeenth century, first at Cuzco (where the monuments of the city centre were rebuilt after the earthquake of 1650) then at Lima, which in 1656 was also partly destroyed by an earthquake. The churches of San Francisco

(Costantino de Vasconcelos, 1657) and of the Desamparados (1669) were rebuilt. The building materials, in this case, were walls of brick supported by a wooden framework and plaster facings, which afforded cheap simulations of the traditional solidity and plastic effects.

A common tendency in the architecture of the Spanish colonies was the independence of the plastic effects from the overall organism; the organisms of churches, palaces and houses remained orthogonal blocks, adhering to the simple geometrical outline of the plot or urban block. But in secondary episodes a desire for complication emerged, a free treatment of traditional models and sometimes an effort to incorporate a potential depth into the surface, fantastical and self-sufficient.

In the churches the two formally and psychologically dominant features were the *retablo* altar and the *retablo* façade, which dominated interior and exterior space respectively. They depended upon seventeenth-century Spanish models – imported to Mexico in the early eighteenth century by Jerónimo Balbas, who designed the altar of the chapel of los Reyes in the cathedral in 1718 – but here acquired a new stylistic coherence and crucial significance.

The two equivalent façades of the Sagrario in Mexico City, designed by Rodríguez about the middle of the century, stand between two unadorned *estípites*, which end at the level of maximum plastic protrusion, and they create an extraordinary play of undercut surfaces, as if a whole space had been compressed and concertinaed in, immediately beyond the plane of the wall. There is no basic plane, but a succession of planes ranged indefinitely, and the plastic forms, now that reference to any unambiguous level has been lost, intertwine in an endless succession of optical references (Figs 1196–8).

Thus in front of the church the faithful found a replica in stone of the internal altar in gilded wood, visible from a great distance,

quite distinct from the smooth surrounding walls and analysable, near to, in the full light of the sun.

The altars and façades of Mexico City were repeated in 1755 at Tepotzotlán (where there is also a *camarín* connected to the conventual church, covered with a Moorish or Guarinian roof with interlacing arches, splendidly decorated in stucco; Figs 1199–1202) and, in the second half of the century, all over Central America. One of the most haunting examples, stylistically provincial but of genuinely popular inspiration, is the shrine of Ocotlán near Tlaxcala (about 1780); here the façade, extremely rich plastically, stands between the shafts of the two bell-towers covered with little red terracotta tiles, in accordance with the custom of the province of Puebla (Fig. 1203).

1195 *(left) The sacristy of the Charterhouse, Granada, 1727–64*
1196–1198 *The façade of the Sagrario next to the cathedral, Mexico City*

1199 *The main* retablo *of the church at Tepotzotlán*

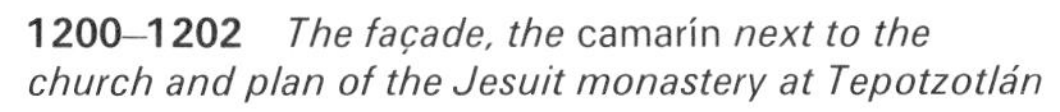

1200–1202 *The façade, the* camarín *next to the church and plan of the Jesuit monastery at Tepotzotlán*

In Peru façades of churches contained within an arched frame were used as early as the late seventeenth century (parish church at Lampa, 1678) and became plastically more elaborate in the early eighteenth century (San Lorenzo at Potosi, 1728); here, too, the effects of undercut isolated the composition from the surrounding structures and emphasized its internal spatial quality, orientated inversely to the naturalistic external space.

In the second half of the eighteenth century the most original architectural experiments were localized in certain mining districts, where, together with Spanish contributions, other artistic tendencies have been documented, especially German ones. At

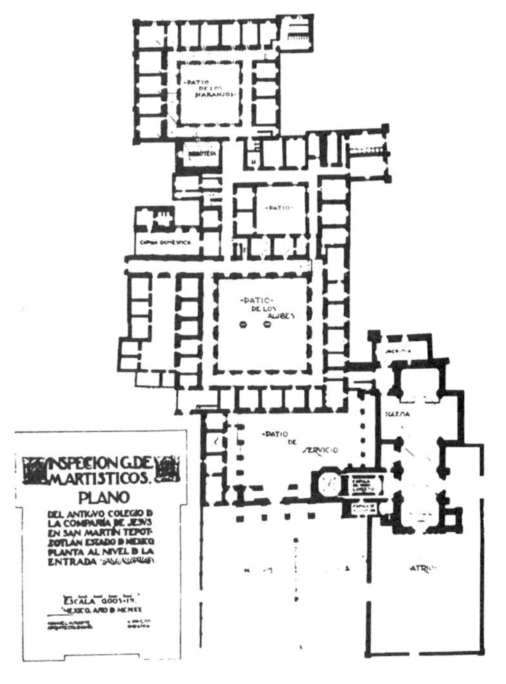

1203 *Façade of the shrine of Ocotlán, Tlaxcala*

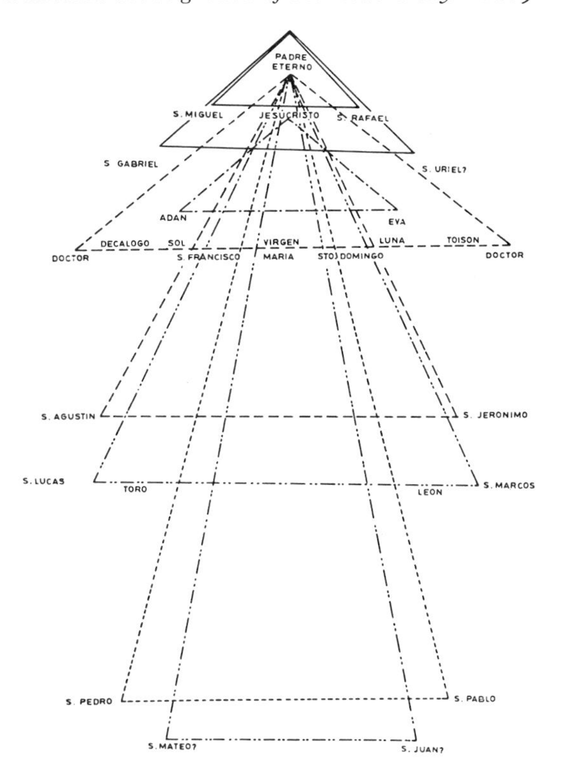

1204, 1205 *View and diagram of the iconographical structure of the façade of Santa Maria Jolalpan, Mexico*

Taxco, in Mexico, the Spaniard Diego Duran Berruecos designed the church of SS. Sebastiano y Prisca, in 1748, with its emphatically vertical façade.

The extraordinary mulatto sculptor and architect Antonio Francisco Lisboa, known as Aleijadinho (1738–1814), was active in the district of Minhas Gerais, in Brazil; he designed the church of San Francisco (1766), and the church of the Rosario (1784) at Ouro Preto, and at the turn of the century, from 1800 to 1805, decorated the façade of the church of Bom Jesús de Matozinhos at Congonhas do Campo, the parapets of its entrance stairway peopled with gesticulating statues (Figs 1210–11).

The organisms of the churches of Ouro Preto reproduced, rather later in time, the geometrically articulated organisms of the German pilgrim churches of the mid-eighteenth century, and the scenario in front of the Bom Jesús was the last great 'baroque' scheme, built at the height of the classical period.

In this final flowering of American colonial architecture, alongside the inevitable European inspiration, there were also obvious signs of the work of native popular artists, who were active as executors and sometimes as designers of the last works mentioned. Two centuries of bureaucratic and conservative colonial administration had made a fruitful exchange of experiences impossible on the level of urban planning, as in the first half of the sixteenth century, and excluded popular participation in organizational choices; the current of popular culture pursued its obstinate course in manifestations on a smaller scale, accepted congenial contributions from Europe and immediately intensified them

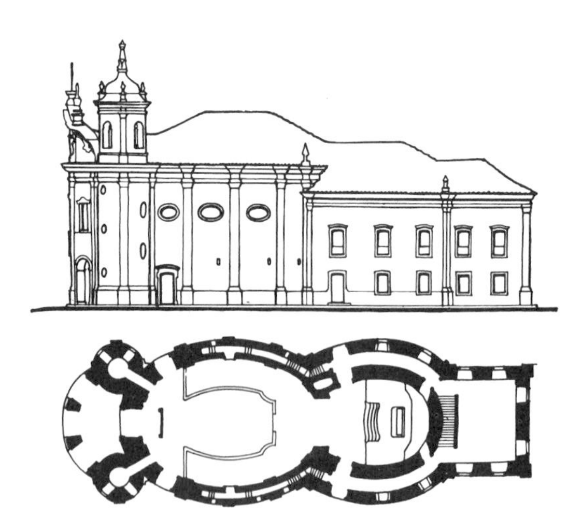

1206–1208 *General view of Ouro Preto and view and plan of the church of the Rosario*

1209 *Church of the Carmine, Sao Joao del Rey*

1210 *Façade of the church of Bom Jesús de Matozinhos, Congonhas do Campo, with the sculptures by Aleijadinho*

1211 *Detail of the entrance stairs to Bom Jesús*

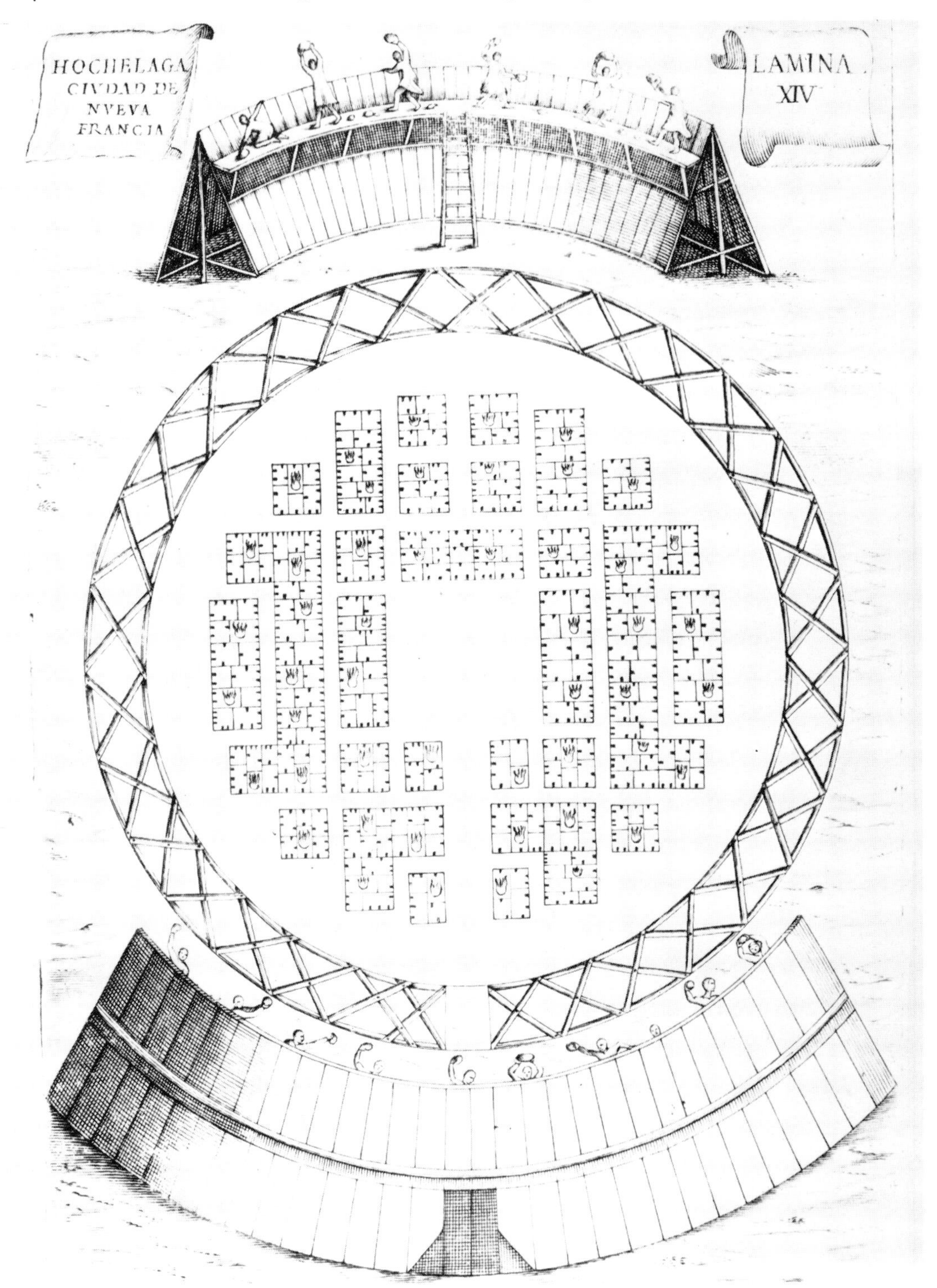

1212 *A plate from the treatise by Caramuel, 1678, showing the city of Hochelaga, occupied by the natives of North America*

with a participation that was already long forgotten in the countries of Europe. This participation gave rise to a further anachronism, because in the meantime in Europe the crisis of traditional artistic culture was coming to a head but, for the same reason, the products of the late eighteenth century in Latin America escaped the doubts and uncertainties of the European debate, and retained a genuine and extremely powerful tone.

The great transformations of the nineteenth century soon obliterated these experiments too, though they seem, because of the brief chronological interval, to be functioning at a short distance from our industrial society, and still retain a uniquely inspiring quality in their own setting.

While the cycle of Spanish and Portuguese colonization was drawing to a close in Central and South America, the colonization of North America was at its height, pursued by the French, Dutch and English.

In chapter 6 we considered the first cities, or rather the fortresses built by the French in Canada in the seventeenth century. In the eighteenth century the French settlers, while extending their control towards the interior of the country, were in a position to found the first real urban organisms: Detroit in 1701 (an organism strangely similar to the medieval *bastides*); Louisburg in 1712 (a fortified town based on the grid plan, similar to those redesigned by Vauban in the previous decades (Fig. 1213)) and, in the plains of the south, Mobile (1711) and New Orleans (1722), which adopted a grid plan system basically not unlike the traditional Spanish one. At the other end of the world, meanwhile, from 1721 to 1735, the governor Lenoir was planning the splendid capital of French possessions in India, Pondichéry (founded in 1677, but at first nothing more than a small fortified

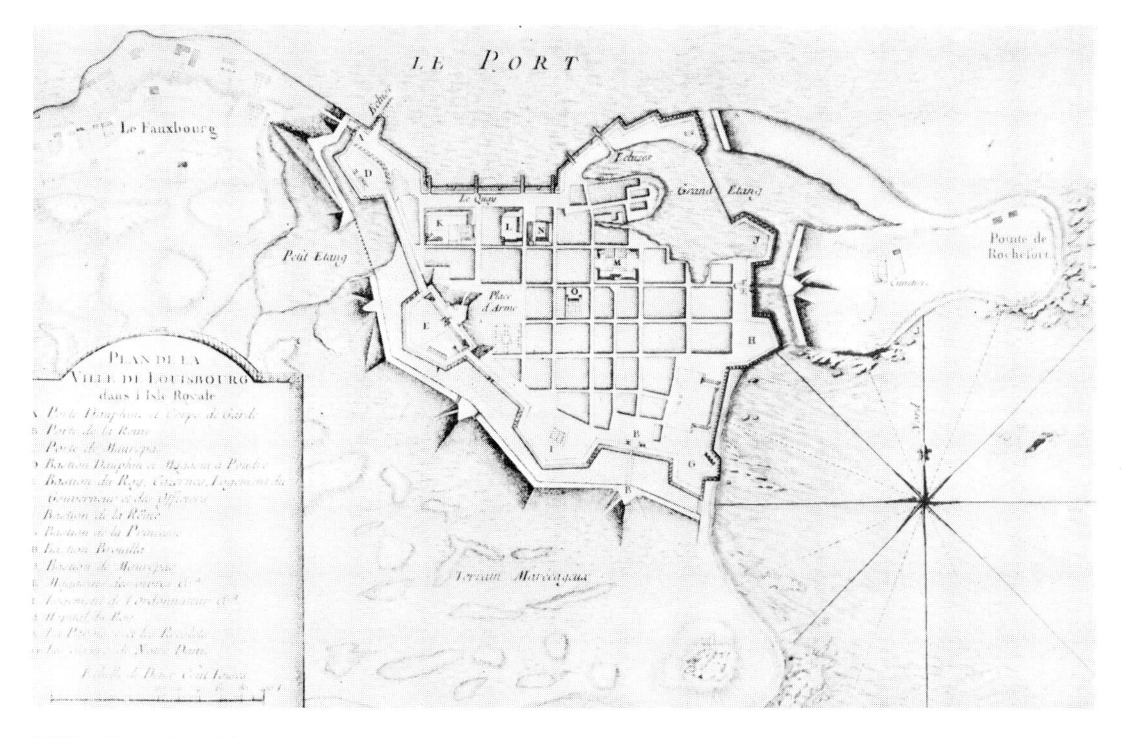

1213 *Plan of Louisburg in 1764*

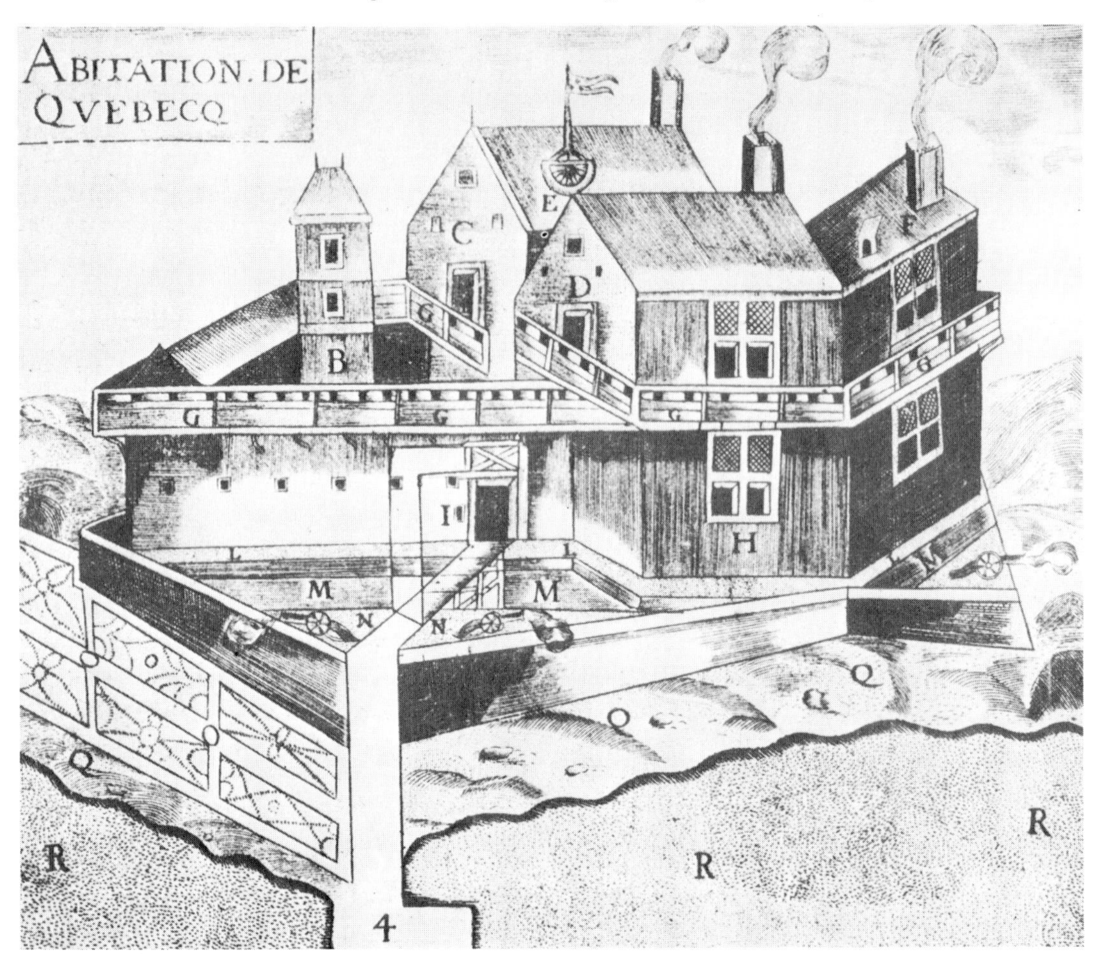

1214 *The first nucleus of Quebec in 1608*

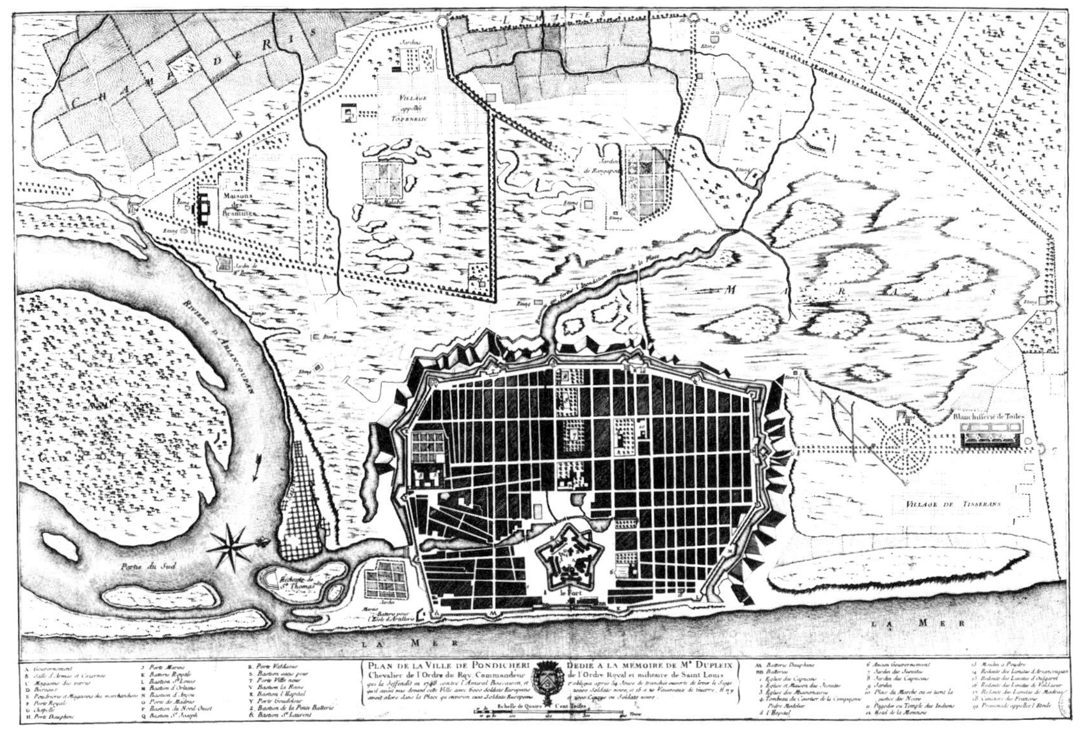

1215 *Plan of Pondichéry in the eighteenth century*

stronghold); here, to impress the Asians, he built a complex of monumental palaces and streets, in accordance with the models of Paris and Versailles (Fig. 1215).

In 1763 most of the French colonial empire, including India and Canada, passed into the possession of the British; just one year earlier the French had founded their last important colonial city, St Louis, in a grid plan along the river bank in the valley of the Mississippi.

English settlement along the coasts of the Atlantic was extremely difficult at first. In New England the Pilgrim Fathers founded the village of Plymouth in 1607, and settled in the surrounding region, in a series of villages; in 1630 the governor John Winthrop founded a new capital on a peninsula at the mouth of the river Charles, Boston, which subsequently became a large city, but retained the regular layout of the original rural nucleus, with its elongated plots perpendicular to the roads (Fig. 1218).

In Virginia the London Company founded Jamestown in 1607, in accordance with the instructions received in the mother country:[51]

'It were necessary that all your carpenters and other such like workmen about building do first build your storehouse and those other rooms of publick and necessary use before any house be set up for private persons, yet let them all work together first for the company and then for private men. . . .

. . . and seeing order is at the same price with confusion it shall be adviseably done to set your houses even and by a line, that your streets may have a good breadth, and be carried square about your market place, and every street's end opening into it, that from thence with a few field pieces you may

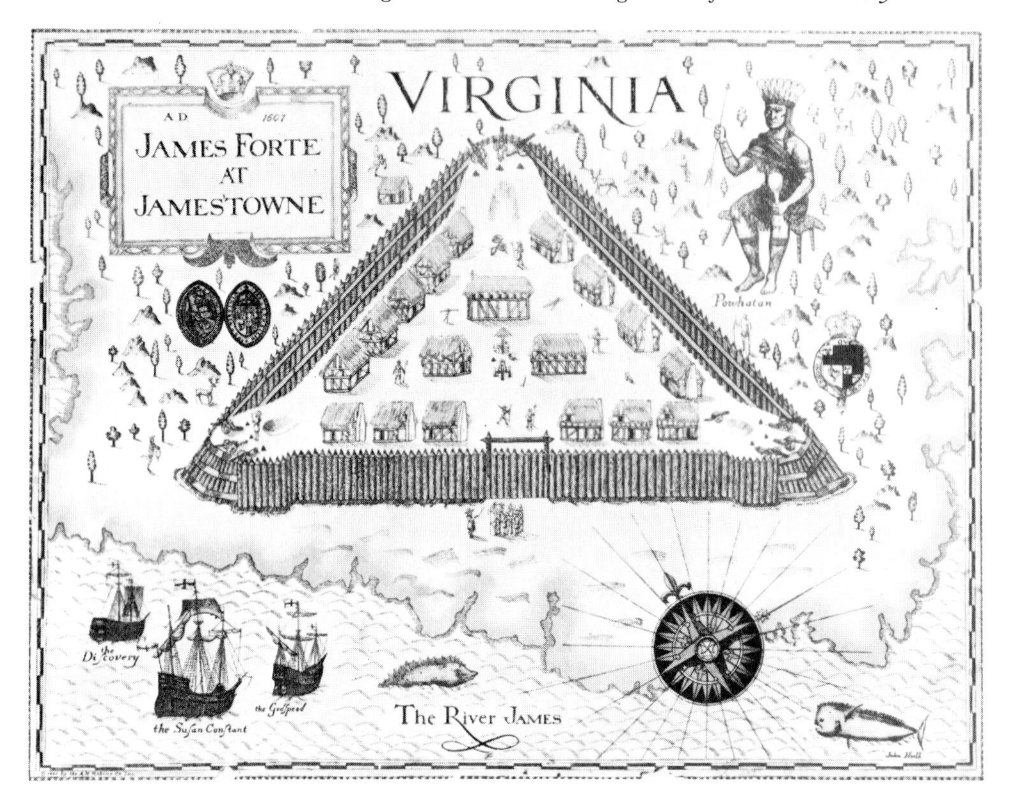

1216 *View of Jamestown in 1607*

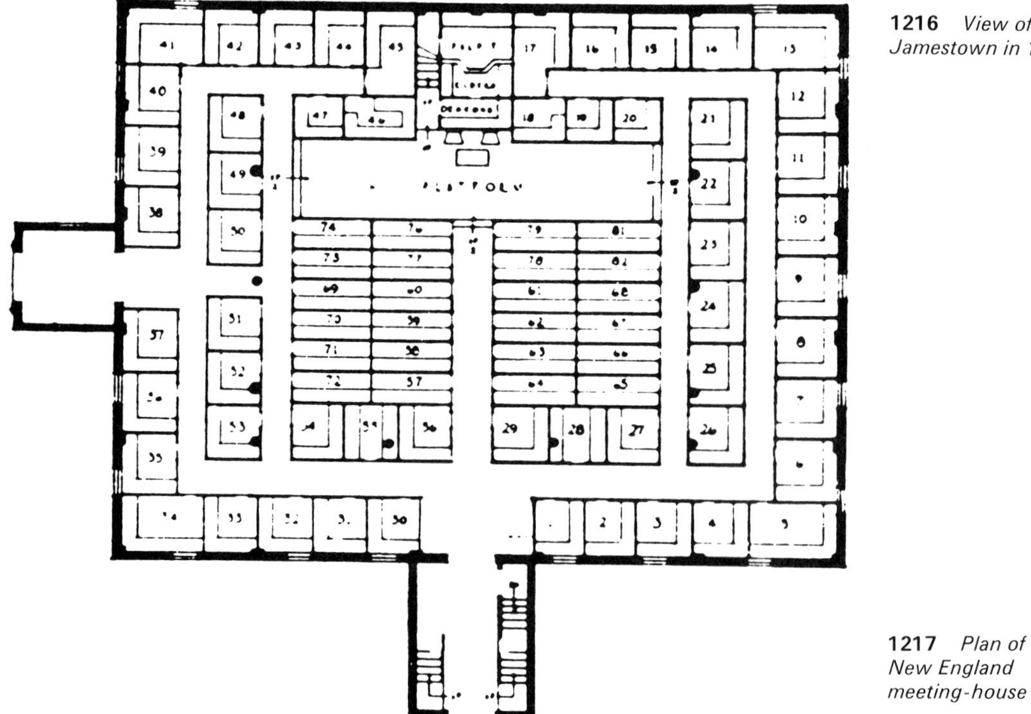

1217 *Plan of a New England meeting-house*

1218 *Plan of Boston in 1640*

command every street throughout, which market place you may also fortify if you feel it need full.'

The first settlement was just a village of tree-trunks; but in 1623 it had to be extended and in 1662 it became a proper town, by means of a law which gave new detailed instructions on the layout of the buildings:[52]

'The towne to be built shall consist of thirty two houses, each house to be built with brick, forty feet long, twenty feet wide, within the walls, to be eighteen feet above the ground, the walls to be two bricks thick to the water table, and a brick and a half thick above the water table to the roof, the roof to be fifteen feet pitch and to be covered with slate or tile.

That the houses shall all be regularly placed one by another in a square or such other form as the honourable Sir William Temple shall appoint most convenient.'

(The reader will have noticed the similarities between these norms and those put out five years later for the rebuilding of the City of London; taking into account the difference in size between the metropolis and the small American outposts, we find the same tendency towards the unification of elements and the same indifference to the geometrical form of the whole; in America, however, on an empty site, the grid plan – already proposed by Hooke and Newcourt for London – appeared the simplest and most economical scheme to give access to a certain number of building plots.)

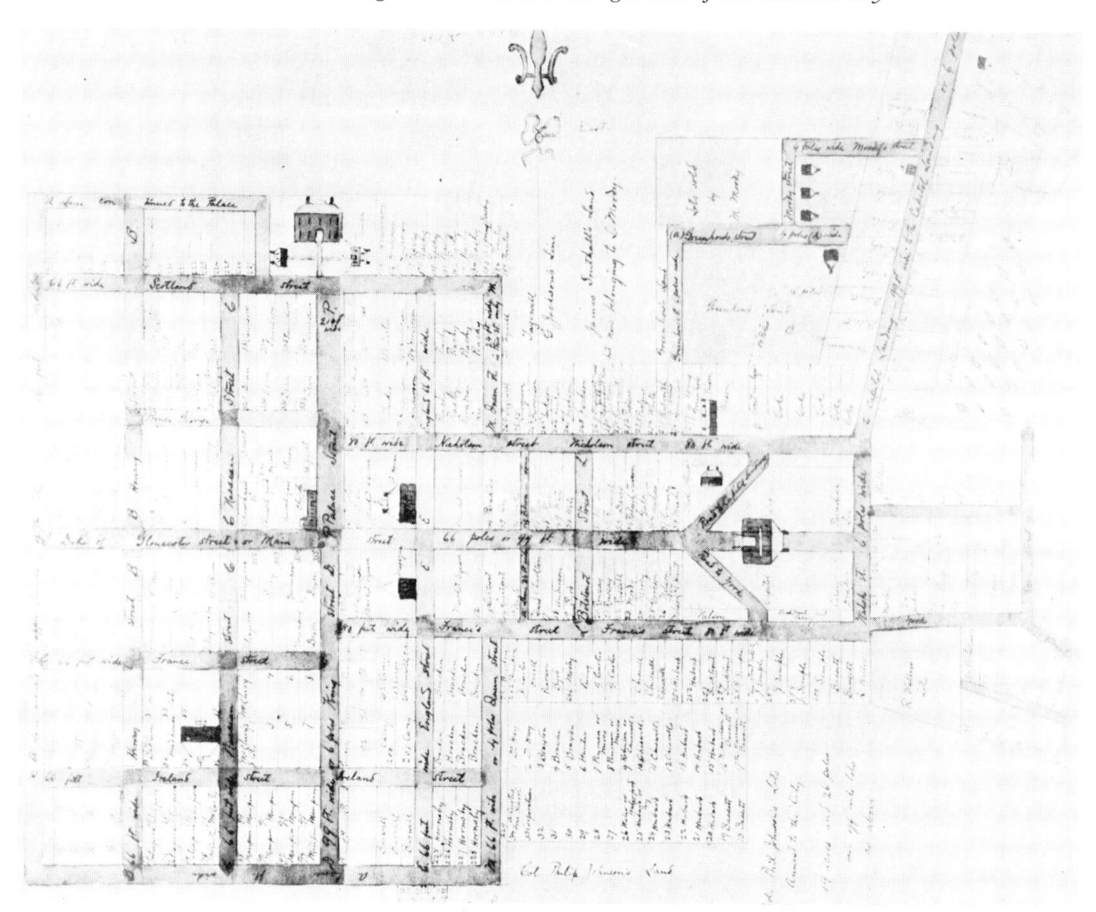

1219, 1220 *Plan and the principal public buildings of Williamsburg in 1740*

Another four centres of this kind were planned in other parts of the colony. This law became the model for the numerous other measures issued for Virginia and Maryland in the late seventeenth century. In Virginia a law of 1680 made provision for the founding of another twenty cities, each on a site of fifty acres (including Yorktown) and was amended by the successive laws of 1691 and 1706. In Maryland – where the first town, St Mary's, had been mapped out in 1633 – a proclamation of 1668, repeated in 1669 and 1671, announced the founding of thirteen cities, but remained inoperative; other laws of 1683, 1684 and 1686, modified in 1692 and 1706, laid down a vast programme of urbanization, which included fifty-seven cities of 100 acres each. After 1706 the period of regional programmes ended, and only special laws for the building of single towns were promulgated: Fredericksburg (1727) and Alexandria (1748) in Virginia, and Charleston in Maryland (1742).

At the end of the seventeenth century when the colonies were developing rapidly, attempts were begun to found more important urban organisms.

Francis Nicholson, governor of Maryland from 1694, resolved to build a new capital for his colony: to this end he founded Annapolis in 1695 (which had an almost monumental plan, with a group of two central circuses and a central square, on to which a series of streets converged) and in 1699 Williamsburg (a grid plan organism, though dominated by a median perspective axis, which framed the Capitol at one end and at the other the William and Mary college, in front of which lay a trident of streets). The building of the city was complete by the first half of the eighteenth century; the elegant Georgian architecture fitted perfectly into this elementary town-planning layout, and some of the more important buildings, such as the governor's house, were surrounded by carefully designed and maintained gardens (Figs 1219–20).

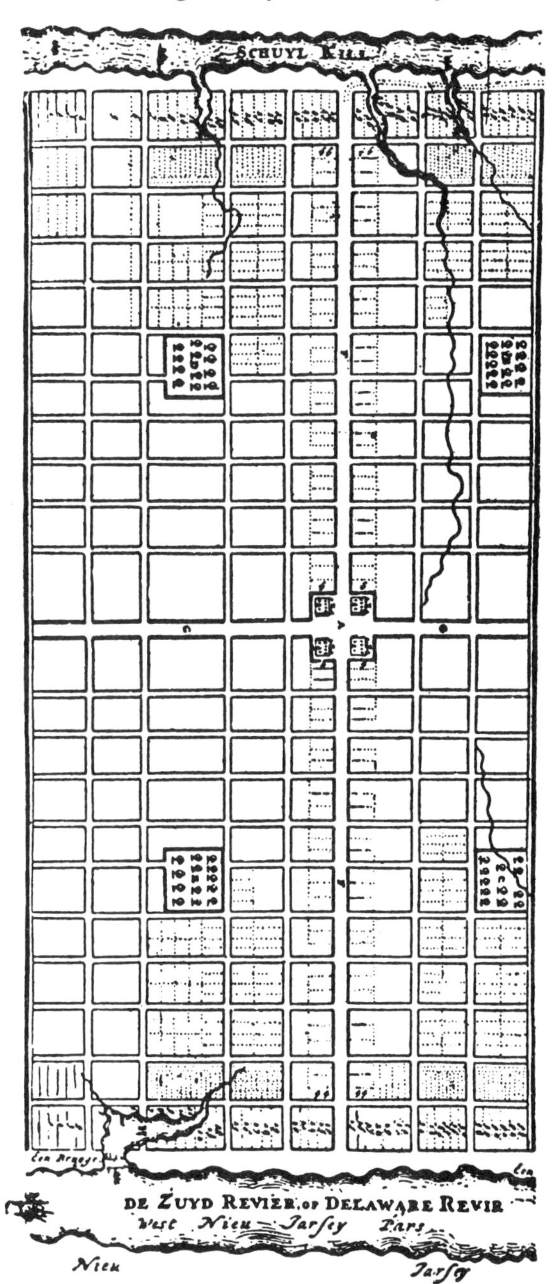

1221 *Penn and Holme's plan for Philadelphia*

Further north in 1664 the English occupied the important Dutch city of New Amsterdam, which was renamed New York. On the other bank of the Hudson, in New Jersey, a Quaker colony was soon established, and in

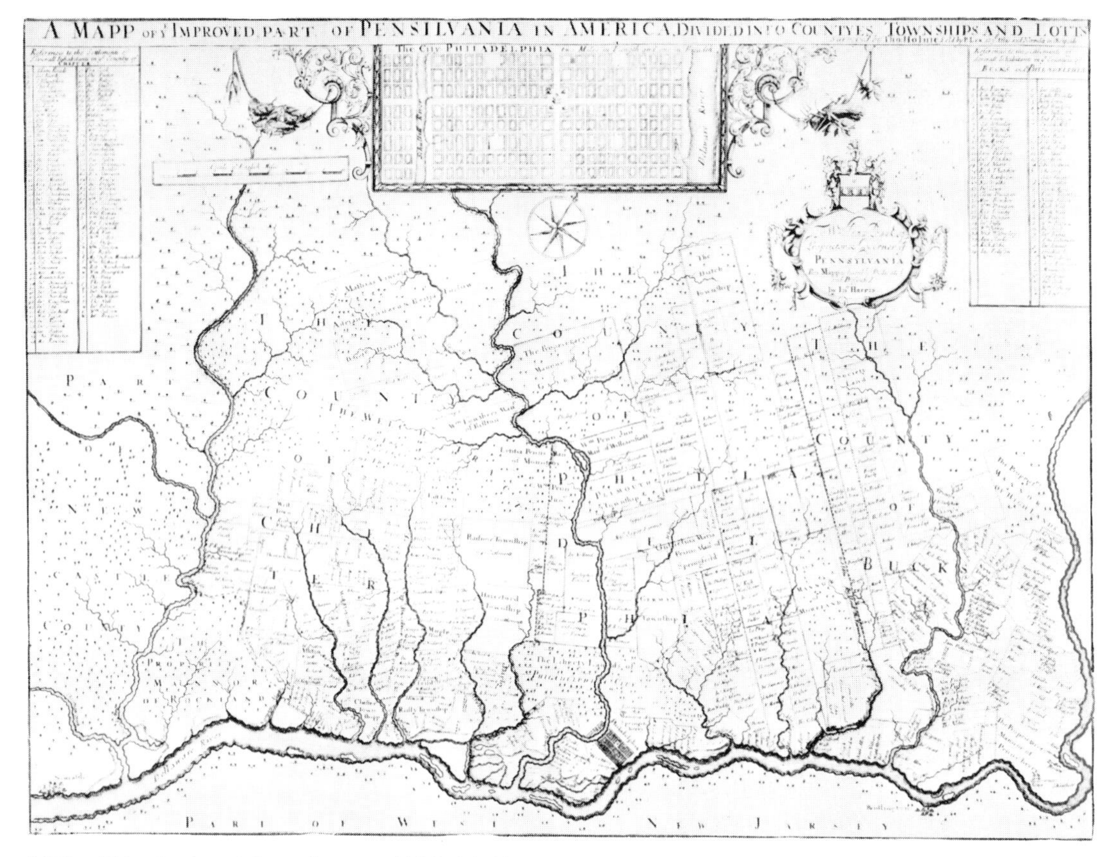

1222 *Urbanization of the region round Philadelphia*

1681 a group of them, led by William Penn (1644–1718), achieved the founding of a new colony further to the west, to be called Pennsylvania.

Penn, the son of an admiral of Cromwell's, was educated at Oxford in the milieu already described in connection with Wren and Hooke, and frequented the court of Louis XIV in Paris before 1665. In 1681 he drew up the instructions for the colonization of the region, which also concerned the planning of the new towns to be built along the navigable rivers of the region:[53]

'Be sure to settle the figure of the town so as that the streets hereafter may be uniform down to the water from the country bounds; let the place for the storehouse be on the middle of the key, which will yet serve for market and statehouse too. . . .

Let every house be placed, if the person pleases, in the middle of its plat [sic], as to the breadth way of it, so that there may be ground on each side for gardens or orchards, or fields, that it may be a green country town, which will never be burnt, and will always be wholesome.'

In 1682 he himself, together with Thomas Holme, prepared the plan for the capital Philadelphia, on a rectangular site between the Schuylkill and Delaware rivers. It was a grid of uniform streets, 50 feet wide, broken by two more important orthogonal axes 100 feet wide which converged on a square, and by four peripheral squares (Fig. 1221).

This design has been compared with Newcourt's plan for London (1666) and may

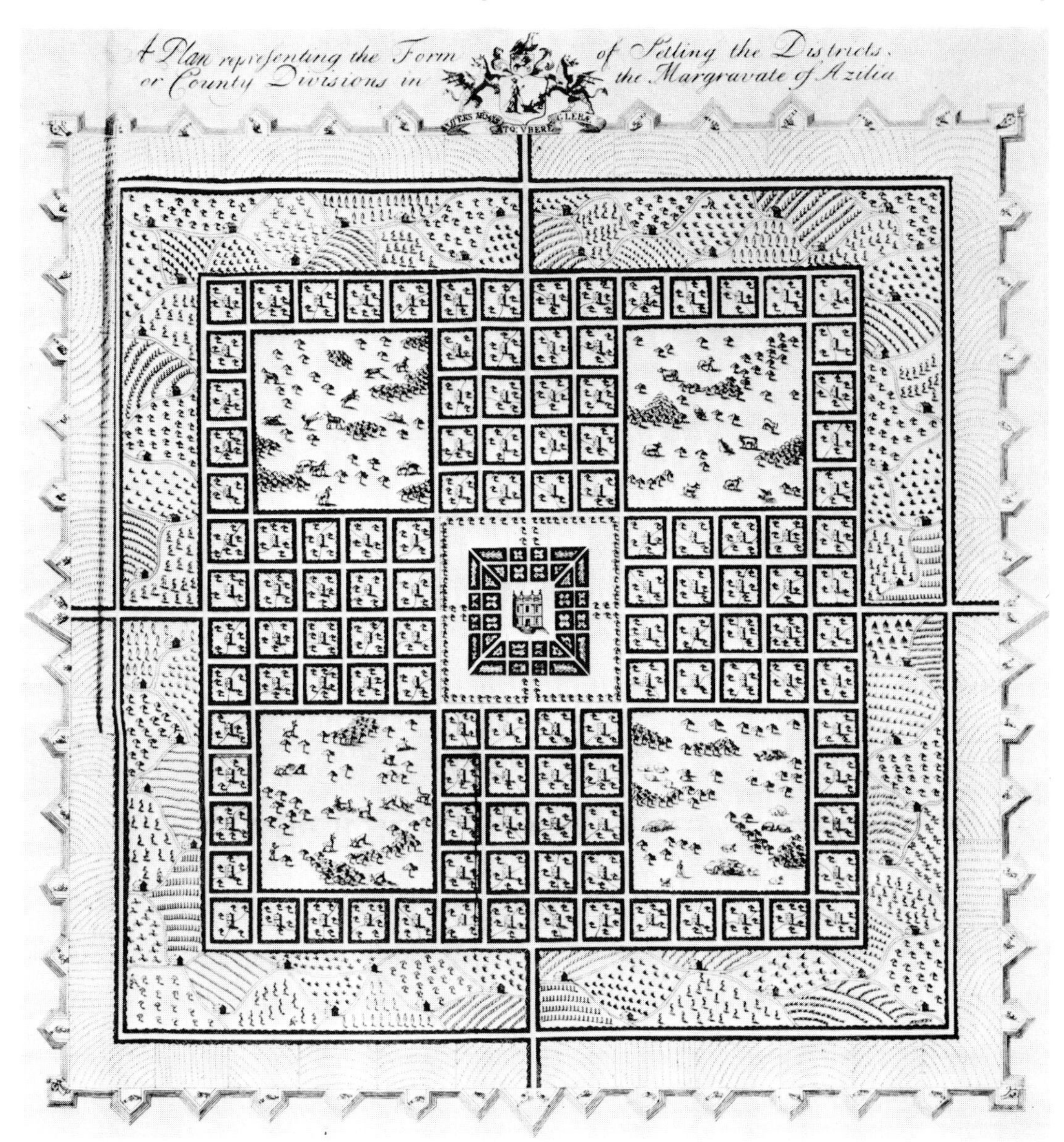

1223 *Plan of the margravate of Azilia in Georgia, 1717*

also be compared with the plan for the new city of Madras in India, drawn up almost at the same time (a little before 1687) by another group of English settlers. What could not be done in England became possible in the empty space of the colonies; but the plan of Penn and Holme differed substantially from every European model hitherto known, and must be considered in the context of the other measures taken for the subdivision of the surrounding agricultural region, which figure on the map published by Holme about 1687, reproduced in Fig. 1222.

Penn's description, published in 1685, explains the criteria followed in the planning of the 'townships', i.e. the rural concerns

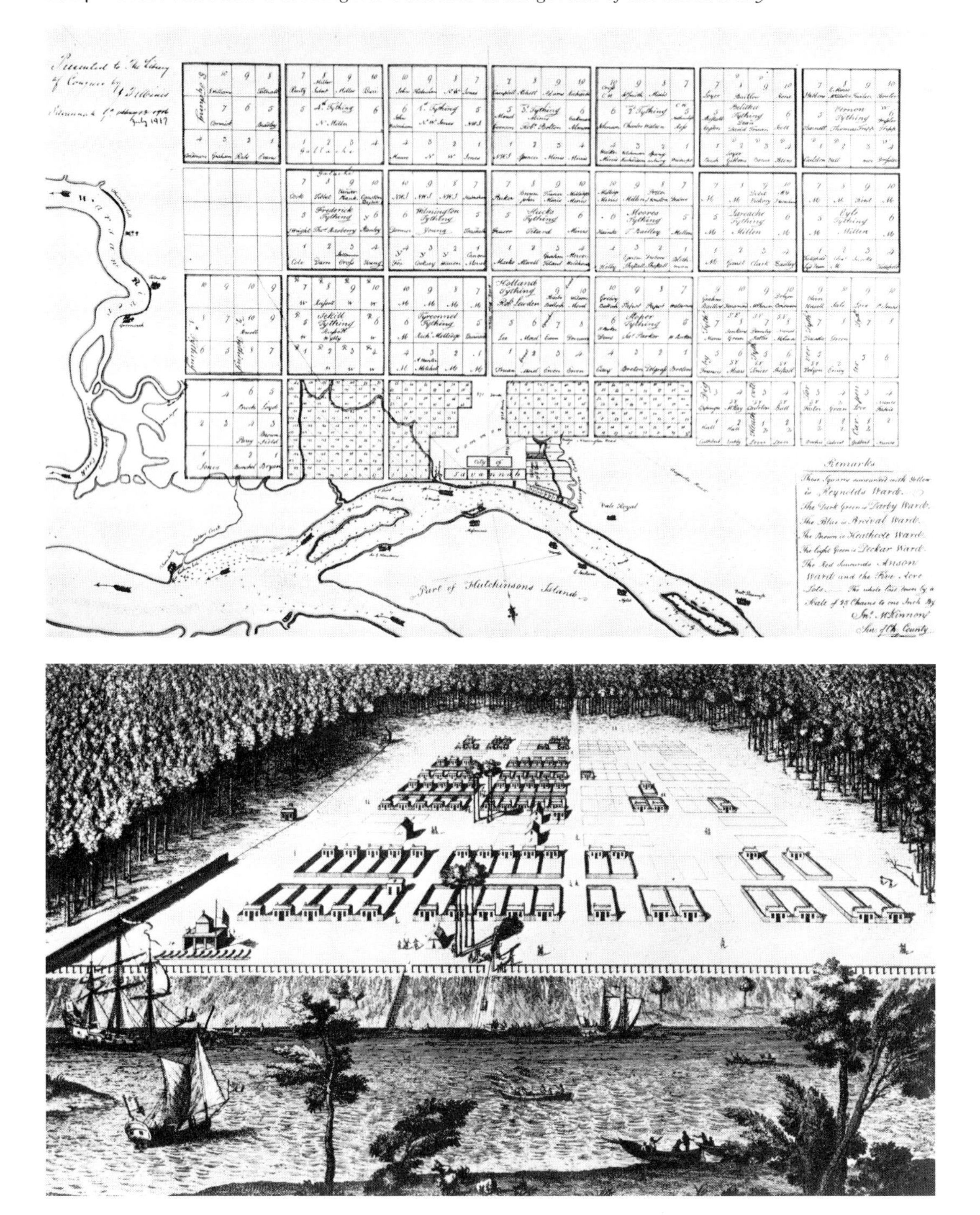

1224, 1225 *The building plots around the city of Savannah in a plan of 1800 and a view of the city under construction in 1734*

installed on the plain to the north of the Delaware:[54]

'Our Townships lie square; generally the village in the Center; the Houses either opposite, or else opposite to the middle, betwixt two houses over the way, for near neighbourhood. We have another method, that though the Village be in the Center, yet after a different manner: five hundred acres are allotted for each Village, which, among ten families, comes to fifty acres each: this lies square, and on the outside of the square stand the Houses with their fifty acres running back. . . . Before the Doors of the Houses lies the high way, and cross it, every man's four hundred Acres of land that makes up the complement of five hundred, so that the Conveniency of the Neighbourhood is made agreeable with that of the land.'

The map of 1687 shows the countryside, on the two sides of the river Schuylkill, divided into plots by means of two orthogonal networks, which reproduced that of the city on a much larger scale in the open countryside. This arrangement – possibly influenced by the agricultural settlements of New Holland, drawn up towards the middle of the seventeenth century – shows that the grid plan system was not associated with any particular scale, but was already used as a generic instrument applicable to any scale.

In 1717 a rich Carolina landowner, Sir Robert Montgomery, planned to realize a large urban and rural settlement, called the margravate of Azilia; it was to be a square region, surrounded by a line of fortification and including a hundred and sixteen farms of one square mile, four large parks of sixteen square miles each, and in the centre the city on a star-shaped plan. This was a Utopian design, which was naturally not translatable into reality, and which was presented as the rationalization of the previous arrangement (Fig. 1223).

In 1732 George II authorized certain Carolina landowners to found the new colony of Georgia, further to the south; their leader was James Oglethorpe (1696–1785), who founded the capital city, Savannah, in 1733. The plan envisaged three types of plots: urban ones for the houses and their services, suburban ones for gardens and rural ones for farms.

The urban plots were grouped into square superplots, which included forty individual residences, a central square and four sites for

Townſhip A.		Townſhip B.		Townſhip C.		Townſhip D.	
1	1	2	2	3	3	4	4
5760 acres wood for the Town A	Commons A Commons	Commons B Commons	Wood for the Town B	Wood for the Town C	Commons C Commons	Commons D Commons	Wood for the Town D
25 lotts of 230 acres 1	1	2	2	3	3	4	4

1226 *Plan of Henry Boucquet's frontier camp in 1765*

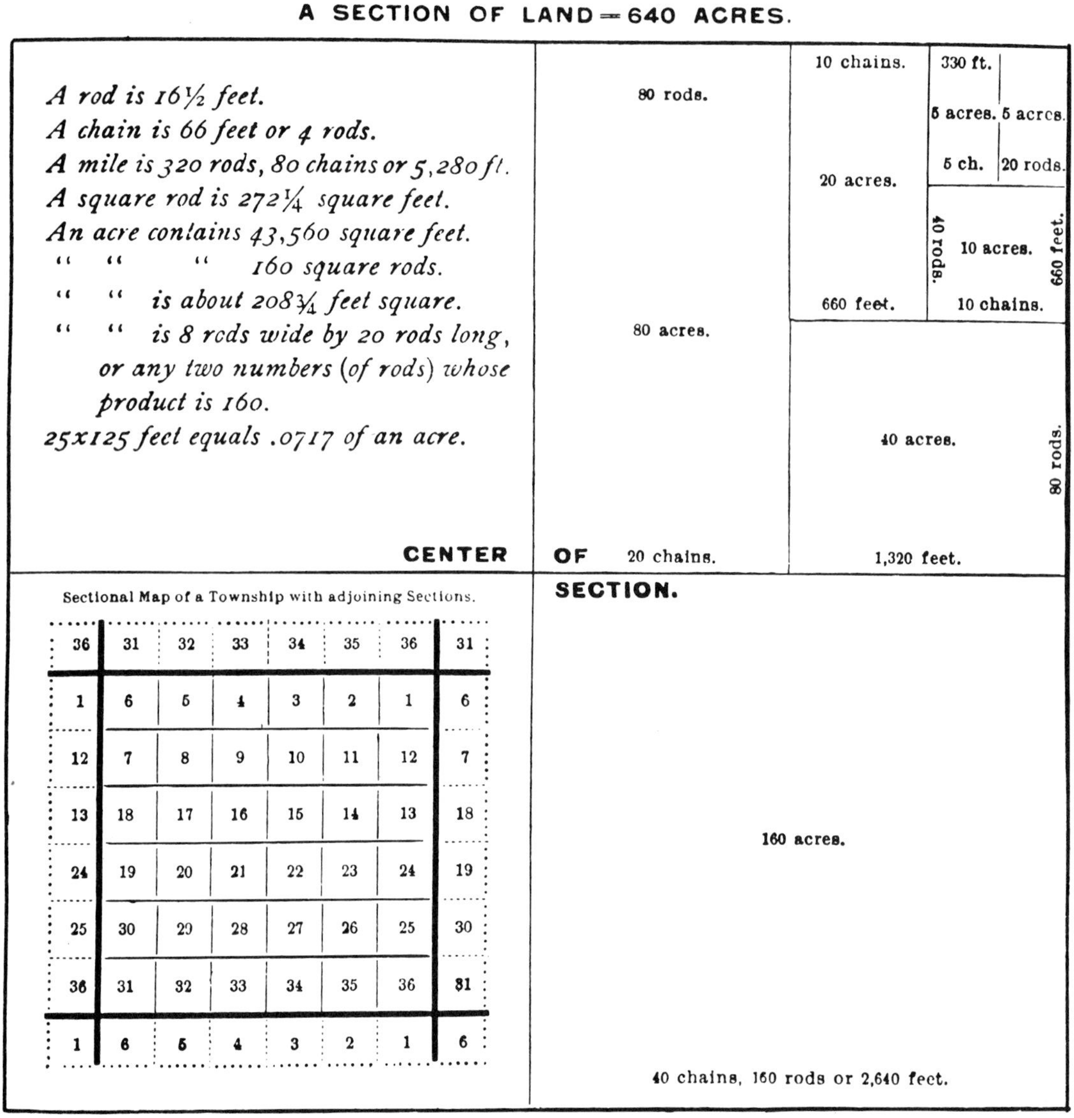

A SECTION OF LAND = 640 ACRES.

A rod is 16½ feet.
A chain is 66 feet or 4 rods.
A mile is 320 rods, 80 chains or 5,280 ft.
A square rod is 272¼ square feet.
An acre contains 43,560 square feet.
" " " 160 square rods.
" " is about 208¾ feet square.
" " is 8 rods wide by 20 rods long, or any two numbers (of rods) whose product is 160.
25x125 feet equals .0717 of an acre.

80 rods.
80 acres.
20 chains.
10 chains.
20 acres.
660 feet.
330 ft.
5 acres. 5 acres.
5 ch. 20 rods.
40 rods.
10 acres.
660 feet.
10 chains.
40 acres.
80 rods.
1,320 feet.

CENTER OF SECTION.

160 acres.

40 chains, 160 rods or 2,640 feet.

Sectional Map of a Township with adjoining Sections.

36	31	32	33	34	35	36	31
1	6	5	4	3	2	1	6
12	7	8	9	10	11	12	7
13	18	17	16	15	14	13	18
24	19	20	21	22	23	24	19
25	30	29	28	27	26	25	30
36	31	32	33	34	35	36	31
1	6	5	4	3	2	1	6

1227 *The territorial grid established by Jefferson with the Land Ordinance of 1785*

public buildings, churches, shops, markets and so on. The city expanded only in whole superplots, and provision was made, around the main nucleus, for a common site to contain future expansion; the plots of the gardens and farms were immediately beyond, but in accordance with the same orientation and the same axes of symmetry. In this case there existed three scales of planning, based on a single network and co-ordinated into a single design (Figs 1224–5).

The historical result of these experiments was the generation of the traditional grid plan, which was no longer an exclusively urban device but could also be applied to the surrounding region, on a landscape or indeed a geographical scale. Ultimately, this process was to lead to Jefferson's Land Ordinance in

1785, which laid down a network for the new territories of the west, orientated according to the meridians and parallels, with meshes of sixteen square miles (Fig. 1227); the submultiples of this grid delimited farms and, at the lower limit, the building plots of the cities; at the upper limit, the multiples served to establish the boundaries between the new states.

Thus the Cartesian network, which guaranteed the measurability of visible forms in the traditional artistic and scientific system, was generalized so as to become applicable on any scale, well beyond the limits that could be embraced by the human eye. The measure of a building plot or structure could be derived, with suitable subdivisions, from the geometrical co-ordinates which ringed the earthly globe; but with this generalization the boundaries of traditional culture were overstepped, for they had been linked precisely to the anthropomorphic scale of human sight and movements, and a completely new cultural universe was opened up. A few years later, in the same spirit, the commission appointed in 1790 by the French National Assembly chose the new units of measurement destined to replace the feet, yards and *braccia* used hitherto: the metre, which was arrived at by dividing the earthly meridian by forty million.

The experiments described in this chapter, considered as a whole, already reveal the degree of disintegration of the traditional artistic system, reached by the end of the eighteenth century. From the American grid plan to the informal curves of Brown's gardens, from the small, precious pilgrim churches of the Zimmermann brothers to the *Mietkasernen* and the *Immediatbauten* of Frederick II, from the furnishings of the princely salons and gardens to the bleak agglomerations of the Sicilian farming villages, from Feichmayr's stuccoes to the indigenous sculptures in the Paraguay *reducciones*, all the variants had been exhausted, all scales of planning experimented with, down to the last ramifications.

The dispersal of the classical figurative heritage, not yet ideologically established, was already statistically complete. In the eighteenth century, for the first time, classicism's universality of intention was echoed by a world-wide circulation; but at this very moment universality emerged as incompatible with unity. It was therefore facts, rather than theoretical speculations, that produced the crisis that the treatise-writers of the second half of the eighteenth century were later to make explicit.

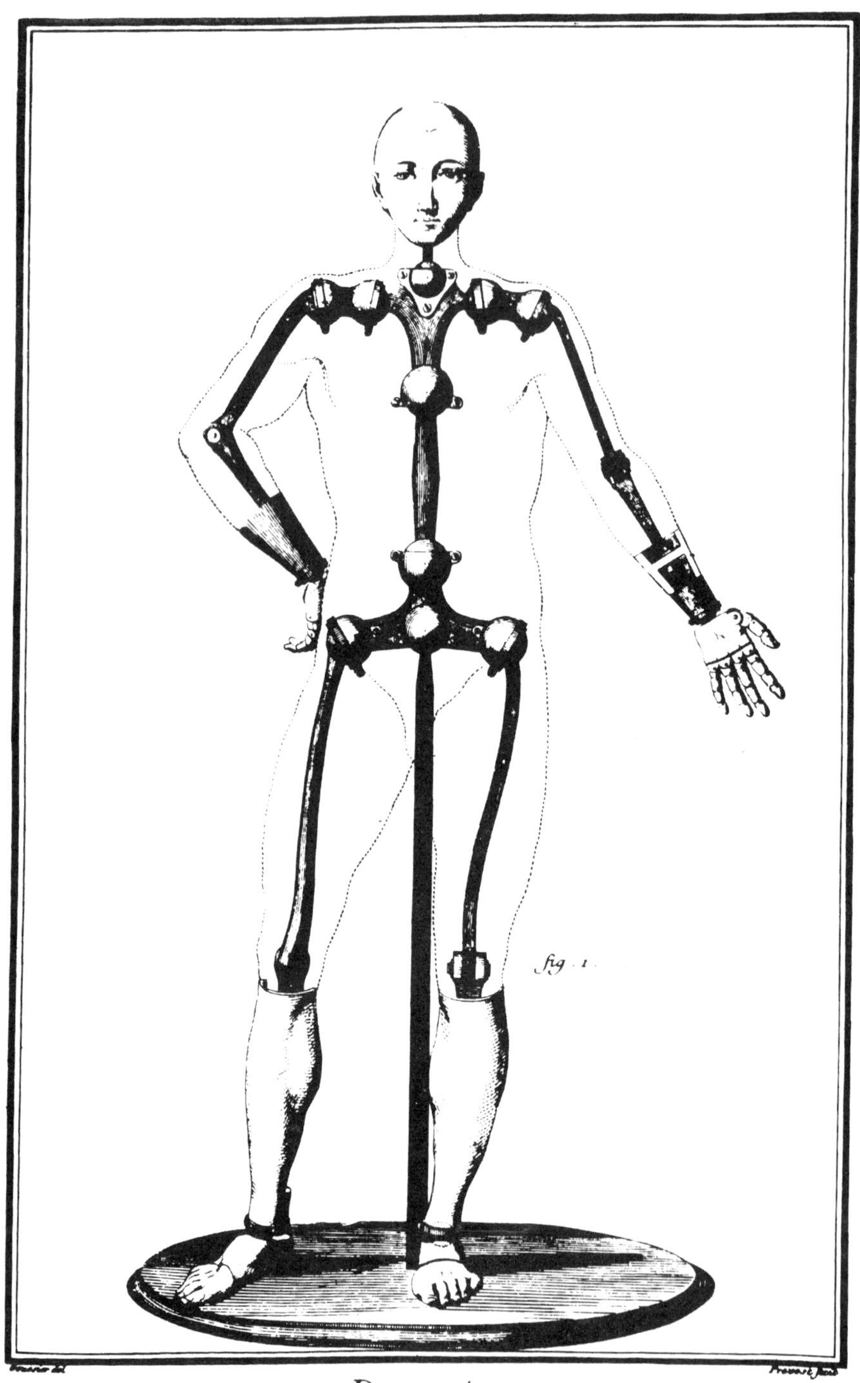

Dessein,

1228 *An illustration from the* Encyclopédie, *1751*

Conclusion: 1750—the turning-point

The period from the Peace of Aix (1748) to the beginning of the Seven Years' War (1756) was only a brief interval of peace between two European conflicts; but this period saw numerous new experiments and ideas emerge, which had a crucial influence on the theory and practice of architecture.

The European economy was now in slow but progressive expansion; England, France and to a lesser degree the other countries were experiencing the combination of growing population and increase in production which was to become an expanding spiral at the end of the eighteenth century. France remained the most highly populated country in Europe and her population, calculated as 28,000,000 on the eve of the Revolution, probably grew by a third during the course of the eighteenth century; England had 5,500,000 inhabitants at the beginning of the century, 6,500,000 in the middle and more than 10,000,000 by the end. Paris and London had over 500,000 inhabitants by the middle of the eighteenth century, but the English capital grew more rapidly and was the first to reach the million mark, as we have said, towards the end of the eighteenth century. Production was increasing everywhere; agriculture was practised with rational methods, emergent industry utilized a series of new technical devices, trade was in full expansion, profiting both from the new organization of credit and from the improvement in transport by land and sea. The new scientific theories and technological experiments connected with the development of science began to be systematically used for the progress of production. In England Kay had patented the fly shuttle in 1733 – the first of the chain of innovations which paved the way for the boom in the textile industry; for a generation the Darbys had been producing cast iron produced with coke, the Newcomen steam engine had been used in the mines since the beginning of the century; in France Vaucanson invented his mechanical loom in 1744; in America Franklin was carrying out his experiments with electricity and invented the lightning conductor in 1751. The traditional arts and techniques, too, were being re-examined with a scientific spirit; theoreticians such as Daniel Bernoulli (in 1738) and Euler (in 1749) established the technique of navigation by sail on a mathematical basis, and in 1750 the composer Rameau wrote the *Démonstration des principes de l'armonie*. Together with the men of science, the technical expert was considered one of the vital protagonists of the productive cycle; d'Alembert sang his praises in the *Discours préliminaire* to the *Encyclo-*

pédie of 1751. In the sectors closer to architecture, in an intermediate position between technician and artist, there appeared a figure now socially well-defined, the engineer; in France the École des Ponts et Chaussées was founded in 1747, to train civil engineers, and in 1748 the École des Ingénieurs de Mézières, which trained military engineers; in England John Smeaton (1725–92) used the title 'civil engineer' about 1750.

The rise in population, the increase in financial means and progress in building technique required and facilitated, more or less everywhere, a large number of building- and town-planning undertakings, both utilitarian and monumental. Some of these have already been mentioned: the Amalienborg complex in Copenhagen (1751–4), the gardens of Sans-Souci (1744) and Schwetzingen (1750), the royal Palace of Caserta (1751) and the great palaces by Rastrelli at St Petersburg (Voronkov, 1749; Stroganov, 1752; the Winter Palace, 1754); some of the most famous Bavarian pilgrim churches, such as Ottobeuren (1748) and the Wies (1754); most of the work by Wood the Elder at Bath (the Circus was begun in 1754); the great public works by Charles III in Spain: the completion of the royal palace in Madrid, the new town of Aranjuez (1748), the industrial villages of El Ferrol (1752) and Barceloneta (1755). To these may be added most of the work of Ferdinando Fuga (1699–1781); the Albergo dei Poveri in Naples dates from 1751 and the Istituto S. Michele in Rome from 1752; of Ventura Rodriguez (1717–85) in Spain and of Jacques-Ange Gabriel (1698–1782) in France.

This heterogeneous list can to some degree be rearranged by distinguishing two main lines: that of despotic absolutism and that of enlightened despotism. Their nature and the meaning of their juxtaposition will emerge more clearly as we consider the most famous text of all where the distinction was stated for the first time: Fénelon's *Les Adventures de Télémaque*, published in 1699 but in fact still widely read and appreciated fifty years later.

More than half the action takes place in Salentum, which may be considered the last urban Utopia of the Renaissance tradition, and which is actually divided into two contrasting Utopias: the city built by Idomeneus before Telemachus' arrival, and the city reformed in accordance with the advice of Mentor, Telemachus' teacher.

Idomeneus' city is a large monumental realization, which the guests found in full expansion on their arrival:[1]

'Telemachus looked upon that rising city with admiration. As a young plant that has been watered with the dews of the night feels the glow of the morning sun, grows under the genial influence, opens its buds, unfolds its leaves, spreads out its odiferous flowers, variegated with a thousand dyes, and discloses every moment some fresh beauty, so flourished this infant city of Idomeneus on the borders of the deep. It rose into greater magnificence every hour, and discovered, in a distant prospect, to the strangers that approached it by sea, new ornaments of architecture, that seemed to reach the clouds. The whole coast resounded with the voices of workmen and the strokes of the hammer, and huge stones were seen suspended from pullies in the air. As soon as morning dawned, the people were animated to their labour by their chiefs, and Idomeneus himself being present to dispense his orders, the works were carried on with incredible expedition.'

The buildings of the city are most sumptuous, for instance the 'Temple of Jupiter, which Idomeneus, who was descended from the god, had adorned with a double range of columns of variegated marble; the capitals of which were silver'.[2] Fénelon's judgment on these marvels is singularly subtle: he describes them poetically, does not blame Idomeneus either for his architectural prodigality or his bellicose policies, indeed he makes Mentor utter words of reproof for

Telemachus, when Telemachus criticizes Idomeneus too eagerly: 'It is common for the inexperience and presumption of youth to indulge a severity of judgment, which leads them to condemn the characters they ought to imitate and produces a hopeless indocility'.[3]

Idomeneus is a good king (and furthermore 'he is judged with the utmost rigour by those who can only guess at his situation; who have not the least sense of the difficulties that attend it'[4]) but has committed certain errors, the result of bad advice from flatterers. Mentor decides to remain in Salentum, to help Idomeneus to remedy these errors, and promotes a series of reforms, which correspond to those principles of eighteenth-century enlightened despotism.

Here are some of them; the census:[5]

'When the army had gone, Idomeneus led Mentor into every quarter of the city. Let us see, said Mentor, how many people you have, as well in the city as in the country: let us number the whole; and let us so examine how many of them are husbandmen. Let us imagine how much corn, wine, oil and other necessaries, your lands will produce one year with another; we shall then know whether it will yield a surplus for foreign trade. . . .'

Disciplining of credit and trade:[6]

'He ordered that bankruptcy should be punished with great severity, because it is generally the effect of rashness and indiscretion, if not of fraud; he also formed regulations, by which bankruptcies might easily be prevented: he obliged the merchants to give an account of their effects, their profits, their expenses and their undertakings, to magistrates established for this purpose: he ordered that they should never be permitted to risk the property of another, nor more than half their own; that they should undertake, by association, what they could not undertake singly: and that the observance of the conditions of such association should be enforced by severe penalties. He ordered that trade should be perfectly open and free, and instead of loading it with imposts, that every merchant, who brought the trade of a new nation to the port of Salentum, should be entitled to a reward.'

Laws on customs:[7]

'Mentor then visited the magazines, warehouses and manufactories of the interior part of the city. He prohibited the sale of all foreign commodities that might introduce luxury or effeminacy; he regulated the dress and the provisions of the inhabitants of every rank; and the furniture, the size, and ornaments of their houses.'

These rules are extremely detailed; the king, the seven classes of free men and the slaves must wear simple clothing, of different colours; only simple food is allowed, and wine in limited quantities; music is forbidden, except in religious services.

The legislation on customs also includes reforms on matters of town-planning, building and the figurative arts:[8]

'To the temples also he confined the superb ornaments of architecture, columns, pediments and porticoes; he gave models, in a simple but elegant style of building, for houses that would contain a numerous family, on a moderate extent of ground, so designed, that they should have a healthful aspect, and apartments sufficiently separated from each other, that order and decency might be easily preserved, and that they might be repaired at a small expense.

He ordered that every house above the middling should have a hall, and a small peristyle, with separate chambers for all the free persons of the family; but he prohibited, under severe penalties, the superfluous number and magnificence of apartments, that ostentation and luxury had introduced. Houses erected upon these models, according to the size of the family, served to embellish one part of the city at a small expense, and gave it a regular appearance; while the other part, which was already finished, according to the caprice and vanity of individuals was, notwithstanding all its magnificence, less pleasing and convenient. This city was built in a very short time; because the neighbouring coast of Greece furnished very skilful architects, and a great number of masons repaired thither from Epirus, and other countries, upon the promise, that, after they finished their work, they should be established in the neighbourhood of Salentum, where land should be granted to them to clear, and where they would contribute to people the country.

Painting and sculpture were arts which Mentor thought should by no means be proscribed; but he permitted the practice of them to few. He established a school, under masters of an exquisite taste, by whom the performances of the pupils were determined: there should be no mediocrity, says he, in the arts which are not necessary to life; and consequently no youth should be permitted to exercise them, but such as have a genius to excel: others were designed by nature for less noble occupations, and may be very usefully employed in supplying the ordinary wants of the community. Sculptors and painters should be employed only to preserve the memory of great men, and great actions; and the representations of whatever has been achieved by heroic virtue, for the service of the public, should be preserved only in public buildings, or the monuments of the dead. But whatever was the moderation of the frugality of Mentor, he indulged the taste for magnificence in the great buildings that were intended for public sports; the races of horses and chariots, combats with the cestus, wrestling, and other exercises which make the body more agile and vigorous.

He suppressed a great number of traders that sold wrought stuffs of foreign manufacture; embroidery at an excessive price; vases of silver and gold, embossed with various figures in bas relief; distilled liquors and perfumes; he ordered also, that the furniture of every house should be plain and substantial, so as not soon to wear out.'

Some of the measures that Fénelon describes at the end of the seventeenth century for his royal pupil, the heir of Louis XIV, became part of the practice of European governments in the following fifty years. The clash with reality naturally eliminated the refinements of the theoretical discussion: despotism or enlightenment, authority and reason, emerged as forces antagonistic one to the other, only partly and temporarily reconcilable. Indeed from 1751 to 1753 Voltaire and Frederick II embarked on an experiment in partnership which did not correspond at all to that of Mentor and Idomeneus. Opulence or the spirit of simplicity were means adaptable to many different political programmes. The eighteenth-century philosophers, furthermore, no longer believed in the educative virtues of a given physical environment, and were no longer interested in representing the ideal city. Fénelon attempts to render his description of Salentum lifelike, but Voltaire makes his description of El Dorado intentionally improbable:[9]

'Meanwhile they took Candide and Cacambo to see the city, the public buildings rising to the clouds, the markets adorned with a thousand columns, the fountains of pure water, the fountains of rose water, those of sugar cane liqueurs which flowed continually into the squares paved with every kind of precious stone, which gave out a perfume similar to that of cloves and cinnamon.'

Discussion on the architecture of absolutism, despotic or enlightened, could only be

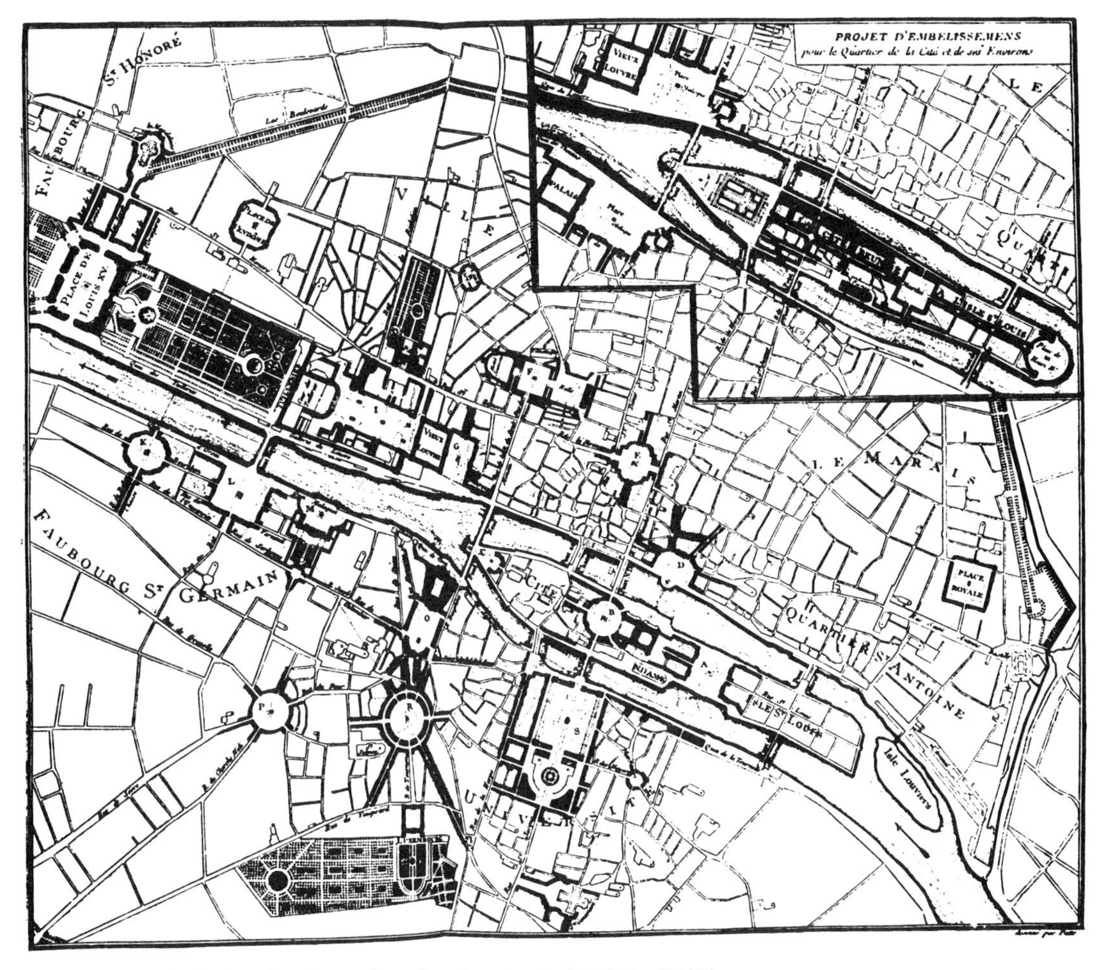

1229 *Plan of Paris showing the projects for place Louis XV (Patte, 1765)*

a survey, not a systematic theoretical exposition, and had to be limited within precise chronological confines. To conclude our historical account, we shall choose three experiments begun around 1750, not included in the previous account and which aptly demonstrate the main aspects of the problems of that time: the royal square in honour of Louis XV in Paris, the plan for Nancy and the rebuilding of Lisbon.

1 On 27 June 1748, immediately after the Peace of Aix, the director of Paris buildings, Tournehem, organized a competition for the architects of the academy, to design a new royal square, 'in the districts of Paris seeming to them most favourable'.[10]

The choice of the site entailed technical and economic decisions of the greatest importance. Land speculation started up, and threatened to be as decisive a factor as the aesthetic choices of the architects; the proposals involved most parts of the historic centre, the Île de la Cité, the surroundings of the Louvre, the faubourg St-Germain, the old medieval nucleus on both banks. They were collected together by Patte in a summarizing plate (Fig. 1229) which is a positive sampler sheet of the models of urban composition current in the middle of the century,

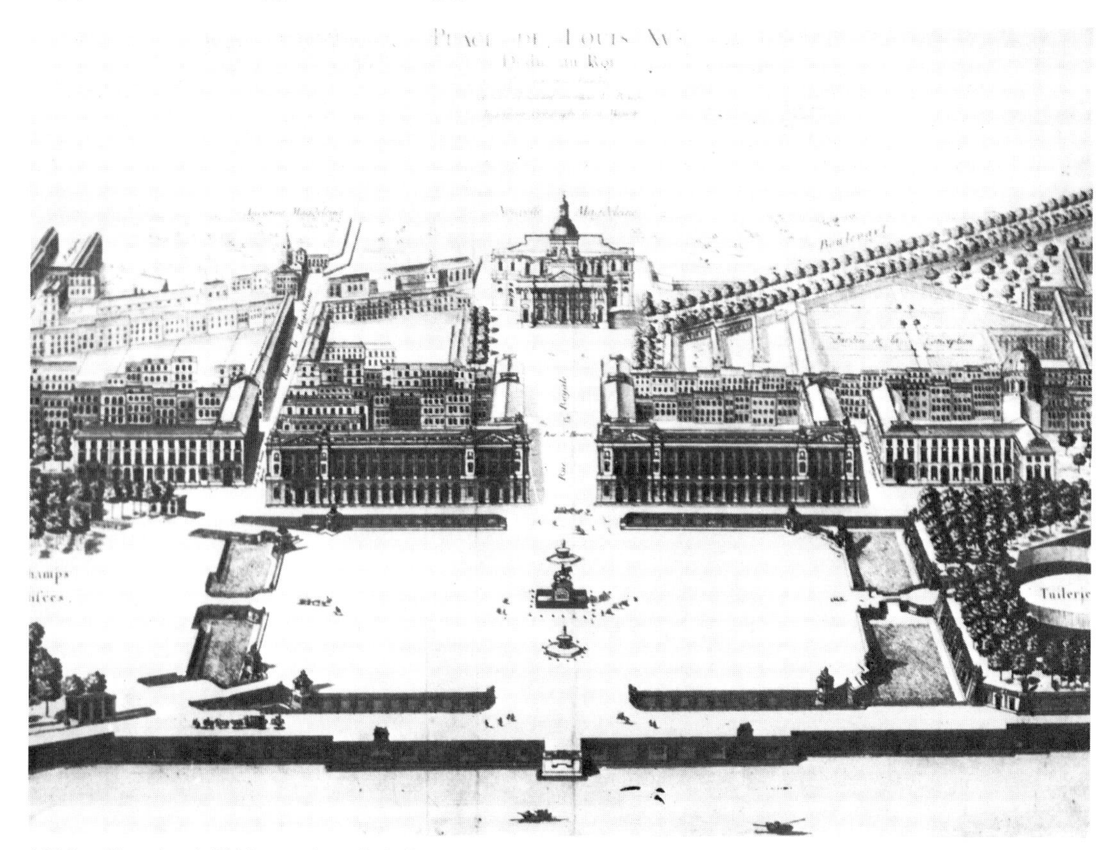

1230 *Place Louis XV (now place de la Concorde) in the eighteenth century*

including the rectangular square open to the river – on the model of the place Royale of Bordeaux, of 1733 – and the round open space, possibly imitated from the English circus.

The king hesitated, realized that the city was not in a position to bear the expenses of an operation in an already built-up district, and at first chose the site of the Hôtel Conti on the left bank, but the price of compulsory purchase was high in this case too. Hence the final solution, which is described as follows by Patte:[11]

'Seeing that it was not possible to execute a suitable square without devastating business districts, and without sacrificing the convenience and interests of a large number of his subjects, by destroying an infinity of houses, the king wished to outdo his people in generosity, and drew the attention of the city to a large site owned by himself, between the mobile bridge of the Tuileries and the Champs Élysées.'

This site was presented to the city, but the majority of those concerned were doubtful about the possibility of realizing a traditional architectural composition in so peripheral a district, and one already characterized by a series of green spaces. A typical judgment is quoted by Lavedan: 'Here no project of any size could be executed without blocking the most beautiful view in the world.'[12] Only in 1757 did Tournehem's successor, Marigny, announce a second competition for academi-

1231, 1232 *Two views of place de la Concorde*

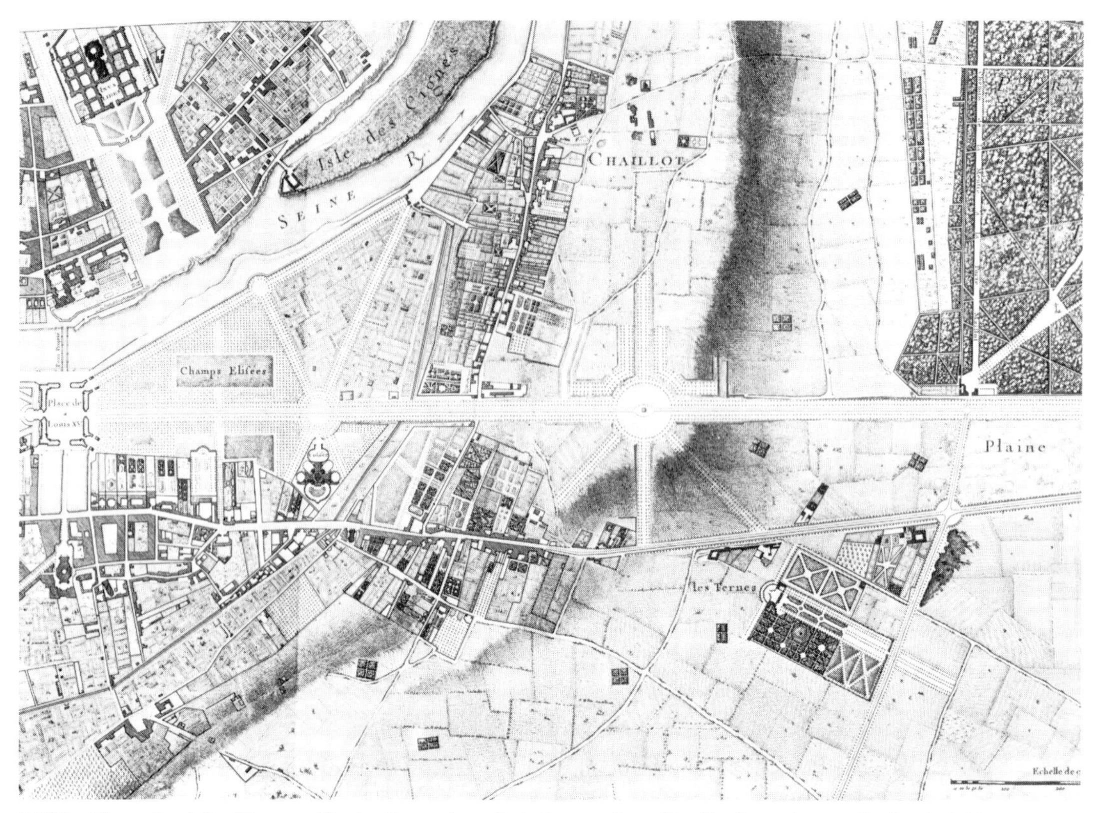

1233 *The axis of the Champs-Elysées from place de la Concorde to Neuilly, from the treatise by J. B. Perronet, 1788*

cians and he himself, in the report, harshly criticized all the plans put forward; it seems that Louis XV preferred the plan by Boffrand, but he died in 1754, and the executive appointment was given to Jacques-Ange Gabriel, who prepared three successive plans in June 1753, August 1753 and the end of 1755.

Gabriel's model was clearly the square in Bordeaux designed by his father Jacques, which is a C-shaped composition open towards the Gironde. In this case, as well as the side nearest the Seine, he had to leave the sides towards the Tuileries and Champs-Élysées open as well. On the fourth side in 1753 he designed a single building, set between the entrance to two roads; but in 1755 – possibly influenced by the plan for the square at Nancy published two years earlier – he envisaged two buildings, framing a street with uniform façades and, at the end, the façade of a great church; in this way a new axis of wide-reaching importance was defined, perpendicular to that of the Champs-Élysées, which brought together the tangential route of the *grands boulevards* and transported it, over a new bridge, across the Seine.

The square, situated at the crossing of the two axes, was simply a ground level scheme; its perimeter was marked by an expanse of water and its extent, given its measure by the statue of the king, stood out freely between the city, the river and the two tree-filled gardens; later the statue was replaced by the guillotine, and finally by the Egyptian obelisk.

This last scheme undertaken by the *ancien régime* was notable precisely for its landscape

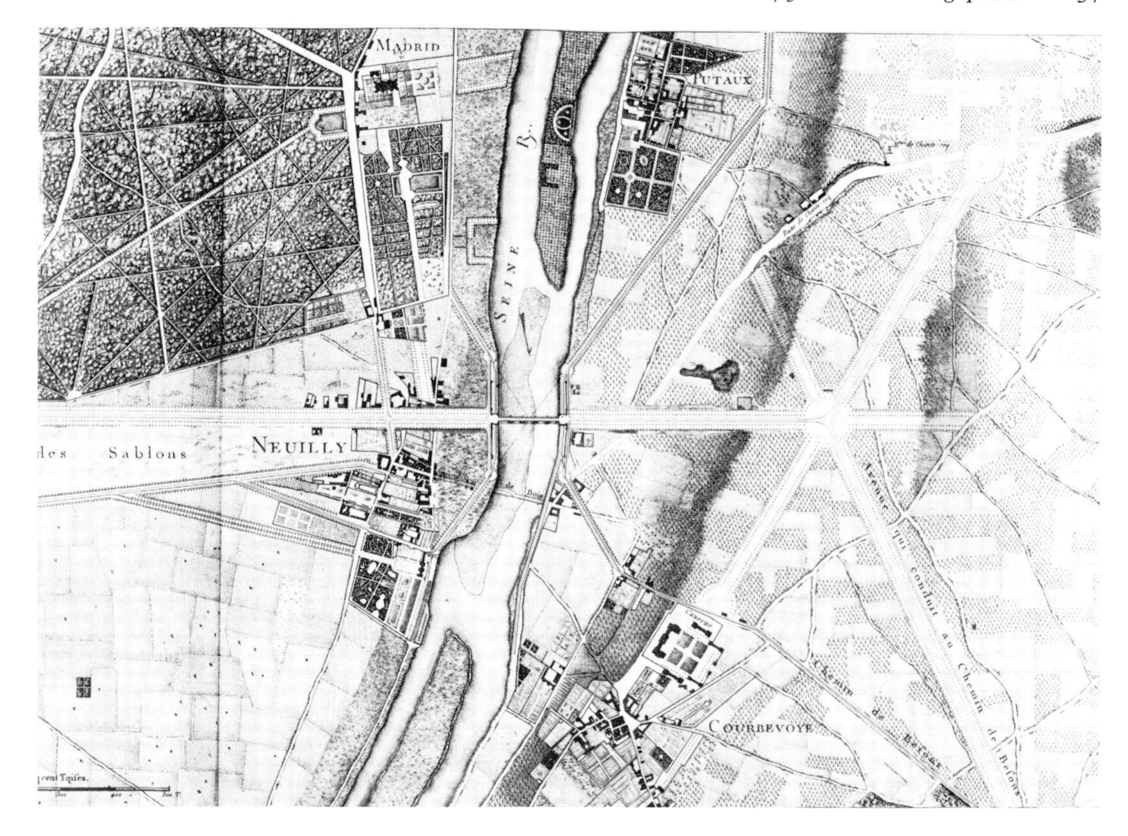

scale and openness; the uncertainties of those responsible, from 1750 and 1753, were ultimately justified by the novelty of the positioning: it avoided the built-up environment within which the other royal squares had been opened, and belonged to the 'green city' of the outskirts, laid out by Le Nôtre. The logic of the park schemes of the *grand siècle* continued to hold sway: only in these circumstances could absolutism avoid the financial, administrative and legal obstacles that obtained within the city, magnified after half a century by the growth of private interests and the chronic weakness of the instruments of public control.

Indeed the realization of the north building wing and of the new road, the rue Royale, was extremely slow and difficult. Metman has published[13] the convention between the city and the heirs of the banker Law, owners of the sites on which the left-hand building and one of the façades of the rue Royale were to stand, almost as far as the crossing with the rue St-Honoré. The city did not acquire the site, but committed itself to building the façades (which in fact were executed between 1758 and 1766), to resell them to the owners for a prearranged price and to pay them an interest, from 1757 onwards, for the occupation of the site. Only in 1766 did the king acquire the Hôtel des Monnaies, and only in 1775 was work begun on the actual buildings, behind independent façades.

The place Louis XV in Paris was in fact the last undertaking of this type realized in France, if one excepts that of Rheims designed between 1755 and 1760 by Legendre and Soufflot. This pattern of operation was by

1234 *View of rue Royale, Paris*

1235 *The urban organism of Paris in the second half of the eighteenth century. The principal spaces opened up in the medieval fabric after the beginning of the seventeenth century are shown in black*

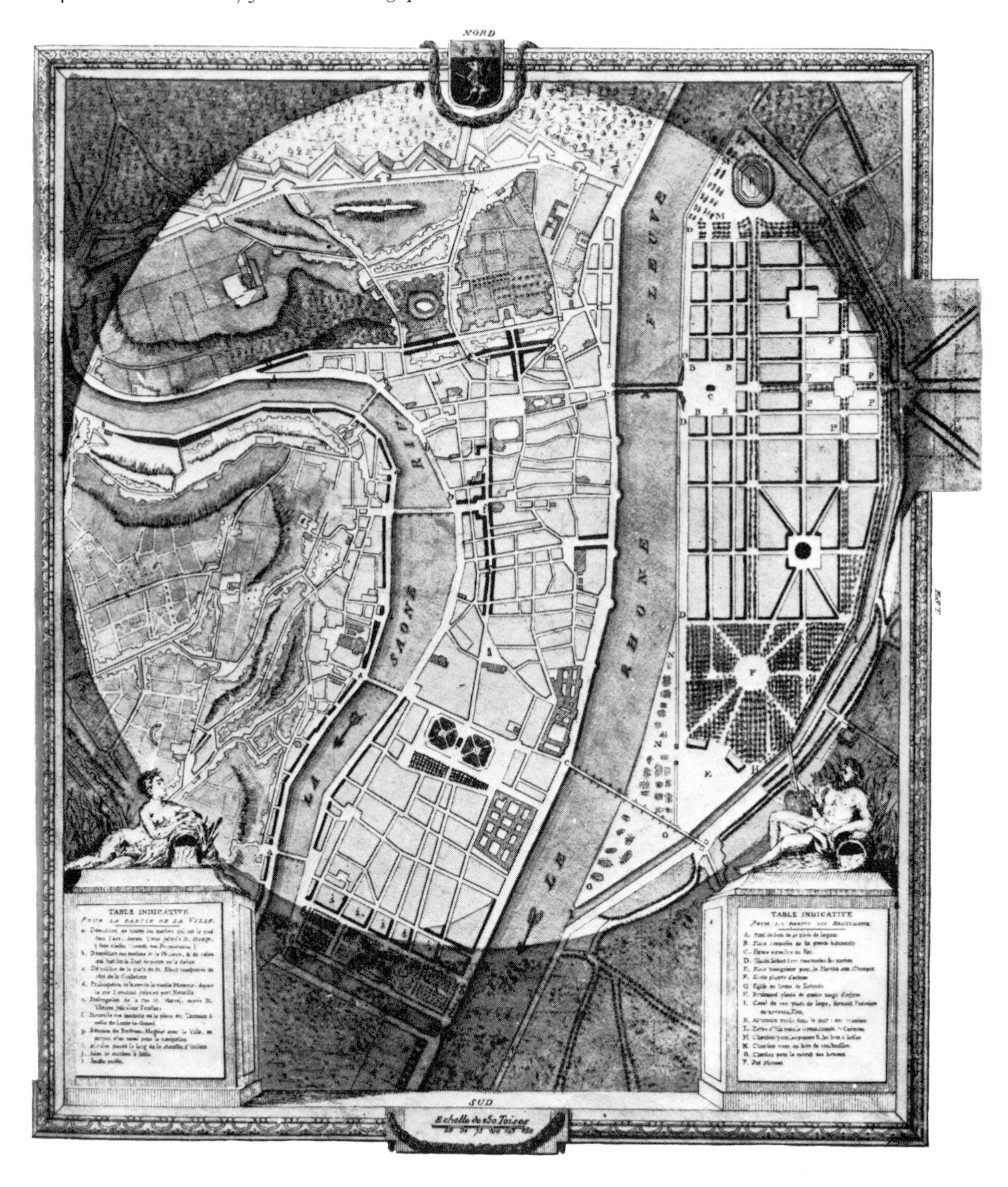

1236 *Morand's plan for the extension of Lyon, 1768*

now aesthetically and administratively outdated. It was in 1755 too that Marigny appointed Jacques-Germain Soufflot (1713–80) *contrôleur des bâtiments du roi* in Paris, and in the twenty-five years that followed this architect, the product of the new rationalist climate, co-ordinated the development of the city, continuing the work of the seventeenth-century *surintendants* in a scientific spirit: he completed the encircling avenues of the left bank, restored Notre Dame, the Louvre, the Tuileries and Luxembourg, repaired the Samaritaine and designed the church of Ste-Geneviève, the manifesto of the new archaeological and technical classicism.

This complex of works, however considerable, was connected only partially with the aristocratic character of the capital, and was echoed – as it had never been in the seventeenth century – in other town-planning programmes conceived and realized in other French cities: the *boulevards* and *quais* by Tourny in Bordeaux (1743–57), the public gardens by Mondran at Toulouse, the new districts of Perrache and Morand in Lyon (1766) (Fig. 1236).

2 The ex-king of Poland, Stanislas Leczinski, Louis XV's father-in-law, was made duke of Lorraine in 1737. The capital of Lorraine, Nancy, was formed of two organisms, the old medieval centre and the *ville neuve* founded by Charles II at the beginning of the seventeenth century, which we have already discussed in chapter 4. The treaty of Ryswick required that the fortifications of the *ville neuve* should be demolished, and the new sovereign – in practice a guest of France, excused from all administrative tasks – devoted himself enthusiastically to the laying out of the new open city: a young local architect, Emmanuel Héré de Corny (1705–63), prepared the plans from 1752 onwards.

The pivot of the new organism was the link between the *ville neuve* and the older nucleus, which retained its bastions and moat. The sovereign decided to bring together the grid plan network of the *ville neuve* with a couple of straight streets and, at a suitable point, to introduce a series of monumental squares, extending into the old city: in front of the moat a first rectangular square with

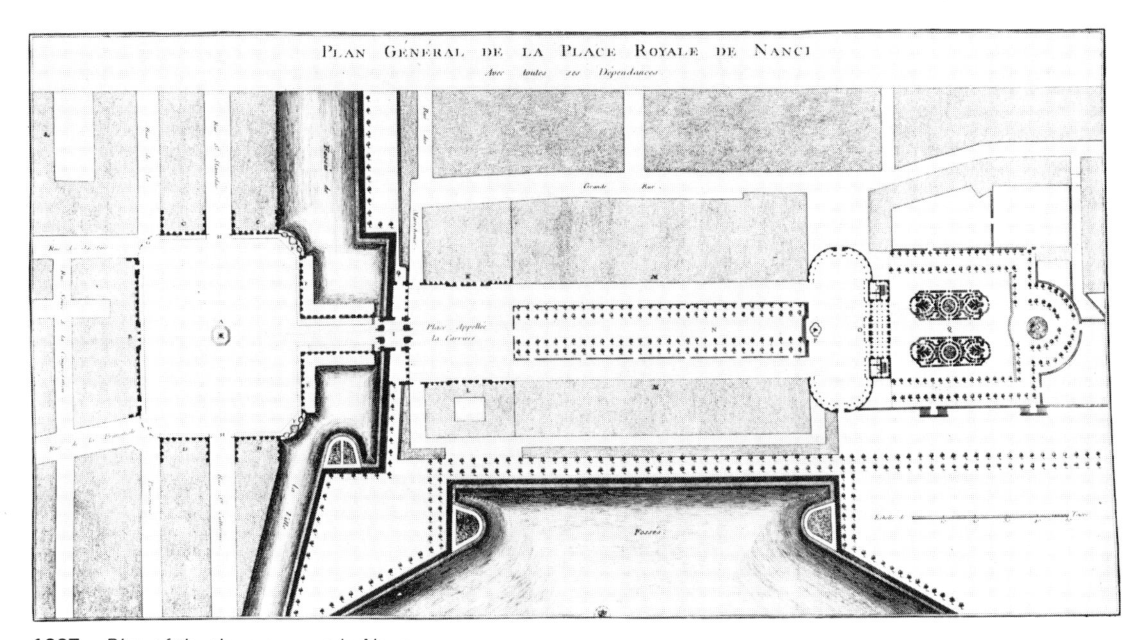

1237 *Plan of the three squares in Nancy*

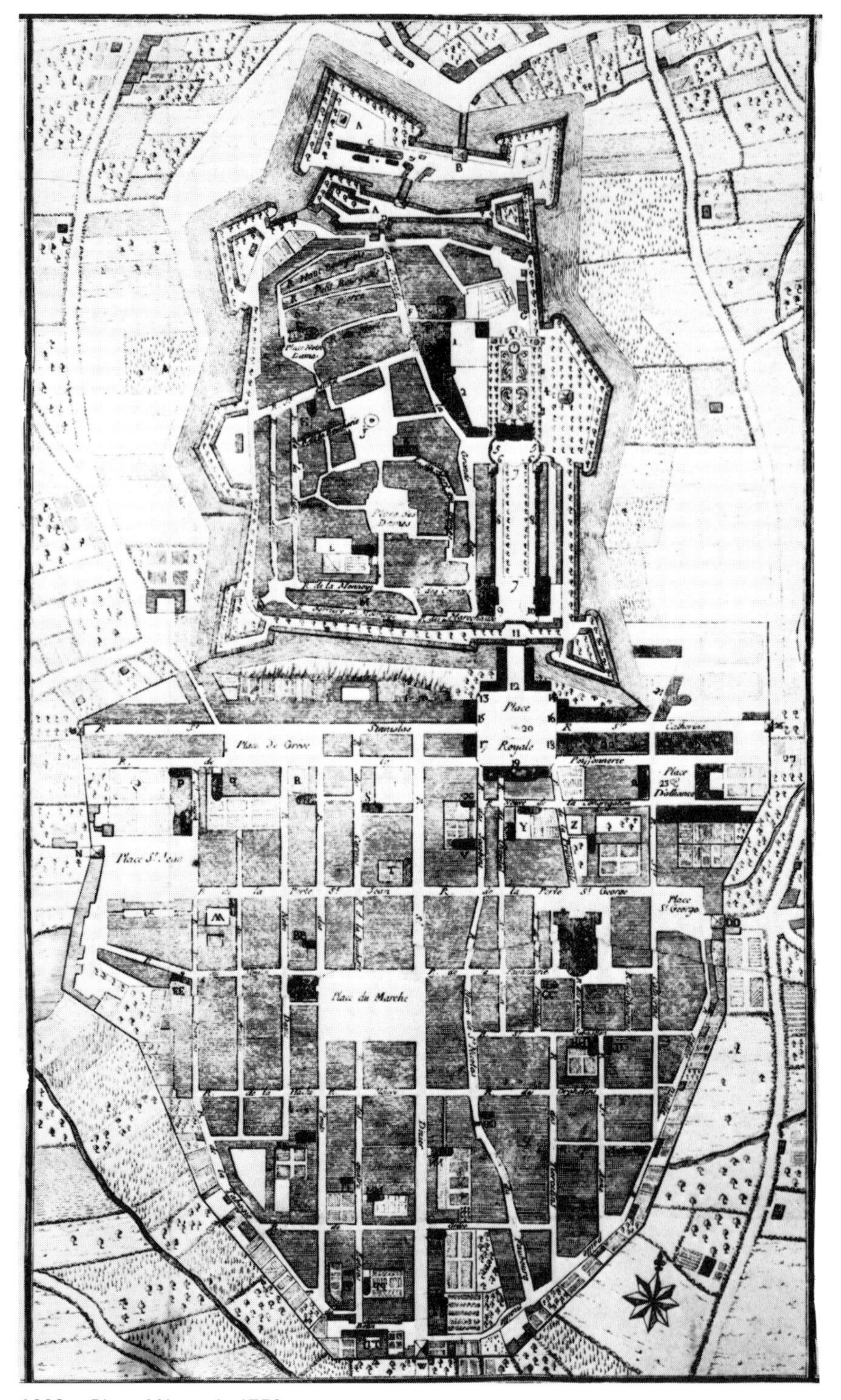

1238 *Plan of Nancy in 1758*

1239 *Aerial view of the three squares in Nancy*

blunted corners, place Royale, where the two straight roads and some secondary crossings of the *ville neuve* converged; here, amid a stately expanse of uniform façades, stood the statue of Louis XV. Beyond the moat there was a long narrow square, with four rows of trees – place de la Carrière – and finally a square with two semi-circular porticoes – the Fer du Cheval – which forms an entrance court in front of the palace of the intendant, the representative of the king of France (Figs 1237–43).

Place Royale is off centre *vis-à-vis* the organism of the *ville neuve*, and its position depends on the existence of the empty space, beyond the moat, where Héré inserted place de la Carrière. To give it a commanding position two lateral squares were envisaged, place d'Alliance – also surrounded by uniform façades – and place de Grève, a simple widening between the two parallel streets mentioned above.

This splendid ensemble, which amounted to a new city centre, intended to unify the two existing cities, was possibly the most perfect achievement of enlightened despotism. In place Royale, which was the pivot of the sequence and architecturally the most important component, the façades were lightened by the spaces at the corners – two opening on to the streets of the *ville neuve* and two on to the moat – screened with the splendid grilles by Jean Lamour (1698–1771); thus the empty space of the square receives not only the axial views of the streets that converge upon the king's statue, but also the diagonal views of the rest of the city fabric and fortifications of the old town.

1240, 1241 *Place de la Carrière, Nancy: aerial view from the tower of St-Epure and general view in an eighteenth-century engraving*

1242 *The Fer du Cheval, Nancy*

Similarly the two semi-circular porticoes isolate the Fer du Cheval only graphically, and the complex of the three squares, grandiosely designed as an enclosed space, is transformed into a filter between the two hitherto isolated urban organisms. The balance of the whole depends both on the perfect technical and financial dimensions of the enterprise, and on the intelligence of the architectural design. The contradictions of absolutism are here minimized by a combination of favourable circumstances: the artistic and political culture of the sovereign, the genius of the designer, the accord, temporary but fruitful, between the reformist aims of public power and the interests of a rich and rising bourgeoisie; houses grand and modest, ceremonial and utilitarian open spaces fit together into a coherent system, and assured the functioning of the city even in its last phases of expansion. In fact at the end of the eighteenth century, when the second ring of fortifications was dismantled too and the new green zones and suburbs were realized at the two sides of the old city, the architectural backbone conceived by Stanislas and Héré de Corny, though no longer the only way through, continued to function as a junction for all the public spaces in the city centre (Fig. 1244).

3 On 1 November 1755 an earthquake destroyed most of the city of Lisbon, which then had 250,000 inhabitants. This unpre-

1243 *Architectural detail from the 1752 layout of Nancy*

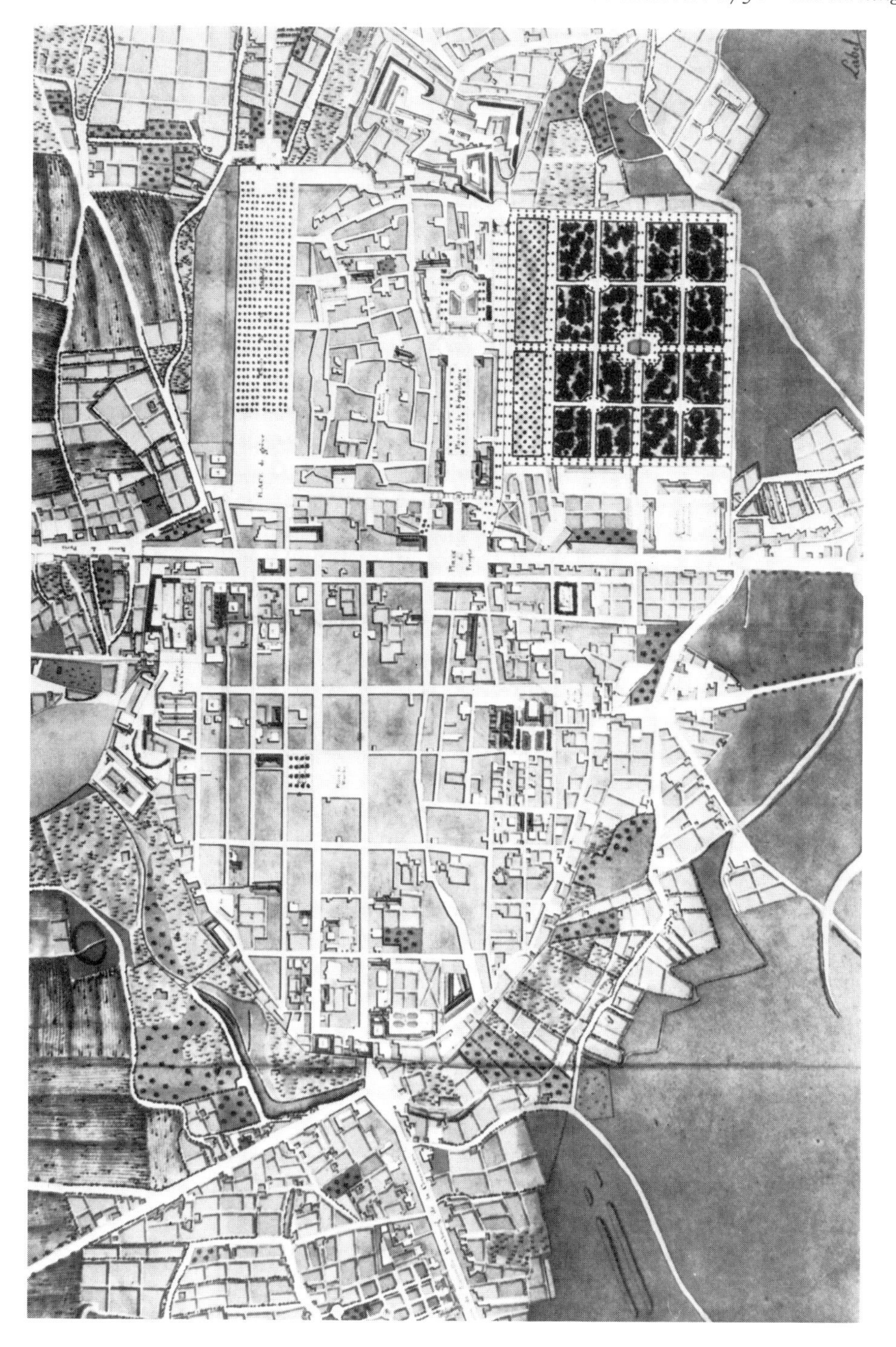

1244 *Plan of Nancy at the end of the eighteenth century*

cedented disaster – which made a deep impression on world public opinion and was discussed from the scientific, philosophical and theological point of view by intellectuals from all Europe – posed Portugal's authorities and technical experts a series of equally unusual problems, because of the extent of the damage and the urgency of the repairs.

The man who organized this work was the minister Sebastiano José de Carvalho y Mello, later made marquis of Pombal (1699–1782), who was in power in 1749 and whom this disaster afforded a complete ascendancy over king Joseph I. From the very beginning he ensured public order, distributed relief, built temporary lodgings for citizens left homeless (for the royal family, a wooden pavilion with a chapel and theatre, designed by Giancarlo Bibbiena); meanwhile he had detailed drawings made of the shattered city, prohibited all new buildings and had plans prepared for its reconstruction.

On 4 December, a month after the earthquake, the *mestre de campo general* Manuel de Maia (1677–1768), the military engineer in charge since 1754, wrote the first report on the criteria for the reconstruction of the city, putting forward four suggested solutions: the rebuilding of the houses according to the old street patterns, the widening of the streets, the creation of a new plan at least for the central districts, or the building of a new city in another position.

The first solution was rendered irrelevant by the very size of the disaster and by the demands for rationalization widespread among the ruling classes; the second – followed in London after the 1666 fire – was inapplicable because of the tortuousness and diminutive scale of the medieval fabric; the fourth, though recommended by Maia and already tried out for some minor towns after similar disasters, raised insurmountable difficulties for a city of this size.

There remained the third solution, i.e. the rebuilding of the central district, the Baixa, lying between the square of the Rossio and

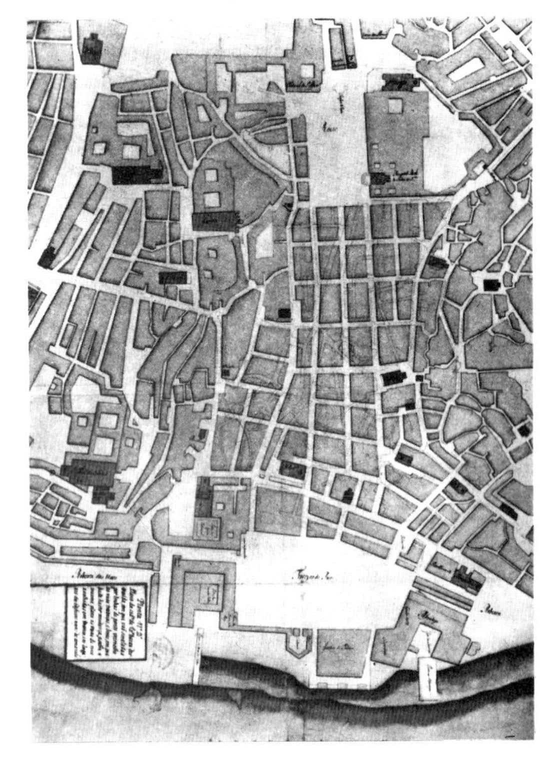

1245 *The second plan for the reconstruction of Lisbon: E. S. and J. D. Poppe (from Franca)*

the Terreiro do Paço, according to a new plan, *regular* and *decoroso*. Maia set up three study commissions: the first, headed by the sub-lieutenant Gualter de Fonseca, proposed an irregular street network which roughly reproduced the old one; the second, headed by captain Poppe, presented a fairly regular grid plan, distorted so as to take into account surrounding points of juncture; the third, led by captain Eugenio dos Santos (1711–60), gave a particular importance to the streets linking the two squares, the Rossio roughly as it had been before and the Terreiro do Paço transformed into a rectangle open on to the water, as in the French examples already mentioned. Maia, not satisfied, wanted a more regular design, and charged the three leaders to prepare other plans, involving a larger area; the six plans were presented to the king in the spring of 1756, and Pombal

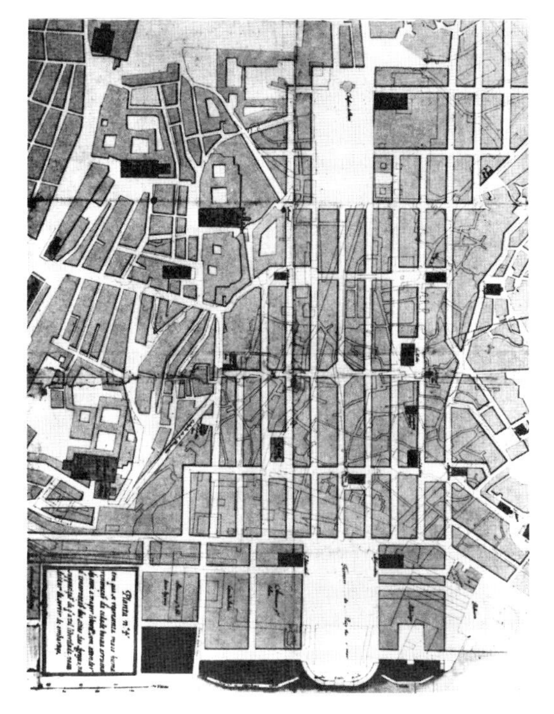

1246 *The fourth plan for the reconstruction of Lisbon: G. de Fonseca (from Franca)*
1247–1249 *Views of the Baixa and praça do Commercio as rebuilt after the earthquake of 1755*

chose that of dos Santos, who envisaged a regular grid plan between two squares, rotated so that it respected a single orientation.

The regularity of the general pattern and the unifying of the measurements of the blocks made the unifying of building types possible, as well as the design of the façades. Between 1758 and 1759 dos Santos provided the designs of a block of houses, distinguishing three types destined for the main roads and two categories for secondary roads. Pombal had prepared other regular plans for the reconstruction of the suburban districts, but he had not power or means to obtain their execution; the rebuilding of the suburbs was realized by private speculators who applied the same criteria of regularity and unification over more limited areas (Figs 1250–4).

1250 *Plan of Lisbon in 1845*

THE ENVIRONS OF LISBON
RIVER TAGUS
THE BAR
Campo de Sta Anna
Praça do Commercio
Arsenal da Marinha
TAGUS
LISBON
LISBOA
SCALES

1251 *View of the Baixa*

The main architectural element of the new Lisbon was the square on the water, which now had a regular architectural aspect and which, after the removal of the royal palace, was renamed praça do Commercio. In the centre was the only monumental feature of the Baixa, the statue of the king sculpted by Machado de Castro.

The rebuilding of Lisbon was carried out at great speed, which amazed contemporary observers. The load-bearing structure of the buildings was the *gaiola*, a wooden cage that could absorb any further earth tremors and that was made non-combustible by a masonry covering; the uniformity of the façades made it possible to unify and mass-produce door and window frames; the balcony balustrades followed a uniform design, with closely set uprights so that they could be produced in strips of any length; the interiors were decorated with the traditional coverings in *azulejos*, their designs produced by the combination of standardized tiles.

This gigantic town-planning and building operation – now studied in an exemplary historical work by José-Augusto Franca[14] – was not the result of the degree of collective maturity of Portuguese society; Portugal was a backward country, the merchant bourgeoisie of Lisbon was a small group, wealthy but culturally undemanding, the court had no part in the works and remained hostile to Pombal, and indeed in 1777, after the death of king Joseph, it removed him from power. The new Lisbon was the illustration, the futurist declaration, Utopian in a sense in comparison with the local situation, of a competent administrator and a series of technical experts, involved in middle-of-the-road European culture. Pombal's political programme was Colbertian in nature, i.e. it was a delayed reproduction of a model

1252–1254 *Three views of the rebuilt streets of Lisbon*

already superseded by the French and English physiocrats and liberals; the town-planning and architectural programmes of Maia and his collaborators followed the current standards of military engineering, simplified by the urgency and extent of its applications. Lastly the legal and administrative means were absolutely authoritarian in nature, though inspired by economy and functionality, rather than by monumental *grandeur*.

In Portugal Lisbon remained an isolated experiment, while in the European field it can be compared to other smaller ventures of enlightened despotism in depressed areas or those outlying the great cultural centres: for instance the extension of Trieste (Figs 1255–6), Charles III's industrial townships in the region of Naples and the agricultural ones in Spain, the new Danish towns of Frederiksvaerck, Cristiansfeld and Söderfors. The regularity of the spatial structures was the result of the disproportion between the strength of the planning authority and the resistance of the environment.

These three examples are enough to show that monumental classicism and technological classicism were two abstract programmes, both inadequate to the solving of the problems of the cities at the dawn of the industrial revolution, and compatible in the case of Nancy, because of certain circumstances not generally obtaining. Classicism, i.e. the complex of formal models, did not retain a distinctive value on its own account: by now it was a matter of custom, which acquired significance in accordance with the political will of those commissioning it and the interpretative ability of those designing it.

The other series of factors to consider, together with the actual experiments, are the statements of intent. As is well known, one climax of the European political and ideological debate came around 1750: in 1748 the *Three Essays* and the *Essay concerning Human Understanding* by Hume came out, and in Geneva *L'Esprit des Lois* by Montesquieu; in

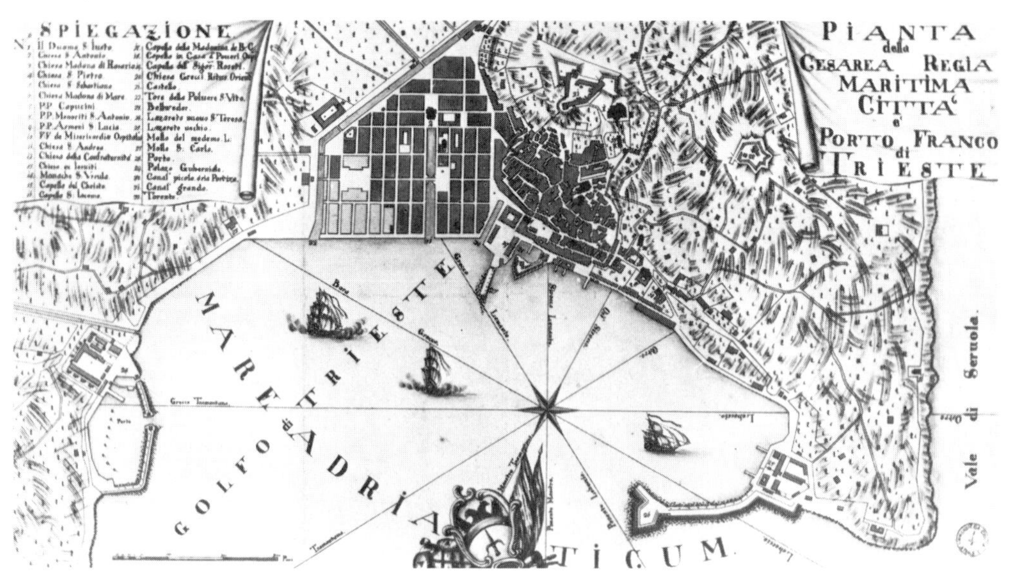

1255, 1256 *View and plan of the* borgo teresiano *of Trieste*

1750 Rousseau rose to fame by winning the competition at the academy of Dijon; in 1751 the publication of the *Encyclopédie* began; in 1752 Adam Smith took up his post as lecturer in moral philosophy at Glasgow.

In the artistic field this was the time of the rationalist polemic. The abbé Laugier published his *Essai sur l'architecture* in 1753, and at the same time padre Lodoli was giving his lectures in Venice, subsequently collected and published by Andrea Memmo;[15] but the crucial problem was the passage from 'arguments' to 'forms', for which, in the last analysis, only the teaching of tradition remained valid, though amended and graded in many different ways. The person responsible for official teaching at the French academy of architecture, Jean-François Blondel, published *L'Architecture française* in 1752, where the body of classical monuments was illustrated and criticized with exemplary balance; he largely accepted the modern arguments on rationality, and suggested combining them with those of formal propriety: 'unity consists in the art of reconciling in one's own plan solidity, convenience and order, without any of these parts being destroyed.'[16] The Vitruvian triad, *firmitas, utilitas, venustas,*[17] utilized hitherto as the description of a single ideal, became an institutional combination of antagonistic criteria, and the hint of its destruction, as Kaufmann observes,[18] revealed an awareness of the impending crisis.

A way of reconciling obedience to tradition with the new rational spirit was that of defining the normative content of tradition with absolute historical exactitude. The actual choice of the repertoire to be imitated remained impossible to lay down, or was laid down with arguments of another type, moral, philosophical or political, but the modes of procedure for imitation could be defined objectively, with the desired degree of exactitude.

In 1748, as we have said, Walpole and his friends started to build his house, Strawberry Hill, and began their experiment in the total resurrection of Gothic models. At the same time the movement for the scientific reconstruction of the classical heritage began: in 1750 James Stuart and Nicholas Revett went to make plans of monuments in Athens, and in 1762 published their book *The Antiquities of Athens*; the comte de Caylus began to publish his *Recueils d'antiquités* in 1752; in 1750 Robert Wood led the expedition which in 1753 published the *Ruins of Palmyra*, and in 1757 the *Ruins of Baalbek*; in 1758 D. Le Roy's book *Les Ruines des plus beaux monuments de la Grèce* appeared, and in the same year Stuart built the first correct copy of a Doric temple at Hagley, near Birmingham (which neither Chambers nor Lord Burlington, nor indeed Goethe at a later date, could bring themselves to appreciate, because of its 'barbaric' heaviness); from 1748 to 1761 Giovanni Battista Piranesi published his views and reconstructions of Roman buildings.[19] Meanwhile from 1748 excavations were begun in Pompeii; in 1754 Robert Adam arrived in Rome from Scotland (and went to Split, where he collected material on Diocletian's palace, published by 1764) and in 1755 Johann J. Winckelmann came to Rome from Germany, publishing his fundamental *Geschichte der Kunst des Altertums* in 1764.

If we were to describe in detail the course of architectural development in the second half of the eighteenth century these facts would have to be examined in every detail, because they constituted without doubt, in the short term, the factor that resolved the debate begun in the first half of the century: the repertoire of classical antiquity, idealized by the humanists of the fifteenth century and thenceforward proposed as an ideal model for modern design, became the object of an objective historical study and was transformed into a system of restrictive, but no longer universal, models.

We are concerned with this only for what it concludes of the past, not for what it opens up for the future. The neoclassical and neo-Gothic movements, when they appeared as scientific hypotheses, had already virtually eliminated the unity of traditional artistic culture, and classicism was no longer the universe in which contemporary practice moved, but a theoretical hypothesis to be put on a par with many others.

Neither current architectural forms nor critical phraseology change much here; but the new exposed condition of the architectural experience can be detected in the tone and the details, for it was losing the shell within which it had moved for four centuries. The authors who were leading the cultural debate about 1750 – Montesquieu, the *Encyclopédists*, the English essayists – talked only incidentally of architecture and then usually in conventional terms (particularly the editors of the *Encyclopédie*, concerned with the fine and applied arts as institutional elements in the dawning political debate). There are frequent observations which make light of the criteria of the traditional court décor, in the name of comfort, for instance that by Voltaire of 1749, in connection with the royal square for Louis XV:[20]

'They talk of a square, and of a statue of the king. It is always a square. Even if this square were built, Paris would still be very irregular and very inconvenient. What is needed is public markets, fountains which really do give water, regular crossroads, halls for entertainment. And the roads need broadening.'

The new, discordant note, which announced the end of the old cultural debate, can be caught with significant emphasis in Rousseau. The discourse on the sciences and arts given at the academy of Dijon in 1750 contains a reference to architecture in the second part:[21]

'One cannot reflect on manners, without pausing to consider the image of the simplicity of the earliest times. This is a beautiful river, untouched except by the hands of nature, to which one's eyes are constantly turned, and from which one moves away with regret. When innocent and virtuous men were pleased to have the Gods as witnesses of their actions, they lived together in the same huts; but soon, when they became wicked, they freed themselves from these inconvenient spectators and relegated them to magnificent temples.

Then they drove them from the temples to settle there themselves, or at least the Temples of the Gods could no longer be distinguished from the houses of the citizens. This was the height of deprivation; and vices were never driven so far away as when they were seen, so to speak, supported at the entrances to the Houses of the Great on columns of marble, and carved on Corinthian capitals.'

The argument against extravagance, and the nostalgia for primitive nature were part of the thesis to be defended, that the arts and sciences had helped to corrupt morals, and were not original themes. But Rousseau's peroration is animated by a powerful new emotion, and found an immediate response among his readers, echoing throughout the whole of the second half of the century down to the time of the Revolution! (Ledoux, in a famous caption, spells out the political consequences of this thesis (Fig. 1258).)

Rousseau was not an expert on architecture. In his *Confessions* he tells of his disappointment and indifference, when he arrived in Paris in 1732:[22]

'How greatly did my first sight of Paris belie the idea I had formed of it! The exterior decoration that I had seen in Turin, the beauty of the streets, the symmetry and alignment of the houses, had led me to expect something even finer in Paris. I had imagined a city of a most imposing appearance, as beautiful as it was large, where nothing was to be seen but splendid streets and palaces of marble or gold. As I entered through the Faubourg St.-Marceau, I saw nothing but dirty, stinking little streets, ugly black houses, a general air of squalor and poverty, beggars, carters, menders of clothes, sellers of herb-drinks and old hats. All this so affected me at the outset that all the real magnificence I have since seen in Paris has not been sufficient to efface my first impression, and I have always retained a secret aversion against living in the capital. I may say that all the time I did, subsequently, reside there was devoted to seeking means which would enable me to live elsewhere. Such is the fruit of an over-lively imagination, which exaggerates beyond the common measure and always sees more than it is told to expect. I had heard such praise of Paris that I imagined it like ancient Babylon, which, had I visited it, I should no doubt have found falling equally short of the picture I had formed of it. The same thing happened to me at the opera, which I hastened to visit on the day after my arrival; the same thing happened later at Versailles; and later still when I saw the sea; and the same thing will always happen to me when I see sights of which I have heard too much. For it is impossible for men, and difficult for Nature herself, to surpass the riches of the imagination.'

His indifference to background is understandable if one considers the new interest in the man who moved against this background; not the generic figure, already brought into harmony with the laws of the universe, of whom everyone had already talked, but the single individual with his single destiny who now emerged, rejecting every recognized model. If sincerity counted more than propriety, the old respect for the traditional forms of society had no further *raison d'être*, and the function of classicism, as a system of visible forms appropriate to civil life, must be regarded as exhausted.

The introduction of the *Confessions*, composed in 1764, still strikes the reader with its desperate attempt to set up a direct communication, by accepting and attributing a meaning to all the miseries of the human condition; this discourse struck the cultural milieu of which we have talked an irremediable blow, and effectively destroyed rhetorical faith in the rules of art:[23]

'I have resolved on an enterprise which has no precedent, and which, once complete, will have no imitator. My purpose is to display to my mind a portrait in every way true to nature, and the man I shall portray is myself.

Simply myself. I know my own heart and understand my fellow man. But I am made unlike any one I have ever met; I will even venture to say that I am like no one in the whole world. I may be no better, but at least I am different. Whether Nature did well or ill in breaking the mould in which she formed me, is a question which can only be resolved after the reading of my book.

Let the last trump sound when it will, I shall come forward with this work in my hand, to present myself before my Sovereign Judge, and proclaim aloud: "Here is what I have done, and if by chance I have used some immaterial embellishment it has been only to fill a void due to a defect of memory. I may have taken for fact what was no more than probability, but I have never put down as true what I knew to be false. I have displayed myself as I was, as vile and despicable when my behaviour was such, as good, generous and noble when I was so. I have bared my secret soul as Thou thyself hast seen it, Eternal Being! So let the numberless legion of my fellow men gather round me, and hear my confessions. Let them groan at my depravities, and blush for my misdeeds. But let each one of them reveal his heart at the foot of Thy throne with equal sincerity, and may any man who dares, say 'I was a better man than he'." '

1257 *Primitive man, from Filarete's treatise, 1460*

Simply a man, with a book in his hand. Any architectural setting was superfluous, and became from now on a fortuitous, interchangeable backdrop. In a distant future, man would have to build a new spatial organization suited to this new condition, but he would have to set aside the vast mass of visible forms inherited from the past, and start again from scratch.

1258 *The poor man's house, from C. N. Ledoux, 1796*

'This vast universe that amazes you is the poor man's house, the house of the rich man who has been despoiled; he has the blue vault of heaven as his dome, and communicates with the assembly of the gods. Son of the same father, he is heir to the same fortune; the rich man's architect is his own. This is a gift for all, cast by the deity upon the earth, and withdrawn only from those who are accursed. Look at everything nature has made for the poor man. Have kings, emperors, even the gods themselves, loftier palaces?

What! The Architect of the earth has treated him so well that he has left nothing to do for the Architects who have succeeded him. The bee has her dwelling, the ant roofs her own house to protect herself from the inclemencies of the seasons. One man utilizes for himself a road where the stone, at vast expense, stretches to the horizon where it merges into its depths. He builds house after house, insolently challenging the clouds, and suffocating the freedom of a people already repressed. Others use up the mountains' granite, and have whole nations of workmen in their pay, building palaces . . .; and the poor man, in the eighteenth century, has not where to lay his head. He runs through the fields, and when he is tired, he lies down on a slab of stone, under a sycamore or a weeping willow, and the fields, so fertile for others, are arid for him alone. Would one not believe that his existence is linked to all these affairs of prestige simply to lock him in the bonds of a humiliating dependence?

Man, whoever he may be, occupies only a small space; however great, he does not fill the immense void of the universe. In whatever situation he stands, he may not challenge nature; art must submit his needs to her possibilities, must submit them to proportion; this is a benefit she renders to all alike.' (C. N. Ledoux, *L'Architecture considérée sous le rapport de l'art, des moeurs et de la législation*, Paris, 1796; cf. L. Benevolo, *History of Modern Architecture*, Routledge & Kegan Paul, London, 1971, p. xix.)

Notes

5 The crisis of sensibility

1 V. Scamozzi, *Dell'idea dell'architettura universale*, Venice, 1615, part I, book I, chapter III.
2 F. Zuccari, *L'idea de' pittori, scultori et architetti*, Turin, 1607, p. 43.
3 L. Venturi, *Storia della critica d'arte* (1936), Turin, 1964, p. 25.
4 G. C. Scaliger, *Exotericarum exercitationum libri ad Hieronymum Cardanum*, Paris, 1557.
5 B. Telesio, *De rerum natura iuxta propria principia*, Naples, 1586, I, p. 25.
6 G. Bruno, *De l'infinito universo et mondi*, 1585, in D. Waley Singer, *Giordano Bruno, his Life and Thought*, Constable, London, 1951, p. 249.
7 F. Patrizi, *Pancosmia*, 1593, p. 65.
8 I. Newton, *Principia mathematica* (1686), English edition, Cambridge University Press, 1934, p. 6.
9 Ibid., p. 8.
10 Venturi, op. cit., p. 125.
11 G. Paleotti, *Discorso intorno le immagini sacre e profane*, Bologna, 1582.
12 F. Borromeo, *De pictura sacra*, Milan, 1634.
13 Pietro da Cortona and Ottonelli, *Trattato della pittura e scultura, uso ed abuso loro*, Florence, 1652.
14 C. Lebrun, *Méthode pour apprendre à dessiner les passions*, *A Method to Learn to Design the Passions*, London, 1734.
15 G. Spini, *Storia dell'età moderna*, Turin, 1965, II, p. 601.
16 Quoted in B. Migliorini, *Storia della lingua italiana*, Florence, 1966, p. 300.
17 G. Morpurgo-Tagliabue, 'Aristotelismo e barocco', in *Retorica e barocco*, Atti del III Congresso Internazionale di Studi Umanistici, Rome, 1955, p. 128.
18 S. Speroni, *Dialogo della retorica*, 1542.
19 F. Patrizi, *Della retorica*, 1562.
20 Morpurgo-Tagliabue, op. cit., pp. 121–43.
21 Matteo Pellegrini, *Trattato delle acutezze*, 1639.
22 Baltasar Gracián, *Agudezas y arte de ingenio*, 1648.
23 Pierre Corneille, *Discours sur le poème dramatique*, 1660.
24 Gian Pietro Bellori, *Vite de' pittori, scultori et architetti moderni*, 1672.
25 Marco Boschini, *Carta de navegar pittoresco*, 1660.
26 Morpurgo-Tagliabue, op. cit., p. 179.
27 *Life of Galileo*, scene XIII.
28 Spini, op. cit., II, pp. 465–6.
29 Don Quixote to Sancho Panza: 'Do not try to turn my real sadness into false comfort.'
30 Biography of Mons. Herrera, quoted in P. Portoghesi, *Roma barocca*, Rome, 1966, pp. 54–5.
31 R. Wittkower, in *Bollettino d'Arte*, 34, 1949, p. 129.
32 C. de Brosses, *Lettres familières sur l'Italie*, 1739.
33 G. C. Argan, *L'architettura barocca in Italia*, Milan, 1957, p. 17.
34 Cf. F. Niceron, *Perspective curieuse*, 1638.
35 Quoted in Portoghesi, op. cit., p. 161.
36 Ibid., p. 223.
37 This is the thesis elaborated by G. C. Argan in the monograph on S. Giovanni in the volume commemorating Borromini's tercentenary.
38 L. Benevolo, 'Il problema dei pavimenti borrominiani in bianco e nero', *Quaderni dell'Istituto di Storia dell'Architettura*, 13, 1956.
39 Bibliography in P. Portoghesi, *Borromini*, Rome, 1967.
40 Quoted in G. Macchia, *Il paradiso della ragione*, Bari, 1960, p. 45.
41 Ibid., p. 48.
42 Italian translation in *La filosofia dell'Encyclopédie*, Bari, 1966, pp. 99–100.
43 Quoted in A. Blunt, *Art and Architecture in France, 1500–1700*, Penguin, Harmondsworth, 1970, p. 133.
44 John Shute, *The First and Chief Groundes of Architecture*, 1563.
45 Let it be noted incidentally that in England – where this notion was introduced so late on – the word *design* was later accepted permanently with a meaning very close to the Italian original, while

elsewhere, Italy included, similar words (*disegno*, *dessin* etc.) acquired a more limited meaning.

46 Quoted in J. Summerson, *Architecture in Britain, 1530–1830*, Penguin, Harmondsworth, 1963, p. 67.
47 Ibid., p. 68.
48 J. Webb, *The Most Notable Antiquity of Great Britain, Vulgarly Called Stone-Heng*; in the polemic that followed Webb intervened again with *Vindication of Stone-Heng Restored*, 1665.
49 This section is partly based on L. Benevolo, 'Breve storia degli edifici teatrali', *Architettura pratica*, vol. III, part II, Turin, 1958, pp. 263 ff.
50 'Two theatres, built at great expense, one oval in shape, the other round, able to hold a large number of persons, for giving plays at carnival time, as is the custom of the city' (F. Sansovino, *Venetia*, Venice, 1581).
51 The eleven London theatres were the following: Theatre (1576), Blackfriars (1576), Curtain (1577), Rose (1587), Swan (1595), Globe (1599), Fortune (1600), Red Bull (c. 1605), Hope (c. 1613), Cockpit (1616), Salisbury Court (1629).
52 G. B. Doni, quoted in *Enciclopedia dello Spettacolo*, vol. II, col. 1566.
53 Preface to the *Euridice*, Florence, 1601.

6 The *grand siècle*

1 Descartes, *The Discourse on Method*, in *Philosophical Works*, ed. E. S. Haldane and G. R. T. Ross, Cambridge University Press, 1967, vol. I, p. 921.
2 F. de Mallevoue, *Les Actes de Sully passées au nom du roi de 1600 à 1610*, Paris, 1911, p. 105; L. Hautecoeur, *Histoire de l'architecture classique en France*, Paris, 1966, vol. I, 3, p. 15.
3 The data on salaries, quoted here and on following pages, are taken from Hautecoeur, op. cit.
4 Letter to Sully of 22 December 1607; Sully, *Mémoires*, II, 206.
5 *Mémoires*, VII, 166; cf. Hautecoeur, op. cit., vol. I, 3, pp. 13–14.
6 This edict is still regarded as operative in French legislation; cf. Hautecoeur, op. cit., vol. I, 3, p. 20.
7 Ibid., p. 196.
8 *Le Menteur*, II, 5.
9 Hautecoeur, op. cit., vol. I, 3, p. 296.
10 *De l'Antiquité, grandeur, richesses, gouvernement de la ville de Paris*, Paris, 1652; Gomboust has calculated that Paris had 900,000 inhabitants.
11 H. Sauval, *Histoire et recherches des antiquités de la ville de Paris* (c. 1676), Paris, 1724.
12 *Le Menteur*, II, 5; cf. note 8, above.
13 P. Lavedan, *Histoire de l'urbanisme: Renaissance et temps modernes*, Paris, 1959, p. 229.
14 La Fontaine, letter to his wife of 1 September 1663; Lavedan, op. cit., p. 230.
15 Vignier: 'a road where the eye never wearies of contemplating, in every house, the same *cimetrie*' (quoted in Lavedan, op. cit., p. 232); Godefroy, in his account of his visit in 1638, admires the symmetry of the houses (quoted in Hautecoeur, op. cit., vol. I, 3, p. 313).
16 Ibid.
17 Pascal, *Pensés*, trans. A. J. Krailsheimer, Penguin, Harmondsworth, 1966, p. 225, n. 580.
18 Ibid., p. 226, n. 585.
19 Aleaume, *Perspective speculative et pratique*, written before 1630 and published by Migon in 1643.
20 Breuil, *Perspective pratique nécessaire à tous peintres, graveurs, sculpteurs, architects . . . et autres qui se meslent de dessiner*, published from 1642 onwards.
21 Desargues, *Exemple de l'une des manières universelles . . . touchant la pratique de la perspective sans employer aucun tiers point de distance ny d'autre nature que ce soit hors du champ de l'ouvrage*, 1636.
22 Pascal, *Essay sur les coniques*, 1640.
23 Derand, *Architecture des voûtes ou l'art des traits et coupes des voûtes*.
24 Bosse, *La Pratique du trait à preuves de m.D. pour la coupe des pierres en l'architecture*.
25 De Caus, *Les Raisons des forces mouvantes avec diverses machines tant utiles que plaisantes, auxquels sont adjoints plusieurs desseins de grottes et fontaines*, Frankfurt, 1615.
26 De Caus, *Nouvelle Manière d'élever l'eau plus haut que la source*, London, 1644.
27 Vernier, *Constructions, usage et propriétés du quadrant nouveau de mathématiques*, Brussels, 1631.
28 Hautecoeur, op. cit., vol. II, 1, pp. 227–48.
29 Sauval, op. cit., vol. II, pp. 173–8.
30 In the preface to *Andromeda*.
31 *Avis nécessaire pour la conduite des feux artificiels*.
32 La Bruyère, *Characters*, trans. Jean Stewart, Penguin, Harmondsworth, 1970, p. 269 (Of Certain Customs).
33 André Mollet, *Jardin de plaisir*, Stockholm, 1651; cf. Hautecoeur, op. cit., vol. II, 1, p. 368.
34 P. Goubert, *Louis XIV and Twenty Million Frenchmen*, Allen Lane, The Penguin Press, London, 1970, p. 96.
35 C. Perrault, *Mémoires*, 196; S. Le Prestre de Vauban, letter to Louvois of 17 July 1685.
36 The Rome academy also guaranteed the prestige of French artistic culture abroad, and it grew rapidly from 1666 onwards; Lebrun was appointed principal of the Roman academy of S. Luca in 1676 and 1677.
37 P. Le Muet, *Traité des cinq ordres d'architecture*, 1645; *Manière de bien bastir pour toutes sortes de personnes*, 1623; J. Marot, *Livre nouveau de l'art d'architecture des cinq ordres*; A. Bosse, *Représentation géometrale des plusieurs parties de bastiment faite par les reigles de l'architecture antique*, 1659; *Traité des manières de dessiner les ordres de l'architecture antique*, 1664. Fréart de Chambray translated Palladio's treatise in 1650.
38 F. Blondel, *Cours*, published in 1675, 1683, 1685, 1688. Claude Perrault, *Dix Livres d'architecture de Vitruve corrigés et traduits*, 1673 and 1684; *Abrégé des dix livres de Vitruve*, 1674; *Ordonnance des cinq ordres de colonnes* 1683; A. Félibien, *Principes de l'architecture*, 1676, 1690, 1697, 1699; *Entretiens sur la vie et sur les ouvrages des plus excellents peintres*, 1666, 1685; *Des Principes de l'architecture, de la sculpture, de la peinture et des autres arts*, 1676, 1690,

1697; *Recueil historique de la vie et des ouvrages des plus célèbres architectes*, 1687; C. A. D'Aviler, *Cinq Ordres d'architecture de Vincent Scamozzi; Cours*, 1691; J. Le Blond, *Deux Exemples des cinq ordres d'architecture antique*, 1683. Also the *procès-verbaux* of the meetings of the academy, edited by Félibien.

39 D'Aviler, *Cours*, I, 5.

40 *Procès-verbaux*, I, 31.

41 Blondel, *Cours*, II, 719.

42 *Mémoire pour servir à l'instruction dans la conduite des sièges*, Leiden, 1740. The other theoretical works by Vauban on this subject are *Traité de l'attaque des places* and *Traité de la défense des fortifications de campagne*, written in the last part of his life.

43 Vauban, *Traité des mines*, Paris, 1740.

44 Quoted in Lavedan, op. cit., p. 228.

45 *Mes Oisivetés*, I, 227.

46 Letter of 28 September 1663.

47 Lavedan, op. cit., pp. 232 ff.

48 A. E. Brinckmann, *Stadtbaukunst des 17. und 18. Jahrhunderts in den romanischen Ländern*, Neubabelsberg, 1919 ff.

49 'Look, Lucillus, at this piece of land, neater and more finely adorned than those that are its neighbours: here you find flowerbeds that are intersected with sheets of water and fountains; there, unending alleys of low-branched trees that shelter you from the north wind; on one side you have a dense wood that gives constant shade, on the other a splendid vista. Lower down a stream, the Yvette or the Lignon, which had flowed obscurely between willows and poplars, has become a walled canal; elsewhere long cool avenues stretch out into the countryside, leading to the house, which is surrounded with water. Will you exclaim: "What a coincidence! how many lovely things are unexpectedly found here together!" No, of course; on the contrary, you will say: "This is finely imagined and well ordered; good taste and great intelligence reign here." I shall say the same, and I'll add that this must be the home of one of these people for whom Le Nôtre comes to make out and measure the ground the very day they settle in. But what are we to think of this plot of land, so carefully laid out, embellished by the cunning of a skilled architect, if the whole earth itself is merely an atom suspended in the air?' (La Bruyère, ed. cit., p. 309 (Of Freethinkers).)

50 P. F. Chantelou, *Journal du voyage du Cavalier Bernini en France*; J. F. Blondel (who made use of Perrault's papers), *L'Architecture française*, 1752.

51 Le Vau's old assistant, François d'Orbay, also worked for the commission; A. Laprade (*François d'Orbay*, Paris, 1960) gives him the main credit for the planning of the Louvre and other works usually attributed to Claude Perrault.

52 Blondel, op. cit.

53 Instructions given by the king, 18 August 1672. Arch. Nat. O I 1854 1.2.

54 Montesquieu, *Lettres persanes*, letter 37.

55 Letter of 1 October 1678.

56 Quoted in Hautecoeur, op. cit., vol. II, 1, p. 398.

57 About 35 metres.

58 Hautecoeur, op. cit., vol. II, 1, p. 438.

59 *Embarras de Paris*, in ibid., p. 440.

60 Letters Patent of 6 August 1676; cf. Lavedan, op. cit., p. 334.

61 Ibid.

62 Voltaire, *Le Siècle de Louis XIV*, 1751, chapter 19.

63 La Bruyère, ed. cit., p. 175 (of the Sovereign and the State, section 24).

64 Haussmann, *Mémoires*, 1891.

65 J. B. Colbert, *Lettres*, published Paris 1861–2, vol. V, p. 337.

66 This first plan, designed or supervised by Blondel, has been lost; there is, however, an executive plan of 1680, attributed to the engineer Decombre which may be a copy, a variant or an alternative to the original.

67 Goubert, op. cit.

68 Saint-Simon, *Mémoires*, 1788–91.

69 E. E. Viollet-le-Duc, *Entretiens sur l'architecture*, I (1863–72).

70 R. Blomfield, *A History of French Architecture*, Bell, London, 1911.

71 Mansart's system was to engage the king in matters apparently negligible, in important or long undertakings, and to show him imperfect designs, particularly of gardens, which infallibly led his finger to the required point. Then Mansart would exclaim that he would never have thought of what the king suggested; he would exclaim in admiration, protest that in comparison with the king he was the merest novice, and brought him where he wanted him without the king ever having the slightest suspicion of it (quoted in Hautecoeur, op. cit., vol. II, 2, p. 539).

72 A. Blunt, *Art and Architecture in France, 1500–1700*, Penguin, Harmondsworth, 1970, p. 237.

73 Nivelon, quoted in Hautecoeur, op. cit., vol. II, 2, p. 544.

74 Dangeau, quoted in ibid., p. 540.

75 Ibid., pp. 151–2.

76 Goubert, op. cit., pp. 173–4.

'*A la Place Royale on a placé ton père*
Parmi les gens de qualité
On voit sur le Pont-Neuf ton aieul débonnaire
Près du peuple qui fut l'objet de sa bonté
Pour toi des partisans le prince tutélaire
A la Place Vendôme entre eux on t'a placé.'
(Hautecoeur, op. cit., vol. II, 2, p. 611.)

78 Letter to the duke of Noailles, 18 September 1713; Hautecoeur, op. cit., vol. II, 2, p. 540.

79 La Bruyère, ed. cit., p. 26 (Of Books, section 15).

80 Blondel's views were put forward in the 1688 edition of the *Cours*; those of Perrault in the preface of the *Ordonnance* of 1683 and in the edition of Vitruvius of 1684.

81 Boileau on music: 'Quoi! par des vains accords et des sons impuissants vous croyez exprimer tous ce que je sais dire' (*Fragments d'un prologue d'opéra*).

82 La Bruyère, ed. cit., p. 149 (Of the Court, section 101).

83 'Descartes has cut poetry's throat' (Boileau). 'I can

say that I have seen literature flourish and die, and have survived' (Huet).

84 *Histoire du renouvellement de l'Académie des sciences* (1708–1722); quoted in R. Mousnier, *Les XVI et XVII Siècles*, Paris, 1967, p. 351.
85 Quoted in G. Macchia, *Il paradiso della ragione*, Bari, 1960, p. 122.
86 Ibid.
87 *Discours sur l'ode*, in ibid., p. 123.
88 *Discours sur Homère*, in *Œuvres*, Paris, 1764, vol. II, p. 117.
89 La Bruyère, ed. cit., p. 26 (Of Books, section 10).
90 Perrault, *Parallèle des anciens et des modernes*, 1688–96; cf. J. B. Bury, *The Idea of Progress*, New York, 1932, p. 84.
91 Perrault, op. cit.; cf. Bury, p. 87.
92 B. Fontenelle, *Digression sur les anciens et les modernes*, 1688.
93 B. Fontenelle, *Éloge de H. Lémery*.
94 P. Hazard, *The European Mind*, London, 1953.
95 V. A. Rebelliau, *Vauban*, Paris, 1962, p. 103.
96 Quoted in Goubert, op. cit., p. 161.
97 *Projet d'une dixième royale* (*A Project for the Royal Tythe*, London, 1708).
98 Voltaire, *Le Siècle de Louis XIV*.

7 Court classicism and bourgeois classicism in the growth of the modern city

1 G. Clark, 'The social foundation of states' in *New Cambridge Modern History*, ed. A. W. Ward, Cambridge University Press, 1970, vol. 5, p. 197.
2 G. Luzzatto, *Storia economica dell'età moderna e contemporanea*, Padua, 1955, vol. I, p. 293.
3 J. Huizinga, *Dutch Civilization in the Seventeenth Century*, Collins, London, 1968, p. 11.
4 Ibid., p. 24.
5 G. Spini, *Storia dell'età moderna*, Turin, 1965, p. 267.
6 Quoted in F. Braudel, 'La vita economica di Venezia nel secolo XVI' in *La civiltà veneziana del Rinascimento*, Florence, 1958, p. 99.
7 Quoted from Huizinga, op. cit., p. 97 (van Campen, 'From our stricken and disfigured face The Gothic squint and squalor did erase').
8 R. Wittkower, 'Art and architecture' in *New Cambridge Modern History*, ed. A. W. Ward, Cambridge University Press, 1970, vol. 5.
9 William Temple, *Observations upon the United Provinces of the Netherlands*, quoted in V. Barbour, *Capitalism in Amsterdam in the Seventeenth Century*, Ann Arbor, Michigan, 1963, p. 60.
10 Huizinga, op. cit., p. 31.
11 M. Passanti, *Architettura in Piemonte*, Turin, 1945, p. 113.
12 Letter of 10 November 1742 to Knobelsdorff, quoted in P. Lavedan, *Histoire de l'urbanisme : Renaissance et temps modernes*, Paris, 1959, p. 398.
13 Ibid., p. 268.
14 Ibid., p. 271.
15 Van der Groen, *Den nederlandischen howenier*, 1668.
16 This tradition is noted by Schopenhauer, who visited Holland in 1812; see M. L. Gothein, *A History of Garden Art*, Hacker, New York, 1966, vol. II, pp. 221–2.
17 N. Pevsner, *An Outline of European Architecture*, Penguin, Harmondsworth, 1963, p. 270.
18 G. Kubler and M. Soria, *Art and Architecture in Spain and Portugal, 1500–1800*, Penguin, Harmondsworth, 1959, p. 38.
19 Blondel, *L'Architecture française*, 1752.
20 Letter from deacon Sancroft to the archbishop of Canterbury and bishops of London and Oxford, quoted in J. Summerson, *Architecture in Britain, 1530–1830*, Penguin, Harmondsworth, 1963, p. 129.
21 Pevsner, op. cit., p. 324.
22 G. Guarini, *Architettura civile*, Turin, 1737, p. 3: 'Architecture is a flattering art, which does not wish to tire the sense with reason.'
23 Published by E. de Ganay, *André le Nostre*, Paris, 1962, p. 107.
24 Quoted in Gothein, op. cit., vol. II, p. 116.
25 Quoted in Summerson, op. cit., p. 159.
26 Ibid., p. 171.
27 *Vitruvius Britannicus*, vol. II, cf. Summerson, op. cit., p. 194.
28 Quoted in K. Clark, *The Gothic Revival*, Penguin, Harmondsworth, 1964, p. 18.
29 Batty Langley, *Gothic Architecture Improved by Rules and Proportions*, London, 1742.
30 Quoted in Gothein, op. cit., vol. II, p. 239.
31 In *The Moralists*; Gothein, op. cit., p. 279.
32 Ibid., pp. 280–1.
33 Quoted in J. S. Berrall, *The Garden – an Illustrated History from Egypt to the Present Day*, Thames & Hudson, London, 1966, p. 250.
34 In 1731 Pope wrote Lord Burlington a letter in verse containing the usual ironies about the current Palladian fashions, but once again taking up the polemic against the formal garden.
35 Burke, *Philosophical Inquiries into the Origin of our Ideas on the Sublime and Beautiful*.
36 Quoted in Gothein, op. cit., vol. II, p. 289.
37 '*Jardins, il faut que je vous fuie Trop d'art me révolte et m'ennuie*' (quoted in Berrall, op. cit., p. 204).
38 Laugier, *Essai sur l'architecture*, Paris 1753.
39 J.-J. Rousseau, *La Nouvelle Eloïse*, quatrième partie, lettre XI.
40 Letter to fraulein von Stein, quoted in P. O. Rave, *Gärten der Goethezeit*, Leipzig, 1941, p. 23.
41 Cf. L. Benevolo, *History of Modern Architecture*, Routledge & Kegan Paul, London, 1971, p. 133.
42 Quoted in I. Brown, *London*, Studio Vista, London, 1965, p. 94.
43 Ibid., p. 68.
44 H. Heine, *English Fragments*, English trans., Edinburgh, 1880, p. 8. Cf. Benevolo, op. cit., p. 133.
45 John Wood, *The Origins of Building, or the Plagiarism of the Heathen Detected*, 1741.
46 Quoted in J. Reps, *The Making of Urban America*, Princeton University Press, 1965, p. 26.
47 H. Cabral, in *Civiltà cattolica*, March 1933.
48 L. A. Muratori, *Il cristianesimo felice nelle missioni del Paraguay*, Venice, 1743.

49 Montesquieu, book VI, chapter 6 (1748).
50 Voltaire, *Candide*, chapter 14 (1759).
51 Reps, op. cit., p. 90.
52 Ibid., p. 93.
53 Penn, in ibid., p. 160.
54 Penn, in ibid., p. 165.

Conclusion: 1750 – the turning-point

1 F. Fénelon, *Telemachus* (1699), English trans, by J. Hawkesworth, Paris, 1850, p. 134.
2 Ibid., p. 138.
3 Ibid., p. 178.
4 Ibid., p. 177.
5 Ibid., p. 180.
6 Ibid., pp. 180 ff.
7 Ibid., p. 181.
8 Ibid., p. 184.
9 Voltaire, *Candide*, chapter 18.
10 P. Patte, *Monuments érigés à la gloire de Louis XV*, Paris, 1765; quoted in P. Lavedan, *Histoire de l'urbanisme : Renaissance et temps modernes*, Paris, 1959, p. 310.
11 Ibid.
12 The lawyer Poncet de la Grave, quoted in ibid., p. 311.
13 *Urbanisme et architecture, études écrites et publiées en l'honneur de Pierre Lavedan*, Paris, 1954, p. 253.
14 J.-A. Franca, *Une Ville de lumières, la Lisbonne de Pombal*, Paris, 1965.
15 *Elementi di architettura lodoliana*, Rome, 1786.
16 *Cours d'architecture*, I, p. 398.
17 Here replaced by the less demanding *ordre*.
18 E. Kaufmann, *Architecture in the Age of Reason*, Harvard University Press, 1955, p. 133.
19 *Prima parte di architettura e prospettiva*, 1743; *Antichità romane*, 1748; *Trofei di Ottaviano Augusto*, 1753; *Della magnificenza ed architettura de' romani*, 1761.
20 Voltaire, *Œuvres*, ed. 1785, XXXIV, p. 174.
21 J.-J. Rousseau, *Œuvres complètes*, ed. NRF, vol. III (1966), p. 22.
22 J.-J. Rousseau, *Confessions*, Penguin, Harmondsworth, 1954, p. 155.
23 Ibid., p. 17.

Bibliographical note

What we understand by architecture of the Renaissance was not considered, in its own time – i.e. in the fifteenth century and the first half of the sixteenth – as a coherent set of data, but as a set of principles; one did not write a history of it, one wrote a treatise on it.

Classical antiquity not only provided the models for the recurrent elements but also transmitted to the men of the Renaissance the text of a treatise of the Augustan age: the work of Vitruvius, which had already been known in the Middle Ages, was reconstructed with historical accuracy for the first time by G. Sulpicio (Rome, 1486). In the sixteenth century there appeared the illustrated editions we listed in chapter 4:

FRA GIOCONDO, Venice, 1511.
C. CESARIANO, Como, 1521 (first Italian translation).
G. B. CAPORALI, Perugia, 1536.
J. MARTIN, Paris, 1547 (first French translation).
W. RIVIUS, Nuremburg, 1548 (first German translation).
D. BARBARO, Venice, 1556.

But soon afterwards, besides the editions of and commentaries on Vitruvius, modern treatises began to be published by many authors: L. B. ALBERTI (finished in 1452, and printed for the first time in Rome in 1485; English edition, *Ten Books on Architecture*, trans. G. Leoni, Tiranti, London, 1955); A. Averlino known as FILARETE (written about 1460; critical edition by L. Grassi, Milan, 1971; complete English edition, Yale University Press, New Haven and London, 1965, with introduction and notes by J. R. Spencer); F. DI GIORGIO MARTINI (written in the 1470s; critical edition by C. Maltese, Milan, 1967); S. SERLIO, published from 1537 to 1547 (first complete edition of the five books, Venice, 1566; of the seven books, Venice, 1588); P. CATANEO (Venice, 1554); PHILIBERT DE L'ORME (Paris, 1561 and 1567); J. BAROZZI DA VIGNOLA (Venice, 1562). Written instructions were gradually replaced by illustrated documentation, which concerned the Vitruvian canonic orders, ancient buildings and modern buildings.

The ancient repertoire and the modern were compared, at the highest level, in the treatise by A. PALLADIO (*I quattro libri di architettura*, Venice, 1570); ancient monuments and those built by the author were documented in a single context, and confirmed one another, excluding any historical analysis which might set them apart.

Almost at the same time, in Florentine circles, G. VASARI was making the first attempt to explain the development of the new artistic activity historically, in the traditional form of the biography (*Vite dei più eccellenti pittori, scultori e architetti*, first edition, Florence, 1550, second edition, Florence, 1568) but in accordance with a theoretical perspective which attributed a dominant function to the figurative arts; hence the successive collections of artists' biographies, including:

G. BAGLIONE, *Le vite dei pittori, scultori ed architetti*, Rome, 1642.
F. BALDINUCCI, *Notizie de' professori del disegno*, Florence, 1681–1728.
A. FÉLIBIEN, *Recueil historique de la vie et des ouvrages des plus célèbres architectes*, Paris, 1687 (the first work where architects were presented separately from painters and sculptors).
F. MILIZIA, *Le vite de' più celebri architetti d'ogni nazione e d'ogni tempo*, Rome, 1678.
A. N. D'ARGENVILLE, *Vies des fameux architectes . . . depuis la Renaissance des arts*, Paris, 1787.

From the second half of the sixteenth century onwards the collections of modern achievements were separated from theoretical treatises; after the imaginary views of the late fifteenth century (H. SCHEDEL, *Liber chronicorum*, Nuremburg, 1493) the first collections of reliable depictions of cities appeared:

S. MÜNSTER, *Cosmographia universalis*, Basle, 1550.
A. ORTELIUS, *Theatrum orbis terrarum*, 1570.
G. BRAUN and F. HOGENBERG, *Civitates orbis terrarum*, Cologne, 1576–1618.

A. LAFRÉRY, the series of engravings published from 1556–72.
G. BLAEU, *Atlas major*, 1641–7.
M. MERIAN, *Topographia Germaniae*, from 1642.

Collections of pictures of modern buildings appeared sporadically alongside the far more numerous ones illustrating ancient buildings. Examples of such works up to the eighteenth century are:

JACQUES I ANDROUET DU CERCEAU, *Plus Excellens Bastiments de France*, 1576–9.
G. B. FAIDA, *Nuovo teatro delle fabbriche di Roma*, Rome, 1665 (followed by *I giardini di Roma*, Rome, 1670, and *Le fontane di Roma*, Rome, 1707).
D. DE ROSSI, *Studio di architettura civile*, Rome, 1702.
C. CAMPBELL, *Vitruvius Britannicus*, London, 1712–25.
J.-F. BLONDEL, *L'Architecture française*, Paris, 1752.

The *querelle des anciens et des modernes*, which emerged in the course of the seventeenth century and reached its pitch, as a general feeling, in the last decades of the century, made it possible to present the results of modern experiment as an autonomous cycle. From this moment, and independently of any theoretical argument, it became justifiable to publish the personal oeuvre of some of the most important European architects, including:

Opera del cavalier Francesco Borromini, Rome, 1720.
F. BORROMINI, *Opus architectonicum*, Rome, 1725.
G. GUARINI, *Architettura civile* (1686), Turin, 1737.
J. B. FISCHER VON ERLACH, *Entwurf einer historischen Architektur*, Vienna, 1721.
W. KENT, *Designs of Inigo Jones*, London, 1727.
O. BERTOTTI-SCAMOZZI, *Le fabbriche e i disegni di A. Palladio*, Vicenza, 1776.

The beginning of critical and historical study of the architecture of the past (from the appearance in 1764 of the *Geschichte der Kunst des Altertums* by J. J. WINCKELMANN) coincided with a decrease of interest in modern architectural classicism, as against both ancient classicism and medieval architecture.

The general condemnation of modern classical architecture, that it was a repetition – and degradation – of the ancient models, was common to most publications of the eighteenth and early nineteenth centuries, from the *Encyclopédie* (1751–72) to the *Dictionnaire historique d'architecture* of M. QUATREMÈRE DE QUINCY (Paris, 1832).

Later, when eclecticism became established both in theoretical discussion and in practice, opposition gave way to classification; writers were concerned to characterize all the periods of the past as so many different styles, since all were regarded freely as models for contemporary design.

In this way the history of architecture accepted and simplified the concepts 'Renaissance' and 'baroque' elaborated by traditional art criticism: and was not able to follow the developments of more recent historical debate, of which the cornerstones, for our period, are: JACOB BURCKHARDT, *Die Kultur der Renaissance in Italien*, Basle, 1860 (English edition, *The Civilization of the Renaissance in Italy*, Phaidon, London, 1945), WALTER PATER, *Studies in the History of the Renaissance*, London, 1873; and the first volume of the *Cambridge Modern History*, 1902; then the extension and hierarchy of the two terms varied as they were applied to the different countries and, in comparative handbooks, according to the importance attributed to one country or another.

J. J. FERGUSSON (*History of Modern Styles of Architecture*, London, 1862; reprinted in the *History of Architecture*, London, 1865–73) calls styles from the Renaissance onwards 'modern styles' precisely because they are based on the imitation of earlier ones (classical antiquity, medieval); B. FLETCHER (*A History of Architecture on the Comparative Method*, London, 1898) and also A. CHOISY (*Histoire de l'Architecture*, Paris 1899) include the Renaissance – or at least Renaissance architecture in their own countries – in 'modern architecture'. This is the terminology current in general history too, which regards the 'modern age' as beginning between the fifteenth and sixteenth centuries.

A critical assessment of Renaissance architecture – i.e. one independent of simplification and which could be utilized as a model for contemporary architecture – began only at the end of the nineteenth century, when *avant-garde* movements reacted to the practice of eclecticism. In our field the debate was opened by H. Wölfflin – *Renaissance und Barock*, Munich, 1888; *Die Klassische Kunst*, Munich, 1899 (English editions, *Renaissance and Baroque*, Fontana, London, 1964 and *Classic Art*, Phaidon, London, 1968) – and led to two consequences: (a) the limiting of the concept of 'Renaissance' to the initial phase of our cycle, i.e. chiefly to Italy from the fifteenth to the mid-sixteenth century; and (b) the reassessment of the originality of subsequent Italian and European experiments and the introduction of a plurality of concepts – 'mannerism', 'baroque', 'rococo', etc. – to distinguish the different experiments.

This debate produced a series of specific studies, mainly German, on the later phases:

G. EBE, *Die Spätrenaissance, Kunstgeschichte der europaischen Länder von der Mitte des XVI zum Ende des XVIII Jahrhunderts*, Berlin, 1886.
C. GURLITT, *Geschichte des Barockstils in Italien*, Stuttgart, 1887; *Geschichte des Barockstils in Belgien, Holland, Frankreich, England*, Stuttgart, 1888; and *Geschichte des Barockstils und des Rococo in Deutschland*, Stuttgart, 1889.
A. SCHMARSOW, *Barock und Rococo*, Leipzig, 1897.
A. RIEGL, *Die Entstehung des Barock-Kunst in Rom*, Vienna, 1908.

Later general works were influenced in varying degrees:

L. MÜNTZ, *Histoire de l'art pendant la Renaissance*, I–III, Paris, 1889–95.
J. BUHLMAN, *Die Architektur der Renaissance*, 1904.
F. M. SIMPSON, *A History of Architectural Development*, vol. III, Longmans, London, 1911.
A. E. BRICKMANN, *Die Baukunst des XVII. und XVIII. Jahrhunders in den romanischen Ländern*, Berlin, 1915.

M. WACKERNAGEL, *Die Baukunst des XVII. und XVIII. Jahrhunderts in den germanischen Ländern*, Berlin, 1915.

See also the following works on various countries:

France: R. BLOMFIELD, *A History of French Architecture, 1494–1774*, Bell, London, 1911–21.
L. HAUTECOEUR, *Histoire de l'architecture classique en France*, so far 11 vols, Paris, 1943–67.
England: M. WHINNEY, *Renaissance Architecture in England*, Longmans, London, 1952.
Spain: F. CHUECA GOITIA, *Arquitectura del siglo XVI* ('Ars Hispaniae', vol. II), Madrid, 1953.
G. KUBLER, *Arquitectura de los siglos XVII y XVIII* ('Ars Hispaniae', vol. XIV), Madrid, 1957.
Germany: W. HAGER, *Die Bauten des deutschen Barock*, Jena, 1941.
Italy: W. J. ANDERSON and A. STRATTON, *The Architecture of the Renaissance in Italy*, Batsford, London, 1927.

Some of the most important of the more recent general books are those published by Penguin Books in the Pelican History of Art series:

R. WITTKOWER, *Art and Architecture in Italy, 1600–1750*, 1958.
A. BLUNT, *Art and Architecture in France, 1500–1700*, 1970.
J. SUMMERSON, *Architecture in Britain, 1530–1830*, 1969.
G. KUBLER and M. SORIA, *Art and Architecture in Spain and Portugal and their American Dominions, 1500–1800*, 1959.
E. HEMPEL, *Baroque Art and Architecture in Central Europe*, 1965.
J. ROSENBERG, S. SLIVE and E. H. TER KUILE, *Dutch Art and Architecture, 1600–1800*, 1966.
H. GERSON and E. H. TER KUILE, *Art and Architecture in Belgium, 1600–1800*, 1960.
W. G. KALNEIN and M. LEVEY, *Art and Architecture of the Eighteenth Century in France*, 1972.

But the new tendency in studies on the history of art has been gradually to reduce the value of general works and to demand particular studies of individual experiments. Definition of the individual has become more important than that of periods and cycles.

The last fifty years have seen the growth of an impressive bibliography on this basis, its cornerstones being the biographies of the most important architects, which have already been largely quoted in the notes. To demonstrate the extent of this trend, here is a list of some of the main monographs on Renaissance architects:

Brunelleschi: C. VON FABRICZY, *Brunelleschi, sein Leben und seine Werke*, Stuttgart, 1892.
H. FOLNESICS, *Brunelleschi*, Vienna, 1915.
L. H. HEYDENREICH, 'Spatwerke Brunelleschis', *Jahrbuch des preussischen Munstsammlung*, 1931, p. 1.
Alberti: G. MANCINI, *L. B. Alberti*, Florence, 1882.
M. PITTALUGA, *L. B. Alberti teorico e architetto del Rinascimento*, Milan, 1939.
Francesco di Giorgio Martini: R. PAPINI, *Francesco di Giorgio architetto*, 3 vols, Florence, 1946.
Giuliano da Sangallo: G. MARCHINI, *Giuliano da Sangallo*, Florence, 1942.
Bramante: O. FÖRSTER, *Bramante*, Vienna, 1956.
Peruzzi: W. W. KENT, *The Life and the Works of Baldassarre Peruzzi of Siena*, New York, 1925.
Raphael: T. HOFMANN, *Raphael in seiner Bedeutung als Architekt*, 4 vols, Leipzig, 1908–11.
Antonio di Sangallo the younger: G. GIOVANNONI, *Antonio da Sangallo il giovane*, Rome, 1959.
Michelangelo: H. VON GEYMÜLLER, *Michelangelo Buonarroti als Architekt*, Munich, 1904.
J. ACKERMAN, *The Architecture of Michelangelo*, Zwemmer, London, 1961.
Palladio: G. C. ARGAN, 'Palladio e la critica neoclassica', *L'Arte*, 1930, p. 327.
R. PANE, *Andrea Palladio*, Turin, 1948.
De l'Orme: H. CLOUZOT, *Philibert de l'Orme*, Paris, 1926.
A. BLUNT, *Philibert de l'Orme*, Zwemmer, London, 1958.
Inigo Jones: J. A. GOTCH, *Inigo Jones*, Methuen, London, 1928.
Herrera: A. RUIZ DE ARCAUTE, *Juan de Herrera*, Madrid, 1936.
Bernini: S. Fraschetti, *Il Bernini*, Milan, 1900.
R. PANE, *Bernini architetto*, Venice, 1953.
Borromini: E. HEMPEL, *Francesco Borromini*, Vienna, 1924.
H. SELDMAYR, *Francesco Borromini*, Munich, 1939.
P. PORTOGHESI, *Borromini*, Milan, 1967.
Guarini: P. PORTOGHESI, *Guarino Guarini*, Milan, 1955.
Juvara: L. ROVERE, F. VIALE and A. E. BRICKMANN, *Filippo Juvara*, Milan, 1937.
Rainaldi: E. HEMPEL, *Carlo Rainaldi*, Munich, 1919.
Fuga: R. PANE, *Ferdinando Fuga*, Naples, 1956.
Vittone: P. PORTOGHESI, *Bernardo Vittone*, Rome, 1967.
François Mansart: A. BLUNT, *François Mansart*, Warburg Institute, London, 1941.
Le Nôtre: E. DE GANAY, *André le Nôtre*, Paris, 1962.
Hardouin-Mansart: P. BOURGET and G. CATTAUI, *Jules Hardouin-Mansart*, Paris, 1960.
Wren: THE WREN SOCIETY'S publications, 20 vols, London, 1924–43.
J. SUMMERSON, *Sir Christopher Wren*, Collins, London, 1953.
Hawksmoor: K. DOWNES, *Nicholas Hawksmoor*, Thames & Hudson, London, 1970.
Vanbrugh: L. WHISTLER, *Sir John Vanbrugh*, Cobden-Sanderson, London, 1938.
Fischer von Erlach: H. SELDMAYR, *Johann Bernhard Fischer von Erlach*, Vienna, 1956.
Neumann: M. H. VON FREEDEN, *Balthasar Neumann*, Munich and Berlin, 1953.
Dientzenhofer: C. NORBERG-SCHULTZ, *Kilan Ignaz Dientzenhofer e il barocco boemo*, Rome, 1968.

Some contemporary writers are working to update judgments on the masters and to complete the exploration of this field with the biographies of artists who have not yet been studied. But this perspective has been complicated by a number of studies on a circle or a period, rather than a person, and which establish a new link between artistic events and the other areas of civil life. The following are of interest:

R. WITTKOWER, *Architectural Principles in the Age of Humanism*, Tiranti, London, 1962.
E. KAUFMANN, *Architecture in the Age of Reason*, Harvard University Press, 1955.
A. CHASTEL, *Art et humanisme à Florence au temps de Laurent le Magnifique*, Paris, 1959; *Italie 1460–1500: Renaissance méridionale*, Paris, 1965 (English edition, *The Golden Age of the Renaissance, Italy 1460–1500*, Thames & Hudson, London, 1965); *Le Grand Atelier d'Italie*, Paris, 1965 (English edition, *The Studios and Styles of the Renaissance*, Thames & Hudson, London, 1966).

The history of town-planning – which from our point of view is inseparable from the history of architecture – still forms a specialized field; here monographs deal with the single towns – usually considered over the entire span of their development – and general works retain the descriptive form typical of general manuals.

The following works should be mentioned:

Florence: R. DAVIDSOHN, *Storia di Firenze*, 7 vols; and no. 12 (1953) of the review *Urbanistica*.
Rome: no. 27 (1959) of the review *Urbanistica*.
Pienza: E. CARLI, *Pienza, la città di Pio II*, Rome, 1966.
Urbino: G. DE CARLO, *Urbino*, Padua, 1967.
Ferrara: B. ZEVI, *Biagio Rossetti*, Turin, 1960.
Mantua: *Mantova, le arti: vol. I, Il Medioevo* by C. PACCAGNINI, Mantua, 1960; *vol. II, Dall'inizio del secolo XV alla metà del XVI* by E. MARANI and C. PERNIA, Mantua, 1961.
Venice: no. 53 (1968) of the review *Urbanistica*.
Naples: G. RUSSO, C. COCCHIA, *Napoli, contributi allo studio della città*, 3 vols, Naples, 1960–1.
Paris: M. POETE, *Paris*, 1932.
London: S. E. RASMUSSEN, *London, the Unique City*, Cape, London, 1937.
I. BROWN, *London*, Studio Vista, London, 1965.
Vienna: F. WALTER, *Wien*, 3 vols, Vienna, 1940.
Berlin: W. HEGEMANN, *Das steinerne Berlin*, Berlin, 1930.
Antwerp: F. PRIMS, *Antwerpen door de eeuwen heen*, Antwerp, 1951.
Lisbon: J.-A. FRANCA, *Une Ville de lumières, La Lisbonne de Pombal*, Paris, 1965.
Bath: W. ISON, *The Georgian Buildings of Bath from 1700 to 1830*, Faber, London, 1948.
Edinburgh: A. J. YOUNGSON, *The Making of Classical Edinburgh*, Edinburgh University Press, 1966.
Dutch towns: G. L. BURKE, *The Making of Dutch Towns*, Cleaver-Hume, London, 1956.
French towns: P. LAVEDAN, *Les Villes françaises*, Paris, 1960.

General works that are still fundamental are:

P. LAVEDAN, *Histoire de l'urbanisme*, vol. II, *Renaissance et temps modernes*, Paris, 1930.
E. A. GUTKIND, *International History of City Development*, Free Press, New York and Collier-Macmillan, London, is in the process of publication, eight volumes having appeared so far:
Urban Development in Central Europe, 1964.
Urban Development in the Alpine and Scandinavian Countries, 1965.
Urban Development in Southern Europe – Spain and Portugal, 1967.
Urban Development in Southern Europe – Italy and Greece, 1969.
Urban Development in Western Europe – France and Belgium, 1971.
Urban Development in Western Europe – Netherlands and Great Britain, 1971.
Urban Development in East/Central Europe – Poland, Czechoslovakia and Hungary, 1972.
Urban Development in Eastern Europe – Bulgaria, Roumania and U.S.S.R., 1973.

On American cities, see the extremely well-documented J. W. REPS, *The Making of Urban America*, Princeton University Press, 1965.

These works and those quoted in the footnotes give only the sketchiest idea of the immense bibliography available on our subject. Since this book is not a general work but a monograph illustrating a historical interpretation, it has necessitated only the merest sounding into this bibliographical sea; during the course of the work we have regularly encountered two problems: that of the superabundance of texts to be consulted and that of the lack of analysis and data essential to our argument, the result of the need to consider these things from a new visual angle.

Thus, *vis-à-vis* current historiography, this book has become an indication of studies still to be made rather than a survey of studies already carried out.

The main figures of our narrative, i.e. the people who with their individual choices decisively influenced the course of the movement – Brunelleschi, Alberti, Bramante, Palladio, Le Nôtre, Vauban, and those responsible for the abandoning of geometry in the planning of the landscaped environment – have yet to be presented with greater clarity, with a more exact evaluation of their historical responsibilities.

Certain equally important and fruitful collective experiments should also be studied together with these individual activities: collaboration between the experts gathered together at the court of Federigo da Montefeltro at Urbino, the work of the teams led by Raphael in Rome and by Giulio Romano in Mantua, the urbanization of the Spanish colonies in America before the middle of the sixteenth century, the extension of Amsterdam in the seventeenth century, artistic organization at the court of Louis XIV and the application of the urban grid plan, on a regional scale, in north America.

More detailed studies on these subjects will either confirm the claims and hypotheses made in this book, or else will modify them, but they will certainly make it possible to pursue the programme we have put forward: to eliminate the metahistorical hypothesis of an immutable arrangement of architectural facts, and to consider them on a par, in the multiplicity of their results and intellectual and institutional settings, with all the others that form the stuff of civil life.

Index

Numbers in italic refer to illustration numbers